INTRODUCTORY

Computer Concepts 2014

Parsons | Oja

COURSE TECHNOLOGY
CENGAGE Learning·

New Perspectives on Computer Concepts, 2014, Introductory

June Jamrich Parsons, Dan Oja

Editor-in-Chief: Marie L. Lee

Director of Development: Marah Bellegarde

Executive Editor: Donna Gridley

Associate Acquisitions Editor: Amanda Lyons

Product Development Manager: Leigh Hefferon

Senior Product Manager: Kathy Finnegan

Product Managers: Katherine C. Russillo, Julia Leroux-Lindsey

Developmental Editor: Katherine C. Russillo

Associate Product Manager: Angela Lang

Editorial Assistant: Melissa Stehler

Brand Manager: Elinor Gregory

Market Development Managers: Gretchen Swann, Kristie Clark

Senior Content Project Manager: Jennifer Goguen McGrail

Photo Research: Bill Smith Group

Art Director: GEX Publishing Services

Cover Designer: GEX Publishing Services

Cover Art: © tratong/Shutterstock

eBook CD Technician: Keefe Crowley

eBook CD Development: MediaTechnics Corp.

Prepress Production: GEX Publishing Services

Copyeditor: Suzanne Huizenga

Indexer: Alexandra Nickerson

For product information and technology assistance, contact us at
Cengage Learning Customer & Sales Support, 1-800-354-9706

For permission to use material from this text or product, submit all requests online at cengage.com/permissions. Further permissions questions can be e-mailed to **permissionrequest@cengage.com.**

Some of the product names and company names used in this book have been used for identification purposes only and may be trademarks or registered trademarks of their respective manufacturers and sellers.

Microsoft and the Office logo are either registered trademarks or trademarks of Microsoft Corporation in the United States and/or other countries. Course Technology, Cengage Learning is an independent entity from the Microsoft Corporation, and not affiliated with Microsoft in any manner. All screenshots are courtesy of Microsoft unless otherwise noted.

Disclaimer: Any fictional data related to persons or companies or URLs used throughout this book is intended for instructional purposes only. At the time this book was printed, any such data was fictional and not belonging to any real persons or companies.

Library of Congress Control Number: 2012923695

ISBN-13: 978-1-285-09768-8
ISBN-10: 1-285-09768-8

Course Technology
20 Channel Center Street
Boston, MA 02210
USA

Cengage Learning is a leading provider of customized learning solutions with office locations around the globe, including Singapore, the United Kingdom, Australia, Mexico, Brazil and Japan. Locate your local office at: **international.cengage.com/global**

Cengage Learning products are represented in Canada by Nelson Education, Ltd.

To learn more about Course Technology, visit **www.cengage.com/coursetechnology**

To learn more about Cengage Learning, visit **www.cengage.com**

Purchase any of our products at your local college store or at our preferred online store **www.cengagebrain.com**

Printed in the United States of America
3 4 5 6 7 17 16 15 14

TABLE OF CONTENTS

CHAPTER 1

COMPUTERS AND DIGITAL BASICS

Africa Studio/Shutterstock.com

NEW PERSPECTIVES LABS

CHAPTER 1
Operating a Personal Computer
Working with Binary Numbers

CHAPTER 2
Benchmarking

CHAPTER 3
Installing and Uninstalling Software

CHAPTER 4
Managing Files
Backing Up Your Computer

CHAPTER 5
Local Area Networks

CHAPTER 6
Tracking Packets
Securing Your Connection

CHAPTER 7
Browser Security & Privacy
Working with Cookies
Working with HTML

CHAPTER 8
Working with Bitmap Graphics
Working with DFDs

New Perspectives on Computer Concepts 2014

Connect the Concepts. We live in a digital world and we are constantly picking up bits and pieces of information about computers and other digital devices. But *understanding* digital devices in a way expected of a college graduate requires a framework of concepts that organizes information into hierarchies and relationships. It is, in a sense, THE SOCIAL NETWORK OF LEARNING.

New Perspectives on Computer Concepts 2014 is designed to help students connect the dots to visualize and internalize a framework for technology concepts that's applicable to academic research, career preparation, and today's digital lifestyles.

Ensure Success. Developed by digital textbook pioneers, NP2014 is a time-tested and fully interactive teaching and learning environment that supplies TOOLS FOR SUCCESS. The printed book, CourseMate Web site, interactive multimedia eBook, and assessment tools offer an engaging, multi-layered technology platform that supports diverse teaching and learning styles.

New for This Edition. What's the most effective study technique: Taking notes? Reviewing? According to researchers, students study most effectively by simply trying to recall the material they've read, seen, or heard. NP2014's new TRY IT! feature helps students recall key concepts as they read and later as they review. TRY IT! questions and activities on just about every page are interactive in digital versions of the textbook. Students using the printed textbook can find answers in the back of the book.

NP2014 is offered in several printed and digital formats. You can use the PRINTED TEXTBOOK alone or bundle it with one of the MULTIMEDIA INTERACTIVE EBOOKS. Or use the interactive eBooks by themselves. They contain page-for-page material from the printed textbook, plus videos, animated diagrams, software tours, computer-scored assessment, and results tracking.

PRINTED TEXTBOOK

- Orientation Chapter
- Section Concept Maps
- Learning Objectives
- Learning Objectives Checkpoints
- TRY IT!s
- Section QuickChecks
- Issues
- Information Tools
- Technology in Context
- Key Terms
- Interactive Summary
- Interactive Situation Questions
- Concept Maps

EBOOK CD

- Page-for-page equivalent to the printed textbook
- Videos and software tours
- Interactive TRY IT!s
- Computer-scored and tracked QuickChecks, Interactive Summaries, Situation Questions, and Concept Maps
- Practice Tests
- New Perspectives Labs with scored and tracked QuickChecks
- WebTrack results tracking
- Instructor annotations
- Chirps

COURSEMATE & EBOOK

- Page-for-page equivalent to the printed textbook
- Videos and software tours
- Interactive TRY IT!s
- Computer-scored and tracked Pre-Quizzes, Quickchecks, Interactive Summaries, Situation Questions, Concept Maps, and Chapter Quizzes
- Audio Overviews
- Audio Flashcards
- Games
- Track results with Engagement Tracker or WebTrack

CREATE YOUR OWN LEARNING PLAN

It's easy! Use the NP2014 printed textbook, NP2014 Online CourseMate, or NP2014 eBook CD in **ANY WAY THAT'S RIGHT FOR YOU**. The Orientation helps you get acquainted with the extensive array of NP2014 technology at your command.

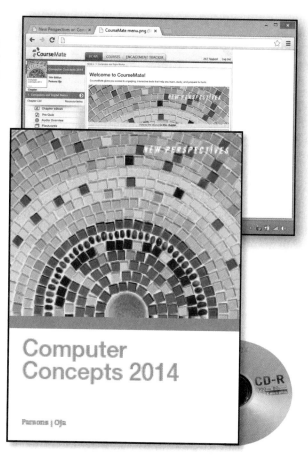

Your eBook CD Plan—Seven Easy Steps

1. Get started with the **EBOOK CD** and work on the Chapter opener **TRY IT! ACTIVITY** for a hands-on introduction to the chapter topics.

2. Read a chapter, answer the embedded **TRY IT!s**, and complete the **QUICKCHECKS**.

3. Use **CHIRPS** while you're reading to send questions to your instructor.

4. Work with **NEW PERSPECTIVES LABS** to apply your knowledge.

5. Complete **REVIEW ACTIVITIES** using your digital textbook.

6. Take **PRACTICE TESTS** to see if you're ready for the exam.

7. Transmit your results to your instructor on **WEBTRACK**.

Your CourseMate Plan—Eight Steps Online

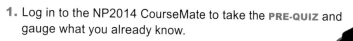

1. Log in to the NP2014 CourseMate to take the **PRE-QUIZ** and gauge what you already know.

2. Listen to an **AUDIO OVERVIEW** of chapter highlights.

3. Read a chapter in the online eBook and answer the embedded **TRY IT!s**.

4. Work with the **EBOOK ACTIVITIES AND PRACTICE TESTS** to assess your understanding. Your instructor can track your progress with WebTrack.

5. Have some fun reviewing with **ONLINE GAMES**.

6. Use **AUDIO AND TECHTERM FLASHCARDS** to review terminology from the chapter.

7. Check the **DETAILED LEARNING OBJECTIVES** to make sure you've mastered the material.

8. Take the **CHAPTER QUIZ** if your instructor is tracking results using Engagement Tracker.

Gladskikh Tatiana/Shutterstock.com

THE BOOK

NP2014 gives you the straight story on today's technology. The style has been carefully honed to be clear, concise, and visual.

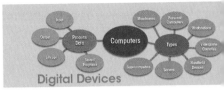

Digital Devices

Easy to read

Each chapter is divided into five **SECTIONS**, beginning with a **CONCEPT MAP** that provides a visual overview of concepts. **FAQS** answer commonly asked questions about technology and help you follow the flow of the presentation.

Keeps you on track

QUICKCHECKS at the end of each section give you a chance to find out if you understand the most important concepts. As you read the chapter, look for the answers to the questions posed as Learning Objectives, then try your hand at the **LEARNING OBJECTIVES CHECKPOINTS** at the end of each chapter to make sure you've retained the key points. Additional review activities include **TRY IT!s**, **KEY TERMS**, **INTERACTIVE CHAPTER SUMMARIES**, **INTERACTIVE SITUATION QUESTIONS**, and **CONCEPT MAPS**.

Helps you explore

The **ISSUE** section in each chapter highlights controversial aspects of technology. In the **TECHNOLOGY IN CONTEXT** section, you'll discover how technology plays a role in careers such as film-making, architecture, banking, and fashion design. The **INFORMATION TOOLS** section helps you brush up on digital research techniques and apps. Work with **ISSUE AND INFORMATION TOOLS TRY IT!s** to apply the concepts you learned as you explore technology controversies and sharpen your information literacy skills.

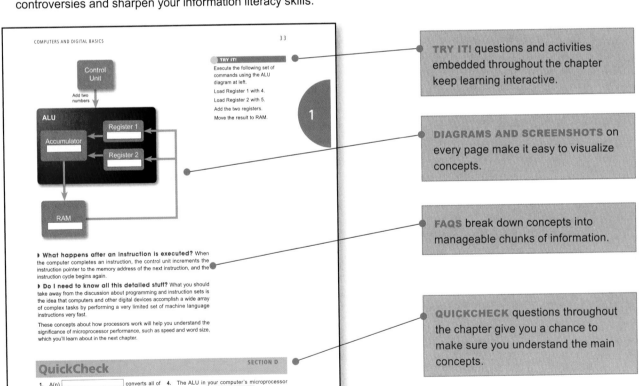

TRY IT! questions and activities embedded throughout the chapter keep learning interactive.

DIAGRAMS AND SCREENSHOTS on every page make it easy to visualize concepts.

FAQS break down concepts into manageable chunks of information.

QUICKCHECK questions throughout the chapter give you a chance to make sure you understand the main concepts.

THE INTERACTIVE MULTIMEDIA EBOOK CD

The NP2014 EBOOK CD is a digital version of your textbook with multimedia and interactive activities designed to enhance your learning experience.

Works alone or with the printed book

Every page of the eBook CD MIRRORS THE PRINTED TEXTBOOK, so use the tool that's most convenient and that best suits your learning style.

Brings concepts to life

In the eBook CD, photos turn into VIDEOS. Illustrations become ANIMATED DIAGRAMS. Screenshots activate guided SOFTWARE TOURS, so you can see how applications and operating systems work even if they aren't installed on your computer.

Makes learning interactive

As you read each chapter, be sure to complete the computer-scored TRY IT!s and the QUICKCHECKS at the end of each section. When you complete a chapter, try the interactive, COMPUTER-SCORED ACTIVITIES. Take some PRACTICE TESTS to gauge how well you'll perform on exams.

You can master hundreds of computer concepts using the NEW PERSPECTIVES LABS. Use WEBTRACK to easily transmit your scores to your instructor. If you have questions as you're reading, use CHIRPS to send questions anonymously to your instructor.

The digital textbook is easy to use. It is packed with MULTIMEDIA, and offers plenty of COMPUTER-SCORED ACTIVITIES.

Interactive NEW PERSPECTIVES LABS give you hands-on experience with concepts and software.

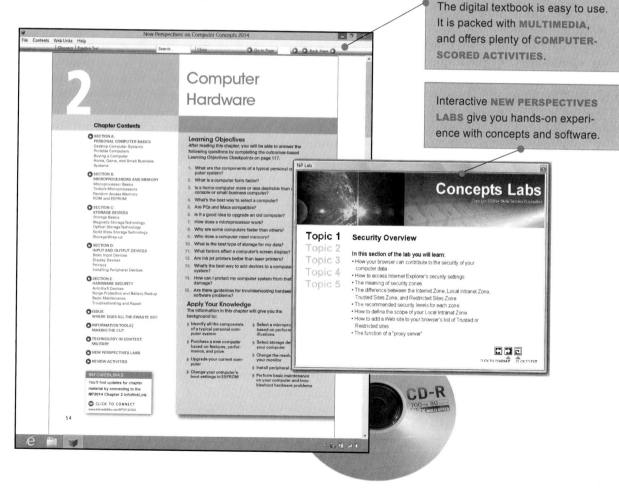

THE NP2014 ONLINE COURSEMATE WITH EBOOK

The NP2014 CourseMate is packed full of information and includes an inter-active, multimedia eBook plus activities to accompany each chapter. Follow the directions in Section D of the Orientation chapter to sign up for an account and access the NP2014 CourseMate.

Lets you study anywhere

CourseMate includes an **ONLINE EBOOK**, so you can access your text-book from any computer that's connected to the Internet. eBook activities can be tracked by instructors using WebTrack.

Gives you options

Want to find out where to focus your study time? Start with a **PRE-QUIZ**. Looking for a fun way to review? Try an **ONLINE GAME** that packages chap-ter concepts into an entertaining quiz show or action game. When you're ready for some serious exam preparation, work with the **CHAPTER QUIZZES** to see how well you understand key concepts. Need some last-minute review? Load up your portable music player with a **CHAPTER OVERVIEW** and **AUDIO FLASHCARDS**.

Now you can listen to Audio Overviews and Flashcards on your computer or study while you are out and about by downloading them to your portable music player.

Reinforces your understanding

DETAILED LEARNING OBJECTIVES help you determine if you've mastered all the requirements for completing a chapter.

Keeps track of your progress

CourseMate's **ENGAGEMENT TRACKER** records the time you spend on various activities, saves your scores, and shares them with your instructor. You can optionally send scores from the activities within the eBook to your instructor's WebTrack.

ONLINE EBOOK lets you access your textbook from any computer that's con-nected to the Internet.

Listen to chapter highlights or practice key terms with handy **AUDIO OVERVIEWS** and **AUDIO FLASHCARDS**.

Quizzes, games, and more provide many ways to explore and review.

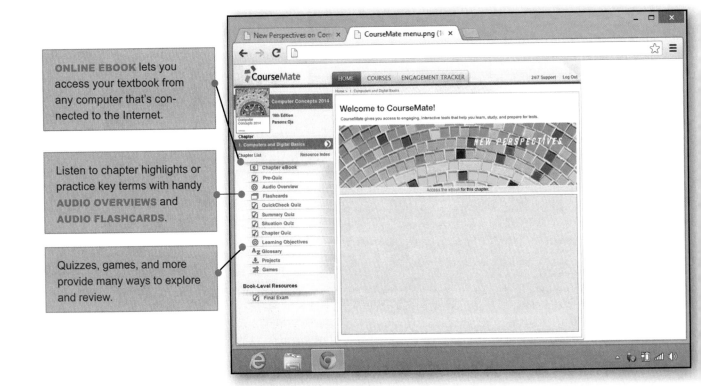

INSTRUCTOR RESOURCES

NP2014 resources provide instructors with a wide range of tools that enhance teaching and learning. These resources and more can be accessed from the NP2014 Instructor Companion Site. Log in by connecting to *www.cengagebrain.com*.

Instructor's Manual: Help is only a few keystrokes away

The NP2014 Instructor's Manual offers the following comprehensive instructional materials:

- Chapter table of contents
- Chapter Objectives
- FastPoll Clicker questions
- Bullet-point lecture notes for each chapter section
- Key terms
- Classroom activities and teaching tips, including how to effectively use and integrate CourseMate online content, interactive multimedia eBook content, and labs.

Tabbing Guide

If you've used previous editions of *New Perspectives on Computer Concepts*, you'll appreciate the Tabbing Guide that lets you see at a glance what's been updated for this edition. Use it to make revisions to your syllabus, as necessary.

Orientation scripts

We can help you introduce students to our technology. We've supplied complete orientation scripts for the NP2014 CD and Online CourseMate.

Solution Files

Your password-protected instructor resources provide answers to all the QuickChecks, Lab Assignments, Interactive Summaries, Interactive Situation Questions, Learning Objective CheckPoints, Concept Maps, Projects, Issue TRY IT!s, and Information Tools TRY IT!s.

Clicker Questions

Did your students read the assignment? Find out by using the FastPoll questions supplied with the Instructor's Manual and included in the NP2014 PowerPoint presentations. Each question is numbered so you can collect results using Chirps or a third-party course polling system. Even if you don't have polling technology, you can use FastPoll questions with a simple show of hands or as a quick paper-and-pencil quiz.

ANNOTATIONS! Instructors can create their own text, graphical, or video annotations that students will see as they read their digital textbook. Find out more about this innovative feature in the Technology Guide.

Course Presenter PowerPoints

Instructors can deliver engaging and visually impressive lectures for each chapter with the professionally designed Course Presenter PowerPoints available from the NP2014 Instructor Companion Site.

Technology Guide

Do you need to learn how to use WebTrack, the eBook CD, and the CourseMate interactive eBook? We now offer instructors a Technology Guide that provides step-by-step instructions for collecting WebTrack data, adding your own annotations to the digital textbook, exporting student scores, and much more.

INSTRUCTIONAL TECHNOLOGY TOOLS

The NP team provides technology assets to help instructors optimize instruction, facilitate learning, and use their time effectively.

ExamView: Testbanks and powerful testing software

With ExamView, instructors can generate printed tests, create LAN-based tests, or test over the Internet. Examview testbanks cover the same material as Practice Tests and Test Yourself testbanks, but the questions are worded differently so the ExamView testbanks contain a unique collection of questions for graded tests and exams. The ExamView software is available from the NP2014 Instructor Companion Site.

WebTrack

Monitoring student progress is easy. With WebTrack's store-and-forward system, a student can transmit scores to an instructor, who can download them at any time. Newly downloaded scores are consolidated with previous scores and can be displayed, printed, or exported in a variety of report formats.

WebTrack setup is easy. We mean it! Simply download one file, start the app, and then create an ID and password. You don't even have to enter your students' names; your student list populates automatically as students submit results. You can link to WebTrack assets from the NP2014 Companion site.

InfoWebLinks

Each chapter has a dedicated InfoWebLinks page containing significant post-publication updates. Be sure to check InfoWebLinks periodically at *www.infoweblinks.com/np2014*.

Chirps

Would you like to know the questions students have while reading their textbooks? Chirps let you find out! Similar to tweets, our Chirps feature allows students to send questions to instructors from within the eBook CD. Instructors can also use Chirps as an in-class polling system, or as an asynchronous polling tool for online students. To learn about this versatile new NP technology, refer to the Technology Guide.

Engagement Tracker

For courses that take advantage of the activities on the NP2014 Online CourseMate, the Engagement Tracker monitors student time on tasks and records scores that help instructors keep track of student progress.

SAM and MindTap Reader eBook

SAM (Skills Assessment Manager) is a robust assessment, training, and project-based system that enables students to be active participants in learning valuable Microsoft Office skills and technology concepts. The MindTap Reader version of New Perspectives on Computer Concepts 2014 works within the SAM environment for courses that combine concepts and Office skills. Let SAM be an integral part of your students' learning experience! Please visit www. cengage.com/samcentral.

WebTrackIII Instructor's Page

WEBTRACKIII is now available as a portable app that instructors can carry on a USB flash drive and use on their classroom, office, or home computer.

FROM THE AUTHORS

Many of today's students have substantially more practical experience with digital devices than their counterparts of 15 years ago, but even these students may lack a cohesive framework for their knowledge. Our Concept Map feature throughout the chapters is designed to help students organize technology-related facts, terms, and experiences. Our new TRY IT! activities are designed to keep students actively learning on every page.

The goal of *New Perspectives on Computer Concepts* is to bring every student up to speed with computer basics, and then go beyond basic computer literacy to provide students with technical and practical information that every college-educated person would be expected to know.

In producing the 2014 edition of this very popular textbook, we incorporated significant technology trends that affect computing and everyday life. Concerns for data security, personal privacy, and online safety, controversy over digital rights management, an explosion of interest in mobile apps and cloud computing, and the skyrocketing sales of Macs are just some of the trends that have been given expanded coverage in this edition of the book.

Whether you are an instructor or a student, we hope that you enjoy the learning experience provided by our text-based and technology-based materials.

ACKNOWLEDGEMENTS

The book would not exist—and certainly wouldn't arrive on schedule—were it not for the efforts of our media, editorial, and production teams. We thank Kate Russillo for her developmental edit and tireless work on every detail of the project; Suzanne Huizenga for a miraculously detailed copy edit; Marie E. Lee and Donna Gridley for their executive leadership of the New Perspectives series; Jennifer Goguen McGrail for managing production; Julia Leroux-Lindsey and Brianna Hawes for managing the book's ancillaries; Elinor Gregory for marketing; and our brilliant sales reps for encouraging instructors to adopt this book for their intro courses.

The MediaTechnics team worked tirelessly and we can't offer enough thanks to Donna Mulder for revising the screentours; Tensi Parsons for her extraordinary devotion to desktop publishing; Keefe Crowley for his versatile skills in producing the online and CD eBooks, creating videos, taking photos, and maintaining the InfoWebLinks site; Chris Robbert for his clear narrations; and Debora Elam, Kevin Lappi, Joseph Smit, Nikki Smit, Marilou Potter, Michael Crowley, and Kelsey Schuch for checking and double-checking the alpha and beta CDs.

We also want to give special thanks to Bob Metcalf for giving us permission to use his original sketch of the Ethernet; and The University of Illinois for supplying photos of PLATO.

In addition, our thanks go to the New Perspectives Advisory Committee members and reviewers listed on the next page, who have made a tremendous contribution to New Perspectives. Thank you all!

June Parsons and Dan Oja

ACADEMIC, TECHNICAL, AND STUDENT REVIEWERS

Thank you to the many students, instructors, Advisory Committee members, and subject-matter experts who provided valuable feedback and who have influenced the evolution of New Perspectives on Computer Concepts:

Dr. Nazih Abdallah, University of Central Florida; Beverly Amer, Northern Arizona University; Ken Baldauf, Florida State University; Dottie Baumeister, Harford Community College; Paula Bell, Lock Haven University of Pennsylvania; Mary Burke, Ocean County College; Barbara Burns, St. Johns River Community College; Mary Caldwell, Rollins College; Chuck Calvin, Computer Learning Centers; Wendy Chisholm, Barstow College; Linda Cooper, Macon State College; Dave Courtaway, Devry University, Ponoma; Becky Curtin, William Rainey Harper College; Eric Daley, University of New Brunswick; Sallie Dodson, Radford University; Leonard Dwyer, Southwestern College of Business; Robert Erickson, University of Vermont; Steven Everding, Fox Valley Technical College; Mark Feiler, Merritt College; Alan Fisher, Walters State Community College; Esther Frankel, Santa Barbara City College; Pat Frederick, Del Mar College; Michael Gaffney, Century College; John Gammell, St. Cloud State University; Ernest Gines, Tarrant Count College SE; Ione Good, Southeastern Community College; Tom Gorecki, College of Southern Maryland; Steve Gramlich, Pasco-Hernando Community College; Safia Gray, Metropolitan Community College: Longview; Michael Hanna, Colorado State University; Dorothy Harman, Tarrant County College Northeast; Bobbye Haupt, Cecil Community College; Heith Hennel, Valencia Community College; Gerald Hensel, Valencia Community College; Patti Impink, Macon State College; Bob Irvine, American River College; Ernie Ivey, Polk Community College; Joanne Lazirko, University of Wisconsin; Stan Leja, Del Mar College; Martha Lindberg, Minnesota State University; Richard Linge, Arizona Western College; Terry Long, Valencia Community College; Karl Smart Lyman, Central Michigan University; Dr. W. Benjamin Martz, University of Colorado, Colorado Springs; Deann McMullen, Western Kentucky Community and Technical College; Dori McPherson, Schoolcraft College; Saeed Molki, South Texas College; Robert Moore, Laredo Community College; Ed Mott, Central Texas College; Rob Murray, Ivy Tech Community College; Cindi Nadelman, New England College; Karen O'Connor, Cerro Coso Community College; Dr. Rodney Pearson, Mississippi State University; Catherine Perlich, St. Thomas; Tonya Pierce, Ivy Tech College; David Primeaux, Virginia Commonwealth University; Ann Rowlette, Liberty University; Joan Shriver, Tarrant County College; Lana Shyrock, Monroe County Community College; Betty Sinowitz, Rockland Community College; Martin Skolnik, Florida Atlantic University; Karl Smart, Central Michigan University; Jerome Spencer, Rowan University; Ella Strong, Hazard Community and Technical College; Gregory Stefanelli, Carroll Community College; Furkan Tari, Anne Arundel Community College; Shane Thomas, Victor Valley College Martha; J. Tilmann, College of San Mateo; Michael Wiemann, Blue River Community College; Kathy Winters, University of Tennessee, Chattanooga; Paul Yaroslaski, Dodge City Community College; John Zamora, Modesto Junior College; Matt Zullo, Wake Tech Community College; Student Reviewers Kitty Edwards and Heather House; Technical Reviewers Jeff Harrow, Barbra D. Letts, John Lucas, Ramachandran Bharath, and Karl Mulder.

Computer Concepts 2014

Parsons | Oja

NEW PERSPECTIVES

Orientation

Chapter Contents

Apply Your Knowledge The information in this chapter will give you the background to:

▶ Start your computer, use the keyboard, and operate the mouse

▶ Work with Windows or Mac OS

▶ Use word processing software

▶ Carry out research on the Web using a search engine and other resources such as Wikipedia

▶ Send e-mail

▶ Take effective steps to guard your privacy and safety online

▶ Access the NP2014 interactive eBook and online CourseMate for labs, quizzes, CourseCasts, and games

▶ Use eBook CD resources, such as pre-assessments, practice tests, labs, and interactive summaries

●TRY IT!

WHAT DO I NEED TO GET STARTED?

To complete the activities in Sections A, B, and C, you'll need access to a computer, Internet access, your e-mail address, and your instructor's e-mail address. To complete optional Sections D and E, you'll need access to the interactive eBook CD or CourseMate eBook.

To be sure you have what you need, use the following checklist. Check off the boxes for each item that you have.

☐ Access to a computer. If you're using your own computer, you might need a user ID and password to log in. Don't write your password down, but make sure you know what it is.

☐ Access to the Internet. You might need a user ID and password if you use your school's network to access the Internet. Check with your instructor or lab manager to learn how your school handles network access.

☐ An interactive, digital version of the textbook, such as the eBook CD or the CourseMate eBook. The eBook CD requires a CD or DVD drive. If your computer does not have this type of drive, check with your instructor. CourseMate eBook versions of your textbook require a browser. Your school network might provide access to the eBook CD or CourseMate eBook from lab computers.

☐ Your e-mail address. Your instructor should explain how you can obtain an e-mail address if you don't already have one. Write your e-mail address here:

_____

☐ Your instructor's e-mail address. To correspond with your instructor, you'll need your instructor's e-mail address. Write it here:

_____

☐ Your instructor's WebTrack address. If your instructor will be collecting your scores with WebTrack, make sure that you have your instructor's WebTrack address. Write it here:

_____

NEW PERSPECTIVES

Computer
Concepts 2014

Parsons | Oja

Getting Started

WHEN YOU USE the *New Perspectives on Computer Concepts* textbook, you will not only learn about computers; you'll also use computers as learning tools. Section A is designed to get computer novices quickly up to speed with computing basics, such as turning on computer equipment, working with Windows or Mac OS, using a mouse and computer keyboard, and accessing Help. Read through this section while at a computer so that you can do the TRY IT! activities.

COMPUTER EQUIPMENT

▶ **What do I need to know about my computer?** Computers come in many packages, including small handheld smartphones, portable tablets and laptops, and stationary desktop models. A computer runs software applications (also called programs and apps) that help you accomplish a variety of tasks. Computer systems consist of several components.

▶ **What are the important components of my computer system?** Your computer is housed in a case called a system unit that contains circuitry, including the microprocessor that is the "brain" of your computer and memory chips that temporarily store data. It also contains storage devices, such as a hard disk drive.

Your computer system includes basic hardware devices that allow you to enter information and commands, view work, and store information for later retrieval. Devices for entering information include a keyboard, mouse, touchpad, or touchscreen. A display device, sometimes called a monitor, allows you to view your work. A printer produces "hard copy" on paper. Speakers output music, movie soundtracks, and various sounds that help you pay attention to what happens on the screen.

▶ **Where are the important components of a desktop computer system?** A desktop computer is designed for stationary use on a desk or table. Figure 1 shows the key components of a desktop computer system.

PC OR MAC?

In addition to being classified as desktops, laptops, tablets, and smartphones, personal computers can be classified by their operating systems.

Microsoft Windows is the world's most popular operating system for desktop and laptop computers. Windows computers are sometimes referred to as PCs.

OS X is the operating system used by desktop and laptop computers called Macs that are manufactured by Apple.

iOS is the operating system for iPhones, iPods, and iPads.

Android is the operating system for many non-Apple smartphones and tablets.

Microsoft Windows RT is the operating system for tablets in the Windows family.

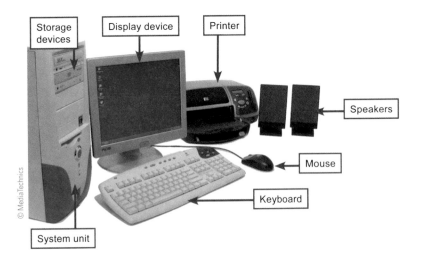

FIGURE 1

A desktop computer system includes several components that can be connected by cables or wirelessly.

Orientation

> **Where are the important components of a laptop computer system?** Laptop computers (sometimes called notebook computers) are small, lightweight computers designed to be carried from place to place. The components of a laptop computer system, except the printer, are housed in a single unit, as shown in Figure 2.

FIGURE 2

A laptop computer includes a flat-panel screen, keyboard, speakers, and touchpad in the same unit that contains the microprocessor, memory, and storage devices. An external mouse is sometimes used instead of the touchpad.

> **How do I identify my computer's storage devices?** Your computer contains a hard disk housed inside the system unit. It might also have a USB connector and some type of drive that works with CDs and DVDs. Figure 3 can help you identify your computer's storage devices and their uses.

DVD drive

DVD drives play CDs and DVDs. Most of today's DVD drives can write data on blank CDs and DVDs.

USB flash drive

A USB flash drive is about the size of a highlighter and plugs directly into the computer system unit.

External drive

External hard drives and DVD drives can be connected to a computer using a USB cable.

FIGURE 3

You should use the hard disk to store most of your data. To transport data, use a USB drive. For backups, use an external hard drive. Use an external DVD drive to run the eBook CD if your computer has no built-in drive to handle CDs and DVDs.

> **Do I have to log in?** Most computers take a minute or two to power up, and you might be required to log in by entering a user ID and password. For security, you should use a password for all your digital devices.

Your computer is ready to use when it displays the Windows 8 Start screen, the Windows 7 desktop, or the Mac OS desktop (refer to the next two pages), and you can move the arrow-shaped pointer with your mouse.

> **Should I turn it off?** After a period of inactivity, most computers are configured to enter a sleep mode that powers down the screen and other components. You can leave your computer in sleep mode if you plan to use it from time to time during the day.

If you're not planning to use your computer for a few days, you can initiate a shutdown sequence. When using a Windows computer, click the on-screen Start button, select Shut Down or Turn Off Computer, and follow the instructions on the screen. If there is no Start button, move the pointer to the lower-left corner of the screen. When the "charms" appear, select ⚙ Settings, and then select the Power icon. To shut down a Mac, click the Apple icon in the upper-left corner of the screen and select Shut Down.

When using computers in a school lab, ask about the shutdown procedure. Your lab manager might want you to log out but leave the computer on.

TRY IT!

Turn your computer on

1. Locate the power switch for any devices connected to your computer and turn them on.

2. Locate the power switch for your computer and turn it on.

3. If a message asks for your user ID and/or password, type them in, and then press the **Enter** key on your computer's keyboard.

4. Wait for the desktop to appear.

WINDOWS BASICS

▶ **What is Windows?** Microsoft Windows is an example of a type of software called an operating system. The operating system controls all the basic tasks your computer performs, such as running application software, manipulating files on storage devices, and transferring data to and from printers, digital cameras, and other devices. The operating system also controls the user interface—the buttons, menus, and controls you see on the screen and how you use them.

▶ **What is the Windows Start screen?** The Windows Start screen offers a quick way to access many computer tools, including apps, e-mail, and social sites (Figure 4).

Desktop tile

FIGURE 4

Windows 8 is ready to use when it displays the Start screen. You can click any of the colored tiles to select tools and apps. To view a Windows desktop similar to the one in Figure 5, click the Desktop tile. Any time you want to get back to the Start screen, press the Windows key on your keyboard.

 Windows key

▶ **What is the Windows desktop?** Windows 7 and earlier versions have no Start screen. Instead, they start by displaying the Windows desktop shown in Figure 5.

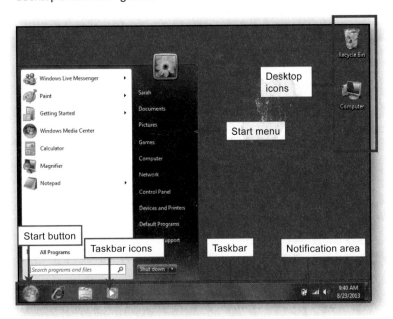

Windows Live Messenger
Paint
Getting Started
Windows Media Center
Calculator
Magnifier
Notepad

Sarah
Documents
Pictures
Games
Computer
Network
Control Panel
Devices and Printers
Default Programs

Desktop icons
Start menu
Recycle Bin
Computer

Start button
All Programs
Taskbar icons
Search programs and files
Shut down
Taskbar
Notification area
9:40 AM
8/23/2013

FIGURE 5

Desktop icons can represent programs, documents, folders, or other electronic tools.
The **taskbar** is the area displayed at the bottom of the desktop.
The **Start button** displays the Start menu, which lists programs installed on your computer. Windows 8 has no Start button or Start menu.
The **Start menu** lists application and utility programs installed on your computer.
The **Notification area** displays the current time and the status of programs, devices, and Internet connections.

MAC OS X BASICS

▶ **What is Mac OS?** Mac OS is the operating system used on many of today's Macintosh computers. The most recent version of this operating system is Mac OS X, featured in Figure 6.

▶ **How similar are the Mac and Windows desktops?** The Mac and Windows desktops have many similarities, such as the use of icons, menus, and rectangular on-screen windows. However, there are notable differences in the two desktops, such as the Mac desktop's dock, Apple icon, and fixed menu bar. If you switch between computers running Windows and Mac OS X, you should be aware of these differences.

▶ **What is the dock?** The dock is a collection of icons that represent programs, files, and other activities. Usually the dock is located at the bottom of the screen, but it can be configured to appear on the left side or right side of the screen if that better suits the way you work. You can add icons to the dock for programs you use frequently so they are easily accessible.

▶ **What is the Apple icon?** The Apple icon is the first icon on the menu bar located at the top of the Mac desktop. It is always visible, regardless of the program you're using. Clicking the Apple icon displays a menu that you can use to configure preferences for your computer display and devices. The Apple icon menu also includes options for logging out and shutting down your computer.

▶ **How does the fixed menu bar work?** The Mac desktop contains a menu bar that remains at the top of the screen. The options on this menu bar change according to the program you are using. In contrast, the menus for Windows programs are incorporated into individual program windows; so if you have more than one window open, each program window displays a menu.

FIGURE 6

The Mac OS X desktop includes icons, a fixed menu bar, and a dock.

Desktop icons can represent devices, programs, documents, folders, or other electronic tools. The **dock** displays icons for frequently used programs and files.

The **menu bar** contains the Apple icon and menu options for the active program.

The **Apple icon** is used to display a menu of options for setting preferences, moving the dock, logging in, and shutting down.

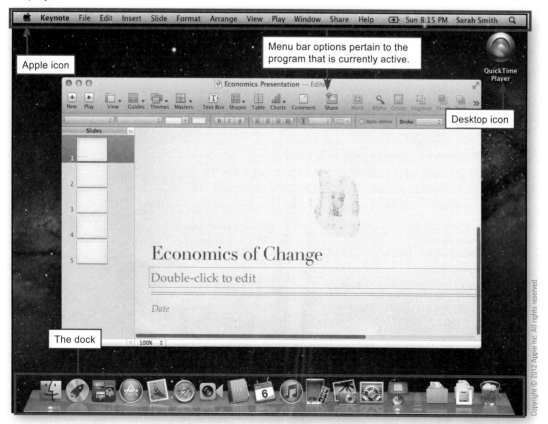

MOUSE BASICS

▶ **What is a mouse?** A mouse is a device used to manipulate items on the screen, such as the buttons and icons displayed on the Windows desktop. The mouse controls an on-screen pointer. The pointer is usually shaped like an arrow ⬉, but it can change to a different shape depending on the task you're doing. For example, when the computer is busy, the arrow shape turns into an hourglass ⌛ or a circle ◯, signifying that you should wait for the computer to finish its current task before attempting to start a new task.

PC-compatible mice have at least two buttons located on top of the mouse. Most mice also include a scroll wheel mounted between the left and right mouse buttons. Your mouse might include additional buttons on the top or sides (Figure 7).

▶ **How do I use a mouse?** Hold the mouse in your right hand as shown in Figure 8. When you drag the mouse from left to right over your mousepad or desk, the arrow-shaped pointer on the screen moves from left to right. If you run out of room to move the mouse, simply pick it up and reposition it. The pointer does not move when the mouse is not in contact with a flat surface.

Spike Mafford/Photodisc/Getty Images

There are several ways you can manipulate on-screen objects. Although you might not be able to manipulate every object in all possible ways, you'll soon learn which mouse actions are allowed for each type of control. The following list describes your repertoire of mouse actions.

Action	How to	Result
Click	Press the left mouse button once, and then immediately release it.	Select an object
Double-click	Press the left mouse button twice in rapid succession without moving the body of the mouse.	Activate an object
Right-click	Press the right mouse button once, and then immediately release it.	Display a shortcut menu
Drag	Hold the left mouse button down while you move the mouse.	Move an object

FIGURE 7

For basic mousing, you only need to use the mouse buttons; but the scroll wheel is also handy.

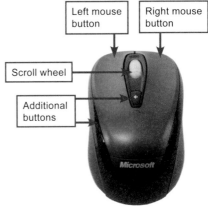

FIGURE 8

Rest the palm of your right hand on the mouse. Position your index finger over the left mouse button and your middle finger over the right mouse button.

▶ **TRY IT!**

Use your mouse

1. With your computer on and the desktop showing on the screen, move your mouse around on the desk and notice how mouse movements correspond to the movement of the arrow-shaped pointer.

2. Move the mouse to position the pointer on the User icon, Start button, or Apple icon.

3. Click the left mouse button to open the User menu, Start menu, or Apple menu.

4. Press the **Esc** key on your keyboard to close the Start menu.

KEYBOARD BASICS

▶ What are the important features of a computer keyboard?

You use the computer keyboard to input commands, respond to prompts, and type the text of documents. An insertion point that looks like a flashing vertical bar indicates where the characters you type will appear. You can change the location of the insertion point by using the mouse or the arrow keys. Study Figure 9 for an overview of important computer keys and their functions.

FIGURE 9

Computer keyboards include special function keys.

[A] **Function** keys activate commands, such as Save, Help, and Print. The command associated with each key depends on the software you are using.

[B] The **Print Screen** key prints the contents of the screen or stores a copy of the screen in memory that you can print or manipulate with graphics software.

[C] The **Esc** (Escape) key cancels an-operation.

[D] The **Windows** key on a PC displays the Windows 8 Start screen.

[E] The **Page Up** key displays the previous screen of information. The **Page Down** key displays the next screen of information.

[F] The **Backspace** key deletes one character to the left of the insertion point.

[G] The **Insert** key switches between insert mode and typeover mode.

[H] The **Home** key takes you to the beginning of a line or the beginning of a document, depending on the software you are using.

© MediaTechnics

[I] The **Tab** key can move your current typing location to the next tab stop or the next text-entry box.

[J] The **Caps Lock** key capitalizes all the letters you type when it is engaged, but does not produce the top symbol on keys that contain two symbols. This key is a toggle key, which means that each time you press it, you switch between uppercase and lowercase modes.

[K] The **Shift** key capitalizes letters and produces the top symbol on keys that contain two symbols.

[L] You hold down the **Ctrl** key while pressing another key. On a Mac, the Command key, marked with an Apple or ⌘ symbol, works the same way. The result of Ctrl or Alt key combinations depends on the software you are using.

[M] You hold down the **Alt** key while you press another key.

[N] The **Enter** key is used to indicate that you have completed a command or want to move your typing position down to the next line.

[O] The **Delete** key deletes the character to the right of the insertion point.

[P] The **End** key takes you to the end of a line or the end of a document, depending on the software you are using.

[Q] The **right-click** key accomplishes the same task as right-clicking a mouse button, and usually opens a shortcut menu.

[R] The **arrow** keys move the insertion point.

[S] The **numeric keypad** produces numbers or moves the insertion point, depending on the status of the Num Lock key shown by indicator lights or a message on the screen.

Orientation

▶ **What's a keyboard shortcut?** A keyboard shortcut allows you to use the keyboard rather than the mouse to select menu commands. If you see <Ctrl X>, Ctrl+X, [Ctrl X], Ctrl-X, or Ctrl X on the screen or in an instruction manual, it means to hold down the Ctrl key while you press X. For example, Ctrl-X is a keyboard shortcut that cuts out text or objects.

▶ **What if I make a mistake?** Everyone makes mistakes. The first rule is don't panic! Most mistakes are reversible. The following hints and tips should help you recover from mistakes.

> **TERMINOLOGY NOTE**
>
> Mac keyboard shortcuts use the Command key ⌘ and the Option key ⌥ instead of the Ctrl or Alt keys.

What Happened	What to Do
Typed the wrong thing	Use the Backspace key to delete the last characters you typed.
Selected the wrong menu	Press the Esc key to close the menu.
Opened a window you didn't mean to	Click the X button in the upper corner of the window.
Computer has "hung up" and no longer responds to mouse clicks or typed commands	Hold down the Ctrl, Shift, and Esc keys, and then follow instructions to close the program.
Pressed the Enter key in the middle of a sentence	Press the Backspace key to paste the sentence back together.

WORKING WITH WINDOWS SOFTWARE

▶ **How do I start Windows applications?** The Windows 8 Start screen includes tiles for many applications. Just click a tile to start the software of your choice. Or you can type the first few characters of the application's name and then select it from a list.

When using earlier versions of Windows, you can click the Start button to display the Start menu, which includes a list of recently accessed programs. Clicking the All Programs option displays a list of every program installed on your computer.

> ## TRY IT!
>
> **Start Microsoft Paint**
>
> **1.** Use the Start screen or Start button.
>
> **Windows 8:** From the Start screen, type **pa** and then select **Paint**.
>
> **Windows 7:** Click the **Start** button to display the Start menu shown on the right.
>
> Click **All Programs** to display a list of all software installed on your computer.
>
> Click **Accessories**, and then click **Paint**.
>
> **2.** Wait a few seconds for your computer to display the main screen for Microsoft Paint, shown below in Windows 7 (top) and Windows 8 (bottom). Leave Paint open for use with the next TRY IT!.

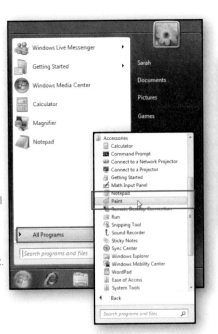

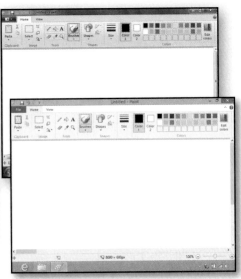

▶ How do I tell the software what I want to do? Word processing, photo editing, and other software designed for use on computers running the Windows operating system is referred to as Windows software. Most Windows software works in a fairly uniform way and uses a similar set of controls.

Each software application appears within a rectangular area called a window, which can include a title bar, a menu bar or ribbon, a workspace, and the various controls shown in Figure 10.

FIGURE 10

The **title bar** displays the title of the software, the name of the current data file, and the window sizing buttons.

The **Minimize button** shrinks the window to a button at the bottom of the screen.

The **Maximize button** stretches the window to fill the screen.

The **Close button** closes the window and exits the program.

A **ribbon**, **menu bar**, or **toolbar** displays the titles of menus and tools that you can click to select commands.

A **scroll bar** can be clicked or dragged to see any material that does not fit in the displayed window.

The **workspace** is the area in which your document or drawing is displayed.

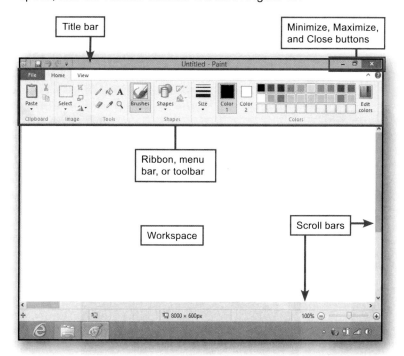

If you're unfamiliar with Windows controls, take a few minutes to complete the steps in the TRY IT! box below.

TRY IT!

Use the toolbar or ribbon

1. As shown below, click the **Brushes** button on the Paint toolbar or ribbon.

2. Move the pointer to the workspace, hold down the left mouse button, and then drag the mouse to paint a shape.

3. Release the mouse button when the shape is complete.

Use the ribbon or menu bar

1. Click the arrow next to **Rotate**, and then click **Flip vertical**.

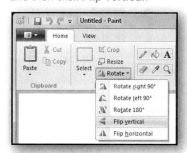

In old versions of Paint, click **Image**, click **Flip/Rotate**, click **Flip Vertical**, then click the **OK** button.

Your shape is now upside down.

Use the sizing buttons

1. Click the 🗕 **Minimize** button.

2. The Paint window shrinks down to a button on the taskbar at the bottom of the screen.

3. Click the taskbar button to make the Paint window reappear.

4. Click the ✖ **Close** button to close the Paint program and remove its window from the screen. If you see a message asking if you want to save changes, click the Don't Save button.

WORKING WITH MAC SOFTWARE

▶ **How do I start programs on the Mac?** When using Mac OS X, you can click icons in the dock to easily start programs. For programs that are not in the dock, you can click the Finder icon and then click the Applications option. If you need to brush up on Mac controls, follow the instructions in the TRY IT! box below.

TRY IT!

Find out which programs are in the dock

1. Position the mouse pointer over each of the icons in the dock and wait for the program name to appear.

Use Finder to start a program

1. Click the Finder icon on the left side of the dock.

2. When the Finder window (similar to the one at right) appears, click the **Applications** option.

3. Double-click the **iCal** option to start the iCal calendar program and display the iCal window shown at right.

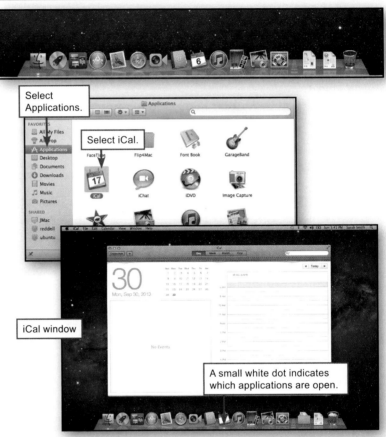

Select Applications.

Select iCal.

iCal window

A small white dot indicates which applications are open.

Use a menu and dialog box

1. Click **iCal** on the menu bar at the top of the screen.

2. Click **Preferences** to display a dialog box.

3. Click the ▼ button next to *Start week on* to change the day to Monday.

4. Click the ⊗ **Close** button to close the Preferences dialog box.

Close a program

1. Click **iCal** on the menu bar.

2. Click **Quit iCal** to close the window and terminate the application.

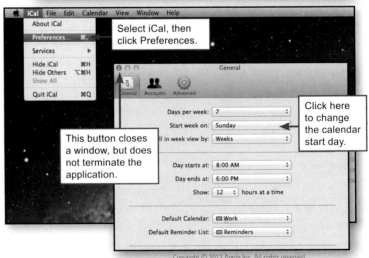

Select iCal, then click Preferences.

This button closes a window, but does not terminate the application.

Click here to change the calendar start day.

HELP

▶ **How can I get help using software?** If you've had problems using software, you're not alone! Everyone has questions at one time or another. Most software offers several sources of help, such as the following:

▶ **Message boxes.** When using software, it is important to pay attention to any message boxes displayed on the screen. Make sure you carefully read the options they present. If the box doesn't seem to apply to what you want to do, click its Cancel button to close it. Otherwise, set the options the way you want them, and then click the OK button to continue.

▶ **User manual.** Whether you're a beginner or a power user, the manual that comes with software can be an excellent resource. User manuals can contain quick-start guides, tutorials, detailed descriptions of menu options, and tips for using features effectively. Many manuals are offered online along with tools you can use to browse through them or look for the answer to a specific question.

▶ **Google it.** If you encounter a software problem, open your browser and use a search engine like Google to enter your question. Be sure to specify the name of the application you are using, along with your computer's operating system.

▶ **Check YouTube.** Connect to YouTube and enter the name of your software. You might find useful videos showing how to use the coolest features.

▶ **Help menu.** The Help menu provides access to on-screen documentation, which can contain detailed instructions, tips, and FAQs. Answers to specific questions can be found by entering search terms, consulting the index, or browsing through a table of contents (Figure 11).

FIGURE 11

Clicking the 🔘 Help button or the Help menu produces a list of help options, where you can enter search terms or browse through topics.

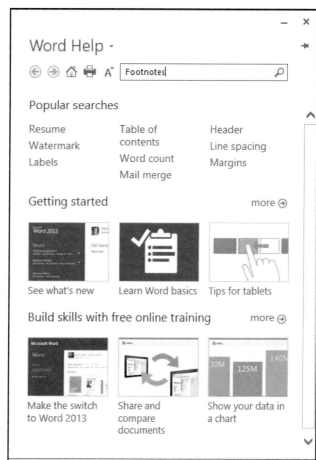

QuickCheck   SECTION A

1. The case that holds a computer's circuitry, memory, and storage devices is called a(n) `System` unit.

2. Instead of using the on/off switch to turn off a computer, you should instead use the Shut Down option. True or false? `True`

3. On the Mac desktop, the `Menu board` displays a row of program icons.

4. Ctrl-X is an example of a keyboard `Short cut`.

5. On a PC the `back Space` key can be used to delete the last character you typed.

▶ CHECK ANSWERS

Documents, Browsers, and E-mail

TO COMPLETE ASSIGNMENTS for your course, you should be able to work with documents, browsers, and e-mail. Section B walks you through the basics.

CREATING DOCUMENTS

▶ **How do I create and save a document?** To create a document, simply type text in the workspace provided by word processing software such as Microsoft Word, OpenOffice Writer, LibreOffice Writer, or Apple iWork Pages. The flashing vertical insertion point (Figure 12) indicates your place in the document. Figure 13 explains how to save a document.

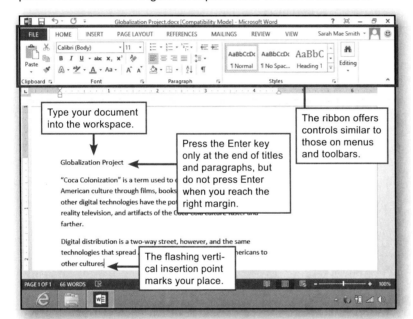

FIGURE 12

When typing text, you can use the following keys to move within a document and make revisions:

▶ **Backspace:** Delete the character to the left of the insertion point. On Macs, hold down the Fn key while pressing the Delete key.

▶ **Delete:** Delete the character to the right of the insertion point.

▶ **Enter:** End a paragraph and begin a new line.

▶ **Arrow keys:** Move the insertion point up, down, right, or left.

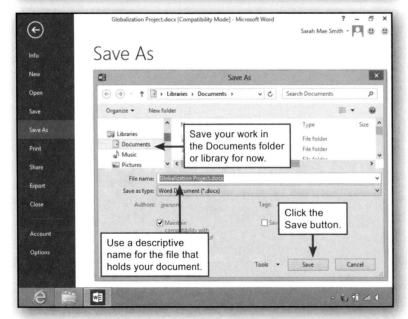

FIGURE 13

It is a good idea to save your document every few minutes, even if it is not finished. When you save a document, use the 💾 Save icon at the top of the screen. Your computer is probably configured to save documents on the hard disk in a library called Documents or a folder called My Documents. There is no need to change that until you gain more experience. File names can be several words long; just do not use the * / \ " ' : symbols in the file name.

▶ How do I print a document? To print a document, simply click the File tab, File menu, or Office button and then select Print. Your computer displays a window containing a series of print options. If you want to print a single copy of your document, these options should be correct, so you can click the Print or OK button to send your document to the printer.

▶ Can I send a document to my instructor? You can e-mail a document by using the Send option accessed from the File tab, File menu, or Office button (Figure 14). To do so, you must know your instructor's e-mail address. Documents that you send along with e-mail messages are referred to as attachments. You'll learn more about e-mail later in the Orientation, but keep this option in mind because it is a handy way to submit assignments, such as projects and term papers.

▶ How do I find my documents again in the future? If you want to revise a document sometime in the future, simply start your word processing software; click the File tab, File menu, or Office button; and then click Open. Your computer should display a list of documents stored in the Documents folder. Locate the one you want to revise and double-click it.

▶ What should I do when I'm done? When you're ready to quit, you can close the document by clicking the Close option from the File tab, File menu, or Office button. When you want to close your word processing software, click the Close button (Windows) or click the program name on the menu bar and then select Quit (Mac).

FIGURE 14

To e-mail a document:
- ▶ In Word 2013, click the File tab, click Share, and then select Email (below).
- ▶ In Word 2010, click the File tab, select Save & Send, and then select Send as Attachment.
- ▶ In Word 2007, click the Office button, point to Send, and then select E-mail.
- ▶ In Word 2003, OpenOffice Writer, or LibreOffice Writer, click File, and then select Send or Send To.
- ▶ In iWork Pages, click the Share tab and then select the e-mail option.

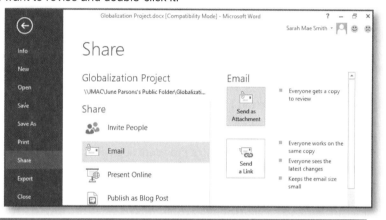

Orientation

TRY IT!

Create a document

1. Windows 8: Click the **Microsoft Word** or **LibreOffice** tile on the Start screen.

Windows 7: Click the **Start** button, and then click the **Microsoft Word** or **LibreOffice** option.

Mac: Click the **Finder** icon, select the **Applications** option, and then click to open iWork Pages or Microsoft Word.

2. Click the word processing workspace to position the insertion point in the upper-left corner.

3. Type a paragraph. Refer to Figure 12 for keys to use while typing and revising your work.

4. When the first paragraph is complete, press the **Enter** key to begin a new paragraph.

5. Type a second paragraph of text.

Save a document

1. Click the Save icon located near the top of the window.

2. Make sure the Documents library or folder is selected, as shown in Figure 13 on the previous page.

3. In the *File name* box, type a name for your document.

4. Click the **Save** button.

5. When the Save As dialog box closes, your document is saved.

Print a document, close it, and exit your word processing application

1. Click the **File** tab, **File** menu, or **Office** button, and then click **Print**.

2. Make sure the page range is set to **All**.

3. Make sure the number of copies is set to **1**.

4. Click the **Print** or **OK** button and wait a few seconds for the printer to produce your document.

5. Close the document by clicking the **File** tab, **File** menu, or **Office** button and then clicking **Close**. The workspace should become blank.

6. Exit your word processing software by clicking the Close button (Windows), or by clicking the program name on the menu bar and then selecting **Quit** (Mac).

INTERNET AND WEB BASICS

▶ What is the Internet? The Internet is the largest computer network in the world, carrying information from one continent to another in the blink of an eye (Figure 15). The computers connected to this network offer many types of resources, such as e-mail, instant messaging, social networking, popular music downloads, and online shopping.

▶ What is the Web? Although some people use the terms *Internet* and *Web* interchangeably, the two are not the same. The Internet refers to a communications network that connects computers all around the globe. The Web—short for World Wide Web—is just one of the many resources available over this communications network.

The Web is a collection of linked and cross-referenced information available for public access. This information is accessible from Web sites located on millions of computers. The information is displayed as a series of screens called Web pages. You'll use the Web for general research and for specific activities designed to accompany this textbook. To use the Web, your computer must have access to the Internet.

▶ How do I access the Internet? Most digital devices can be configured to connect to the Internet over telephone, cell phone, satellite, or cable television systems. Internet access can be obtained from school computer labs, local service providers such as your cable television company, and national Internet service providers such as AOL, AT&T, Comcast, Verizon, and EarthLink.

To expedite your orientation, it is assumed that your computer has Internet access. If it does not, consult your instructor, or ask an experienced computer user to help you get set up.

▶ How do I know if my computer has Internet access? The easiest way to find out if your computer can access the Internet is to try it. You can quickly find out if you have Internet access by starting software called a browser that's designed to display Web pages.

Browser software called Internet Explorer is supplied with Microsoft Windows. Mac OS X includes a browser called Safari. Other browsers, such as Firefox and Chrome, are also available. Follow the steps in the TRY IT! box to start your browser.

HOW TO USE A WEB BROWSER AND SEARCH ENGINE

▶ How do I use a browser? A browser lets you enter a unique Web page address called a URL, such as *www.google.com*. You can also jump from one Web page to another by using links. Links are usually underlined; and when you position the arrow-shaped mouse pointer over a link, it changes to a hand shape.

FIGURE 15

The Internet communications network stretches around the globe.

Courtesy of Stephen G. Eick

TRY IT!

Start your browser

1. Click the [icons] icon for your browser. It is usually located on the Start screen, near the Start button, or on the dock.

2. Your computer should soon display the browser window.

If your computer displays a *Connect to* box, click the **Dial** button to establish a dial-up connection over your telephone line.

You'll need to cancel the browser command and consult an experienced computer user if:

- Your computer displays a "working off line" message.
- Your computer displays an Internet Connection Wizard box.

Although browsers offer many features, you can get along quite well using the basic controls shown in Figure 16.

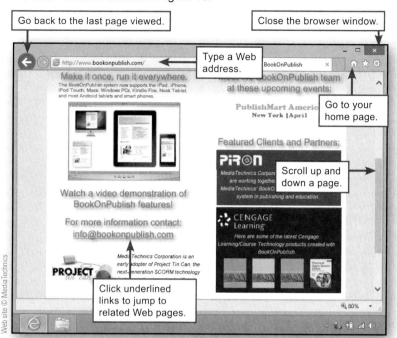

Go back to the last page viewed.

Close the browser window.

Type a Web address.

Go to your home page.

Scroll up and down a page.

Click underlined links to jump to related Web pages.

Web site © MediaTechnics

FIGURE 16

Using a Browser

A full Web address might look like this:
http://www.mediatechnicscorp.com
It is not necessary to type the *http://*. So to access the MediaTechnics Corporation page shown here, you would type:
www.mediatechnicscorp.com
When typing a Web address, do not use any spaces, and copy uppercase and lowercase letters exactly.

▶ **How do I find specific information on the Web?** If you're looking for information and don't know the Web site where it might be located, you can use a search engine to find it. Follow the steps in the TRY IT! box to "google it" by using the Google search engine.

TRY IT!

Use a search engine

1. Make sure the browser window is open.

2. Click the Address box and type:

3. Press the **Enter** key. Your browser displays the Web page for the Google search engine.

4. Click the blank search box and then type **national parks**.

5. Press the **Enter** key. Google displays a list of Web pages that relate to national parks.

6. Click the underlined **U.S. National Park Service** link. Your browser displays the Park Service's home page.

7. Leave your browser open for the next TRY IT!.

Type **national parks**.

Select the link to *www.nps.gov*.

Search results © 2012 Google

Courtesy of the U.S. Park Service

▶ What are the best sources of information on the Web?

The best sources of information are easy to access, dependable, and preferably free. Sites such as Wikipedia, Answers.com, WhatIs.com, and HowStuffWorks are great sources for general information and researching topics for computer courses.

When you're looking for information on the Web, remember that virtually anyone can post anything. Consequently, some information you encounter might not be accurate.

To check the quality of information provided by a Web site, you can cross-check facts with other sites. Be sure to check when the material was posted or updated to determine if it is current. You might also consider the information source. Blogs, tweets, Facebook posts, and YouTube videos often express opinions rather than facts.

▶ How does Wikipedia work?

Wikipedia is an encyclopedia that is written and maintained by the people who use it. More than 23 million articles on a vast range of topics have been submitted and updated by users, many of them experts. Wikipedia information tends to be accurate because users are continually reading the articles and correcting inaccurate or biased information. However, some vandalism occurs and from time to time a few articles contain false or misleading information.

Most Wikipedia articles include a View history tab that tracks changes. Check the date of the last change to determine if the information is current. Articles also include a Discussion tab that can help you spot controversial aspects of the information. Use the TRY IT! below to see how Wikipedia works.

TRY IT!

Check out Wikipedia

1. In the Address bar of your browser, type **www.wikipedia.org** and then press the **Enter** key.

2. When the Wikipedia window appears, enter **cyberspace** in the search box and then press **Enter**.

3. Read a bit of the article to get an idea of its scope and detail. Do you detect any bias in the article?

4. Click the **View history** tab. Look at the last few updates. Does this article seem up to date?

5. Click the **Discussion** tab. What is the status of the article? Does it contain controversial statements? Can you envision how you might use Google or other Web resources to explore specific controversies?

6. Click the **Article** tab to return to the Cyberspace article.

7. You can leave your browser open for the next TRY IT!.

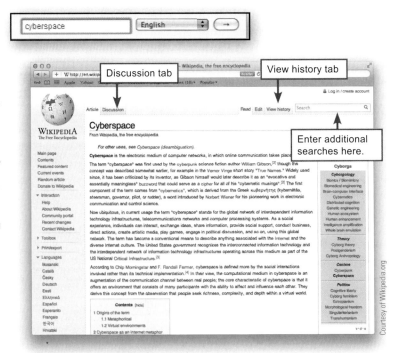

WORKING WITH E-MAIL

▶ **What is e-mail?** E-mail is a form of communication that relies on computer networks, such as the Internet, to transmit messages from one computer to another. Like regular mail, e-mail messages are sent to a mailbox where they are kept until the recipient retrieves them. Messages might arrive at their destination within seconds, or might not arrive for a few hours. Once sent, e-mail messages cannot be recalled.

▶ **What do I need to use e-mail?** To send and receive e-mail, you need an Internet connection, an e-mail account, and software that enables you to compose, read, and delete e-mail messages. An e-mail account consists of an e-mail address (Figure 17), a password, and a mailbox. You can usually obtain an e-mail account from your Internet service provider, your school, or a Webmail provider, such as Hotmail, Yahoo! Mail, or Gmail.

Webmail providers store your mail online. To access your mail, simply use your browser. In contrast, local mail, such as Microsoft Outlook, transfers mail to your computer and requires you to use special e-mail software instead of a browser.

▶ **How do I get a Webmail account?** Registering for a Webmail account is easy and many online e-mail providers offer free basic service. Work with the TRY IT! below to see how.

FIGURE 17

E-mail Addresses

An e-mail address consists of a user ID followed by an @ symbol and the name of a computer that handles e-mail accounts. Ask your instructor for his or her e-mail address. It is likely similar to the following:

instructor@school.edu

When typing an e-mail address, use all lowercase letters and do not use any spaces.

TRY IT!

Get a Web-based e-mail account

1. In the Address bar of your browser, enter **www.gmail.com**.

2. When the Gmail window appears, click the button labeled **CREATE AN ACCOUNT**.

3. Follow the directions to enter your first name, last name, and username.

4. The login name you select is checked for uniqueness. If it is already in use, you'll have to try a different one.

5. When you've selected a valid username, continue down the page to create a password. Try not to use a name, a date, or any dictionary word as your password.

6. Continue down the page to complete the rest of the registration form.

7. Before finalizing your registration, review the information you've entered and jot down your login name and password.

8. Read the Terms of Service. If you agree, click the **Next step** button. That's it! You now have a Gmail account.

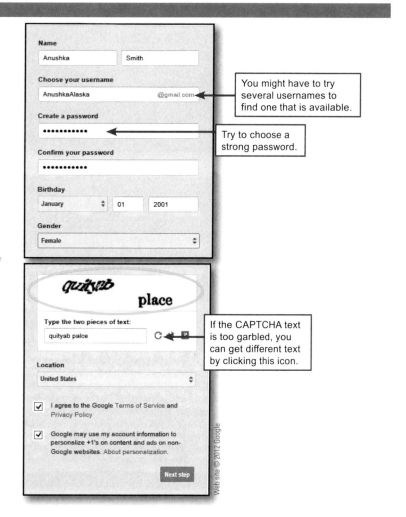

You might have to try several usernames to find one that is available.

Try to choose a strong password.

If the CAPTCHA text is too garbled, you can get different text by clicking this icon.

▶ **Is Webmail better than local e-mail?** Both Web-based and local e-mail have their advantages and disadvantages. Webmail accounts are definitely easier to set up and you can use them from any computer with an Internet connection. Webmail accounts are also ideal for "throw-away" accounts.

▶ **What is a throw-away e-mail account?** Whether you use local mail or Webmail for your regular correspondence, you might consider creating one or two throw-away accounts for occasions when you have to give an e-mail address, but you don't want any continued correspondence from that source. Later in the chapter, you'll learn more about how e-mail scams and online marketing contribute to all the junk e-mail you receive. Your throw-away e-mail address can become the recipient for lots of those messages, and eventually you can simply delete the throw-away account and all the junk it contains.

▶ **How do I create and send an e-mail message?** Many e-mail systems are available, and each uses slightly different software, making it impossible to cover all options in this short orientation. You might want to enlist the aid of an experienced computer user to help you get started. The steps in the TRY IT! box pertain to Gmail, but other e-mail packages work in a similar way.

E-MAIL PRIVACY

E-mail messages are not necessarily private; their contents might be seen during system maintenance or repair, and commercial e-mail archives are subject to search by government agencies.

Free Web-based mail is typically searched as you write it by digital bots that look for keywords, like *vacation* or *pet*, to display related advertising. If you want more privacy, consider private e-mail providers and local e-mail software.

TRY IT!

Create and send e-mail

1. If Gmail is not open, open your browser and type **www.gmail.com** in the address box. Log in to your Gmail account.

2. Click the **Compose** button to display a form like the one below.

3. Follow steps 4 through 6 as shown below.

7. When your message is complete, click the **SEND** button and Gmail sends the message.

8. You can continue to experiment with e-mail. When done, use the **Sign out** option under the link for your account (circled), then close your browser.

Note: With some local e-mail configurations, the Send button places the e-mail in an Outbox and you have to click the **Send/Receive** button on the toolbar to ship the message out from your computer.

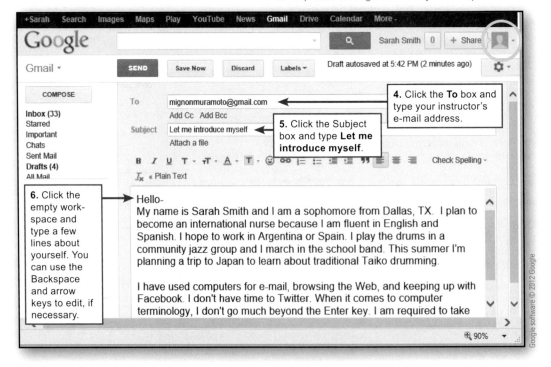

▶ How do I get my e-mail?

As with sending mail, the way you get mail depends on your e-mail system. In general, clicking the Send/Receive button collects your mail from the network and stores it in your Inbox. Your e-mail software displays a list of your messages. The new ones are usually highlighted or shown in bold type. You can click any message to open it, read it, and reply to it, as shown in Figure 18.

▶ How do I log off?

When working with a Webmail account, it is important to use the Log out or Sign out link before you close your browser. Taking this extra step makes your e-mail less vulnerable to hackers.

FIGURE 18

When e-mail software displays your Inbox, you can:

▶ Open a message and read it.

▶ Reply to a message.

▶ Delete unwanted messages (a good idea to minimize the size of your mailbox).

▶ Forward a message to someone else.

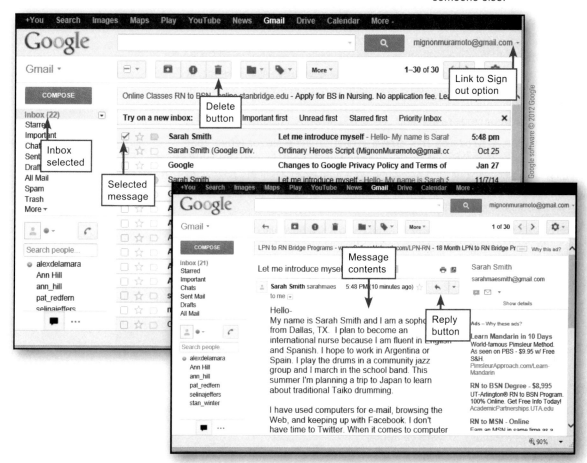

QuickCheck

1. Documents that you send along with e-mail messages are referred to as ☐ *attachment*.

2. Popular ☐ *browser* software includes Internet Explorer, Chrome, and Firefox.

3. When looking for information on the Web, you can use a(n) ☐ *search* engine to produce a list of links to Web pages that might contain the information you seek.

4. An e-mail ☐ *address* looks something like student@school.edu.

5. To access Webmail, you use a browser; but to access ☐ *local* e-mail, you use e-mail software such as Microsoft Outlook.

 CHECK ANSWERS

Security and Privacy

AS WITH MOST OTHER facets of modern life, the digital world has its share of troublemakers, scam artists, and identity thieves. Section C offers some tips on navigating through the sometimes rough neighborhoods of cyberspace, while keeping your data safe and your identity private.

SECURING YOUR DIGITAL DEVICES AND DATA

▶ What's at risk if my computer or phone is stolen? The value of a stolen computer or phone is not so much in the hardware as in the data it contains. With stolen data such as your bank account numbers and PINs, a thief can wipe out your checking and savings accounts. With your credit card numbers, a thief can go on a spending spree. Even worse, a criminal can use stolen data to assume your identity, run up debts, get into legal difficulties, ruin your credit rating, and cause you no end of trouble.

▶ How can I protect my data from theft? Never leave your devices unattended. If a thief steals your computer or phone, you can make it difficult to access your data by setting up a password. Until the password is entered, your data is off limits. Thieves will not be able to get beyond the login screen and should not be able to easily access your data.

Use security tools to protect your phone. Keep it locked while not in use and consider subscribing to a tracking service that allows you to use a Web site to find your phone, lock it, or erase it.

Many new computers are shipped with a standard administrator password that everyone knows. If you are the only person using your computer, you can use the administrator account for your day-to-day computing, but create a secure password (Figure 19) for this account as soon as you can.

Your computer might also include a preset guest account with a nonsecure password such as *guest*. You should disable this guest account or assign it a secure password.

FIGURE 19

To create a secure password:

> ▶ Use at least eight characters, mixing numbers with letters, as in *2by4lumber*.
>
> ▶ Do not use your name, the name of a family member, or your pet's name.
>
> ▶ Do not use a word that can be found in the dictionary.
>
> ▶ Do not forget your password!

TRY IT!

Check the accounts on your computer

1. Access user accounts.

Windows 8: From the Start screen, type **c** and then select **Control Panel**. Select **User Accounts** and then select **Manage another account**.

Windows 7: Click the **Start** button, and then select **Control Panel**. Select **User Accounts and Family Safety**, select **User Accounts**, and then select **Manage another account**. (You might be required to enter an administrator password.)

Mac: Click the **Apple** icon, select **System Preferences**, and then select **Accounts**.

2. Check the password protection on all accounts. If you are working on a school lab computer, do not make changes to the account settings. If you are using your own computer, click the Administrator account and make sure it has a secure password.

AVOIDING VIRUSES

▶ **What's so bad about viruses?** The term *virus* has a technical meaning, but is loosely used when referring to malicious programs that circulate on infected downloads, in e-mail attachments, and on the Internet. This malware, as it is sometimes called, can steal your data, destroy files, or create network traffic jams. It might display an irritating message to announce its presence, or it might surreptitiously spread itself to various files or mail itself out to everyone in your e-mail address book.

After a virus takes up residence in a computer or phone, it is often difficult to disinfect all your files. Rather than wait for a virus attack, you can take steps to keep your digital devices virus free.

▶ **How can I steer clear of malware?** It helps to avoid risky behaviors, such as downloading pirated software, opening e-mail attachments from unknown senders, installing random social networking plug-ins, installing non-approved apps, and participating in illegal file sharing.

Antivirus software protects digital devices from malware (Figure 20). Because fewer viruses target Macs, OS X users who don't engage in risky online activities sometimes opt to work without antivirus software.

If you use antivirus software, configure it to run continuously whenever your computer is on. You should make sure your antivirus software is set to scan for viruses in incoming files and e-mail messages. At least once a week, your antivirus software should run a full system check to make sure every file on your computer is virus free.

As new viruses emerge, your antivirus software needs to update its virus definition file. It gets this update as a Web download. If you've selected the auto update option, your computer should automatically receive updates as they become available.

FIGURE 20

Popular Antivirus Software

Windows Defender
Norton AntiVirus
McAfee AntiVirus Plus
Kaspersky Anti-Virus
F-Secure Anti-virus
Panda Antivirus
Trend Micro Antivirus+
AVG AntiVirus FREE
Avast! Free Antivirus

TRY IT!

Get familiar with your antivirus software

1. Look for antivirus software (refer to Figure 20 for a list). In Windows 7, click the **Start** button, and then select **All Programs**. In Windows 8, scroll through the tiles on the Start screen. On the Mac, use **Finder** to access the Applications folder.

Can't find any? If you are using your own computer and it doesn't seem to have antivirus software, you can connect to an antivirus supplier's Web site and download it.

2. Open your antivirus software. Each antivirus program has unique features.

3. Explore your antivirus software to find out if it offers options to:

• Scan incoming e-mail.

• Run continuously in the background—a feature sometimes called Auto Protect.

• Block malicious scripts.

4. Check the date of your last full system scan. If it was more than one week ago, you should check the settings that schedule antivirus scans.

5. Check the date when your computer last received virus definitions. If it was more than one week ago, you should make sure your antivirus software is configured to receive automatic live updates.

Windows Defender is included with Windows 8. You can access it from the Start screen by typing **w**.

PREVENTING INTRUSIONS

▶ **Is the Internet risky?** The Internet offers lots of cool stuff: music, movies, online shopping and banking, and much more. Most Internet offerings are legitimate, but some downloads contain viruses, and shady characters called hackers control programs that lurk about waiting to infiltrate your digital devices. If a hacker gains access to your phone or computer, he or she can view your files and steal personal information.

An infiltrated computer can be used as a launching platform for viruses and network-jamming attacks, or turned into a server for pornography and other unsavory material. Hackers have even found ways to turn thousands of infiltrated computers into "zombies," link them together, and carry out coordinated attacks to disrupt online access to Microsoft, Bank of America, and other Internet businesses.

▶ **How do hackers gain access?** Intruders gain access by exploiting security flaws in your device's operating system, browser, and e-mail software. Companies such as Microsoft, Apple, and HTC constantly produce software updates to fix these flaws. As part of your overall security plan, you should download and install security updates as they become available.

▶ **Do I need a firewall?** Firewall software and Internet security suites, such as those listed in Figure 21, provide a protective barrier between a computer and the Internet. If your computer is directly connected to the Internet, it should have active firewall software. If your computer connects to a local area network for Internet access, the network should have a device called a router to block infiltration attempts.

When a firewall is active, it watches for potentially disruptive incoming data called probes. When a probe is discovered, your firewall displays a warning and asks what to do. If the source looks legitimate, you can let it through; if not, you should block it (Figure 22).

▶ **Where do I get a firewall?** Mac OS X and Windows include built-in firewalls. Third-party Internet security suites also include firewall modules.

FIGURE 21

Popular Firewall Software and Internet Security Suites

Emsisoft Online Armor

McAfee Internet Security

ZoneAlarm Free Firewall

Norton Internet Security

Mac OS X Firewall

Agnitum Outpost Firewall

Windows Firewall

Comodo Firewall

Kaspersky Internet Security

Trend Micro Internet Security

FIGURE 22

When your firewall software encounters new or unusual activity, it asks you what to do.

TRY IT!

Check your Windows computer's firewall

1. Access the **Control Panel** and then click the **Windows Firewall** link.

2. If the Windows firewall is not active, you should check to see if a third-party firewall is protecting your computer. To do so in Windows 7, click the **Start** button, select **All Programs**, and then look through the program list for firewalls such as those in Figure 21. In Windows 8, scroll through the tiles on the Start screen. If you find a firewall listed, start it and explore to see if it has been activated.

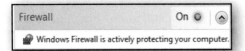

Check your Mac computer's firewall

1. Click the **Apple** icon, and then select **System Preferences**.

2. Click the **Security** icon, and then click the **Firewall** button.

3. If the firewall is off, click the **Start** button if you want to activate it.

4. If the Start button is grayed out, click the lock at the bottom of the page and then enter an administrator name and password.

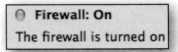

SAFE BROWSING

▶ **Are some Web sites dangerous?** When you access Web sites, data is transferred to your device and displayed by your browser. Most of this data is harmless, but Web-based malware and spyware have the potential to search your device for passwords and credit card numbers, monitor your Web-browsing habits for marketing purposes, block your access to legitimate Web sites, or surreptitiously use your device as a staging area for illicit activities.

▶ **How can I block spyware?** The first line of defense is to never click pop-up ads—especially those with dire warnings, such as the ad in Figure 23, about your computer being infected by a virus or spyware! To close an ad, right-click its button on the taskbar at the bottom of your screen, and then select the Close option from the menu that appears.

Most browsers can be configured to block spyware and pop-up ads. Your antivirus software might offer similar options.

▶ **What other steps can I take to browse the Web safely?** Browsers include security features. You should take some time to become familiar with them. For example, Internet Explorer allows you to specify how you want it to deal with potentially dangerous ActiveX components, HTML scripts, spyware, and cookies. If you don't want to be bothered by these details, however, Internet Explorer offers several pre-defined configurations for Medium, Medium-High, and High security. Most Internet Explorer users set security and privacy options to Medium-High.

Your browser might also offer features such as private browsing, do not track, and delete browser history that can make your Web experience safer and more private.

FIGURE 23

Some pop-up ads contain fake warnings about viruses, spyware, and intrusion attempts.

> **WARNING! Your computer may be infected with spyware**
>
> If your computer has been running slower than usual, it may be infected with adware or spyware! To scan your comptuer for such infections, click OK below.
>
> Cancel   OK

TRY IT!

Check Internet security and privacy options

1. Start your browser and look for its security settings.

Internet Explorer: Click **Tools**, and then select **Internet Options**. Click the **Security** tab. Normally, your security setting should be Medium High. Click the **Privacy** tab. Your privacy setting should be Medium. If your version of IE offers a Pop-up Blocker, make sure its box contains a check mark so that it is activated.

Firefox: Click the **Firefox** tab or menu, select **Options** or **Preferences**, and then click **Content**. Make sure there is a check mark in the box for **Block pop-up windows**.

Safari: Click **Safari** on the menu bar. Make sure there is a check mark next to **Block Pop-Up Windows**.

Chrome: Click the **Chrome menu** icon, select **Settings**, and then click **Show advanced settings**. Click the **Content settings** button. Under Pop-ups, make sure that the **Do not allow** option is selected.

2. Use your browser's Help to find out if the following features are available:

Private browsing

Do not track

Delete browser history

PROTECTING E-COMMERCE TRANSACTIONS

▶ **Is online shopping safe?** Online shopping is generally safe. From time to time, shoppers encounter fake storefronts designed to look like legitimate merchants but that are actually set up to steal credit card information. You can avoid these fakes by making sure you enter correctly spelled URLs when connecting to your favorite shopping sites.

▶ **How safe is my credit card information when I'm shopping online?** Online shopping has about the same level of risk as using your credit card for a telephone order or giving it to a server when you've finished eating in a restaurant.

That's not to say that credit cards are risk free. Credit cards are surprisingly vulnerable both online and off. Anyone who handles your card can copy the card number, jot down the expiration date, and try to make unauthorized charges. Thieves can break in to merchant computers that store order information. Thieves might even pick up your credit card information from discarded order forms. Despite these risks, we continue to use credit cards.

Many people are concerned about their credit card data getting intercepted as it travels over the Internet. As you wrap up an online purchase and submit your credit card information, it is transmitted from your computer to the merchant's computer. Software called a packet sniffer, designed for legitimately monitoring network traffic, can be used by unscrupulous hackers to intercept credit card numbers and other data traveling over the Internet.

▶ **How can I keep my credit card number confidential?** When you submit credit card information, make sure the merchant provides a secure connection for transporting data. Normally, a secure connection is activated when you're in the final phases of checking out—as you enter your shipping and credit card information into a form and click a Submit button to send it.

A secure connection encrypts your data. Even if your credit card number is intercepted, it cannot be deciphered and used. To make sure you have a secure connection, look for the lock icon. The Address box should also display a URL that begins with *https://*.

TRY IT!

Identify a secure connection

1. Start your browser and connect to the site **bookstore.gpo.gov**.

2. Select any book and place it in your online shopping cart.

3. Click the **Go to Checkout** button to reach step 1 of the checkout process.

4. At the checkout screen, do you see any evidence that you're using a secure connection?

5. Close your browser so that you don't complete the transaction.

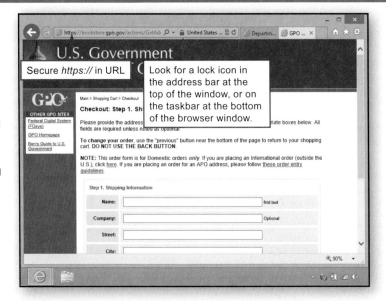

AVOIDING E-MAIL SCAMS

▶ **What are e-mail scams?** From time to time, you hear about con artists who have bilked innocent consumers out of their life savings. The Internet has its share of con artists, too, who run e-mail scams designed to collect money and confidential information from unsuspecting victims. E-mail scams are usually distributed in mass mailings called spam.

▶ **What do I need to know about spam?** The Internet makes it easy and cheap to send out millions of e-mail solicitations. In the United States, the CAN-SPAM Act requires mass-mail messages to be labeled with a valid subject line. Recipients are supposed to be provided with a way to opt out of receiving future messages.

Legitimate merchants and organizations comply with the law when sending product announcements, newsletters, and other messages. Unscrupulous spammers ignore the law and try to disguise their solicitations as messages from your friends, chat room participants, or co-workers (Figure 24).

FIGURE 24

Some e-mail systems use spam filters to flag suspected spam by adding [SPAM] to the subject line. Spam filters are not perfect, however. Some spam is not flagged and occasionally legitimate mail is mistaken for spam.

▶ **Is spam dangerous?** Some mass mailings contain legitimate information, including daily or weekly newsletters to which you've subscribed. Many mass mailings, however, advertise illegal products. Others are outright scams to get you to download a virus, divulge your bank account numbers, or send in money for products you'll never receive.

Beware of e-mail containing offers that seem just too good to be true. Messages about winning the sweepstakes or pleas for help to transfer money out of Nigeria (Figure 25) are scams to raid your bank account.

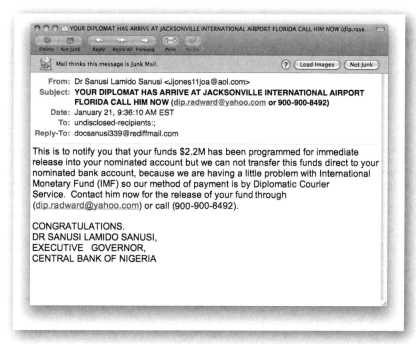

FIGURE 25

Many variations of this African money-transfer fraud—complete with deliberate grammatical errors—have circulated on the Internet for years. Victims who respond to these preposterous e-mails have found their bank accounts raided, their credit ratings destroyed, and their reputations ruined. According to the FBI, some victims have even been kidnapped!

▶ What's phishing? Phishing (pronounced "fishing") is a scam that arrives in your e-mailbox looking like official correspondence from a major company, such as Microsoft, PayPal, eBay, UPS, Yahoo!, or AOL. The e-mail message is actually from an illegitimate source and is designed to trick you into divulging confidential information or downloading a virus.

Links in the e-mail message often lead to a Web site that looks official, where you are asked to enter confidential information such as your credit card number, Social Security number, or bank account number.

The following are examples of phishing scams you should be aware of:

▶ A message from Microsoft with an attachment that supposedly contains a security update for Microsoft Windows. Downloading the attachment infects your computer with a virus.

▶ A message that appears to come from PayPal, complete with official-looking logos, that alerts you to a problem with your account. When you click the Billing Center link and enter your account information, it is transmitted to a hacker's computer.

▶ A message from UPS or the postal service informing you that a package cannot be delivered until you click a link to print or download a mailing label. Clicking the link installs malware on your computer.

▶ How do I avoid e-mail scams? If your e-mail software provides spam filters, you can use them to block some unsolicited mail from your e-mailbox. Spam filters are far from perfect, however, so don't assume everything that gets through is legitimate. Use your judgment before opening any e-mail message or attachment.

Never reply to a message that you suspect to be fraudulent. If you have a question about its legitimacy, check whether it's on a list of known scams. Never click a link provided in an e-mail message to manage any account information. Instead, use your browser to go directly to the company's Web site and access your account as usual. Microsoft never sends updates as attachments. To obtain Microsoft updates, go to the Control Panel and click the Windows Update option.

TRY IT!

Arm yourself against e-mail scams

1. Start your browser and connect to the site **www.millersmiles.co.uk**. Browse through the list of recent phishing attacks.

2. Open your e-mail software and find out if it includes spam filters. You can usually find this information by clicking **Help** on the menu bar and then typing **spam filter** in the search box.

3. Explore how your e-mail software handles messages that might be spam. Can you create customized spam filters, or does your software have automatic filtering?

4. Spam filters sometimes catch legitimate mail and group it with junk mail. Check your Trash, Spam, or Junk folder. Does it contain any legitimate messages that were automatically labeled as spam and blocked from your Inbox?

PROTECTING YOUR PRIVACY

▶ **How much information about me has been collected online?** Information about you is stored in many places and has the potential to be consolidated by government agencies, private businesses, and criminals. Some databases are legitimate—those maintained by credit bureaus and medical insurance companies, for example. By law, you have the right to ask for a copy of these records and correct any errors you find. Many other databases, such as those maintained at e-commerce sites and those illegally acquired by hackers, are not accessible, and you have no way of checking the data they contain.

▶ **What's the problem with having my personal information in a few databases?** The problem is that many companies share their databases with third parties. Your personal data might start in a single legitimate database, but that data can be sold to a continuous chain of third parties who use it to generate mass mailings that clog up your Inbox with marketing ploys, unwanted newsletters, and promotions for useless products.

▶ **Can I control who collects information about me?** To some extent, you can limit your exposure to future data collection by supplying personal data only when absolutely necessary. When filling out online forms, consider whether you want to or need to provide your real name and address. Avoid providing merchants with your e-mail address even if you're promised a $5 coupon or preferred customer status. A small reward might not be worth the aggravation of an Inbox brimming with spam and e-mail scams. You should also be careful when using public computers (Figure 26).

▶ **Can I opt out?** Some mass e-mailings give you a chance to opt out so that you don't receive future messages. Opting out is a controversial practice. On mailings from reputable businesses, clicking an opt-out link might very well discontinue unwanted e-mail messages. However, opting out does not necessarily remove your name from the database, which could be sold to a third party that disregards your opt-out request.

Scammers use opt-out links to look for "live" targets, perhaps in a database that contains lots of fake or outdated e-mail addresses. By clicking one of these opt-out links, you've played right into the hands of unscrupulous hackers—this action lets them know that your e-mail address is valid.

Most experts recommend that you never use opt-out links, but instead go to the sender's Web site and try to opt out from there. If you are tempted to use an opt-out link directly from an e-mail message, carefully examine the link's URL to make sure you'll connect to a legitimate Web site.

FIGURE 26

Using public computers poses security risks from people looking over your shoulder, spyware that collects your keystrokes, and the footprint you leave behind in cookies and temporary Internet pages.

AP Photo/Darren Hauck

To minimize risks when using public computers:

▶ Be sure to log out from all sites and close all browser windows before quitting.

▶ Delete cookies and browser history.

▶ Avoid using public computers for financial transactions such as filing your taxes.

▶ Reboot the computer before you quit.

▶ If you're using your own portable apps from a USB drive, make sure your computer is running antivirus software.

TRY IT!

Check your privacy

1. Start your browser and go googling by connecting to **www.google.com**. Enter your name in the Search box. What turns up?

2. Connect to **www.peoplefinders.com**. Enter your name and state of residence. Click the **Search** button. Notice all the information that's offered.

3. Connect to **www.ciadata.com** and scroll down the page to view the kind of information anyone can obtain about you for less than $100.

4. Read about your rights to view credit reports at the Federal Trade Commission site:

www.ftc.gov/bcp/menus/consumer/credit/rights.shtm

Orientation

SAFE SOCIAL NETWORKING

▶ **What's the risk at sites like Twitter, Facebook, and LinkedIn?** A prolific Twitter user with 650 followers had a nasty surprise one morning. She discovered that private messages she'd sent to specific friends were showing up on her public feed for everyone to see. Although this is an extreme example of how things can go wrong on social networking sites, embarrassing incidents are all too frequent.

The more information you reveal at social networking sites, the more you increase your susceptibility to identity theft, stalking, and other embarrassing moments, such as when a prospective employer happens to see those not-so-flattering photos of you on your spring break.

▶ **How do I stay safe and keep my stuff private when using social networking sites?** The first rule of social networking safety is never share your Social Security number, phone number, or home address. Unfortunately, everyone has access to Web-based tools for finding addresses and phone numbers, so withholding that information provides only a thin security blanket.

Most social networking sites depend on references and friends-of-friends links to establish a trusted circle of contacts. *Trusted* is the key word here. When using social networking sites, make sure you understand what information is being shared with friends, what information is available to strangers on the site, and what data is available publicly to search engines.

Be careful about revealing personal information at social networking sites, blogs, chat rooms, and Twitter. Many online participants are not who they appear to be. Some people are just having fun with fantasy identities, but others are trying to con people by telling hard luck stories and faking illnesses. Resist the temptation to meet face to face with people you've met online without taking precautions, such as taking along a group of friends.

▶ **And what about the site itself?** Social networking sites, like any online business, are always looking for ways to make a profit. Every participant is a valuable commodity in a database that can be used for marketing and research. Before you become a member, read the site's privacy policy to see how your personal data could be used. Remember, however, that privacy policies can change, especially if a site goes out of business and sells its assets.

You should also find out if you can remove your data from a site. Although most sites allow you to deactivate your information, some sites never actually remove your personal information from their databases, leaving it open to misuse in the future.

> **TRY IT!**

Check your social networking sites

1. Log in to any social networking site you use.

2. Locate the site's privacy policy and read it. Are you comfortable with the ways in which the site protects your personal information?

3. If you are not familiar with the site's options for designating who can view your personal data, find out how you can limit its public exposure.

4. Find out if you can delete your data from the site.

ONLINE PRIVACY AND SAFETY GUIDELINES

▶ **What should I do?** Online safety and online privacy are important aspects of computer use today. The average consumer must remain constantly vigilant to detect if his or her personal data has been misused or has fallen into the wrong hands.

Cyberthreats are becoming more troubling. Who would imagine that the webcam at the top of your laptop computer screen could be remotely controlled by hackers to capture video of you without your knowledge?

If you recognize that anything on the Web or in e-mail messages is not necessarily private, you've got the right outlook. You can use the guidelines in Figure 27 to keep track of your personal data and stay safe online.

FIGURE 27

Online Privacy and Safety Guidelines

▶ Use a password to protect your data in case your computer is stolen.

▶ Don't leave your digital devices unattended in public places.

▶ Run antivirus software and keep it updated.

▶ Install software service packs and security patches as they become available, but make sure they are legitimate.

▶ Install and activate firewall software, especially if your computer is directly connected to the Internet by an ISDN, DSL, satellite, or cable connection.

▶ Do not publish or post personal information, such as your physical address, passwords, Social Security number, phone number, or account numbers, on your Web site, in your online resume, in your blog, or in other online documents.

▶ Be wary of contacts you make in public chat rooms and social networking sites.

▶ Don't click pop-up ads.

▶ Install and activate antispyware and ad-blocking software.

▶ Do not reply to spam.

▶ Ignore e-mail offers that seem too good to be true.

▶ Establish a throw-away e-mail account and use it when you have to provide your e-mail address to marketers and other entities whom you don't want to regularly correspond with.

▶ Make sure you control who has access to the data you post at social networking sites.

▶ Do not submit data to a social networking site until you've read its privacy policy and have made sure that you can remove your data when you no longer want to participate.

▶ Avoid using opt-out links in mass mailings unless you are certain the sender is legitimate.

▶ When using public computers, avoid financial transactions if possible. Make sure you log out from password-protected sites. Delete cookies and Internet history. Reboot the computer at the end of your session.

▶ Regard e-mail messages as postcards that can be read by anyone, so be careful what you write!

▶ Cover the webcam on your computer with a sticky note when it is not in use.

▶ Use the private browsing feature offered by your browser when you don't want to store a record of sites you've visited.

▶ Activate your browser's Do Not Track feature if you don't want Web sites to collect information about your visit.

QuickCheck

1. Internet security suites usually include antivirus and antispyware tools. True or false? ☐ True

2. ☐ Anti Virus software can block intrusion attempts such as hacker probes.

3. Most Web browsers include settings for blocking pop-up ads. True or false? ☐ True

4. E-mail scams are usually distributed in mass mailings called ☐ .

5. Using opt-out links is the most secure and dependable way to reduce the amount of spam you receive. True or false? ☐ True

 CHECK ANSWERS

NP2014 Online CourseMate

THE INTERNET offers access to information that's useful to just about everyone, and New Perspectives students are no exception. When you purchase access to the New Perspectives 2014 Online CourseMate, you'll find targeted learning materials to help you understand key concepts and prepare for exams.

COURSEMATE RESOURCES

▶ **What's on CourseMate?** The New Perspectives 2014 CourseMate includes a digital version of your textbook loaded with videos, software tours, and activities. The CourseMate menu includes even more goodies such as quizzes, games, and audio files that you can download to your iPod or other portable device. Figure 28 highlights the features you'll find on the NP2014 CourseMate.

FIGURE 28

NP2014 CourseMate Features

eBook
The NP2014 interactive, multimedia eBook gives you access to your textbook from any computer connected to the Internet.

Detailed Objectives
Access an expanded version of the Learning Objectives that are included at the beginning of each chapter.

Pre-Quiz
Before starting a chapter, take the pre-quiz to find out how to best focus your study time.

TechTerm Flashcards
Make sure you understand all of the technical terms presented in the chapter.

Audio Overview
Listen to a five-minute audio presentation of chapter highlights on your computer or download the files to your MP3 player to study on the go.

Audio Flashcards
Interact with downloadable audio flashcards to review key terms.

Projects
Get ideas for term papers, group projects, and assignments.

Quizzes
Check your understanding and ability to apply concepts.

Student Edition Labs
Get hands-on practice with key topics presented in a chapter.

Games
Have some fun while refreshing your memory about key concepts that might appear on the exam.

Glossary
Get a quick overview of all the key terms presented in each chapter.

COURSEMATE ACCESS

▶ How do I access the NP2014 CourseMate? CourseMate is hosted on the CengageBrain Web site, *www.cengagebrain.com*. The first time you connect to CengageBrain, sign up for an account. When you have completed the short registration process, you can search for materials by logging in (Figure 29).

FIGURE 29

Open your browser to connect to CengageBrain.

▶ How do I add NP2014 to my dashboard? After you've logged in to CengageBrain, enter the ISBN for your book. If you have an access code, enter it, too.

There are several digital and print options for the NP2014 textbook, as well as bundles that include both print and digital versions. Make your selection carefully. Complete the purchase process, as necessary, and the NP2014 CourseMate will appear on your CengageBrain dashboard (Figure 30).

FIGURE 30

The Home page of your CengageBrain dashboard displays the course materials you've selected.

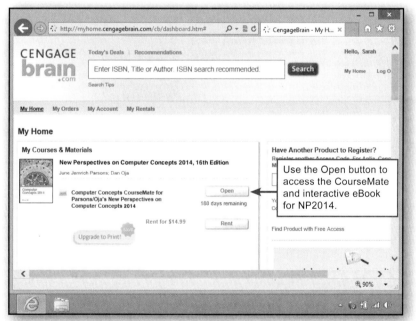

TRY IT!

Get started with CourseMate

1. Start your browser and connect to *www.cengagebrain.com*.

2. If you are accessing CengageBrain for the first time, click the **Sign Up** link and follow the instructions to create your account.

3. Once you've created a CengageBrain account, you can log in by entering your user name and password, and then clicking the **Log In** button.

4. Add the NP2014 title that's used in your course. Choose carefully to make sure you get the correct edition, version, and electronic format.

5. Open the NP2014 CourseMate.

COURSEMATE ACTIVITIES

▶ **How do I use CourseMate?** The NP2014 CourseMate includes two major assets: an interactive, multimedia textbook and a set of activities designed to help you review chapter material, prepare for tests, and extend your understanding of various topics. Let's take a look at the activities first because you might want to use some of them even before you begin reading a chapter.

CourseMate activities are displayed in a list on the left side of the screen, as shown in Figure 31.

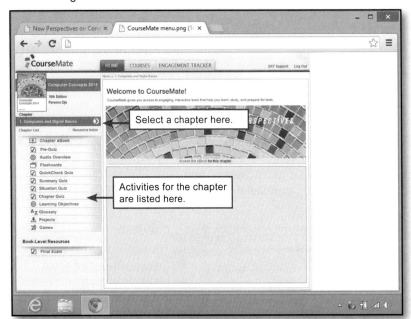

FIGURE 31

CourseMate offers activities you can use before and after reading a chapter.

▶ **Where do I start?** Consider the following tips for using CourseMate activities as an effective study tool:

▶ Before beginning a chapter, try the Pre-Quiz activity to find out where to focus your study time.

▶ The Audio Overview presents a high-level introduction to chapter highlights. Use it as an orientation or as a quick refresher before an exam.

▶ If you like a challenge, use the online games as a review activity; you'll get high scores if you understand the chapter material.

▶ Quizzes are a great way to make sure that you understand and can apply key concepts presented in a chapter.

▶ For last-minute review, load up your iPod with the Audio Flashcards. You can listen to them for a quick refresher on your way to the test!

▶ **Can I submit scores from CourseMate activities to my instructor?** Your results from various CourseMate activities are automatically recorded for your instructor using the Engagement Tracker.

TROUBLE?

If your computer has trouble properly displaying CourseMate or your online eBook, try using a different browser.

Google Chrome seems to be the browser that offers the most consistent browsing experience for PCs and Macs. You can download Chrome for free from *www.google.com/chrome*.

TRY IT!

Explore CourseMate

1. Select **Chapter 1** and then try some CourseMate activities.

2. Be sure to check out the Audio Overview, Flashcards, and Games.

ONLINE INTERACTIVE EBOOK

▶ **What is the NP2014 interactive eBook?** The digital version of NP2014 uses an advanced eBook technology that's chock full of activities designed to help readers focus on important concepts and remember them when it is time to take a test.

Each page of the eBook looks exactly like the printed book, so students and instructors are literally all on the same page for assignments and discussions.

▶ **How do I access the NP2014 interactive eBook?** You can access the eBook from the list on the left side of the CourseMate screen. Select the Chapter eBook option. The NP2014 eBook opens in a new tab or new browser window, depending on how your browser is configured (Figure 32).

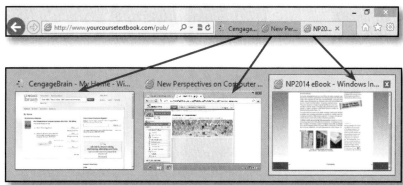

CengageBrain screen   CourseMate screen   eBook screen

FIGURE 32

Remain aware of the windows and tabs that hold the CourseMate and eBook so that you don't mistakenly close one or the other during a session.

▶ **How do I navigate through the interactive eBook?** You can turn pages using the arrows at the top and bottom of each page. Use the Contents link at the top of each page to jump to the first page of the chapter. Use the links on the first page to jump to any section of a chapter or to end-of-chapter activities.

▶ **How do I work with videos and software tours?** You can click the ▶ Video button to open a video window or software tour. Then use the control buttons to play, pause, or stop playback (Figure 33).

Video controls start, pause, and stop playback.

FIGURE 1-47

Password managers help you keep track of all your passwords. ▶ If you've never used a password manager and want to see how one works, start the guided tour for this figure in your interactive eBook.

FIGURE 33

Most videos play within the page, whereas software tours play in a separate window. Look for the playback controls on the left side of the video or software tour window.

▶ Are my eBook activities tracked? Quizzes and Practice tests in the NP2014 eBook are computer scored. You have the option of saving your results and sending them to your instructor.

The first time you start a quiz or practice test, you'll see a message box like the one in Figure 34. If you want to send your scores, fill in the box. If you do not want to send your scores, click the *Do not track results for this session* check box.

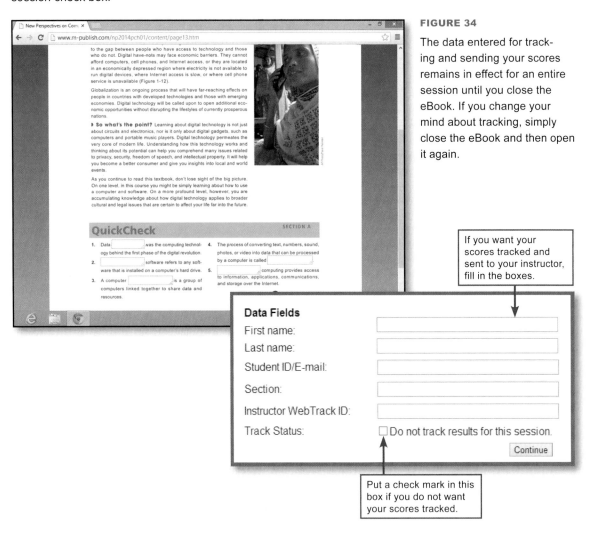

FIGURE 34

The data entered for tracking and sending your scores remains in effect for an entire session until you close the eBook. If you change your mind about tracking, simply close the eBook and then open it again.

If you want your scores tracked and sent to your instructor, fill in the boxes.

Put a check mark in this box if you do not want your scores tracked.

QuickCheck   SECTION D

1. To access the NP2014 CourseMate, you need a user name and password. True or false? [   ]

2. The [   ] Tracker automatically records your scores for quiz activities listed on the CourseMate main screen.

3. Audio Flashcards can be loaded on an iPod. True or false? [   ]

4. The Audio [   ] is a five-minute audio presentation of chapter highlights.

5. The interactive eBook opens in a new [   ] or window of your browser.

▶ CHECK ANSWERS

Interactive eBook CD

IF YOU CAN'T DEPEND ON your Internet connection, you might consider the interactive, digital version of your textbook that is available on CD. This section describes its features.

EBOOK CD BASICS

▶ **How do I start the eBook CD?** To start the eBook CD on any Windows computer, follow the instructions in the TRY IT! box below.

▶ **What if I have a Mac?** If you have a Mac that runs Parallels or Boot Camp, that means you have access to the Windows operating system on your Mac. Boot up your Mac in Windows mode and then use the eBook CD just as you would on a Windows computer.

If your Mac runs only OS X, you can still access the digital textbook by performing a simple conversion process. For instructions on how to convert the eBook CD for your Mac, connect to *www.infoweblinks.com/np2014* and look for the MacPac link.

▶ **What if my computer has no CD drive?** You can use an external CD drive or install the eBook CD on a local drive. Refer to the NP2014 technical support link at *www.infoweblinks.com/np2014*.

QUESTIONS?

Additional FAQs about the eBook CD are posted at *www. infoweblinks.com* under the Technical Support link. You'll find information on topics such as what to do if the CD doesn't start, and how to use the eBook CD in a computer without a CD drive.

TRY IT!

Start the eBook CD

1. Insert the eBook CD into your computer's CD or DVD drive, label side up.

2. Wait a few seconds until the eBook CD has loaded.

3. When the main Computer Concepts screen appears, proceed to step 4.

- If an Autoplay box appears, select *Run eBook CD.exe*.

- If the CD does not start automatically, click the Start button, click Computer, and then double-click the CD or DVD drive icon.

The eBook CD allows you to save your scores for QuickChecks, practice tests, and other activities. But for this session, you do not need to track this data.

4. Click the **File** menu, and then select **Change Tracking Options**.

5. To disable tracking for now, make sure the box next to *Save Tracking data* is empty. If the box contains a check mark, click the box to empty it.

6. Click the **OK** button to close the Tracking Options dialog box.

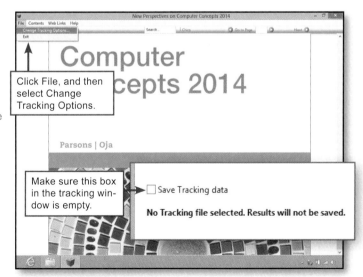

Click File, and then select Change Tracking Options.

Make sure this box in the tracking window is empty.

▶ **How do I navigate through the book?** The eBook CD menu and toolbar near the top of the screen contain tools you can use for navigation. The Next and Back buttons turn one page at a time. To get to the first page of any chapter, you can select it from the Contents menu.

The eBook CD pages mirror the pages in the printed book. So if you want to take the QuickCheck that's on page 21 of your printed textbook, for example, you can use the Go to Page option on the toolbar to jump right to it.

▶ **What are the other menu and navigation options?** The menu bar includes a Web Links menu that opens your browser and connects to InfoWebLinks. The menu bar also includes a Help menu where you can access instructions and troubleshooting FAQs. The Glossary button provides access to definitions for key terms. An Annotation button appears when your instructor has posted comments or lecture notes. If your instructor has not posted annotations, the button will not appear.

▶ **How do I exit the eBook CD?** When you have completed a session and want to close the eBook CD, you can click the [✕] button in the upper-right corner of the title bar (Windows). On Mac OS X, you can click *NP2014 eBook CD* on the menu bar and select Quit. Figure 35 helps you locate the Close button and eBook CD navigation tools.

> **TERMINOLOGY NOTE**
>
> The eBook CD requires Adobe Flash Player for displaying labs. The Flash Player is installed on most computers. If the eBook CD cannot find your Flash Player when it starts, you'll be directed to go online to download and install it.

FIGURE 35

Key Features of the eBook CD Menu Bar and Toolbar

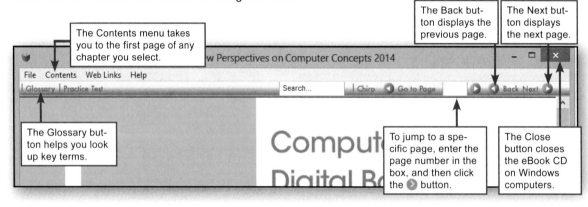

> **TRY IT!**

Open a chapter and navigate the eBook CD

1. Click **Contents** on the menu bar. The Contents menu appears.

2. Click **Chapter 2**.

3. When Chapter 2 appears, click the **Next** button twice until you see page 56.

4. Click the **Back** button twice to go back to the first page of Chapter 2.

5. Click the white box on the right side of *Go to Page*. Type **89**, and then click the **Go to Page** ❯ button.

6. Click the ❮ **Go to Page** button. Now you should be back at the first page of Chapter 2.

7. Scroll down the page until you can see the Chapter Contents listing. As shown at right, you can use this list to quickly jump to Sections A, B, C, D, or E; Issues; Technology in Context; NP Labs; and Review Activities.

8. Click ❯ **Section D** to jump to Section D.

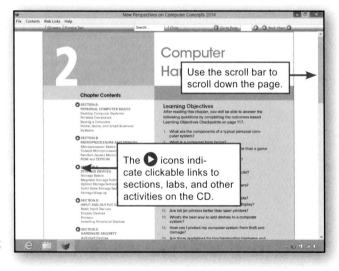

MULTIMEDIA AND COMPUTER-SCORED ACTIVITIES

▶ **What kinds of multimedia are included in the eBook CD?** Figures in your book marked with the ▶ icon morph into multimedia tours, animations, and videos. A tour takes you on a guided software tour—even if you don't have the software installed on your computer! Animations and videos visually expand on the concepts presented in the text.

▶ **How do I access software tours and other multimedia?** To access multimedia elements, simply click the ▶ icon while using the eBook CD.

▶ **Which activities are computer scored?** Figure 36 lists the eBook CD activities that are computer scored. You can use these activities to gauge how well you remember and understand the material you read in the textbook.

Suppose you're reading Chapter 2. Work with the TRY IT! below to see how multimedia and computer-scored activities work.

FIGURE 36

eBook CD Computer-scored Activities

> Interactive Summary
>
> Interactive Situation Questions
>
> Interactive Practice Tests
>
> Concept Map
>
> QuickChecks
>
> Lab QuickChecks

TRY IT!

Explore multimedia and computer-scored activities

1. Use the **Go to Page** control to jump to page 79.

2. On page 79, Figure 2-27 contains an ▶ icon. Click any line of the figure caption to launch the video.

3. When you want to stop the video, click any blank area of the eBook CD page. To restart the video, click the ▶ icon again.

4. Now, try a computer-scored QuickCheck. Use the **Go to Page** control to get to page 87 and scroll down the page until you can see the entire set of QuickCheck questions.

5. Click the answer box for question 1, and then type your answer. Most answers are a single word. Upper- and lowercase have no effect on the correctness of your answer.

6. Press the **Tab** key to jump to question 2, and then type your answer. Don't worry if you don't know the answer; you haven't actually read Chapter 2 yet. Just make a guess for now.

7. When you have answered all the questions, click the ▶ CHECK ANSWERS icon. The computer indicates whether your answer is correct or incorrect.

8. Continue to click **OK** to check the rest of your answers.

9. When you've reviewed all your answers, the computer presents a score summary. Click **OK** to close the dialog box.

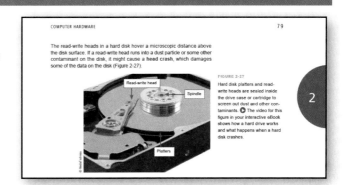

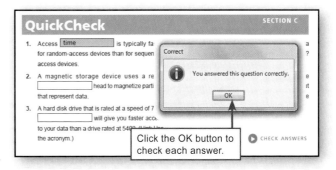

NEW PERSPECTIVES LABS

▶ **What about labs?** Your eBook CD includes New Perspectives Labs that give you hands-on experience applying concepts and using software discussed in each chapter. Labs in the eBook CD are divided into topics, and each topic ends with a QuickCheck so that you can make sure you understand key concepts.

In addition to lab QuickChecks, each New Perspectives Lab also includes a set of assignments located on the Lab page of each chapter. Your instructor might require you to complete these assignments. You can submit them on paper, as an e-mail message, or as a document in your Blackboard drop box according to your instructor's directions.

▶ **How do I launch a lab?** First, navigate to the lab page using the New Perspectives Labs option from the Chapter Contents list, or type in the corresponding page number from the printed book. Click the lab's ▶ icon to start it, as explained in the TRY IT! below.

TRY IT!

Open a lab

1. Click **Contents** on the eBook CD menu bar and select **Chapter 1**.

2. Scroll down to the Chapter Contents list and click ▶ **New Perspectives Labs**.

3. When the New Perspectives Labs page appears, click ▶ **OPERATING A PERSONAL COMPUTER**.

4. The lab window opens. Click the 🔁 button to view objectives for Topic 1.

5. Click the 🔁 button again to view page 1 of the lab. Read the information on the page, and then continue through the lab, making sure to follow any numbered instructions.

6. After page 8, you will encounter the first QuickCheck question. Click the correct answer, and then click the **Check Answer** button. After you find out if your answer was correct, click the 🔁 button to continue to the next question. Complete all the QuickCheck questions for Topic 1.

7. For this TRY IT!, you don't have to complete the entire lab. When you are ready to quit, click the 🔁 button.

8. Click the 🔁 button again. Your Lab QuickCheck results are displayed.

9. Click the **OK** button to return to the eBook CD.

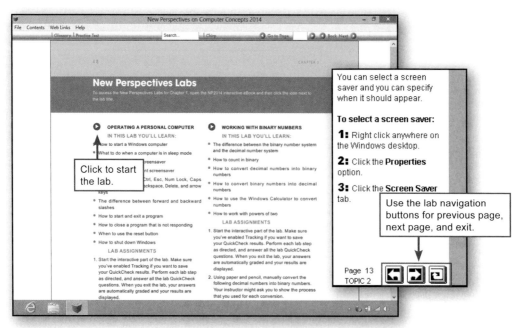

TRACKING YOUR SCORES

▶ **Can I save scores from QuickChecks, labs, and other activities?** To save your scores, you have to create a Tracking file. The file can be located on a rewritable CD, your computer's hard disk, a USB flash drive, or a network drive where you have permission to store files.

▶ **How do I make a Tracking file?** The Tracking Options dialog box lets you create a Tracking file and designate where you want to store it. Work with the TRY IT! below to create a Tracking file.

TRY IT!

Create a Tracking file

1. Make sure your eBook CD is open.

2. Click **File** on the eBook CD menu bar, and then click **Change Tracking Options**.

3. When the Tracking Options dialog box appears, click the **Create** button.

4. When the Create Tracking File dialog box appears, enter the requested data (see illustration at right), and then click **Continue**. The Save As (Windows) or Save (Mac) dialog box appears.

5. Use the dialog box to specify the location and name for your Tracking file. (See the illustration at right for Windows or the illustration below for Macs.)

6. After selecting a name and location for your Tracking file, click the **Save** button.

7. Back at the Tracking Options dialog box, make sure there is a check mark in the box labeled *Save Tracking data*, and then click the **OK** button. Now your Tracking file is ready to receive your scores.

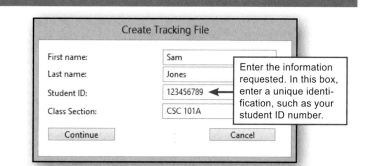

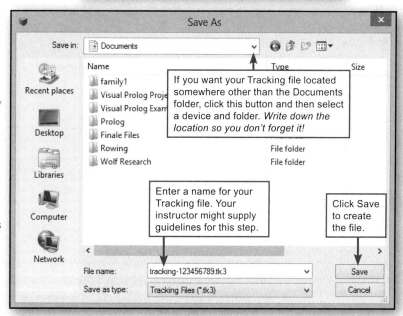

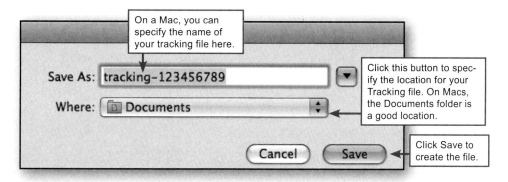

How do I get scores into my Tracking file? Whenever the *Save Tracking data* box is checked, all scored activities are automatically saved in your Tracking file. In the previous TRY IT!, you activated tracking; so until you go back into Tracking Options and remove the check mark from *Save Tracking data*, your scores will be saved.

What happens if I do an activity twice? While tracking is active, all your scores are saved. If you do an activity twice, both scores are saved. Your scores are dated, so you and your instructor can determine which scores are the most recent.

Can I review my scores? You can see all your scores in a Tracking Report.

Can I delete or change my scores? No. Your Tracking data is encrypted and cannot be changed.

Work with the TRY IT! below to see how easy it is to save scores and view your Tracking Report.

TRY IT!

Complete a Practice Test

To start tracking your scores, you can complete a Practice Test.

1. Click the **Practice Test** button located on the eBook CD toolbar.

2. The first question of a ten-question Practice Test appears. Answer the question, and then click the **Next** button.

3. Answer the remaining questions, and then click the **Check Answers** button.

4. When you see your score summary, click the **OK** button. You can then step through each of your answers or view a study guide.

5. Click the **Study Guide** button. A browser window opens to display each Practice Test question, your answers, and the corresponding page numbers in your textbook.

6. Close the Study Guide by clicking the [X] button on your browser window (Windows), or by clicking the browser name in the Mac menu bar and then selecting **Quit** (Mac).

7. Click the **Close** button on the Practice Test window to close it and save your scores.

View the contents of your Tracking file

1. Click **File** on the eBook CD menu bar.

2. Click **View Tracking Report**. Your computer opens your browser and displays a summary score for the Practice Test you completed. The list of summary scores grows as you save additional Practice Tests, QuickChecks, Interactive Summaries, Interactive Situation Questions, and Lab QuickChecks.

3. To close the Tracking Report, close the browser window (Windows) or the TextEdit window (Mac).

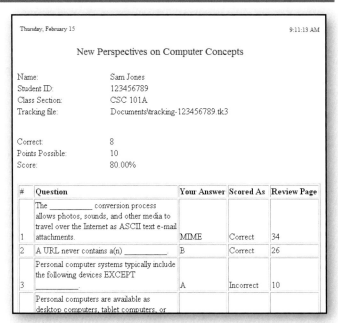

Thursday, February 15   9:11:13 AM

New Perspectives on Computer Concepts

Name:	Sam Jones
Student ID:	123456789
Class Section:	CSC 101A
Tracking file:	Documents\tracking-123456789.tk3

Correct:	8
Points Possible:	10
Score:	80.00%

#	Question	Your Answer	Scored As	Review Page
1	The _____ conversion process allows photos, sounds, and other media to travel over the Internet as ASCII text e-mail attachments.	MIME	Correct	34
2	A URL never contains a(n) _____.	B	Correct	26
3	Personal computer systems typically include the following devices EXCEPT _____.	A	Incorrect	10
	Personal computers are available as desktop computers, tablet computers, or			

Sunday, August 24   7:16:33 PM

Tracking Report

New Perspectives on Computer Concepts

Name:	Sam Jones
Student ID:	123456789
Class Section:	CSC 101A
Tracking file:	Macintosh HD:Users Sam:Documents:tracking-123456789.tk3

#	Activity	Date	Time	Points Earned	Points Possible	Score
1	NP2014 Chapter 01 Practice Test	8/24	7:16 PM	8	10	80.00%

▶ **How do I submit scores from my Tracking file?** You can use the Submit Tracking Data option on the File menu to send your scores to your instructor. The files are sent over an Internet service called WebTrack.

▶ **Are the scores erased from my Tracking file when they are sent?** No. Your scores remain in your file—a copy is sent to your instructor. If your instructor's computer malfunctions and loses your data, you can resubmit your Tracking file. It is a good idea to back up your Tracking file using the Back Up Tracking File option on the File menu.

▶ **What are chirps?** A chirp is a short message, similar to a Twitter-style tweet. You can use chirps to send queries to your instructor. Your instructor might also use chirps as a classroom polling system. Chirps work through WebTrack.

TRY IT!

Send your Tracking data and send a chirp

1. Click **File** on the eBook CD menu bar, and then click **Submit Tracking Data**.

2. Make sure your instructor's WebTrack address is correctly displayed in the Tracking Data Destination dialog box, and then click **Continue**.

3. Your computer opens a browser window, makes an Internet connection, and contacts the WebTrack server.

4. When the WebTrack screen appears, make sure the information displayed is correct, and then click the **Submit** button.

5. When you see a message that confirms your data has been submitted, you can close the browser window.

6. To send a chirp, click the **Chirp** button on the eBook CD toolbar.

7. When the Chirps panel appears, enter your message in the box labeled *Your message*.

8. Click the **Send** button.

9. Close your eBook CD.

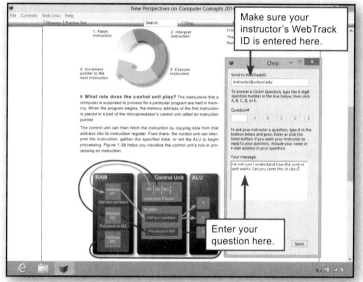

QuickCheck

SECTION E

1. Figures in the book marked with an & sign morph into multimedia software tours, animations, and videos. True or false? [＿＿＿＿]

2. When you use the NP2014 eBook CD, a(n) [＿＿＿＿＿＿] button appears if your instructor has posted comments or lecture notes.

3. To save your scores, you have to create a(n) [＿＿＿＿＿＿] file.

4. New Perspectives [＿＿＿＿＿＿] are divided into topics and each topic ends with a QuickCheck.

5. WebTrack provides a way to submit scores to your instructor. True or false? [＿＿＿＿]

 CHECK ANSWERS

Computer Concepts 2014

Parsons | Oja

NEW PERSPECTIVES

1

Computers and Digital Basics

> **INFOWEBLINKS**
>
> You'll find updates for chapter
> material by connecting to the
> **NP2014 Chapter 1** InfoWebLink.
>
> ⓦ CLICK TO CONNECT
> www.infoweblinks.com/np2014/ch01

Learning Objectives

After reading this chapter, you will be able to answer the
following questions by completing the outcomes-based
Learning Objectives Checkpoints on page 53.

1. What are the four phases of the digital revolution?
2. What is convergence and how does it apply to the digital revolution?
3. How does digital technology affect society?
4. How do computers work with input, output, processing, storage, and stored programs?
5. What's the difference between an operating system and application software?
6. How do personal computers differ from servers, mainframes, and supercomputers?
7. Are portable media players and mobile phones classified as computers?
8. Why are microcontrollers the computers no one sees?
9. Aren't data and information the same thing?
10. What's the difference between analog and digital?
11. How do digital devices use 1s and 0s to work with numbers, text, images, and sound?
12. Why is there so much jargon pertaining to bits and bytes?
13. What hardware components manipulate the bits that represent data?
14. Why do computers need programs?
15. How do a microprocessor's ALU and control unit work?
16. How do hackers steal passwords?
17. How can I create secure passwords?

Apply Your Knowledge

The information in this chapter will give you the
background to:

▶ Inventory the digital devices
you own

▶ Put digital technology in
the context of history, pop
culture, and the global
economy

▶ Read computer ads with an
understanding of technical
terminology

▶ Select secure passwords for
protecting your computer
and Internet logins

▶ Use a password manager
to keep track of all your
passwords

▶ Use digital devices with an
awareness of how they might
infringe on your privacy

TRY IT!

WHAT'S MY DIGITAL PROFILE?

The average American consumer owns more than 24 digital devices. Before you begin Chapter 1, take an inventory of your digital equipment to find the brands, models, and serial numbers. Tuck this information in a safe place. It can come in handy when you need to call technical support, arrange for repair services, or report missing equipment.

1. Fill in the following table for any digital equipment you own, rent, lease, or use.

	BRAND	MODEL	SERIAL NUMBER
COMPUTER			
KEYBOARD			
MOUSE			
MONITOR			
PRINTER			
DIGITAL CAMERA			
DIGITAL MUSIC PLAYER			
INTERNET OR NETWORK DEVICE			
MOBILE PHONE			
GAME CONSOLE			
OTHER (LIST)			

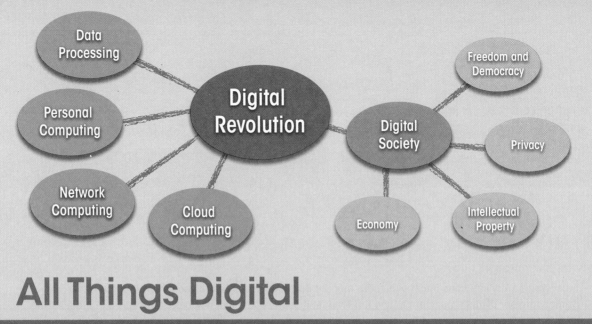

All Things Digital

WE LIVE IN THE INFORMATION AGE: a period in history when information is easy to access and affects many aspects of everyday life, from the economy to politics and social relationships. The importance of information is not new. It has always been a powerful tool. Scrolls treasured by monks during the Middle Ages, scientific knowledge collected during the Renaissance, and intelligence data collected during the Cold War were all critical in shaping world events. The Information Age is unique because of its underlying technology based on digital electronics. Section A offers an overview of the digital revolution that ushered in the Information Age.

THE DIGITAL REVOLUTION

▶ **What is the digital revolution?** The **digital revolution** is an ongoing process of social, political, and economic change brought about by digital technology, such as computers and the Internet.

Like the agricultural and industrial revolutions, the digital revolution offers advantages, but requires adaptations. Digital innovations challenge the status quo and require societies to make adjustments to traditions, lifestyles, and legislation.

The technology driving the digital revolution is based on digital electronics and the idea that electrical signals can represent data, such as numbers, words, pictures, and music. Without digital electronics, computers would be huge machines, priced far beyond the reach of individuals; your favorite form of entertainment would probably be foosball, and you'd be listening to bulky vacuum tube radios instead of carrying sleek iPods (Figure 1-1).

> **TERMINOLOGY NOTE**
>
> The word *digital* comes from the root *digit*. In Latin, the word *digitus* means finger or toe. The modern use of the term *digital* is probably derived from the idea of counting on your fingers.

FIGURE 1-1

From Victrolas to stereos, and from boomboxes to iPods, music is only one aspect of life that's been affected by technology.

▶ What is the significance of digitization? **Digitization** is the process of converting text, numbers, sound, photos, and video into data that can be processed by digital devices. The significant advantage of digitization is that things as diverse as books, movies, songs, conversations, documents, and photos can all be distilled down to a common set of signals that do not require separate devices.

Before digitization, a phone conversation required a telephone handset and dedicated phone lines. Viewing photos required a slide projector and screen. Reading required a paper book. Viewing movies required a film projector. Once digitized, however, conversations, photos, books, and movies can all be managed by a single device or transmitted over a single set of communication lines.

You can pull a photo down from a Web site, store it on your computer's hard disk, make a copy of it on a flash drive, send it to a friend as an e-mail attachment, add it to a report, print it, combine it with other photos to make a slide show, burn the slide show to a CD, and watch the slide show on your home theater system.

You can use a digitized photo in so many ways. In contrast, if you just have a photo print, you can make a copy of it with a photo copier, send it by snail mail, or frame it, but not much else. Digitization creates versatility.

The digital revolution has evolved through four phases, beginning with big, expensive, standalone computers, and progressing to today's digital world in which small, inexpensive digital devices are everywhere (Figure 1-2).

TRY IT!

According to Figure 1-2, AOL and CompuServe were popular when:

○ data processing was the main digital technology

○ most people had dial-up Internet access and used desktop computers

○ smartphones and tablets were introduced

○ people stopped using cloud computing

FIGURE 1-2

As the digital revolution progressed, technology changed, as did the way we use it.

Expired	Tired	Uninspired	Desired
Data processing	Personal computing	Network computing	Cloud computing
Big corporate and government computers	Desktop computers	Laptop computers	Smartphones and tablets
Custom applications	Standalone applications	Monolithic software suites	Handheld apps and cloud-based apps
CB radios	Dial-up Internet access	Cable and satellite Internet access	4G and Wi-Fi Internet access
ARPANET	AOL and CompuServe	The Web and virtual worlds	Social media
Arcade games	2-D action games	3-D multiplayer games	Touchscreen micro-games

DATA PROCESSING

▶ **When did the digital revolution begin?** Some historians mark the 1980s as the beginning of the digital revolution, but engineers built the first digital computers during World War II for breaking codes and calculating missile trajectories. In the 1950s, computers were marketed for business applications, such as payroll and inventory management.

▶ **What was computing like back then?** In this first phase of the digital revolution, computers were huge, complex, and expensive devices. They existed in limited numbers, primarily housed in big corporations and government agencies. Computers were operated by trained technicians. Each computer installation required specialized software. The idea that computers might be used by ordinary people in their homes was only a glimmer of an idea in the minds of science fiction writers.

Back then, processing components for computers were housed in closet-sized cabinets that did not usually include a keyboard or display device. Computers were accessed using the keyboard and display screen of a terminal. Terminals had little processing capability of their own, so they were simply used to enter data and view results produced by software that ran on the main computer.

During the antiestablishment era of the 1960s, the digital revolution was beginning to transform organizations, but ordinary people had little direct contact with computers. As with many new technologies, computers were initially viewed with suspicion by consumers, who were uncomfortable with the idea of giant machine "brains." Computers seemed remote. They were housed out of sight in special facilities and were inaccessible to ordinary people. Computers also seemed impersonal. Instead of names, computers used Social Security numbers to uniquely identify people (Figure 1-3).

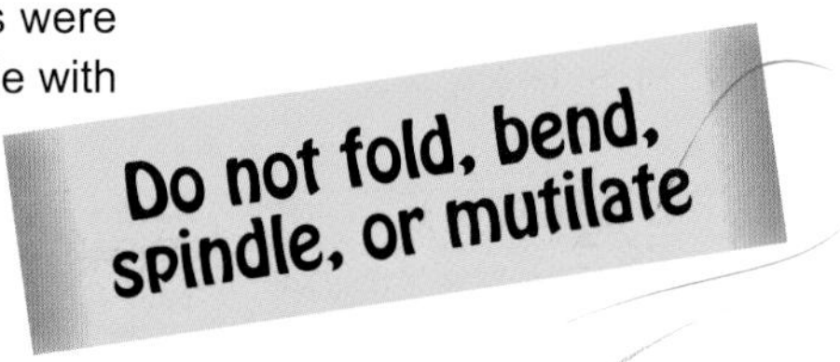

Throughout the first phase of the digital revolution, businesses adopted computers with increasing enthusiasm as benefits for cutting costs and managing mountains of data became apparent. Computers and data processing became crucial tools for effective business operations.

▶ **What is data processing?** **Data processing** is based on an input-processing-output cycle. Data goes into a computer, it is processed, and then it is output. For example, a batch of employee time cards are entered into a payroll computer system; the payroll data is processed to calculate take-home pay, deductions, and taxes; paychecks are output (Figure 1-4).

FIGURE 1-3

In the 1950s and 1960s, data used by government and business computers was coded onto punched cards that contained the warning "Do not fold, tear, or mutilate this card." Similar slogans were used by protesters who were concerned that computers would have a dehumanizing effect on society.

Do not fold, bend, spindle, or mutilate

FIGURE 1-4

Data processing is the computing model for the first phase of the digital revolution. The concept of large computers performing tasks based on the input-processing-output cycle represents the primary way computers were used from the 1940s through the 1970s. Data processing installations still exist today, but other technologies emerged, making computing available to a more diverse group of users. ▶ See an example of data processing.

Input   ⟶   Process   ⟶   Output

PERSONAL COMPUTING

▶ **When did digital devices become available to consumers?** Digital devices were first available to consumers in the 1970s when handheld calculators and digital watches hit store shelves. The first personal computers made their debut in 1976, but sales got off to a slow start. Without compelling software applications, personal computers, such as the Apple II, seemed to offer little for their $2,400 price.

As the variety of software increased, however, consumer interest grew. In 1982, *TIME* magazine's Man of the Year award went to the computer, an indication that these digital machines had finally gained a measure of popular acceptance.

▶ **What is personal computing?** The model for the second phase of the digital revolution, **personal computing** is characterized by small, standalone computers powered by local software. **Local software** refers to any software that is installed on a computer's hard drive.

During this phase of the digital revolution, computers were not connected to networks, so they were essentially self-contained units that allowed users to interact only with installed software. On the business front, large computers continued to run payroll, inventory, and financial software. Some managers used personal computers and spreadsheet software to crunch numbers for business planning.

If you owned a computer back in the second phase of the digital revolution, it was probably a small standalone machine with a display device that looked like an old-fashioned television (Figure 1-5).

Courtesy of Blake Patterson

FIGURE 1-5

The most popular uses for personal computers were word processing and gaming; sound systems and graphics capabilities were primitive. The Internet wasn't open to public use, so computing was not a social experience.

▶ **How long was the second phase of the digital revolution?** In 1982, computers had gained recognition in *TIME* magazine, but fewer than 10% of U.S. households had a computer. Working on a standalone computer wasn't for everyone.

People without an interest in typing up corporate reports or school papers, crunching numbers for accounting, or playing computer games weren't tempted to become active soldiers in the digital revolution. Social scientists even worried that people would become increasingly isolated as they focused on computer activities rather than social ones. Computer ownership increased at a gradual pace until the mid-1990s, and then it suddenly accelerated into the third phase of the digital revolution.

TRY IT!

During the second phase of the digital revolution, which one of the following was making news headlines?

○ A new band called The Beatles

○ The first space flights

○ President Bill Clinton

◐ Apple II computers

NETWORK COMPUTING

▶ What caused the sudden upswing in computer ownership during the 1990s? The third phase of the digital revolution materialized as computers became networked and when the Internet was opened to public use. A **computer network** is a group of computers linked together to share data and resources.

Network technology existed before the Internet became popular, but those networks were mainly deployed to connect computers within a school or business. Networks were complicated to set up and unreliable. As the third phase of the digital revolution unfolded, network technology became consumer-friendly, allowing homeowners to connect multiple computers, exchange files, and, most importantly, share an Internet connection.

The **Internet** is a global computer network originally developed as a military project, and was then handed over to the National Science Foundation for research and academic use. When restrictions on commercial use of the Internet were lifted in 1995, companies such as AOL and CompuServe became popular services for access to e-mail and the World Wide Web. Internet access was a major factor contributing to the upswing in computer ownership during the 1990s.

▶ What about the Web? When historians look back on the digital revolution, they are certain to identify the Web as a major transformative influence. The **Web** (short for *World Wide Web*) is a collection of linked documents, graphics, and sounds that can be accessed over the Internet.

A key aspect of the Web is that it adds content and substance to the Internet. Without the Web, the Internet would be like a library without any books or a railroad without any trains. Online storefronts, auction sites, news, sports, travel reservations, and music downloads made the Web a compelling digital technology for just about everyone.

▶ So what was computing like? During the period from 1995–2010, computing was characterized by the Web, e-mail, multiplayer games, music downloads, and enormous software applications, such as Microsoft Office, Norton's Internet Security Suite, and Corel Digital Studio (Figure 1-6).

TRY IT!

The Web and the Internet are not the same. Why?

○ The Internet is a communications network; but the Web consists of content that is distributed by the Internet

○ The Internet consists of sites like Twitter and Facebook, whereas the Web links devices like iPods and computers

FIGURE 1-6

Computers were the primary devices for accessing the Internet prior to 2010, but applications, media, and data remained on the local hard disk.

Internet connections provided access to e-mail and the Web.

Computers included multimedia equipment for music and video.

Computers stored most data locally on the hard disk or flash drives.

Application software was typically stored locally.

Multiplayer games

Word processor

E-mail

© MediaTechnics

CLOUD COMPUTING

▶ **Is the Web dead?** A 2010 *Wired* magazine cover announced "The Web is Dead." That pronouncement was premature, but Facebook, Twitter, and Google Apps have sent computing in new directions. Local applications are being eclipsed by cloud computing, which characterizes the fourth phase of the digital revolution.

▶ **What is cloud computing?** Cloud computing provides access to information, applications, communications, and storage over the Internet. Before cloud computing, most computers ran software based locally. For example, to use a word processor, you might fire up the latest edition of Microsoft Word, which you'd installed on your computer's hard disk. Prior to the cloud, you stored data locally, too. E-mail, documents, photos, and music all resided on your computer's hard disk or flash drive.

With cloud computing, all that changes. You can use your browser to access word processing applications that run from the Internet, instead of software that you have installed on your local hard disk. You can use online applications to manage your e-mail, create floor plans, produce presentations, and carry out a host of other activities. You can store your data in the cloud, too, making it available no matter what computer you're using as long as it has an Internet connection.

The cloud gets its name from diagrams like the one in Figure 1-7, which shows Internet-based applications, storage, and other services outlined by a cloud-like shape designed to help you visualize the idea that cloud services are "out there" somewhere on the Internet.

▶ **What is convergence?** The expansion of cloud computing is due in part to **convergence**, a process by which several technologies with distinct functionalities evolve to form a single product. Your computer plays movies. Your cell phone has a camera. Your clock has a radio. Your watch functions as a compass. You can store data on your iPod touch. All these are examples of technological convergence.

Convergence worked its magic on cell phones, computers, portable media players, digital cameras, GPSs, watches, and ebook readers. Now you get features from all of them by purchasing a single digital device. Whether you purchase a full-size computer, a sophisticated mobile phone, or even a game console, you generally have access to software, music, photos, ebooks, movies, communications, and the Web (Figure 1-8).

Convergence is important to the digital revolution because it created sophisticated mobile devices whose owners demand access to the same services available from full-size computers on their desks.

Your smartphone isn't usually in range of the cable modem in your house, so it needs a different way to access the Internet. Your iPad is too small for a huge hard disk, so it needs an alternative place to store data and applications. Touchscreen devices are not great for typing tasks, so cloud-based apps can be specially designed to suit the use of gestures, rather than the use of a mouse and keyboard. You can see how these mobile devices require a solution such as cloud computing to provide a full spectrum of digital services.

FIGURE 1-7

The "cloud" represents Internet-based services, such as applications and social media, that are available from computers and handheld digital devices.

FIGURE 1-8

Smartphones such as the iPhone and Droid offer a huge selection of applications and Internet access.

▶ What role do social media play? The fourth phase of the digital revolution turned the worry of social isolation on its head; instead of computers decreasing human interaction, social media encourage interpersonal communications and relationships. **Social media** are cloud-based applications designed for social interaction and consumer-generated content. They include social networking services, wikis, blogging services, photo sharing services, and microblogging sites (Figure 1-9).

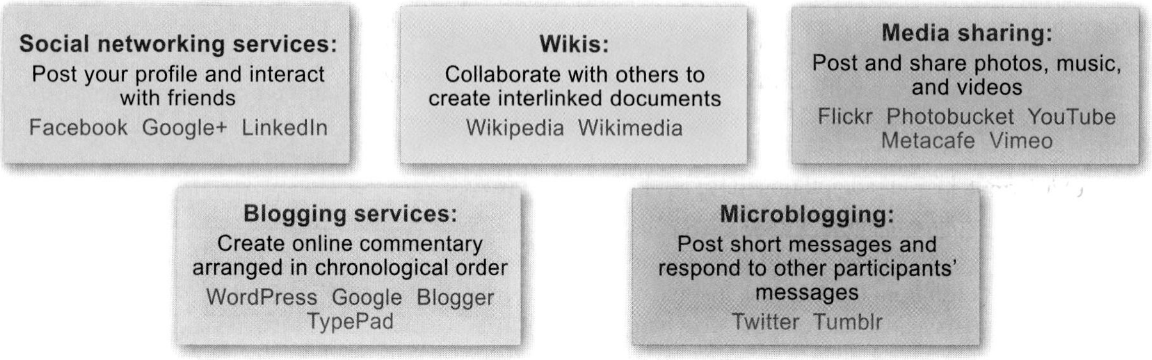

FIGURE 1-9

Social media include many popular services.

| Social networking services: Post your profile and interact with friends Facebook Google+ LinkedIn | Wikis: Collaborate with others to create interlinked documents Wikipedia Wikimedia | Media sharing: Post and share photos, music, and videos Flickr Photobucket YouTube Metacafe Vimeo |

| Blogging services: Create online commentary arranged in chronological order WordPress Google Blogger TypePad | Microblogging: Post short messages and respond to other participants' messages Twitter Tumblr |

Myspace, Facebook, and Twitter became some of the first popular social networking services. Myspace lost steam in 2008, but Facebook and Twitter marched ahead by attracting millions of users. Many factors influenced the popularity of these sites, but one important factor is their ease of use. As cloud-based services, there is no software to install and there are no updates to worry about. Getting started is as simple as registering your name and creating a password.

▶ How is today's computing different from the past? Using computers during the fourth phase of the digital revolution, you're likely to have a mobile device that accesses the Internet using a cell phone service provider.

The touchscreen on your mobile device gives you access to apps that play music, show movies, report news and sports scores, help you find the nearest Starbucks, and all kinds of other fun stuff. You occasionally use Google or Wikipedia to access information; and when you need to produce a document, you head over to Google to access its cloud-based word processor. You spend lots of time maintaining your profiles on social networking services and interacting with friends through cloud-based social media.

DIGITAL SOCIETY

▶ How does digital technology affect freedom and democracy? Freedom of speech is the cornerstone of democracy. It can be defined as being able to speak freely without censorship or fear of reprisal. The concept is not limited to speaking, but includes all forms of expression, such as writing, art, and symbolic actions. The more inclusive term *freedom of expression* is sometimes used instead of *freedom of speech*.

Freedom of speech is not an absolute. Most societies prohibit or repress some types of expression, such as hate speech, libel, pornography, and flag burning. Although freedom of expression is guaranteed under the U.S. Constitution, the European Convention on Human Rights, and the Universal Declaration of Human Rights, these documents recognize the necessity for some restrictions, which might vary from one society to the next.

Incidents ranging from the controversy over teaching evolution in schools to the Arab world's fury over cartoons of Mohammed illustrate that societies

TRY IT!

Which social media site has more users: Facebook or Twitter? Do a Google search and find out.

○ Facebook

○ Twitter

draw the freedom of speech line in different places. The types of expression that are allowed or prohibited in a particular country are, in many respects, a reflection of its culture.

Digital technologies and communications networks make it easy to cross cultural and geographic boundaries. News, television shows, music, and art from all over the globe are accessible on the Internet. The Internet has the potential to expand freedom of speech by offering every person on the planet a forum for personal expression using personal Web sites, blogs, chat groups, social media, and collaborative wikis. Anonymous Internet sites such as Freenet and **anonymizer tools** that cloak a person's identity even make it possible to exercise freedom of speech in situations where reprisals might repress it.

Internet information that seems innocuous in some cultures is not acceptable in others. Governments, parents, and organizations sometimes find it necessary to censor the Internet by limiting access and filtering content.

Despite attempts to censor and filter speech on the Internet, it seems clear that digital technology opens the door to freedom of expression in unprecedented ways. Limitations on Internet speech are likely to change, too, as technology evolves and as societies come to grips with the balance between freedom and responsibility.

▶ **Has digital technology changed the way we view privacy?** Citizens of free societies have an expectation of privacy, which in the words of Supreme Court Justices Warren and Brandeis is "the right to be let alone." Digital technology use has exerted substantial pressure to diminish privacy by making it possible to easily collect and distribute data about individuals without their knowledge or consent.

Privacy also encompasses confidentiality—the expectation that personal information will not be collected or divulged without permission. Internet marketers have a whole bag of tricks for surreptitiously getting personal information, and hackers are adept at breaking into sensitive databases to obtain confidential information (Figure 1-10).

Surveillance is viewed by many people as an invasion of privacy. Tracking technologies embedded in cars, clothing, passports, and devices such as cell phones make it much too easy to track people without their knowledge.

In the United States, the expectation of privacy is derived from Fourth Amendment protections against unreasonable searches and seizures. The Fourth Amendment was formulated long before the digital revolution. Today's lawmakers struggle to strike the right balance between privacy and competing principles, such as free speech or free trade, but the Internet and other digital technologies are slowly being used to chip away at the wall that protects our private lives.

Some individuals dismiss the erosion of privacy saying, "I have nothing to hide, so I don't care." Many other people don't want stores, hackers, and curious onlookers to have access to data about what they buy, read, and watch; who they call; where they travel; and what they say.

Social media, however, encourage participants to reveal personal details online, and that information is being captured, aggregated, reposted, and distributed publicly. Privacy advocates fear that these digital technologies are fundamentally changing our expectation of what is private and what is not.

TRY IT!

Which country has the most Draconian Internet censorship? Search the Web to find out.

○ United States

○ Russia

○ Iran

○ Greece

FIGURE 1-10

Is your location private information? Many applications and social media sites want to know your location. Do you want to reveal it? If not, turn location off.

▶ How does digital technology affect intellectual property? **Intellectual property** refers to the ownership of certain types of information, ideas, or representations. It includes patented, trademarked, and copyrighted material, such as music, photos, software, books, and films. In the past, such works were difficult and expensive to copy.

Digital technology has made it easy to produce copies with no loss in quality from the original. Pirating—illegal copying and distribution of copyrighted material—is simple and inexpensive. It has caused significant revenue loss for software publishers, recording studios, and film producers. The fight against piracy takes many forms, from passing strict anti-piracy laws; to scrambling, encryption, and digital rights management schemes that physically prevent copying; to anti-piracy videos (Figure 1-11).

Digital technology adds complexity to intellectual property issues. For example, artists used to think nothing of cutting out various photos from magazines and pasting them together to form a collage. It is even easier to download digital images from the Web and paste them into reports, add them to Web pages, and incorporate them into works of art. Without permission, however, such digital cut and paste is not allowed.

Don't copy that (what? what? why?)

FIGURE 1-11

Most moviegoers have seen the rock-video style "Don't Copy" trailer. Consumer education is one front in the war against piracy. ▶ You can view this video from your interactive eBook.

Some films contain scenes that parents would rather their children not see. Even some scenes from family-oriented Harry Potter films might be too intense for young viewers. So, why not simply edit them out digitally to make a new DVD that even preschoolers can watch? Such modifications are not allowed under current U.S. law, even for private viewing.

In the U.S., it is legal to make a backup copy of software CDs or DVDs that you own. However, if a software CD is copy protected to prevent you from making a copy, it is against the law to break the copy protection. So, legally you have a right to a backup, but you don't have the right to circumvent the copy protection to legally create one!

Bucking protectionist trends are **open source** projects that promote copying, free distribution, peer review, and user modification. Linux is an open-source computer operating system that can be modified and freely distributed. Open source application software includes the popular LibreOffice suite, Firefox Web browser, and Thunderbird e-mail.

Digital technology makes it possible to copy and modify films, music, software, and other data, but a tricky balancing act is required to allow consumers flexibility to use data while protecting the income stream to artists, performers, and publishers.

▶ What effect does digital technology have on the economy? Digital technology is an important factor in global and national economies, in addition to affecting the economic status of individuals. **Globalization** can be defined as the worldwide economic interdependence of countries that occurs as cross-border commerce increases and as money flows more freely among countries.

▶ TRY IT!

The United Nations declared that Internet access is a human right, along with food and clean water. Visit the Internet World Stats site to find out what percent of the world's population has Internet access.

○ 10-25%

○ 25-50%

○ 50-75%

○ 75-100%

In a global economy, consumers gain access to a wide variety of products, including technology products manufactured in locations scattered all over the globe.

Global communications technology offers opportunities for teleworkers in distant countries. Customer service lines for U.S.-based companies, such as IBM, Dell, and Hewlett-Packard, are often staffed by offshore technicians who earn far more than they could if working for a company that is based in their home country.

Globalization, fueled by digital technology, has controversial aspects, however. Worker advocates object to the use of cheap offshore labor that displaces onshore employees.

Some individuals are affected by the **digital divide**, a term that refers to the gap between people who have access to technology and those who do not. Digital have-nots may face economic barriers. They cannot afford computers, cell phones, and Internet access, or they are located in an economically depressed region where electricity is not available to run digital devices, where Internet access is slow, or where cell phone service is unavailable (Figure 1-12).

Globalization is an ongoing process that will have far-reaching effects on people in countries with developed technologies and those with emerging economies. Digital technology will be called upon to open additional economic opportunities without disrupting the lifestyles of currently prosperous nations.

▶ **So what's the point?** Learning about digital technology is not just about circuits and electronics, nor is it only about digital gadgets, such as computers and portable music players. Digital technology permeates the very core of modern life. Understanding how this technology works and thinking about its potential can help you comprehend many issues related to privacy, security, freedom of speech, and intellectual property. It will help you become a better consumer and give you insights into local and world events.

As you continue to read this textbook, don't lose sight of the big picture. On one level, in this course you might be simply learning about how to use a computer and software. On a more profound level, however, you are accumulating knowledge about how digital technology applies to broader cultural and legal issues that are certain to affect your life far into the future.

FIGURE 1-12

The digital divide is narrowing as the prices of digital devices fall, and as inexpensive handheld devices acquire more features.

AP Photo/Pavel Rahman

QuickCheck

1. Data ⟨processing⟩ was the computing technology behind the first phase of the digital revolution.

2. ⟨Local⟩ software refers to any software that is installed on a computer's hard drive.

3. A computer ⟨network⟩ is a group of computers linked together to share data and resources.

4. The process of converting text, numbers, sound, photos, or video into data that can be processed by a computer is called ⟨digitization⟩ .

5. ⟨Cloud⟩ computing provides access to information, applications, communications, and storage over the Internet.

 CHECK ANSWERS

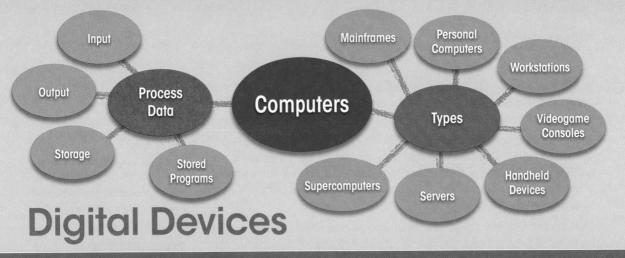

Digital Devices

WHETHER YOU REALIZE IT or not, you already know a lot about the devices produced by the digital revolution. You've picked up information from commercials and news articles, from books and movies, from friends and coworkers—even from using a variety of digital devices and trying to figure out why they don't always work! Section B provides an overview that's designed to help you start organizing what you know about digital devices, beginning with computers.

COMPUTER BASICS

▶ **What is a computer?** The word *computer* has been part of the English language since 1646; but if you look in a dictionary printed before 1940, you might be surprised to find a computer defined as a person who performs calculations! Prior to 1940, machines designed to perform calculations were usually referred to as calculators and tabulators, not computers. The modern definition and use of the term *computer* emerged in the 1940s, when the first electronic computing devices were developed.

Most people can formulate a mental picture of a computer, but computers do so many things and come in such a variety of shapes and sizes that it might seem difficult to distill their common characteristics into an all-purpose definition. At its core, a **computer** is a multipurpose device that accepts input, processes data, stores data, and produces output, all according to a series of stored instructions (Figure 1-13).

FIGURE 1-13

A computer can be defined by its ability to accept input, process data, store data, and produce output, all according to a set of instructions from a computer program.

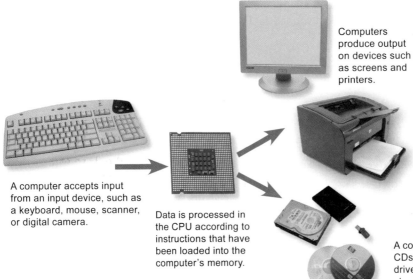

Computers produce output on devices such as screens and printers.

A computer accepts input from an input device, such as a keyboard, mouse, scanner, or digital camera.

Data is processed in the CPU according to instructions that have been loaded into the computer's memory.

A computer uses disks, CDs, DVDs, and flash drives to permanently store data.

14

▶ What is input? Computer **input** is whatever is typed, submitted, or transmitted to a computer system. Input can be supplied by a person, by the environment, or by another computer. Examples of the kinds of input that computers can accept include words and symbols in a document, numbers for a calculation, pictures, temperatures from a thermostat, audio signals from a microphone, and instructions from a computer program. An input device, such as a keyboard or mouse, gathers data and transforms it into a series of electronic signals for the computer to store and manipulate.

▶ What is output? **Output** is the result produced by a computer. Some examples of computer output include reports, documents, music, graphs, and pictures. Output devices display, print, or transmit the results of processing.

▶ What does *process data* mean? Technically speaking, **data** refers to the symbols that represent facts, objects, and ideas. Computers manipulate data in many ways, and this manipulation is called **processing**. Some of the ways that a computer can process data include performing calculations, modifying documents and pictures, keeping track of your score in a fast-action game, drawing graphs, and sorting lists of words or numbers (Figure 1-14).

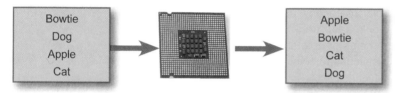

FIGURE 1-14

An unsorted list is input into the computer, where it is processed in the CPU and output as a sorted list.

In a computer, most processing takes place in a component called the **central processing unit** or **CPU**. The CPU of most modern computers is a **microprocessor**, which is an electronic component that can be programmed to perform tasks based on data it receives. You'll learn more about microprocessors later in the chapter. For now, visualize a microprocessor as the little black box that's the brain of a digital device.

▶ How do computers store data? A computer stores data so that it will be available for processing. Most computers have more than one place to put data, depending on how the data is being used. **Memory** is an area of a computer that temporarily holds data waiting to be processed, stored, or output. **Storage** is the area where data can be left on a permanent basis when it is not immediately needed for processing.

Data is typically stored in files. A computer file, usually referred to simply as a **file**, is a named collection of data that exists on a storage medium, such as a hard disk, CD, DVD, or flash drive. A file can contain data for a term paper, Web page, e-mail message, or music video. Some files also contain instructions that tell the computer how to perform various tasks.

▶ What's so significant about a computer's ability to store instructions? The series of instructions that tells a computer how to carry out processing tasks is referred to as a **computer program**, or simply a program. These programs form the **software** that sets up a computer to do a specific task. When a computer "runs" software, it performs the instructions to carry out a task.

Take a moment to think about the way you use a simple handheld calculator to balance your checkbook each month. You're forced to do the calculations in stages. Although you can store data from one stage and use it in the next stage, you cannot store the sequence of formulas—the program—required to balance your checkbook. Every month, therefore, you have to

TRY IT!

Suppose you see an iPad advertised with a 64-GB capacity. Does that specification refer to memory or storage?

○ memory

○ storage

perform a similar set of calculations. The process would be much simpler if your calculator remembered the sequence of calculations and just asked you for this month's checkbook entries.

The idea of a **stored program** means that a series of instructions for a computing task can be loaded into a computer's memory. These instructions can easily be replaced by a different set of instructions when it is time for the computer to perform another task. This ability to switch programs makes computers multipurpose machines.

The stored program concept allows you to use your computer for one task, such as word processing, and then easily switch to a different type of computing task, such as editing a photo or sending an e-mail message. It is the single most important characteristic that distinguishes a computer from other simpler and less versatile digital devices, such as watches, calculators, and pocket-sized electronic dictionaries.

▶ **What kinds of software do computers run?** Computers run two main types of software: application software and system software. A computer can be applied to many tasks, such as writing, number crunching, video editing, and online shopping. **Application software** is a set of computer programs that helps a person carry out a task. Word processing software, for example, helps people create, edit, and print documents. Personal finance software helps people keep track of their money and investments. Video editing software helps people create home movies and professional films. Software applications are sometimes referred to as **apps**, especially in the context of handheld devices.

Whereas application software is designed to help a person carry out a task, the primary purpose of **system software** is to help the computer system monitor itself in order to function efficiently. An example of system software is a computer **operating system** (OS), which is essentially the master controller for all the activities that take place within a computer. Although an operating system does not directly help people perform application-specific tasks, such as word processing, people do interact with the operating system for certain operational and storage tasks, such as starting programs and locating data files.

COMPUTER TYPES AND USES

▶ **Are computers categorized in any way?** At one time it was possible to define three distinct categories of computers. Mainframes were housed in large, closet-sized metal frames. Minicomputers were smaller, less expensive, and less powerful computers that were able, nevertheless, to support multiple users and run business software. Microcomputers were clearly differentiated from computers in other categories because they were dedicated to a single user and their CPUs consisted of a single microprocessor chip.

Today, microprocessors are no longer a distinction between computer categories because just about every computer uses one or more microprocessors as its CPU. The term *minicomputer* has fallen into disuse, and the terms *microcomputer* and *mainframe* are used with less and less frequency.

Computers are versatile machines, but some computers are better suited than others for certain tasks. Categorizing computers is a way of grouping them according to criteria such as usage, cost, size, and capability. Experts don't necessarily agree on the categories or the devices placed in each category, but commonly used computer categories include personal computers, servers, mainframes, and supercomputers.

▶ TRY IT!

Do you know the difference between the apps you use and your computer's operating system? Which of the following are operating systems?

○ Microsoft Windows

○ Microsoft Word

○ Apple iOS

○ Mac OS X

○ iWork

○ iTunes

TERMINOLOGY NOTE

The term *personal computer* is sometimes abbreviated as *PC*. However, *PC* can also refer to a specific type of personal computer that descended from the original IBM PC and runs Windows software.

In this book, *PC* refers to IBM PC descendants. It is not used as an abbreviation for *personal computer*.

▶ **What is a personal computer?** A **personal computer** is a microprocessor-based computing device designed to meet the computing needs of an individual. It commonly includes a keyboard and screen, and provides access to a wide variety of local and cloud-based applications.

Personal computers are available as desktop or portable models, and in a variety of shapes, sizes, and colors. You'll learn more about the wide variety of personal computers in the Hardware chapter. For now, simply remember that computers like those pictured in Figure 1-15 are classified as personal computers.

FIGURE 1-15

Personal computer designs run the gamut from drab gray boxes to colorful curvy cases.

▶ **Are handheld devices computers?** Handheld digital devices include familiar gadgets such as iPhones, iPads, iPods, Garmin GPSs, Droids, and Kindles. These devices incorporate many computer characteristics. They accept input, produce output, process data, and include storage capabilities. Handheld devices vary in their programmability and their versatility.

Handheld devices can be divided into two broad categories: those that allow users to install software applications (apps) and those that do not. Handheld devices that allow you to install applications can be classified as personal computers; devices that are not programmable cannot.

iPads and Droid phones, for example, offer access to a wide range of apps that include games, ebook readers, maps, comics, recipes, and news, which are tasks also performed by personal computers that sit on a desk or table (Figure 1-16).

FIGURE 1-16

Tablet computers, high-end mobile phones, and similar handheld devices allow you to install your choice of application software.

▶ **Is an Xbox a computer?** A **videogame console**, such as Nintendo's Wii, Sony's PlayStation, or Microsoft's Xbox, is a computer, but would not generally be referred to as a personal computer because of its history as a dedicated game device. Videogame consoles originated as simple digital devices that connected to a television and provided only a pair of joysticks for input.

Today's videogame consoles contain microprocessors that are equivalent to any found in a fast personal computer, and they are equipped to produce graphics that rival those on dedicated technical and scientific computers. Add-ons such as keyboards, DVD players, and Internet access make it possible to use a videogame console for activities similar to those for which you'd use a personal computer. Despite these features, videogame consoles like the one in Figure 1-17 fill a specialized niche and are not considered a replacement for a personal computer.

FIGURE 1-17

A videogame console includes circuitry similar to a personal computer's, but its input and output devices are optimized for gaming.

▶ **What is a workstation?** The term **workstation** has two meanings. It can simply refer to an ordinary personal computer that is connected to a network. A second meaning refers to powerful desktop computers used for high-performance tasks, such as medical imaging and computer-aided design, that require a lot of processing speed. Workstations, such as the one pictured in Figure 1-18, typically cost a bit more than an average personal computer.

▶ **What makes a computer a server?** In the computer industry, the term *server* has several meanings. It can refer to computer hardware, to a specific type of software, or to a combination of hardware and software. In any case, the purpose of a **server** is to serve computers on a network (such as the Internet or a home network) by supplying them with data.

Any software or digital device, such as a computer, that requests data from a server is referred to as a **client**. For example, on the Internet, a server might respond to a client's request for a Web page. Servers also handle the steady stream of e-mail that travels among clients from all over the Internet. A server might also allow clients within a home, school, or business network to share files or access a centralized printer.

Client computers can download and upload files from servers. The term **download** refers to the process of copying a file from a server to your own client computer. For example, you can say "I had to download the file before I could install it." The term can also refer to the file that you download, as in "I had to delete the download because it was infected with a virus."

Upload refers to the process of copying files from your client computer to a server. As with the term *download*, *upload* can also refer to the file you have uploaded.

Remarkably, just about any personal computer, workstation, mainframe, or supercomputer can be configured to perform the work of a server. That fact should emphasize the concept that a server does not require a specific type of hardware. Nonetheless, computer manufacturers such as IBM, SGI, HP, and Dell offer devices called servers (Figure 1-19) that are especially suited for storing and distributing data on a network.

FIGURE 1-18

A workstation resembles a desktop computer, but typically features more processing power and storage capacity.

© 2011 Hewlett-Packard Development Company, LP

TRY IT!

How would you classify the computer in this diagram?

○ A server

○ A client

○ Both

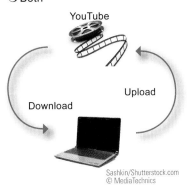

YouTube

Upload

Download

Sashkin/Shutterstock.com
© MediaTechnics

© MediaTechnics

© John Kershaw/Alamy

FIGURE 1-19

Some servers look like personal computer tower units, whereas others are housed in industrial-looking cases.

Server prices vary, depending on configuration, but tend to be more similar to workstation prices than personal computer prices. Despite impressive performance on server-related tasks, these machines do not offer features such as sound cards, DVD players, and other fun accessories, so they are not a suitable alternative to a personal computer.

▶ **What's so special about a mainframe computer?** A **mainframe computer** (or simply a mainframe) is a large and expensive computer capable of simultaneously processing data for hundreds or thousands of users. Mainframes are generally used by businesses or governments to provide centralized storage, processing, and management for large amounts of data. Mainframes remain the computer of choice in situations where reliability, data security, and centralized control are necessary.

The price of a mainframe computer typically starts at $100,000 and can easily exceed $1 million. Its main processing circuitry is housed in a closet-sized cabinet (Figure 1-20); but after large components are added for storage and output, a mainframe computer system can fill a good-sized room.

FIGURE 1-20

This IBM z9 mainframe computer weighs 2,807 pounds and is about 6.5 feet tall.

Courtesy of International Business Machines Corporation. Unauthorized use not permitted.

1

▶ **How powerful is a supercomputer?** A computer falls into the **supercomputer** category if it is, at the time of construction, one of the fastest computers in the world (Figure 1-21).

Because of their speed, supercomputers can tackle complex tasks and compute-intensive problems that just would not be practical for other computers. A **compute-intensive** problem is one that requires massive amounts of data to be processed using complex mathematical calculations. Molecular calculations, atmospheric models, and climate research are all examples of projects that require massive numbers of data points to be manipulated, processed, and analyzed.

Common uses for supercomputers include breaking codes, modeling worldwide weather systems, and simulating nuclear explosions. One impressive simulation, which was designed to run on a supercomputer, tracked the movement of thousands of dust particles as they were tossed about by a tornado.

At one time, supercomputer designers focused on building specialized, very fast, and very large CPUs. Today, most supercomputer CPUs are constructed from thousands of microprocessors. Of the 500 fastest supercomputers in the world, the majority use microprocessor technology.

Lawrence Livermore National Laboratory

FIGURE 1-21

In 2012, IBM's Blue Gene/Q became the fastest supercomputer in the world. With a speed of 16.32 petaflops, the number of calculations this computer can perform in one hour would require 300 years if every person on Earth used a handheld calculator.

MICROCONTROLLERS

▶ What is a microcontroller? Have you ever wondered how a guided missile reaches its target or how your refrigerator knows when to initiate a defrost cycle? What controls your microwave oven, digital video recorder, washing machine, and watch? Many common appliances and machines are controlled by embedded microcontrollers. A **microcontroller** is a special-purpose microprocessor that is built into the machine it controls. A microcontroller, such as the one in Figure 1-22, is sometimes called a computer-on-a-chip or an embedded computer because it includes many of the elements common to computers.

FIGURE 1-22

A microcontroller is a self-contained chip that can be embedded in an appliance, vehicle, or other device.

▶ How does a microcontroller work? Consider the microcontroller in a Sub-Zero refrigerator. It accepts user input for desired temperatures in the refrigerator and freezer compartments. It stores these desired temperatures in memory. Temperature sensors collect additional input of the actual temperatures. The microcontroller processes the input data by comparing the actual temperature to the desired temperature. As output, the microcontroller sends signals to activate the cooling motor as necessary. It also generates a digital readout of the refrigerator and freezer temperatures.

▶ Is a microcontroller really a computer? Recall that a computer is defined as a multipurpose device that accepts input, produces output, stores data, and processes it according to a stored program. A microcontroller seems to fit the input, processing, output, and storage criteria that define computers. Some microcontrollers can even be reprogrammed to perform different tasks.

Technically, a microcontroller could be classified as a computer. Despite this technicality, however, microcontrollers tend to be referred to as processors rather than as computers because in practice they are used for dedicated applications, not as multipurpose devices.

TRY IT!

Which one of the following would you most likely use to add and use apps such as games and weather tracking?

○ A microcontroller

○ Any handheld digital device

○ A handheld computer

▶ **Why are microcontrollers significant?** Microcontrollers can be embedded in all sorts of everyday devices, enabling machines to perform sophisticated tasks that require awareness and feedback from the environment (Figure 1-23).

FIGURE 1-23

A microcontroller is usually mounted on a circuit board and then installed in a machine or an appliance using wires to carry input and output signals.

TRY IT!

Where's the microcontroller in this figure? Click it to see if you're right.

When combined with wireless networks, devices with embedded processors can relay information to Web sites, cell phones, and a variety of data collection devices. Machines and appliances with embedded processors tend to be smarter about their use of resources—such as electricity and water—which makes them environmentally friendly.

Perhaps the most significant effect of microcontrollers is that they are an almost invisible technology, one that doesn't require much adaptation or learning on the part of the people who interact with microcontrolled devices. However, because microcontrollers remain mostly out of sight and out of mind, it is easy for their use to creep into areas that could be detrimental to quality of life, privacy, and freedom.

The GPS chip in your cell phone, for example, can be useful if you're lost and need 911 assistance, but it could potentially be used by marketers, law enforcement, and others who want to track your location without your consent.

QuickCheck

1. A computer is a digital device that processes data according to a series of Stored instructions called a program or software.

2. Computer data is temporarily stored in Memory , but is usually transferred to Storage where it can be left on a more permanent basis.

3. Personal computers are available in desktop and portable models.

4. A digital device, such as a computer, is called a(n) host when it requests data from a server.

5. A(n) Microcontroller is a special-purpose microprocessor that is built into the machine it controls.

 CHECK ANSWERS

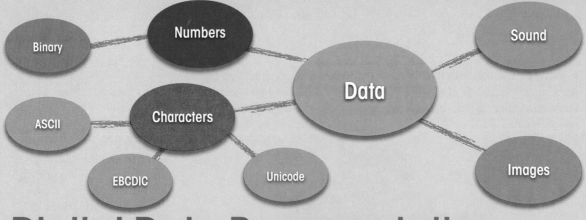

Digital Data Representation

SECTION C

COMPUTERS AND OTHER DIGITAL DEVICES work with all sorts of "stuff," including text, numbers, music, images, speech, and video. The amazing aspect of digital technology is that it distills all these different elements down to simple pulses of electricity and stores them as 0s and 1s. Understanding the data representation concepts presented in Section C will help you grasp the essence of the digital world and get a handle on all the jargon pertaining to bits, bytes, megahertz, and gigabytes.

DATA REPRESENTATION BASICS

▶ **What is data?** As you learned earlier in the chapter, *data* refers to the symbols that represent people, events, things, and ideas. Data can be a name, a number, the colors in a photograph, or the notes in a musical composition.

▶ **Is there a difference between data and information?** In everyday conversation, people use the terms *data* and *information* interchangeably. Nevertheless, some technology professionals make a distinction between the two terms. They define data as the symbols that represent people, events, things, and ideas. Data becomes information when it is presented in a format that people can understand and use. As a general rule, remember that (technically speaking) data is used by machines, such as computers; information is used by humans.

▶ **What is data representation? Data representation** refers to the form in which data is stored, processed, and transmitted. For example, devices such as smartphones, iPods, and computers store numbers, text, music, photos, and videos in formats that can be handled by electronic circuitry. Those formats are data representations. Data can be represented using digital or analog methods.

▶ **What's the difference between analog and digital?** For a simple illustration of the difference between analog and digital, consider the way you can control the lights in a room using a traditional light switch or a dimmer switch (Figure 1-24).

A traditional light switch has two discrete states: on and off. There are no in-between states, so this type of light switch is digital. A dimmer switch, on the other hand, has a rotating dial that controls a continuous range of brightness. It is, therefore, analog.

Digital data is text, numbers, graphics, sound, and video that have been converted into discrete digits such as 0s and 1s. In contrast, **analog data** is represented using an infinite scale of values.

FIGURE 1-24

A computer is a digital device, more like a standard light switch than a dimmer switch.

▶ How does digital data work? Imagine that you want to send a message by flashing a light. Your light switch offers two states: on and off. You can use sequences of ons and offs to represent various letters of the alphabet. To write down the representation for each letter, you can use 0s and 1s. The 0s represent the off state of your light switch; the 1s indicate the on state. For example, the sequence *on on off off* would be written as 1100, and you might decide that sequence represents the letter *A*.

Digital devices are electronic and so you can envision data flowing within these devices as pulses of light. In reality, digital signals are represented by two different voltages, such as +5 volts and +.2 volts. They can also be represented by two different tones as they flow over a phone line. Digital data can also take the form of light and dark spots etched onto the surface of a CD or the positive and negative orientation of magnetic particles on the surface of a hard disk.

The 0s and 1s used to represent digital data are referred to as binary digits. It is from this term that we get the word *bit—bi*nary digi*t*. A **bit** is a 0 or 1 used in the digital representation of data.

REPRESENTING NUMBERS, TEXT, IMAGES, AND SOUND

▶ How do digital devices represent numbers? **Numeric data** consists of numbers that can be used in arithmetic operations. For example, your annual income is numeric data, as is your age. Digital devices represent numeric data using the binary number system, also called base 2.

The **binary number system** has only two digits: 0 and 1. No numeral like 2 exists in this system, so the number two is represented in binary as 10 (pronounced "one zero"). You'll understand why if you think about what happens when you're counting from 1 to 10 in the familiar decimal system. After you reach 9, you run out of digits. For ten, you have to use the digits 10—zero is a placeholder and the 1 indicates one group of tens.

In binary, you just run out of digits sooner—right after you count to 1. To get to the next number, you have to use the 0 as a placeholder and the 1 indicates one group of twos. In binary, then, you count 0 (zero), 1 (one), 10 (one zero), instead of counting 0, 1, 2 in decimal. If you need to brush up on binary numbers, refer to Figure 1-25 and to the lab at the end of the chapter.

← don't need to know

Decimal (Base 10)	Binary (Base 2)
0	0
1	1
2	10
3	11
4	100
5	101
6	110
7	111
8	1000
9	1001
10	1010
11	1011
1000	1111101000

FIGURE 1-25

The decimal system uses ten symbols to represent numbers: 0, 1, 2, 3, 4, 5, 6, 7, 8, and 9. The binary number system uses only two symbols: 0 and 1.

TRY IT!

The table shows the binary equivalent of numbers 1 through 11. What is the binary for the number 12?

○ 10111

○ 1100

○ 10000

○ 1111

The important point to understand is that the binary number system allows digital devices to represent virtually any number simply by using 0s and 1s. Digital devices can then perform calculations using these numbers.

▶ How do digital devices represent words and letters?

Character data is composed of letters, symbols, and numerals that are not used in arithmetic operations. Examples of character data include your name, address, and hair color. Just as Morse code uses dashes and dots to represent the letters of the alphabet, a digital computer uses a series of bits to represent letters, characters, and numerals.

Digital devices employ several types of codes to represent character data, including ASCII, EBCDIC, and Unicode. **ASCII** (American Standard Code for Information Interchange, pronounced "ASK ee") requires only seven bits for each character. For example, the ASCII code for an uppercase *A* is 1000001. ASCII provides codes for 128 characters, including uppercase letters, lowercase letters, punctuation symbols, and numerals.

EBCDIC (Extended Binary-Coded Decimal Interchange Code, pronounced "EB seh dick") is an 8-bit code used only by older, mainframe computers.

Extended ASCII is a superset of ASCII that uses eight bits to represent each character. For example, Extended ASCII represents the uppercase letter *A* as 01000001. Using eight bits instead of seven bits allows Extended ASCII to provide codes for 256 characters. The additional Extended ASCII characters include boxes and other graphical symbols. Figure 1-26 lists the Extended ASCII character set.

TRY IT!

Write out **Hi!** in Extended ASCII code. (Hint: Use an uppercase *H*, but a lowercase *i*.)

H [ ]

i [ ]

! [ ]

FIGURE 1-26

The Extended ASCII code uses eight 1s and 0s to represent letters, symbols, and numerals. The first 32 ASCII characters are not shown in the table because they represent special control sequences that cannot be printed. The two blank entries are space characters.

char	code	char	code	char	code	char	code	char	code	char	code	char	code	char	code
	00100000	>	00111110	\	01011100	z	01111010	ÿ	10011000	‖	10110110	╘	11010100	≥	11110010
!	00100001	?	00111111	]	01011101	{	01111011	Ö	10011001	╖	10110111	╒	11010101	≤	11110011
"	00100010	@	01000000	^	01011110	|	01111100	Ü	10011010	╕	10111000	╓	11010110	⌠	11110100
#	00100011	A	01000001	_	01011111	}	01111101	¢	10011011	╣	10111001	╫	11010111	⌡	11110101
$	00100100	B	01000010	`	01100000	~	01111110	£	10011100	║	10111010	╪	11011000	÷	11110110
%	00100101	C	01000011	a	01100001	⌂	01111111	¥	10011101	╗	10111011	┘	11011001	≈	11110111
&	00100110	D	01000100	b	01100010	Ç	10000000	₧	10011110	╝	10111100	┌	11011010	°	11111000
'	00100111	E	01000101	c	01100011	ü	10000001	ƒ	10011111	╜	10111101	█	11011011	∙	11111001
(	00101000	F	01000110	d	01100100	é	10000010	á	10100000	╛	10111110	▄	11011100	·	11111010
)	00101001	G	01000111	e	01100101	â	10000011	í	10100001	┐	10111111	▌	11011101	√	11111011
*	00101010	H	01001000	f	01100110	ä	10000100	ó	10100010	└	11000000	▐	11011110	ⁿ	11111100
+	00101011	I	01001001	g	01100111	à	10000101	ú	10100011	┴	11000001	▀	11011111	²	11111101
,	00101100	J	01001010	h	01101000	å	10000110	ñ	10100100	┬	11000010	α	11100000	■	11111110
-	00101101	K	01001011	i	01101001	ç	10000111	Ñ	10100101	├	11000011	ß	11100001		11111111
.	00101110	L	01001100	j	01101010	ê	10001000	ª	10100110	─	11000100	Γ	11100010		
/	00101111	M	01001101	k	01101011	ë	10001001	º	10100111	┼	11000101	π	11100011		
0	00110000	N	01001110	l	01101100	è	10001010	¿	10101000	╞	11000110	Σ	11100100		
1	00110001	O	01001111	m	01101101	ï	10001011	⌐	10101001	╟	11000111	σ	11100101		
2	00110010	P	01010000	n	01101110	î	10001100	¬	10101010	╚	11001000	µ	11100110		
3	00110011	Q	01010001	o	01101111	ì	10001101	½	10101011	╔	11001001	τ	11100111		
4	00110100	R	01010010	p	01110000	Ä	10001110	¼	10101100	╩	11001010	Φ	11101000		
5	00110101	S	01010011	q	01110001	Å	10001111	¡	10101101	╦	11001011	Θ	11101001		
6	00110110	T	01010100	r	01110010	É	10010000	«	10101110	╠	11001100	Ω	11101010		
7	00110111	U	01010101	s	01110011	æ	10010001	»	10101111	═	11001101	δ	11101011		
8	00111000	V	01010110	t	01110100	Æ	10010010	░	10110000	╬	11001110	∞	11101100		
9	00111001	W	01010111	u	01110101	ô	10010011	▒	10110001	╧	11001111	φ	11101101		
:	00111010	X	01011000	v	01110110	ö	10010100	▓	10110010	╨	11010000	ε	11101110		
;	00111011	Y	01011001	w	01110111	ò	10010101	│	10110011	╤	11010001	∩	11101111		
<	00111100	Z	01011010	x	01111000	û	10010110	┤	10110100	╥	11010010	≡	11110000		
=	00111101	[	01011011	y	01111001	ù	10010111	╡	10110101	╙	11010011	±	11110001		

Unicode (pronounced "YOU ni code") uses sixteen bits and provides codes for 65,000 characters—a real bonus for representing the alphabets of multiple languages. For example, Unicode represents an uppercase *A* in the Russian Cyrillic alphabet as 0000010000010000.

▶ **Why do ASCII and Extended ASCII provide codes for 0, 1, 2, 3, 4, 5, 6, 7, 8, and 9?** While glancing at the table of ASCII codes in Figure 1-26, you might have wondered why the table contains codes for 0, 1, 2, 3, and so on. Aren't these numbers represented by the binary number system? A computer uses Extended ASCII character codes for 0, 1, 2, 3 , etc. to represent numerals that are not used for calculations.

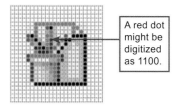

1	**0**		**B**	**S**	**T**
			01000010	00100000	

▶ **How can bits be used to store images?** Images, such as photos, pictures, line art, and graphs, are not small, discrete objects like numbers or the letters of the alphabet. Images have to be digitized in order for digital devices to work with them.

Images can be digitized by treating them as a series of colored dots. Each dot is assigned a binary number according to its color. For example, a green dot might be represented by 0010 and a red dot by 1100, as shown in Figure 1-27. A digital image is simply a list of color numbers for all the dots it contains.

▶ **How can bits be used to store sound?** Sound, such as music and speech, is characterized by the properties of a sound wave. You can create a comparable wave by etching it onto a vinyl platter—essentially how records were made in the days of jukeboxes and record players. You can also represent that sound wave digitally by sampling it at various points, and then converting those points into digital numbers. The more samples you take, the closer your points come to approximating the full wave pattern. This process of sampling, illustrated in Figure 1-28, is how digital recordings are made.

FIGURE 1-27

An image can be digitized by assigning a binary number to each dot.

A red dot might be digitized as 1100.

FIGURE 1-28

A sound wave can be sampled at fraction-of-a-second time intervals. Each sample is recorded as a binary number and stored.

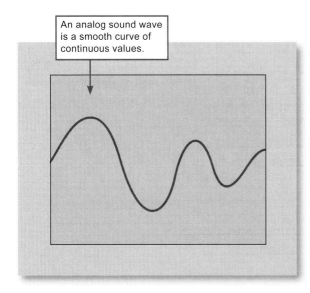

An analog sound wave is a smooth curve of continuous values.

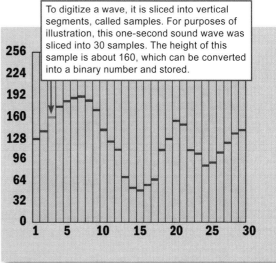

To digitize a wave, it is sliced into vertical segments, called samples. For purposes of illustration, this one-second sound wave was sliced into 30 samples. The height of this sample is about 160, which can be converted into a binary number and stored.

QUANTIFYING BITS AND BYTES

▶ How can I tell the difference between bits and bytes?

The ads for digital devices often include lots of abbreviations relating to bits and bytes. A few key concepts can help you understand what these abbreviations mean. Even though the word *bit* is an abbreviation for *binary digit*, it can be further abbreviated, usually as a lowercase *b*.

On older digital devices, bits were handled in groups, and terminology from that era is still used. A group of eight bits is called a **byte** and is usually abbreviated as an uppercase *B*.

Transmission speeds are usually expressed in bits, whereas storage space is typically expressed in bytes. For example, a cable Internet connection might transfer data from the Internet to your computer at 8 mega*bits* per second. In an iPod ad, you might notice that it can store up to 60 giga*bytes* of music and video.

▶ What do the prefixes *kilo-, mega-, giga-,* and *tera-* mean?

When reading about digital devices, you'll frequently encounter references such as 50 kilobits per second, 1.44 megabytes, 2.8 gigahertz, and 2 terabytes. *Kilo*, *mega*, *giga*, *tera*, and similar terms are used to quantify digital data as shown in Figure 1-29.

Bit	One binary digit	Gigabit	2^{30} bits
Byte	8 bits	Gigabyte	2^{30} bytes
Kilobit	1,024 or 2^{10} bits	Terabyte	2^{40} bytes
Kilobyte	1,024 or 2^{10} bytes	Petabyte	2^{50} bytes
Megabit	1,048,576 or 2^{20} bits	Exabyte	2^{60} bytes
Megabyte	1,048,576 or 2^{20} bytes		

FIGURE 1-29

Quantifying Digital Data

In common usage, *kilo*, abbreviated as K, means a thousand. For example, $50K means $50,000. In the context of computers, however, 50K means 51,200. Why the difference? In the decimal number system we use on a daily basis, the number 1,000 is 10 to the third power, or 10^3. For digital devices where base 2 is the norm, a kilo is precisely 1,024, or 2^{10}. A **kilobit** (abbreviated Kb or Kbit) is 1,024 bits. A **kilobyte** (abbreviated KB or Kbyte) is 1,024 bytes. Kilobytes are often used when referring to the size of small computer files.

The prefix *mega* means a million, or in the context of bits and bytes, precisely 1,048,576 (the equivalent of 2^{20}). A **megabit** (Mb or Mbit) is 1,048,576 bits. A **megabyte** (MB or MByte) is 1,048,576 bytes. Megabytes are often used when referring to the size of medium to large computer files.

In technology lingo, the prefix *giga* refers to a billion, or precisely 1,073,741,824. As you might expect, a **gigabit** (Gb or Gbit) is approximately 1 billion bits. A **gigabyte** (GB or GByte) is 1 billion bytes. Gigabytes are commonly used to refer to storage capacity.

Computers—especially mainframes and supercomputers—sometimes work with huge amounts of data, and so terms such as *tera* (trillion), *peta* (thousand trillion), and *exa* (quintillion) are also handy.

TRY IT!

Fill in the correct abbreviation (B, MB, KB, or GB):

My iPhone has 8 [   ] of storage space.

I uploaded a high-resolution 8- [   ] graphic.

You can download my resume; the file is only 8 [   ] .

CIRCUITS AND CHIPS

▶ **How do digital devices store and transport all those bits?** Because most digital devices are electronic, bits take the form of electrical pulses that can travel over circuits in much the same way that electricity flows over a wire when you turn on a light switch. All the circuits, chips, and mechanical components that form a digital device are designed to work with bits.

At the simplest level, you can envision bits as two states of an electric circuit; the state used for a 1 bit would be on and the state for a 0 bit would be off. In practice, the 1 bit might be represented by an elevated voltage, such as +5 volts, whereas a 0 bit is represented by a low voltage, such as 0.2.

VOLTS | +0.2 | +5 | +0.2 | +5 | +0.2 | +0.2 | +5 | +5

▶ **What's inside?** If it weren't for the miniaturization made possible by digital electronic technology, computers, cell phones, and portable media players would be huge and contain a complex jumble of wires and other electronic gizmos. Instead, today's digital devices contain relatively few parts—just a few wires, some microchips, and one or more circuit boards.

▶ **What's a computer chip?** The terms *computer chip*, *microchip*, and *chip* originated as technical jargon for integrated circuit. An **integrated circuit** (IC), such as the one pictured in Figure 1-30, is a super-thin slice of semiconducting material packed with microscopic circuit elements, such as wires, transistors, capacitors, logic gates, and resistors.

Semiconducting materials (or semiconductors), such as silicon and germanium, are substances with properties between those of a conductor (like copper) and an insulator (like wood). To fabricate a chip, the conductive properties of selective parts of the semiconducting material can be enhanced to essentially create miniature electronic pathways and components, such as transistors.

Integrated circuits are packaged in protective carriers that vary in shape and size. Figure 1-31 illustrates some chip carriers, including small rectangular DIPs (dual in-line packages) with caterpillar-like legs protruding from a black, rectangular body; and pincushion-like PGAs (pin-grid arrays).

FIGURE 1-30

The first computer chips contained fewer than 100 miniaturized components, such as diodes and transistors. The chips used as the CPUs for today's computers and cutting-edge graphics cards contain billions of transistors.

A DIP has two rows of pins that connect the IC circuitry to a circuit board.

A PGA is a square chip package with pins arranged in concentric squares, typically used for microprocessors.

FIGURE 1-31

Integrated circuits can be used for microprocessors, memory, and support circuitry. They are housed within a ceramic carrier. These carriers exist in several configurations, or chip packages, such as DIPs and PGAs.

▶ **How do chips fit together?** The electronic components of most digital devices are mounted on a circuit board called a system board, motherboard, or main board. The **system board** houses all essential chips and provides connecting circuitry between them. Figure 1-32 illustrates circuit boards for two digital devices. Although one device is a full-size computer and the other is an iPhone, they both have chips for processing, memory, input, and output.

FIGURE 1-32

The electronic components of computers and handheld devices have many similar elements, including microchips and circuit boards. Circuit boards are usually green, whereas microchips are usually black.

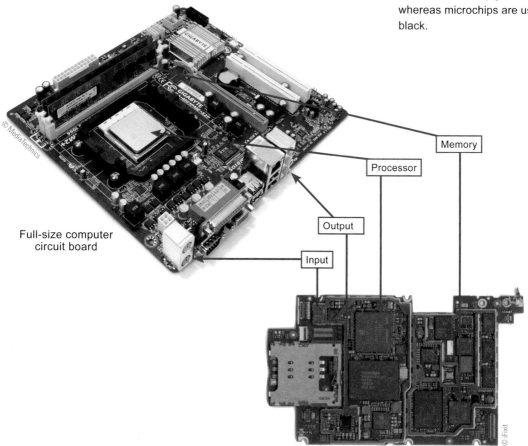

Full-size computer circuit board

Memory

Processor

Output

Input

iPhone circuit board (enlarged)

QuickCheck   SECTION C

1. Data [＿＿＿＿＿] refers to the format in which data is stored, processed, and transferred.

2. Digital devices often use the [＿＿＿＿＿] number system to represent numeric data.

3. Most computers use Unicode or Extended [＿＿＿＿＿] code to represent character data. (Hint: Use the acronym.)

4. KB is the abbreviation for [＿＿＿＿＿].

5. Integrated circuits are fabricated from [＿＿＿＿＿] materials that have properties of a conductor and an insulator.

▶ CHECK ANSWERS

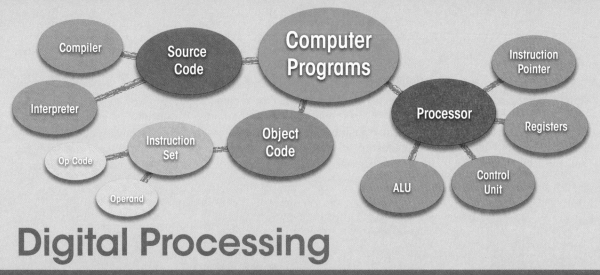

Digital Processing

COMPUTERS AND OTHER DIGITAL DEVICES process data, but how do they know what to do with it? The instructions you issue aren't 0s and 1s that a digital device can work with. So what goes on inside the box? Section D explains the programs that make digital devices tick. You'll discover that although digital devices appear to perform very complex tasks, under the hood they are really performing some very simple operations, but doing them at lightning speed.

PROGRAMS AND INSTRUCTION SETS

▶ **How do digital devices process data?** Computers and dedicated handheld devices all work with digital data under the control of a computer program. Let's take a closer look at programs to see how they are created and how digital devices work with them.

▶ **Who creates programs?** Computer programmers create programs that control digital devices. These programs are usually written in a high-level **programming language**, such as C, BASIC, COBOL, or Java.

Programming languages use a limited set of command words such as *Print*, *If*, *Write*, *Display*, and *Get* to form sentence-like statements designed as step-by-step directives for the processor chip. An important characteristic of most programming languages is that they can be written with simple tools, such as a word processor, and they can be understood by programmers. A simple program to select a song on your iPod might contain the statements shown in Figure 1-33.

Was the first computer programmer a man or a woman? There is controversy surrounding the answer to this question. Check online to find the name of the person who is often cited as the first computer programmer.

○ Bill Gates

○ Ada Lovelace

○ Grace Hopper

○ Charles Fortran

FIGURE 1-33

The program for an iPod displays a list of songs that the user can choose to play. A program works behind the scenes to display the list, get your selection, process it, and play the song.

The human-readable version of a program, like the one above, created in a high-level language by a programmer is called **source code**. However, just as a digital device can't work directly with text, sounds, or images until they have been digitized, source code has to be converted into a digital format before the processor can use it.

29

▶ How does source code get converted? The procedure for translating source code into 0s and 1s can be accomplished by a compiler or an interpreter. A **compiler** converts all the statements in a program in a single batch, and the resulting collection of instructions, called **object code**, is placed in a new file (Figure 1-34). Most of the program files distributed as software contain object code that is ready for the processor to execute.

FIGURE 1-34

A compiler converts statements written in a high-level programming language into object code that the processor can execute. ▶ Watch a compiler in action.

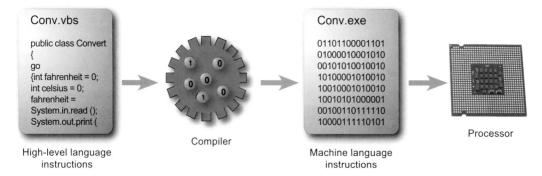

High-level language instructions — Compiler — Machine language instructions — Processor

As an alternative to a compiler, an **interpreter** converts and executes one statement at a time while the program is running. After a statement is executed, the interpreter converts and executes the next statement, and so on (Figure 1-35).

FIGURE 1-35

An interpreter converts high-level statements one at a time as the program is running. ▶ Watch an interpreter in action.

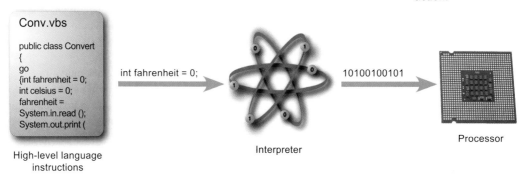

High-level language instructions — Interpreter — Processor

Compilers and interpreters don't simply convert the characters from source code into 0s and 1s. For example, in the first line of the iPod program, Display Playlist, a compiler would not simply convert the *D* into its ASCII equivalent. No, computers are a little trickier than that.

▶ What does the conversion process produce? A microprocessor is hard-wired to perform a limited set of activities, such as addition, subtraction, counting, and comparisons. This collection of preprogrammed activities is called an **instruction set**. Instruction sets are not designed to carry out any specific task, such as word processing or playing music. Instead, an instruction set is designed to be general purpose so that programmers can use it in creative ways for the wide variety of tasks performed by all kinds of digital devices.

Each instruction has a corresponding sequence of 0s and 1s. For example, 00000100 might correspond to *Add*. The list of codes for a microprocessor's instruction set, called **machine language**, can be directly executed by the processor's circuitry. A set of machine language instructions for a program is called **machine code**.

◀ TRY IT!

Suppose a programmer wants to distribute the object code for an iPhone app. After creating the program as source code, the programmer needs to use a(n):

○ interpreter

○ compiler

○ COBOL

○ ASCII code

A machine language instruction has two parts: the op code and the operands. An **op code**, which is short for *operation code*, is a command word for an operation such as add, compare, or jump. The **operand** for an instruction specifies the data, or the address of the data, for the operation. In the following instruction, the op code means add and the operand is 1, so the instruction means add 1.

```
          00000100    00000001
            ADD          1
```

A single high-level instruction very often converts into multiple machine language instructions. Figure 1-36 illustrates the number of machine language instructions that correspond to a simple high-level program.

TRY IT!

Label the operand and the op code.

```
#include <stdio.h>
int main ()
{
int i;

for (i=1; i<=100; i=i+1)
  printf("%d\t",i);
return(0);
}
```

```
001001111011110111111111111100000
101011111011111100000000000010100
101011111010010000000000000100000
101011111010010100000000000100100
101011111010000000000000000011000
101011111010000000000000000011100
100011111010111000000000000011100
100011111011100000000000000011000
000000011100111000000000000011001
001001011100100000000000000000001
001010010000000100000000001100101
101011111010101000000000000011100
000000000000000000111100000010010
000000110000111111001000001000001
000101000010000011111111111110111
101011111011100100000000000011000
001111000000001000001000000000000
100011111010010010000000000011000
000011000001000000000000011101100
001001001000001000000001000011000
```

To summarize what you should now know about programs and instruction sets, a programmer creates human-readable source code using a programming language. A compiler or an interpreter converts source code into machine code. Machine code instructions are a series of 0s and 1s that correspond to a processor's instruction set.

PROCESSOR LOGIC

▶ **What happens inside a computer chip?** A microprocessor contains miles of microscopic circuitry and millions of miniature components divided into different kinds of operational units, such as the ALU and the control unit.

The **ALU** (arithmetic logic unit) is the part of the microprocessor that performs arithmetic operations, such as addition and subtraction. It also performs logical operations, such as comparing two numbers to see if they are the same. The ALU uses **registers** to hold data that is being processed, just as you use a mixing bowl to hold the ingredients for a batch of cookies.

The microprocessor's **control unit** fetches each instruction, just as you get each ingredient out of a cupboard or the refrigerator. Data is loaded into the ALU's registers, just as you add all the ingredients to the mixing bowl. Finally, the control unit gives the ALU the green light to begin processing, just as you flip the switch on your electric mixer to begin blending the cookie ingredients. Figure 1-37 illustrates a microprocessor control unit and an ALU preparing to add 2 + 3.

FIGURE 1-37

The control unit fetches the ADD instruction, then loads data into the ALU's registers where it is processed.

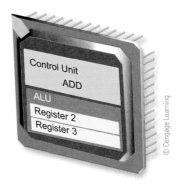

▶ What happens when a computer executes an instruction?

The term **instruction cycle** refers to the process in which a computer executes a single instruction. Some parts of the instruction cycle are performed by the microprocessor's control unit; other parts of the cycle are performed by the ALU. The steps in this cycle are summarized in Figure 1-38.

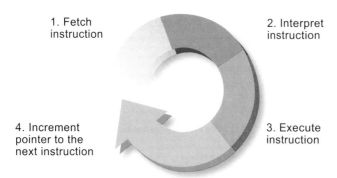

1. Fetch instruction

2. Interpret instruction

4. Increment pointer to the next instruction

3. Execute instruction

FIGURE 1-38

The instruction cycle includes four activities.

▶ What role does the control unit play?

The instructions that a computer is supposed to process for a particular program are held in memory. When the program begins, the memory address of the first instruction is placed in a part of the microprocessor's control unit called an instruction pointer.

The control unit can then fetch the instruction by copying data from that address into its instruction register. From there, the control unit can interpret the instruction, gather the specified data, or tell the ALU to begin processing. Figure 1-39 helps you visualize the control unit's role in processing an instruction.

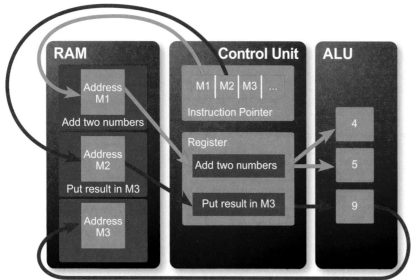

RAM
Address M1
Add two numbers
Address M2
Put result in M3
Address M3

Control Unit
M1 | M2 | M3 | ...
Instruction Pointer
Register
Add two numbers
Put result in M3

ALU
4
5
9

FIGURE 1-39

The control unit's instruction pointer indicates M1, a location in memory. The control unit fetches the "Add two numbers" instruction from M1. This instruction is then sent to the ALU. The instruction pointer then changes to M2. The processor fetches the instruction located in M2, moves it to a register, and executes it.
▶ See how it works.

▶ When does the ALU swing into action?

The ALU is responsible for performing arithmetic and logical operations. It uses registers to hold data ready to be processed. When it gets the go-ahead signal from the control unit, the ALU processes the data and places the result in an accumulator. From the accumulator, the data can be sent to memory or used for further processing. The TRY IT! on the next page helps you visualize what happens in the ALU as the computer processes data.

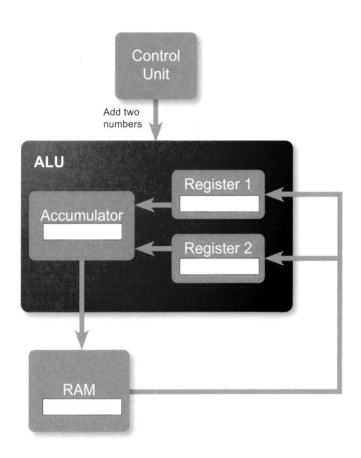

TRY IT!

Execute the following set of commands using the ALU diagram at left.

Load Register 1 with 4.

Load Register 2 with 5.

Add the two registers.

Move the result to RAM.

▶ **What happens after an instruction is executed?** When the computer completes an instruction, the control unit increments the instruction pointer to the memory address of the next instruction, and the instruction cycle begins again.

▶ **Do I need to know all this detailed stuff?** What you should take away from the discussion about programming and instruction sets is the idea that computers and other digital devices accomplish a wide array of complex tasks by performing a very limited set of machine language instructions very fast.

These concepts about how processors work will help you understand the significance of microprocessor performance, such as speed and word size, which you'll learn about in the next chapter.

QuickCheck

1. A(n) [   ] converts all of the source code instructions into a new file containing [   ] code.

2. A microprocessor is hard-wired to perform a set of activities called a(n) [   ] set.

3. A machine language instruction has two parts: a(n) [   ] code and an operand.

4. The ALU in your computer's microprocessor holds data in [   ].

5. The microprocessor's control unit contains a(n) [   ] pointer that holds the address of the instruction being executed.

▶ CHECK ANSWERS

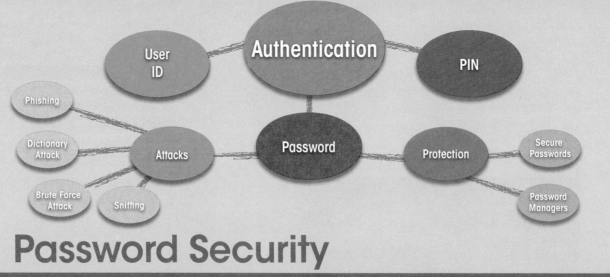

Password Security

SECTION **E**

USER IDS, passwords, and personal identification numbers (PINs) are a fact of everyday life in the information age. They are required for activities such as using ATMs and debit cards, logging in to Windows, accessing wireless networks, making an iTunes purchase, instant messaging, reading e-mail, and file sharing. Many Web sites encourage you to sign up for membership by choosing a user ID and password. Section E provides information about selecting secure passwords and managing the mountain of passwords you collect and tend to forget.

AUTHENTICATION PROTOCOLS

▶ **What is an authentication protocol?** Security experts use the term **authentication protocol** to refer to any method that confirms a person's identity using something the person knows, something the person possesses, or something the person is. For example, a person might know a password or PIN. A person might possess an ATM card or a credit card. A person can also be identified by **biometrics**, such as a fingerprint, facial features (photo), or a retinal pattern (Figure 1-40).

Authentication protocols that use more than one means of identification are more secure than others. Two-factor authentication, which verifies identity using two independent elements of confirmation such as an ATM card and a PIN, is more secure than single-factor authentication, such as a password. Computer-related security is primarily based on passwords associated with user IDs. The level of protection offered by single-factor authentication depends on good password selection and management on the part of users.

▶ **What is a user ID?** A **user ID** is a series of characters—letters and possibly numbers or special symbols—that becomes a person's unique identifier, similar to a Social Security number. It is also referred to as a user name, login, screen name, online nickname, or handle. User IDs are public. Because they are not secret, they do not offer any level of security.

The rules for creating a user ID are not consistent throughout all applications, so it is important to read instructions carefully before finalizing your user ID. For example, spaces might not be allowed in a user ID. Hence, the underline in brunhilde_jefferson is used instead of a space. There might be a length limitation, so Ms. Jefferson might have to choose a short user ID, such as bjeffe. It is becoming common to use your e-mail address as a user ID; it is unique and easy to remember.

FIGURE 1-40

Biometric authentication protocols include retinal scans that identify unique patterns of blood vessels in the eye.

© Brand X Pictures/Alamy

TRY IT!

When you use a debit card, you have to enter your PIN. This is an example of:

○ single-factor authentication

○ single user ID

○ two-factor authentication

○ password security

34

Some computers that host password-protected resources don't differentiate between uppercase and lowercase letters, and would consider the user IDs B_Jefferson and b_jefferson to be the same. Other computers are **case sensitive** and differentiate between uppercase and lowercase. On such computers, if Ms. Jefferson selected Brun_Jeff as her user ID, she would not be able to gain access by typing brun_jeff.

▶ **What is a password?** A **password** is a series of characters that verifies a user ID and guarantees that you are the person you claim to be. Although you might be assigned a password, more commonly you are asked to provide your own. In some situations, you might be given a temporary password and then be asked to change it as soon as you successfully log in for the first time. Passwords and user IDs are created on a registration or enrollment screen similar to the one in Figure 1-41.

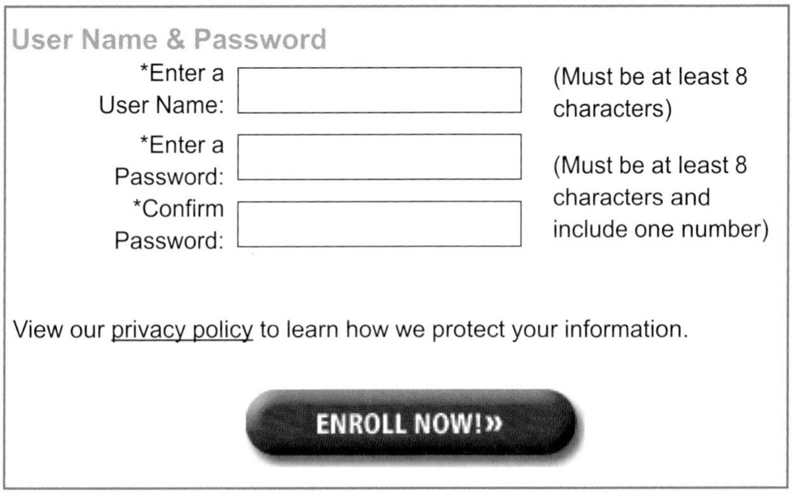

FIGURE 1-41

When you create an account, you are usually required to enter a user ID and password. Then you are required to confirm the password to make sure you typed it correctly.

User Name & Password

*Enter a User Name: [_____] (Must be at least 8 characters)

*Enter a Password: [_____] (Must be at least 8 characters and include one number)

*Confirm Password: [_____]

View our privacy policy to learn how we protect your information.

ENROLL NOW! »

▶ **What if I forget my password?** Login screens for many applications provide a "forgot my password" link. Clicking this link checks your identity using your answer to a personal question. If your identity checks out, your password is e-mailed to you. A personal question provides an alternative authentication protocol to ensure that you are not a hacker pretending to be a legitimate user who has lost a password.

Personal questions and answers are usually set up at the same time you create an account. After selecting a password, you are required to choose a question that you must answer before your forgotten password is e-mailed to you. This question might be something like: *What is your mother's maiden name?*, *What is your favorite color?*, or *Where were you born?* You should be careful about the question you choose because public information like your mother's maiden name or the town of your birth can be researched by any hacker.

▶ **What is the difference between a password and a PIN?** Both passwords and PINs are classified as *something-the-user-knows* authentication methods. In practice, PINs tend to be a short sequence of numbers that can be entered using a numeric keypad, whereas passwords tend to be longer sequences of letters, numbers, and special characters that require a full qwerty keyboard for entry. PINs are commonly used with two-factor authentication protocols, whereas passwords are used in conjunction with single-factor authentication protocols.

For example, ATMs require a bank card (something you possess) and a PIN (something you know). In contrast, passwords are associated with single-factor authentication used for networks, Web sites, and other situations in which the hardware for dealing with ID cards is not available.

PASSWORD HACKS

▶ **How serious is password theft?** To a hacker, obtaining the password for a specific user ID can be even more rewarding than a burglar figuring out the combination to a house safe. Once hackers get into a user account, a wealth of personal information can be at their fingertips. This information could be anything from juicy e-mail gossip to Social Security numbers, credit card numbers, bank account numbers, health data, and other private details. When someone gains unauthorized access to your personal data and uses it illegally, it is called **identity theft**. Victims of this increasingly common crime often don't realize what has happened until it's too late.

Armed with your password and other personal data, a cybercriminal can rack up bills using your credit card, apply for a mortgage using your financial data, create fake accounts in your name, send embarrassing e-mail messages, or wreak havoc on your bank account. Once a thief breaks into an online account, he or she can also change your password and you will no longer be able to log in. Password theft is serious and pervasive, so it is important to understand how hackers get passwords and how you can protect yours.

▶ **How can hackers get my password?** Hackers employ a whole range of ways to steal passwords. Some primitive means include shoulder surfing, which is looking over your shoulder as you type in your password, and dumpster diving, which is going through your trash.

Password thieves can easily find your password if you write it down on a yellow sticky note hidden under your keyboard or in plain sight on top of your monitor. If a hacker doesn't have physical access to your work area but your computer is connected to a network, your password can be discovered by a hacker using a remote computer and software tools that systematically guess your password, intercept it, or trick you into revealing it.

A **dictionary attack** helps hackers guess your password by stepping through a dictionary containing thousands of the most commonly used passwords. Password dictionaries can be found on black hat sites and packaged with password-cracking software, such as John the Ripper. Unfortunately, dictionary attacks are often enough to break a password because many users choose passwords that are easy to remember and likely to be in the most commonly used list (Figure 1-42).

> **TERMINOLOGY NOTE**
>
> *Hacker* can refer to a skilled programmer or to a person who manipulates computers with malicious intent. The terms *black hat* and *cracker* are also used to refer to a malicious or criminal hacker.

FIGURE 1-42

Some of the most commonly used passwords are included in the dictionaries packaged with password-cracking software. These passwords (listed in order of popularity) should not be used.

12345	internet	jordan	alex	newyork	jonathan
abc123	service	michael	apple	soccer	love
password	canada	michelle	avalon	thomas	marina
computer	hello	mindy	brandy	wizard	master
123456	ranger	patrick	chelsea	Monday	missy
tigger	shadow	123abc	coffee	asdfgh	monday
1234	baseball	andrew	dave	bandit	monkey
a1b2c3	donald	bear	falcon	batman	natasha
qwerty	harley	calvin	freedom	boris	ncc1701
123	hockey	changeme	gandalf	dorothy	newpass
xxx	letmein	diamond	golf	eeyore	pamela
money	maggie	matthew	green	fishing	pepper
test	mike	miller	helpme	football	piglet
carmen	mustang	ou812	linda	george	poohbear
mickey	snoopy	tiger	magic	happy	pookie
secret	buster	trustno1	merlin	iloveyou	rabbit
summer	dragon	12345678	molson	jennifer	rachel

The **brute force attack** also uses password-cracking software, but its range is much more extensive than the dictionary attack. Because it exhausts all possible combinations of letters to decrypt a password, a brute force attack can run for days to crack some passwords.

If hackers can't guess a password, they can use another technique called **sniffing**, which intercepts information sent out over computer networks. Sniffing software is used legitimately by network administrators to record network traffic for monitoring and maintenance purposes. The same software can also be used for illicit activities. If your user ID and password travel over a network as unencrypted text, they can easily fall into the hands of a password thief.

An even more sophisticated approach to password theft is **phishing**, in which a hacker poses as a legitimate representative of an official organization such as your ISP, your bank, or an online payment service in order to persuade you to disclose highly confidential information. Mostly through e-mail or instant messaging, a fake customer representative or administrator asks you to visit a Web page to confirm billing information or verify your account by providing your password, credit card number, or Social Security number.

If you examine phishing messages more closely, you might realize that the Web sites referred to are fake. However, seasoned hackers try to make the URLs look as close as possible to the official Web sites they claim to represent (Figure 1-43).

TRY IT!

How fast can you guess the password for this account?

Log in

User name:

Mickey@gmail.com

Password:

FIGURE 1-43

A fake Web site can look very similar to the real thing, but this fraudulent site originates in Korea. Do you notice that the URL is www.paypvl.com.kr instead of the legitimate *www. paypal.com*? You should avoid clicking links in e-mail messages that attempt to get you to confirm or renew account data.

As users became better at identifying phishing messages, password thieves resorted to the use of keyloggers. Short for *keystroke logging*, a **keylogger** is software that secretly records a user's keystrokes and sends the information to a hacker. A keylogger is a form of malicious code called a Trojan horse, or Trojan. Trojans are computer programs that seem to perform one function while actually doing something else. They can be embedded in e-mail attachments, software downloads, and even files. Trojans are discussed in more detail in the security section of the Software chapter.

SECURE PASSWORDS

▶ **How do I create a secure password?** With password theft becoming more and more widespread, security experts recommend using a strong, secure password for financial transactions such as those that involve PayPal, iTunes, or bank accounts. A strong, secure password is one that is easy to remember but difficult to crack. Figure 1-44 offers guidelines for selecting secure passwords and avoiding ones that are easily crackable.

FIGURE 1-44

Tips for Creating Secure Passwords

▶ Use passwords that are at least eight characters in length. The longer the password, the tougher it is to crack.

▶ Use a combination of letters, numbers, and special characters such as $, #, if permitted.

▶ Use uppercase and lowercase letters if the hosting computer is case sensitive.

▶ Use a passphrase based on several words or the first letters of a verse from a favorite poem or song. For example, the words from the nursery rhyme "Jack and Jill went up the hill" can be converted to jjwuth. You can then insert special characters and numbers, and add some uppercase letters to create a password that still makes sense to you personally, such as J&J w^th!ll. This type of password appears random to anyone else but you.

▶ Do not use a password based on public information such as your phone number, Social Security number, driver's license number, or birthday. Hackers can easily find this information, and other personal facts such as names of your spouse, children, or pets.

▶ Avoid passwords that contain your entire user ID or part of it. A user ID of bjeffe coupled with a password of bjeffe123 is an easy target for password thieves.

▶ Steer clear of words that can be found in the dictionary, including foreign words. Dictionary attacks can utilize foreign language dictionaries. Even common words spelled backwards, such as drowssap instead of password, are not tricky enough to fool password-cracking software.

▶ **How do I protect my password?** Once you have selected a strong password, you must take steps to keep it safe. Do not share your password with anyone. Avoid writing down a password. If possible, memorize it. If you must write down a password, do not leave it in an obvious place such as under your keyboard or mouse pad. Recording passwords in an unencrypted file stored on your computer is risky, too, especially if you have more than one password. A hacker who gains access to that file can use the passwords to access all your accounts.

If you think one of your passwords has been compromised, change it immediately. Even if you have no evidence of password tampering, security experts recommend that you change passwords periodically, say every six months. When you change your passwords, do not just make a slight variation to your current one. For example, do not change just4Me1 to just4Me2. You should not reuse your old passwords either, so it's best to keep a password history list.

TRY IT!

Which password for Dave Meyers is most secure?

○ DaveBMeyers

○ Dave12345

○ Gilgamesh

○ Ih2gtg8pw

○ HomeGilgamesh

Aside from good password maintenance habits, computer maintenance is also essential. Make sure that your entire computer is protected by security software, which is explained in the Software chapter.

▶ **How do I deal with all my passwords and user IDs?** You can accumulate many passwords and user IDs—for logging in to Windows, accessing online banking, using e-mail, shopping online, downloading music, and getting into your Facebook account. The more passwords and user IDs you have, the more difficult they become to remember.

How many times have you had to click the "I forgot my password" link when you logged in to an online account? Your passwords provide the most protection if they are unique, but accessing even 25 different Web sites that require 25 different user IDs and 25 corresponding passwords requires quite a memory. To add to the confusion, you must also regularly change passwords to your critical accounts!

Instead of using 25 different user IDs and passwords, you need some way to reduce the number of things you have to memorize. First, strive to select a unique user ID that you can use for more than one site. Remember that people with your name who selected user IDs before you might have already taken the obvious user IDs. For example, when John Smith selects a user ID, you can bet that other people have already used johnsmith, jsmith, and john_smith. To keep his user ID unique, John might instead select jsl2wm (the first letters in "John Smith loves 2 watch movies").

Next, you can maintain two or three tiers of passwords—the top level for high security, the second level for medium security, and the third level for low security. If you do not have too many accounts, you can opt for just two tiers—for high and low security. You can then select two passwords. Use the high-security password for accessing critical data, such as online banking, for managing an online stock portfolio, or for your account at an online bookstore that stores a copy of your billing and credit card information.

Use your low-security password in situations where you don't really care if your security is compromised. Some places on the Internet want you to establish an account with a user ID and password just to add your name to a mailing list. At other sites, your user ID and password provide access to information, but none of your critical personal or financial data is stored there. It is not necessary to change your low-security password very often. Figure 1-45 provides more information about tiered passwords.

FIGURE 1-45

Tiered passwords reduce the number of user IDs and passwords that you have to remember; however, the disadvantage is that a hacker who discovers one of your passwords will be able to use it to access many of your accounts.

▶ Can my computer help me to remember passwords?

Your computer's operating system, Web browser, or other software might include a password manager to help you keep track of user IDs and passwords. A **password manager** (sometimes called a keychain) stores user IDs with their corresponding passwords and automatically fills in login forms. For example, when you register at a Web site while using a browser such as Internet Explorer, the browser stores your new ID and password in an encrypted file on your computer's hard disk. The next time you visit the Web site, your ID and password are automatically filled in on the login screen (Figure 1-46).

The drawback to password managers that are built into browsers, operating systems, or other software is that if you switch to different software or to a different computer, you will not have access to the stored passwords. For example, if you usually work with the Safari browser on your MacBook Air, it stores your passwords; but if you use a public computer in a coffee shop, your passwords are not accessible from that machine.

Standalone password manager software offers a more inclusive approach to creating and retrieving passwords.

▶ What is password manager software?

A standalone password manager is a software application that feeds passwords into login forms regardless of the software you're using. As with built-in password managers, a standalone password manager stores user IDs and passwords in an encrypted file. You can access this file using a master password. This type of password manager can be moved from one computer to another, for example, if you purchase a new computer.

A standalone password manager can also generate secure "nonsense passwords." You don't have to worry if the passwords are difficult to remember because the password manager software can keep track of them (Figure 1-47).

FIGURE 1-46

Checking the *Remember me* box saves your user ID and password for the next time you log in, but you have to be using the same browser.

FIGURE 1-47

Password managers help you keep track of all your passwords. ▶ If you've never used a password manager and want to see how one works, start the guided tour for this figure in your interactive eBook.

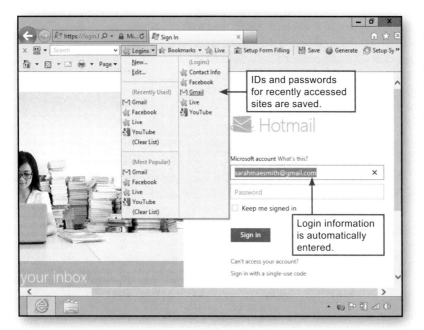

In addition to generating and tracking your passwords, most password manager software provides other features, such as password strength meters and form fillers.

A password strength meter indicates whether your passwords are secure enough—a feature that is useful if you've created your own passwords, rather than using your password manager to generate them.

Form fillers automatically enter data into online Web forms such as those that request billing data when you order at an online shopping site. Many form fillers also match a Web form's URL against a set of valid URLs that you have provided in order to avoid sending data to a fake Web site that you have been lured to visit by a phishing message. When entering passwords, form fillers are not collecting your password from the keyboard; therefore, a hacker's keylogger cannot secretly record keystrokes.

There are several free, shareware, or open source password managers, such as KeePass, RoboForm, DataVault, and Kaspersky Password Manager. Some password manager software is portable, which means that it does not have to be installed on a computer before it is used. Instead, you can carry it around on a USB flash drive so that your passwords are available wherever you use a computer, such as in your school lab, at the library, or at work. When you remove the flash drive, your portable password manager leaves no traces of passwords behind (Figure 1-48).

For extra protection against intruders who might search your computer for passwords, a flash drive that contains a password manager can be unplugged when you are not accessing password-protected sites. You can also remove the flash drive from your computer when you're out so that your nosy roommate can't snoop through your computer files.

▶ **Should I store passwords in the cloud?** New password management techniques are being developed, but some offer their own set of potential security problems. For example, Web-based password managers can be attractive targets for password thieves. By breaking into a single site, a password thief could harvest thousands of passwords. As new password management technologies appear, make sure you evaluate them carefully before trusting them with your valuable data.

TRY IT!

Smartphone access can be controlled by a password. Would you recommend a password manager to your friend with an iPhone?

○ No. The phone's password is all my friend will need

○ Yes, especially if my friend wants to access Facebook or other subscription sites from the phone

QuickCheck   SECTION E

1. An authentication [   ] is any method that confirms a person's identity using something the person knows, something the person possesses, or something the person is.

2. On a(n) [   ]-sensitive server, the user ID BJP is different from bjp.

3. A(n) [   ] attack can guess your password if you are using common passwords or everyday words.

4. A(n) [   ] scam looks like a request from your bank or an online payment service, but is actually a hacker who wants you to disclose your user ID and password.

5. Most browsers include a built-in password [   ] that remembers the user IDs and passwords you use when logging in to Web sites or online e-mail.

 CHECK ANSWERS

Issue: What Is the Value of Information?

THE GUERILLA Open Access Manifesto begins, "Information is power. But like all power, there are those who want to keep it for themselves. The world's entire scientific and cultural heritage, published over centuries in books and journals, is increasingly being digitized and locked up by a handful of private corporations."

Written by Aaron Swartz, the manifesto makes a case for free access to information, particularly scientific information that has the potential to benefit society. To publicize his views, Swartz took action, allegedly downloading nearly 5 million articles, editorials, reviews, and other material from the prestigious JSTOR academic database. He was arrested on felony charges.

Shortly after the Swartz story broke, another open access advocate, Gregg Maxwell, uploaded more than 18,000 articles from Philosophical Transactions of the Royal Society to a file sharing site. The articles, all dated prior to 1923 and previously available by subscription, became accessible to the general public for free.

In explaining his actions, Maxwell wrote, "The liberal dissemination of knowledge is essential to scientific inquiry. More than in any other area, the application of restrictive copyright is inappropriate for academic works: there is no sticky question of how to pay authors or reviewers, as the publishers are already not paying them. And unlike 'mere' works of entertainment, liberal access to scientific work impacts the well-being of all mankind. Our continued survival may even depend on it."

Certainly there are expenses associated with operating academic databases such as JSTOR, but the researchers who write academic articles are typically not paid for their contributions. Money to support their research often comes from public funding collected from taxpayers. Yet academic databases often charge access fees to read full-text articles.

Schools and libraries often pay a per-year fee that provides students and faculty with free access to academic publications, but members of the general public trying to access such information from their home or work computers hit a paywall that becomes a barrier to access. Open access advocates want information to be freely available, and technologies of the Information Age seem on the way to making that a reality.

Information purveyors such as JSTOR and *The New York Times* argue that free data is unsustainable. Gathering, storing, and distributing information entail costs that need to be passed on to consumers. Information has value that consumers should be willing to pay for.

A U.S. Department of the Navy report suggests that information has value whether or not it is free; however, the value of information increases when it is easy to access, organized, current, and reliable.

On the surface, information available from the Web might seem free, but there are hidden costs such as intrusive advertising, surreptitious tracking, and personal data collection that erode privacy.

Information from the Web might seem free, but there are hidden costs…

Public release of massive numbers of documents onto the Internet is becoming more common as open access advocates take action. Sometimes information, such as Sarah Palin's e-mails and FBI files on the Roswell UFO incident, can be obtained through the Freedom of Information Act (FOIA) and other legitimate channels.

When legitimate routes fail, documents and databases are sometimes released through backdoor channels. Climategate and WikiLeaks are notorious examples of leaked data.

Open access is a complex concept that requires intelligent compromise among the interests of individuals, businesses, and government agencies. Individuals want to retain their privacy, businesses want to retain their income stream, and governments want to maintain security. Yet, all parties would like as much information as possible in order to make informed decisions and take constructive action.

TRY IT! Explore the value of information, paywalls, and data leaks by working on the following activities.

1 Despite the widespread belief that digital information should be free, the popularity of iTunes and ebook readers, such as the Kindle, demonstrate that consumers are willing to pay for some digital content accessed from the Internet. Make a list of digital content that you currently pay for.

2 A paywall blocks access to documents, news articles, and other content until the consumer pays an access or registration fee. Notable publications such as *The New York Times* and *The Wall Street Journal* have instituted paywalls with varying degrees of success. Use a search engine to answer two questions about paywalls:

a. What is the reason that premium newspapers and magazines believe that paywalls are necessary?

b. How successful are paywalls based on the number of consumers who actually pay for access to content in online newspapers and magazines?

3 Paywalls are not the only barrier that blocks access to information. Individuals, corporations, and governments hold personal, proprietary, and classified information that is not available for public access. That information sometimes goes public. Explore some of the most notorious data leaks by filling in the following table.

LEAK	CONTENTS	DATE	NUMBER OF DOCUMENTS
CRU CLIMATE DATA			
U.S. DIPLOMATIC CABLES			
WAR DIARY: AFGHANISTAN WAR LOGS			
WAR DIARY: IRAQ WAR LOGS			

4 Many countries have legislation similar to the United States Freedom of Information Act, which provides a legitimate channel for requesting the release of proprietary and classified information. Declassified data is posted on Web sites for public access. The FBI maintains a fascinating site called The Vault, where you can read dossiers about Marilyn Monroe, Malcolm X, and the Roswell UFO incident.

Head over to The Vault (*vault.fbi.gov*), browse through the documents for a topic that interests you, and record the most surprising piece of information you find.

INFOWEBLINKS

You can check the **NP2014 Chapter 1** InfoWebLink for updates to these activities.

W CLICK TO CONNECT
www.infoweblinks.com/NP2014/ch01

What Do You Think?

ISSUE

1. From what you have learned, do you think that academic research articles should be available for free?

2. Do you agree with magazine and news companies that quality content requires a paywall?

3. Do you support efforts to make information accessible through back channels such as WikiLeaks?

Information Tools: Finding the Right Stuff

You're looking for information. Where you start depends on how you plan to use the information. The sources you need for a class research paper often differ from information sources for personal use.

Information sources can be roughly divided into two categories: those that serve academic audiences and those that serve consumers.

Scholarly and academic sources

Find these sources using Google Scholar and academic databases/directories such as DOAJ

- Written by experts
- Intended for academic or professional readers
- Peer-reviewed by other experts before publication
- Contain original research, theoretical analysis, or best practices
- Carefully documented by footnotes or endnotes
- Published by academic publishers, professional associations, or university presses
- Include academic books, academic journals, papers, conference proceedings, dissertations, textbooks, and monographs in printed or digital format

Use these sources for class papers, theses, essays, and dissertations

Consumer-level sources

Find these sources using Google Web, Google News, and product Web sites

- Written by reporters, bloggers, or practitioners
- Intended for the general public
- Usually reviewed by an editor before publication
- Sometimes open to public comment after publication   👍 Like
- Printed or displayed in color with included photos
- Often published in for-profit publications that include advertising
- Include trade books, magazines, encyclopedias, press releases, trade journals, blogs, news sites, and online forums

Use these sources for product information, troubleshooting, news, and topic overviews

HELP!

Can't access what you need for a research project? Here are some common problems encountered by students, and solutions that help you find the resources you need for a paper that earns you an A.

PROBLEM: Web search engines, such as Google, sometimes miss many of the articles most relevant for a college-level research project because articles are often locked behind paywalls or firewalls that don't allow search engine access. **SOLUTION:** Go directly to a journal's Web site and search there.

PROBLEM: Many scholarly journals display only abstracts to the general public; viewing the full text of articles requires a subscription or download fee. **SOLUTION:** Use your library's online database to locate articles that are included in the physical collection. You might have to go to the library to read the articles or ask for the full article from inter-library loan.

PROBLEM: Access to academic search engines and databases, such as LexisNexis, requires subscriptions. **SOLUTION:** Your school might provide registered students with free access to journal databases if you log in from a computer on the school network or from within the library.

⬤TRY IT! Research about computers and technology relies on information from a broad base of sources. Let's explore these sources by comparing what they offer. Some searches will produce information suitable for academic projects, such as term papers, while other searches tend to produce information suitable for personal use, such as figuring out if someone is hacking into your home network.

To record the results of this comparison, write down (or screen capture) one example that you get from each source, and then describe an academic project or personal use for which that information would be suitable. As an example, suppose that you search for "cloud computing" using Google Scholar and one of the results is

> **Introduction to parallel algorithms and architectures**
> T Leighton - sce.uhcl.edu
> ... Catalog Description: This course covers parallel computations using popular interconnection networks such as arrays, trees, hypercubes, and permutation networks such as the star and the pancake networks, as well as grid and **cloud computing**. ...
> Cited by 2996 - Related articles - View as HTML - Library Search - All 5 versions

This information is academic and could be suitable as one of the sources for a term paper about cloud computing for a computer science course. Okay, now see what you can do with the rest.

1 Check Wikipedia for general information about "cloud computing" and then look at the list of references.

2 Search for academic and trade books about cloud computing at Amazon Books.

3 Search for conference proceedings about cloud computing at the ACM Digital Library.

4 Search an open access database such as DOAJ (see sidebar) for a recent paper about cloud computing.

5 Search an academic database (see sidebar) for an abstract about cloud computing.

6 Search Science.gov for a full text article about cloud computing.

7 Search an online computer magazine, such as *Wired*, for a recent article about cloud computing.

8 Use a search engine, such as Google or Bing, to locate a recent press release about cloud computing.

9 Search Amazon Electronics for cloud computing products and customer reviews.

10 Search a technology news site (see sidebar) for the latest industry news about cloud computing.

Computer and Technology Academic Databases

Odysci Academic Search

DOAJ (Directory of Open Access Journals)

Science.gov

TDG Scholar

Microsoft Academic Search

IEEE Xplore

CiteSeerX

ACM (Association for Computing Machinery) Digital Library

Computer and Technology News Sites

Huffington Post Tech

Engadget

TechCrunch

Ars Technica

Google News Technology

WSJ All Things Digital

CNET News

Tom's Hardware

1

Technology in Context: Marketing

WALKING OUT THE GATE of ancient Pompeii, you might have come across an eye-catching sign extolling the virtues of a popular tavern in the next town. The sign was a clever bit of marketing designed to target thirsty travelers and drum up business. Throughout the centuries, handbills, newspaper ads, television commercials, radio spots, and mass mail campaigns were all important tools of the marketing industry. Now, computers have opened new vistas for communicating with consumers.

The American Marketing Association defines marketing as an organizational function and a set of processes for creating, communicating, and delivering value to customers and for managing customer relationships in ways that benefit the organization and its stakeholders. A person-in-the-street definition might simply be that marketing is an attempt to sell products.

Computers first played a role in marketing as a research tool for quickly crunching numbers from consumer surveys and sales figures. Statistics derived from that data helped companies focus development efforts on the most promising products and market them effectively. Marketing research data made one fact very clear: Even the most effective advertising cannot convince everyone to buy a particular product. A costly prime-time television ad, for example, might be seen by millions of viewers, but many of them have no interest in the advertised product. To better target potential buyers, marketers turned to direct marketing.

Direct marketing attempts to establish a one-to-one relationship with prospective customers rather than waiting for them to learn about a product from general, impersonal forms of advertising, such as billboards, radio spots, television commercials, and newspaper ads. The first direct marketing techniques included personalized let-

ters, catalogs, and telemarketing. Customer names, addresses, and phone numbers were mined from computer databases maintained by mailing list brokers. Lists could be tailored in rudimentary ways to fit target markets. Selling snow tires? Get a list of consumers in northern states. Looking for Peace Corps volunteers? Get a list of college students.

"Dear Carmen Smith, you might already have won…" Just about everyone in America has received a personalized sweepstakes mailing. Initially, personalized names were crudely inserted using dot matrix printers, but today high-speed laser printers dash off thousands of personalized letters per hour and use graphics capabilities to affix signatures that appear to have been hand-signed in ink.

Telemarketing is a technique for telephone solicitation. Computerized autodialers make it possible for telemarketers to work efficiently. An autodialer is a device that can dial telephone numbers stored in a list. It can also generate and dial telephone numbers using a random or sequential number generator.

Image Courtesy of The Advertising Archives

A smart autodialer, called a predictive dialer, increases a telemarketer's efficiency even more by automatically calling several numbers at the same time and only passing a call to the marketer when a person answers.

If you've picked up the telephone only to hear silence or a disconnect, it was likely an autodialer that connected to more than one person at the same time and dropped your call. Predictive dialers eliminate telemarketing time that would be otherwise wasted with busy signals, answering machines, and so on.

The Internet opened up dramatic new horizons in direct marketing by providing an inexpensive conduit for collecting information about potential customers and distributing targeted direct marketing. According to author Jim Sterne, "The Internet and the World

Wide Web have become the most important new communication media since television, and ones that are fundamentally reshaping contemporary understanding of sales and marketing." Today, a vast amount of information flows over the Internet and marketers are trying to harness that information to most efficiently communicate their messages to prospective customers.

E-commerce Web sites offer a global distribution channel for small entrepreneurs as well as multinational corporations. Consumers can locate e-commerce sites using a search engine. Some search engines allow paid advertising to appear on their sites. Clever marketers use search engine optimization techniques to get their Web sites to the top of search engine lists.

Another way to drive traffic to an e-commerce site is banner advertising that clutters up Web pages with inviting tag lines for free products. Clicking the ad connects consumers to the site. The cost of placing a banner ad depends on the click-through rate—the number of consumers who click an ad. Sophisticated banner ad software displays the banner ad across an entire network and monitors click-through rates. Not only does this software keep track of clickthroughs for billing purposes, it can automatically adjust the sites that carry each ad to maximize click-through rates.

Internet marketing is often associated with the tidal wave of spam that's currently crashing into everyone's Inbox. These mass spam e-mails, however bothersome, are a very crude form of direct marketing. Typically, spammers use unscrubbed mailing lists containing many expired, blocked, and invalid e-mail addresses. This hit-or-miss strategy is cheap. Ten million e-mail addresses can be rented for as low as $100 and server bandwidth provided by e-mail brokers costs about $300 per million messages sent.

Marketing professionals regard massive e-mail spamming with some degree of scorn because most lists don't narrow the focus to the most promising

customers. Worse yet, consumers react by installing spam filters. Some spammers try to evade spam filters. More than one Web site offers marketers a free service that analyzes mass e-mail solicitations using a spam filter simulator. If the solicitation can't get through the filter, the service offers suggestions on what to change so the message slips through.

In contrast to gratuitous spammers, marketing professionals have learned that opt-in mailing lists have much higher success rates. Consumers who have asked for information more often appreciate receiving it and act on it. Opt-in consumers are also more willing to divulge information that develops an accurate profile of their lifestyle so marketers can offer them the most appropriate products.

When given a choice, however, consumers tend to opt out, and marketers responded by surreptitiously collecting data from free apps, Web sites, Facebook pages, and the content of Web-based e-mail messages. Privacy advocates attacked this practice, and savvy consumers have found tools and techniques to minimize the amount of personal data that is harvested behind the scenes.

Most consumers would agree that the marketing industry needs professionals who are socially responsible. In describing the qualifications for marketing professionals, the Bureau of Labor Statistics states the obvious when it says, "Computer skills are vital because marketing, product promotion, and advertising on the Internet are increasingly common."

In preparing for a marketing career, a knowledge of computers, the Web, and the Internet are important. Equally important is preparation in statistical analysis, psychology, and ethics, along with coursework that covers legal and regulatory aspects of the technology-driven marketing industry.

1

New Perspectives Labs

To access the New Perspectives Labs for Chapter 1, open the NP2014 interactive eBook and then click the icon next to the lab title.

▶ OPERATING A PERSONAL COMPUTER

IN THIS LAB YOU'LL LEARN:

- How to start a Windows computer
- What to do when a computer is in sleep mode
- How to deactivate a screensaver
- How to select a different screensaver
- How to use the Alt, Ctrl, Esc, Num Lock, Caps Lock, Windows, Fn, Backspace, Delete, and arrow keys
- The difference between forward and backward slashes
- How to start and exit a program
- How to close a program that is not responding
- When to use the reset button
- How to shut down Windows

LAB ASSIGNMENTS

1. Start the interactive part of the lab. Make sure you've enabled Tracking if you want to save your QuickCheck results. Perform each lab step as directed, and answer all the lab QuickCheck questions. When you exit the lab, your answers are automatically graded and your results are displayed.

2. Make a note of the brand and location of the computer you're using to complete these lab assignments.

3. Use the Start button to access your computer's Control Panel folder. Describe the status of your computer's power saver settings.

4. Preview the available screensavers on the computer you use most frequently. Select the screensaver you like the best and describe it in a few sentences.

5. What is the purpose of an Fn key? Does your computer keyboard include an Fn key? Explain why or why not.

6. In your own words, describe what happens when you (a) click the Close button; (b) hold down the Ctrl, Alt, and Del keys; (c) press the reset button; and (d) select the Shut Down option.

▶ WORKING WITH BINARY NUMBERS

IN THIS LAB YOU'LL LEARN:

- The difference between the binary number system and the decimal number system
- How to count in binary
- How to convert decimal numbers into binary numbers
- How to convert binary numbers into decimal numbers
- How to use the Windows Calculator to convert numbers
- How to work with powers of two

LAB ASSIGNMENTS

1. Start the interactive part of the lab. Make sure you've enabled Tracking if you want to save your QuickCheck results. Perform each lab step as directed, and answer all the lab QuickCheck questions. When you exit the lab, your answers are automatically graded and your results are displayed.

2. Using paper and pencil, manually convert the following decimal numbers into binary numbers. Your instructor might ask you to show the process that you used for each conversion.

   a. 100   b. 1,000   c. 256
   d. 27   e. 48   f. 112
   g. 96   h. 1,024

3. Using paper and pencil, manually convert the following binary numbers into decimal numbers. Your instructor might ask you to show the process that you used for each conversion.

   a. 100   b. 101   c. 1100
   d. 10101   e. 1111   f. 10000
   g. 1111000   h. 110110

4. Describe what is wrong with the following sequence:

   10 100 110 1000 1001 1100 1110 10000

5. What is the decimal equivalent of 2^0? 2^1? 2^8?

Key Terms

Make sure you understand all the boldfaced key terms presented in this chapter. With the NP2014 interactive eBook, you can use this list of terms as an interactive study activity. First, try to define a term in your own words, and then click the term to compare your definition with the definition presented in the chapter.

1

ALU, 31
Analog data, 22
Anonymizer tools, 11
Application software, 16
Apps, 16
ASCII, 24
Authentication protocol, 34
Binary number system, 23
Biometrics, 34
Bit, 23
Brute force attack, 37
Byte, 26
Case sensitive, 35
Central processing unit, 15
Character data, 24
Client, 18
Cloud computing, 9
Compiler, 30
Compute-intensive, 19
Computer, 14
Computer network, 8
Computer program, 15
Control unit, 31
Convergence, 9
CPU, 15
Data, 15
Data processing, 6
Data representation, 22
Dictionary attack, 36
Digital data, 22
Digital divide, 13
Digital revolution, 4
Digitization, 5

Download, 18
EBCDIC, 24
Extended ASCII, 24
File, 15
Gigabit, 26
Gigabyte, 26
Globalization, 12
Identity theft, 36
Input, 15
Instruction cycle, 32
Instruction set, 30
Integrated circuit, 27
Intellectual property, 12
Internet, 8
Interpreter, 30
Keylogger, 37
Kilobit, 26
Kilobyte, 26
Local software, 7
Machine code, 30
Machine language, 30
Mainframe computer, 19
Megabit, 26
Megabyte, 26
Memory, 15
Microcontroller, 20
Microprocessor, 15
Numeric data, 23
Object code, 30
Op code, 31
Open source, 12
Operand, 31
Operating system, 16

Output, 15
Password, 35
Password manager, 40
Personal computer, 17
Personal computing, 7
Phishing, 37
Processing, 15
Programming language, 29
Registers, 31
Semiconducting materials, 27
Server, 18
Sniffing, 37
Social media, 10
Software, 15
Source code, 29
Storage, 15
Stored program, 16
Supercomputer, 19
System board, 28
System software, 16
Unicode, 25
Upload, 18
User ID, 34
Videogame console, 17
Web, 8
Workstation, 18

Interactive Summary

To review important concepts from this chapter, fill in the blanks to best complete each sentence. When using the NP2014 interactive eBook, click the Check Answers buttons to automatically score your answers.

SECTION A: The [Digital] revolution is an ongoing process of social, political, and economic change brought about by technologies such as computers and networks. The [Internet] is a global computer network originally developed as a military project, adapted for research and academic use, and then for commercial use. [＿＿＿＿＿＿], a form of electronic communication, was an application for the masses and finally a reason to buy a computer and join the digital revolution. Another aspect of the digital revolution is [＿＿＿＿＿＿], a process by which several technologies with distinct functionalities evolve to form a single product. Technology has the potential to spread ideas, such as freedom and democracy, but it might have a chilling effect on [＿＿＿＿＿＿], or "the right to be left alone." It might also affect intellectual [＿＿＿＿＿＿] because digital technology has made it easy to produce copies with no loss in quality from the original. Technology-driven [＿＿＿＿＿＿] has an effect on the economy, as consumers gain access to products and services from countries other than their own. Activists worry about the digital [＿＿＿＿＿＿] that separates people who have access to technology and those who do not.

▶ CHECK ANSWERS

SECTION B: A(n) [＿＿＿＿＿＿] is a multipurpose device that accepts input, processes data, stores data, and produces output according to a series of stored instructions. The data a computer is getting ready to process is temporarily held in [＿＿＿＿＿＿]. This data is then processed in the central processing [＿＿＿＿＿＿]. The series of instructions that tells a computer how to carry out processing tasks is referred to as a computer [＿＿＿＿＿＿], which forms the [＿＿＿＿＿＿] that sets up a computer to do a specific task. Data is typically stored in a(n) [＿＿＿＿＿＿], which is a named collection of data that exists on a storage medium, such as a hard disk, CD, DVD, Blu-ray disc, or USB flash drive. The idea of a(n) [＿＿＿＿＿＿] program means that a series of instructions for a computing task can be loaded into a computer's memory. [＿＿＿＿＿＿] software is a set of computer programs that helps a person carry out a task. [＿＿＿＿＿＿] software helps the computer system monitor itself in order to function efficiently. For example, a computer [＿＿＿＿＿＿] system (OS) is essentially the master controller for all the activities that take place within a computer. Computers can be grouped into categories. A(n) [＿＿＿＿＿＿] computer is a type of microcomputer designed to meet the needs of an individual. The term [＿＿＿＿＿＿] can refer to an ordinary personal computer that is connected to a network or to a powerful desktop computer designed for high-performance tasks. A(n) [＿＿＿＿＿＿] is, at the time of its construction, one of the fastest computers in the world. A(n) [＿＿＿＿＿＿] computer is large, expensive, and capable of simultaneously processing data for hundreds or thousands of users. Small, portable digital devices that allow you to install apps can be classified as [＿＿＿＿＿＿] computers. A(n) [＿＿＿＿＿＿] is a special-purpose microprocessor that can control a device, such as a refrigerator or microwave oven.

▶ CHECK ANSWERS

SECTION C:

_____ data is processed, stored, and transmitted as a series of 1s and 0s. Each 1 or 0 is called a(n) _____ . A series of eight 0s and 1s, called a(n) _____ , represents one character—a letter, number, or punctuation mark. Data becomes _____ when it is presented in a format that people can understand and use. _____ data consists of numbers that might be used in arithmetic operations. It can be represented digitally using the _____ number system. _____ data is composed of letters, symbols, and numerals that are not used in arithmetic operations. Computers represent this type of data using _____ , EBCDIC, or Unicode. Data is quantified using terms such as _____ or kibibyte (1024 bytes), and prefixes, such as _____ or mebi (1,048,576), and giga or _____ (1,073,741,824). The bits that represent data travel as electronic pulses through _____ circuits, sometimes called computer chips. These chips are made from _____ materials and are housed in chip carriers that can be plugged into the _____ board of a digital device. ▶ CHECK ANSWERS

SECTION D:

Software is usually written in high-level languages, such as C, BASIC, COBOL, and Java. The human-readable version of a program, created in a high-level language by a programmer, is called _____ code. A(n) _____ or an interpreter converts this high-level code into _____ code. A microprocessor is hard-wired to perform a limited set of activities, such as addition, subtraction, counting, and comparisons. This collection of preprogrammed activities is called a(n) _____ set. Each instruction begins with a(n) _____ code, which is a command word for an operation such as add, subtract, compare, or jump. Most instructions also include a(n) _____ that specifies the data, or the address of the data, for the operation. The processor's ALU uses _____ to hold data that is being processed. The processor's _____ unit fetches each instruction, sends data to the registers, and then signals the ALU to begin processing. ▶ CHECK ANSWERS

SECTION E:

Passwords and user IDs are the most common authentication _____ . Password theft has become a serious security problem that has led to many cases of _____ theft, when unauthorized individuals gain access to personal data. Hackers guess, discover, and steal passwords using a variety of techniques. A(n) _____ attack tries passwords from a list of commonly used passwords. A(n) _____ force attack tries every possible combination of letters and numbers. _____ intercepts information sent out over computer networks. _____ uses fraudulent Web sites or e-mail messages to fool unsuspecting readers into entering passwords and other personal information. A(n) _____ is software that secretly records a user's keystrokes and sends them to a hacker. To keep passwords safe, you should consider using tiered passwords or standalone password _____ software that generates secure passwords and keeps track of which password corresponds to each site you access. ▶ CHECK ANSWERS

Interactive Situation Questions

Apply what you've learned to some typical computing situations. When using the NP2014 interactive eBook, you can type your answers, and then use the Check Answers button to automatically score your responses.

1. Suppose that you walk into an office and see the devices pictured to the right. You would probably assume that they are the screen, keyboard, and mouse for a(n) ___Personal___ computer, workstation, or server.

2. You receive an e-mail message asking you to join a circle of friends. You assume that the message was generated in conjunction with an online ___Social___ network, such as Facebook, and if you become a member, you will be able to socialize online.

3. You're planning a trip to Finland, but when you access the hotel site, the prices are listed in euros. To find the price in U.S. dollars, you access a currency converter from your mobile phone. That's an example of _____ computing, representative of the fourth phase of the digital revolution.

4. You're visiting an antique shop and notice a collection of old-fashioned radios. They actually feature a dial for tuning in different radio stations. You immediately recognize this as a(n) _____ device because it deals with an infinite scale of values, rather than discrete values.

5. While attending a meeting at work, you hear one of the executives wondering if "unit code" would be helpful. After a moment of puzzlement, you realize that the executive really meant _____, and that it would allow your company software to be translated into the Cyrillic alphabet used by the Russian language.

6. You have a storage device that offers 2 GB of storage space. It is currently empty. Your friend wants to give you a large digital photo that's 16 MB. Will it fit on your storage device? ____

7. Your bank is giving customers the choice of using a four-digit PIN or a password that can contain up to ten letters and numbers. The _____ is more secure, so that's what you decide to use.

8. You need to select a password for your online PayPal account. Which of the following passwords would be the LEAST secure: jeff683, hddtmrutc, gargantuan, fanhotshot, bb#ii22jeffry, or high348? _____

 CHECK ANSWERS

Interactive Practice Tests

Practice tests that consist of ten multiple-choice, true/false, and fill-in-the-blank questions are available in your NP2014 interactive eBook. Test questions are selected at random from a large test bank, so each time you take a test, you'll receive a different set of questions. Your tests are scored immediately, and you can print study guides that help you find the correct answers for any questions that you missed.

CLICK TO START

Learning Objectives Checkpoints

Learning Objectives Checkpoints are designed to help you assess whether you have achieved the major learning objectives for this chapter. You can use paper and pencil or word processing software to complete most of the activities.

1. List the four phases of the digital revolution.

2. Define the term *convergence* and provide examples of at least five devices that are converging.

3. Describe at least two social, political, and economic effects of the digital revolution.

4. Draw a diagram to explain how a computer makes use of input, processing, storage, memory, output, and stored programs.

5. Describe the difference between system software, an operating system, application software, and a computer program.

6. List, briefly describe, and rank (in terms of computing capacity) the characteristics of each computer category described in Section B of this chapter.

7. List three handheld devices that would be classified as personal computers and three that would not be.

8. Define the term *microcontroller* and provide three examples of devices in which microcontrollers are found.

9. Explain the technical difference between data and information.

10. Provide three examples of digital devices and three examples of analog devices.

11. List the ASCII representation for *B* and the binary representation for 18; draw a stepped waveform showing a digital sound; and draw a diagram showing how color is represented in a graphic.

12. List and define all the chapter terms, such as *bit*, *byte*, and *kibibyte*, that pertain to quantifying data.

13. Use the terms *integrated circuits*, *microprocessor*, and *system board* in a meaningful sentence.

14. Describe how compilers and interpreters work with high-level programming languages, source code, and object code.

15. Make a storyboard showing how a microprocessor's ALU would add the numbers 2 and 8.

16. Explain how hackers use dictionary and brute force attacks.

17. Provide examples of five secure passwords and five passwords that might be easy to crack.

Study Tip: Make sure you can use your own words to correctly answer each of the purple focus questions that appear throughout the chapter.

1

Concept Map

Fill in the blanks to show that you understand the relationships between programming concepts presented in the chapter.

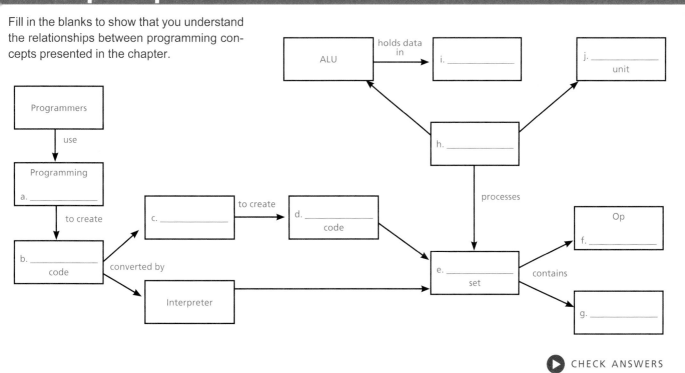

▶ CHECK ANSWERS

2

Computer Hardware

Chapter Contents

> ### INFOWEBLINKS
>
> You'll find updates for chapter material by connecting to the **NP2014 Chapter 2** InfoWebLink.
>
> Ⓦ CLICK TO CONNECT
> www.infoweblinks.com/NP2014/ch02

Learning Objectives

After reading this chapter, you will be able to answer the following questions by completing the outcomes-based Learning Objectives Checkpoints on page 117.

1. What are the components of a typical personal computer system?
2. What is a computer form factor?
3. Is a home computer more or less desirable than a game console or small business computer?
4. What's the best way to select a computer?
5. Are PCs and Macs compatible?
6. Is it a good idea to upgrade an old computer?
7. How does a microprocessor work?
8. Why are some computers faster than others?
9. Why does a computer need memory?
10. What is the best type of storage for my data?
11. What factors affect a computer's screen display?
12. Are ink jet printers better than laser printers?
13. What's the best way to add devices to a computer system?
14. How can I protect my computer system from theft and damage?
15. Are there guidelines for troubleshooting hardware and software problems?

Apply Your Knowledge

The information in this chapter will give you the background to:

▶ Identify all the components of a typical personal computer system

▶ Purchase a new computer based on features, performance, and price

▶ Upgrade your current computer

▶ Change your computer's boot settings in EEPROM

▶ Select a microprocessor based on performance specifications

▶ Select storage devices for your computer

▶ Change the resolution of your monitor

▶ Install peripheral devices

▶ Perform basic maintenance on your computer and troubleshoot hardware problems

2

⬤TRY IT!

HOW POWERFUL IS MY COMPUTER?

As you read Chapter 2, you'll learn that some computers are more powerful than others because they can store more data and process data faster. To find out how your home, work, or lab computer stacks up, you'll need to know a few of its specifications. Check your computer's specifications by starting your computer and then doing the following:

1. Access your computer's system information.

   Windows 7: Click the **Start** button, then click **Control Panel**. Follow links to System where you can view basic information about your computer.

   Windows 8: From the Start screen, type **Control** and then click **Control Panel**. Follow links to System where you can view basic information about your computer.

   MAC OS X: Click the  **Apple** icon on the menu bar located at the top of the desktop. Select **About this Mac**.

2. Record information about your computer similar to the information provided for the sample computer in the table at right.

3. Next, find the list of devices that are attached to your computer.

   Windows 7 and 8: Click the link or icon for **Device Manager**.

   Mac OS X: Click the **More Info** button.

4. Make a note of five devices connected to your computer. When you're done, close the window that lists your devices.

5. If you have a PC, click the **Windows Experience Index**. Make a note of your computer's base score and subscores.

	SAMPLE COMPUTER	YOUR COMPUTER
COMPUTER MANUFACTURER	DELL	
COMPUTER MODEL	INSPIRON 17	
PROCESSOR MANUFACTURER	INTEL	
PROCESSOR TYPE	CORE I7	
PROCESSOR SPEED	3.1 GHZ	
OPERATING SYSTEM	WINDOWS 7	
RAM CAPACITY	8 GB	
WINDOWS EXPERIENCE INDEX	5.4	

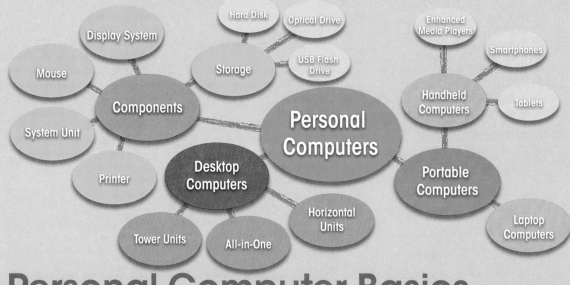

Personal Computer Basics

WHETHER YOU ARE SHOPPING for a new computer, using your trusty laptop, or troubleshooting a system glitch, it is useful to have some background about computer system components and how they work. Section A begins with a framework for understanding the vast number of options available for putting together a personal computer system, and then wraps up with some tips on interpreting the jargon in computer ads and negotiating the digital marketplace.

DESKTOP COMPUTER SYSTEMS

▶ What are the components of a typical desktop computer system? A **desktop computer** fits on a desk and runs on power from an electrical wall outlet. The main component of a typical desktop computer is a system unit that houses the processor, memory, storage devices, display circuitry, and sound circuitry.

In addition, most desktop systems include peripheral devices. The term **peripheral device** designates input, output, and storage equipment that might be added to a computer system to enhance its functionality. Popular peripheral devices include printers, digital cameras, scanners, game controllers, and speakers (Figure 2-1).

FIGURE 2-1

A personal computer system includes the system unit and a variety of storage, input, and output devices. ▶ The components of a typical desktop system are shown here. To compare the components of desktops with portable computers, watch the video for this figure in your interactive eBook.

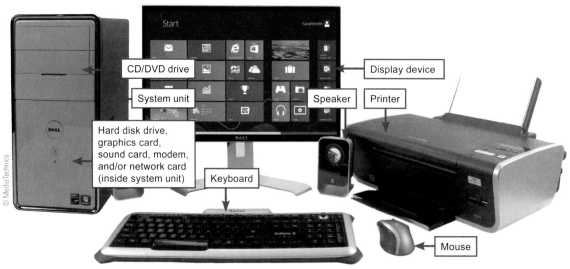

A typical desktop computer system includes several components. Many of these components can also be found in portable computers.

▶ **System unit.** The **system unit** is the case that holds the computer's main circuit boards, microprocessor, memory, power supply, and storage devices. Depending on the computer design, the system unit might also include other built-in devices, such as a keyboard and speakers.

▶ **Keyboard.** Most desktop computer systems are equipped with a keyboard as the primary input device.

▶ **Mouse.** A mouse is an input device designed to manipulate on-screen graphical objects and controls.

▶ **Hard disk drive.** A hard disk drive is the main storage device on many computer systems. It is usually mounted inside the computer's system unit and can store billions of characters of data. Some portable computers use a solid state drive as an alternative for main storage.

▶ **Optical drive.** An optical drive is a storage device that works with CDs, DVDs, Blu-ray discs, or some combination of these storage media. Optical drives are handy for playing audio CDs, DVD movies, and Blu-ray movies. They can also be used to store computer data on writable CDs, DVDs, and Blu-ray discs.

▶ **Removable storage.** In the past, personal computers included a low-capacity storage device called a floppy disk drive that accepted removable storage disks. Today, floppy disks have been replaced by solid state storage options, such as USB flash drives and memory cards (Figure 2-2).

FIGURE 2-2

Computers provide sockets called ports for solid state storage such as these SD cards and USB flash drives.

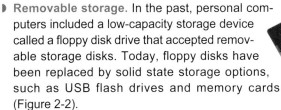

© MediaTechnics

▶ **Sound system.** The sound system for a personal computer can output digital music, digitally recorded speech, and a variety of sound effects called system sounds designed to draw your attention to various messages and events. To produce sounds, a computer uses a circuit board called a sound card, which is housed in the system unit. A computer's sound card sends signals to speakers, which can be external devices or built into the system unit.

▶ **Display system.** A personal computer display system consists of two parts. Circuitry, called a graphics card, converts raw digital data into images that can be shown on a display device. Display devices, often called computer screens or monitors, present visual output, such as documents, photos, and videos. Display devices are usually integrated with the system unit of portable computers, but exist as standalone devices for computers that spend most of their time on a desk.

▶ **Network and Internet access.** Many personal computer systems include built-in circuitry for wired or wireless connections to a computer network. Networking circuitry is useful for constructing a home network or connecting to public networks in coffee shops and airports.

▶ **Printer.** A computer printer is an output device that produces computer-generated text or graphical images on paper.

TERMINOLOGY NOTE

The word *peripheral* is a relatively old part of computer jargon that dates back to the days of mainframes when the CPU was housed in a giant box and all input, output, and storage devices were housed separately. Technically speaking, a peripheral is any device that is not part of the CPU.

In the world of personal computers, however, the use of the term *peripheral* varies and it is often used to refer to any components that are not housed inside the system unit. Many personal computer owners do not think of a hard disk drive as a peripheral device, but technically it is one.

▶ What is the significance of different computer designs?

The industrial design principle that "form follows function" applies to computers. If you need a computer that's functional for mobile applications, you would not consider hauling around a large, heavy unit designed to remain on a desk. Instead, you would look for a computer "form" that suits your mobile "function."

In the computer industry, the term form factor refers to the size and dimensions of a component, such as a system board or system unit. Personal computers are available in all sorts of form factors; some are small and some are large; some are designed to remain on a desk, whereas others are designed to be portable.

▶ What are the options for desktop computer form factors?

A desktop computer's keyboard, mouse, and display screen are typically separate components that are connected to the main unit by cables or wireless technology. A desktop computer's system unit can be housed in a vertical case, a horizontal case, or the display device (Figure 2-3).

FIGURE 2-3

Desktop computer form factors include horizontal, tower, and all-in-one units.

A tower unit can be placed on the desk or on the floor.

A horizontal unit is often placed under the monitor

The circuitry for this desktop all-in-one model is integrated into the case that holds the screen.

Most horizontal units are placed under the display device to save desk space. A vertical system unit can be placed on a desk, on the floor, or in a cubbyhole beneath the desk. The case for a vertical system unit is often referred to as a tower.

A **tower case** provides plenty of space for gamers and "modders" who want to enhance their machines by adding storage devices, lighted power cables, or accelerated graphics cards. Tower units are also the form factor of choice for computer owners who might want to upgrade components in the future because it is easy to get inside the case and swap out parts.

Some manufacturers eliminate the separate system unit by incorporating computer circuitry in the back of a flat-panel screen. Dubbed an **all-in-one computer**, this form factor is handy, but has limited space for expansion.

The first personal computers were desktop models, and this style remains popular for offices, schools, and homes. Because their components can be manufactured economically, desktop computers generally provide the most computing power for your dollar. The price of an entry-level desktop computer starts at US$300 or a bit less. Desktops with average performance cost $500–$700 and a souped up desktop equipped for gaming can cost over $3,000.

TRY IT!

Visit the Dell Web site. What is the price of the least expensive desktop computer?

PORTABLE COMPUTERS

▶ **How do portable computers differ from desktops?** A **portable computer** is a small, lightweight personal computer with input, output, storage, and processing components integrated into a single unit that runs on power supplied by an electrical outlet or a battery.

Portable computers are ideal for mobile uses because they are easy to carry and can be used outdoors, in airports, and in classrooms without the need for a nearby electrical outlet. Portable computer form factors include clamshell styles and slate styles (Figure 2-4).

FIGURE 2-4

Portable computers can have a clamshell or slate form factor.

Clamshell units are hinged with a screen on top and a keyboard below. The advantage of this form factor is that the screen is protected when the unit is closed.

Slate units have a screen, but no physical keyboard. The screen accepts touch input. These units are lighter and smaller than their clamshell counterparts.

▶ **What is a laptop computer?** A **laptop computer** (also referred to as a notebook computer) is a small, lightweight portable computer that opens like a clamshell to reveal a screen and keyboard. Laptop computers tend to cost a bit more than desktop computers with similar computing power and storage capacity.

Laptops are popular with students because they don't take up too much space in crowded dorm rooms and they are fairly easy to carry around campus. On average, a laptop computer weighs about five pounds. The price of an entry-level laptop computer starts around $400. Consumers often spend between $700 and $1,000, however, to get the features and performance they want. A fully loaded laptop computer with widescreen display can cost more than $2,000 (Figure 2-5).

TRY IT!

Check the Web for information on the MacBook Air and Dell Ultrabook. What do these computers have in common?

FIGURE 2-5

A laptop computer is small and lightweight, giving it the advantage of portability. It can be plugged into an electrical outlet, or it can run on battery power.

▶ What types of computers are available in the slate form factor? Three types of computers are available in the slate form factor: enhanced media players, smartphones, and tablets. These computers are sometimes referred to as "mobile devices" because they are so easy to carry and they can access the Internet using wireless connections.

▶ What is an enhanced media player? An **enhanced media player** is a handheld device designed for playing music and videos. These devices offer a camera, access to the Internet, and a variety of apps. Enhanced media players do not ordinarily include mobile phone capabilities.

Media players are great for listening to music and watching videos on the go. They're handy entertainment devices for traveling because you can use them without worrying that you're depleting the battery in your mobile phone. Enhanced media players feature a 3.5" screen, with overall dimensions about the size of an index card (Figure 2-6).

▶ What is a smartphone? A **smartphone** is an enhanced mobile phone that also functions as a portable media player and has the capability to access the Internet. Smartphones, such as Apple's iPhone and Motorola's Droid, are similar in size and appearance to enhanced media players, but generally cost a bit more and require a mobile service contract for voice calls.

▶ What is a tablet computer? A **tablet computer** is a handheld computer that is essentially a large version of an enhanced media player. First popularized by the Apple iPad, tablets are also offered by other companies, including Samsung and Motorola. Tablet prices range upward from $250 depending on brand and features.

Tablets are smaller than most laptop computers and weigh considerably less, in part because they have no keyboard, trackpad, or DVD drive. A virtual keyboard, displayed on the screen, can be supplemented by an auxiliary keyboard. A trackpad and mouse are not necessary; the touchscreen handles most input and provides output (Figure 2-7).

Tablets can generally access the Internet using Wi-Fi networks or cellular data service. Many people use a tablet as a second computer; one that's handy for a quick Web search. In the business world, tablets are used by insurance adjusters who do most of their work at the scene of accidents and natural disasters, real estate agents who need access to data while out with clients, and health care workers who are moving quickly from one patient to the next.

FIGURE 2-6

Enhanced media players, such as this iPod Touch, can be as small as a set of car keys, and range in price from $150–$400, depending on storage capacity.

TRY IT!

In what ways do tablet computers differ from enhanced media players?

○ Size

○ Touchscreen

○ Slate form factor

○ Mobile phone service

FIGURE 2-7

Tablet computer prices start at $250 and can exceed $1,200, depending on storage capacity. Most tablets feature a 10" touchscreen and weigh about one pound.

BUYING A COMPUTER

How do I get started? The process of buying your own computer system is not cut and dried. Some experts advocate assessing your computing needs first, whereas other experts suggest researching features and prices. The trick is to do your homework for the entire system before jumping into a purchase of any one component. Remember that you will be purchasing peripherals, software, and accessories in addition to a computer. To prepare for a computer purchase, you should complete the following activities:

- Browse through computer magazines and online computer stores to get a general idea of features and prices.

- Decide on a budget and stick to it.

- Make a list of the ways you plan to use your computer.

- Select a platform.

- Decide on a form factor.

- Select peripherals, software, and accessories.

Where can I find product information? You can start by looking at ads in current computer magazines, such as *Wired*, *PCWorld*, and *Macworld*. You might visit computer stores online or in a nearby mall to get a general idea of prices and features.

How can I make sense of all the jargon in computer ads? Computer ads are loaded with jargon and acronyms, such as RAM, ROM, GHz, GB, and USB. You're sure to spot lots of this computer lingo in ads like the one in Figure 2-8.

When you complete this chapter, you should be able to sort out the terminology used in a typical computer ad. For terms you encounter that are not covered in this textbook, you can google the term or refer to online dictionaries and encyclopedias, such as Webopedia, Whatis.com, or Wikipedia.

What can I expect to pay for a new computer? The price tag for a smartphone is $200–$500, whereas tablet computer prices range from $200–$1,200. Desktop and laptop computers usually cost a bit more, with price points roughly grouped into three categories: above $1,200, $500–$1,200, and under $500.

A desktop or laptop computer priced higher than $1,200 is the computer equivalent of a luxury automobile. Computers in this price range contain one or more fast processors, a generous amount of RAM, and a copious amount of disk space. These computers contain state-of-the-art components and should not have to be replaced as quickly as less expensive computers. Computer game enthusiasts and anyone planning to work extensively with video editing, graphics, and desktop publishing are likely to require a high-end computer.

Desktops and laptops that retail for between $500 and $1,200 might be considered the four-door sedans of the computer marketplace because a majority of buyers select computers in this price range. These popular computers lack the flashy specifications of their state-of-the-art cousins, but provide ample computing power to meet the needs of an average user.

FIGURE 2-8

A typical computer ad provides specifications and lots of computer jargon.

- Intel Core i7-2630M processor 2.0 GHz 1066 MHz FSB
- 6 MB L2 cache
- 6 GB DDR3-800 MHz dual channel SDRAM
- 750 GB SATA HD (7200 rpm)
- 8x CD/DVD burner (Dual Layer DVD+/-R)
- 15.6" High Def (720p) LCD display screen
- 1 GB NVIDIA GeForce graphics card
- Harman/Kardon speakers
- Integrated 1.3 megapixel webcam
- 4 USB ports
- 1 IEEE 1394 port
- HDMI graphics ports
- 5-in-1 media card reader
- Wireless networking 802.11 g/n
- 1 GB Ethernet
- Windows 8 64-bit operating system
- Home/small business software bundle
- 1-year limited warranty

© MediaTechnics

In the computer industry, the equivalent of a compact car is a sub-$500 computer. The technology in these computers is usually a year or two old and you can expect reduced processor speed, memory capacity, and drive capacity. Nevertheless, budget computers feature many of the same components that owners coveted in their state-of-the-art computers a few years back. You might have to replace a budget computer sooner than a more expensive computer, but it should be serviceable for typical applications.

▶ Why is it important to figure out how I'm going to use my new computer? Although it is impossible to predict all the ways you might use your new machine in the future, you can make a list of the ways you plan to immediately use your computer and that list can help you think about the features you'll need.

Some computer-based activities require more processing or storage capacity than others. Therefore, if you have some ideas about your computer usage, you're more likely to buy the right computer and not have to purchase expensive upgrades for it later. Figure 2-9 offers some guidelines to help you evaluate how your plan for using a computer might affect your purchase decision.

TRY IT!

The majority of desktop and laptop buyers spend how much on a computer?

○ $100–$250

○ $250–$500

○ $500–$1,200

○ $800–$1,500

FIGURE 2-9

Consider these factors to narrow down the mind-boggling number of choices offered to computer shoppers.

Usage Plan	Purchase Recommendation
You plan to use your computer for popular activities such as e-mail and Facebook, browsing the Web, playing a few games, managing your finances, downloading digital music, and writing school papers.	A mid-priced computer with standard features might meet your needs.
You're on a budget.	A budget-priced computer will handle the same applications as a mid-priced computer, but some tasks might run more slowly.
You plan to work on accounting and budgeting for a small business.	Consider one of the business systems offered by a local or an online computer vendor.
You spend lots of time playing computer games.	Buy a computer with the fastest processor and graphics card you can afford.
You plan to work extensively with video editing or desktop publishing.	Select a computer system with a fast processor, lots of hard disk capacity, and a graphics card loaded with memory.
Someone who will use the computer has special needs.	Consider purchasing appropriate adaptive equipment, such as a voice synthesizer or one-handed keyboard.
You plan to use specialized peripheral devices.	Make sure the computer you purchase can accommodate the devices you plan to use.
Your work at home overlaps your work at school or on the job.	Shop for a computer that's compatible with the computers you use at school or work.
You want to work with specific software, such as a game or graphics tool.	Make sure you select a computer that meets the specifications listed on the software box or Web site.
You're buying a new computer to replace an old one.	If you have a big investment in software, you should select a new computer that's compatible with the old one.
You want a 3-D display for games and movies.	Make sure the monitor is rated for 3-D display.
You need a computer that is easy to transport.	Consider a tablet computer or small laptop computer.

▶ **How important is compatibility?** Suppose that you want to do some assignments at home using the same software provided by your school lab. Maybe you want to transport data back and forth between your job and home. Or, perhaps your children want to use a computer at home that is similar to those they use at school.

Computers that operate in essentially the same way and use the same software are said to be **compatible**. They can also be described as having the same "platform." To assess whether two computers are compatible, check their operating systems. Computers with the same operating systems can typically use the same software and peripheral devices.

Currently, there are three popular platforms for desktop and laptop computers: PC, Mac, and Linux.

▶ The **PC platform** is based on the original IBM PC. The great-grand-children of the IBM PC are on computer store shelves today—a huge selection of personal computer brands and models manufactured by companies such as Lenovo, Hewlett-Packard, Dell, Toshiba, and Sony. The Windows operating system was designed specifically for these personal computers and, therefore, the PC platform is sometimes called the Windows platform.

▶ The **Mac platform** is based on a proprietary design for a personal computer called the Macintosh (or Mac), manufactured almost exclusively by Apple Inc. The Mac lineup includes the iMac, MacBook Air, MacBook Pro, and Mac mini, all running the Mac OS operating system.

▶ The **Linux platform** uses a standard PC or Mac to run the Linux operating system. A variety of software is available for this platform, though it tends to be more specialized but not as polished as software for Windows and Mac operating systems.

At one time, the PC, Mac, and Linux platforms were not compatible because of hardware and operating system differences. Application software designed for Macs did not work on other platforms and vice versa.

The compatibility situation has changed because most Mac computers now use the same microprocessor as PCs. If you have a Mac computer with an Intel processor (sometimes called an Intel Mac), you can install Windows on it and run Windows software. You can also configure it to run Linux software.

The ability to run Windows offers Mac owners access to software from the PC and Mac platforms, and makes it possible to use the Mac OS to run one application, then switch to Windows to run another application. This capability can come in handy, for example, if a parent who uses Windows software is sharing a computer with an elementary-school student who is working with Macs at school.

▶ **Are there compatibility issues with handheld computers?** As with full-size computers, the world of handheld computers includes several non-compatible platforms that affect your selection of apps.

When purchasing apps, you are limited to those designed for your device. Android apps do not work on iPhones, iPods, or iPads. Windows Phone apps run on many Nokia phones, but not on iPhones, Droids, or BlackBerry devices. Handheld computer platforms are summarized in Figure 2-10 on the next page.

2

TERMINOLOGY NOTE

Computers that are compatible with the PC platform are usually referred to simply as PCs. Computers in the Mac platform are referred to as Macs.

TRY IT!

If you want to run Mac and Windows software, what can you do?

○ Buy a Mac and install Windows on it

○ Buy a PC and install Mac OS on it

○ Buy an iPad and access Windows on the Internet

○ Forget it; it can't be done

Platform	Source	Devices
iOS	Apple	iPhone, iPad, iPod Touch
Android	Google	Droid, ATRIX, HKC, HTC phones Samsung Galaxy, Acer ICONIA, Motorola XOOM, Toshiba Excite tablets
Windows Phone	Microsoft	Nokia smartphones
Windows 8 RT	Microsoft	Windows tablet computers
BlackBerry OS	Research In Motion	BlackBerry smartphones

FIGURE 2-10

Handheld Computer Platforms

▶ **What about software?** Most computers are sold with a preinstalled operating system and a Web browser. Some computers are bundled with application software that you can use to create documents, crunch numbers, and produce presentations. Check the software offerings carefully; they might include applications that you can use for free only for a few months. To continue using the software beyond the trial period, however, you have to pay for it. Such software is "included" but not "free." Buyer beware.

If you're purchasing a computer to do a task that requires specialized software, you should factor its price into the cost of your computer system. Check the specifications listed on the software box to make sure your new computer has enough memory and processing speed to run it.

HOME, GAME, AND SMALL BUSINESS SYSTEMS

▶ **What's the significance of designations, such as home, small business, or game systems?** When studying computer ads and browsing vendor Web sites, you're likely to see some computer systems designated as home systems, whereas others are designated as game systems or small business systems. These designations are created by computer vendors to help consumers sort through the sometimes mind-boggling variety of configuration options.

▶ **What differentiates a home computer from other types?** The idea of a home computer system probably developed because Microsoft offered Home and Professional versions of the Windows operating system. Windows Home version targeted less sophisticated users and originally was not meant to be used extensively for networking.

Today, the term **home computer system** encompasses a vast array of desktop and laptop computer configurations designed to accommodate consumers who use computers for personal tasks. These systems also work for dual-use environments where a computer might be needed for general computing activities and also for home office tasks.

TRY IT!

Which platform supports the widest variety of handheld devices?

○ iOS

○ Android

○ Windows 8 RT

○ BlackBerry OS

The prices and features of home computer systems vary. Basic, inexpensive home systems offer adequate, but not super-charged, support for most computer applications, including Web browsing, e-mail, working with photos, downloading music, and working with general productivity applications, such as word processing. Software applications run at an acceptable speed, but graphics and games might be a bit slow.

A basic home computer system can also function for home office tasks with the addition of accounting software or other business applications.

Upscale home computer systems include cutting-edge computers, large-screen displays, 3-D Blu-ray players, and entertainment components to stream music throughout the house and display movies in a home theater (Figure 2-11).

FIGURE 2-11

Many high-end home computers are configured to function as the command center for watching movies and listening to music.

Movies, games, and music come to life with cutting-edge 3-D graphics and mind-blowing audio. Experience amazing visuals and incredible sound.

- 3-D Blu-ray at home or on the go
- 2nd generation Intel Core processors
- Razor-sharp graphics
- High-fidelity JBL speakers and Waves MaxxAudio
- Hi-def webcam

Maximum Entertainment Experience.

▶ What's so great about a gaming computer? Some of the most cutting-edge computers are designed for gaming. Not only do these machines feature the fastest processors, they are also stuffed with memory, include state-of-the-art sound capabilities, and feature multiple graphics processors.

Although some manufacturers produce gaming laptop computers, most serious gamers tend to select desktop models because they are easier to customize and offer a little more power per dollar. The technophile features of a gaming computer come with a steep price premium. Game systems start at $1,000 and quickly climb past the $3,000 price point (Figure 2-12).

FIGURE 2-12

Game systems are high-powered and expensive.

Aurora: Alienware Built. Gamer Approved.

The new Alienware Aurora: Overwhelm the enemy with overclocked power and expandability with the most upgradable desktop in its class.

Factory-overclocked, liquid-cooled processors
Ultraperformance dual graphics and optional high-definition (HD) 3-D gaming
Chassis designed for easy and optional thermal control

▶ What are the characteristics of small business computers?

Computers marketed for small business applications tend to be middle-of-the-line models pared down to essentials. A medium-speed processor, moderate amount of RAM, and sensible disk capacity are adequate for basic business applications, such as word processing, spreadsheet analysis, accounting, and e-mail. Easy networking options allow small business computers to connect with other computers in an office environment.

Tower and all-in-one units are popular for in-office use, whereas laptop computers are a practical solution for employees who are on the go.

With price tags under $1,000, small business computers like those advertised in Figure 2-13 remain cost-effective because they are not loaded with memory, fancy graphics cards, or audio systems, which are typical on home computers. Small business computers might not include a CD or DVD drive and often do not include speakers.

FIGURE 2-13

Small business owners want a cost-effective solution without bells and whistles.

BusinessClass 400 Desktop.

Reliable, Expandable Solution for Small Businesses

From its scalable design to its versatility, the latest MTC BusinessClass computers can be configured to meet all your business requirements. Whether your business is migrating to the cloud or staying anchored to the ground, the BusinessClass 400 provides a strong foundation for a wide range of business applications.

- Scalable design: Just the right size for the modern office, with choices of network options

- Business dedicated: No extraneous software, no demoware—just the basic operating system, which allows your tech team to easily install your business desktop

- Affordable: Put your investment where you need it: in processing power, storage, and connectivity

- Backed by solid MTC service and warranty

mmaxer/Shutterstock.com

QuickCheck

1. A computer [＿＿＿＿] unit houses the main circuit board, microprocessor, storage devices, and network card.

2. Personal computers are available in a variety of [＿＿＿＿] factors, such as tower units and all-in-one units.

3. The iPad is an example of a computer with a(n) [＿＿＿＿] form factor.

4. Small [＿＿＿＿] computers are middle-of-the-line models that are not loaded with memory, fancy graphics cards, or audio systems.

5. Desktop and laptop computer [＿＿＿＿] include PC, Mac, and Linux.

▶ CHECK ANSWERS

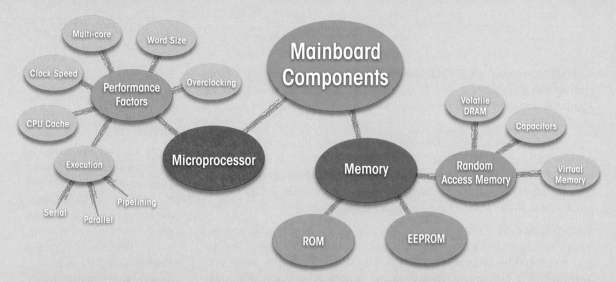

Mainboard Components
- Microprocessor
  - Performance Factors
    - Multi-core
    - Word Size
    - Clock Speed
    - Overclocking
    - CPU Cache
  - Execution
    - Serial
    - Parallel
    - Pipelining
- Memory
  - Random Access Memory
    - Volatile DRAM
    - Capacitors
    - Virtual Memory
  - ROM
  - EEPROM

Microprocessors and Memory

SECTION B

A TYPICAL COMPUTER AD contains a long list of specifications that begin with microprocessor speed and memory capacity (Figure 2-14). Section B explains how microprocessors and memory affect computer performance and price.

MICROPROCESSOR BASICS

▶ **What exactly is a microprocessor?** As you learned in Chapter 1, a microprocessor (sometimes simply referred to as a processor) is an integrated circuit designed to process instructions. It is the most important, and usually the most expensive, component of a computer.

▶ **What does it look like?** Looking inside a computer, you can easily identify the microprocessor because it is the largest chip on the system board, although it might be hidden under a cooling fan. Most of today's microprocessors are housed in a pin grid array chip package, as shown in Figure 2-15.

▶ **What makes one microprocessor perform better than another?** A microprocessor's performance is affected by several factors, including clock speed, bus speed, word size, cache size, instruction set, number of cores, and processing techniques.

▶ **What do MHz and GHz have to do with computer performance?** A specification, such as 3.4 GHz, that you see in a computer ad indicates the speed of the **microprocessor clock**—a timing device that sets the pace for executing instructions. Most computer ads specify the speed of a microprocessor in gigahertz. **Gigahertz** (GHz) means a billion cycles per second.

A cycle is the smallest unit of time in a microprocessor's universe. Every action a processor performs is measured by these cycles. It is important, however, to understand that the clock speed is not equal to the number of instructions a processor can execute in one second. In many computers, some instructions occur within one cycle, but other instructions might require multiple cycles. Some processors can even execute several instructions in a single clock cycle.

FIGURE 2-14

Most computer ads specify the amount and type of RAM.

- Intel Core i7 processor 3.4 GHz 1600 MHz FSB
- 8 MB L3 cache
- 4 GB DDR3-1800 MHz dual channel SDRAM
- 2 TB SATA HD (7200 rpm)
- 16X max. DVD+/-R/RW SuperMulti drive

FIGURE 2-15

Although a microprocessor is sometimes mistakenly referred to as a computer on a chip, it can be more accurately described as a CPU on a chip because it contains—on a single chip—circuitry that performs essentially the same tasks as the central processing unit of a classic mainframe computer.

67

A specification such as 2.13 GHz means that the microprocessor's clock operates at a speed of 2.13 billion cycles per second. If you are curious about the speed of the processor in your computer, Figure 2-16 can help you find it.

You might expect a computer with a 2.13 GHz processor to perform slower than a computer with a 3.4 GHz processor. This is not necessarily the case. Clock speed comparisons are only valid when comparing processors within the same chip family. As you might expect, a 1.87 GHz i7 processor is faster than a 1.6 GHz i7 processor.

Suppose, however, that you're shopping for a laptop computer and you have the option of an Intel i7 1.6 GHz processor or an i5 2.4 GHz processor. You might be surprised that the i7 1.6 GHz processor is faster than the i5 2.4 GHz processor. Why? Because factors other than clock speed contribute to the overall performance of a microprocessor. In multi-core processors, the number of cores affects performance.

FIGURE 2-16

You can discover your computer processor's specs using operating system utilities or third-party software, such as HWiNFO64. If you are using a Mac, click the Apple icon and then select About This Mac. When using Windows, link to the Control Panel to access System Information.

▶ **What's a multi-core processor?** A microprocessor that contains circuitry for more than one processing unit is called a **multi-core processor**. More cores usually produce faster performance. The 2.4 GHz i5 processor has two cores, giving it the equivalent of 4.8 GHz performance (2.4 x 2). The 1.6 GHz i7 processor has four cores, giving it the equivalent of 6.4 GHz performance (1.6 x 4).

▶ **What is FSB?** FSB stands for **front side bus**, a term that refers to the circuitry that transports data to and from the microprocessor. A fast front side bus moves data quickly and allows the processor to work at full capacity. FSB speed (technically its frequency) is measured in megahertz. **Megahertz** means one million cycles per second. Today's computers have FSB speeds ranging from 1000 MHz to 1800 MHz. Higher numbers indicate faster FSB speeds.

TERMINOLOGY NOTE

Other terms for *front side bus* include *system bus* and *memory bus*.

▶ **How does the cache size affect performance?** CPU cache (pronounced "cash") is special high-speed memory that allows a microprocessor to access data more rapidly than from memory located elsewhere on the system board. A large cache can increase computer performance.

CPU cache is structured into several levels. Level 1 cache (L1) is the fastest, whereas Level 2 (L2) and Level 3 (L3) are slightly slower, but still faster than accessing main memory or disk storage. Cache capacity is usually measured in megabytes.

▶ **What impact does word size have on performance?** **Word size** refers to the number of bits that a microprocessor can manipulate at one time. Word size is based on the size of registers in the ALU and the capacity of circuits that lead to those registers. A **64-bit processor**, for example, has 64-bit registers and processes 64 bits at a time.

TRY IT!

Is bigger always better? Which one of the following will NOT increase computer performance?

○ Higher GHz clock speed

○ More cycles per instruction

○ Higher MHz front side bus speed

○ More cores

A large word size gives processors the ability to handle more data during each processing cycle—a factor that leads to increased computer performance. Today's personal computers typically contain 32-bit or 64-bit processors.

▶ How does an instruction set affect performance? As chip designers developed various instruction sets for microprocessors, they added increasingly complex instructions, each requiring several clock cycles for execution. A microprocessor with such an instruction set uses **CISC** (complex instruction set computer) technology. A microprocessor with a limited set of simple instructions uses **RISC** (reduced instruction set computer) technology.

A RISC processor performs most instructions faster than a CISC processor. It might, however, require more of these simple instructions to complete a task than a CISC processor requires for the same task.

Most processors in today's desktop and laptop computers use CISC technology. Many processors used in handheld devices, such as iPods, Droids, and BlackBerrys, are ARM (advanced RISC Machine) processors.

▶ Can a microprocessor execute more than one instruction at a time? Some processors execute instructions "serially"—that is, one instruction at a time. With **serial processing**, the processor must complete all steps in the instruction cycle before it begins to execute the next instruction. However, using a technology called **pipelining**, a processor can begin executing an instruction before it completes the previous instruction. Many of today's microprocessors also perform **parallel processing**, in which multiple instructions are executed at the same time. Pipelining and parallel processing, illustrated in Figure 2-17, enhance processor performance.

FIGURE 2-17

Microprocessor designers have developed techniques for serial processing, pipelining, and parallel processing.

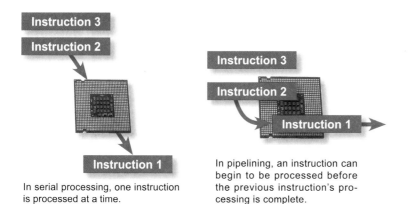

In serial processing, one instruction is processed at a time.

In pipelining, an instruction can begin to be processed before the previous instruction's processing is complete.

In parallel processing, multiple instructions can be processed at the same time.

To get a clearer picture of serial, pipelining, and parallel processing technology, consider an analogy in which computer instructions are pizzas. Serial processing executes only one instruction at a time, just like a pizzeria with one oven that holds only one pizza.

Pipelining is similar to a pizza conveyor belt. A pizza (instruction) starts moving along the conveyor belt into the oven; but before it reaches the end, another pizza starts moving along the belt.

Parallel processing is similar to a pizzeria with a large oven. Just as this oven can bake more than one pizza at a time, a parallel processor can execute more than one instruction at a time.

TRY IT!

Which processing method is slowest?

◯ Serial processing

◯ Pipelining

◯ Parallel processing

▶ **With so many factors to consider, how can I compare microprocessor performance?** Various testing laboratories run a series of tests to gauge the overall speed of a microprocessor. The results of these tests—called **benchmarks**—can then be compared to the results for other microprocessors. The results of benchmark tests are usually available on the Web and published in computer magazine articles.

FIGURE 2-18

To access the Windows Experience Index, search for it in the Control Panel.

Windows 7 and 8 offer a set of benchmarks called the Windows Experience Index that scores a computer's overall performance, and the performance of components such as its processor, memory, graphics, and storage system (Figure 2-18).

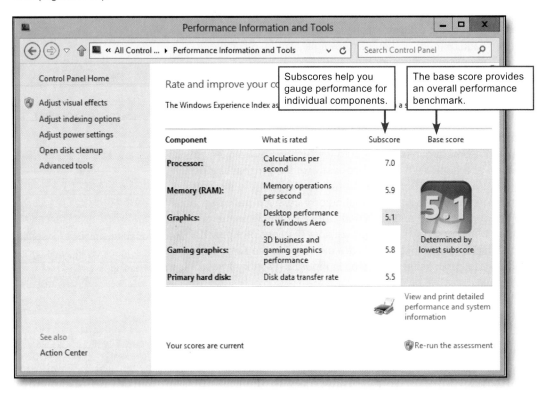

▶ **What do the Windows Experience Index scores mean?** Windows determines the performance subscores for five computer components: processor speed, memory transfer speed, ability to display graphics for the Aero desktop, 3-D animated graphics performance, and disk drive data transfer rate. Scores range from a low of 1.0 to a high score of 7.9.

The base score is determined by the lowest subscore because the component with the worst performance sets the limit on overall performance. Computers with a base score lower than 3.0 might be fine for basic applications, but base scores above 6.0 are desirable for computers used for multiplayer and 3-D games, teleconferencing, and HDTV playback.

TRY IT!

In Figure 2-18, click the component that has the lowest subscore.

TODAY'S MICROPROCESSORS

▶ **Which companies produce most of today's popular microprocessors?** Intel is the world's largest chipmaker and supplies a sizeable percentage of the microprocessors that power computers of all types. In 1971, Intel introduced the world's first microprocessor—the 4004. Intel's 8088 processor powered the original IBM PC. Since the debut of the IBM PC in 1985, Intel has introduced numerous microprocessors that have been used by most major computer manufacturers.

AMD (Advanced Micro Devices) is Intel's chief rival in the PC chip market. AMD's Phenom processors are direct competitors to Intel's Core 2 Quad line; AMD's Athlon X2 processors compete directly with Intel's Core 2 Duo processors (Figure 2-19). AMD processors are less expensive than comparable Intel models and have a slight performance advantage according to some benchmarks.

ARM processors are designed and licensed by ARM Holdings, a British technology company founded by Acorn Computers, Apple Inc., and VLSI Technology. Its RISC processors are manufactured by companies that include Apple, NVIDIA, Samsung, and Nintendo. ARM processors are used in many mobile phones and other handheld devices, such as the Apple iPad.

▶ **Which microprocessor is best?** The microprocessor that's best for you depends on your budget and the type of work and play you plan to do. The microprocessors marketed with the current crop of desktop and laptop computers can handle most business, educational, and entertainment applications. You'll want to consider the fastest processor offerings if you engage in processing-hungry activities, such as 3-D animated computer games, desktop publishing, multitrack sound recording, or video editing.

▶ **Can I replace my computer's microprocessor with a faster one?** It is technically possible to upgrade the microprocessor in a desktop computer, but computer owners rarely do so. The price of the latest, greatest microprocessor can often get you more than halfway to buying an entirely new computer system.

Technical factors also discourage microprocessor upgrades. A microprocessor operates at full efficiency only if all components in the computer can handle the faster speeds. In many cases, installing a new processor in an old computer can be like attaching a huge outboard engine to a canoe. In both cases, too much power can lead to disaster.

▶ **What is overclocking?** Overclocking is a technique for increasing the speed of a computer component, such as a processor, graphics card, system board, or memory. When successful, overclocking can increase the processing power of a slow component to match that of a faster, more expensive component. Overclocking is popular with gamers who want to squeeze every bit of processing speed out of their computers.

▶ **Why doesn't everyone overclock?** Overclocking is very risky. Additional electrical power pumped into a component increases heat output. Overclocked components can overheat and even catch fire. To maintain safe operating temperatures, an overclocked computer might require a supplemental cooling system.

FIGURE 2-19

Today's Popular Server, Desktop, and Mobile Microprocessor Families

2

Processor	Application
INTEL	
Core i7 and i5	Desktops and Laptops
Pentium	Desktops
Celeron	Desktops and Laptops
Xeon	Servers and Workstations
Itanium	Servers
Atom	Tablets and Handhelds
AMD	
Phenom	Desktops
Athlon	Desktops and Laptops
Sempron	Desktops and Laptops
Turion	Laptops
Opteron	Servers and Workstations
Fusion	Tablets
ARM	
ARM7	Analog Phones
ARM9	Digital Phones
Cortex-A	Handhelds
Apple A5X	iPad 2

RANDOM ACCESS MEMORY

▶ **What is RAM? RAM** (random access memory) is a temporary holding area for data, application program instructions, and the operating system. In a personal computer, RAM is usually several chips or small circuit boards that plug into the system board within the computer's system unit. A computer's RAM capacity is invariably included in the list of specifications in personal computer ads (Figure 2-20).

The amount of RAM in a computer can affect the overall price of a computer system. To understand how much RAM your computer needs and to understand computer ad terminology, it is handy to have a little background on how RAM works and what it does.

▶ **Why is RAM so important?** RAM is the "waiting room" for the computer's processor. It holds raw data waiting to be processed as well as the program instructions for processing that data. In addition, RAM holds the results of processing until they can be stored more permanently on a hard disk, CD, or flash drive.

In addition to data and application software instructions, RAM also holds operating system instructions that control the basic functions of a computer system. These instructions are loaded into RAM every time you start your computer, and they remain there until you turn off your computer.

▶ **How does RAM work?** In RAM, microscopic electronic parts called **capacitors** hold the bits that represent data. You can visualize the capacitors as microscopic lights that can be turned on or off. A charged capacitor is "turned on" and represents a "1" bit. A discharged capacitor is "turned off" and represents a "0" bit. Each bank of capacitors holds eight bits—one byte of data. A RAM address on each bank helps the computer locate data, as needed, for processing (Figure 2-21).

FIGURE 2-20

A computer ad typically specifies the amount and type of RAM.

■ Intel Core i7 processor 3.4 GHz 1600 MHz FSB
■ 8 MB L3 cache
■ 4 GB DDR3-1800 MHz dual channel SDRAM
■ 2 TB SATA HD (7200 rpm)
■ 16X max. DVD+/-R/RW SuperMulti drive

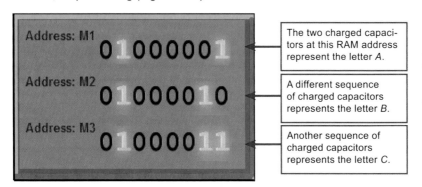

FIGURE 2-21

Each RAM location has an address and uses eight capacitors to hold the eight bits that represent a byte. ▶ Your interactive eBook shows you how RAM works with bits that represent data.

The two charged capacitors at this RAM address represent the letter *A*.

A different sequence of charged capacitors represents the letter *B*.

Another sequence of charged capacitors represents the letter *C*.

In some respects, RAM is similar to a chalkboard. You can use a chalkboard to write mathematical formulas, erase them, and then write an outline for a report. In a similar way, RAM can hold numbers and formulas when you balance your checkbook, and then can hold the outline of your English essay when you use word processing software. RAM contents can be changed just by changing the charge of the capacitors.

Unlike disk storage, most RAM is **volatile**, which means it requires electrical power to hold data. If the computer is turned off, if the battery runs out of juice, or if a desktop computer is accidentally unplugged or experiences a power failure, all data stored in RAM instantly and permanently disappears. This type of RAM is technically classified as **dynamic RAM** (DRAM) but it is commonly referred to simply as RAM.

TRY IT!

Which statement is true?

○ Computers usually have more memory than storage

○ RAM is a data holding area between the processor and disk storage

○ Volatile RAM holds data even when the computer is turned off

▶ **How much RAM does my computer need?** RAM capacity is expressed in gigabytes. Today's personal computers typically feature 2–8 GB of RAM. For good basic performance, a computer running Windows should have at least 1 GB of RAM. Games, desktop publishing, graphics, and video applications tend to run more smoothly with at least 2 GB of RAM.

The amount of RAM your computer needs depends on the software you use. RAM requirements are routinely specified on the outside of a software package (Figure 2-22).

▶ **Can my computer run out of memory?** Suppose that you want to work with several programs and large graphics at the same time. Will your computer eventually run out of memory? The answer is "probably not." Today's personal computer operating systems are quite adept at allocating RAM space to multiple programs.

If a program exceeds its allocated space, the operating system uses an area of the hard disk, called **virtual memory**, to store parts of programs or data files until they are needed. By selectively exchanging the data in RAM with the data in virtual memory, your computer effectively gains almost unlimited memory capacity.

Too much dependence on virtual memory can slow down your computer's performance, however, because getting data from a mechanical device, such as a hard disk drive, is much slower than getting data from an electronic device, such as RAM. To minimize virtual memory use, load up your computer with as much RAM as possible.

▶ **How do I add RAM?** First, check how much RAM is currently installed, and then check the maximum RAM limit to make sure RAM can be added. Check your computer documentation or the manufacturer's Web site for information on the type and speed of RAM required.

Most of today's personal computers use SDRAM (synchronous dynamic RAM), which is fast and relatively inexpensive. SDRAM (shown in Figure 2-23) is further classified as DDR, DDR2, or DDR3. Make sure that you purchase the right type.

FIGURE 2-22

Minimum RAM requirements are usually displayed on the package of a software product.

Minimum System Requirements:
- Windows 7 or 8
- 1 GB of RAM
- 450 MB hard drive space
- CD drive for installation
- Mouse
- Internet connection (optional)
- Printer (optional)
- Scanner or digital camera

2

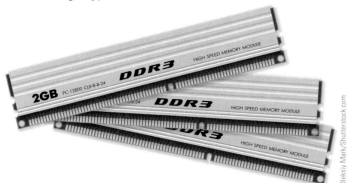

FIGURE 2-23

SDRAM is the most popular type of RAM in today's computers. It is sold as a small circuit board. When adding memory to a computer, follow the manufacturer's instructions carefully.

▶ **What about RAM for handheld computers?** Handheld computers commonly have about 512 MB–1 GB of RAM, which is far less than the amount in desktop or laptop computers. Handheld apps are simpler than the applications designed for more powerful devices, so they require less memory. Apps run within the standard memory limits, so there is no need to add RAM to handheld devices.

ROM AND EEPROM

▶ **What is ROM?** **ROM** (read-only memory) is a type of memory circuitry that is housed in a single integrated circuit—usually a fairly large, caterpillar-like DIP package—which is plugged into the system board.

Whereas RAM is temporary and volatile, ROM is permanent and non-volatile. The contents of ROM are "hard-wired" in the circuitry and remain in place even when the computer power is turned off.

Early ROM technologies were not modifiable; updating ROM meant physically replacing the chip. Newer EEPROM technologies now offer more versatility.

▶ **What is EEPROM?** **EEPROM** (electrically erasable programmable read-only memory) is a type of ROM that is non-volatile but user-modifiable. EEPROM technology has replaced non-modifiable ROMs on most modern computers. Today, the term *ROM* is used when referring to either ROMs or EEPROMs.

▶ **What does a computer store in ROM?** ROM contains a small set of instructions and data called the **bootstrap loader**. In a PC, the contents of ROM are sometimes referred to as the **BIOS** (basic input/output system).

The bootstrap loader's instructions tell the computer how to access the hard disk, find the operating system, and load it into RAM. After the operating system is loaded, the computer can understand your input, display output, run software, and access data files.

The bootstrap loader requires some basic information about storage, memory, and display configurations. That data is stored in ROM along with the bootstrap loader instructions.

▶ **Why isn't the bootstrap loader stored in RAM?** RAM requires power to hold data. When your computer is off, RAM is empty. When you turn on your computer, RAM is still empty and doesn't contain any instructions for the microprocessor to execute. ROM, on the other hand, holds data even when the power is off. So when you press the power button, your computer can immediately access the instructions in ROM and proceed with the startup routine.

▶ **How do I change the contents of ROM?** In rare cases, the bootstrap loader instructions must be changed in ROM. This process is called "flashing" and it is performed by running a program supplied by your computer manufacturer. Be sure to carefully follow instructions for this procedure. If the flash fails, your computer will not start until you get the ROM chip replaced.

If you change basic hardware—for example, by adding RAM or changing your hard drive—the bootstrap loader data must be updated. Unlike an update to the bootstrap loader instructions, the configuration data stored in ROM can usually be changed without the perilous flashing procedure.

Some operating systems recognize hardware changes and automatically update the configuration data stored in ROM. Alternatively, you can use a setup utility to manually change the data in ROM as shown in Figure 2-24 on the next page.

TERMINOLOGY NOTE

A ROM or EEPROM chip along with its instructions is commonly referred to as firmware; a sort of melding of hardware and software.

TRY IT!

When a computer is turned on, what happens first?

○ The microprocessor gets the operating system from the hard disk

○ ROM is cleared to make space for the operating system

○ The bootstrap loader is copied into RAM and then executed by the microprocessor

```
                    PhoenixBIOS Setup Utility
  Main   Advanced    Power    Boot    Exit

    System Time:       [10:40:48]              Item Specific Help
    System Date:       [03/03/2013]
    Language:          [English  [US]]      <Tab>, <Shift-Tab>, or
                                            <Enter> selects field.
    CPU Type:          Intel [R] Core [TM] i7 CPU

    CPU Speed:         1.60GHz

    HDD1/SSD1:         TOSHIBA MK5055GSX [S2]
    ODD:               MATSHITADVD-RAM UJ890ES

    Total Memory Size: 4096 MB

    System BIOS Version: 1.20
    EC Version:          5.30




  F1   Help      ↑↓ Select Item    -/+    Change Values    F5   Setup Defaults
  Esc  Exit      ←→ Select Menu    Enter  Select Submenu   F10  Save and Exit
```

FIGURE 2-24

On a PC, you can access the BIOS setup utility by holding down the F1 key as your computer boots. But be careful! If you make a mistake with these settings, your computer might not be able to start.

2

If you mistakenly enter the setup program, follow the on-screen instructions to exit and proceed with the boot process. The Esc (Escape) key allows you to exit the setup program without making any changes to the configuration settings.

▶ **What information about memory performance is most important?** Even though ROM has important roles in the operation of a personal computer, RAM capacity really makes a difference you can notice. With lots of RAM, you'll find that documents scroll faster, games respond more quickly, and many graphics operations take less time than with a computer that has a skimpy RAM capacity.

Most ads specify RAM capacity, speed, and type. Now when you see the specification "2 GB Dual Channel DDR2 SDRAM (max. 4 GB)" in a computer ad, you'll know that the computer's RAM capacity is 2 gigabytes (enough to run Windows 8) and that it uses dual-channel, double data rate SDRAM. You'll also have important information about the maximum amount of RAM that can be installed in the computer—4 GB, which is more than enough for the typical computer owner who does a bit of word processing, surfs the Web, and plays computer games.

QuickCheck

1. A personal computer with an Intel Core i7 microprocessor is likely to operate at a speed of 3.4 [_____]. (Hint: Use the abbreviation.)

2. A(n) [_____] side bus is circuitry that transports data to and from the processor.

3. 4004, 8088, Athlon, and Pentium are all types of [_____].

4. *DDR2*, *virtual*, and *volatile* are terms that apply to [_____]. (Hint: Use the acronym.)

5. The instructions for loading the operating system into RAM when a computer is first turned on are stored in [_____]. (Hint: Use the acronym.)

▶ CHECK ANSWERS

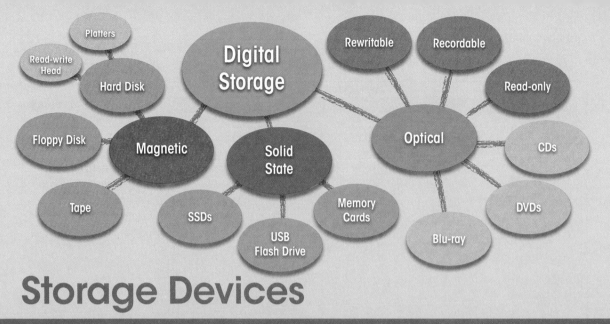

Storage Devices

COMPUTER MANUFACTURERS commonly try to entice consumers by configuring computers with a variety of storage devices, such as a hard disk drive, solid-state card readers, and some sort of CD or DVD drive. What's the point of having so many storage devices? As it turns out, none of today's storage technologies is perfect.

In this section, you'll find guidelines that can make you a smart storage technology buyer and owner. The storage technologies you'll learn about are now used in a variety of devices—from digital cameras to player pianos—so an understanding of storage technology can be useful even outside the boundaries of personal computing.

STORAGE BASICS

▶ **What are the basic components of a data storage system?** A data storage system has two main components: a storage medium and a storage device. A **storage medium** (*storage media* is the plural) is the disk, tape, CD, DVD, paper, or other substance that contains data. A **storage device** is the mechanical apparatus that records and retrieves data from a storage medium. Storage devices include hard disk drives, CD drives, DVD drives, Blu-ray drives, and flash drives. The term *storage technology* refers to a storage device and the media it uses.

▶ **How does a storage device interact with other computer components?** You can think of your computer's storage devices as having a direct pipeline to RAM. Data gets copied from a storage device into RAM, where it waits to be processed. After data is processed, it is held temporarily in RAM, but it is usually copied to a storage medium for more permanent safekeeping.

As you know, a computer's processor works with data that has been coded into bits that can be represented by 1s and 0s. When data is stored, these 1s and 0s must be converted into some kind of signal or mark that's fairly permanent, but can be changed when necessary.

Obviously, the data is not literally written as "1" or "0." Instead, the 1s and 0s must be transformed into something that can remain on the surface of a storage medium. Exactly how this transformation happens depends on the storage technology. For example, hard disks store data in a different way than CDs. Three types of storage technologies are commonly used for personal computers: magnetic, optical, and solid state.

TERMINOLOGY NOTE

The process of storing data is often referred to as writing data or saving a file because the storage device writes the data on the storage medium to save it for later use.

The process of retrieving data is often referred to as reading data, loading data, or opening a file.

TRY IT!

Data stored on a hard disk:

○ has a direct pipeline to the microprocessor

○ goes to RAM before it is transferred to the processor

○ can be remotely processed without leaving the storage device

---

▶ **Which storage technology is best?** Each storage technology has its advantages and disadvantages. If one storage system was perfect, we wouldn't need so many storage devices connected to our computers! To compare storage devices, it is useful to apply the criteria of versatility, durability, speed, and capacity.

▶ **How can one storage technology be more versatile than another?** The hard disk drive sealed inside a computer's system unit is not very versatile; it can access data only from its fixed disk platters. More versatile devices can access data from several different media. For example, a DVD drive is versatile because it can access computer DVDs, DVD movies, audio CDs, computer CDs, and CD-Rs.

▶ **What makes a storage technology durable?** Most storage technologies are susceptible to damage from mishandling or environmental factors, such as heat and moisture. Some technologies are more susceptible than others to damage that could cause data loss. CDs and DVDs tend to be more durable than hard disks, for example.

▶ **What factors affect storage speed?** Quick access to data is important, so fast storage devices are preferred over slower devices. **Access time** is the average time it takes a computer to locate data on the storage medium and read it. Access time for a personal computer storage device, such as a disk drive, is measured in milliseconds (thousandths of a second). One millisecond (ms) is one-thousandth of a second. Lower numbers indicate faster access times. For example, a drive with a 6 ms access time is faster than a drive with an access time of 11 ms.

Access time is best for random-access devices. **Random access** (also called direct access) is the ability of a device to "jump" directly to the requested data. Hard disk, CD, DVD, Blu-ray, and solid state drives are random-access devices, as are the memory cards used in digital cameras. Old-fashioned tape drives, on the other hand, used slower **sequential access** by reading through the data from the beginning of the tape. The advantage of random access becomes clear when you consider how much faster and easier it is to locate a song on a CD (random access) than on a cassette tape (sequential access).

Data transfer rate is the amount of data a storage device can move per second from the storage medium to the computer. Higher numbers indicate faster transfer rates. For example, a hard disk drive with a 57 MBps (megabytes per second) data transfer rate is faster than one with a 50 MBps transfer rate.

▶ **What's important about storage capacity?** In today's computing environment, higher capacity is almost always preferred. Storage capacity is the maximum amount of data that can be stored on a storage medium, and it is measured in bytes; usually in gigabytes (GB) or terabytes (TB).

Storage capacity is directly related to **storage density**, the amount of data that can be stored in a given area of a storage medium, such as the surface of a disk. The higher the storage density, the more data is stored. Storage density can be increased by making the particles representing bits smaller, by layering them, packing them closer together, or standing them vertically (Figure 2-25).

Most computer storage devices locate and retrieve data by:

○ random access

○ sequential access

FIGURE 2-25

Vertical storage produces higher storage capacities than horizontal storage.

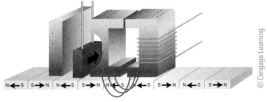

With horizontal storage, particles are arranged end to end, and use of the disk surface is not optimized.

With vertical storage, particles stand on end so that many more can be packed on the disk surface.

MAGNETIC STORAGE TECHNOLOGY

‣ **What is magnetic storage technology?** Magnetic storage stores data by magnetizing microscopic particles on a disk or tape surface. The particles retain their magnetic orientation until that orientation is changed, thereby making disks fairly permanent but modifiable storage media.

Data stored magnetically can be easily changed or deleted simply by changing the magnetic orientation of the appropriate particles on the disk surface. This feature of magnetic storage provides lots of flexibility for editing data and reusing areas of a storage medium containing unneeded data.

‣ **How does a hard disk drive work?** As the main storage device on most computers, a **hard disk drive** contains one or more platters and their associated read-write heads. A **hard disk platter** is a flat, rigid disk made of aluminum or glass and coated with magnetic iron oxide particles.

More platters mean more data storage capacity. The platters rotate as a unit on a spindle, making thousands of rotations per minute. Hard disk platters are typically 3.5" in diameter, with storage capacities ranging from 40 GB to 2 TB.

Each platter has a read-write head that hovers just a few microinches above the surface. A **read-write head** mechanism in the disk drive magnetizes particles to write data, and senses the particles' polarities to read data. Figure 2-26 shows how a computer stores data on magnetic media.

> **TERMINOLOGY NOTE**
>
> You might hear the term *fixed disk* used to refer to hard disks. You often see the terms *hard disk* and *hard disk drive* used interchangeably, although technically *hard disk* refers to the platters sealed inside the hard disk drive.

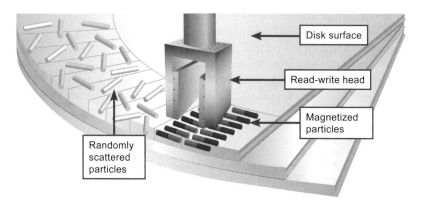

FIGURE 2-26

Before data is stored, particles on the surface of the disk are scattered in random patterns. The disk drive's read-write head magnetizes the particles, and orients them in a positive (north) or negative (south) direction to represent 0 and 1 bits, respectively.

‣ **Why are hard disk drives so popular?** Hard disk technology is the preferred type of main storage for most personal computers for three reasons. First, it provides lots of storage capacity. Second, it provides fast access to files. Third, a hard disk is economical. The cost of storing 1 gigabyte of data is about five cents.

‣ **What's the downside of hard disk storage?** Hard disks are not as durable as many other storage technologies. Data stored on magnetic media can be unintentionally altered by magnetic fields, dust, mold, smoke particles, heat, and mechanical problems with a storage device. Over time, magnetic media gradually lose their magnetic charge, resulting in lost data. Some experts estimate that the reliable life span of data stored on magnetic media is about three years. They recommend that you refresh your data every two years by recopying it.

> **TRY IT!**
>
> Check online. What's the average price for a 2 TB hard drive?

The read-write heads in a hard disk hover a microscopic distance above the disk surface. If a read-write head runs into a dust particle or some other contaminant on the disk, it might cause a **head crash**, which damages some of the data on the disk (Figure 2-27).

Read-write head

Spindle

Platters

© MediaTechnics

FIGURE 2-27

Hard disk platters and read-write heads are sealed inside the drive case or cartridge to screen out dust and other contaminants. ▶ The video for this figure in your interactive eBook shows how a hard drive works and what happens when a hard disk crashes.

2

To help prevent contaminants from contacting the platters and causing head crashes, a hard disk is sealed in its case. A head crash can be triggered by jarring the hard disk while it is in use. Although hard disks have become considerably more rugged in recent years, you should handle and transport them with care. You should also make backup copies of the data stored on your hard disk in case of a head crash.

▶ What should I know about selecting a hard disk drive?

Computer ads commonly specify the capacity, access time, and speed of a hard disk drive. So "2 TB 8 ms 7200 RPM HD" means a hard disk drive with 2 terabyte capacity, access time of 8 milliseconds, and speed of 7,200 revolutions per minute. Ads rarely specify the amount of data that a hard drive can transfer, but the average data transfer rate is about 57,000 KBps (also expressed as 57 MBps or MB/s).

Hard disk access times of 6 to 11 ms are not uncommon, whereas a CD takes about 500 ms to spin up to speed and find data. Hard disk drive speed is sometimes measured in revolutions per minute (rpm). The faster a drive spins, the more rapidly it can position the read-write head over specific data. For example, a 7,200 rpm drive is able to access data faster than a 5,400 rpm drive.

Computer ads use acronyms such as ATA, EIDE, SCSI, and DMA to describe the type of circuitry used to transfer data between the hard disk and other components on the computer's system board. Some are slightly faster than others, but for most buyers this specification is not a significant factor.

TERMINOLOGY NOTE

Data transfer rates can be specified in bits or bytes, so read the specifications carefully.

50 Mbps or Mb/s means 50 mega*bits* per second.

50 MBps or MB/s means 50 mega*bytes* per second.

Also stay alert for the difference between kilo (K) and mega (M), remembering that mega is 1,000 times more than kilo.

● **TRY IT!**

If you see an ad for a computer with a 6 ms hard drive, you can assume that 6 ms refers to:

○ the drive's access time

○ the drive's capacity

○ the drive's rotational speed

○ the drive's data transfer rate

◗ Can I use a second hard disk drive to increase storage space?

You can increase the storage capacity of your desktop or laptop computer by adding a second hard disk drive, which can also provide a backup for your primary drive. Hard disk drives are available as internal or external units. Internal drives are inexpensive and can be easily installed in a desktop computer's system unit. External drives are slightly more expensive and connect to a desktop or laptop computer using a cable (Figure 2-28).

FIGURE 2-28

External hard drives offer a low-cost way to beef up the storage capacity of a personal computer.

◗ Do computers still store data on tapes?

Next time you watch a movie from the 1950s or 1960s that shows a computer, look for the big reels of tape used as storage devices. Tape storage, once used to store mainframe data and also used for personal computer backups, is too slow for modern computing.

◗ What is floppy disk technology?

At one time, just about every personal computer included a floppy disk drive (Figure 2-29) that stored data on **floppy disks** (also called floppies or diskettes). This storage technology is no longer used because a floppy disk's 1.44 MB capacity is not sufficient for today's media-intensive applications.

Many MP3 music files and photos are too large to fit on a floppy. In the past, floppy disks were extensively used to distribute software. CDs and DVDs offer more capacity for distributing the huge files for today's software applications. Web downloads offer more convenience.

FIGURE 2-29

A standard floppy disk drive reads and writes data on a 3.5" floppy disk.

TRY IT!

Which device does NOT use magnetic storage technology?

◯ Hard disk

◯ Floppy disk

◯ USB flash drive

◯ Tape drive

OPTICAL STORAGE TECHNOLOGY

▶ How do CD, DVD, and Blu-ray technologies differ? Today, most desktop and laptop computers come equipped with one or more drives designed to work with CD, DVD, and Blu-ray technologies.

▶ **CD** (compact disc) technology was originally designed to hold 74 minutes of recorded music. The original CD standard was adapted for computer storage with capacity for 650 MB of data. Later improvements in CD standards increased the capacity to 80 minutes of music or 700 MB of data.

▶ **DVD** (digital video disc or digital versatile disc) is a variation of CD technology that was originally designed as an alternative to VCRs, but was quickly adopted by the computer industry to store data. The initial DVD standard offered 4.7 GB (4,700 MB) of data storage; that's about seven times as much capacity as a CD. Subsequent improvements in DVD technology offer even more storage capacity. A double layer DVD has two recordable layers on the same side and can store 8.5 GB of data.

▶ **Blu-ray** is a high-capacity storage technology with a 25 GB capacity per layer. The name *Blu-ray* is derived from the blue-violet colored laser used to read data stored on Blu-ray discs. DVD technology uses a red laser; CD technology uses a near infrared laser.

▶ How do CD, DVD, and Blu-ray drives work? CD, DVD, and Blu-ray technologies are classified as **optical storage**, which stores data as microscopic light and dark spots on the disc surface. The dark spots, shown in Figure 2-30, are called **pits**. The lighter, non-pitted surface areas of the disc are called **lands**.

Optical drives contain a spindle that rotates the disc over a laser lens. The laser directs a beam of light toward the underside of the disc. The dark pits and light lands on the disc surface reflect the light differently. As the lens reads the disc, these differences are translated into the 0s and 1s that represent data (Figure 2-31).

FIGURE 2-30

As seen through an electron microscope, the pits on an optical storage disc look like small craters. Each pit is less than 1 micron (one-millionth of a meter) in diameter—1,500 pits lined up side by side are about as wide as the head of a pin.

Courtesy of IBM

FIGURE 2-31

CD, DVD, and Blu-ray drives use a laser to read data from the underside of a disc.

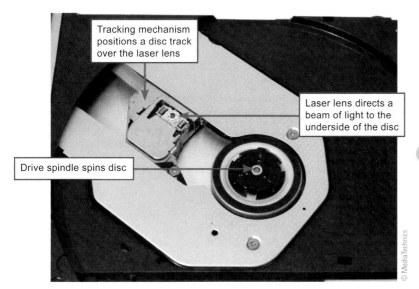

Tracking mechanism positions a disc track over the laser lens

Laser lens directs a beam of light to the underside of the disc

Drive spindle spins disc

© MediaTechnics

TRY IT!

How does the capacity of a Blu-ray disc compare to a standard DVD?

○ It has about half the capacity

○ It has double the capacity

○ It has about five times the capacity

▶ **How durable are optical drives?** The surface of an optical disc is coated with clear plastic, making the disc quite durable and less suscep-tible to environmental damage than data recorded on magnetic media. An optical disc, such as a CD, is not disrupted by humidity, fingerprints, dust, magnets, or spilled soft drinks. Scratches on the disc surface can inter-fere with data transfer, but a good buffing with toothpaste can erase the scratch without damaging the underlying data. An optical disc's useful life is estimated to be more than 30 years. Figure 2-32 illustrates the layers of an optical disc.

▶ **How fast are CD, DVD, and Blu-ray drives?** In the past, opti-cal drives were used to store computer data, such as software and document files. Today, the trend is to use optical storage primarily for watching movies on your computer screen.

The CD and Blu-ray drives built into today's computers are fast enough to stream video and audio data for movies.

Most optical drives permit you to also store computer data on blank CDs, DVDs, and BDs using recordable or rewritable technologies.

▶ **What's the significance of ROM, R, and RW?** Optical technolo-gies are grouped into three categories: read-only, recordable, and rewritable.

▶ **Read-only technology** (ROM) stores data permanently on a disc, which cannot be subsequently added to or changed. Read-only discs, such as CD-ROMs, CDDAs, DVD-Video, and DVD-ROMs, are mass produced and used to distribute software, music, and movies.

▶ **Recordable technology** (R) uses a laser to change the color in a dye layer sandwiched beneath the clear plastic disc surface. The laser cre-ates dark spots in the dye that are read as pits. The change in the dye is permanent, so data cannot be changed once it has been recorded.

▶ **Rewritable technology** (RW) uses phase change technology to alter a crystal structure on the disc surface. Altering the crystal structure cre-ates patterns of light and dark spots similar to the pits and lands on a CD. The crystal structure can be changed from light to dark and back again many times, making it possible to record and modify data much like on a hard disk. The term *rerecordable* (RE) is sometimes used instead of *rewritable*.

FIGURE 2-32

CDs, DVDs, and Blu-ray discs are constructed with one or more layers of recording sur-face sandwiched between protective plastic.

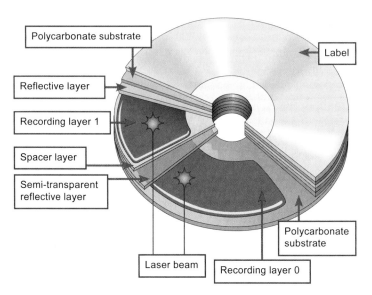

Polycarbonate substrate
Label
Reflective layer
Recording layer 1
Spacer layer
Semi-transparent reflective layer
Polycarbonate substrate
Laser beam
Recording layer 0

TERMINOLOGY NOTE

The letter *D* in acronyms for optical media such as CDs and DVDs formally means *disc*. In common usage, however, you will often see it spelled *disk*.

TRY IT!

Which optical technology performs most similarly to a hard disk drive?

○ RAM
○ ROM
○ R
○ RW

▶ What are my choices for CD, DVD, and Blu-ray media?

Several CD and DVD formats are currently popular for use in personal computers. Figure 2-33 summarizes available optical media formats.

FIGURE 2-33

Optical Storage Media

2

CDDA	(compact disc digital audio)	The format for commercial music CDs. Music is recorded on audio CDs by the manufacturer, but can't be changed by the consumer. Commonly known as audio CDs.
DVD-Video	(digital versatile disc video)	The format for commercial DVDs that contain feature-length films.
CD-ROM	(compact disc read-only)	The original optical format for computer data. Data is stamped on the disc at the time it is manufactured. Data cannot be added, changed, or deleted from these discs.
DVD-ROM	(digital versatile disc read-only)	Contains data stamped onto the disc surface at the time of manufacture. Like CD-ROMs, the data on DVD-ROMs is permanent, so you cannot add or change data.
CD-R	(compact disc recordable)	Stores data using recordable technology. The data on a CD-R cannot be erased or modified once you record it. However, most CD-R drives allow you to record your data in multiple sessions. For example, you can store two files on a CD-R disc today, and add data for a few more files to the disc at a later time.
DVD+R DVD-R	(digital versatile disc recordable)	Stores data using recordable technology similar to a CD-R, but with DVD storage capacity.
CD-RW	(compact disc rewritable)	Stores data using rewritable technology. Stored data can be recorded and erased multiple times, making it a very flexible storage option.
DVD+RW DVD-RW	(Digital versatile disc rewritable)	Stores data using rewritable technology similar to CD-RW, but with DVD storage capacity.
BD-ROM	(Blu-ray disc read-only memory)	Used to store commercial movies.
BD-R	(Blu-ray disc recordable)	Stores data using recordable technology; can be written to once.
BD-RE	(Blu-ray disc rerecordable)	Stores data using rewritable technology so data can be recorded and erased multiple times.

▶ Are rewritable CD, DVD, or Blu-ray drives an acceptable replacement for a hard disk?

A rewritable CD, DVD, or Blu-ray drive is a fine addition to a computer system, but is not a good replacement for a hard disk drive. Unfortunately, the process of accessing, saving, and modifying data on a rewritable disc is relatively slow compared to the speed of hard disk access.

▶ Can I use a single drive to work with any CD, DVD, or Blu-ray media?

Most CD drives can read CD-ROM, CD-R, and CD-RW discs, but cannot read DVDs or BDs. Most DVD drives can read CD and DVD formats. Storing computer data and creating music CDs require a recordable or rewritable device.

TRY IT!

In the table above, click the row that contains the technology used to play movies from an optical drive on your computer.

SOLID STATE STORAGE TECHNOLOGY

▶ What is solid state storage? **Solid state storage** (sometimes called flash memory) is a technology that stores data in erasable, rewritable circuitry, rather than on spinning disks or streaming tape. It is widely used in portable consumer devices, such as digital cameras, portable media players, iPads, and cell phones. It is also used as an alternative for hard disk storage in some laptop computers.

Some solid state storage is removable and provides fairly fast access to data. It is an ideal solution for storing data on mobile devices and transporting data from one device to another.

▶ How does solid state storage work? Solid state storage contains a gridwork of circuitry. Each cell in the grid contains two transistors that act as gates to hold the 1s and 0s that represent data (Figure 2-34).

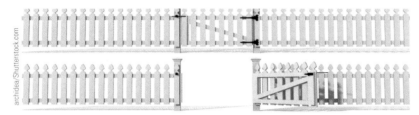

FIGURE 2-34

When the gates are closed by a process called Fowler-Nordheim tunneling, the cell has a value that represents a "0" bit. When the gates are open, current can flow and the cell has a value that represents a "1" bit.

Very little power is required to open or close the gates, which makes solid state storage ideal for battery-operated devices, such as digital cameras and media players. Once the data is stored, it is **non-volatile**—the chip retains the data without the need for an external power source.

Solid state storage provides fast access to data because it includes no moving parts. This storage technology is very durable—it is virtually impervious to vibration, magnetic fields, or extreme temperature fluctuations. On the downside, the capacity of solid state storage does not currently match that of hard disks. The cost per megabyte of solid state storage is slightly higher than for magnetic or optical storage.

▶ What are my options for solid state storage? Several types of solid state storage are available to today's consumers: memory cards, solid state drives, and USB flash drives.

▶ When should I use memory cards? A **memory card** is a flat, solid state storage medium commonly used to transfer files from digital cameras and media players to computers. The term *memory card* might lead you to believe that it is similar to random access memory (RAM), but these cards are non-volatile, so they retain data even when they are disconnected from computers and other devices.

The formats for memory cards include CompactFlash, MultiMedia, Secure Digital (SD), xD-Picture Cards, and SmartMedia. A **card reader** is a device that reads and writes data on solid state storage. Sometimes referred to as 5-in-1, 7-in-1, or all-in-one card readers, these combination devices work with multiple types of solid state storage formats (Figure 2-35).

Because digital photography is so popular, many laptop and desktop computers have a built-in card reader to make it simple to transfer photos from your camera to your computer. Moving data in the other direction, a computer can download MP3 or iTunes music files and store them on a solid state memory card. That card can be removed from the computer and inserted into a portable media player, so you can listen to your favorite tunes while you're on the go.

TRY IT!

Both solid state storage and RAM store data in integrated circuits. What is the main difference between the circuits used for RAM and for solid state storage?

○ RAM is volatile

○ Solid state storage is more temporary

○ RAM is more easily removable

○ Solid state storage has less capacity

FIGURE 2-35

Most personal computers are equipped with a card reader for transferring data to and from solid state memory cards.

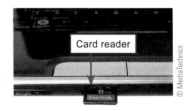

Card reader

Memory card

❱ **Do I need a solid state drive?** A **solid state drive** (SSD) is a package of flash memory that can be used as a substitute for a hard disk drive. Some solid state drives are about the same size as a microprocessor chip, whereas others are about the size of a small hard disk drive (Figure 2-36).

SSDs are widely used as the main storage device in handheld devices, such as iPhones and iPads. Some laptop computers also include an SSD instead of a hard disk drive.

When shopping for a laptop computer, you might have the choice of a hard disk drive or an SSD. An SSD is an attractive option for customers who use computers in rugged conditions. Currently, solid state drives are not a popular option for adding storage capacity to existing computers.

❱ **What is the best use for USB flash drives?** A **USB flash drive** is a portable storage device that plugs directly into a computer's system unit using a built-in connector.

Also called thumb drives, pen drives, jump drives, keychain drives, or UFDs, USB flash drives are about the size of a highlighter pen and so durable that you can literally carry them on your key ring. USB flash drives have capacities ranging from 16 MB to 256 GB.

USB flash drive data transfer speeds average 10–35 MBps (10,000–35,000 KBps). At these speeds, flash drives are slower than hard disk drives, so you might notice a bit of hesitation, especially when working with large files.

Files stored on a USB flash drive can be opened, edited, deleted, and run just as though those files were stored on magnetic or optical media. You might say that USB flash drives are the new floppy disks because not only can you access files as if they were stored on disks, but you can carry them from one computer to another and you can run software from them, too.

A USB flash drive is used for storing data files and programs that you want to use on various computers; for example, on your home computer and at work or in a school lab. When a USB flash drive is inserted, your computer automatically detects it. Macs display a flash drive icon on the desktop. Windows detects the flash drive and displays the AutoPlay window shown in Figure 2-37 so that you can quickly access files.

FIGURE 2-36

Like hard disk drives, SSDs offer fast data transfer rates and are fixed in place. Although they use the same technology as USB flash drives, SSDs cannot be easily removed from a computer.

FIGURE 2-37

To view the files and programs stored on a USB flash drive, insert it into the computer. Windows displays the AutoPlay window that you can use to quickly view the files stored on the USB device.

Removable Disk (E:)

Choose what to do with removable drives.

 Speed up my system
Windows ReadyBoost

 Configure this drive for backup
File History

 Open folder to view files
Windows Explorer

 Take no action

STORAGE WRAP-UP

▶ Can I add storage to my computer? You can increase storage capacity in a desktop or laptop computer by adding hard drives, and you can add storage flexibility by installing additional types of storage devices.

External storage devices, such as external hard disk drives, CD drives, DVD drives, and USB flash drives, simply plug into connectors built into your computer's system unit. They can be easily detached when you want to move your computer or if your external drive contains a backup that you want to store away from your computer.

Before you disconnect any storage device, make sure you understand the manufacturer's instructions for doing so. On PCs, you usually have to use the Safely Remove Hardware icon on the Windows taskbar. Macs usually provide an eject icon next to the drive listing.

As an alternative to an external drive, you can install storage devices inside a desktop or laptop system unit case in "parking spaces" called **drive bays**. An external drive bay provides access from outside the system unit—a necessity for a storage device with removable media, such as floppy disks, CDs, and DVDs.

Internal drive bays are located deep inside the system unit and are designed for hard disk drives, which don't use removable storage media. Most desktop computers include several internal and external bays. Laptop computers may include a drive bay for a CD/DVD drive (Figure 2-38).

An empty drive bay located on the side of a laptop computer

© MediaTechnics

Which one of the following can be installed in an internal drive bay?

○ Solid state drive

○ CD drive

○ USB flash drive

○ Blu-ray player

FIGURE 2-38

Some laptop computers provide bays for one hard disk drive and one CD or DVD drive.

Most desktop computers have several drive bays: some accessible from outside the case, and others—designed for hard disk drives—without any external access. Empty drive bays are often hidden from view with a face plate.

▶ Watch the video for this figure to find out how to install internal and external drives.

© MediaTechnics

What are the relative advantages and disadvantages of each type of computer storage device? Earlier in the chapter, you read that no storage technology is perfect. While hard disk drives offer fast and inexpensive access, they are not the most durable technology. CD and DVD technology is durable, but slow, and flash drive storage is expensive when compared per gigabyte to other storage media. The table in Figure 2-39 summarizes the relative advantages and disadvantages of each storage technology covered in this section.

FIGURE 2-39

Storage Technology Comparison

Storage Type	Cost of Device	Capacity	Data Transfer Rate	Technology	Removable
USB Flash Drive	$$	2–256 GB	Medium	Solid state	Yes
CD-RW	$	700 MB	Slow	Optical	Yes
DVD+RW	$	8.5 GB	Slow	Optical	Yes
Blu-ray	$$$$	50 GB	Slow	Optical	Yes
Floppy Disk	$	1.44 MB	Glacial	Magnetic	Yes
Hard Drive (Internal)	$$$	80 GB–2 TB	Fast	Magnetic	No
Hard Drive (External)	$$$	80 GB–2 TB	Fast	Magnetic	Yes
Solid State Drive (Internal)	$$$	32 GB–256 GB	Fast	Solid state	No

QuickCheck

1. Access [＿＿＿＿＿＿] is typically faster for random-access devices than for sequential-access devices.

2. A magnetic storage device uses a read-[＿＿＿＿＿＿] head to magnetize particles that represent data.

3. A hard disk drive that is rated at a speed of 7200 [＿＿＿＿＿＿] will give you faster access to your data than a drive rated at 5400. (Hint: Use the acronym.)

4. CD-R technology allows you to write data on a disc, and then change that data. True or false? [＿＿＿＿]

5. A(n) [＿＿＿＿＿＿] uses the same storage technology as a USB flash drive, but is not designed to be removable. (Hint: Use the acronym.)

▶ CHECK ANSWERS

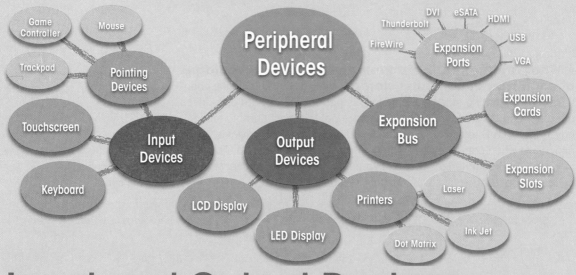

Input and Output Devices

THIS SECTION provides an overview of the most popular input and output devices for personal computers. After a survey of input devices, display devices, and printers, you'll take a look at the computer's expansion bus so that you'll be able to select, install, and use all kinds of peripherals.

BASIC INPUT DEVICES

▶ What devices can I use to get data into a computer?
Most computer systems include a keyboard and pointing device, such as a mouse, for basic data input. Touch-sensitive screens offer an additional input option. Other input devices, such as scanners, digital cameras, and graphics tablets, are handy for working with graphical input. Microphones and electronic instruments provide input capabilities for sound and music.

▶ What's special about a computer keyboard's design?
The design of most computer keyboards is based on the typewriter's qwerty layout, which was engineered to keep the typewriter's mechanical keys from jamming. In addition to a basic typing keypad, desktop and laptop computer keyboards include a collection of keys such as Alt, Ctrl, and Print Screen, designed for computer-specific tasks.

Most desktop computer keyboards include a calculator-style numeric keypad, plus an editing keypad with keys such as End, Home, and Page Up, to efficiently move the screen-based insertion point. You can even find tiny keyboards on handheld devices—entering text and numbers is an important part of most computing tasks.

▶ What does a pointing device do? A **pointing device** allows you to manipulate an on-screen pointer and other screen-based graphical controls. The most popular external pointing devices for personal computers include mice and game controllers. External pointing devices, such as the mouse in Figure 2-40, can be connected to the computer with a cable or with a wireless connection.

▶ Which pointing device should I choose? Most desktop computer systems include a **mouse** as the primary pointing device. Many computer owners also add a mouse to their laptop computers.

Game controllers come in many styles, such as joysticks, steering wheels, and wands. Game controllers also serve as adaptive devices for people with physical disabilities who cannot use a keyboard or mouse.

TRY IT!

Desktop and laptop computers have QWERTY keyboards. Check your tablet or smartphone. Is its on-screen keyboard layout QWERTY or ABCD?

FIGURE 2-40

An optical mouse uses an onboard chip to track a light beam as it bounces off a surface, such as a desk, clipboard, or mouse pad.

© MediaTechnics

▶ When do I need a trackpad? A **trackpad** (or touchpad) is a touch-sensitive surface on which you can slide your fingers to move the on-screen pointer. Trackpads also include buttons that serve the same function as mouse buttons. Trackpads are located just beneath the keyboard of most laptop computers so that it is not necessary to carry a mouse as an extra component.

The act of moving your fingers on the surface of a trackpad is called a gesture. On a standard trackpad, sliding a single finger moves the pointer. With a multi-touch trackpad, additional gestures are possible (Figure 2-41).

FIGURE 2-41

Touchpad Gestures

Zoom in: Move two fingers apart to zoom in and enlarge photos or documents.

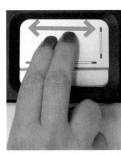
Zoom out: Move two fingers closer to each other to reduce the size of images or documents.

Horizontal scrolling: Move two fingers to the right or left.

Vertical scrolling: Move two fingers up or down.

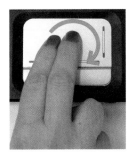
Rotate: Turn two fingers on the trackpad to rotate an image.

Tap: Tapping the trackpad performs the same function as clicking a mouse button.

Two-finger tap: Tapping the trackpad with two fingers generates a right-click.

Swipe: Move three fingers horizontally to step through a series of photos, album covers, or windows.

© MediaTechnics

▶ How does a touchscreen work? Tablet computers, handheld devices, retail store self-checkouts, and information kiosks collect input from a **touchscreen**, which overlays a display screen. The most commonly used touchscreen technology is a transparent panel coated with a thin layer of electrically conductive material that senses a change in the electrical current when touched. This "resistive" technology is fairly durable. It is not susceptible to dust or water, but it can be damaged by sharp objects. Processing technology can interpret a single touch or more complex input such as handwriting.

The coordinates for a touch event are processed in essentially the same way as a mouse click. For example, if you touch your iPad screen at the location of a button labeled Calendar, the area you touch generates coordinates and sends them to the processor. The processor compares the coordinates to the image displayed on the screen to find out what is at the coordinates, and then responds—in this case, by opening your appointment calendar. A popular use for touchscreens is to display a **virtual keyboard** on the screen of a handheld device, as shown in Figure 2-42.

FIGURE 2-42

A virtual keyboard can be displayed on a touchscreen to collect typed input.

© MediaTechnics

DISPLAY DEVICES

▶ **What are my options for display devices?** A computer display device that simply displays text and images is classified as an output device. Touch-sensitive screens, however, can be classified as both input and output devices because they accept input and display output.

Standalone display devices, sometimes called monitors, are popular for desktop computers. Display devices for laptops, tablets, and handheld devices are built into the system units. Two technologies are commonly used for computer display devices: LCD and LED.

LCD (liquid crystal display) technology produces an image by filtering light through a layer of liquid crystal cells (Figure 2-43). The advantages of LCD screens include display clarity, low radiation emission, portability, and compactness. The source of the light that filters through the LCD is referred to as backlighting. In a standard LCD screen, the source of this light is a series of cold cathode fluorescent lamps (CCFLs), which are not environmentally friendly. Gradually, CCFL backlighting is being replaced by **LED** (light-emitting diode) technology.

FIGURE 2-43

An LCD screen is composed of a grid arrayed with liquid crystal cells.

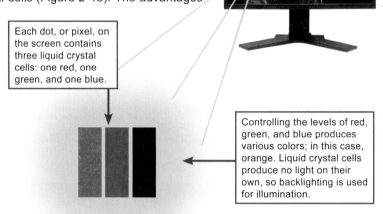

Andrey Burmakin/Shutterstock.com

Each dot, or pixel, on the screen contains three liquid crystal cells: one red, one green, and one blue.

Controlling the levels of red, green, and blue produces various colors; in this case, orange. Liquid crystal cells produce no light on their own, so backlighting is used for illumination.

▶ **What factors affect image quality?** Image quality is a factor of screen size, dot pitch, width of viewing angle, response rate, resolution, and color depth. Screen size is the measurement in inches from one corner of the screen diagonally across to the opposite corner. Screen sizes range from 3" on smartphones to 60" or more for home entertainment systems.

Dot pitch (dp) is a measure of image clarity. A smaller dot pitch means a crisper image. Technically, dot pitch is the distance in millimeters between like-colored **pixels**—the small dots of light that form an image. A dot pitch between .26 and .23 is typical for today's display devices. Dot pitch can also be expressed as dots per inch, with higher numbers indicating better image quality.

A display device's **viewing angle width** indicates how far to the side you can still clearly see the screen image. With a wide viewing angle of 170 degrees or more, you can view the screen from various positions without compromising image quality.

Response rate is the time it takes for one pixel to change from black to white then back to black. Display devices with fast response rates display a crisp image with minimal blurring or "ghosting" of moving objects. Response rate is measured in milliseconds (ms). For gaming systems, a response rate of 5 ms or less is desirable.

The number of colors a monitor can display is referred to as **color depth** or bit depth. Most PC display devices have the capability to display millions of colors. When set at 24-bit color depth (sometimes called True Color), your PC can display more than 16 million colors—and produce what are considered photographic-quality images.

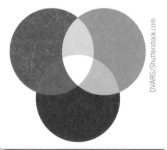

DVARG/Shutterstock.com

TRY IT!

The colors above show what happens when you blend red, green, and blue. Which combination of liquid crystal cells creates a yellow pixel?

○ Blue and red

○ Red and green

○ Green and blue

○ Red, green, and blue

▶ **What should I know about screen resolution?** The number of horizontal and vertical pixels that a device displays on the screen is referred to as **screen resolution**. Standard resolutions are optimized for a 4:3 aspect ratio in which the width is slightly larger than the height. Widescreen displays with 16:9 aspect ratios carry a W designation. Common screen resolutions are listed in Figure 2-44.

HDTV (high-definition TV) broadcast systems use resolutions of 1280 x 720 (720p) or 1920 x 1080 (1080p). For HDTV compatibility and viewing movies, your computer display should be compatible with one of these formats.

▶ **Should I set my computer on its highest resolution?** At higher resolutions, text and other objects appear smaller, but the computer can display a larger work area, such as an entire page of a document. At lower resolutions, text appears larger, but the work area is smaller. Enlarged text sometimes looks blurry because a letter that required one row of dots might now require additional dots to fill it in. Most displays have a recommended resolution at which images are clearest and text is crispest.

The two screens in Figure 2-45 help you compare a display set at 1280 x 800 resolution with a display set at 800 x 600 resolution.

FIGURE 2-44

Common Screen Resolutions

VGA	640 x 480
SVGA	800 x 600
XGA	1024 x 768
SXGA	1280 x 1024
UXGA	1600 x 1200
WUXGA	1920 x 1200
WQXGA	2560 x 1600

FIGURE 2-45

The screen on the left shows 1280 x 800 resolution. Notice the size of text and other screen-based objects. The screen on the right shows 800 x 600 resolution. Text and other objects appear larger on the low-resolution screen, but you see a smaller portion of the screen desktop.

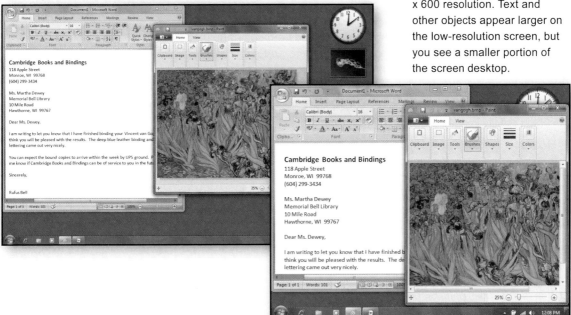

▶ **What are the components of a typical computer display system?** In addition to a display device, such as a monitor, a computer display system also requires graphics circuitry that generates the signals for displaying an image on the screen. One type of graphics circuitry, referred to as **integrated graphics**, is built into a computer's system board. A second option, called **dedicated graphics**, is graphics circuitry mounted on a small circuit board called a **graphics card** (or video card) like the one in Figure 2-46.

A graphics card contains a **graphics processing unit** (GPU) and special video memory, which stores screen images as they are processed but before they are displayed. Lots of video memory is the key to lightning-fast screen updating for fast action games, 3-D modeling, and graphics-intensive desktop publishing. In addition to video memory, most graphics cards contain special graphics accelerator technology to further boost performance.

FIGURE 2-46

A graphics card is a small circuit board that plugs into the system board.

Lusoimages/Shutterstock.com

PRINTERS

▶ **What printer technologies are available for personal computers?** Printers are one of the most popular output devices available for personal computers. Today's best-selling printers use ink jet or laser technology in multifunction devices that can also serve as scanners, copiers, and fax machines.

▶ **How does an ink jet printer work?** An **ink jet printer** has a nozzle-like print head that sprays ink onto paper to form characters and graphics. The print head in a color ink jet printer consists of a series of nozzles, each with its own ink cartridge. Most ink jet printers use CMYK color, which requires only cyan (blue), magenta (pink), yellow, and black inks to create a printout that appears to have thousands of colors. Alternatively, some printers use six or eight ink colors to print midtone shades that create slightly more realistic photographic images.

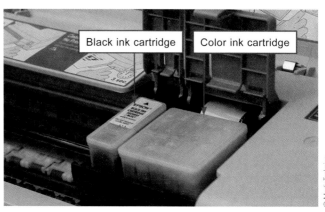

FIGURE 2-47

Ink jet printers spray ink from a series of ink cartridges.

Black ink cartridge   Color ink cartridge

Ink jet printers, such as the one in Figure 2-47, outsell all other types of printers because they are inexpensive and produce both color and black-and-white printouts. They work well for most home and small business applications. Small, portable ink jet printers meet the needs of many mobile computer owners.

Ink jet technology also powers many photo printers, which are optimized to print high-quality images produced by digital cameras and scanners.

▶ **How do laser printers compare to ink jet printers?** A **laser printer** uses the same technology as a photocopier to paint dots of light on a light-sensitive drum. Electrostatically charged ink is applied to the drum and then transferred to paper. A laser printer prints faster than an ink jet printer, but laser technology is more complex than ink jet technology, which accounts for the higher price of laser printers.

TRY IT!

Digital devices use various color models. Whereas display devices use the RGB model, printers use what color model?

A basic laser printer like the one in Figure 2-48 produces only black-and-white printouts. Color laser printers are available, but are somewhat more costly than basic black-and-white models. Laser printers are often the choice for business printers, particularly for applications that produce a high volume of printed material.

Toner cartridge

FIGURE 2-48

Laser printers electrostatically collect toner on a drum, then the toner is transferred onto paper. ▶ Find out more about laser printers by watching the video for this figure in your interactive eBook.

What is a dot matrix printer? When PCs first appeared in the late 1970s, dot matrix printers were the technology of choice, and they are still available today. A **dot matrix printer** produces characters and graphics by using a grid of fine wires. As the print head noisily clatters across the paper, the wires strike a ribbon and paper in a pattern prescribed by your PC (Figure 2-49).

FIGURE 2-49

Unlike laser and ink jet technologies, a dot matrix printer actually strikes the paper and, therefore, can print multipart carbon forms.

The print head contains a matrix of thin wires.

© MediaTechnics

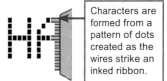

Characters are formed from a pattern of dots created as the wires strike an inked ribbon.

Dot matrix printers can print text and graphics—some even print in color using a multicolored ribbon. Today, dot matrix printers are used primarily for "back-office" applications that demand low operating cost and dependability, but not high print quality.

What features should I look for in a printer? Printers differ in resolution, print speed, duty cycle, operating costs, duplex capability, memory, and networkability.

- **Resolution.** The quality or sharpness of printed images and text depends on the printer's resolution—the density of the gridwork of dots that create an image. Printer resolution is measured by the number of dots printed per linear inch, abbreviated as dpi. At normal reading distance, a resolution of about 900 dpi appears solid to the human eye, but a close examination reveals a dot pattern. If you want magazine-quality printouts, 900 dpi is sufficient resolution. If you are aiming for resolution similar to expensive coffee-table books, look for printer resolution of 2,400 dpi or higher.

- **Print speed.** Printer speeds are measured either by pages per minute (ppm) or characters per second (cps). Color printouts typically take longer than black-and-white printouts. Pages that contain mostly text tend to print more rapidly than pages that contain graphics. Typical speeds for personal computer printers range between 6 and 30 pages of text per minute. A full-page 8.5 x 11 photo can take about a minute to print.

- **Duty cycle.** In addition to printer speed, a printer's **duty cycle** determines how many pages a printer is able to churn out. Printer duty cycle is usually measured in pages per month. For example, a personal laser printer has a duty cycle of about 3,000 pages per month (ppm)—that means roughly 100 pages per day. You wouldn't want to use it to produce 5,000 campaign brochures for next Monday, but you would find it quite suitable for printing ten copies of a five-page outline for a meeting tomorrow.

- **Operating costs.** The initial cost of a printer is only one of the expenses associated with printed output. Ink jet printers require frequent replacements or refills for relatively expensive ink cartridges. Laser printers require toner cartridge refills or replacements. Dot matrix printers require replacement ribbons. When shopping for a printer, you can check online resources to determine how often you'll need to replace printer supplies and how much they are likely to cost.

TRY IT!

Which type of printer is slower, but less expensive to operate?

○ Laser printer

○ Ink jet printer

▶ **Duplex capability.** A **duplex printer** can print on both sides of the paper. This environmentally friendly option saves paper but can slow down the print process, especially on ink jet printers that pause to let the ink dry before printing the second side.

▶ **Memory.** A computer sends data for a printout to the printer along with a set of instructions on how to print that data. **Printer Command Language** (PCL) is the most widely used language for communication between computers and printers, but **PostScript** is an alternative printer language that many publishing professionals prefer. Data that arrives at a printer along with its printer language instructions requires memory. Laser printers do not start printing until all the data for a page is received. You can add memory to most laser printers if necessary for your print jobs.

▶ **Networkability.** A network-enabled printer can connect directly to a computer network, rather than to a single computer. The network connection can be wired or wireless. The advantage of a network-ready printer is that it can be placed in a location convenient for all the network users. Network-enabled printers are essential for printing from handheld devices that can't be connected to a printer by cable. For example, to print from an iPad or iPhone, you can use an AirPrint compatible printer that's part of your home Wi-Fi network.

▶ **Should I refill or recycle?** Ink and toner cartridges are expensive and you can save some money by refilling them yourself or taking them to an ink refilling station at a local office store. Remanufactured and discount printer supplies are available online, too. Before you try one of these options, read the instructions and warranty for your printer. Inexpensive printer supplies don't always get stellar ratings from consumers. If cartridge and toner refills are not available, find out how to responsibly recycle them (Figure 2-50).

FIGURE 2-50

When you replace printer components, check to see if the manufacturer has a recycle program.

INSTALLING PERIPHERAL DEVICES

▶ **How does a computer move data to and from peripheral devices?** When you install a peripheral device, you are basically creating a connection for data to flow between the device and the computer. Within a computer, data travels from one component to another over circuits called a **data bus**.

One part of the data bus, referred to as the local bus or internal bus, runs between RAM and the microprocessor. The segment of the data bus to which peripheral devices connect is called the **expansion bus** or external bus. As data moves along the expansion bus, it can travel through expansion slots, expansion cards, ports, and cables (Figure 2-51).

FIGURE 2-51

The expansion bus connects the computer system board to peripheral devices.

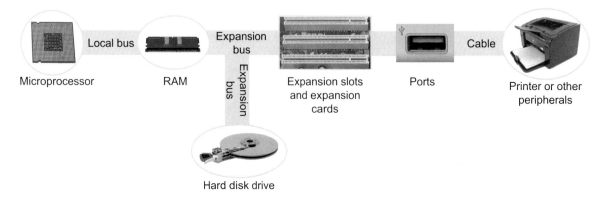

Microprocessor   Local bus   RAM   Expansion bus   Expansion slots and expansion cards   Ports   Cable   Printer or other peripherals

Hard disk drive

▶ **What's an expansion slot?** An **expansion slot** is a long, narrow socket on the system board into which you can plug an expansion card. An **expansion card** is a small circuit board that gives a computer the capability to control a storage device, an input device, or an output device. Expansion cards are also called expansion boards, controller cards, or adapters.

Expansion slots can be used for installing high-end graphics cards in desktop computers configured for gaming, desktop publishing, and graphics applications. Figure 2-52 shows how to plug an expansion card into an expansion slot.

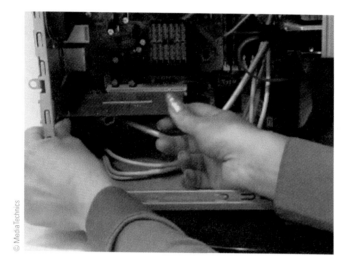

FIGURE 2-52

An expansion card simply slides into an expansion slot. Before you install an expansion card, be sure to unplug the computer and ground yourself—that's technical jargon for releasing static electricity by using a special grounding wristband or by touching both hands to a metal object. ▶ Your interactive eBook explains how to install expansion cards in a desktop computer.

▶ **What is an expansion port?** An **expansion port** is any connector that passes data into and out of a computer or peripheral device. It is similar to an electrical outlet because you can plug things in to make a connection.

Expansion ports are usually incorporated in the system board. Computer system units are designed with openings that make these ports accessible from outside the case.

As shown in Figure 2-53, the built-in ports supplied with today's desktop and laptop computers usually include graphics ports for connecting display devices, an Ethernet port for connecting to a wired network, eSATA and FireWire ports for high-speed external data storage, audio ports for microphone and speakers, and USB ports for connecting a mouse, keyboard, printer, and other peripheral devices.

FIGURE 2-53

When this system board is installed in a computer, the expansion ports will be accessible from outside the system unit.

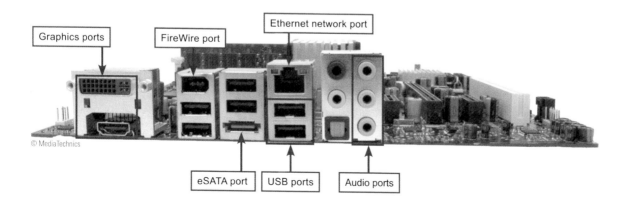

Graphics ports

FireWire port

Ethernet network port

eSATA port

USB ports

Audio ports

Is it difficult to install a new peripheral device? At one time, installing computer peripherals required a screwdriver and extensive knowledge of ports, slots, boards, and various electronic gizmos. Today, most peripheral devices connect to an external **USB** (universal serial bus) port, located on the front, sides, or back of the computer system unit (Figure 2-54).

Many kinds of peripheral devices—including mice, scanners, and joysticks—are available with USB connections. Transmitters for wireless devices, such as wireless mice, also plug into USB slots. Several types of storage devices, such as USB flash drives and external hard disk drives, use USB connections, too.

What if I run out of USB ports? You can easily add USB ports to your computer by using an inexpensive **USB hub**, which contains several auxiliary USB ports. The hub plugs into one of your computer's USB ports and you can then insert multiple USB devices into the ports supplied by the hub.

Self-powered USB hubs require power from an external power supply, such as a wall outlet. Bus-powered USB hubs (sometimes called unpowered hubs) draw their power from the computer. A bus-powered USB hub can be used for low-power devices, such as card readers and mice. A self-powered USB hub is required if the hub is used for connecting scanners, printers, and some external hard drives. Figure 2-55 illustrates how a USB hub can be used to connect several devices to a single USB port on a computer.

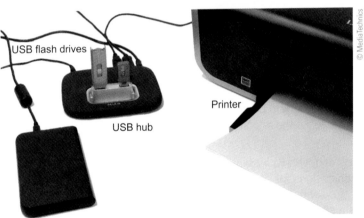

USB flash drives

USB hub

Printer

External hard drive

When do I use other kinds of ports? **FireWire** ports (also called IEEE 1394 ports) are used for external storage devices and for transferring data from digital video cameras to a computer. **eSATA** is a high-speed port used for connecting external storage devices. **Thunderbolt** is a very high-speed port for connecting display or storage devices.

VGA (Video Graphics Array), **DVI** (Digital Visual Interface), and **HDMI** (High-Definition Multimedia Interface) ports are designed for audiovisual devices. They are primarily used for connecting a monitor to a desktop computer, and for connecting an external monitor to a laptop computer. Figure 2-56 illustrates ports that can be used for connecting display devices.

VGA

DVI

HDMI

FIGURE 2-54

A USB connector is shaped like a flat rectangle. Make sure you know which side of the plug is up; the top is usually labeled with the USB logo.

FIGURE 2-55

This self-powered USB hub connects two USB flash drives, an external hard drive, and a printer to a single USB port that is connected to a computer.

FIGURE 2-56

A variety of ports are available for connecting an external monitor to a desktop or laptop computer.

▶ **What is hot-plugging?** When you connect or disconnect a peripheral device while the computer is operating, you are **hot-plugging**, a practice that's allowed with USB and FireWire devices. Before you unplug a device, such as a USB flash drive, however, your computer might require notification. In Windows, you can give notification using the Safely Remove Hardware icon in the notification area of the taskbar. With a Mac, hold down the Control key, click the device icon, and then select Eject.

Windows

Macs

TRY IT!

Click the icons on the Windows and Mac toolbars to find out which ones remove a USB flash drive from your computer.

▶ **Why do some peripheral devices include a CD?** Some devices require software to establish communication with your computer. The directions supplied with your peripheral device include instructions on how to install the software. Typically, you use the installation CD one time to get everything set up, and then you can put the CD away in a safe place. You'll learn more about this software, called a device driver, in the next chapter.

FIGURE 2-57

After your computer detects a newly connected device, it might take a few seconds to set up communication.

Long-time computer techies probably remember the days when installing a peripheral device meant messing around with little electronic components called dip switches and a host of complex software settings called IRQs.

Fortunately, USB, FireWire, and Thunderbolt ports can auto-detect a newly connected device and attempt to establish the settings necessary for sending data between it and the computer (Figure 2-57).

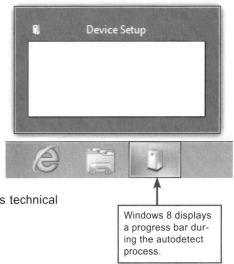

Autodetect, sometimes called "plug and play," works quite well for most popular peripheral devices. If your computer does not recognize a newly connected device or is unable to correctly exchange data with it, check the manufacturer's Web site for a device driver update, or call the manufacturer's technical support department.

Windows 8 displays a progress bar during the autodetect process.

QuickCheck

SECTION D

1. On a multi-touch trackpad, you can use various [_____] to move the pointer, zoom, and scroll.

2. A widescreen computer display has a 16:9 [_____] ratio.

3. One type of graphics circuitry, referred to as [_____] graphics, is built into a computer's system board.

4. Most ink jet printers use [_____] color that requires four ink colors. (Hint: Use the acronym.)

5. A(n) [_____] port provides one of the fastest, simplest ways to connect peripheral devices. (Hint: Use the acronym.)

 CHECK ANSWERS

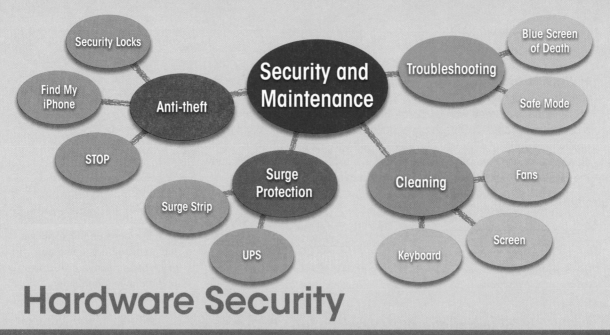

Security Locks

Find My iPhone

Anti-theft

STOP

Surge Strip

Surge Protection

UPS

Security and Maintenance

Troubleshooting

Blue Screen of Death

Safe Mode

Cleaning

Fans

Keyboard

Screen

Hardware Security

THE INFORMATION that computers contain and process has become practically priceless to every PC owner. Just about everyone depends on a computer for information and communication. A stolen computer, even if it's low-priced, can be a huge loss if it holds valuable financial data or months of research. A broken PC can easily cost hundreds of dollars to repair, especially if the data is damaged and needs to be recovered. For trouble-free computer use, it is important to secure and regularly maintain your computer equipment, just as you would your home and car.

ANTI-THEFT DEVICES

▶ What can I do to prevent my computer from being stolen?

Computers are prime targets for thieves. Many security breaches have been traced to stolen computers. The portability of laptop and tablet computers makes them particularly easy for a thief to grab, just as a wallet or a handbag would be. Figure 2-58 contains important tips for protecting your portable computer from theft.

> ▶ Never leave your portable computer unattended, especially when you are at a coffee shop, the library, or the airport.
>
> ▶ If you have to leave your portable computer in your car, never leave it in plain view. Lock it up in the trunk or cover it up.
>
> ▶ Carry your portable computer in an inconspicuous carrying case.
>
> ▶ Record your portable computer's make, model, and serial number and store them away from the computer. Many recovered computers cannot be returned to their owners because this tracking information is not supplied to police.
>
> ▶ Consider securing your portable computer with an anti-theft device.

FIGURE 2-58

Tips for Preventing Computer Theft

FIGURE 2-59

The Kensington Security Slot is an industry standard way to secure a computer to a desk.

▶ **How do computer anti-theft devices work?** Several computer anti-theft devices are available. Most can be used for both desktop and laptop computers.

The Kensington Security Slot is a security mechanism that's factory-installed on many personal computers. It is a small, reinforced oblong hole into which you can insert a special lock that can be attached to a cable. The cable can be fastened to a desk to prevent theft as shown in Figure 2-59.

© MediaTechnics

▶ If my computer is stolen, can authorities recover it? Your chances of recovering a stolen computer improve if you have taken some steps in advance, such as recording the computer's serial number, affixing a tracking label, or installing tracking software.

STOP (Security Tracking of Office Property) plates leave an indelible tattoo on your computer equipment, which contains a unique ID number registered in the international STOP database.

Tracking and recovery software, such as CyberAngel and LoJack for Laptops, secretly sends a message as soon as a thief uses a stolen computer to log on to the Internet. This message contains the computer's exact location and is directed to a tracking or monitoring center.

Apple's Find My iPhone system can be used to track missing iPhones, iPods, and iPads (Figure 2-60).

FIGURE 2-60

Find My iPhone can locate a missing phone and remotely lock it or delete its contents.

SURGE PROTECTION AND BATTERY BACKUP

▶ What is a power surge? To ensure that your computer stays in good running condition, it is essential to protect it from power surges. A **power surge** is a sudden increase in electrical energy affecting the current that flows to electrical outlets. Power surges often occur before or after power failures, which also put your computer and data at risk.

Computers and peripheral devices require stable current and are particularly sensitive to sudden bursts of electrical energy. A powerful surge can ruin computer circuitry. Smaller surges can slowly damage your computer's circuit boards and other electrical components. Over time, even small, repeated power surges can shorten your PC's life.

Power surges originate from a number of sources: downed power lines, power grid switching by the electric company, faulty wiring, and large appliances like refrigerators and air conditioners powering on and off. Lightning causes extremely large power surges and consequently poses a real threat to your computer equipment.

▶ How can I protect my computer from power surges? You can protect your computer equipment from power surges by plugging it into a surge strip instead of directly into a wall outlet. For added protection during thunderstorms, shut down your computer, turn off all your peripheral devices, and unplug the surge strip and all computer-related cables from wall outlets, including the cable for your modem.

TRY IT!

You're recharging your iPad. Which is safest?

○ Plug the charger into a wall outlet

○ Plug the charger into a surge strip

▶ **What is a surge strip and how does one work?** A **surge strip** (also called a surge suppressor or surge protector) is a device that contains electrical outlets protected by circuitry that blocks surges. Some surge strips also have sockets for modem connections that prevent surges from traveling down telephone or cable lines and into your computer.

A surge strip like the one in Figure 2-61 monitors the electrical current that passes from an outlet to all the devices plugged into the strip. When it detects a surge, it redirects the extra current to a grounded circuit.

© MediaTechnics

FIGURE 2-61

Surge strips should be connected directly to a wall outlet. Plugging one surge strip into another surge strip reduces their effectiveness.

A big power surge can burn out a surge strip while it tries to protect your equipment. Some surge strips have an indicator light that warns you if the surge strip is no longer functioning properly. Check the manufacturer's documentation to determine if you should discard the depleted strip, reset it, or install a new fuse.

▶ **What is a UPS?** A **UPS** (uninterruptible power supply) is a device that not only provides surge protection, but also furnishes desktop computers and network devices with battery backup power during a power outage.

If your desktop computer is connected to a UPS when a power outage occurs, the battery backup allows you to save what you're doing and properly shut down your computer. Depending on your system's configuration, a UPS with a high-performance battery might give you enough backup power to keep your computer up and running for several hours, allowing you to continue to work during the entire power outage.

Portable computers run on battery power and so the data you're working on is not immediately affected by a power outage. However, if you want to access your local area network or Internet connection, you might consider plugging your network devices and Internet modem into a UPS so that they continue to operate during an outage.

As shown in Figure 2-62, most UPSs have two types of sockets: one type offers battery backup plus surge protection, and the other offers only surge protection. The surge-only sockets are for printers, which use so much power that they can quickly drain the battery. At the Web site for American Power Conversion, you'll find tips for choosing a UPS based on your system's configuration and the amount of run time you want during a power outage.

TRY IT!

A UPS is NOT particularly useful for which of the following devices?

○ A desktop computer

○ A laptop computer

○ The router for your home network

○ Your Internet modem

Surge and battery backup outlets

Surge-only outlets

© MediaTechnics

FIGURE 2-62

An uninterruptible power supply (UPS) not only protects electronic equipment from power surges, it also provides battery power during power outages.

BASIC MAINTENANCE

▶ **Can I prevent hardware problems?** Computer component failures can be caused by manufacturing defects and other circumstances beyond your control. You can, however, undertake some preventive maintenance to extend the life of your computer equipment, just as regular tune-ups lengthen the life of your car.

Preventive maintenance can save you more than the cost of repairs; you also save the time you would've lost while tracking down problems and arranging for repairs. Regularly cleaning your computer components and peripheral devices helps to keep them in good condition.

▶ **How do I clean the keyboard?** Always shut down your computer before you clean your keyboard so that you don't inadvertently type in commands that you don't want your system to execute. Also, disconnect the keyboard and remember where the connection is located. Flip the keyboard over and shake it gently to get rid of debris that became lodged between the keys. A can of compressed air is also effective for removing debris. A vacuum cleaner can suck away the keys on your keyboard, so be very careful if you use one to clean your keyboard.

You can use cotton swabs just slightly moistened with a mild cleaning fluid to clean the sides of keys. Wipe the tops of the keys with a soft cloth, again slightly dampened with a mild cleaning solution. Allow your keyboard to dry before you reconnect it. Keep drinks away from your computer to avoid spilling liquids onto the keyboard. Figure 2-63 provides more information on cleaning your computer keyboard.

© MediaTechnics

FIGURE 2-63

Carefully use a cotton swab and a can of compressed air or a vacuum cleaner to remove dust and debris from your keyboard. Sticky liquids are difficult to remove. That can of pop? Keep it away from your keyboard. ▶ Watch the video in your interactive eBook to see how to safely clean your computer keyboard.

▶ **How do I get dust and fingerprints off my computer screen?** Dust and fingerprint smudges can easily accumulate on display screens and make them quite difficult to read. You should clean screens, especially touchscreens, on a regular basis. It's always best to turn off your display device before you clean because a blank screen will reveal all the smudges, dust, and dirt.

Follow the manufacturer's instructions for cleaning your display screens, using the recommended cleaning product. Spray the cleaner on a lint-free, soft cloth, but never directly on the screen. Don't scrub. The membrane covering many screens is delicate and can be easily damaged.

▶ Should I be concerned about my computer's operating temperature? High-performance processors, hard drives, graphics cards, and several other computer components generate a lot of heat. Overheating can shorten the lifespan of internal components and chips.

Most desktop computers have a fan mounted on the power supply that runs continuously to maintain the proper temperature inside of the system unit. Additional cooling fans might also be used to cool the microprocessor or graphics card. Laptop computers also have cooling fans, but the fans come on only after the processor reaches a certain temperature (Figure 2-64).

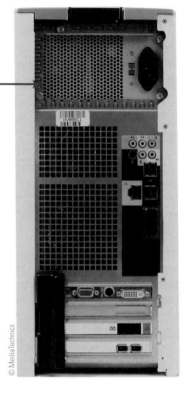

Desktop system unit fans

Laptop computer fans

It is important to be aware of the ventilation around your computer system and ensure that the fans are able to draw air from the room and blow it across the internal components. If your desktop's system unit is in an enclosed space, such as a cabinet, you might need to cut out a hole at the back to give your PC some room to "breathe."

Dust particles, dirt, and pet hair can collect on and around a computer's cooling fans and impede their performance. You should regularly use a can of compressed air or a vacuum cleaner hose to clean out debris from the vents and fans.

Exercise extreme caution when cleaning inside your computer's system case. First, make sure that you've turned off the computer and all connected devices. Do not touch the system board, and be sure not to knock any cables loose.

You should also be aware of the temperature in the room in which your computer resides. Several vendors sell cooling mats containing fans that can be placed under your laptop computer (Figure 2-65).

FIGURE 2-65

If your laptop computer case usually feels warm, consider placing it on a chill mat containing fans that can lower the computer's temperature and potentially increase its lifespan.

▶ Are there any other components that need TLC? To avoid read or write errors, you want your optical drives to function properly. Retailers provide cleaning kits for many types of storage devices and media. Also examine your CDs and DVDs for scratches and fingerprints. Clean them with a soft cloth slightly dampened with water. If the smudges don't come off, a little isopropyl alcohol might help.

▶ **What is a good computer maintenance routine?** Aside from cleaning your computer equipment on a regular basis, you should do the preventive maintenance tasks listed in Figure 2-66. You'll learn how to do these tasks in later chapters.

▶ Back up your files regularly, particularly those that are most important to you. You might want to perform daily backups of critical data and monthly backups of all your files. You should also test your backup procedures periodically.

▶ Run utilities that ensure peak performance for your hard disk drive. In Windows, these utilities include Disk Cleanup and Disk Defragmenter. It's best to do this maintenance on a weekly basis.

▶ Delete your browser's history and cache files on a monthly basis in order to free up space for your temporary files. The free space results in faster downloads from the Internet.

▶ Apply the latest operating system, driver, and security updates.

▶ Scan your computer for viruses and spyware once a week.

▶ Keep antivirus and spyware definitions updated.

FIGURE 2-66

Tips for Regular Computer Maintenance

TROUBLESHOOTING AND REPAIR

▶ **How can I tell if something is wrong with my computer?** There are several telltale signs that your computer is in trouble. The most obvious one is failure to power up. A loud beep at startup time can also indicate a problem. If your computer's screen remains blank or error messages appear, you might have a hardware problem (Figure 2-67).

FIGURE 2-67

Windows 8 displays this Recovery message when it detects a hardware problem during startup.

Hardware problems can also show up as unexpected restarts at random intervals, or as a peripheral device that stops working. Some problems are intermittent and might seem to be resolved only to come back when they are least convenient to deal with.

▶ **What is the blue screen of death?** Many seasoned Windows users have encountered the **blue screen of death** (also called BSoD) that suddenly replaces the usual graphical screen display with an enigmatic error message written in white text against a blue background. The blue screen of death indicates that the operating system has encountered an error from which it cannot recover, and the computer no longer accepts any commands.

Hardware problems can quickly escalate and some can eventually make your computer non-functional or make your data impossible to access. Any computer problem that prevents you from working as usual should be taken seriously. A little time spent troubleshooting can save you lots of annoyance down the road.

❱ **How do I troubleshoot a hardware problem?** You might be able to solve many hardware problems by simply following the basic guidelines for troubleshooting listed in Figure 2-68.

❱ Stay calm and don't jump to any conclusions until you've thought everything through.

❱ Write down all error messages and any other information that goes with them.

❱ Make sure all components are plugged in and that there are no loose cables. For example, if your display device's cable is loose, the indicator light will be off and your screen will be blank.

❱ If you can, try to duplicate the problem by going through the same steps that led you to it.

❱ Look for troubleshooting and repair tips in your user's manual, on your vendor's Web site, or even through a search engine. If you search the Internet by typing in the error message number or keywords in the error message, you might discover that at least one person has already found a solution to your problem.

❱ Run your antispyware and antivirus software. Lurking viruses, worms, Trojan horses, and spyware (discussed in the next chapter) can cause strange and unexplainable occurrences in your computer system. For example, spyware can cause your computer to keep displaying a pop-up ad no matter how you try to close it.

❱ Restarting your computer can clear up many minor operational problems. Windows always requires a reboot when it displays the blue screen of death. However, a more serious problem underlying the BSoD will not be resolved with a reboot. To reboot a PC, hold down the Ctrl, Alt, and Del keys at the same time. When the next screen appears, select the Shut Down button.

FIGURE 2-68

Troubleshooting Tips

TRY IT!

What is one of the simplest steps to take if your computer seems to have an operational problem?

○ Access the BSoD

○ Activate its safe mode

○ Restart your computer

○ Plug it into a surge strip

Troubleshooting and diagnostic tools can help you find the source of a problem and fix it. For example, Windows offers interactive troubleshooting tools formatted as a series of simple questions, answers, and recommendations (Figure 2-69). You might have to borrow a computer to run these tools if your computer is totally out of commission.

FIGURE 2-69

To access Windows troubleshooters, go to the Control Panel.

▶ **What is safe mode?** Whether you use a PC or a Mac, your computer probably has a special **safe mode** designed for professional troubleshooting. On Macs this mode is referred to as Safe Boot, whereas Windows calls it Safe Mode. When operating in these modes, your computer uses a limited version of the operating system that allows you to use your mouse, screen, and keyboard, but no other peripheral devices. Safe Mode and Safe Boot can be used to track down and uninstall programs or hardware that might be causing operational problems (Figure 2-70).

FIGURE 2-70

When your computer is in a "safe" mode, it can be used for troubleshooting, but not normal computing.

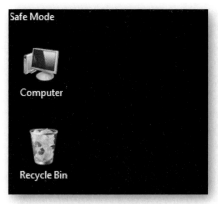

Windows Safe Mode

Mac Safe Boot Mode

▶ **What if I can't solve the problem myself?** If you are unable to fix a hardware problem yourself, you might have to call the technical support center for the device or component that is malfunctioning. You can also consider asking for help from a knowledgeable person or from computer repair professionals like the Geek Squad.

When seeking outside technical help, make sure you've checked your warranty, and know the purchase date, serial number, brand, model, and operating system. You should also have a written copy of error messages and a description of the steps that led to the problem.

Once the problem is resolved, write down the solution. You never know when you might need it again!

QuickCheck

1. A power [＿＿＿＿＿] is a sudden increase or spike in electrical energy, affecting the current that flows to electrical outlets.

2. A(n) [＿＿＿＿＿] can provide power to keep your desktop computer, network, and Internet connection operational during a power outage. (Hint: Use the acronym.)

3. If your computer's built-in fans don't provide an adequate level of cooling, you can place it on a chill mat. True or false? [＿＿＿＿＿]

4. When using Windows, you can troubleshoot hardware problems by logging in to the BSoD. True or false? [＿＿＿＿＿]

5. [＿＿＿＿＿] Mode is a stripped-down version of Windows that is designed for troubleshooting.

▶ CHECK ANSWERS

Issue: Where Does All the Ewaste Go?

IN THE WEST AFRICAN nation of Ghana, smoldering piles of discarded computers and monitors ring a mucky river, polluted beyond recovery. Teenage boys play soccer in a toxic haze. When their break is over, they get back to work smashing monitors, ripping out the innards, and tossing the plastic cases into a smoking pyre of oozing plastic.

In Guiyu, China, thousands of women huddle over primitive stoves "cooking" circuit boards to retrieve trace amounts of gold. Toxic fumes from the cooking process cloud the air; a toddler showing symptoms of lead poisoning plays listlessly with the carcasses of discarded mice and cell phones.

It is called ewaste, e-garbage, or technotrash—all the unwanted and outdated computers, monitors, printers, cell phones, disk drives, disks, CDs, and DVDs. According to the Environmental Protection Agency (EPA), 3 million tons of it is discarded every year. In the United States alone, almost eight printer cartridges are discarded every second, and millions of CDs and DVDs end up in landfills every year.

Computers and other electronic gear contain toxic substances such as lead, cadmium, and mercury. When discarded equipment is buried in landfills, these substances can leach into groundwater and streams. When burned, electronic components can emit toxic dioxin.

Ewaste is a global problem. As countries struggle to deal with discarded electronic components, an alarming amount of ewaste is shipped to developing countries where villagers, working for pennies a day, are exposed to toxic chemicals as they attempt to reclaim resalable metals from discarded equipment. Throughout the emerging world, ugly ewaste dumps defile the landscape and have yet unknown health effects.

Where does all this ewaste originate? Every country generates ewaste, but the bulk of it comes from prosperous, technology-forward countries such as the United States, Great Britain, Germany, Japan, France, and China. Despite laws that ban ewaste transhipping, loopholes allow discarded but work-ing electronics to be shipped as "donations." Tons of donations arrive every day in port cities, such as Hong Kong, where they follow a shadowy route to unregulated workshops and dump sites.

Some illegal ewaste originates in legitimate recycling centers, where consumers assume electronic components will be handled in environmentally friendly ways. Many recycling centers do not process materials on site. Instead, they ship the ewaste to third parties. Without careful monitoring, that ewaste can be diverted to offshore locations where it piles up, waiting to be disassembled by backstreet laborers ungoverned by environmental protection regulations.

Developed countries have strict environmental regulations designed to prevent toxic substances from polluting air, land, and water. Proper disposal is expensive, however. In countries with high labor costs and stringent environmental regulations, the value of compounds retrieved from ewaste does not cover the cost of extraction.

Some illegal ewaste originates in legitimate recycling centers...

The high cost of properly processing ewaste makes gray market options attractive. Ewaste can be handled more cost-effectively in emerging countries where environmental regulations are ignored, wages are pitiful, and workers are not covered by health and safety laws.

So, who is responsible for ewaste sweatshops and pollution? Is it consumers in developed countries who deposit unwanted gear at recycling stations that don't carry out the recycling process in-house, or is it the recycling firms that ship ewaste to third parties? Is it the firms that ship ewaste to emerging countries or the governments that can't close the loopholes on ewaste transhipping?

Perhaps the responsibility lies with emerging countries that are unable to control ewaste sweatshops and ignore the resulting environmental and human casualties.

Wherever the blame lies, consumers who are aware of the problem can become more responsible in the way they dispose of unwanted gear to keep it out of landfills at home and offshore.

TRY IT! Explore the ewaste issue. Watch a video of the Ghana crisis and explore the steps you can take to minimize the number of electronic components that end their life in landfills and toxic waste dumps.

1 A group of graduate journalism students from the University of British Columbia investigated the illicit ewaste industry. Their story is presented in a Frontline World report located at *www.pbs.org/frontlineworld/stories/ghana804/video/video_index.html*. Watch the video. Where do the researchers drop off the ewaste and where does it end up?

2 Many computers, mobile phones, and other electronic components pile up in landfills because their owners are unaware of potential environmental hazards and simply toss them in the garbage. Use Web sites such as Earth911.com, or search for "recycling computers" and add your city name as in "recycling computers Chicago." Where is the nearest drop-off location for old laptop computers? Would you be charged a fee, and if so, how much?

3 Before donating or discarding a computer, you should erase all the data it contains. Simply deleting files is not sufficient to prevent data from being recovered. Connect to *www.pcworld.com* and search for "erase hard drive." Locate the how-to video and watch it. What are three ways you can securely prevent access to the data on a hard disk?

4 Consumers can select "green" products and purchase equipment from environment-friendly manufacturers. Check out Greenpeace's Green Ranking. What is the ranking for the company that manufactured your computer?

5 You might wonder if the computer you are currently using is environmentally friendly. The Green Electronics Council rates specific computer models as bronze, silver, or gold. Connect to the EPEAT site (*www.epeat.net*), click Search the Registry, and then drill down to find your computer. What is the rating for your computer brand and model?

	BRONZE	SILVER	GOLD	Total
Desktops	1	83	132	216
Displays	0	352	308	660
Integrated Desktop Computers	0	51	27	78
Notebooks	50	635	1018	1703
Thin Clients	0	21	4	25
Workstation Desktops	0	0	20	20
Workstation Notebooks	0	2	7	9
Totals	51	1144	1516	2711

INFOWEBLINKS

You can check the **NP2014 Chapter 2** InfoWebLink for updates to these activities.

W CLICK TO CONNECT
www.infoweblinks.com/NP2014/ch02

What Do You Think?

ISSUE

1. Have you ever thrown away an old computer or other electronic device?

2. Do you research products before you purchase them to find out if they are environmentally friendly throughout their life cycle?

3. Would it be fair for consumers to pay a recycling tax on electronic equipment that they purchase?

Information Tools: Making the Cut

Searching Bing, Google Scholar, or academic databases produces mountains of links. How do you select and save the most relevant bits of information? The first step is to decide which information is relevant enough to make the cut. To decide, ask yourself the following three questions:

1. IS IT RELEVANT? Read the search engine synopsis carefully. With Google and other search engines, the synopsis shows your search terms in the context of the article. Academic databases display a standard synopsis. Don't waste your time linking to articles that are not relevant to your research topic.

The zen of **overclocking**

B Colwell - Computer, 2004 - ieeexplore.ieee.org
Every once in a while, some- thing comes along in the computer industry that really surprises me. The first time this happened was in the early 1980s, when the first personal computing stores showed up in shop- ping malls. The second time was when I took the first Internet browser ...
Cited by 13 - Related articles - All 4 versions

2. WHAT'S THE MAIN IDEA? Link to articles that seem relevant and skim them to pick up the main idea. Academic databases typically connect you to an abstract that provides a short summary. You can get an overview of an article's key terms using Web apps such as Wordle to create a word cloud.

3. ARE THERE LINKS TO ADDITIONAL MATERIAL?
The first part of a full-text journal article summarizes historical research and may include lots of citations. Some of these ideas might be worth tracking down for your own research. The bibliography can help you locate specific material mentioned in the article.

> Overclocked parts that are pushed to their limits also tend to have a reduced functional lifespan or even worse, if improperly done, can be destroyed completely [1]. In this experiment we will overclock an Intel processor. Its original frequency is 2.13 GHz, we will try to hit 3.20 GHz which is about 50% increase in CPU frequency

> Bibliography
> [1]http://compreviews.about.com/od/cpus/l/aaOverclock.htm

For more sources, jump to resources mentioned in the bibliography.

NOTE-TAKING TIPS

Use a word processor or bookmarking tool.

Be sure to identify information that is not your own; one technique is to put it inside quotation marks. Another technique is to apply a highlight color.

Always capture the URL of a source document so that you can return to it if you eventually include it in your paper and need a full citation.

Make sure that you add your own identifier to each piece of information; use your notes as topic headers, which will help you group and organize the information.

Articles most relevant to your research topic require careful reading and note taking. For less relevant articles, simply make a note of the main idea and URL, just in case it becomes relevant later in your research process.

TRY IT! As you find information that is relevant to your research topic, you need a way to record it and keep track of it. Note-taking tools help you record important ideas; the trick is to keep your notes in good order. Many students use word processors to take notes. Bookmarking tools offer another option. Here's a chance to explore these tools and make a word cloud.

Many scholars record their notes in a word processing document. This method offers flexibility for copying snippets of text as well as entering summary notes.

1 Use your favorite word processing software to create a blank document called Project [Your Name] Chapter 2, then complete the rest of the steps.

2 Use an academic database to search for a journal article about ewaste. Read the conclusion, highlight the most important idea, and copy it to your Project document using quotation marks to show that it is original material. Capture the Web address (URL) in your Project document. Add a phrase in your own words that summarizes the main idea.

3 Find three pieces of information that support the idea you selected in step 2. This information can be found in the journal article or another source. Copy the passages into your Project document (don't forget the quotation marks) along with the corresponding URLs.

4 Use a search engine, such as Google or Bing, to locate a magazine article about ewaste. Read the article, highlight the paragraph containing the most important idea, copy it to your Project document, and put it in quotation marks. Also capture the URL.

5 Search for ewaste in Wikipedia. Highlight one of the main ideas. Copy the text, add quotation marks, and capture the URL in your Project document.

A bookmarking tool helps you collect and recall key pieces of information by storing the source URL and important snippets that you highlight. Dedicated bookmarking apps offer tools that automate the process of collecting information and URLs from online sources. Many bookmarking services are Web apps, so your data remains in the cloud and is accessible to you from any computer connected to the Internet.

6 Register for a free account on a bookmarking service such as WebNotes or Diigo. Use that tool to capture the same information as you collected in steps 2–5. Don't forget to add your own tags that summarize each idea. Export your bookmarks if the tool offers a way to do so, then import the bookmarks into your Project document. If you can't export and import, then instead take a screenshot of your bookmarks and paste it into your Project document.

7 Search Wikipedia for the article about ewaste. Copy the entire article, then go to *www.wordle.com* and paste the text to create a word cloud. Take a screenshot of your word cloud and paste it into your Project document.

Technology in Context: Military

© Bettmann/CORBIS

IN THE BOOK ENGINES OF THE MIND, Joel Shurkin writes, "If necessity is the mother of invention, then war can be said to be its grandmother." The military, an early pioneer in computer and communication technologies, continues to be the driving force behind technologies that have revolutionized everyday life.

During World War II, the U.S. military initiated a classified research program, called Project PX, to develop an electronic device to calculate artillery firing tables; by hand, each table required weeks of grueling calculations.

Project PX produced ENIAC (Electronic Numerical Integrator And Computer), one of the first general-purpose electronic computers. When ENIAC was completed in 1946, the war was over, but ENIAC's versatile architecture could be used for other calculations, such as designing hydrogen bombs, predicting weather, and engineering wind tunnels. ENIAC's technology evolved into the computers used today.

After Project PX, the military continued to support computer research. Like most large corporations, the military used mainframe computers to maintain per-

sonnel, inventory, supply, and facilities records. This data was distributed to terminals at other locations through rudimentary networks.

Because all data communication flowed through the mainframe, a single point of failure for the entire system was a possible risk. A malfunction or an enemy "hit" could disrupt command and control, sending the military into chaos. Therefore, the armed forces created the Advanced Research Projects Agency (ARPA) to design a distributed communications system that could continue operating without a centralized computer.

The result was ARPANET, which paved the way for the data communications system we know today as the Internet. ARPANET was activated in 1967, but the .mil domain that designates U.S. military Web sites was not implemented until 1984.

The U.S. Department of Defense (DoD) currently maintains several data communications networks, including SIPRNet, a classified (secret-level) network, and NIPRNet, which provides unclassified services. The DoD's public Web site provides official information about defense policies, organizations, budgets, and operations.

Computers and communications technology have also become an integral part of high-tech military operations. U.S. Apache helicopters, for example, are equipped with computer-based Target Acquisition Designation Sights, laser range finder/designators, and Pilot Night Vision Sensors.

The U.S. Army's BCT Modernization project includes high-tech vehicles, sensors, and equipment, coordinated by a network of computers, software, and radios. According to United States Army General George W. Casey Jr., "The network links Soldiers on the battlefield with space-based and aerial sensors, robots, and command posts. This provides the situational awareness necessary to apply lethal and non-lethal force with the precision demanded by the security environment."

BCT, which stands for Brigade Combat Team, includes "software-defined" radios that are less vulnerable to cyberthreats than conventional radios. Soldiers can use these radios to communicate voice and data.

A small handheld device with a touch-sensitive screen allows soldiers to control unmanned robots and drones. A solar backpack supplements the battery-powered device. BCT equipment also includes wearable devices, such as helmet-mounted displays and communications devices.

The military has conducted research in computer simulations that are similar to civilian computer games. "Live" military training is dangerous— weapons are deadly and equipment costs millions of dollars. With computer simulations, however, troops can train in a true-to-life environment without physical harm or equipment damage.

Flying an F-16 fighter, for example, costs thousands of dollars an hour, but flying an F-16 simulator costs only a few hundred dollars per hour. The military uses simulators to teach Air Force pilots to fly fighter jets, Navy submarine officers to navigate in harbors, and Marine infantry squads to handle urban combat. Military trainers agree that widespread use of computer games helps prepare troops to adapt quickly to simulations.

A 24-year-old preflight student at Pensacola Naval Air Station modified the Microsoft Flight Simulator game to re-create a T-34C Turbo Mentor plane's controls. After logging 50 hours on the simulator, the student performed so well on a real plane that the Navy used his simulation to train other pilots.

Today, a growing cadre of computer and communications specialists is needed to create and maintain increasingly complex military systems such as the Defense Department's Distributed Common Ground System (DCGS) for sharing surveillance imagery and intelligence.

Photo Courtesy of U.S. Army

Armies once depended primarily on their infantry divisions, but today's high-tech armies also depend on database designers, computer programmers, and network specialists. Even previously low-tech military jobs, such as mechanics and dietitians, require some computer expertise. Happily, new recruits are finding military computer systems easy to learn, based on their knowledge of civilian technologies, such as the Internet and computer games.

Although most citizens recognize that an adequate national defense is necessary, the cost of defense-related equipment, personnel, and cutting-edge research remains controversial. In a 1961 speech, President Dwight Eisenhower warned "We must guard against the acquisition of unwarranted influence, whether sought or unsought, by the military-industrial complex."

Some socially motivated citizens and pacifists tried to withhold tax dollars from the military-industrial complex that Eisenhower cautioned against. In retrospect, however, military funding contributed to many technologies we depend on today.

For example, detractors tried to convince the government that Project PX was doomed to failure; but without ENIAC research, computers might not exist today. Skeptics saw no future for the fruits of ARPANET research; but it led to the Internet, which has changed our lives significantly.

New Perspectives Labs

To access the New Perspectives Lab for Chapter 2, open the NP2014 interactive eBook and then click the icon next to the lab title.

 BENCHMARKING

IN THIS LAB YOU'LL LEARN:

- Which computer performance factors can be measured by benchmark tests

- How to run a test that identifies a computer's processor type, RAM capacity, and graphics card type

- How to run benchmarking software that analyzes a computer's processor speed and graphics processing speed

- How to interpret the results of a benchmark test

- How to compare results from benchmark tests that were performed on different system configurations

- When benchmark tests might not provide accurate information on computer performance

LAB ASSIGNMENTS

1. Start the interactive part of the lab. Make sure you've enabled Tracking if you want to save your QuickCheck results. Perform each lab step as directed, and answer all the lab QuickCheck questions. When you exit the lab, your answers are automatically graded and your results are displayed.

2. Use the System Information utility to analyze the computer you typically use. If you are using a Windows 7 or 8 computer, also check the results of the Windows Experience Index. Provide the results of the analysis along with a brief description of the computer you tested and its location (at home, at work, in a computer lab, and so on).

Processor Benchmarks		
Processor	Quake III Arena	PCMark
"Supernova EE"	548	5198
"Pulsar FX"	551	5020

3. Based on the Processor Benchmarks table above, which fictional processor appears to be faster at graphics processing? Which processor appears to be better at overall processing tasks?

4. Explain why you might perform a benchmark test on your own computer, but get different results from those stated in a computer magazine, which tested the same computer with the same benchmark test.

5. Use a search engine on the Web to find benchmark ratings for one of Intel's Core processors and one of AMD's Athlon 64 processors. Are the benchmarks different? What would account for the benchmark results?

Key Terms

Make sure you understand all the boldfaced key terms presented in this chapter. With the NP2014 interactive eBook, you can use this list of terms as an interactive study activity. First, try to define a term in your own words, and then click the term to compare your definition with the definition presented in the chapter.

64-bit processor, 68
Access time, 77
All-in-one computer, 58
Benchmarks, 70
BIOS, 74
Blue screen of death, 103
Blu-ray, 81
Bootstrap loader, 74
Capacitors, 72
Card reader, 84
CD, 81
CISC, 69
Color depth, 90
Compatible, 63
CPU cache, 68
Data bus, 94
Data transfer rate, 77
Dedicated graphics, 91
Desktop computer, 56
Dot matrix printer, 93
Dot pitch, 90
Drive bays, 86
Duplex printer, 94
Duty cycle, 93
DVD, 81
DVI, 96
Dynamic RAM, 72
EEPROM, 74
Enhanced media player, 60
eSATA, 96
Expansion bus, 94
Expansion card, 95
Expansion port, 95
Expansion slot, 95
FireWire, 96
Floppy disks, 80
Form factor, 58
Front side bus, 68
Game controllers, 88
Gigahertz, 67

Graphics card, 91
Graphics processing unit, 91
Hard disk drive, 78
Hard disk platter, 78
HDMI, 96
Head crash, 79
Home computer system, 64
Hot-plugging, 97
Ink jet printer, 92
Integrated graphics, 91
Lands, 81
Laptop computer, 59
Laser printer, 92
LCD, 90
LED, 90
Linux platform, 63
Mac platform, 63
Magnetic storage, 78
Megahertz, 68
Memory card, 84
Microprocessor clock, 67
Mouse, 88
Multi-core processor, 68
Non-volatile, 84
Optical storage, 81
Overclocking, 71
Parallel processing, 69
PC platform, 63
Peripheral device, 56
Pipelining, 69
Pits, 81
Pixels, 90
Pointing device, 88
Portable computer, 59
PostScript, 94
Power surge, 99
Printer Command Language, 94
RAM, 72
Random access, 77
Read-only technology, 82

Read-write head, 78
Recordable technology, 82
Response rate, 90
Rewritable technology, 82
RISC, 69
ROM, 74
Safe mode, 105
Screen resolution, 91
Sequential access, 77
Serial processing, 69
Smartphone, 60
Solid state drive, 85
Solid state storage, 84
Storage density, 77
Storage device, 76
Storage medium, 76
Surge strip, 100
System unit, 57
Tablet computer, 60
Thunderbolt, 96
Touchscreen, 89
Tower case, 58
Trackpad, 89
UPS, 100
USB, 96
USB flash drive, 85
USB hub, 96
VGA, 96
Viewing angle width, 90
Virtual keyboard, 89
Virtual memory, 73
Volatile, 72
Word size, 68

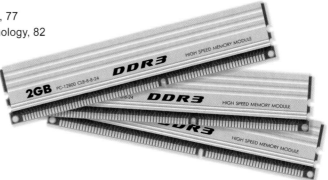

Interactive Summary

To review important concepts from this chapter, fill in the blanks to best complete each sentence. When using the NP2014 interactive eBook, click the Check Answers buttons to automatically score your answers.

SECTION A: The core of a personal computer system includes the computer system [_____], display device, keyboard, and mouse. Personal computers come in several varieties of [_____] factors. A(n) [_____] computer fits on a desk, runs on power from an electrical wall outlet, and can be housed in a horizontal case or vertical [_____] case. A(n) [_____] computer is a small, lightweight personal computer designed to run on battery power. Three categories of these computers include tablet computers, smartphones, and [_____] computers, which have the screen, keyboard, storage, and processing components integrated into a single clamshell-style system unit. At one time, Macs and PCs were not compatible, but today's Macs can run Windows because they use the same [_____] as PCs. The apps you can install on a slate-style handheld tablet or smartphone depend on its [_____]; for example, if it is an Android or iOS device. Personal computers are sometimes designated as home, small business, or game systems to help consumers select the computer that's right for their needs. Consumers can sometimes save money by installing upgrades after purchase; however, replacing a(n) [_____] is difficult and not recommended.

▶ CHECK ANSWERS

SECTION B: The microprocessor and memory are two of the most important components in a computer. The microprocessor is a(n) [_____] circuit, which is designed to process data based on a set of instructions. Microprocessor performance can be measured by the speed of the microprocessor [_____]. A specification such as 3.33 GHz means that the microprocessor operates at a speed of 3.33 [_____] cycles per second. Other factors affecting overall processing speed include word size, cache size, instruction set complexity, parallel processing, and pipelining. Most personal computers only contain one main microprocessor, but today's multi-[_____] processors contain the circuitry for multiple microprocessors.

Computers contain various kinds of memory. Random [_____] memory is a special holding area for data, program instructions, and the [_____] system. It stores data on a temporary basis until the processor makes a data request. RAM is different from disk storage because it is [_____], which means that it can hold data only when the computer power is turned on. Computers also contain read-[_____] memory, which is a type of non-volatile memory that provides a set of "hard-wired" instructions that a computer uses to boot up. A type of user-modifiable ROM, called by its acronym [_____], is used to store the bootstrap loader instructions and data in most modern computers.

▶ CHECK ANSWERS

SECTION C: Today's personal computers use a variety of storage technologies. [_____] storage technologies, such as hard disks, store data as magnetized particles. A hard disk drive provides multiple [_____] for data storage that are sealed inside the drive case to prevent airborne contaminants from interfering with the read-write heads. Hard disks are less durable than many other types of storage, so it is important to make a copy of the data they contain. [_____] storage technologies store data as a series of [_____] and lands on the surface of CDs, DVDs, or BDs. Storage technologies, such as CD-[_____], are often used for distributing software, but you cannot alter the disc's contents. [_____] technology allows you to write data on a CD, DVD, or BD, but you cannot delete or change that data. Rerecordable or [_____] technology allows you to write and erase data on a CD, DVD, or BD. [_____] state storage technologies, such as USB flash drives, store data by activating electrons in a microscopic grid of circuitry.

▶ CHECK ANSWERS

SECTION D: Most computer systems include a keyboard and some type of [_____] device, such as a mouse, for basic data [_____]. For output, most computers include a display device. [_____] technology produces an image by filtering light through a layer of liquid crystal cells. Image quality for a display device is a factor of resolution, screen size, dot [_____], viewing angle width, response [_____], and color [_____]. A typical computer display system consists of the display device and a(n) [_____] card. For printed output, most personal computer owners select [_____] jet printers, although [_____] printers are a popular option when low operating costs and high duty cycle are important. A(n) [_____] matrix printer is sometimes used for back-office applications and printing multipart forms. Installing a peripheral device is not difficult when you remember that it uses the [_____] bus to make a connection between the computer and peripheral device. Many of today's peripherals connect to a(n) [_____] port. If the right type of port is not built into your computer, you might have to add a(n) [_____] card.

▶ CHECK ANSWERS

SECTION E: For trouble-free computer use, it is important to secure and regularly [_____] your computer equipment. Anti-theft devices include computer locks and tie-down brackets. Computers can be protected from power [_____] by connecting to a surge strip. A(n) [_____] power supply can also protect against surges, plus it can supply backup power in case of a power outage. Keeping your computer's [_____] vents free of dust can help to keep its temperature within operational levels. You can also clean dust off the screen and shake dirt out of the keyboard. Problems such as the blue screen of [_____] require troubleshooting. Windows offers interactive troubleshooting tools formatted as a series of simple questions, answers, and recommendations. Booting into [_____] mode can also be a helpful step in the troubleshooting process.

▶ CHECK ANSWERS

Interactive Situation Questions

Apply what you've learned to some typical computing situations. When using the NP2014 interactive eBook, you can type your answers, and then use the Check Answers button to automatically score your responses.

1. Suppose you're reading a computer magazine and you come across the ad pictured to the right. By looking at the specs, you can tell that the microprocessor was manufactured by which company? [   ]

2. The capacity of the hard disk drive in the ad is [   ] GB and the memory capacity is [   ] GB.

3. The computer in the ad appears to have a(n) [   ] controller card for the hard disk drive.

4. You are thinking about upgrading the microprocessor in your four-year-old computer, which has a 2.6 GHz Core i3 microprocessor and 512 MB of RAM. Would it be worthwhile to spend $500 to install an Intel Core 7 processor? Yes or no? [   ]

5. You're in the process of booting up your computer and suddenly the screen contains an assortment of settings for date and time, hard disk drive, and memory capacity. From what you've learned in this chapter, you surmise that these settings are stored in [   ] , and that they are best left unmodified.

6. You're looking for a portable storage device that you can use to transport a few files between your home computer and your school computer lab. The school lab computers have no floppy disk drives, but do have USB ports. You should be able to transport your files using a USB [   ] drive.

SUP-R GAME DESKTOP MODEL EEXL

- Intel® Core™ i7
- 6 GB Tri-Channel DDR3
- 500 GB SATA-II (7200 rpm)
- 16x CD/DVD burner
- 21.5" HD widescreen monitor
- NVIDIA® GeForce™
- Creative Sound Blaster® X-Fi Titanium
- Altec Lansing speakers
- Gigabit Ethernet port
- 3-year limited warranty
- Windows 8

$949

7. You're frustrated about using the keys on your cell phone to enter long e-mail addresses, so you decide to get a new smartphone with a touchscreen that displays a(n) [   ] keyboard.

8. Suppose that you want to purchase a new monitor. A(n) [   ] screen offers a more environmentally friendly choice than a(n) [   ] screen.

9. Suppose that you volunteer to produce a large quantity of black-and-white leaflets for a charity organization. It is fortunate that you have access to a(n) [   ] printer with a high duty cycle and low operating costs.

▶ CHECK ANSWERS

Interactive Practice Tests

Practice tests that consist of ten multiple-choice, true/false, and fill-in-the-blank questions are available in the NP2014 interactive eBook. Test questions are selected at random from a large test bank, so each time you take a test, you'll receive a different set of questions. Your tests are scored immediately, and you can print study guides that help you find the correct answers for any questions that you missed.

▶ CLICK TO START

Learning Objectives Checkpoints

Learning Objectives Checkpoints are designed to help you assess whether you have achieved the major learning objectives for this chapter. You can use paper and pencil or word processing software to complete most of the activities.

1. Draw a sketch of your computer system and label at least six of its components. Make a table with three columns, labeled Input, Output, and Storage/Memory. Skim through the chapter and for each device you encounter, place it in one or more of the columns as appropriate.

2. Draw a set of quick sketches that show each of the following form factors: desktop tower, desktop horizontal, all-in-one, clamshell, slate. List the advantages of each form factor.

3. Create a short consumer brochure that lists five characteristics that would help consumers choose among a home, game, or small business computer system.

4. List important factors to consider when shopping for a new computer. Describe the three price points for personal computers and indicate which price point best fits your computing needs.

5. Explain how Intel Macs are changing the old idea that PCs and Macs are not compatible.

6. List at least six computer upgrades and rank each as easy, moderate, or difficult for computer owners to perform.

7. Refer to Section D of Chapter 1 and create a sequence of sketches that shows what happens in a microprocessor's ALU and control unit when an instruction is processed.

8. List and describe the factors that affect microprocessor performance. Name three popular microprocessors, and list some of the models in each family.

9. List four types of memory and briefly describe how each one works.

10. Describe the advantages and disadvantages of magnetic storage, optical storage, and solid state storage using criteria such as versatility, durability, capacity, access time, and transfer rate.

11. Summarize what you know about how a graphics card can affect a display device's resolution.

12. Compare and contrast the technologies and applications for ink jet, laser, and dot matrix printers.

13. Create your own diagram to illustrate how the data bus connects RAM, the microprocessor, and peripheral devices. Explain the hardware compatibility considerations, device drivers, and procedures involved in installing a peripheral device.

14. List ways you can protect your computer system hardware from theft and damage.

15. Think about the last time you had a problem with computer hardware or software. Would any of the steps in Figure 2-68 have helped you solve the problem faster? If not, what guidelines would you add to the list in the figure?

Study Tip: Make sure you can use your own words to correctly answer each of the purple focus questions that appear throughout the chapter.

2

Concept Map

Fill in the blanks to show the hierarchy of system unit components.

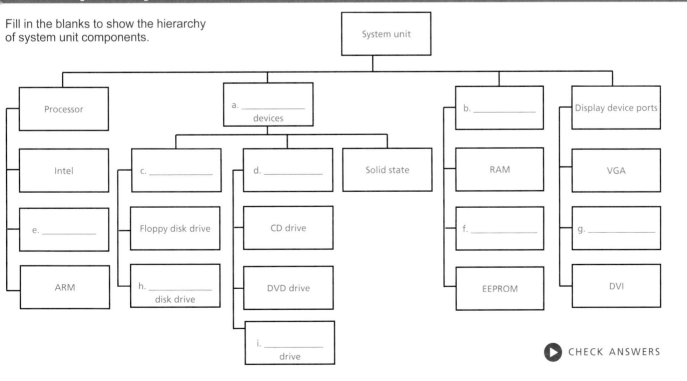

CHECK ANSWERS

3

Software

Chapter Contents

Learning Objectives

After reading this chapter, you will be able to answer the following questions by completing the outcomes-based Learning Objectives Checkpoints on page 181.

1. What are the most popular types of application software?
2. What basic utilities are included with Windows and Mac operating systems?
3. How do iPhones provide adaptive utilities for people who can't see the screen?
4. Why is it important to know where to locate the version numbers for device drivers?
5. How can word processing software help improve your writing?
6. How does spreadsheet software work?
7. How is the data in a database stored and accessed?
8. What are key features of presentation software?
9. What is the difference between Web apps and mobile apps?
10. What kinds of files are included in local applications software?
11. Is installing downloaded software different from installing software from a distribution CD?
12. What are software patches and service packs?
13. How do I uninstall software on Windows and Macs?
14. What is a EULA?
15. What are the differences between proprietary software, commercial software, shareware, open source software, freeware, and public domain software?
16. What's malware?
17. How does antivirus software work?

Apply Your Knowledge

The information in this chapter will give you the background to:

- Find and update device drivers for printers and other devices
- Use word processing software
- Use a spreadsheet
- Use Web apps
- Install mobile apps
- Download and install local software
- Work with portable application software
- Find open source software
- Read a EULA so that you know how to use software legally
- Uninstall software
- Install and use antivirus software

TRY IT!

IS MY SOFTWARE UP TO DATE?

The average American consumer owns more than 24 digital devices. Before you begin Chapter 1, take an inventory of your digital equipment to find the brands, models, and serial numbers. Tuck this information in a safe place. It can come in handy when you need to call technical support, arrange for repair services, or report missing equipment.

1. Find the list of installed software.

   Windows 7: Click the **Start** button. Click the **All Programs** option to display a list of installed software. Point to items in the list that have a ▸ symbol to see a sublist of software programs.

   Windows 8: Make sure you are viewing the Start screen. Use the horizontal scroll bar, if necessary, to view the application tiles on the right side of the screen.

   Mac: Click the Finder icon and then click **Applications** from the list on the left side of the Finder window.

   Tablet or smartphone: Swipe the screen to scroll through pages of icons that represent apps.

2. As you look through the list of installed software, jot down the names of any that you're not familiar with. When you read the chapter, you might find out what they do.

3. Open any one of your applications.

4. Find the current version of the application.

   Windows 7 and 8: Click the **Help** menu, then click **About**. For Microsoft Office 2010, click **File**, then click **Help**; for Office 2013, click **File**, then click **Account**.

   Mac: Click the program name from the menu bar at the top of the screen, then select About.

   Tablet or smartphone: Press the **Home** button to display the main screen. Touch the **Settings** icon. On some devices you might have to select Apps or Apps Manager. Select an app from the list.

   Version numbers are displayed in a format like 1.4.5 or 7.0. Version information might also include a service pack number like SP2. You'll learn the significance of version numbers and service packs when you read the chapter.

5. Check the version numbers for other software that is installed on your computer. Do some programs provide more information than others in the About window?

Desktop and laptop applications display version numbers in a window accessed through Help.

Tablets and smartphones provide access to version numbers through Settings.

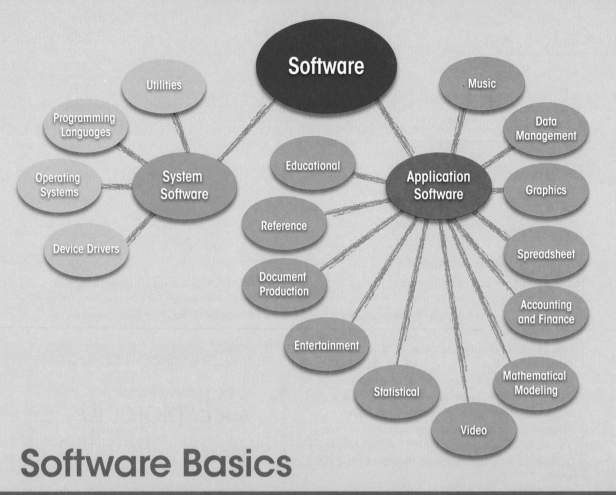

Software Basics

SOFTWARE determines the tasks a digital device can help you accomplish. Some software helps you create documents, while other software helps you block viruses or fine-tune computer performance. Section A helps you categorize application software, utilities, and device drivers.

SOFTWARE CATEGORIES

▶ **What is software?** As you learned in Chapter 1, the instructions that tell a computer how to carry out a task are referred to as a computer program. These programs form the software that prepares a computer to do a specific task, such as document production, photo editing, virus protection, file management, or Web browsing.

▶ **How is software categorized?** The two main categories are system software and application software. Operating systems, which are covered in the next chapter, are classified as system software. Device drivers, utilities, and programming languages are also system software. Application software categories include music, graphics, mapping, finance, and entertainment.

Application software is designed to help people accomplish real-world tasks, whereas system software is designed for computer-centric tasks. For example, you would use application software to edit a photo, write a term paper, or play a game, but you would use system software to diagnose a problem with your hard disk drive or Internet connection. Let's take a look at some of the applications you might have on your digital devices.

TERMINOLOGY NOTE

The term *software* was once used for all non-hardware components of a computer. In this context, *software* referred to computer programs and to the data the programs used. It could also refer to any data that existed in digital format, such as documents or photos. Using today's terminology, however, the documents and photos you create are usually referred to as data files rather than as software.

MUSIC SOFTWARE

▶ What are the basic capabilities of music software?

Music software offers many ways to work with music, sound effects, and narration from your desktop, laptop, or handheld computer. The most popular music software capabilities are listed in Figure 3-1.

▶ Download music and other sound files

▶ Play music and sound files

▶ Create playlists

▶ Transfer music to handheld devices

▶ Convert audio CDs into digital music

▶ Record music and narrations

▶ Edit volume, speed, and quality of digital recordings

▶ Crop and mix recordings

▶ Stream radio music to your computer

▶ Identify songs playing on the radio

▶ Voice training

FIGURE 3-1

Music software may offer some, but not all, of these features. For example, some music software offers extensive playback features, but no way to make recordings. You might have to use more than one music software product to complete a project.

▶ What's the most popular music software?

The premier music software, iTunes, can be used by anyone who wants to listen to digital music (Figure 3-2).

FIGURE 3-2

iTunes helps you collect digital music and arrange it into playlists; you can also use it to pull music from audio CDs and convert it into a format supported by your portable media player.

If you want tools that allow you to record, edit, and mix digital audio, you can turn to **audio editing software**, also called recording or mixing software. Your operating system might supply audio editing software, such as Windows Sound Recorder, or you can download software, such as the ProStudio app or open source Audacity (Figure 3-3).

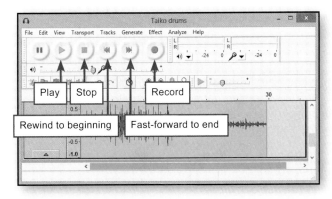

FIGURE 3-3

Audio editing software provides controls much like those on a DVD player. Menus offer additional digital editing features, such as speed control, volume adjustments, clipping, and mixing.

VIDEO SOFTWARE

▶ **What do I need to work with video on my digital devices?**
The most popular video software plays movies on your computer or hand-held device. As with digital music, the source of videos is usually an online store such as iTunes or Netflix, or a video sharing site such as YouTube. Another popular video application is video editing software.

▶ **What can video editing software do?** Video editing software provides a set of tools for creating video productions from raw footage. Professional versions are used by video production studios, whereas simpler, consumer-level software is designed for the casual user.

The popularity of video editing can be attributed to consumer-level video editing software, such as Windows Movie Maker and Apple iMovie, included with many new computers. Consumer-level video editing software provides a set of tools for video production tasks, such as these:

▶ Transfer footage from camera to computer hard disk

▶ Split video into smaller clips

▶ Rearrange clips

▶ Add still photos

▶ Add transitions between clips

▶ Add soundtracks

▶ Add titles and captions

▶ Add special effects

▶ Alter colors

▶ Zoom in and out

▶ Export in formats for e-mail, Web pages, or desktop viewing

Despite an impressive array of features, video editing software is relatively easy to use, as explained in Figure 3-4.

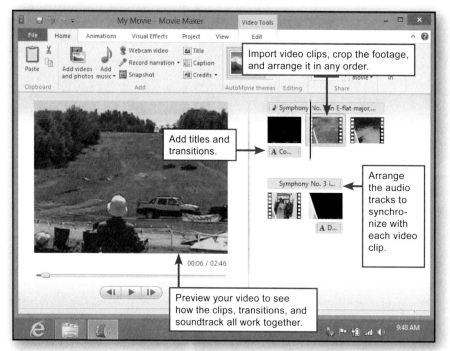

FIGURE 3-4

Video editing software helps you import a series of video clips from a camera or other video source, arrange the clips in the order of your choice, add transitions between clips, and add an audio track.

▶ **Can it produce discs for DVD players?** After producing a video that plays on your computer, you might want to transfer it to a DVD that you can use in a standard DVD or Blu-ray player connected to a television or projector. **DVD authoring software** offers tools for creating DVDs with Hollywood-style menus. You can obtain this software as a standalone product or in a collection of video editing tools.

TRY IT!

Check the Web. What software would you use to create your own DVDs?

GRAPHICS SOFTWARE

▶ **What kind of software do I need to work with drawings, photos, and other pictures?** In computer lingo, the term **graphics** refers to any picture, drawing, sketch, photograph, image, or icon that appears on your computer screen. **Graphics software** is designed to help you create, manipulate, and print graphics.

Some graphics software products specialize in a particular type of graphic, while others allow you to work with multiple graphics formats. If you are really interested in working with graphics, you will undoubtedly end up using more than one graphics software product.

The graphics captured by digital cameras and smartphones can be best edited using paint or photo editing software (Figure 3-5). To create graphics from scratch, you can use drawing software, 3-D graphics software, or CAD software.

Paint software (sometimes called a raster graphics editor) provides a set of electronic pens, brushes, and paints for painting images on the screen. A simple program called Microsoft Paint is included with Windows. More sophisticated paint software products are also available. Many graphic artists, Web page designers, and illustrators use paint software as their primary computer-based graphics tool.

Photo editing software, such as Adobe Photoshop, includes features specially designed to fix poor-quality photos by modifying contrast and brightness, cropping out unwanted objects, and removing red eye. Photos can also be edited using paint software, but photo editing software commonly offers tools and wizards that simplify common photo editing tasks.

Drawing software provides a set of lines, shapes, and colors that can be assembled into diagrams, corporate logos, and schematics. The drawings created with tools such as Adobe Illustrator, CorelDRAW, and Autodesk SketchBook tend to have a flat cartoon-like quality, but they are very easy to modify and look good at just about any size. Figure 3-6 illustrates a typical set of tools provided by drawing software.

FIGURE 3-5

Use paint or photo editing software for working with images from digital cameras, smartphones, or scanners.

TRY IT!

Suppose that you want to create a logo for your local softball team. What kind of graphics software would give you the most flexibility for using the final design on uniforms, Web sites, and printed materials?

○ Paint software

○ Photo editing software

○ Drawing software

FIGURE 3-6

Drawing software provides tools for creating and manipulating graphics.

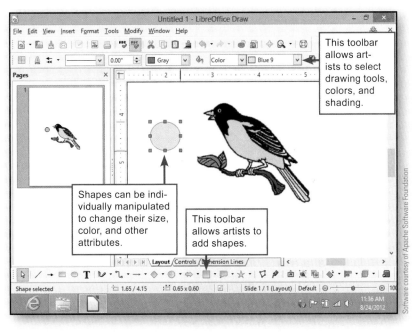

This toolbar allows artists to select drawing tools, colors, and shading.

Shapes can be individually manipulated to change their size, color, and other attributes.

This toolbar allows artists to add shapes.

3-D graphics software provides a set of tools for creating wireframes that represent three-dimensional objects. A wireframe acts much like the framework for a pop-up tent. Just as you would construct the framework for the tent and then cover it with a nylon tent cover, 3-D graphics software can cover a wireframe object with surface texture and color to create a graphic of a 3-D object (Figure 3-7).

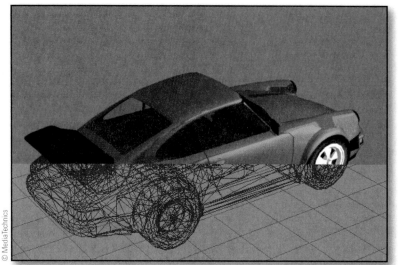

FIGURE 3-7

3-D graphics software provides tools for creating a wireframe that represents a 3-D object. Some 3-D software specializes in engineering-style graphics, while other 3-D software specializes in figures.

CAD software (computer-aided design software) is a special type of 3-D graphics software designed for architects and engineers who use computers to create blueprints and product specifications. AutoCAD is one of the best-selling professional CAD products. TurboCAD is a low-cost favorite. Scaled-down versions of professional CAD software provide simplified tools for homeowners who want to redesign their kitchens, examine new landscaping options, or experiment with floor plans (Figure 3-8).

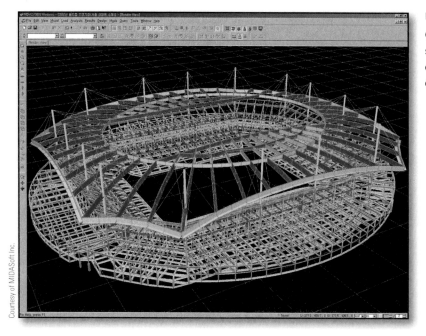

FIGURE 3-8

CAD software is used extensively for architectural, engineering, and mechanical drawings.

MAPPING AND LOCATION-BASED SOFTWARE

▶ **What are mapping applications?** A **mapping application** displays satellite, aerial, or street maps used to locate places and get directions between two addresses. Google Maps is one of the most extensive mapping applications, and its core technology is the basis for many other mapping and location-based products (Figure 3-9).

FIGURE 3-9

With Google Maps, you can view a street map, satellite image, or street view.

▶ **What is location-based software?** **Location-based software** is able to access your current location and use it to show you the closest shops, restaurants, and theaters, as well as information about each location. Want to find the nearest ATM? Need turn-by-turn directions to the airport? Want to hook up with friends who are nearby? Would you like some user reviews about the Mexican restaurant you just spotted? There are location-based apps designed to answer those questions and more (Figure 3-10).

Location-based software is available for desktop, laptop, and handheld computers. Mobile devices can pinpoint your location using the built-in GPS (Global Positioning System) or by triangulating your distance from nearby cell towers. Desktop and laptop computers can determine your location based on your Internet service provider and nearby private computer networks.

▶ **Is it safe?** When devices record your location, there is the possibility of abuse. Stay alert for devices and software applications that track your location. In some cases, you can turn tracking off temporarily or permanently. In other cases, tracking may not be under your control; you'll have to decide whether the service you receive from the device or software is worth relinquishing your privacy.

FIGURE 3-10

Yelp uses the GPS signal built into your mobile phone to pinpoint your position and offer suggestions for nearby restaurants, banks, museums, and other attractions.

BUSINESS AND "NUMBER CRUNCHING" SOFTWARE

▶ **Do businesses use specialized software?** *Business software* is a broad term that includes vertical and horizontal market software.

▶ **What is vertical market software?** **Vertical market software** is designed to automate specialized tasks in a specific market or business. Examples include hospital patient management and billing software, construction industry job estimating software, and student record management. Today, almost every business has access to some type of specialized vertical market software designed to automate, streamline, or computerize key business activities.

▶ **What is horizontal market software?** **Horizontal market software** is generic software that just about any kind of business can use. For example, many small and medium-size businesses use QuickBooks to keep track of income and expenses, pay bills, and track inventory.

Payroll software is another example of horizontal market software. Almost every business has employees and must maintain payroll records. No matter what type of business uses it, payroll software must collect similar data and make similar calculations to produce payroll checks and W-2 forms.

Accounting software and project management software are additional examples of horizontal market software. **Accounting software** helps a business keep track of the money flowing into and out of various accounts. **Project management software** is an important tool for planning large projects, scheduling project tasks, and tracking project costs.

▶ **How about other "number crunching" software?** Businesses use a variety of "number crunching" software applications for planning and analysis. Spreadsheets, featured in Section B, are an important tool that can be used to create numeric models by simply entering values, labels, and formulas.

Statistical software is designed for analyzing large sets of data to discover relationships and patterns. Products such as IBM SPSS Statistics and StatSoft STATISTICA are helpful tools for summarizing survey results, test scores, sales data, experiment results, or population data. Most statistical software includes graphing capability so that you can display and explore your data visually.

Mathematical modeling software provides tools for solving a wide range of math, science, and engineering problems. Students, teachers, mathematicians, and engineers, in particular, appreciate how products such as Mathcad and Mathematica help them recognize patterns that can be difficult to identify in columns of numbers (Figure 3-11).

Retail businesses use point-of-sale software systems to keep track of transactions at checkout registers. This software would be classified as:

○ vertical market software

○ horizontal market software

○ project management software

○ CAD software

FIGURE 3-11

Mathematical modeling software helps you visualize complex formulas. Here the points from a sphere are graphed onto a plane to demonstrate the principles behind the Astronomical Clock of Prague.

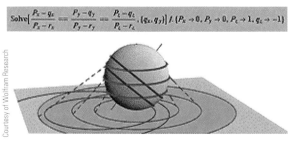

DESKTOP PUBLISHING SOFTWARE

▶ **What is desktop publishing software? Desktop publishing software** (DTP software) takes word processing to the next level by providing professional tools for producing typeset-quality documents.

DTP software is available in consumer-level and professional-level versions. Adobe InDesign is the choice of professional layout artists, with Scribus and QuarkXPress as alternatives. Microsoft Publisher is an example of a consumer-level option.

▶ **How does DTP software differ from word processing software?** The main difference is that word processing software is document-based, whereas DTP software is frame based. When you use word processing software, each page is basically one box into which you enter text and paste images. When the box becomes full, your software adds another page and the text flows onto it.

DTP software allows you to create a page using multiple frames; some frames can hold text, while other frames can hold titles, graphics, and tables. To achieve a pleasing layout, you can move, resize, and overlap frames. You can also link frames so that text flows seamlessly from one frame to another on the same page or over to a different page. Because this software maximizes the flexibility for placing elements on a page, it is sometimes referred to as page layout software.

▶ **Do I need DTP software?** Today's word processing software provides an adequate feature set for the document production needs of most individuals.

DTP software is usually used in a production environment for publishing paperback and hardcover books. In a typical production environment, an author uses word processing software to create a document, edit it, and check spelling. The electronic version of the document then goes to a desktop publishing technician who imports the document into desktop publishing software, where the text can be formatted into columns and linked to flow from one page to another (Figure 3-12).

3

▶ **TRY IT!**

How many frames are used in the layout of the Launching page shown in Figure 3-12?

○ 1

○ 3

○ 5

○ 7

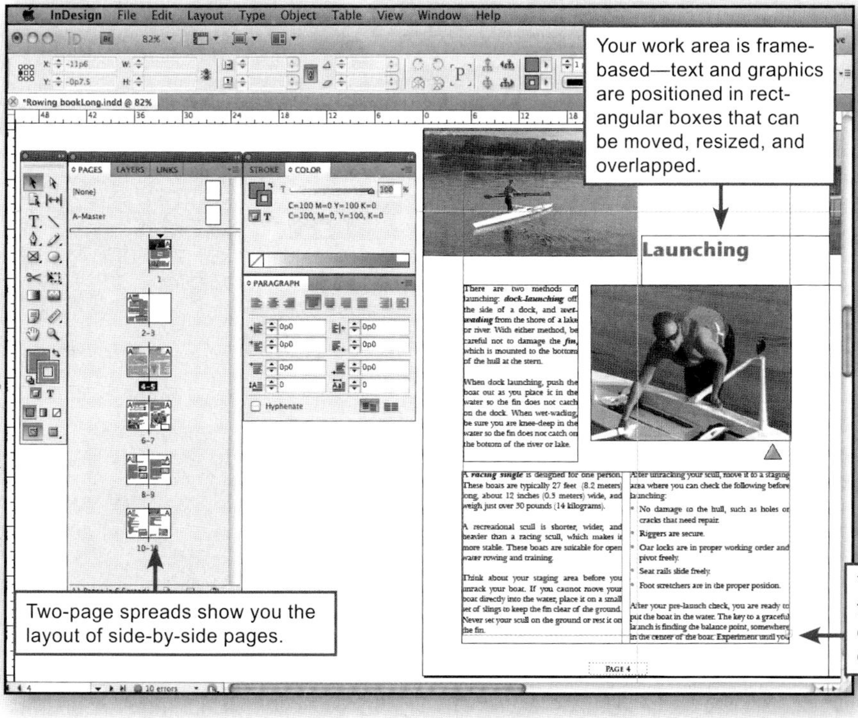

Your work area is frame-based—text and graphics are positioned in rectangular boxes that can be moved, resized, and overlapped.

Two-page spreads show you the layout of side-by-side pages.

You can link text from one frame to another so it is easy to continue an article on a different page.

FIGURE 3-12

DTP frames give you exact control over the position of text and graphical elements on a page. ▶ Want to see how desktop publishing software works? Start the tour for this figure in your interactive eBook.

PERSONAL FINANCE SOFTWARE

▶ What software is available for managing my money?

Money management software offers a variety of tools for tracking cash flow and investments. In this software category, **personal finance software**, such as Intuit Quicken, is designed to keep track of income, expenses, assets, and liabilities using a simple checkbook-like user interface. Options for handhelds include Checkbook HD and PocketMoney.

Personal finance software also automates routine tasks, such as budgeting, investing, check writing, and bill paying. Many personal financial software products provide direct links to online banking services, so you can use them to check account balances, transfer funds, and pay bills.

Personal finance software produces reports and graphs that show you where your money goes. For example, you can analyze various aspects of your cash flow, such as how much you spent on entertainment last month and how that compares to previous months (Figure 3-13).

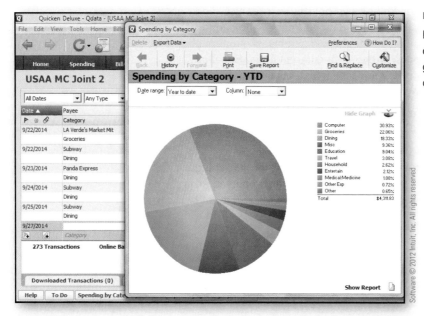

FIGURE 3-13

Personal finance software offers lots of tools to help you get a handle on the money that comes in and goes out.

Tax preparation software is a specialized type of personal finance software designed to help you gather your annual income and expense data, identify deductions, and calculate tax payments. Popular products, such as Intuit TurboTax, even accept data directly from personal finance software to eliminate hours of tedious data entry.

When using tax preparation software, make sure you have the current version and updates. Tax laws are constantly changing; you don't want to miss out on any changes that let you keep more of the money you earn. Before submitting your return, proofread it to make sure the numbers make sense.

Your tax preparation software includes a feature that files your return electronically. That option not only eliminates paper forms and the late night trip to the post office on April 15, but it speeds up your refund, too.

TRY IT!

Check the IRS Web site for information on e-file. What is the name of the software that individuals can use to file their U.S. tax returns online?

UTILITY SOFTWARE

❱ **What is utility software?** A type of system software called **utility software** is designed to help you monitor and configure settings for your digital gear, its operating system, or application software.

Like all system software, utilities focus on computer-centric tasks such as blocking viruses or diagnosing hard disk errors, rather than real-world tasks such as document production or accounting.

A set of basic utilities is included with your device's operating system. Your iPhone utilities are accessed from the Settings icon. With a Mac, click the Apple icon and select System Preferences (Figure 3-14):

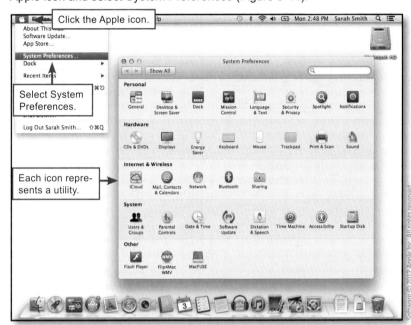

FIGURE 3-14

Mac utilities are listed in the System Preferences window.

In Windows, all the utilities supplied by Microsoft can be accessed from the Control Panel. To open the Control Panel from the Start screen, type "Control" and then click the Control Panel option (Figure 3-15).

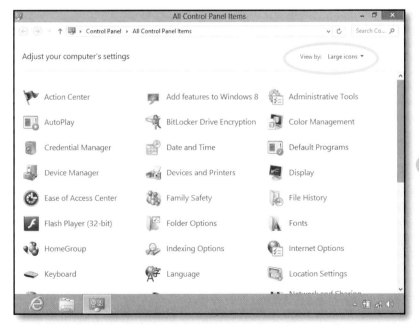

FIGURE 3-15

Windows utilities are listed in the Control Panel. To easily find a utility, set the view to Large icons.

TRY IT!

The following are bundled with the Windows operating system, but which one would NOT be considered a utility?

○ Disk Defragmenter

○ Paint

○ Sync Center

○ Power Options

❯ What are must-have utilities? Third-party software companies offer additional products that extend and improve upon those supplied by the operating system. You can download these products from the Web or from an app store. A PDF reader, such as Adobe Reader, is an essential utility that displays documents stored in standard PDF files. **PDF** (Portable Document Format) is a standard format for exchanging files, so most people will assume that your computer has PDF capability (Figure 3-16).

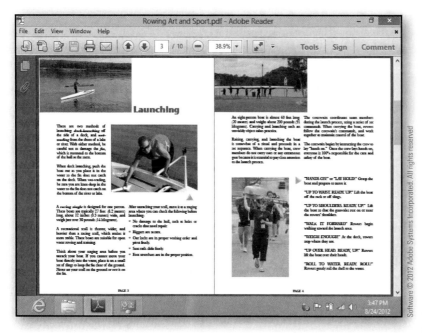

FIGURE 3-16

Documents from expensive DTP software and other applications can be output in PDF format. You don't have to own the DTP software to view these documents; you can simply open them using a PDF reader.

❯ How about adaptive utilities? Computers offer opportunities for individuals with physical challenges. **Adaptive utilities** alter a device's user interface to create an accessible environment by providing closed captions, text-to-speech, speech-to-text, or large screen text. These capabilities are usually included with operating system utilities.

Individuals who cannot read the screen have the biggest challenge when it comes to computers. Screen readers that narrate the text displayed on a computer screen offer only rudimentary accessibility. Imagine the jumble of text, advertising, and sidebars displayed on a typical Web page; making sense out of a narrated version of that chaos is not easy.

Touchscreen capabilities, combined with screen readers, are a next step toward better accessibility. For example, the iPhone includes an accessibility feature for people who can't see the screen (Figure 3-17).

❯ What else? Another popular category of utility software is **system utilities** that can track down and fix disk errors, repair corrupted files, and give your device a performance-enhancing tune-up.

System utilities for handheld computers include apps such as System Activity Monitor, which displays memory usage, available storage space, CPU usage, Wi-Fi and cellular addresses, and battery level. Similar utilities for desktops and laptops include TuneUp Utilities, System Mechanic, and Advanced System Optimizer.

FIGURE 3-17

The iPhone Accessibility screen includes a VoiceOver option that speaks a description of anything you touch on the screen.

DEVICE DRIVERS

What is a device driver? A **device driver** is software that helps a peripheral device establish communication with a computer. This type of system software is used by printers, monitors, graphics cards, sound cards, network cards, modems, storage devices, mice, and scanners. Once installed, a device driver automatically starts when it is needed. Device drivers usually run in the background, without opening a window on the screen.

Suppose you connect a new printer to your computer. You might also have to install a printer driver or select a preinstalled driver. After the device driver is installed, it runs in the background to send data to the printer whenever you initiate a print job. The printer driver signals you only if it runs into a problem, such as if the printer is not connected or it runs out of paper.

On a Mac, you can click the Apple icon, select About this Mac, and then select More info to look at a list of devices connected to your computer. By selecting a device, you can view information about it, including the driver version number. Check the manufacturer's Web site to find out if your version is current.

On a PC, if you need to update a device driver or change its settings, you can usually view driver information by accessing the Control Panel and selecting System (or System and Security). Then use the Device Manager option to view a list of your computer system hardware and corresponding device drivers, as shown in Figure 3-18.

FIGURE 3-18

The Windows Device Manager offers access to device drivers. You can check if they are working and change settings. You can also check the device driver's version number and compare it with the most recent version posted online.

TRY IT!

System software includes all of the following EXCEPT:

○ device drivers

○ adaptive utilities

○ system utilities

○ DTP software

QuickCheck   SECTION A

1. The category of software that is designed for computer-centric tasks is ⟨System Software⟩ software.

2. ⟨Application⟩ software helps you carry out tasks such as creating documents, editing graphics, and locating nearby restaurants.

3. ⟨Vertical⟩ market software is designed to automate specialized business tasks, such as hospital billing.

4. System ⟨utilities⟩ software can help you track down and fix disk errors, repair corrupted files, and improve device performance.

5. A(n) ⟨device⟩ driver is designed to help a peripheral device establish communication with a computer.

 CHECK ANSWERS

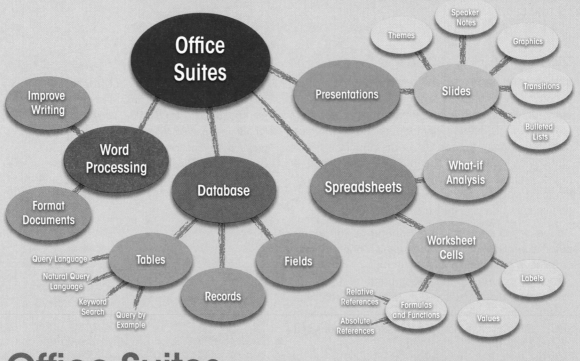

Office Suites

OFFICE SUITES, such as Microsoft Office and Google Docs, are popular with individual computer owners and in business environments. They are sometimes referred to as **productivity software** because they offer features that really help get work done. Section B highlights productivity software applications in office suites.

OFFICE SUITE BASICS

▶ **What is an office suite?** An **office suite** is a collection of programs that typically include word processing, spreadsheet, presentation, and database modules. Suites may also include e-mail and contact managers, calendars, project management, and drawing modules.

In the context of office suites, the term **module** refers to a component, such as a word processing module. Modules can be run as individual programs, but all of the modules in an office suite have a standard set of controls, making it easy to transfer your expertise on one module to the others.

▶ **What are the most popular office suites?** Popular office suites include Google Docs, iWork, LibreOffice, Microsoft Office, Microsoft Office 365, and Zoho Office Suite (Figure 3-19).

FIGURE 3-19

Popular office suites contain a similar set of modules.

Name	Modules	Platform
Google Docs	Word processing, spreadsheet, presentation	Online (Free)
iWork	Word processing, spreadsheet, presentation	Mac ($$)
LibreOffice	Word processing, spreadsheet, presentation, database, drawing	Windows, Mac, Linux (Free)
Microsoft Office	Word processing, spreadsheet, presentation, database, mail/calendar	Windows, Mac, Linux ($$)
Microsoft Office 365	Word processing, spreadsheet, presentation	Online (Free)
Zoho Office Suite	Word processing, spreadsheet, presentation, calendar, and more	Online (Free)

WORD PROCESSING

▶ How can my computer help me with my writing? Whether you are writing a ten-page paper, generating software documentation, designing a brochure for your new startup company, or writing a dissertation, you will probably use the word processing module of an office suite.

Word processing software has replaced typewriters for producing many types of documents, including reports, letters, memos, papers, and book manuscripts. Word processing packages, such as Microsoft Word, iWork Pages, and LibreOffice Writer, give you the ability to create, spell-check, edit, and format a document on the screen before you commit it to paper.

A typical word processor window displays a work area, called a workspace, that represents a blank piece of paper. The window also includes controls for viewing and formatting the document (Figure 3-20).

FIGURE 3-20

No matter which word processor you use, it includes elements similar to those shown in this Microsoft Word example.

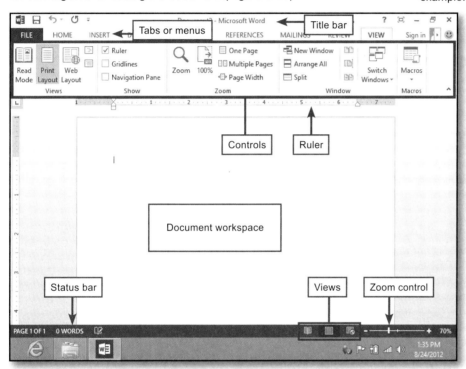

▶ How does word processing software help me turn my ideas into sentences and paragraphs? Word processing software makes it easy to let your ideas flow because it automatically handles many tasks that might otherwise distract you. For example, you don't need to worry about fitting words within the margins. A feature called **word wrap** determines how your text flows from line to line by automatically moving words down to the next line as you reach the right margin.

Imagine that the sentences in your document are ribbons of text; word wrap bends the ribbons. Changing the margin size just means bending the ribbon in different places. Even after you type an entire document, adjusting the size of your right, left, top, and bottom margins is simple.

▶ Can word processing software help me break bad writing habits? You can use the **Search and Replace** feature to hunt down mistakes that you habitually make in your writing. For example, if you tend to overuse the word *typically*, you can use Search and Replace to find each occurrence of *typically*, and then decide whether you should substitute a different word, such as *usually* or *ordinarily*.

❱ Can word processing software improve my writing?

Because word processing software tends to focus on the writing process, it offers several features that can improve the quality of your writing.

Your word processing software is likely to include a **thesaurus**, which can help you find a synonym for a word so that you can make your writing more varied and interesting. A **grammar checker** reads through your document and points out potential grammatical trouble spots, such as incomplete sentences, run-on sentences, and verbs that don't agree with nouns.

Your word processing software might also be able to analyze the reading level of your document using a standard **readability formula**, such as the Flesch-Kincaid reading level. You can use this analysis to find out if your writing matches your target audience, based on sentence length and vocabulary.

Most word processing software includes a **spelling checker** that marks misspelled words in a document. You can easily correct a misspelled word as you type, or you can run the spelling checker when you finish entering all the text. Some software even has autocorrecting capability as you type that automatically changes a typo, such as *teh*, to the correct spelling (*the*).

Although your software's spelling checker helps you correct misspellings, it cannot guarantee an error-free document. A spelling checker works by comparing each word from your document to a list of correctly spelled words stored in a data file called a **spelling dictionary**. If the word from your document is in the dictionary, the spelling checker considers the word correctly spelled. If the word is not in the dictionary, the word is counted as misspelled.

Spelling checkers can't tell if you misuse a word, such as if you use the phrase *pear of shoes* instead of *pair of shoes*. Also, spelling checkers flag many proper nouns and scientific, medical, and technical words because they are not included in the spelling checker's dictionary. Make sure you proofread, even after using a spelling checker (Figure 3-21).

TRY IT!

You can depend on your word processor's spelling checker to:

○ flag words that are not in its dictionary

○ catch all your misspellings

○ identify words that you misuse

○ correct grammar errors

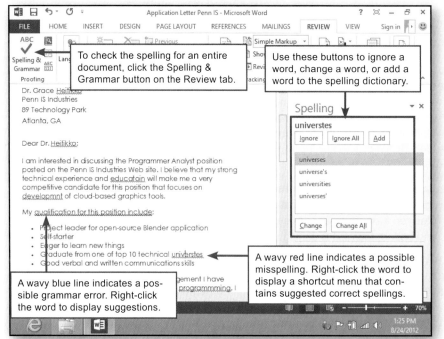

FIGURE 3-21

Word processing software can check your spelling and grammar. ⏵ Refer to your interactive eBook for an overview of using your word processor's thesaurus, spelling checker, grammar checker, and readability statistics.

How do I get my documents to look good? The term **document formatting** refers to the way that all the elements of a document—text, pictures, titles, and page numbers—are arranged on the page.

The final format of your document depends on how and where you intend to use it. A school paper, for example, simply needs to be printed in standard paragraph format—perhaps double spaced and with numbered pages. A brochure, newsletter, or corporate report, on the other hand, might require more ambitious formatting, such as columns, headers, and graphics.

The look of your final document depends on several formatting factors, such as page layout, paragraph style, and font.

▶ **Page layout** refers to the physical position of each element on a page. In addition to paragraphs of text, these elements might include margins, page numbers, **header** text that you specify to automatically appear in the top margin of every page, and **footer** text that you specify to automatically appear in the bottom margin of every page.

▶ **Paragraph style** includes the alignment of text within the margins and the space between each line of text. The spacing between lines of text is called **leading** (pronounced "LED ding"). Most documents are single spaced or double spaced, but you can adjust line spacing in 1 pt. increments. **Paragraph alignment** refers to the horizontal position of text—whether it is aligned at the left margin, aligned at the right margin, or **fully justified** so that the text is aligned evenly on both the right and left margins (Figure 3-22).

▶ A **font** is a set of letters that share a unified design. Font size is measured as **point size**, abbreviated pt. One point is about 1/72 of an inch.

Instead of individually selecting font and paragraph style elements, word processing software allows you to select a **style** that lets you apply several font and paragraph characteristics with a single click (Figure 3-23).

FIGURE 3-22

Your document looks more formal if it is fully justified than if it has an uneven, ragged-right margin.

> The study in question produced results that appear consistent with the findings from earlier research, with the exception of Miller and Candlewood's classic experiment with digital and genetic markers.

Fully justified text

> Once upon a time, very long ago, a motley crew of pirates sailed into a sheltered Caribbean harbor ringed with jagged rocks and scrubby vegetation.

Left-aligned text

3

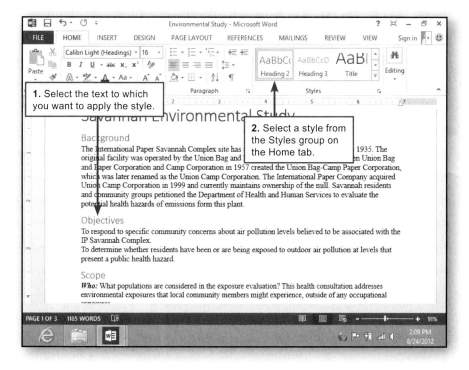

FIGURE 3-23

In this document, headings were formatted by selecting a style with a single click instead of individually selecting a font color, font size, and font style. Now if the Heading style is changed to green, for example, all the headings will automatically change from black to green. ▶ Your interactive eBook walks you through the process of defining and using styles.

SPREADSHEETS

▶ What is a spreadsheet? A **spreadsheet** uses rows and columns of numbers to create a model or representation of a real situation. For example, your bank statement is a type of spreadsheet because it is a numerical representation of cash flowing into and out of your bank account.

Spreadsheet software, such as Microsoft Excel, iWork Numbers, Google Docs Spreadsheets, or LibreOffice Calc, provides tools to create electronic spreadsheets. It is similar to a smart piece of paper that automatically adds up columns of numbers written on it.

You can make other calculations, too, based on simple equations that you create or more complex, built-in formulas. As an added bonus, spreadsheet software can turn your data into colorful graphs. It also includes special data-handling features that allow you to sort data, search for data that meets specific criteria, and print reports.

Spreadsheet software was initially popular with accountants who dealt with paper-based spreadsheets, but found the electronic version far easier to use and less prone to errors than manual calculations. Other people soon discovered the benefits of spreadsheets for projects that require repetitive calculations, such as budgeting, computing grades, tracking investments, calculating loan payments, and estimating project costs.

Because it is so easy to experiment with different numbers, spreadsheet software is particularly useful for **what-if analysis**. You can use what-if analyses to answer questions such as "What if I get an A on my next two economics exams? But what if I get only Bs?" or "What if I invest $100 a month in my retirement plan? But what if I invest $200 a month?"

▶ What does a computerized spreadsheet look like? You use spreadsheet software to create an on-screen **worksheet**. A worksheet is based on a grid of columns and rows. Each **cell** in the grid can contain a value, label, or formula. A **value** is a number that you want to use in a calculation. A **label** is any text used to describe data (Figure 3-24).

Is the worksheet in Figure 3-24 an example of a what-if analysis?

○ Yes

○ No

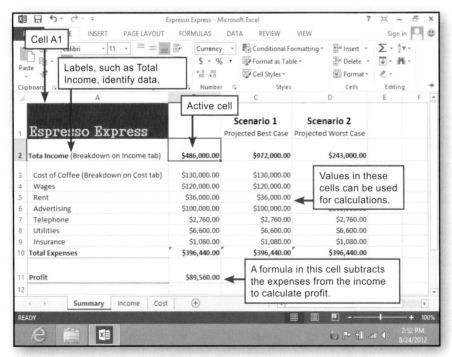

FIGURE 3-24

In a worksheet, each column is lettered and each row is numbered. The intersection of a column and a row is called a cell. Each cell has a unique cell reference, or address, derived from its column and row location. For example, A1 is the cell reference for the upper-left cell in a worksheet because it is in column A and row 1. You can designate the active cell by clicking it. Once a cell is active, you can enter data into it.

▶ Click for an overview of spreadsheet software.

▶ **Are there formatting options?** You can format the labels and values on a worksheet in much the same way as you would format text in a word processing document. You can change fonts and font size, select a font color, and select font styles, such as bold, italics, and underline.

▶ **How does spreadsheet software work?** The values contained in a cell can be manipulated by formulas placed in other cells. A **formula** works behind the scenes to tell the computer how to use the contents of cells in calculations. You can enter a simple formula in a cell to add, subtract, multiply, or divide numbers. More complex formulas can be designed to perform just about any calculation you can imagine. Figure 3-25 illustrates how a formula might be used in a simple spreadsheet to calculate savings.

3

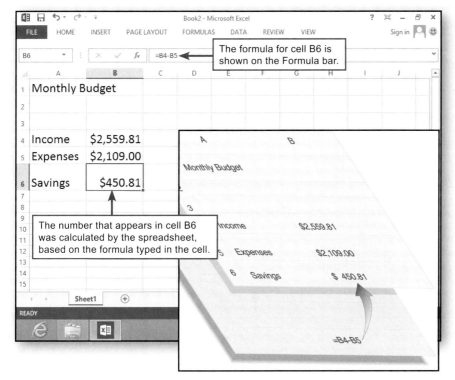

FIGURE 3-25

When a cell contains a formula, it displays the result of the formula rather than the formula itself. To view and edit the formula, you use the Formula bar. You can think of the formula as working behind the scenes to perform calculations and then to display the result.

▶ Why is it important to use a formula such as =B4-B5 instead of a formula with the actual numbers? To find out, start the tour for this figure in your interactive eBook.

FIGURE 3-26

Functions are special formulas provided by spreadsheet software.

A formula, such as =D4-D5+((D8/B2)*110), can contain **cell references** (like D4 and D5), numbers (like 110), and **mathematical operators**, such as the multiplication symbol (*), the division symbol (/), the addition symbol, and the subtraction symbol. Parts of a formula can be enclosed in parentheses to indicate the order in which the mathematical operations should be performed. The operation in the innermost set of parentheses—in this case, (D8/B2)—should be performed first.

You can enter a formula from scratch by typing it into a cell, or you can use a built-in preset formula called a **function**, provided by the spreadsheet software. To use a function, you simply select one from a list, as shown in Figure 3-26, and then indicate the cell references of any values you want to include in the calculation.

❯ What happens when I modify a worksheet? When you change the contents of any cell in a worksheet, all the formulas are recalculated. This **automatic recalculation** feature ensures that the results in every cell are accurate for the information currently entered in the worksheet.

Your worksheet is also automatically updated to reflect any rows or columns that you add, delete, or copy within the worksheet. Unless you specify otherwise, a cell reference is a **relative reference**—that is, a reference that can change from B4 to B3, for example, if row 3 is deleted and all the data moves up one row.

If you don't want a cell reference to change, you can use an absolute reference. An **absolute reference** never changes when you insert rows, or copy or move formulas. Understanding when to use absolute references is one of the key aspects of developing spreadsheet design expertise. Figure 3-27 and its associated tour provide additional information about relative and absolute references.

FIGURE 3-27

As shown in the examples, a relative reference within a formula can change when you change the sequence of a worksheet's rows and columns. An absolute reference is anchored so that it always refers to a specific cell. ▶ For some dynamic examples of absolute and relative references, watch the tour for this figure in your digital textbook.

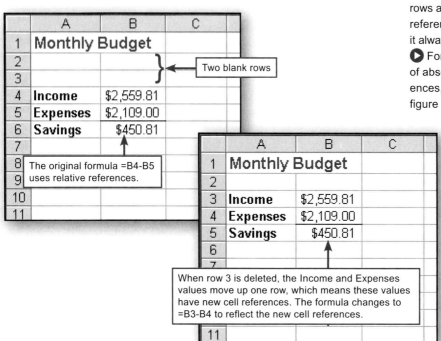

❯ How will I know which formulas and functions to use when I create a worksheet? To create an effective and accurate worksheet, you must understand the calculations and formulas that are involved. If, for example, you want to create a worksheet that calculates your final grade in a course, you need to know the grading scale and understand how your instructor plans to weight each assignment and test.

Most spreadsheet software includes a few templates or wizards for pre-designed worksheets, such as invoices, income-expense reports, balance sheets, and loan payment schedules. Additional templates are available on the Web. These templates are designed by professionals and contain all the necessary labels and formulas. To use a template, you simply plug in the values for your calculation.

TRY IT!

In Figure 3-27, the formula in cell B5 is =B3-B4. Are B3 and B4 relative references or absolute references?

○ Relative

○ Absolute

3

DATABASES

▶ **What is a database?** The term *database* has evolved from a specialized technical term into a part of our everyday vocabulary. In the context of modern usage, a **database** is simply a collection of data that is stored on one or more computers.

A database can contain any sort of data, such as a university's student records, a library's card catalog, a store's inventory, an individual's address book, or a utility company's customers. Databases can be stored on personal computers, network servers, Web servers, mainframes, and even handheld computers.

▶ **What is database software?** **Database software** helps you enter, find, organize, update, and report information stored in a database. Microsoft Access, FileMaker Pro, and LibreOffice Base are three examples of popular database software for personal computers. Oracle and MySQL are popular server database software packages.

▶ **How does a database store data?** Database software stores data as a series of records, which are composed of fields that hold data. A **record** holds data for a single entity—a person, place, thing, or event. A **field** holds one item of data relevant to a record. You can envision a record as a Rolodex card or an index card. A series of records is often presented as a table arranged in rows and columns (Figure 3-28).

TERMINOLOGY NOTE

Database software is also referred to as database management software (DBMS).

FIGURE 3-28

A single database record is similar to a Rolodex card or an index card. A series of records is usually depicted in table format.

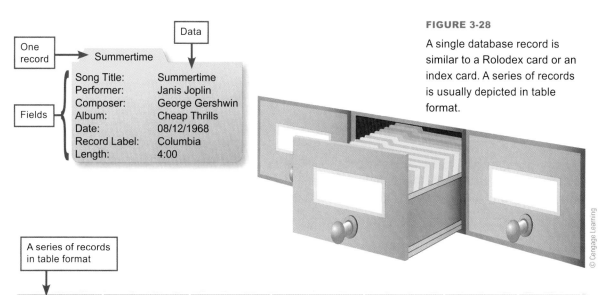

© Cengage Learning

Song Title	Performer	Composer	Album	Date	Label	Length
Take It Back	Norah Jones	Jones	Little Broken Hearts	05/01/2012	Blue Note	4:05
Even Though	Norah Jones	Jones and Harris	The Fall	11/17/2009	Blue Note	3:52
Summertime	Janis Joplin	Gershwin	Cheap Thrills	08/12/1968	Columbia	4:00
Summertime	Sarah Vaughan	Gershwin	Compact Jazz	06/22/1987	PolyGram	4:34

▶ Can a database hold different kinds of records? Some database software provides tools to work with more than one collection of records, as long as the records are somehow related to each other.

For example, suppose MTV maintains a database pertaining to jazz music. One series of database records might contain data about jazz songs. It could contain fields such as song title, performer, and length. Another series of records might contain biographical data about jazz performers, including the performer's name, birth date, and hometown. It might even include a field for the performer's photo.

These two sets of records can be related by the name of the performing artist, as shown in Figure 3-29.

JAZZ PERFORMERS Performer	Birth Date	Hometown
Ella Fitzgerald	04/25/1917	Newport News, VA
Norah Jones	03/30/1979	New York, NY
Billie Holiday	04/07/1915	Baltimore, MD
Lena Horne	06/30/1917	Brooklyn, NY

JAZZ SONGS Song Title	Performer	Composer	Album	Date	Label	Length
Take It Back	Norah Jones	Jones	Little Broken Hearts	05/01/2012	Blue Note	4:05
Even Though	Norah Jones	Jones and Harris	The Fall	11/17/2009	Blue Note	3:52
Summertime	Janis Joplin	Gershwin	Cheap Thrills	08/12/1968	Columbia	4:00
Summertime	Sarah Vaughan	Gershwin	Compact Jazz	06/22/1987	PolyGram	4:34

TRY IT!

Figure 3-29 shows a table of jazz performers and a table of jazz songs. How many databases do these tables represent?

○ 1

○ 2

○ 4

○ 8

FIGURE 3-29

The two sets of records are related by the Performer field. The relationship allows you to select Norah Jones from the Jazz Performers table and locate two of her songs in the Jazz Songs table.

▶ How do I create a database? Database software provides the tools you need to define fields for a series of records. Figure 3-30 shows a simple form you might use to specify the fields for a database.

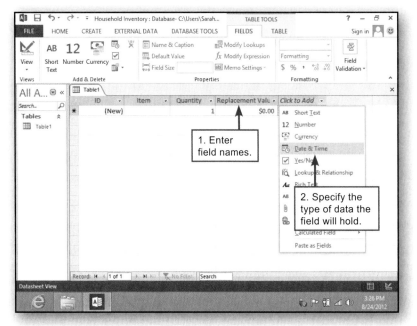

FIGURE 3-30

Database software provides tools for specifying fields for a series of records. ▶ Your interactive eBook shows you how to use database software to create a handy household database.

When can I enter data? After you've defined fields for a series of records, you can enter the data for each record. Your database software provides a simple-to-use data entry form that allows you to easily fill in the data for each field.

Instead of typing data into a database, you can also import data from a commercial database, such as a customer mailing list. You can even download databases from the Web, and then import the data into fields you have defined with your database software.

How do I locate specific data? Many databases contain hundreds or thousands of records. If you want to find a particular record or a group of records, scrolling through every record would take a very long time. Instead, you can enter a **query** that describes the information you want to find. Queries can take several forms:

- A **query language**, such as SQL (Structured Query Language), provides a set of commands for locating and manipulating data. To locate all performances of *Summertime* before 1990 from a Jazz Songs database, you might enter a query such as:

  Select * from JazzSongs where SongTitle = 'Summertime' and Date < '1990'

- A **natural language query** is a question stated in a language such as English, rather than an esoteric query language.

  Who performed Summertime before 1990?

- A **keyword search**, popular with search engines such as Google, is simply a collection of words relevant to your search:

  Summertime song performer <1990

- A **query by example** (QBE) simply requires you to fill out a form with the type of data you want to locate. Figure 3-31 illustrates a query by example for *Summertime* performances before 1990.

How can I use database search results? Your database software can help you print reports, export data to other programs (such as to a spreadsheet where you can graph the data), convert the data to other formats (such as HTML so that you can post the data on the Web), and transmit data to other computers.

Whether you print, import, copy, save, or transmit the data you find in databases, it is your responsibility to use it appropriately. Never introduce inaccurate information into a database.

Respect copyrights, giving credit to the person or organization that compiled the data. You should also respect the privacy of the people who are the subject of the data. Unless you have permission to do so, do not divulge names, Social Security numbers, or other identifying information that might compromise someone's privacy.

TRY IT!

What kind of query do most people use when searching for data on the Web?

❍ A query language

❍ A natural language query

❍ A keyword search

❍ A query by example

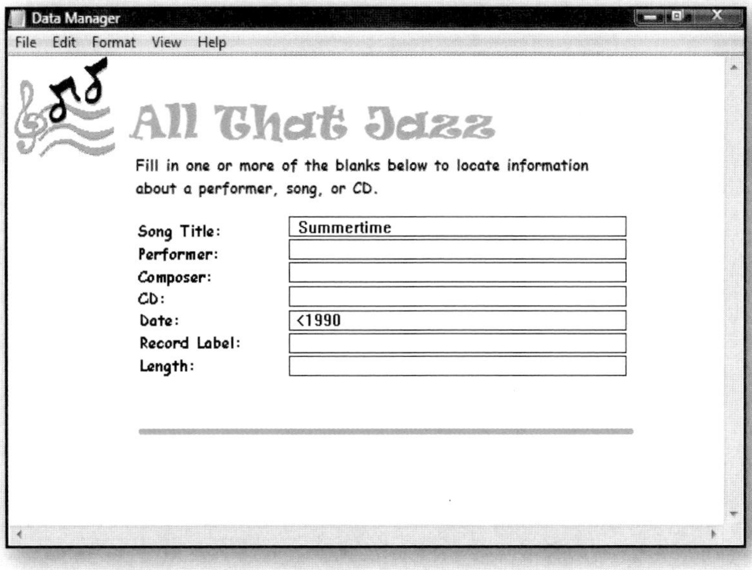

FIGURE 3-31

When you query by example, your database software displays a blank form on the screen, and you enter examples of the data that you want to find.

PRESENTATIONS

▶ What is presentation software? Presentation software supplies the tools for combining text, photos, clip art, graphs, animations, and sound into a series of electronic slides that can be shown on a computer screen or projector (Figure 3-32).

Popular presentation software products include Microsoft PowerPoint, iWork Keynote, LibreOffice Impress, and Google Docs Presentations.

▶ What are the best features of presentation software? Presentation software highlights include:

- ▶ Bulleted lists to summarize the points in your presentation

- ▶ Graphics to make your presentation visually interesting

- ▶ Transitions between slides to keep your audience's attention

- ▶ Speaker notes to help you remember what to say

- ▶ Themes and templates to give your slides a professional appearance

- ▶ Conversion routines to package presentations as PDF files and YouTube videos

FIGURE 3-32

A computer-based presentation consists of a series of slides created with presentation software. ▶ Click to find out how to use presentation software.

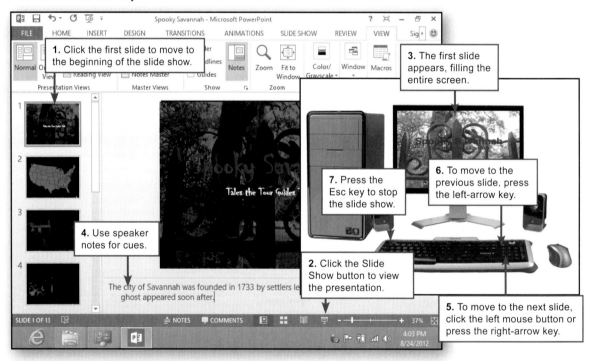

QuickCheck

1. Word processing applications offer _____ style options including margins, leading, and alignment.

2. _____ software is useful for performing "what-if" analyses.

3. When entering formulas, you can use relative references and _____ references.

4. When using database software, you can search for data by entering a keyword or natural language _____ .

5. Each database record is composed of many _____ .

 CHECK ANSWERS

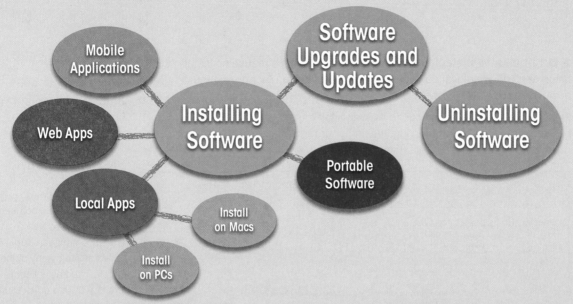

Installing Software and Upgrades

IT'S SURPRISING HOW QUICKLY your collection of software can grow as you discover new applications for school, work, and play. You can use some software without installing it, but other software has to be installed before you can use it. **Software installation** is the process of placing a program into a computer so that it can be run or executed. As you read Section C, you'll find out how to access and install software on desktops and laptops, as well as handheld computers. You'll also learn how to eliminate software you no longer need.

WEB APPS

▶ **What are Web apps?** A **Web application** (or Web app) is software that is accessed with a Web browser. Instead of running locally, much of the program code for the software runs on a remote computer connected to the Internet or other computer network.

Web apps are examples of cloud computing. You might be familiar with some frequently used Web apps, such as Hotmail, Google Docs, and Turnitin, but there are thousands more.

Many Web apps are associated with consumer sites, such as the Color Visualizer at the Sherwin-Williams Web site that uses a photo of your house to help you select paint colors. Other Web apps, such as the XE Universal Currency Converter, have dedicated sites.

Remote computer   Local computer   Web browser

TRY IT!

In this diagram, which component runs a Web app?

143

▶ Do I have to install Web apps? Most Web apps require no installation at all on your local computer or handheld device. Your device must,
however, have a Web browser and an Internet connection.

To access a Web app, simply go to its Web site. You might have to register
before your first use, and then log in using your registered user name and
password for subsequent visits (Figure 3-33).

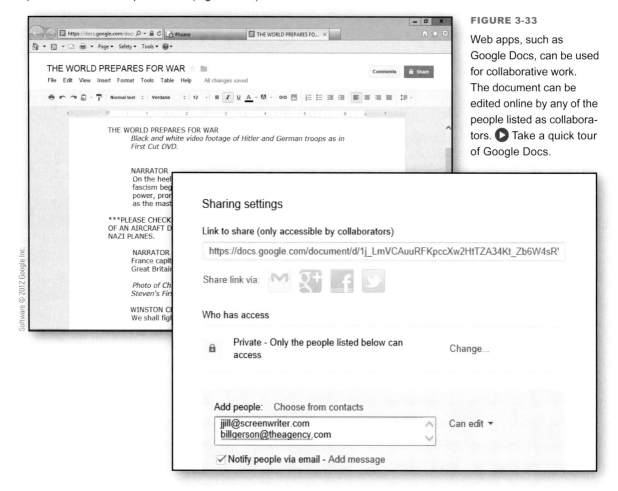

FIGURE 3-33

Web apps, such as
Google Docs, can be used
for collaborative work.
The document can be
edited online by any of the
people listed as collabora-
tors. ▶ Take a quick tour
of Google Docs.

**▶ What are the advantages and disadvantages of Web
apps?** Web apps are truly handy, but consider their advantages and disadvantages before entrusting them with your work:

➕ You can access Web apps from any device that has a
browser and an Internet connection, including full-
size computers, smartphones, tablet computers, and
enhanced media players.

➕ Your data is usually stored on the app's Web site, so you
can access data even when you are away from your main
computer.

➕ Web apps are always up to date; you don't have to install
updates because the latest version is the one posted at
the Web site where you access the app.

➕ Web apps don't require local storage space, so you don't
have to worry about them accumulating on your hard disk
or SSD.

➖ Web apps tend to have fewer features than applications
that require installation.

➖ If the site hosting the app shuts down, you will not be able
to access the application or your data.

➖ Your data might be more vulnerable to exposure or loss
because it is out of your control; make local backups, if
possible.

MOBILE APPS

▶ **What are mobile apps?** A **mobile app** is designed for a handheld device, such as a smartphone, tablet computer, or enhanced media player. They are generally small, focused applications sold through an online app store. Many apps are free or cost less than US$5.00. There are lots of them, and they are fun (Figure 3-34)!

FIGURE 3-34

Mobile apps range from simple utilities that turn the device into a flashlight, to more sophisticated apps for entertainment and learning.

3

▶ **How do mobile apps differ from Web apps?** Most handheld devices can use both Web apps and mobile apps. The difference between the two is that Web apps run on a remote computer, whereas mobile apps run from the handheld device, so they have to be downloaded and installed. Games and entertainment seem to dominate mobile apps, whereas shopping and social apps dominate the Web apps category.

▶ **How do I install mobile apps?** The first step is to head over to the app store for your device. iPhone, iPad, and iPod Touch owners can find apps for their devices at the online Apple App Store; Droid owners can go to the Android Market. Most handheld devices have an icon that takes you directly to the app store for your device's platform.

At the app store, select an app and pay for it, if necessary. Touching the Download button retrieves the file and installs it automatically. The installation process places the app's program file on the storage device and creates an icon that you can use to launch the app (Figure 3-35).

▶ **What is jailbreaking?** iPads, iPhones, and iPods are only allowed to download apps from the official iTunes App Store. Apps are available from other sources, but using them requires an unauthorized change to the device's software called a **jailbreak**.

Software that helps you jailbreak a device is available from several Web sites. After downloading and installing the jailbreak software, your device will be able to install apps from a variety of sources other than the iTunes App Store.

The jailbreak lasts until you accept a software update from Apple. Updates wipe out the jailbreak software, forcing you to reinstall it.

▶ **Can I jailbreak an Android device?** Android phones are not limited to a single app store, so there is no need to jailbreak them to access more apps. There are various ways to make unauthorized modifications to any mobile device to overcome limitations imposed by mobile service providers. The process is called **rooting**, but most consumers have no need to root their mobile devices.

FIGURE 3-35

Once an app is downloaded, an icon automatically appears on the start screen. You can start the app by touching the icon. Some apps require an Internet connection to run.

LOCAL APPLICATIONS

▶ **How do local applications work?** Local applications are installed on a computer's hard disk. When you install a local application, all of its files are placed in the appropriate folders on your computer's hard disk, and then your computer performs any software or hardware configurations necessary to make sure the program is ready to run.

▶ **What's included in a typical software package?** The main component of a software package is an **executable file** designed to be started by users or automatically launched by the operating system.

On PCs, these programs are sometimes referred to as EXE files (pronounced "E-X-E") because of the .exe file extension appended to the program name. For example, the main executable file for Microsoft Word would be called Word.exe.

For Macs, the executable program usually has an .app file extension. Microsoft Word running on a Mac would be called Word.app.

▶ **Are there additional files?** Many Mac applications consist of a single application file. Other Mac applications require more than one file.

Most applications for PCs consist of multiple files. Additional files contain support modules called "application extensions," data files, and text files as shown in Figure 3-36.

▶ **Are all the software files installed in the same folder?** Most executable files and data files for new software are placed in the folder you specify. Some support programs for the software, however, might be stored in other folders. The location for these files is determined by the software installation routine.

The process of installing software on PCs often sprinkles files in various folders, including the System folder, where they can be shared with other programs. This technique complicates the process of locating all the files associated with an application that you want to delete because they are not all in one place. You'll learn more about this topic later in the chapter.

FIGURE 3-36

Blender is an example of software installed on a PC that requires executable, support, and data files.

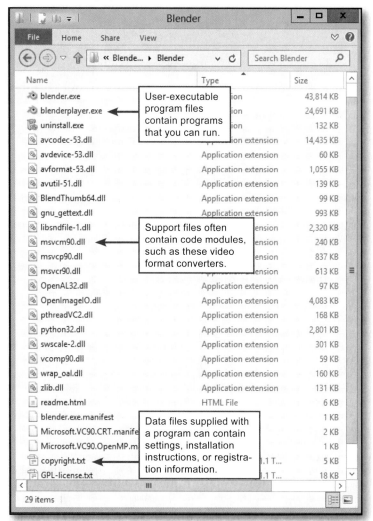

In Figure 3-36, how many executable files were installed for the Blender software?

○ 1

○ 2

○ 3

○ 22

▶ How do I install software on a Mac? Mac software is easy to install. Downloads are ordinarily supplied as .dmg files, commonly referred to as "disk images." When you download software from the Apple App Store, the software's .dmg file is installed automatically, just like installing apps for your mobile device.

Software downloaded from other sources often requires a manual step or two. You might have to open the .dmg file from the Downloads folder and then drag it to your Applications folder as shown in Figure 3-37.

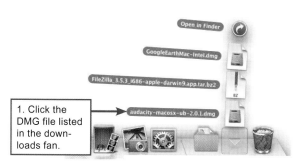

1. Click the DMG file listed in the downloads fan.

FIGURE 3-37

If a Mac download doesn't automatically install, you can manually drag the program icon to the Applications folder. ▶ Use your interactive eBook to see how it works.

2. Drag the program icon or folder to the Applications folder.

▶ How do I access Mac software after it is installed? On a Mac, you can access most software from the Launchpad at the bottom of the screen. Clicking an icon tells the computer to start the .app executable file. You can drag an icon from the Launchpad to the Dock if you use it frequently (Figure 3-38).

The Launchpad displays each software application as an icon.

Open the Launchpad to see icons for all the software you've installed.

You can drag an icon to the Dock for easy access.

FIGURE 3-38

After an application is installed, you can start it from the Launchpad.

TRY IT!

Mac users should be able to identify executable and disk image files. On a Mac, software downloads are usually packaged as:

○ .app files

○ .exe files

○ .dmg files

○ .dwl files

❯ What about installing software on PCs? Software for PCs contains a **setup program** that guides you through the installation process. The setup program makes installation easy because it handles a variety of behind-the-scenes technical details. During the installation process, the setup program usually performs the following activities:

❯ Copies application files from distribution media (CDs or DVDs) or downloads files to specified folders on the hard disk

❯ Reconstitutes files that have been distributed in compressed format

❯ Analyzes the computer's resources, such as processor speed, RAM capacity, and hard disk capacity, to verify that they meet or exceed the minimum system requirements

❯ Analyzes hardware components and peripheral devices to select appropriate device drivers

❯ Looks for any system files and players, such as Internet Explorer or Windows Media Player, that are required to run the program but are not supplied on the distribution media or download

❯ Updates necessary system files, such as the Windows Registry and the Windows 7 Start menu, with information about the new software

❯ Places an icon for the new software on the Windows desktop or the Windows 8 Start screen (Figure 3-39)

TERMINOLOGY NOTE

The Windows Registry is a database that keeps track of your computer's peripheral devices, software, preferences, and settings. You'll learn more about the Registry in the operating system chapter. The important concept to understand is that when you install software on a computer with the Windows operating system, information about the software is recorded in the Registry.

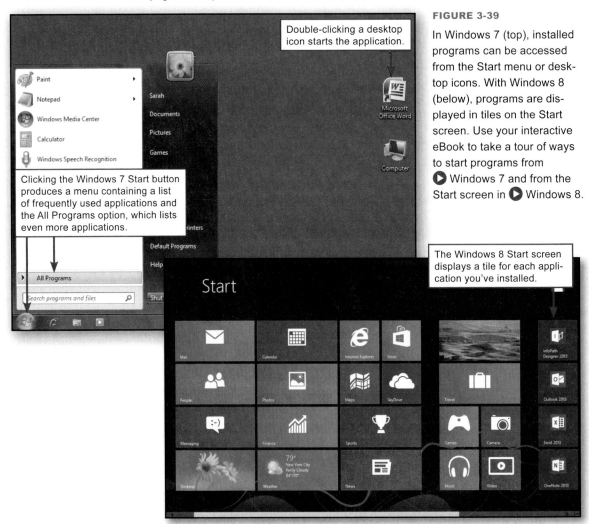

Double-clicking a desktop icon starts the application.

Clicking the Windows 7 Start button produces a menu containing a list of frequently used applications and the All Programs option, which lists even more applications.

The Windows 8 Start screen displays a tile for each application you've installed.

FIGURE 3-39

In Windows 7 (top), installed programs can be accessed from the Start menu or desktop icons. With Windows 8 (below), programs are displayed in tiles on the Start screen. Use your interactive eBook to take a tour of ways to start programs from ▶ Windows 7 and from the Start screen in ▶ Windows 8.

How do I install PC applications from CDs and DVDs?

The process of installing a local application from distribution CDs or DVDs is very straightforward. You insert the CD or DVD and close the tray. A setup program should autostart and then guide you through the process of selecting the hard disk location for the program files and acknowledging the license agreement. Figure 3-40 shows what to expect when you use a setup program to install local applications from CDs or DVDs.

FIGURE 3-40

Installing from Distribution Media

3

1 Insert the first distribution CD or DVD. The setup program should start automatically. If it does not, look for a file called *Setup.exe* and then run it.

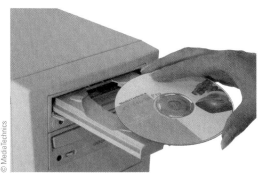

© MediaTechnics

2 Read the license agreement, if one is presented on the screen. By agreeing to the terms of the license, you can proceed with the installation.

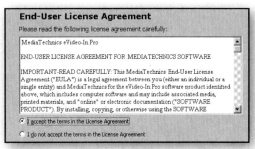

3 Select the installation option that best meets your needs. If you select a full installation, the setup program copies all files and data from the distribution medium to the hard disk of your computer system. A full installation gives you access to all features of the software.

If you select a custom installation, the setup program displays a list of software features for your selection. After you select the features you want, the setup program copies only the selected program and data files to your hard disk. A custom installation can save space on your hard disk.

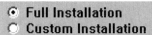

4 Follow the prompts provided by the setup program to specify a folder to hold the new software program. You can use the default folder specified by the setup program or a folder of your own choosing. You can also create a new folder during the setup process.

5 If the software includes multiple distribution CDs, insert each one in the specified drive when the setup program prompts you to do so.

6 When the setup is complete, start the program you just installed to make sure it works.

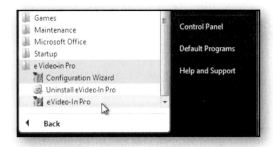

▶ How do I install downloaded Windows software? The installation process is slightly different for Windows software that you download. Usually all the files needed for the new software are **zipped** to consolidate them into one large file, which is compressed to decrease its size and reduce the download time. As part of the installation process, this downloaded file must be reconstituted, or **unzipped**, into the original collection of files.

It is a good idea to store original unzipped files for downloaded software on a CD or in a hard disk folder that you back up periodically. If your computer's hard drive malfunctions, you can use these files to reconstitute your software without having to download all of it again. Figure 3-41 maps out the process of downloading and installing local apps.

FIGURE 3-41

Installing Downloaded Software

1 At the distribution Web site, locate any information pertaining to installing the software. Read it. You might also want to print it. ⟶ **2** Click the download link.

3 If you are downloading from a trusted site and have antivirus software running, click the Run button in the File Download dialog box. ⟶ **4** Wait for the download to finish. Usually, the setup program included in the download starts automatically.

5 Use the setup program to specify a folder to hold the new software program. You can use the default folder specified by the setup program or a folder of your own choosing. You can also create a new folder during the setup process. ⟶ **6** Wait for the setup program to uncompress the downloaded file and install the software in the selected directory. During this process, respond to the license agreement and other prompts. When the installation is complete, test the software to make sure it works.

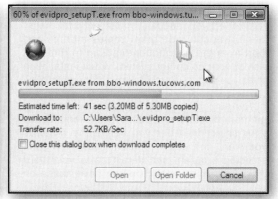

PORTABLE SOFTWARE

▶ **What is portable software?** **Portable software** is designed to run from removable storage, such as a CD or USB flash drive. Program files are not installed on the hard disk, no configuration data is stored on the hard disk, and no entries need to be made in the Windows Registry. When the device containing the portable software is removed from the computer, no trace of it is left there.

The CD version of this textbook is an example of portable software. To use it, you simply insert the CD containing the program files. Other examples of portable applications include LibreOffice Portable, Thunderbird (e-mail), Firefox (browser), and FileZilla (upload and download), which are designed to run from USB flash drives.

▶ **How do I install portable software?** Portable software is so simple to install that it is sometimes referred to as install-free software. Installation is simply a matter of getting program files to the media on which they are supposed to run. For example, suppose that you want to run LibreOffice Portable from a USB flash drive. You can download the LibreOffice Portable zip file and then simply unzip it so that the files end up on the USB flash drive (Figure 3-42).

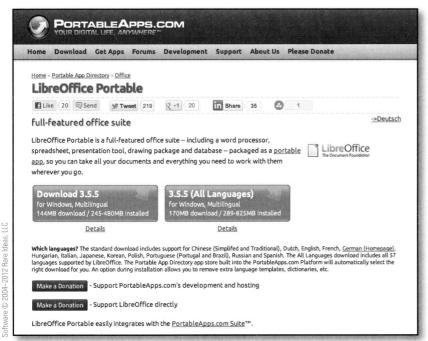

FIGURE 3-42

Portable software is designed so that you can simply copy files to a hard disk or flash drive and run the program without additional installation. ▶ Find out how to work with portable software from your USB flash drive.

Download the program files to your flash drive.

TRY IT!

The key aspect of using portable software with a PC is:

○ it runs from the hard disk

○ it uses an easy setup program for installation

○ it runs from the cloud

○ it does not require an entry in the Windows Registry

SOFTWARE UPGRADES AND UPDATES

▶ **What are updates, patches, and service packs?** Periodically, software publishers replace older versions of a software product with a new version that's sometimes referred to as a **software upgrade**. To keep these upgrades straight, each one carries a version or revision number. For example, version 1.0 might be replaced by a newer version, such as version 2.0. Upgrading to a new version usually involves a fee, but it is usually less costly than purchasing the new version off the shelf.

A **software update** (sometimes called a software patch) is a small section of program code that replaces part of the software you currently have installed. The term **service pack**, which usually applies to operating system updates, is a set of updates. Updates and service packs are designed to correct problems and address security vulnerabilities. Software updates and service packs are usually free. They are typically numbered using decimal places; for example, an update might change version 2.0 to version 2.01.

▶ **How do I get updates?**
Many software applications allow you to set your preferences for how you would like to receive notifications and updates. You can periodically check for updates at the publisher's Web site, or use the software's Automatic Update option that downloads and installs updates without user intervention. The advantage of Automatic Update is convenience. The disadvantage is that changes can be made to your computer without your knowledge.

Most popular software can be configured to check the Web to see if an update is available and gives you the option of downloading and installing it (Figure 3-43).

▶ **When should I update or upgrade my software?** It is always a good idea to install updates and service packs when they become available. The revised code they contain often addresses security vulnerabilities, and the sooner you patch up those holes, the better.

Version upgrades are a slightly different story. Many savvy computer owners wait to upgrade for a few weeks or months after new software versions become available. The reason they wait is to find out how other users like the new version. If Internet chatter indicates some major flaws, it can be prudent to wait until the publisher is able to address them with patches.

▶ **How do I install an upgrade?** A new version upgrade usually installs in a similar way as you installed the original version: by activating a setup program, displaying a license agreement, and adding updated entries to your computer's Start menu. To combat piracy, many software publishers require users to enter a validation code to complete an upgrade.

TRY IT!

A service pack is most similar to:

○ a software upgrade

○ a software update

○ a portable app

○ a Web app

UNINSTALLING SOFTWARE

▶ **How do I know what software is installed on my computer?** Mac users can find a list of installed software by opening the Applications folder from the Dock. When working with a PC, there are several places you can look to see what software is installed. The All Programs menu lists most installed applications. A few applications might not appear on this list if they were installed in a non-standard way.

▶ **How do I get rid of software?** The Windows operating system includes an **uninstall routine**, which deletes the software's files from various folders on your computer's hard disk. The uninstall routine helps you decide what to do with shared files that are used by more than one program. As a rule, you should leave the shared files in place.

The uninstall routine also removes references to the program from the desktop and from operating system files, such as the file system and the Windows Registry (Figure 3-44).

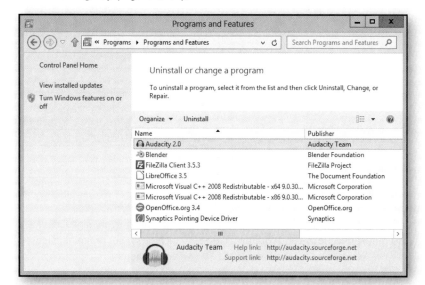

FIGURE 3-44

To make sure all files are properly deleted, always use the Uninstall utility when removing software from a PC. ▶ Make sure you know how to uninstall software by watching the tour for this figure in your interactive eBook.

▶ **What about uninstalling Mac software?** Most Mac users simply use Finder to locate the program's .app file and move it to the trash. This process can leave some support files on the hard disk, however. Some Mac programs include a more thorough uninstall routine, which is usually listed in the Utilities folder.

QuickCheck   SECTION C

1. Most _____ applications require no installation and are accessed through a browser.

2. On a PC, a(n) _____ program guides you through the installation process.

3. Usually the files for downloaded software are _____ into one compressed file.

4. _____ software can be copied to a flash drive and run without additional installation.

5. A(n) _____ pack is a set of patches that correct problems and address security vulnerabilities.

▶ CHECK ANSWERS

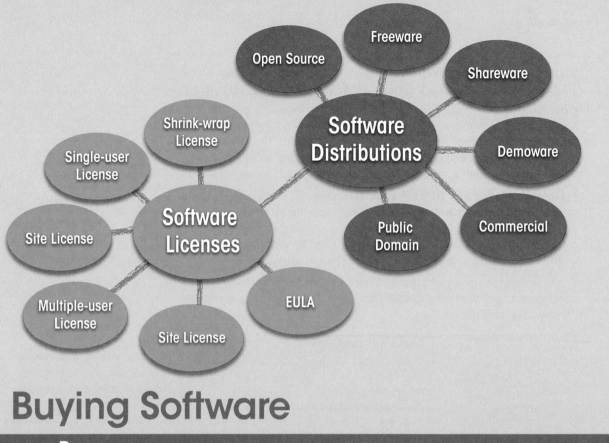

Buying Software

SAVVY SOFTWARE SHOPPERS have a good sense of what to buy and where to find it. Section C offers some shopping tips for expanding the software accessible from your handheld or full-size computer. The section ends with a discussion of software copyrights—important information that will help you understand the difference between legal and illegal software use.

CONSUMER BASICS

▶ **What are the most essential applications and utilities to have on a handheld device?** Most smartphones and other handheld computers include a basic set of apps including a calendar, clock, calculator, notepad, and browser, as well as e-mail. Your device might also supply social networking, photo, video, music, and game apps (Figure 3-45).

▶ **What about a full-size computer?** In addition to an operating system, your desktop or laptop computer should have browser software, an e-mail client, word processing software, a security suite, a graphics viewer, and software that lets you burn files onto CDs and DVDs.

You will probably also want compression software that lets you shrink big graphics files before e-mailing them, graphics software for editing photos, and some type of diagnostic software for troubleshooting hardware and software problems. For entertainment, you might want music software, as well as a few computer games.

FIGURE 3-45

Just about every digital device includes a set of preinstalled applications.

▶ Should I use the apps and utilities that come with the operating system?

Most operating systems include a handful of small applications and a good variety of useful utility software. You'll want to thoroughly explore what your operating system has to offer before you spend money on third-party software. Figure 3-46 contains a list of the most frequently used apps and utilities offered by the Microsoft Windows operating system.

Software	Function
Internet Explorer	Browse the Web
File Explorer	Keep track of files and folders; shrink file size
WordPad	Perform basic word processing
Notepad	Perform basic text editing
Calculator	Add, subtract, and calculate basic functions
Paint	Edit bitmap images, such as photos
Sound Recorder	Digitize music and voice input from a microphone
Windows Media Player	Play music and videos
File History	Make backups of hard disk files
Disk Defragmenter	Arrange data on hard disk for optimal efficiency
Windows Defender	Protect your computer from viruses and spyware
Windows Firewall	Block intrusion attempts
Magnifier and Narrator	Improve accessibility
Windows Photo Viewer	View digital photos

FIGURE 3-46

The Windows 8 operating system includes many useful applications and utilities. You can evaluate these offerings before considering whether to supplement them with third-party versions.

▶ How do I know if an application will work on my device?

If you're like the majority of digital device owners, you want more applications and utilities than those supplied out of the box. You can choose from any applications that are compatible with your device.

Most Web apps work on any device with a compatible browser. Mobile, local, and portable apps specify device requirements, such as model number, memory capacity, and storage space. **System requirements** specify the operating system and minimum hardware capacities necessary for a software product to work correctly (Figure 3-47).

FIGURE 3-47

System requirements can be found on the software box or on the download site.

System Requirements

Operating Systems: Windows 8/7/Vista/XP
Processor: Intel Pentium or Core or equivalent
Memory: 1 GB or more
Hard Disk Space: 50 MB for installation
Screen Resolution: 1024 x 768 or better
Internet Connection

eCourse Internet Works
2014 eCourseWare Corp. All rights reserved. eCourse is a registered trademark of eCourseWare Corp.

SOFTWARE COPYRIGHTS AND LICENSES

▶ **What is a software copyright?** After you purchase a software package, you might assume that you can install it and use it in any way you like. In fact, your purchase entitles you to use the software only in certain prescribed ways. In most countries, computer software, like a book or movie, is protected by a copyright.

A **copyright** is a form of legal protection that grants the author of an original work an exclusive right to copy, distribute, sell, and modify that work. Purchasers do not have this right except under the following special circumstances described by copyright laws:

▶ The purchaser has the right to copy software from distribution media or a Web site to a computer's hard disk in order to install it.

▶ The purchaser can make an extra, or backup, copy of the software in case the original copy becomes erased or damaged, unless the process of making the backup requires the purchaser to defeat a copy protection mechanism designed to prohibit copying.

▶ The purchaser is allowed to copy and distribute sections of a software program for use in critical reviews and teaching.

Most software displays a **copyright notice**, such as © *2014 eCourse Corporation*, on one of its screens. This notice is not required by law, however, so programs without a copyright notice are still protected by copyright law. People who circumvent copyright law and illegally copy, distribute, or modify software are sometimes called software pirates, and their illegal copies are referred to as **pirated software**.

▶ **Can I tell if software is pirated?** Software pirates are getting more and more aggressive, and pirated software is not always easy to identify. Some unsuspecting consumers have inadvertently obtained pirated software, even when paying full price from a reputable source. Widespread pirating of Microsoft products has led to preventive measures such as Certificates of Authenticity and expensive-to-duplicate holographic images on CD labels.

If you suspect that software is pirated, it is best not to buy it or install it. If you have questions about a product's authenticity, you can contact the Software & Information Industry Association (SIIA) or the legitimate software publisher. According to the SIIA, the following characteristics can help you spot pirated software:

▶ Software sold at Web sites for prices well below retail

▶ Software sold in a clear CD-ROM jewel case with no accompanying documentation, license, registration card, or Certificate of Authenticity

▶ Software marked as an "Academic" product, but not purchased through an authorized dealer

▶ Software marked as "OEM" or "For Distribution Only With New PC Hardware"

▶ Software marked "NFR" (not for resale)

▶ Software CD-ROMs with handwritten labels

▶ Backup discs that you receive from a computer retailer containing handwritten labels

▶ Poor graphics and coloring of labels, disc jackets, or documentation

▶ Multiple programs from many different publishers on a single CD-ROM (commonly referred to as compilation CDs)

▶ Software loaded on your PC by a computer retailer, with no manuals; when you request the original manual, the dealer responds by telling you to purchase a third-party book (e.g., *Photoshop for Dummies*)

▶ Photocopied manuals

TRY IT!

Suppose you download a free app for your smartphone and the main screen contains no copyright notice. What should you assume?

◯ The software is copyrighted

◯ The software is pirated

◯ The software has a virus

◯ The software is defective

▶ **What is a software license?** In addition to copyright protection, computer software is often protected by the terms of a software license. A **software license**, or license agreement, is a legal contract that defines the ways in which you may use a computer program.

Software licenses can impose additional restrictions on software use, or they can offer additional rights to consumers. For example, most software is distributed under a **single-user license** that limits use to one person at a time. However, some software publishers offer volume licenses for multiple users to schools, organizations, and businesses.

A **site license** is generally priced at a flat rate and allows software to be used on all computers at a specific location. A **multiple-user license** is priced per copy and allows the allocated number of copies to be used simultaneously.

▶ **Where is the license?** For personal computer software, you can find the license on the outside of the package, on a separate card inside the package, on the CD packaging, in one of the program files, or at the software publisher's Web site.

Most legal contracts require signatures before the terms of the contract take effect. This requirement becomes unwieldy with software—imagine having to sign a license agreement and return it before you can use new software. To circumvent the signature requirement, software publishers use two techniques to validate a software license: shrink-wrap licenses and EULAs.

▶ **What is a shrink-wrap license?** When you purchase boxed computer software, the distribution media are usually sealed in an envelope, a plastic box, or shrink wrapping. A **shrink-wrap license** goes into effect as soon as you open the packaging.

▶ **What is a EULA?** A **EULA** (end-user license agreement) is displayed on the screen when you first install software. After reading the software license on the screen, you can indicate that you accept the terms of the license by clicking a designated button—usually labeled OK, I agree, or I accept. If you do not accept the terms, the software does not load and you will not be able to use it (Figure 3-48).

3

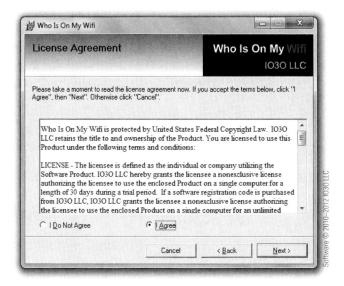

FIGURE 3-48

When you agree to the terms of an on-screen license agreement, you are essentially signing a contract to abide by the terms stated in the agreement.

▶ When I accept a software license, what am I agreeing to do? Software licenses are often lengthy and written in legalese, but your legal right to use the software continues only as long as you abide by the terms of the software license. Therefore, you should understand the software license for any software you use. To become familiar with a typical license agreement, you can read through the one in the TRY IT! below.

TRY IT!

Read the EULA and answer the following questions:

○ Am I buying the software or licensing it?

○ When does the license go into effect?

○ Under what circumstances can I make copies?

○ Can I loan the software?

○ Can I sell the software?

○ Does the software publisher provide a warranty?

▶ Are all software licenses similar? From a legal perspective, there are two categories of software: public domain and proprietary. **Public domain software** is not protected by copyright because the copyright has expired, or the author has placed the program in the public domain, making it available without restriction. Public domain software may be freely copied, distributed, and even resold. The primary restriction on public domain software is that you are not allowed to apply for a copyright on it.

Proprietary software has restrictions on its use that are delineated by copyright, patents, or license agreements. Some proprietary software is distributed commercially, whereas some of it is free. Based on licensing rights, proprietary software is distributed as commercial software, demoware, shareware, freeware, and open source software.

▶ **What is commercial software?** **Commercial software** is usually sold in retail stores or at Web sites. Although you buy this software, you actually purchase only the right to use it under the terms of the software license. Most licenses for commercial software adhere closely to the limitations provided by copyright law, although they might give you permission to install the software on a computer at work and on a computer at home, provided that you use only one of them at a time.

▶ **How about free apps?** Some commercial software is free. The next time you download a free app for your tablet or smartphone, take a look at the license agreement. Your use of the app is usually restricted to the device on which it was downloaded.

▶ **What is demoware?** Some commercial software is available as a trial version, sometimes called demoware. **Demoware** is distributed for free and often comes preinstalled on new computers, but it is limited in some way until you pay for it.

Demoware publishers can use a variety of techniques to limit the software. It might remain functional for a set number of days before expiring and requiring payment. It might run for a limited amount of time—for example, 60 minutes—each time you launch it. Demoware could be configured so that you can run it for only a limited number of times. Or, key features, such as printing, might be disabled.

Demoware publishers usually take steps to prevent users from uninstalling and reinstalling the demo to circumvent time limitations. Users who want to unlock the full version of a demo can do so by following links to the software publisher's Web site and using a credit card to purchase a registration code. The software can then be restarted and used without further interruption after the registration code is entered.

▶ **Is shareware the same as demoware?** The characteristics of shareware sound very similar to those of demoware. **Shareware** is copyrighted software marketed under a try-before-you-buy policy. It typically includes a license that permits you to use the software for a trial period. To use it beyond the trial period, you are supposed to pay a registration fee. Unlike feature- or time-limited demoware, shareware is supposed to be fully-functioning software.

Shareware was conceived as a low-cost marketing and distribution channel for independent programmers. A shareware license usually encourages you to make copies of the software and distribute them to others. Copying—considered a bad thing by commercial software publishers—can work to the advantage of shareware authors, but only if users pay for the product. Unfortunately, many shareware authors collect only a fraction of the money they deserve for their programming efforts.

Today, many shareware authors use demoware techniques to limit their programs until payment is received. The term *shareware* is used today to refer to programs distributed by independent programmers, whereas *demoware* tends to be used when referring to trial versions of software from big software firms, such as Microsoft, Adobe Systems, and Symantec.

TRY IT!

What is the main difference between shareware and demoware?

○ Shareware is distributed by independent programmers

○ Shareware is not copyrighted

○ Shareware is free

○ Shareware is distributed through app stores

▶ **What is open source software?** Open source software makes uncompiled program instructions—the source code—available to programmers who want to modify and improve the software. Open source software may be sold or distributed free of charge in compiled form, but it must, in every case, also include the source code.

Linux is an example of open source software, as are programs such as Blender and FileZilla. LibreOffice—a full-featured productivity suite—is another popular example of open source software. You can search for open source applications at the *sourceforge.net* Web site (Figure 3-49).

Despite the lack of restrictions on distribution and use, open source software is copyrighted and is not in the public domain. Many open source characteristics also apply to free software (not to be confused with freeware, which you are not supposed to modify or resell). Both open source and free software can be copied an unlimited number of times, distributed for free, sold, and modified.

The philosophies behind open source and free software are slightly different, but their licenses are really quite similar. Two of the most common open source and free software licenses are BSD and GPL. The **BSD license** originated as the Berkeley Software Distribution license for a UNIX-like operating system. The license is simple and short (Figure 3-50).

The **GPL** (General Public License) was developed for a free operating system called GNU. The GPL is slightly more restrictive than the BSD license because it requires derivative works to be licensed. That means if you get a really cool computer game that's licensed under a GPL and you modify the game to create a new level, you have to distribute your modification under the GPL. You cannot legally market your modification under a commercial software license. There are currently three versions of the GPL. Their differences are of interest primarily to software developers.

FIGURE 3-49

Open source and free software applications are plentiful. ▶ Click to find out how to participate in open source software development projects and download free open source software.

Software	Function
LibreOffice	Productivity
Thunderbird	E-mail
Firefox	Browser
GIMP	Graphics editing
Gallery	Photo viewer
Blender	3-D modeling and game design
Audacity	Sound editing and effects
7-Zip	Compression
FileZilla	FTP download

FIGURE 3-50

The BSD license for open source software is short and easy to understand.

Copyright (c) 2014, [Publisher]

All rights reserved.

Redistribution and use in source and binary forms, with or without modification, are permitted provided that the following conditions are met:

* Redistributions of source code must retain the above copyright notice, this list of conditions, and the following disclaimer.

* Redistributions in binary form must reproduce the above copyright notice, this list of conditions and the following disclaimer in the documentation and/or other materials provided with the distribution.

* Neither the name of the Publisher nor the names of its contributors may be used to endorse or promote products derived from this software without specific prior written permission.

THIS SOFTWARE IS PROVIDED BY THE PUBLISHER AND CONTRIBUTORS "AS IS" AND ANY EXPRESS OR IMPLIED WARRANTIES, INCLUDING, BUT NOT LIMITED TO, THE IMPLIED WARRANTIES OF MERCHANTABILITY AND FITNESS FOR A PARTICULAR PURPOSE ARE DISCLAIMED. IN NO EVENT SHALL THE PUBLISHER AND CONTRIBUTORS BE LIABLE FOR ANY DIRECT, INDIRECT, INCIDENTAL, SPECIAL, EXEMPLARY, OR CONSEQUENTIAL DAMAGES (INCLUDING, BUT NOT LIMITED TO, PROCUREMENT OF SUBSTITUTE GOODS OR SERVICES; LOSS OF USE, DATA, OR PROFITS; OR BUSINESS INTERRUPTION) HOWEVER CAUSED AND ON ANY THEORY OF LIABILITY, WHETHER IN CONTRACT, STRICT LIABILITY, OR TORT (INCLUDING NEGLIGENCE OR OTHERWISE) ARISING IN ANY WAY OUT OF THE USE OF THIS SOFTWARE, EVEN IF ADVISED OF THE POSSIBILITY OF SUCH DAMAGE.

TRY IT!

The first clause of the BSD license permits what?

○ Breaking copy protection

○ Distribution of the source code

○ Pirating

○ Modifying the copyright

▶ **What about freeware?** **Freeware** is copyrighted software that—as you might expect—is available for free. It is fully functional and requires no payment for its use. A freeware license permits you to use the software, copy it, and give it away, but does not permit you to alter it or sell it. Many utility programs, most device drivers, and some games are available as freeware.

▶ **What if my software requires activation?** **Product activation** is a means of protecting software from illegal copying by requiring users to enter a product key or activation code before the software can be used. Activation is usually part of the software installation process, but it can also occur when demoware times out. Failure to enter a valid code prohibits the program from launching. The information you enter is either checked against a database or used to create a hash value.

Checking an activation code against a database makes sure that the code you've entered has not been used before. If the code is a duplicate, the license for that copy of the software is being used by someone else and you will have to call customer service to straighten out the problem.

A **hash value** is a unique number derived from encoding one or more data sets, such as names, serial numbers, and validation codes. Product validation can create a hash value based on your validation code and your computer's internal serial number, effectively tying the software to use on one specific computer.

Validation codes are very important. You should keep a list of them in a safe place, along with other configuration information for your computer system.

▶ **Should a software license affect my purchase decision?** Before purchasing software, make sure the license allows you to use the software the way you want to. If you plan to install the software on more than one computer or introduce modifications, make sure the license allows you to do so.

Some commercial software, such as security software, requires annual renewal. If you don't want to pay the fee every year, you might consider freeware or open source security software instead. Informed consumers tend to make better buying decisions. Just remember that many software programs exist and you can usually find alternatives with similar features offered under various licensing terms.

3

QuickCheck

1. Before purchasing software, you should check the [_____] requirements.

2. [_____] law allows you to make an extra, or backup, copy of software as long as you do not defeat any copy protection mechanisms.

3. [_____] licenses include site licenses and multiple-user licenses.

4. [_____] that expires after a set period of time is often factory-installed on new computers.

5. LibreOffice, Firefox, and Linux are examples of [_____] source software that can be legally modified and redistributed.

▶ CHECK ANSWERS

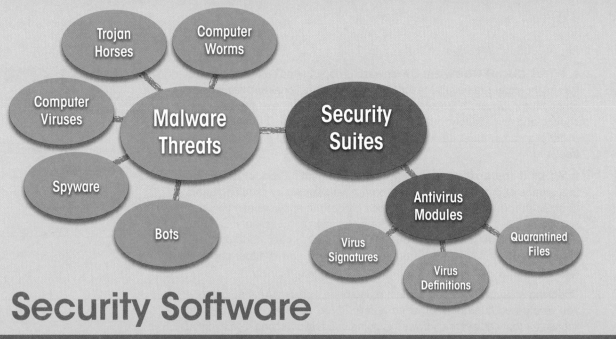

Security Software

THE DAYS WHEN VIRUSES were the greatest threat to computers are long gone. Today, a virus is just one of many categories of malicious software, or malware, that can wreak havoc on computer systems, networks, and even handheld devices. Section E explains how you can use security software to combat malicious software that threatens your computer.

SECURITY SOFTWARE BASICS

▶ **What is security software?** **Security software** is designed to protect computers from various forms of destructive software and unauthorized intrusions. Security software can be classified into various types: antivirus, antispyware, anti-spam, and firewalls. Each type focuses on a specific security threat.

▶ **What devices are at risk?** Windows computers have the highest risk of unwanted intrusions or contracting a virus, but any device that receives e-mail, accesses the Web, and runs apps is potentially vulnerable.

Apple computers and handheld devices are not targeted as often as Windows and Android devices, but the incidence of attacks is growing across all platforms. Jailbreaking or rooting a phone increases its vulnerability (Figure 3-51).

▶ **What are malware threats?** The terms **malicious software** and **malware** refer to any computer program designed to surreptitiously enter a computer, gain unauthorized access to data, or disrupt normal processing operations. Malware includes viruses, worms, Trojans, bots, and spyware.

Malware is created and unleashed by individuals referred to as hackers, crackers, black hats, or cybercriminals. Some malware is released as a prank. Other malware is created to distribute political messages or to disrupt operations at specific companies.

In an increasing number of cases, malware is unleashed for monetary gain. Malware designed for identity theft or extortion has become a very real threat to individuals and corporations.

FIGURE 3-51

This smartphone's security was breached, letting a hacker surreptitiously record conversations.

▶ **What is a virus?** A **computer virus** is a set of program instructions that attaches itself to a file, reproduces itself, and spreads to other files. A common misconception is that viruses spread themselves from one computer to another. They don't. Viruses can replicate themselves only on the host computer.

A key characteristic of viruses is their ability to lurk in a computer for days or months, quietly replicating themselves. While this replication takes place, you might not even know that your computer has contracted a virus; therefore, it is easy to inadvertently spread infected files to other people's computers.

In addition to replicating itself, a virus usually delivers a payload, which can be as harmless as displaying an annoying message or as devastating as trashing the data on your computer's storage device. It can corrupt files, destroy data, or otherwise disrupt computer operations. A trigger event, such as a specific date, can unleash some viruses. Viruses that deliver their payloads on a specific date are sometimes referred to as time bombs. Viruses that deliver their payloads in response to some other system event are referred to as logic bombs.

Viruses spread when people exchange infected files on disks and CDs, as e-mail attachments, and on file sharing networks, social networking sites, and download sites.

▶ **What is a worm?** A **computer worm** is a self-replicating program designed to carry out some unauthorized activity on a victim's computer. Worms can spread themselves from one computer to another without any assistance from victims.

Worms can enter a computer through security holes in browsers and operating systems, as e-mail attachments, and by victims clicking on infected pop-up ads or links contained in e-mails. For example, a mass-mailing worm called Ackantta is hidden in an attachment to an e-mail message that's a fake Twitter invitation. Clicking the attachment activates the worm.

A **mass-mailing worm** spreads by sending itself to every address in the address book of an infected computer. Your friends receive these messages and, thinking that they are from a trusted source, open the infected attachment, spreading the worm to their computers and on to their friends.

Although e-mail is currently the primary vehicle used to spread worms, hackers have also devised ways to spread worms over file sharing networks, instant messaging links, and mobile phones.

▶ **What is a Trojan horse?** A **Trojan horse** (sometimes simply called a Trojan) is a computer program that seems to perform one function while actually doing something else. Unlike a worm, a Trojan is not designed to spread itself to other computers. Also differing from viruses and worms, most Trojans are not designed to replicate themselves. Trojans are stand-alone programs that masquerade as useful utilities or applications, which victims download and install unaware of their destructive nature.

Trojans are notorious for stealing passwords using a keylogger that records keystrokes as you log in to your computer and various online accounts. Another type of Trojan called a **Remote Access Trojan** (RAT) has back-door capabilities that allow remote hackers to transmit files to victims' computers, search for data, run programs, and use a victim's computer as a relay station for breaking into other computers.

3

TERMINOLOGY NOTE

A spoofed address is one that is misleading or incorrect. In the case of e-mail, it is not the actual address of the person or computer that sent the e-mail message. Spoofed addresses make it difficult or impossible to trace mail back to the sender.

▶ **What is a bot?** Any software that can automate a task or autonomously execute a task when commanded to do so is called an intelligent agent. Because an intelligent agent behaves somewhat like a robot, it is often called a **bot**.

Good bots perform a variety of helpful tasks such as scanning the Web to assemble data for search engines like Google. Some bots offer online help, while others monitor online discussions for prohibited behavior and language. Bad bots, on the other hand, are controlled by hackers and designed for unauthorized or destructive tasks. They can be spread by worms or Trojans. Most bad bots are able to initiate communications with a central server on the Internet to receive instructions. A computer under the control of a bad bot is sometimes referred to as a **zombie** because it carries out instructions from a malicious leader.

Like a spider in its web, the person who controls many bot-infested computers can link them together into a network called a **botnet**. Experts have discovered botnets encompassing more than 1 million computers. Botmasters who control botnets use the combined computing power of their zombie legions for many types of nefarious tasks such as breaking into encrypted data, carrying out denial-of-service attacks against other computers, and sending out massive amounts of spam.

▶ **What is spyware?** **Spyware** is a type of program that secretly gathers personal information without the victim's knowledge, usually for advertising and other commercial purposes. Once it is installed, spyware starts monitoring Web-surfing and purchasing behavior, and sends a summary back to one or more third parties. Just like Trojans, spyware can monitor keystrokes and relay passwords and credit card information to cybercriminals.

Spyware can get into a computer using exploits similar to those of Trojans. It can piggyback on seemingly legitimate freeware or shareware downloads. You can also inadvertently allow spyware into your computer by clicking innocuous but infected pop-up ads or surfing through seemingly valid and secure Web sites that have been compromised by hackers.

▶ **What does malware do?** Once viruses, worms, bots, Trojans, and spyware enter your computer, they can carry out a variety of unauthorized activities, such as those listed in Figure 3-52.

FIGURE 3-52

Malware Activities

▶ Display irritating messages and pop-up ads

▶ Delete or modify your data

▶ Encrypt your data and demand ransom for the encryption key

▶ Upload or download unwanted files

▶ Log your keystrokes to steal your passwords and credit card numbers

▶ Propagate malware and spam to everyone in your e-mail address book or your instant messaging buddy list

▶ Disable your antivirus and firewall software

▶ Block access to specific Web sites and redirect your browser to infected Web sites

▶ Cause response time on your system to deteriorate

▶ Allow hackers to remotely access data on your computer

▶ Allow hackers to take remote control of your machine and turn it into a zombie

▶ Link your computer to others in a botnet that can send millions of spam e-mails or wage denial-of-service attacks against Web sites

▶ Cause network traffic jams

Michael D Brown/Shutterstock.com

▶ How do I know if my computer is infected? Watch out for the symptoms of an infected computer listed in Figure 3-53.

FIGURE 3-53

Symptoms of Infection

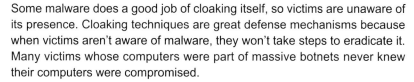

- Irritating messages or sounds
- Frequent pop-up ads, at times with pornographic content
- The sudden appearance of a new Internet toolbar on your browser's home page
- An addition to your Internet favorites list that you didn't put there
- Prolonged system startup
- Slower than usual response to mouse clicks and keyboard strokes
- Browser or application crashes
- Missing files
- Your computer's security software becomes disabled and cannot be restarted
- Periodic network activity when you are not actively browsing or sending e-mail
- Your computer reboots itself frequently

Some malware does a good job of cloaking itself, so victims are unaware of its presence. Cloaking techniques are great defense mechanisms because when victims aren't aware of malware, they won't take steps to eradicate it. Many victims whose computers were part of massive botnets never knew their computers were compromised.

Some hackers cloak their work using rootkits. The term **rootkit** refers to software tools used to conceal malware and backdoors that have been installed on a victim's computer. Rootkits can hide bots, keyloggers, spyware, worms, and viruses. With a rootkit in place, hackers can continue to exploit a victim's computer with little risk of discovery. Rootkits are usually distributed by Trojans.

▶ How do I avoid security threats? The Orientation section at the beginning of this book listed some techniques for safe computing. That list is worth repeating (Figure 3-54).

FIGURE 3-54

Avoiding Security Threats

- Install and activate security software on any digital device that is at risk.
- Keep software patches and operating system service packs up to date.
- Do not open suspicious e-mail attachments.
- Obtain software only from reliable sources; and before running it, use security software to scan for malware.
- Do not click pop-up ads—to make an ad go away, right-click the ad's taskbar button and select the Close option.
- Avoid unsavory Web sites.
- Disable the option *Hide extensions for known file types in Windows* so you can avoid opening files with more than one extension, such as a file called *game.exe.zip*.

▶ **What's a virus hoax?** Some virus threats are very real, but you're also likely to get e-mail messages about so-called viruses that don't really exist. A **virus hoax** usually arrives as an e-mail message containing dire warnings about a supposedly new virus on the loose. When you receive an e-mail message about a virus or any other type of malware, don't panic. It could be a hoax.

You can check one of the many hoaxbuster or antivirus software Web sites to determine whether you've received a hoax or a real threat. The Web sites also provide security or virus alerts, which list all of the most recent legitimate malware threats. If the virus is a real threat, the Web site can provide information to determine whether your computer has been infected. You can also find instructions for eradicating the virus. If the virus threat is a hoax, by no means should you forward the e-mail message to others.

▶ **What if my computer gets infected?** If you suspect that your computer might be infected by a virus or other malware, you should immediately use security software to scan your computer and eradicate any suspicious program code.

SECURITY SUITES

▶ **What is a security suite?** A **security suite** integrates several security modules to protect against the most common types of malware, unauthorized access, and spam. Security suites might include additional features such as Wi-Fi detection that warns of possible intrusions into your wireless network, and parental controls for monitoring and controlling children's Internet usage. A security suite, like the one in Figure 3-55, typically includes antivirus, firewall, and antispyware modules.

FIGURE 3-55

The Norton 360 security suite includes modules for scanning viruses, detecting spyware, and activating a firewall against unauthorized intrusions.
▶ Take a tour of these modules by using your interactive eBook.

▶ **What are the advantages and disadvantages of a security suite?** A security suite costs less than purchasing standalone security modules. In addition, a single interface for accessing all of the security suite's features is much less complex than having to learn how to configure and run several different products.

When installing a security suite, you might be required to uninstall or disable all other antivirus, antispyware, and firewall software on your computer. Most security suites cannot run concurrently with standalone security products, and overlapping security coverage from two similar products can cause glitches. Therefore, one disadvantage of security suites is that you become dependent on your security package's vendor, which becomes the sole protector of your computer from malicious code.

▶ **Where can I purchase a security suite?** The most popular security suites include Norton 360, McAfee Internet Security Suite, avast!, and Trend Micro Titanium Maximum Security. They can be purchased in most office, electronics, and computer stores, or downloaded from the Web.

It is also worth looking into your Internet service provider's free security offerings. For example, Comcast provides its customers with Norton security products, all accessible through Comcast's Security Web page.

A security suite is often preinstalled on new desktop and laptop computers. However, the suite is usually demoware, so you have the option of purchasing it after the trial period, normally 60 days. Commonly, there is also an annual subscription fee for continued use and regular updates. When you renew your subscription, you might have an option to upgrade to a newer version for an extra $10–$20. There are also open source and freeware versions of security software, which do not require annual subscription fees.

ANTIVIRUS MODULES

▶ **What is antivirus software?** **Antivirus software** is a type of utility software that looks for and eradicates viruses, Trojan horses, worms, and bots. Some antivirus software also scans for spyware, although several security software publishers offer spyware detection as a separate module. Antivirus software is included in security suites or available as a standalone module. Antivirus software is available for all types of computers and data storage devices, including handhelds, personal computers, USB flash drives, servers, PCs, and Macs (Figure 3-56).

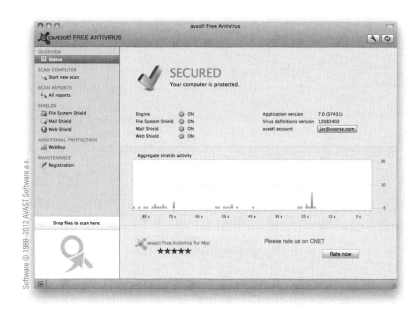

FIGURE 3-56

Free antivirus software is available, so computer owners have no excuse for leaving their computers unprotected.

TRY IT!

What is the name of the antivirus software installed on the computer you usually use? (Hint: On a PC, look in the Programs folder; on a Mac, look in the Utilities folder; on a handheld device, look in Settings.)

▶ **How does antivirus software work?** Modern antivirus software attempts to identify malware by searching your computer's files and memory for virus signatures. A **virus signature** is a section of program code, such as a unique series of instructions, that can be used to identify a known malicious program, much as a fingerprint is used to identify an individual.

Antivirus software scans for virus signatures in programs, data files, incoming and outgoing e-mail and attachments, and inbound instant message attachments. Antivirus software can also watch for unusual activity such as a large number of e-mail messages being sent out from your computer by a mass-mailing worm or bot.

Most antivirus programs can also scan for virus signatures in zip files, which is important when downloading zipped software and receiving zipped e-mail attachments.

▶ **How do I activate and deactivate my antivirus software?** Installation and activation procedures vary for each virus protection product. However, once you have installed your antivirus software, the best and safest practice is to keep it running full time in the background so that it checks every e-mail message as it arrives and scans all files the moment you access them. The scanning process requires only a short amount of time, which creates a slight delay in downloading e-mail and opening files.

When installing some application or utility software, you might be instructed to deactivate your antivirus software. You can usually right-click the icon on your computer's taskbar that corresponds to your antivirus software and then select the exit or disable option. Do not forget to reactivate your antivirus software as soon as the installation is completed.

▶ **How should I configure my antivirus software?** For the most extensive protection from malware, you should look for and enable the following features of your antivirus software:

▶ Start scanning when the computer boots.

▶ Scan all programs when they are launched and document files when they are opened.

▶ Scan other types of files, such as graphics, if you engage in some risky computing behaviors and are not concerned with the extra time required to open files as they are scanned.

▶ Scan incoming mail and attachments.

▶ Scan incoming instant message attachments.

▶ Scan outgoing e-mail for worm activity such as mass-mailing worms.

▶ Scan zipped (compressed) files.

▶ Scan for spyware, sometimes called pups (potentially unwanted programs).

▶ Scan all files on the computer's hard disk at least once a week.

▶ **How do I keep my antivirus software up to date?** Two aspects of your antivirus software periodically need to be updated. First, the antivirus program itself might need a patch or an update to fix bugs or improve features. Second, the list of virus signatures must be updated to keep up with the latest malware developments.

Virus signatures and other information that antivirus software uses to identify and eradicate malware are stored in one or more files usually referred to as **virus definitions** (or a virus database). Antivirus program updates and revised virus definitions are packaged into a file that can be manually or automatically downloaded. If your antivirus software is part of a security suite, the update might also include patches for other security software modules, such as the spyware module or firewall.

Most antivirus products are preconfigured to regularly check for updates, download them, and install them without user intervention. If you would rather control the download and installation process yourself, you can configure your antivirus software to alert you when updates are ready. In any case, you should manually check for updates periodically just in case the auto-update function has become disabled.

TRY IT!

When were the virus definitions for your antivirus software last updated?

▶ **How often should I run a system scan?** Most experts recommend that you configure your antivirus software to periodically scan all the files on your computer. With the proliferation of malware attacks, it's best to schedule a weekly system scan. Because a full system scan can significantly slow down your computer, schedule the scan for a time when you are not usually using your computer, but it is turned on.

You can also run a manual scan of your entire computer or of specific files. For example, suppose you download a program and you want to make sure it is virus-free before you install and run it. Depending on your antivirus software, you might be able to simply right-click the file name to start the scan (Figure 3-57). Otherwise, open your antivirus software and select the manual scan option.

▶ **What does** *quarantine* **mean?** If, during the scanning process, your virus protection software identifies a virus, worm, Trojan horse, or bot in a file or an attachment, it can try to remove the infection, put the file into quarantine, or simply delete the file.

In the context of antivirus software, a **quarantined file** contains code that is suspected of being part of a virus. For your protection, most antivirus software encrypts the file's contents and isolates it in a quarantine folder, so it can't be inadvertently opened or accessed by a hacker. If the infected file ends up on a quarantine list, your antivirus software might give you the option of trying to disinfect the file or deleting it.

▶ **How dependable is antivirus software?** Today's antivirus software is quite dependable, but not infallible. A fast-spreading worm can reach your computer before a virus definition update arrives, some spyware can slip through the net, and cloaking software can hide some viral exploits.

Despite occasional misses, however, antivirus software and other security software modules are constantly weeding out malware that would otherwise infect your computer. It is essential to use security software, but also important to take additional precautions, such as making regular backups of your data.

FIGURE 3-57

Before installing and running a downloaded file, you can scan it by right-clicking the file name and selecting the Scan option.

Name ▲	Size	Type
audacity-win-1.2.4b.exe	2,273 KB	Application
Building Secure Software - Co...	768 KB	Microsoft PowerPoi...
color.log	1 KB	Text Document
color.ps	8 KB	PostScript File
cpu-z-135.zip	412 KB	WinZip File
Eudora_7.0.1.0.exe	16,801 KB	Application
ffasetup.exe	2,457 KB	Application
FreePrimoS		

Open
Run as...
🗐 Add to Zip
🗐 Add to FreePrimoSetup.zip
🗐 Zip and E-Mail FreePrimoSetup.zip
Upload using WS_FTP Upload Wizard
Pin to Start menu
Scan

Send To ▶

Cut
Copy

Create Shortcut
Delete
Rename

Properties

iPodderUser ... be Acrobat 7.0 ...
Juice22Setu ... plication
lame-3.96. ... Zip File
lj1010series ... plication
np9demowe ... Zip File
pfbackup.e ... plication
QuickTimeIn ... plication
R115321.EX ... plication
setupeng.e ... plication
smartdraw_ ... plication
Thunderbird ... plication
WebTrack.e ... plication
winzip100.e ... plication
WSFTP_Pro ... plication

TRY IT!

Has your antivirus software quarantined any files? (Hint: Open your antivirus software and check the History tab.)

QuickCheck

1. A computer _____ can lurk in a computer for days or months, quietly replicating itself.

2. A mass-mailing _____ spreads to other computers by sending itself to all the addresses stored in the local e-mail client.

3. A group of zombie computers controlled by a hacker is called a(n) _____ .

4. A virus _____ is a unique section of malicious code that can be identified by antivirus software.

5. A(n) _____ file is suspected of containing a virus, so your antivirus software usually encrypts the file and stores it in a special folder.

 CHECK ANSWERS

Issue: How Serious Is Software Piracy?

SOFTWARE IS EASY TO STEAL. You don't have to walk out of a Best Buy store with a box of expensive software under your shirt. You can simply copy the software from your friend's computer. It seems so simple that it couldn't be illegal. But it is.

Piracy takes many forms. End-user piracy includes friends loaning distribution discs to each other and installing software on more computers than the license allows. Although it is perfectly legal to lend a physical object, such as a sweater, to a friend, it is not legal to lend digital copies of software and music. Unlike a sweater that can be worn by only one person at a time, copies of digital things can be simultaneously used by many people.

Software counterfeiting is the large-scale illegal duplication of software distribution media, and sometimes even its packaging. According to Microsoft, many software counterfeiting groups are linked to organized crime and money-laundering schemes that fund a diverse collection of illegal activities, such as smuggling, gambling, extortion, and prostitution. Counterfeit software is sold in retail stores and through online auctions—often the packaging looks so authentic that buyers have no idea they have purchased illegal goods.

Internet piracy uses the Web as a way to illegally distribute unauthorized software. In Net jargon, the terms *appz* and *warez* (pronounced as "wares" or "war EZ") refer to pirated software. Some warez have even been modified to eliminate serial numbers, registration requirements, expiration dates, or other forms of copy protection. Web sites, file sharing networks, and auction sites sell or distribute hundreds of thousands of pirated software products.

In many countries, including the United States, software pirates are subject to civil lawsuits for monetary damages and criminal prosecution, which can result in jail time and stiff fines. Nonetheless, software piracy continues to have an enormous impact. According to a Business Software Alliance (BSA) and IDC Piracy Study, $130 billion of software was legiti-

Web sites, file sharing networks, and auction sites sell or distribute hundreds of thousands of pirated software products.

mately purchased worldwide, but software worth a whopping $53 billion was pirated.

Is software piracy really damaging? Who cares if you use a program without paying for it? According to industry experts, software piracy has a negative effect on the economy. Software production makes a major contribution to the United States economy, employing more than 250,000 people and accounting for billions of dollars in corporate revenue. It fuels economic development in countries such as India and China. A BSA economic impact study concluded that lowering global piracy by 10 percentage points over a four-year period would add more than 500,000 jobs and $141 billion in worldwide economic growth.

Decreases in software revenues can have a direct effect on consumers, too. When software publishers are forced to cut corners, they tend to reduce customer service and technical support. As a result, you, the consumer, get put on hold when you call for technical support, find fewer free technical support sites, and encounter customer support personnel who are only moderately knowledgeable about their products. The bottom line—software piracy negatively affects customer service.

As an alternative to cutting support costs, some software publishers might build the cost of software piracy into the price of the software. The unfortunate result is that those who legitimately license and purchase software pay an inflated price.

TRY IT! What is the extent of piracy and is there any way to stop it? Explore the issue by completing the TRY IT! activities. Your instructor can specify how to submit your findings.

1 Analysts fear that the Internet is a major factor in piracy growth. As Internet access becomes more widely available, piracy is likely to increase, rather than decrease. Access to high-speed Internet connections makes it much easier to quickly download large software files. To find out if piracy is increasing, connect to *www.bsa.org* and look at the most recent Global Piracy Study, and then answer the following questions:

a. What time period does the study cover?

b. Did software piracy increase or decrease during this time period, and if so, by how much?

c. Which regions had the highest and lowest piracy rates?

d. Which countries had the three highest piracy rates, and what percentage of software is pirated in these countries?

2 As a justification of high piracy rates, some observers point out that people in many countries simply might not be able to afford software priced for the U.S. market. Find the current retail price for Microsoft Office in the United States. Next, find the average annual income for Bangladesh. Divide the price by the average annual income to calculate the percentage of a Bangladeshi's income that would be required to purchase Microsoft Office. What percentage of a Bangladeshi's income would he or she have to pay to get Microsoft Office at full retail U.S. price?

3 The incidence of piracy seems to be higher among small businesses and individual users than corporations and government agencies. According to one study, two-thirds of college and university students see nothing unethical about swapping or downloading digital copyrighted software, music, and movie files without paying for them, and more than half of the people surveyed for the study believe it is acceptable to do so in the workplace. Perhaps education is part of the solution; more publicity about the cost of piracy might encourage people to stop using illegal software. Search YouTube for "software piracy" or "anti-piracy ads," and then complete the following:

a. List the titles and links for three of the ads that you consider most effective.

b. List the title and link for an anti-piracy video that college students would consider "lame."

4 The software industry wants you to report piracy. Do a Web search for "report piracy" and list five sites where you can report individuals or businesses that use or distribute illegal copies of software.

INFOWEBLINKS

You can check the **NP2014 Chapter 3** InfoWebLink for updates to these activities.

W CLICK TO CONNECT
www.infoweblinks.com/NP2014/ch03

What Do You Think?

ISSUE

1. Do you believe that software piracy is a serious issue?

2. Do you know of any instances of software piracy?

3. Do you think that most software pirates understand that they are doing something illegal?

4. Should software publishers try to adjust software pricing for local markets?

Information Tools: Organizing Your Writing

You can organize a research paper, a report, or an essay simply by rearranging entries you made in the document containing your research notes. Your bookmarking application might include a feature to arrange your bookmarks and accompanying notes. These tools can be clumsy, however, if your notes are extensive. Dealing with hundreds of notes, you might have trouble seeing the big picture.

Organization tools help you visualize relationships between important pieces of information and supporting detail. They also help you determine the order in which you'll present concepts when you begin to write. Tools that writers find useful include outlines, concept maps, and SmartArt shapes.

OUTLINES. Most word processors include an outline feature that you can use to devise the basic structure of a research paper. You can rearrange outline points using your word processor's Move function. Pay attention to make sure the outline numbering adjusts correctly.

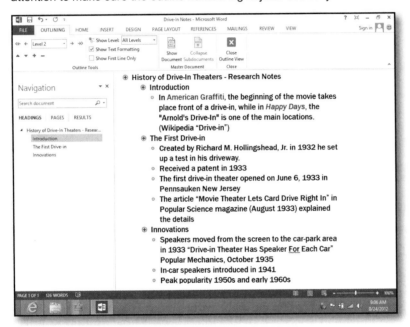

Microsoft Word offers an Outline view in which you can collapse or expand outline levels. This feature is useful for long outlines. For example, suppose you want to organize main ideas; you can collapse the detail so that supporting points are not displayed. Dedicated outline apps, such as OmniOutliner and ThinkBook, offer similar features.

CONCEPT MAPS. If you like to work with concepts visually, check out concept mapping software, such as SimTech MindMapper, Tufts' VUE, and SmartDraw, or Web apps, such as Cacoo and bubbl.us.

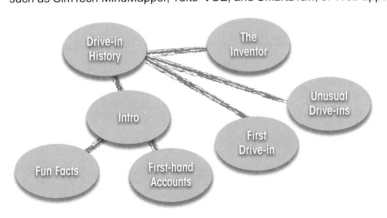

Concept maps use bubbles to represent ideas. Lines connect the bubbles to show related concepts. You can customize your concept maps to show a sequence by mapping from left to right.

SMARTART SHAPES.

You can use Microsoft Excel's SmartArt shapes to organize the structure for a research paper. Just looking through the SmartArt options can give you ideas about the overall structure and the structure of subsections.

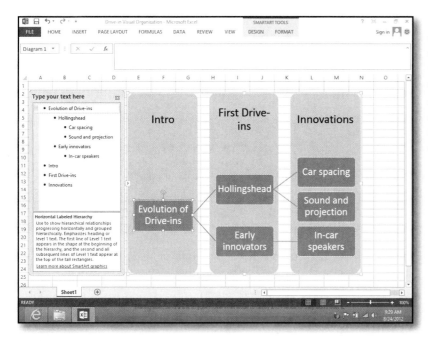

Excel's SmartArt Tools feature contains a variety of pre-designed diagrams that you can use to visualize how the pieces of your report fit together. You can enter text directly on the shapes, or in the outline box located on the left side of the screen.

TRY IT! Suppose you are working with a team to improve the organization of a Wikipedia article on gray wolves. To begin this project, copy the entire Wikipedia article on gray wolves into a new document named Wolf Project [Your Name] Chapter 3.

1 Use outline view and make each of the headings an outline level.

2 Add or modify headings and move material so that the article is organized into the sections listed in the sidebar.

3 Enter the headings as nodes in a concept map created with the diagramming tool of your choice. Add three subpoints to each node.

4 Use an Excel SmartArt diagram to show how you visualize the points made in the "Relation with humans" section.

New Organization for Gray Wolves Article

Naming and etymology

Range and habitat

Physical characteristics

Behavior

Conservation efforts

Relation with humans

Technology in Context: Journalism

IN THE ANCIENT WORLD, news spread by word of mouth, relayed by bards and merchants who traveled from town to town—in essence, they were the first reporters to broadcast the news. The news business is all about gathering and disseminating information quickly. Technology has played a major role in news reporting's evolution from its bardic roots to modern 24-hour news networks and Web sites.

Johann Gutenberg's printing press (ca. 1450), the first technological breakthrough in the news business, made it feasible to publish news as printed notices tacked to walls in the town square. As paper became more economical, resourceful entrepreneurs sold broadsheets to people eager for news, and the concept of a newspaper was born. The first regularly published newspapers appeared in Germany and Holland in 1609, and the first English newspaper, the *Weekly News*, was published in 1622.

But the news spread slowly. In the early 1800s, it took four weeks for newspapers in New York to receive reports from London. With the advent of the telegraph in 1844, however, reporters from far-flung regions could wire stories to their newspapers for publication the next day. The first radio reporters in the 1920s offered live broadcasts of sports events, church services, and variety shows. Before the 1950s, black-and-white newsreels shown in movie theaters provided the only visual imagery of news events, but television gave viewers news images on a nightly basis.

Technology has benefited print journalism, too. For decades, typesetters transferred reporters' handwritten stories into neatly set columns of type. Today, reporters use computers and word processing software to tap out their stories and run a preliminary check of spelling and grammar.

Stories are submitted by computer network to editors, who also use word processing software to edit stories to fit time and space constraints. The typesetting process has been replaced by desktop publishing software and computer to plate (CTP) technology. Digital pages produced with desktop publishing software are sent to a raster image processor (RIP), which converts the pages into dots that form words and images. After a page has been RIPed, a plate-

setter uses lasers to etch the dots onto a physical plate, which is then mounted on the printing press to produce printed pages. CTP is much faster and more flexible than typesetting, so publishers can make last-minute changes to accommodate late-breaking stories.

Personal computers have also added a new dimension to the news-gathering process. Reporters were once limited to personal interviews, observation, and fact gathering at libraries, but can now make extensive use of Internet resources and e-mail. Web sites and online databases provide background information on all sorts of topics. Other resources include newsgroups and chat rooms, where reporters can monitor public opinion on current events and identify potential sources.

Most major networks maintain interactive Web sites that offer online polls and bulletin boards designed to collect viewers' opinions. Although online poll respondents are not a representative sample of the population, they can help news organizations gauge viewer opinions and determine whether news coverage is comprehensive and effective.

Blogs and Web sites can be a source of news, in addition to reporting it. An online newspaper called *The Huffington Post* is a frequently cited source of stories reported on cable news networks. And even CNN now reports on news stories that originate on blogs such as *Slashdot*.

E-mail has changed the way reporters communicate with colleagues and sources. It's often the only practical method for contacting people in remote locations or distant time zones, and it's useful with reluctant sources, who feel more comfortable providing information under the cloak of anonymous Hotmail or Yahoo! accounts. Vetting e-mail sources—verifying credentials such as name, location, and occupation—can be difficult, however, so reporters tend not to rely on these sources without substantial corroboration.

For broadcast journalism, digital communications play a major role in today's live-on-the-scene television reporting. Most news organizations maintain remote production vans, sometimes called satellite news gathering (SNG) trucks, that travel to the site of breaking news, raise their antennas, and begin to broadcast. These complete mobile production facilities include camera control units, audio and video recording equipment, and satellite or microwave transmitters.

On-the-scene reporting no longer requires a truck full of equipment, however. Audiovisual editing units and video cameras have gone digital, making them easier to use and sized to fit in a suitcase. A new breed of backpack journalists carry digital video cameras, notebook computers, and mobile phones.

Backpack journalists can transfer video footage to their notebook computers and then edit the footage with consumer-level video editing software. The resulting video files are compressed and sent to newsroom technicians, who decompress the videos and then broadcast them—all in a matter of seconds.

One drawback of backpack journalists' use of digital cameras and compression is that the video quality usually isn't as crisp as images filmed with studio cameras. News organizations with high standards were once hesitant to use this lower quality video, but have found that viewers would rather see a low-quality image now than a high-quality image later. To many viewers, a few rough edges just make the footage seem more compelling—more like you are there.

A memorable tour de force in SNG was the brainchild of David Bloom, an NBC reporter embedded with the U.S. Army 3rd Infantry Division during Operation Iraqi Freedom. He helped modify an M-88 tank recovery vehicle into a high-tech, armored SNG vehicle. The $500,000 Bloommobile featured a gyrostabilized camera that could produce jiggle-free video as the tank blasted over sand dunes at 50 mph. Tragically, Bloom died while covering the conflict; but viewers vividly remember his exhilarating reports as the Bloommobile raced down desert roads, trundled along with Army supply convoys, and narrowly escaped enemy fire.

Video-enabled mobile phones ushered in another era of news gathering. Citizen journalists who are on the spot during news-making events simply point, shoot, and e-mail footage to media Web sites, such as CNN.com and FOXNews.com. During the tragic 2008 terrorist attacks in Mumbai, eyewitness accounts and updates flooded over social networking sites such as Facebook and Twitter. The first images of the attacks spread through social networking sites minutes before they appeared on mainstream news channels.

Computers, the Internet, and communications technology make it possible to instantly broadcast live reports across the globe, but live reporting is not without controversy. Reporters and amateur journalists who arrive at the scene of a disaster with microphones, cameras, or cell phones in hand have little time for reflection, vetting, and cross-checking, so grievous errors, libelous images, or distasteful video footage sometimes find their way into news reports.

Jeff Gralnick, former executive producer for ABC News, remarks, "In the old days, we had time to think before we spoke. We had time to write, time to research and time to say, 'Hey, wait a minute.' Now we don't even have the time to say, 'Hey, wait a nanosecond.' Just because we can say it or do it, should we?" Technology has given journalists a powerful arsenal of tools for gathering and reporting the news, but has also increased their accountability for accurate, socially responsible reporting.

3

New Perspectives Labs

To access the New Perspectives Lab for Chapter 3, open the NP2014 interactive eBook and then click the icon next to the lab title.

 INSTALLING AND UNINSTALLING SOFTWARE

IN THIS LAB YOU'LL LEARN:

- How to use a setup program to install Windows application software from a distribution CD

- The difference between typical, compact, and custom installation options

- How to specify a folder for a new software installation

- How to install downloaded software

- How to install an upgrade

- How to uninstall a Windows application

- What happens, in addition to deleting files, when you uninstall a software application

- How to locate the program that will uninstall a software application

- Why you might not want to delete all of the files associated with an application

LAB ASSIGNMENTS

1. Start the interactive part of the lab. Make sure you've enabled Tracking if you want to save your QuickCheck results. Perform each lab step as directed, and answer all the lab QuickCheck questions. When you exit the lab, your answers are automatically graded and your results are displayed.

2. Browse the Web and locate a software application that you might like to download. Use information supplied by the Web site to answer the following questions:

   a. What is the name of the program and the URL of the download site?

   b. What is the size of the download file?

   c. According to the instructions, does the download file appear to require manual installation, or does it automatically install itself when the download is complete?

3. On the computer you regularly use, look through the list of installed programs. List the names of any programs that include their own uninstall routines.

4. (Windows only) On the computer you regularly use, open the Control Panel and then select the Uninstall a Program option. List the first ten programs shown.

Key Terms

Make sure you understand all the boldfaced key terms presented in this chapter. With the NP2014 interactive eBook, you can use this list of terms as an interactive study activity. First, try to define a term in your own words, and then click the term to compare your definition with the definition presented in the chapter.

*See page 180 for a list of key software applications.

3

© Ralf Juergen Kraft/shutterstock

Interactive Summary

To review important concepts from this chapter, fill in the blanks to best complete each sentence. When using the NP2014 interactive eBook, click the Check Answers buttons to automatically score your answers.

SECTION A: Computer software can be grouped into two main categories. _____ software is designed for computer-centric tasks, whereas _____ software is designed to help people accomplish real-world tasks. These two main categories can be further divided into subcategories. Popular software categories include music, video, and graphics. Mapping and _____-based software on desktop and mobile computing devices helps consumers find the nearest ATM or turn-by-turn directions to the airport. For businesses, _____ market software is designed to automate specialized tasks in a specific market or business. _____ market soft-

ware is generic software that can be used by just about any kind of business. _____ software is designed to help you monitor and configure settings for your computer system equipment, the operating system, or application software. A(n) _____ reader is an essential utility that displays documents in a standard format for exchanging files. _____ utilities alter a device's user interface to create an accessible environment for people who cannot see the screen or have other barriers to access. Device _____ are a type of system software that helps a computer establish communication with peripheral devices.

▶ CHECK ANSWERS

SECTION B: Office suites are sometimes referred to as _____ software because they offer features that really help get work done. Word _____ software assists you with composing, editing, designing, printing, and electronically publishing documents. When you want to change margins, headers, and footers, you can use _____ layout tools. To change the spacing between lines or the alignment of text, you can use tools to adjust _____ style. _____ software is similar to a smart piece of paper that automatically adds up the columns of numbers you write on it. You can use it to make other calculations, too, based on simple equations that you write or more complex, built-in formulas. Because it is so

easy to experiment with different numbers, this type of software is particularly useful for _____ analyses. _____ software helps you store, find, organize, update, and report information stored in one or more tables. Data is stored in _____, which form records. When two sets of records are _____, database software allows you to access data from both tables at the same time. A(n) _____ language such as SQL describes the information you want to find in a set of records. _____ software supplies tools for creating a series of electronic slides that can be shown on a computer screen or projector.

▶ CHECK ANSWERS

SECTION C:

The process of _____ software places a program into a computer so that it can be executed or run. _____ apps are examples of cloud computing and are accessed from a browser. _____ apps are installed on a local handheld device by downloading from an app store. Some Apple devices have to use a designated app store unless they are _____ by an unauthorized change to the device's software. Most local applications include a(n) _____ program that guides you through the installation process. The main program is stored in a(n) _____ file that might call additional programs as necessary. For downloaded software, the first step in the installation process is usually to _____ the distribution file that was compressed to conserve space and reduce download time. In contrast to local applications, _____ software is designed to run from removable storage, such as a CD or USB flash drive. On PCs, these apps require no entries in the Windows Registry. Software publishers regularly update their software to add new features, fix bugs, and update its security. A software _____ is a small section of program code that replaces part of the software you currently have installed. The term *service* _____, which usually applies to operating system updates, is a set of patches that correct problems and address security vulnerabilities. To remove software from a Windows PC, it is important to use a(n) _____ routine, rather than simply deleting program files.

▶ CHECK ANSWERS

SECTION D:

Most new computers include an operating system, essential utilities, and some basic application software. When shopping for additional utilities and apps, check the system _____ to make sure your device has the correct operating system and necessary hardware capacity. Software is protected by _____, and illegal copying or distribution is sometimes referred to as software _____. _____ software, such as commercial software, is protected by copyright that grants to its author an exclusive right to copy, distribute, sell, and modify that work. Public _____ software is not protected by copyright. A software _____ can extend or limit the rights granted by copyright. Demoware and _____ are distributed free of charge, but require payment for continued use. Freeware is copyrighted software that can be used for free, but cannot be altered or resold. _____ source software is distributed with its source code, and can be modified, sold, and redistributed.

▶ CHECK ANSWERS

SECTION E:

Security software can be classified into various types: antivirus, antispyware, anti-spam, and firewalls. Each type focuses on a specific security threat. A computer _____ is a set of program instructions that attaches itself to a file, reproduces itself, and spreads to other files. A computer _____ is a self-replicating program designed to carry out some unauthorized activity on a victim's computer. In the context of computing, a Trojan _____ is a computer program that seems to perform one function while actually doing something else. For example, it might steal passwords using a type of program called a _____ that records keystrokes. A Remote Access Trojan sets up _____ capabilities that allow remote hackers to access files on victims' computers. _____ programs can turn computers into zombies and link them together into _____. _____ is a type of program that secretly gathers personal information without the victim's knowledge, usually for advertising and other commercial purposes. To combat malware, it is important to use _____ software that looks for virus signatures. Most computer owners obtain this software as one module in a security _____.

▶ CHECK ANSWERS

Software Key Terms

Interactive Situation Questions

Apply what you've learned to some typical computing situations. When using the NP2014 interactive eBook, you can type your answers, and then use the Check Answers button to automatically score your responses.

1. You're using an app on your iPhone to find the nearest bike repair shop. This _____ -based app works because it can triangulate your whereabouts based on the built-in GPS or your distance from nearby cell towers.

2. Suppose that you've been hired to organize a professional skateboard competition. When you consider how you'll need to use computers, you realize that you must collect information on each competitor and keep track of every competitive event. With at least two types of related records, you'll probably need to use _____ software.

3. Imagine that you just purchased a new software package. You insert the distribution CD, but nothing happens. No problem—you can manually run the _____ program, which will start the install routine.

4. Your friend has an iPod Touch that's loaded with all kinds of applications; but every time there's a software update, your friend grumbles about "redoing stuff." You guess that your friend's iPod is _____ .

5. You download an open source software program from the Web. You assume that the download includes the uncompiled _____ code for the program as well as the _____ version.

6. You're in the process of receiving some e-mail messages when your antivirus software displays an alert. You assume that it has discovered a virus _____ in an attachment for one of the e-mail messages. The message also states that the file has been _____ ; that is, moved to an area where it cannot cause more harm.

 CHECK ANSWERS

Interactive Practice Tests

Practice tests that consist of ten multiple-choice, true/false, and fill-in-the-blank questions are available in the NP2014 interactive eBook. Test questions are selected at random from a large test bank, so each time you take a test, you'll receive a different set of questions. Your tests are scored immediately, and you can print study guides that help you find the correct answers for any questions that you missed.

▶ CLICK TO START

Learning Objectives Checkpoints

Learning Objectives Checkpoints are designed to help you assess whether you have achieved the major learning objectives for this chapter. You can use paper and pencil or word processing software to complete most of the activities.

1. List seven categories of application software.

2. List at least ten functions performed by utilities included with Windows and Mac operating systems.

3. Provide an example of an adaptive utility on the iPhone.

4. Explain why you might want to locate the version number for a device driver.

5. Describe three ways that word processing software can help improve your writing.

6. Draw a sketch of a simple worksheet and label the following: columns, rows, cell, active cell, values, labels, formulas, and Formula bar. Explain the difference between an absolute reference and a relative reference, giving an example of each.

7. Describe four ways to query a database.

8. List at least six key features of presentation software.

9. Describe the difference between Web apps and mobile apps.

10. List and describe the two main types of files included in a local software installation.

11. Write a set of step-by-step instructions for installing software from a distribution CD, and another set of instructions for installing downloaded software.

12. Explain the purpose of a software patch and describe how it differs from a service pack.

13. Describe the difference between uninstalling software on Macs and on Windows.

14. Find a EULA for an application installed on your computer and use it to answer each of the questions posed in the TRY IT! on page 158.

15. Explain the differences between proprietary software, commercial software, shareware, open source software, freeware, and public domain software.

16. Create a table that summarizes the differences between various types of malware based on their method of distribution and exploits.

17. Draw a storyboard to illustrate how antivirus software works.

Study Tip: Make sure you can use your own words to correctly answer each of the purple focus questions that appear throughout the chapter.

Concept Map

Fill in the blanks to show the hierarchy of software described in this chapter.

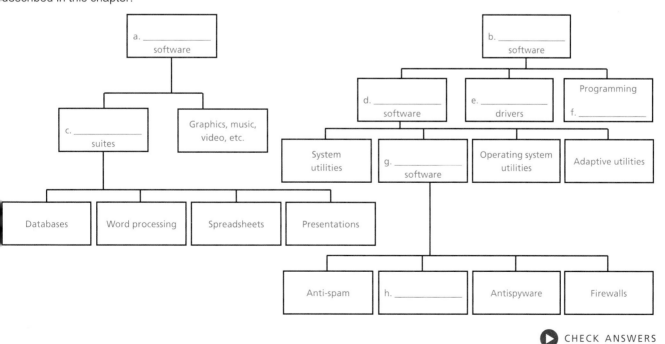

CHECK ANSWERS

4

Operating Systems and File Management

Chapter Contents

INFOWEBLINKS

You'll find updates for chapter material by connecting to the **NP2014 Chapter 4** InfoWebLink.

W CLICK TO CONNECT
www.infoweblinks.com/np2014/ch04

Learning Objectives

After reading this chapter, you will be able to answer the following questions by completing the outcomes-based Learning Objectives Checkpoints on page 243.

1. What are system resources?
2. How do multitasking, multithreading, and multiprocessing work?
3. What is a memory leak?
4. What happens during the boot process?
5. When do users interact with the operating system?
6. How do GUIs differ from command line interfaces?
7. Which operating systems are typically used on personal computers, on servers, and on handheld devices?
8. What is a virtual machine?
9. Do operating systems put limits on the names that can be used for files?
10. What is a file specification or path?
11. What is a native file format?
12. Are there guidelines for managing files so that they are easy to locate and back up?
13. What happens behind the scenes when a computer stores a file?
14. What is the best backup device?
15. How do synchronization and backup software differ?
16. How do restore points, bare-metal restore, disk imaging, virtual machines, boot disks, and recovery disks relate to backup?
17. Is it possible to back up data on handheld devices?

Apply Your Knowledge

The information in this chapter will give you the background to:

▶ Find out which processes are running on your computer

▶ Use operating systems, such as Windows, Mac OS, iOS, Android, and Linux

▶ Maintain an efficient organization of files

▶ Identify file name extensions

▶ Convert files from one format to another

▶ Open, save, rename, move, copy, and delete files

▶ Burn a CD, DVD, or BD

▶ Shred computer files so they cannot be read

▶ Back up important data

▶ Get up and running after a hard disk failure

TRY IT!

IS MY COMPUTER'S HARD DISK GETTING FULL?

Your computer's hard disk stores a high percentage of the programs you use and the data files you create. You might wonder if your hard disk is getting full. To find out, follow the steps below.

Windows 7:

1. Start your computer and make sure you can see the Windows desktop.
2. Click the **Start** button, and then select Computer.
3. Right-click your **(C:)** drive to display a pop-up menu.
4. Click **Properties**. A Local Disk Properties dialog box should appear containing statistics about your computer's hard disk.
5. For the properties indicated by red underlines in the figure at right, jot down the statistics for used space, free space, and capacity. Then sketch in the slices of the pie chart for your computer.
6. Also, use the blank provided to jot down the file system used by your computer. You'll learn the significance of your computer's file system when you read the chapter.

Windows 8:

1. From the Start screen, click the **Desktop** tile.
2. Click the **File Explorer** folder at the bottom of the screen.
3. Follow instructions 3–6 for Windows 7.

Mac:

1. Click the **Finder** icon, located on the dock at the bottom of the screen.
2. Right-click the **Macintosh HD** link. (If your mouse has only one button, hold down the **Ctrl** key and click it.)
3. Select **Get Info** from the pop-up menu.
4. For the properties indicated by red underlines in the figure at right, jot down the statistics for capacity, available space, and used space in GB and bytes.
5. Also, jot down the file system shown on the Format line. You'll learn the significance of the file system when you read the chapter.

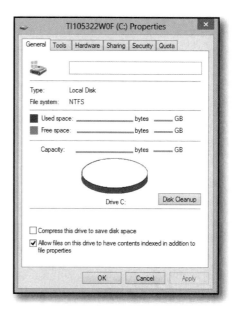

Finder icon

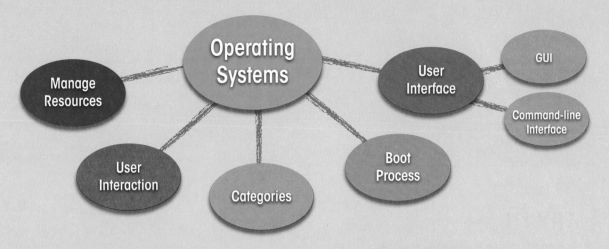

Operating System Basics

AN OPERATING SYSTEM is an integral part of virtually every computer system. It fundamentally affects how you can use your computer. Can you run two programs at the same time? Can you connect your computer to a network? Does your computer run dependably? Does it have a touchscreen? To answer questions like these, it is helpful to have a clear idea about what an operating system is and what it does. Section A provides an overview of operating system basics.

OPERATING SYSTEM TASKS

▶ **What is an operating system?** An operating system (abbreviated OS) is a type of system software that acts as the master controller for all activities that take place within a computer system. It is one of the factors that determines your computer's compatibility and platform.

Most computers are sold with a preinstalled operating system, such as Microsoft Windows or Mac OS (Figure 4-1). A third operating system called Linux is customarily used for high-end workstations and servers, but can also be installed on personal computers. Tablet computers and smartphones use operating systems such as Windows RT, iOS, and Android.

FIGURE 4-1

Windows (left) is preinstalled on IBM-compatible computers manufactured by companies such as Dell and Hewlett-Packard. Mac OS (middle) is preinstalled on Apple Macintosh computers. Linux (right) is an open source operating system that's available as a free download.

▶ What does an operating system do? Your computer's operating system provides an environment for running software and controlling peripheral devices.

The operating system, application software, and device drivers are organized similar to the chain of command in an army. You issue a command using application software. Application software tells the operating system what to do. The operating system tells the device drivers, the device drivers tell the hardware, and the hardware actually does the work. Figure 4-2 illustrates this chain of command for printing a document or photo.

FIGURE 4-2

A command to print a document is relayed through various levels of software, including the operating system, until it reaches the printer.

4

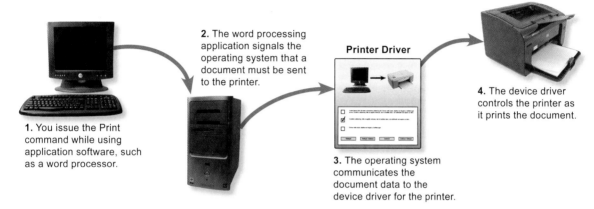

2. The word processing application signals the operating system that a document must be sent to the printer.

Printer Driver

4. The device driver controls the printer as it prints the document.

1. You issue the Print command while using application software, such as a word processor.

3. The operating system communicates the document data to the device driver for the printer.

The operating system interacts with application software, device drivers, and hardware to manage a computer's resources. In the context of a computer system, the term **resource** refers to any component that is required to perform work.

The processor is a computer's main resource. RAM (random access memory), storage space, and peripheral devices are also resources. While you interact with application software, your computer's operating system is busy behind the scenes with resource management tasks such as those listed in Figure 4-3.

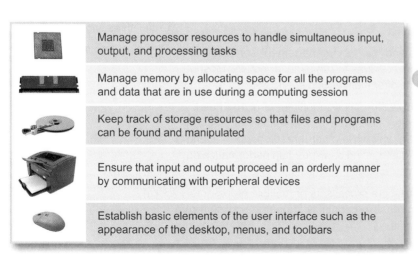

Manage processor resources to handle simultaneous input, output, and processing tasks

Manage memory by allocating space for all the programs and data that are in use during a computing session

Keep track of storage resources so that files and programs can be found and manipulated

Ensure that input and output proceed in an orderly manner by communicating with peripheral devices

Establish basic elements of the user interface such as the appearance of the desktop, menus, and toolbars

FIGURE 4-3

Operating System Tasks

TRY IT!

Click the resource in Figure 4-3 that stores data on a temporary basis.

▶ How do operating systems manage processor resources?

Every cycle of a computer's microprocessor is a resource for accomplishing tasks. Many activities—called processes—compete for the attention of your computer's microprocessor. Commands are arriving from programs you're using, while input is arriving from the keyboard, mouse, and other devices. At the same time, data is being sent to the display device or printer, and Web pages could be arriving from your Internet connection.

To manage all these competing processes, your computer's operating system must ensure that each process receives its share of microprocessor cycles. You can check the processes that are being executed by the microprocessor if you suspect that a program did not close properly or that malware is working behind the scenes (Figure 4-4).

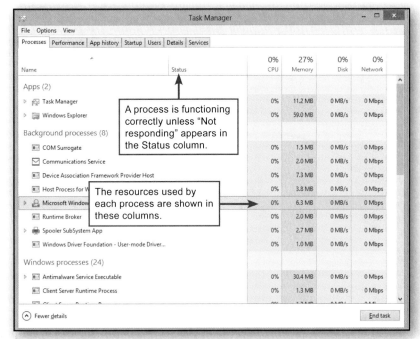

FIGURE 4-4

The Windows operating system displays a list of processes when you hold down the Ctrl, Shift, and Esc keys. On the Mac, look for the Activity Monitor in the Utilities folder listed under Applications. Most processes are legitimate programs that run in the background to carry out tasks for the operating system, device drivers, and applications. Occasionally a bot or worm launches rogue processes. If you want to know if a process is legitimate, you can google it. ▶ Use your interactive eBook to find out how to access information about the processes on your computer.

▶ How do operating systems handle so many processes?

During a typical computing session, your computer might run an average of 50 processes. Ideally, the operating system should be able to help the microprocessor switch seamlessly from one process to another. Depending on the capabilities of the operating system and computer hardware, processes can be managed by multitasking, multithreading, and multiprocessing.

Multitasking provides process and memory management services that allow two or more tasks, jobs, or programs to run simultaneously. Most of today's popular operating systems offer multitasking services.

Within a single program, **multithreading** allows multiple parts, or threads, to run simultaneously. For example, one thread for a spreadsheet program might be waiting for input from the user while other threads perform a long calculation in the background. Multithreading can speed up performance on single- or multiple-processor computers.

Many new computers include multi-core processors or multiple processors. An operating system's **multiprocessing** capability supports a division of labor among all the processing units.

TRY IT!

When an operating system allocates tasks to various cores of a microprocessor, it is called:

○ multitasking

○ multithreading

○ multiprocessing

▶ How does an operating system manage memory? A

microprocessor works with data and executes instructions stored in RAM—one of your computer's most important resources. When you want to run more than one program at a time, the operating system has to allocate specific areas of memory for each program, as shown in Figure 4-5.

Sometimes an application requests memory but never releases it—a condition called a **memory leak**. Memory "leaks" away into this application's reserved area, eventually preventing other programs from accessing enough memory to function properly. Those programs can crash, and the operating system might display error messages, such as "General Protection Fault" or "Program Not Responding." Your computer can sometimes recover from a memory leak if you access Task Manager (PCs) or Activity Monitor (Macs) to close the corrupted program.

▶ How does the OS keep track of storage resources?

Behind the scenes, an operating system acts as a filing clerk that stores and retrieves files from your computer's hard drive and other storage devices. It remembers the names and locations of all your files and keeps track of empty spaces where new files can be stored. Later in the chapter, you'll explore file storage in more depth and learn how the operating system affects the way you create, name, save, and retrieve files.

▶ Why does the operating system get involved with peripheral devices?

Every device connected to a computer is regarded as an input or output resource. Your computer's operating system communicates with device driver software so that data can travel smoothly between the computer and peripheral resources. If a peripheral device or driver is not performing correctly, the operating system makes a decision about what to do—usually it displays an on-screen message to warn you of the problem.

Your computer's operating system ensures that input and output proceed in an orderly manner, using **buffers** to collect and hold data while the computer is busy with other tasks. By using a keyboard buffer, for example, your computer never misses one of your keystrokes, regardless of how fast you type or what else is happening in your computer at the same time.

▶ Are different operating systems needed for different computing tasks?

One operating system might be better suited to some computing tasks than others. To provide clues to their strengths and weaknesses, operating systems are informally categorized and characterized using one or more of the following terms:

A **single-user operating system** deals with one set of input devices—those that can be controlled by one user at a time. Operating systems for tablet computers and smartphones fit into this category. DOS is an example of a single-user operating system designed for desktop computers.

A **multiuser operating system** allows a single, centralized computer to deal with simultaneous input, output, and processing requests from many users. One of its most difficult responsibilities is to schedule all the processing requests that a centralized computer must perform.

A **server operating system** provides tools for managing distributed networks, e-mail servers, and Web hosting sites. Mac OS X Server, Windows Server 2012, and Linux are examples of server operating systems. Server operating systems typically route data and programs to each user's local computer where the actual processing takes place. They might also provide multiuser capabilities.

FIGURE 4-5

The operating system allocates a specific area of RAM for each program that is open and running. The operating system is itself a program, so it requires RAM space, too.

4

TERMINOLOGY NOTE

The term *buffer* is technical jargon for a region of memory that holds data waiting to be transferred from one device to another.

TRY IT!

Is Windows 8 a multiuser operating system?

○ Yes

○ No

A **desktop operating system** is designed for a desktop or laptop personal computer. The computer you use at home, at school, or at work is most likely configured with a desktop operating system, such as Microsoft Windows or Mac OS. These operating systems are designed to accommodate one user at a time, but also provide networking capability. Today's desktop operating systems invariably provide multitasking capabilities so that users can run more than one application at a time.

A **mobile operating system** is designed for devices such as smartphones and tablet computers. Mobile OSs support touchscreens, but tend to limit multitasking and user access to local storage devices.

Operating systems for handheld and desktop devices provide many similar services, such as scheduling processor resources, managing memory, loading programs, managing input and output, and establishing the user interface. But because handheld devices tend to be used for less sophisticated tasks, their operating systems are somewhat simpler and significantly smaller.

THE BOOT PROCESS

▶ **Where is the operating system stored?** In some digital devices, such as handheld media players, ebook readers, and games, the entire operating system is small enough to be stored in ROM. For most other computers, the operating system program is quite large, so most of it is stored on a hard disk.

During the boot process, the operating system kernel is loaded into RAM. The **kernel** provides essential operating system services, such as memory management and file access. The kernel stays in RAM all the time your computer is on. Other parts of the operating system, such as customization utilities, are loaded into RAM as they are needed.

▶ **What is the boot process?** The sequence of events that occurs between the time that you turn on a computer and the time that it is ready for you to issue commands is referred to as the **boot process**, or booting your computer.

Your computer's small **bootstrap program** is built into special ROM circuitry housed in the computer's system unit. When you turn on a computer, the ROM circuitry receives power and begins the boot process by executing the bootstrap program. Six major events happen during the boot process:

❶ **Power up.** When you turn on the power switch, the power light is illuminated, and power is distributed to the computer circuitry.

❷ **Start boot program.** The microprocessor begins to execute the bootstrap program that is stored in ROM.

❸ **Power-on self-test.** The computer performs diagnostic tests of several crucial system components.

❹ **Identify peripheral devices.** The computer identifies any peripheral devices that are connected and checks their settings.

❺ **Load operating system.** If necessary, the operating system is copied from the hard disk to RAM.

❻ **Check configuration and customization.** The microprocessor reads configuration data and executes any customized startup routines specified by the user.

TERMINOLOGY NOTE

Some operating system vendors characterize their products as home or professional versions. The home version usually has fewer network management tools than the professional version.

TERMINOLOGY NOTE

The term *boot* comes from the word *bootstrap*, which is a small loop on the back of a boot. Just as you can pull on a big boot using a small bootstrap, your computer boots up by first loading a small program into memory, and then it uses that small program to load a large operating system.

TRY IT!

During the boot process on a desktop computer, what part of the operating system is loaded into RAM?

○ Bootstrap loader

○ Kernel

○ ROM

○ Desktop

▶ Why doesn't a computer simply leave the operating system in memory? Most of a computer's memory is volatile DRAM, which cannot hold any data when the power is off. Although a copy of the operating system is housed in RAM while the computer is in operation, this copy is erased as soon as the power is turned off.

In addition to RAM, computers have non-volatile memory circuitry, such as ROM, which can store data even when the power is off. Typically, ROM is not large enough to store an entire operating system.

Given the volatility of RAM and the insufficient size of ROM, computer designers decided to store the operating system on a computer's hard disk or solid state drive. During the boot process, a copy of the operating system is transferred into RAM, where it can be accessed quickly whenever the computer needs to carry out an input, output, or storage operation (Figure 4-6).

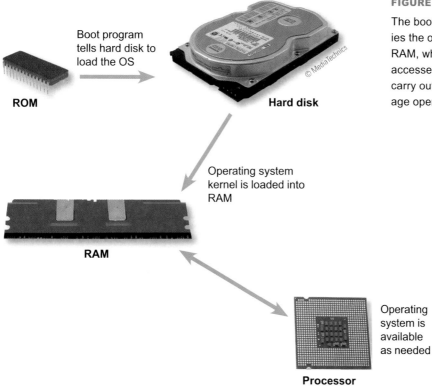

Boot program tells hard disk to load the OS

ROM

Hard disk

Operating system kernel is loaded into RAM

RAM

Operating system is available as needed

Processor

FIGURE 4-6

The bootstrap program copies the operating system into RAM, where it can be directly accessed by the processor to carry out input, output, or storage operations.

▶ How do I know when the operating system is loaded?
The operating system is loaded and the boot process is complete when the computer is ready to accept your commands. Usually, the computer displays an operating system prompt or a main screen. For example, Windows 8 displays the Start screen when the boot process is complete; Mac OS X displays the desktop and dock.

USER INTERFACES

▶ Do I ever interact directly with the OS? Although its main purpose is to control what happens behind the scenes, you can interact with the operating system to launch programs, manage files, configure your computer equipment, and customize your work environment.

The programs you use to accomplish these tasks are called utilities, but the general way you interact with an operating system and application software is referred to as the user interface.

▶ What is a user interface? A **user interface** can be defined as the combination of hardware and software that helps people and computers communicate with each other. A personal computer's user interface includes a display device, mouse, and keyboard that allow you to view and manipulate your computing environment. It also includes software elements, such as icons, menus, and toolbar buttons.

▶ How does the operating system affect the user interface? The operating system's user interface defines the so-called look and feel of compatible software. For example, application software that runs under Mac OS uses a standard set of menus, buttons, and toolbars based on the operating system's user interface. Originally, computers had a **command-line interface** that required users to type memorized commands to run programs and accomplish tasks.

Command-line user interfaces can be accessed from most operating systems, including Windows and Mac OS. Experienced users and system administrators sometimes prefer to use a command-line interface for troubleshooting and system maintenance. Figure 4-7 illustrates the use of a command-line interface.

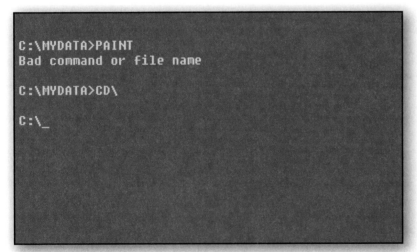

FIGURE 4-7

A command-line user interface requires users to type commands. Here the prompt C:\MYDATA> means the computer is looking at the MYDATA folder of drive C. The user has tried to start a program called Paint, but that program does not exist in the current folder, so the computer has produced the error message "Bad command or file name."

▶ What kind of UIs do modern computers have? Most computers today feature a graphical user interface, abbreviated as GUI and pronounced as "gooey" or "gee you eye." A **graphical user interface** provides a way to select menu options and manipulate graphical objects displayed on the screen using a mouse or gesture.

GUIs were originally conceived at the prestigious Xerox PARC research facility. In 1984, Apple turned the idea into a commercial success with the launch of its popular Macintosh computer, which featured a GUI operating system and applications. Graphical user interfaces didn't really catch on in the PC market until the 1992 release of Windows 3.1.

TRY IT!

How long have computers had GUIs?

○ About 5 years

○ About 10 years

○ About 20 years

○ More than 25 years

▶ What are the basic control elements of a GUI? GUIs are
based on graphical objects that can be manipulated using a touchscreen, mouse, or other input device. Each graphical object represents a computer task, command, or real-world object.

Desktops and windows. A **desktop** is a visual work area that covers the entire screen and remains in the background throughout a computing session. A desktop includes a **taskbar** or **dock** for launching applications, which are displayed in rectangular **application windows** on the desktop. These application windows can be resized and repositioned so you can simultaneously work on multiple projects (Figure 4-8).

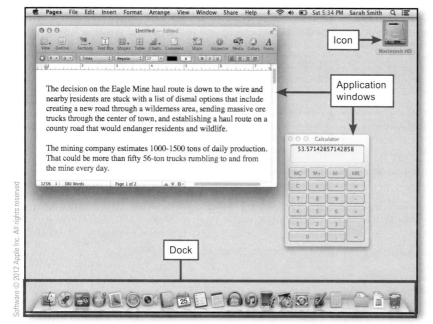

FIGURE 4-8

This Mac desktop stretches over the entire screen and displays windows, icons, and a dock for launching applications.

Start screens. A **Start screen**, popular on handheld devices, appears at the end of the boot process and whenever it is invoked by the user, commonly by pressing the Home button. Start screens display icons or tiles for apps, so that you can select the one you want to use (Figure 4-9).

FIGURE 4-9

This Start screen is displayed when the iPad starts, and any time the user presses the Home button.

Icons. An **icon** is a small picture that represents a program, file, or hardware device. Some icons are designed as **tiles**, which can display information feeds of live data (Figure 4-10).

FIGURE 4-10

Icons (left) and Tiles (right)

Buttons, toolbars, and taskbars. A **button** is a graphic—usually rectangular in shape—that can be clicked to make a selection. Buttons can be arranged in a **toolbar** or displayed on a taskbar (Figure 4-11).

FIGURE 4-11

Buttons can be arranged on a taskbar (top) or on a toolbar (bottom).

Menus and ribbons. A **menu** displays a list of commands or options on a **menu bar**. Each line of the menu is referred to as a menu option or a menu item. Menus were developed in response to the difficulties many people experienced trying to remember command words and syntax for command-line user interfaces. Menus are popular because you simply choose the command you want from a list. Also, because all the commands on the list are valid, it is not possible to invoke invalid commands that generate errors (Figure 4-12).

FIGURE 4-12

Clicking a command word on the menu bar displays a list of menu options.

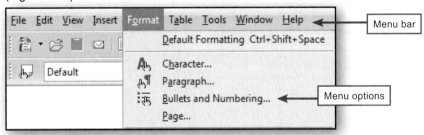

A **ribbon** is an alternative type of menu that is arranged as rows of tools on a succession of tabs. Microsoft pioneered the ribbon interface element, which was incorporated in the last several editions of Microsoft Office (Figure 4-13).

FIGURE 4-13

Each tab on the ribbon contains a series of command options.

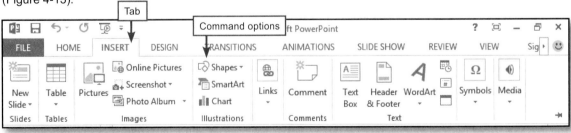

You might wonder how a menu can present all the commands you might want to use. Obviously, there are many possibilities for combining command words so there could be hundreds of menu options. Two methods are generally used to present a reasonably sized list of options: submenus and dialog boxes.

A **submenu** is an additional set of commands that the computer displays after you make a selection from the main menu. Sometimes a submenu displays another submenu, providing even more command choices (Figure 4-14).

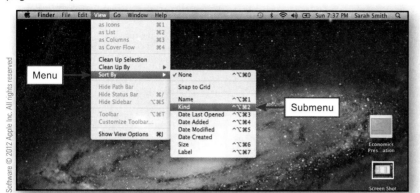

FIGURE 4-14

Menu options with a ▶ symbol lead to submenus.

4

Some menu and ribbon options lead to a dialog box. A **dialog box** displays the options associated with a command. You fill in the dialog box to indicate specifically how you want the command carried out. Dialog boxes, like the one shown in Figure 4-15, appear when you click a dialog box launcher or when you click a menu item that ends with the three dots of an ellipsis.

FIGURE 4-15

A dialog box contains controls to specify settings for a task.

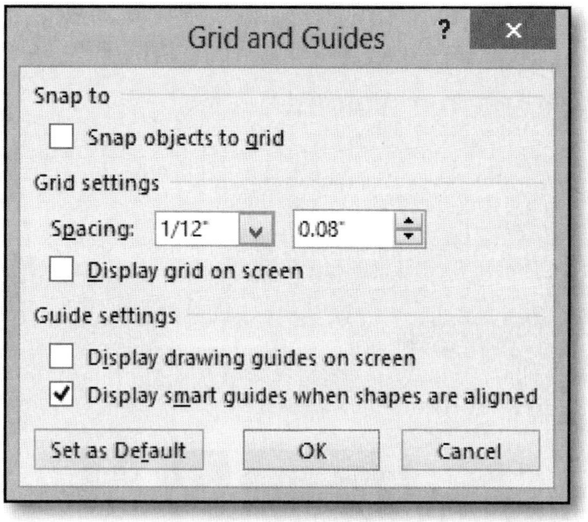

▶ How similar are the user interfaces for Windows, Mac OS, and Linux? All of the popular desktop operating systems use graphical user interfaces that are more similar than they are different. Regardless of whether you use Windows, Mac OS, or Linux, you'll encounter a fairly standard set of on-screen controls. They might differ in their visual design, but it is easy to determine how to use them. In the next section of the chapter, you'll learn more about the similarities and differences in today's popular operating systems.

QuickCheck

SECTION A

1. An operating system manages a computer's [   ], such as RAM, storage, and peripherals.

2. Most personal computer operating systems have [   ] capabilities so that they can simultaneously run two or more tasks, jobs, or programs.

3. The core part of an operating system is called its [   ].

4. During the [   ] process, a program stored in ROM tells the hard disk to load the operating system into RAM.

5. Most computers today have [   ] user interfaces.

⏵ CHECK ANSWERS

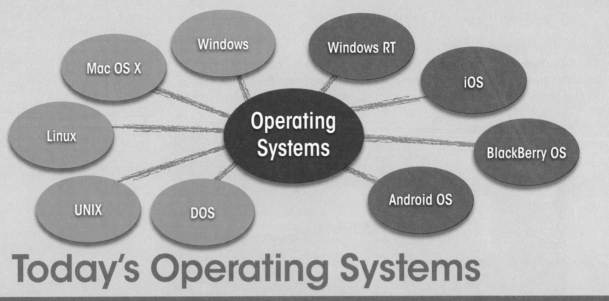

Today's Operating Systems

CONSUMERS HAVE A CHOICE of computer operating systems. What makes these operating systems different? What are their strengths and weaknesses? Section B offers an operating system overview designed to give you a basic familiarity with their features.

MICROSOFT WINDOWS

▶ **What's the best-selling operating system?** Microsoft **Windows** is installed on more than 80% of the world's personal computers. It features a Start screen with colorful tiles that can be used to launch applications, connect to Internet-based sites and services, or access a multitasking desktop environment (Figure 4-16).

FIGURE 4-16

Microsoft Windows is the world's most popular operating system. The Start screen is displayed on startup. Clicking a tile launches an application. To redisplay the Start screen, press the Windows key on the keyboard or the Start button on a Windows smartphone or tablet. ▶ Tour the Windows desktop and find out how to set up live tiles.

▶ **What do I need to know about the evolution of Windows?** From its inception, the Windows operating system was designed to run on Intel or Intel-compatible microprocessors. The first PCs used a command-line operating system called **DOS** (Disk Operating System).

To create Microsoft Windows, developers used the DOS kernel, but added a point-and-click graphical user interface. Since its introduction in 1985, Windows has evolved through several versions, listed in Figure 4-17 on the next page.

TRY IT!

Before Windows, PCs used a command-line user interface called [ ] .

▶ **Why "Windows"?** The Windows operating system got its name from the rectangular work areas on the screen-based desktop. Each window can display a different document or program, which provides a visual model of the operating system's multitasking capabilities (Figure 4-18).

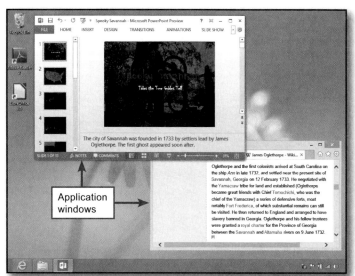

FIGURE 4-18 The Windows desktop can display multiple application windows.

Through many editions, the Windows user interface was characterized by a colorful Start button in the lower-left corner of the screen (Figure 4-19). Clicking the Start button produced a menu for quickly accessing programs, files, and settings. The Start button was replaced by the Start screen with the release of Windows 8.

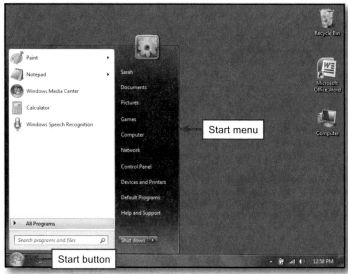

FIGURE 4-19 Legacy versions of Windows featured a Start button and Start menu.

FIGURE 4-17

Windows Timeline

2012 Windows 8
Replaced the Start button with a Start screen.

2009 Windows 7
Featured 64-bit support, enhanced desktop and taskbar features, and touchscreen capabilities.

2007 Windows Vista
Featured 64-bit support, enhanced security, and more flexible file management.

2001 Windows XP
Featured an updated user interface, used the Windows 2000 32-bit kernel, and supported FAT32 and NTFS file systems.

2000 Windows Me
The last Windows version to use the original Windows kernel that accesses DOS.

2000 Windows 2000
Billed as a "multipurpose network OS for businesses of all sizes" and featured enhanced Web services.

1998 Windows 98
Increased stability was a big feature of this Windows version, which also included the Internet Explorer browser.

1995 Windows 95
Featured a revised user interface. Supported 32-bit processors, dial-up networking, and long file names.

1993 Windows NT
Provided management and security tools for network servers and the NTFS file system.

1992 Windows for Workgroups
Provided peer-to-peer networking, e-mail, group scheduling, and file and printer sharing.

1992 Windows 3.1
Introduced program icons and the file folder metaphor.

1990 Windows 3.0
Introduced graphical controls.

1987 Windows 2.0
Introduced overlapping windows and expanded memory access.

1985 Windows 1.0
Divided the screen into rectangular windows that allowed users to work with several programs at the same time.

4

▶ Does Windows 8 run on tablets and phones, too? Microsoft offers several editions of Windows 8 designed for desktop and laptop computers. In addition to basic Windows 8, consumers can purchase Windows 8 Pro and Windows 8 Enterprise editions, designed for power users and businesses. Windows 8 Pro also runs on a select group of Intel-based tablet computers, offering the complete Windows 8 experience and access to the vast array of Windows software.

FIGURE 4-20

Microsoft offers several versions of Windows designed for different computing tasks and equipment.

Windows RT is designed as a mobile operating system for tablet devices with ARM processors (Figure 4-20). It does not include a full-featured desktop and will not run Windows desktop applications. Like other mobile operating systems, Windows RT limits software to apps obtained through an authorized online store.

© MediaTechnics

Windows Phone 8 is designed for smartphones. It features a Start screen and live tiles similar to Windows RT.

▶ What are the strengths of Windows? The number and variety of programs that run on Windows are unmatched by any other operating system. For the best selection of software, especially for games and business software, Windows is the operating system of choice.

The Windows user community is also a strength. Comprehensive tutorials and troubleshooting guides can be found online and on the shelves of most bookstores. Microsoft's official site, *www.microsoft.com*, includes thousands of pages of easily searchable information.

With the largest user base of any platform, Windows computer owners can select from a vast array of peripheral devices. Many of the fastest graphics cards and the coolest joysticks are offered exclusively for the Windows platform.

▶ What are Windows' weaknesses? Windows has been criticized for two major weaknesses: reliability and security. The reliability of an operating system is usually gauged by the length of time it operates without glitches. Windows tends to become unstable with more frequency than other operating systems.

Slow system response, programs that stop working, and error messages can be symptoms of a Windows malfunction. Rebooting usually clears the error condition and returns a computer to normal functionality, but the time wasted shutting down and waiting for a reboot adds unnecessary frustration to the computing experience.

Of the major desktop operating systems, Windows has the reputation for being the most vulnerable to viruses, worms, and other attacks. One reason for Windows' vulnerability is because its huge user base makes it the biggest target for hackers. Although Microsoft is diligent in its efforts to patch security holes, its programmers are often one step behind the hackers; and while users wait for patches, their computers are vulnerable.

TRY IT!

Which edition of Windows 8 is installed on ARM tablets?

○ Windows RT

○ Windows Pro

○ Windows Server 2012

○ Windows Enterprise

MAC OS

▶ **What's unique about Mac OS? Mac OS** stands for Macintosh Operating System and it is the operating system designed for Apple's Macintosh line of computer systems. As a desktop operating system, Mac OS features a GUI with beautifully designed icons and multiple rectangular work areas to reflect multitasking capabilities.

Unique features of the Mac desktop include the Apple icon, the Dock, and an application menu bar fixed at the top of the screen. Figure 4-21 illustrates some basic features of the Mac desktop.

FIGURE 4-21

You can tell when you're using Mac OS by the Apple logo that appears on the menu bar.
▶ Tour the Mac OS desktop and compare it to the Windows desktop.

4

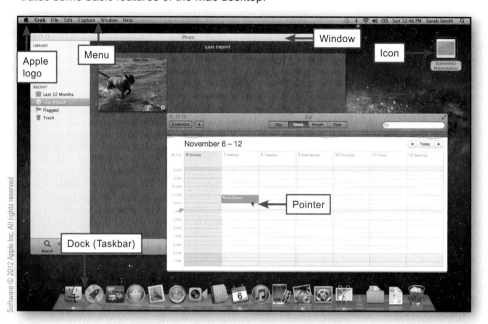

▶ **What do I need to know about the evolution of Mac OS?** Like Windows, Mac OS has been through a number of revisions. The original Classic Mac OS was introduced in 1984 and designed for a line of Macintosh computers based on the Motorola 68000 microprocessor.

In 2001, Classic Mac OS was rewritten to run on Macintosh computers containing PowerPC microprocessors produced by IBM. The new Mac OS was called Mac OS X (the X can be pronounced as either "ten" or the letter "X"). Mac OS X was much more sophisticated than its predecessor, with better memory management and multitasking capabilities.

In 2006, Macintosh hardware changed significantly with the switch from PowerPC to Intel processors. Mac OS X was again rewritten. The first version of Mac OS X to support the Intel architecture was Mac OS X version 10.4.4, sometimes referred to as Tiger. In 2012, Apple released Mac OS X 10.8 (Mountain Lion). A timeline of Mac OS development is detailed in Figure 4-22.

FIGURE 4-22

Mac OS X Timeline

2012	**Mac OS X 10.8 (Mountain Lion)** Offered support for storing files in iCloud, an Internet-based cloud storage and computing service.
2011	**Mac OS X 10.7 (Lion)** Integrated iPad-style gestures and App Store.
2009	**Mac OS X 10.6 (Snow Leopard)** Enhanced version to increase efficiency and reliability.
2007	**Mac OS X 10.5 (Leopard)** Supported both Intel and PowerPC processors; full support for 64-bit applications.
2006	**Mac OS X 10.4.4 (Tiger Intel)** First OS for Intel Macs.
2001	**Mac OS X 10.1 - 10.4 (Cheetah)** Desktop editions for PowerPC; new kernel based on UNIX-like, open source code.

▶ What are the strengths of Mac OS? Mac OS X has a reputation for being an easy-to-use, reliable, and secure operating system. Back when PC owners were struggling with an inscrutable command-line operating system, Macintosh owners were breezing along with a point-and-click GUI. According to industry observers, Macintosh developers have always been in the lead when it comes to intuitive user interface design.

The operating system kernel of Mac OS X is based on UNIX and includes industrial-strength memory protection features that contribute to a low incidence of errors and glitches. Mac OS X inherited a strong security foundation from UNIX that tends to limit the number of security holes and the damage that can be done by hackers who manage to slip in.

Another factor that contributes to the security of computers running Mac OS is that fewer viruses are designed to target Macs because the user base is much smaller than the Windows user base.

Regardless of the relative security of computers running Mac OS X, Macintosh owners should practice safe computing by applying software and OS patches as they become available, activating wireless network encryption, not opening suspicious e-mail attachments, and not clicking links embedded in e-mail messages.

In addition to reliability and security, Mac OS X offers dual boot options and a good virtual machine platform.

▶ What is dual boot? Mac OS X on an Intel Mac offers the ability to run Windows and Windows application software in addition to software designed for the Macintosh. Software called Boot Camp is a **dual boot** utility that can switch between Mac OS X and Windows. When booting, you can select either Mac OS X or Windows (Figure 4-23). To change operating systems, you have to reboot.

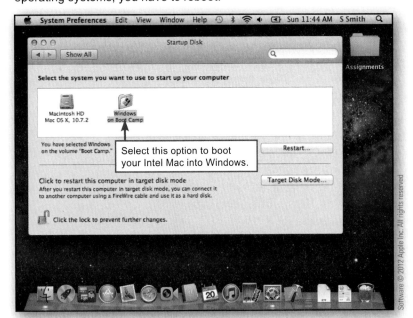

FIGURE 4-23

On a Macintosh computer with Boot Camp, you can boot into Mac OS X or into Windows.
▶ See how it works!

▶ What is a virtual machine? Mac OS X is also a good platform for **virtual machine** (VM) technologies that allow you to use one computer to simulate the hardware and software of another. Each virtual machine has its own simulated processor (or core processor), RAM, video card, input and output ports, and operating system. Each machine can run most software that's compatible with the virtual OS platform.

TRY IT!

Dual boot or _____ machine technology can be used to run two different operating systems on a single computer.

Popular virtual machine software such as VMware and Parallels Desktop can run on most computers with Intel microprocessors, including Intel Macs, PCs, and generic Linux computers. The computer boots into its native OS such as Mac OS, but users can create a virtual machine running guest operating systems, such as Windows. The virtual machine's desktop appears in a window on the host desktop (Figure 4-24).

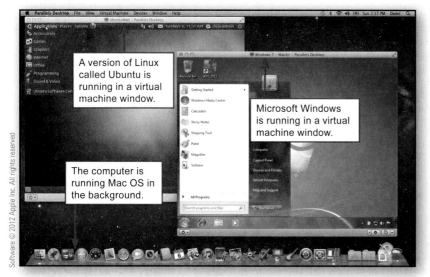

A version of Linux called Ubuntu is running in a virtual machine window.

Microsoft Windows is running in a virtual machine window.

The computer is running Mac OS in the background.

FIGURE 4-24

On a Mac with virtual Windows and Linux, switching from one operating system to another is as simple as selecting a window. When switched to the Windows work area, you can run games, business software, and other applications designed for the Windows OS. By clicking the Linux work area, you could run Linux applications from its vast collection of open source software. After returning to the Mac OS X desktop, you could run your collection of high-end graphics and multimedia iLife software designed exclusively for the Macintosh.

▶ **What are the weaknesses of Mac OS?** The weaknesses of Mac OS include a somewhat limited selection of software and its use of resource forks. A decent collection of software is available for computers that run Mac OS, although the selection is not as vast as the Windows collection. Many of the most prolific software publishers produce one version of their software for Windows and another, similar version for Mac OS.

Macintosh computer owners might find that many popular software titles are not available for Mac OS X. The selection of games, for example, is much sparser than for Windows, although it should be noted that the selection of graphics software for Mac OS X is as good as or better than the selection available for Windows.

▶ **What is a resource fork?** In most operating systems, a file is a single unit that contains data or program code. Files maintained by the Macintosh operating system, however, can have two parts, called forks. The **data fork** is similar to files in other operating systems. It contains data, such as the text for a document, the graphics for a photo, or the commands for a program. The **resource fork** is a companion file that stores information about the data in the data fork, such as the file type and the application that created it.

Although resource forks have advantages on their native Macintosh platform, they can be a nuisance when files are transferred to other platforms. When you copy a file from a Mac to a Windows computer, for example, you end up with two files: one for the data fork and one for the resource fork. The resource fork begins with a period and can usually be ignored or deleted from the Windows directory.

TRY IT!

OS X files have data and resource [_____] .

iOS

▶**What is iOS?** Because Mac OS X was designed for desktop and laptop computers, Apple developed **iOS** as an operating system for the Apple iPhone, which launched in 2007. iOS was subsequently used for the iPod Touch and iPad. All iOS devices use ARM-based microprocessors.

▶**Is iOS related to Mac OS X?** iOS is derived from the Mac OS X code, and shares its UNIX roots. The appearance of iOS has similarities to Mac OS X. Both operating systems feature icons that look three-dimensional.

▶**How does iOS work?** iOS displays a home screen containing application icons. At the bottom of the screen, a dock holds icons for frequently used apps. Touching an app launches it. Pressing the physical Home button located on the device returns the user to the home screen (Figure 4-25).

FIGURE 4-25

iPhones, iPod Touches, and iPads use the iOS operating system.

▶ See how it works!

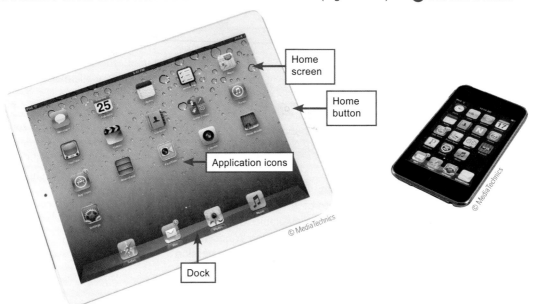

Home screen

Home button

Application icons

Dock

Apps can be grouped into folders to save space on the Home screen. Touching and holding an app icon produces "Jiggle mode" in which icons vibrate to indicate they are in a modifiable state. From Jiggle mode, icons can be deleted or dragged on top of each other to put them into a folder.

iOS was the first operating system to offer routines to manage touchscreen gesture inputs, such as using your fingers to "squeeze" an on-screen graphic into a smaller size.

As a mobile operating system, iOS provides connectivity options, such as 3G and 4G cell phone connections, as well as local networking. Though all iOS devices have Wi-Fi and Bluetooth capability, only iPhones and some iPads have cellular capabilities.

▶**What are the limitations of iOS?** iOS limits your selection of apps to those provided by the online Apple App store, unless you jailbreak the phone. Jailbreaking also overcomes other limitations, such as access to the file system. Unlike full desktop operating systems, iOS does not include a file manager. The only way to access a data file is through the app that was used to create it.

You won't find a desktop with application windows on an iOS device. Each app fills the entire screen. Background processes, such as music, voice calls, and notifications, provide very limited multitasking.

TRY IT!

Which device does NOT use iOS?

○ iPhone

○ MacBook Air

○ iPad

○ iPod Touch

4

ANDROID

▶**What is Android?** **Android** is a mobile operating system that is a popular platform for tablet computers, smartphones, and ebook readers. Android was developed by a consortium of technology companies and unveiled in 2007. It is an open source operating system under the project leadership of Google. As with other popular mobile operating systems, Android is designed for ARM processors.

▶**How does Android work?** Android displays a home screen containing icons that represent software applications. Touching an icon launches the app.

Unlike iOS and Windows RT devices, Android devices have a screen-based home button, rather than a physical button. Touching the on-screen home button recalls the home screen (Figure 4-26).

FIGURE 4-26

All the Android controls can be accessed from the screen.

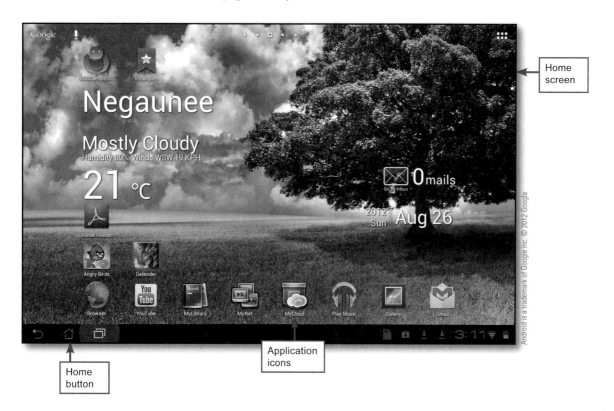

Home screen

Application icons

Home button

▶**What's unique about Android?** In addition to touchscreen input, the Android OS supports voice input for Google searching, voice dialing, navigation, and other applications.

The Android OS contains basic network and routing routines that allow Android devices to become Wi-Fi hotspots. For example, activating the Network utility on an Android-based smartphone transforms the phone into a router, and the phone's data connection can be used by a nearby desktop, laptop, or tablet computer to access the Internet.

Android gives you access to the file system and provides a utility that lets you view the files stored internally or on external SD cards. A third-party file manager utility is required to manipulate files.

TRY IT!

Where can you find the Home button on an Android device?

○ On the Start menu

○ On the system unit

○ Next to the Apple icon

○ At the bottom of the screen

UNIX AND LINUX

▶ **Are UNIX and Linux the same?** The **UNIX** operating system was developed in 1969 at AT&T's Bell Labs. It gained a good reputation for its dependability in multiuser environments, and many versions of it became available for mainframes and microcomputers.

In 1991, a young Finnish student named Linus Torvalds developed the **Linux** (pronounced "LIH nucks") operating system. Linux was inspired by and loosely based on a UNIX derivative called MINIX, created by Andrew Tanenbaum. Linux is frequently used as an operating system for servers. It is not as popular for desktop applications as Windows or Mac OS.

▶ **What are the strengths of Linux?** Linux is rather unique because it is distributed along with its source code under the terms of a GPL (General Public License), which allows everyone to make copies for their own use, to give to others, or to sell. This licensing policy has encouraged programmers to develop Linux utilities, software, and enhancements. Linux is primarily distributed over the Web.

Linux shares several technical features with UNIX, such as multitasking and multiuser capabilities. It is also secure and reliable. Android OS, iOS, and Mac OS are based on UNIX and Linux kernels.

▶ **What are the weaknesses of Linux?** Linux requires more tinkering than the Windows and Mac desktop operating systems. The comparatively limited number of programs that run under Linux also discourages many nontechnical users. A constantly growing collection of high-quality open source software is becoming available for the Linux platform, but many of these applications are targeted toward business and technical users.

▶ **How do I get Linux?** A **Linux distribution** is a download that contains the Linux kernel, system utilities, graphical user interface, applications, and an installation routine. Beginner-friendly Linux distributions include Fedora, Mint, Debian, openSUSE, and Ubuntu (Figure 4-27).

What is significant about UNIX?

○ It is the most dependable mobile operating system

○ It is the basis for Linux, Android, iOS, and Mac OS

○ It is part of the PC platform

○ It is the newest operating system

FIGURE 4-27

Linux users can choose from several graphical interfaces. Pictured here is the popular Ubuntu graphical desktop. ▶ With your interactive eBook, you can tour Linux and compare it to using Windows and Mac OS.

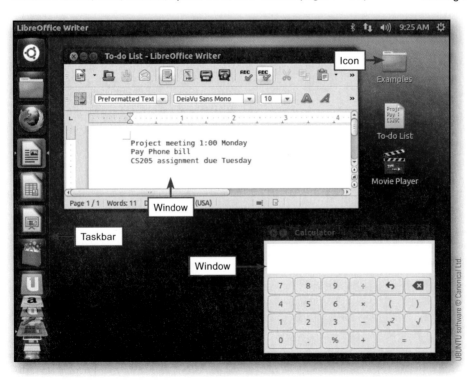

UBUNTU software © Canonical Ltd

4

BLACKBERRY OS

▶ **What's BlackBerry OS?** **BlackBerry OS** is a proprietary operating system produced by RIM, the Canadian company that developed the BlackBerry smartphone. A key feature of BlackBerry OS is its ability to work with corporate e-mail software systems produced by Microsoft and IBM.

▶ **What's unique about BlackBerry OS?** RIM pioneered the idea of **push technology** in which notifications are automatically sent to a device. For example, rather than collect e-mail using a Get Mail button, push technology automatically sends new messages to your device and notifies you when they arrive (Figure 4-28).

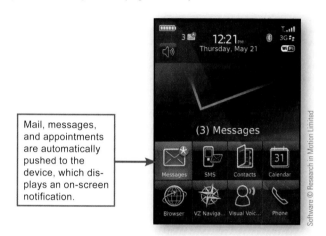

Mail, messages, and appointments are automatically pushed to the device, which displays an on-screen notification.

FIGURE 4-28

BlackBerry devices are known for push technology.

BlackBerry devices can be integrated into a wireless platform designed for corporate-wide secure exchange of encrypted e-mail, calendars, and text messages. The exchange is handled by the BlackBerry Enterprise Server, a software package that can be deployed by independent corporations.

RIM also offers direct Internet connections, which don't require a third-party carrier, such as AT&T or Verizon. As with the enterprise platform, data is encrypted before being sent over secure connections. The significance of encrypted data is that it cannot be intercepted by corporate spies or government censors. In recent years, RIM has been challenged by several governments to establish censorship mechanisms that pierce through the veil of encryption.

QuickCheck   SECTION B

1. Microsoft Windows featured the first graphical user interface. True or false? [   ]

2. A resource [   ] is a companion file created by Mac OS to store information about a file and its data.

3. VMware and Parallels Desktop are examples of [   ] machine technology that can be used to run Windows software on a Mac.

4. The operating system for iPads, iPod Touches, and iPhones is called [   ].

5. Tablets and smartphones with the [   ] operating system have a screen-based home button, rather than a physical button.

 CHECK ANSWERS

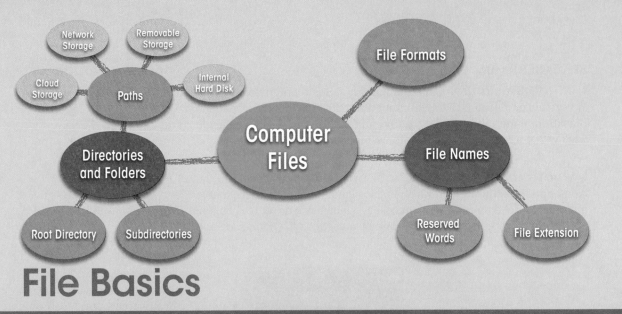

File Basics

COMPUTER FILES IN DIGITAL format offer a compact and convenient way to store documents, photos, videos, and music. Computer files have several characteristics, such as a name, format, location, size, and date. To make effective use of computer files, you'll need a good understanding of these file basics, and that is the focus of Section C.

FILE NAMES AND EXTENSIONS

▶ **What is a computer file?** As you learned in Chapter 1, a computer file—or simply a file—is defined as a named collection of data that exists on a storage medium, such as a hard disk, CD, DVD, or USB flash drive. A file can contain a group of records, a document, a photo, music, a video, an e-mail message, or a computer program.

▶ **What are the rules for naming files?** Every file has a name and might also have a file extension. When you save a file, you must provide a valid file name that adheres to specific rules, referred to as **file-naming conventions**. Each operating system has a unique set of file-naming conventions. Figure 4-29 lists file-naming conventions for the current versions of Windows and Mac OS.

▶ **Is there a maximum length for file names?** Current versions of Windows and Mac OS support file names up to 255 characters long. In practice, some of the 255 characters are used for the file's drive letter, folder designation, and extension, so the name you assign to a file should be much shorter. A file name limitation of 255 characters gives you the flexibility to use descriptive file names, such as *Household Budget 2014*, so that you can easily identify what a file contains.

▶ **What is a file extension?** A **file extension** (sometimes referred to as a file name extension) is an optional file identifier that is separated from the main file name by a period, as in *Paint.exe*. File extensions provide clues to a file's contents. For example .exe files (Windows) and .app files (Mac OS) contain computer programs.

▶ **Why are certain characters not allowed in a file name?** If an operating system attaches special significance to a symbol, you might not be able to use it in a file name. For example, Windows uses the colon (:) character to separate the device letter from a file name or folder, as in

FIGURE 4-29

Windows File-naming Conventions

Case sensitive	No
Maximum length of file name	File name, path, and extension cannot exceed 255 characters
Spaces allowed	Yes
Numbers allowed	Yes
Characters not allowed	* \ : < > | " / ?
File names not allowed	Aux, Com1, Com2, Com3, Com4, Con, Lpt1, Lpt2, Lpt3, Prn, Nul

Macintosh File-naming Conventions

Case sensitive	No
Maximum length of file name	File name, path, and extension cannot exceed 255 characters
Spaces allowed	Yes
Numbers allowed	Yes
Characters not allowed	: (the colon)

C:Music. A file name that contains a colon, such as *Report:2014*, is not valid because the operating system would become confused about how to interpret the colon. When you use Windows applications, avoid using the symbols : * \ < > | " / and ? in file names.

▶ **What are reserved words?** Some operating systems also contain a list of **reserved words** that are used as commands or special identifiers. You cannot use these words alone as a file name. You can, however, use these words as part of a longer file name. For example, under Windows, the file name *Nul* would not be valid, but you could name a file something like *Nul Committee Notes.docx* or *Null Set.exe*.

▶ **What else should I know about creating file names?** Some operating systems are case sensitive, but not those you regularly work with on personal computers. Feel free to use uppercase and lower-case letters in file names that you create on PCs and Macs.

You can also use spaces in file names. That's a different rule than for e-mail addresses, where spaces are not allowed. You've probably noticed that people often use underscores or periods instead of spaces in e-mail addresses such as Madi_Jones@msu.edu. That convention is not necessary in file names, so a file name such as *Letter to Madi Jones* is valid.

FILE DIRECTORIES AND FOLDERS

▶ **How do I designate a file's location?** To designate a file's location, you must first specify the device where the file is stored. As shown in Figure 4-30, you can store files on a hard drive, removable storage, a network computer, or cloud-based storage.

4

FIGURE 4-30

Files can be stored on local devices, on a network, or in the cloud. Before storing files on a network, you might need permission. To store files using a cloud-based service, such as Microsoft's SkyDrive, you'll have to sign up for an account.

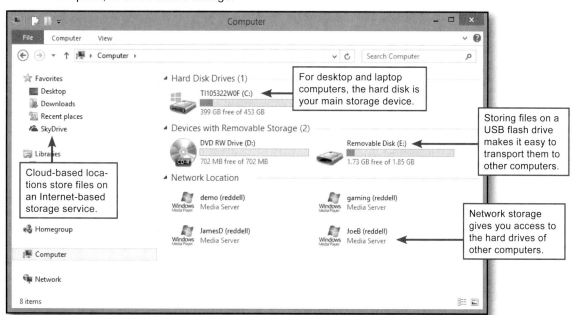

▶ **What does C: mean?** When working with Windows, each local storage device is identified by a device letter. The main hard disk drive is referred to as drive C. A device letter is usually followed by a colon, so C: is typically the designation for a hard disk drive. See if you can spot it in the figure above. Removable storage devices are assigned drive letters when they are inserted.

Macs do not use drive letters. Every storage device has a name. The main hard disk is called Macintosh HD, for example.

▶ **What is a disk partition?** A **disk partition** is a section of a hard disk drive that is treated as a separate storage unit. Most computers are configured with a single hard disk partition that contains the operating system, programs, and data. However, it is possible to create more than one hard disk partition. For example, a PC owner might set up one partition for operating system files and another partition for programs and data. This arrangement sometimes can speed up the process of disinfecting a computer that has been attacked by malicious software.

Partitions can be assigned drive letters. In the example above, the operating system files would be stored in partition C. The program and data file partition would probably be designated as drive D. Partitions are not the same thing as folders. Partitions are more permanent, and a special utility is required to create, modify, or delete them.

▶ **Do I have to remember where I put each file?** Every storage device has a **directory** containing a list of its files. The main directory is referred to as the **root directory**. On a PC, the root directory is identified by the device letter followed by a backslash. For example, the root directory of the hard disk would be C:\. A root directory can be subdivided into smaller lists. Each list is called a **subdirectory**.

▶ **What is a folder?** When you use Windows, Mac OS, or a Linux graphical file manager, each subdirectory is depicted as a **folder**. Folders help you envision your files as if they were stored in a filing cabinet. Each folder can hold related items; for example, a set of documents, sound clips, financial data, or photos for a school project. Windows provides a folder called My Documents that you might use to hold reports, letters, and so on. You can also create and name folders to meet your needs, such as a folder called QuickBooks to hold your personal finance data.

Folders can be created within other folders. You might, for example, create a Jazz folder within your Music folder to hold a collection of jazz tracks, and another folder named Reggae to hold your reggae music collection.

A folder name is separated from a drive letter and other folder names by a special symbol. In Microsoft Windows, this symbol is the backslash (\). For example, the folder for your reggae music (within the Music folder on drive C) would be written as C:\Music\Reggae. Other operating systems use a forward slash (/) to separate folders.

A computer file's location is defined by a **file specification** (sometimes called a **path**), which on a PC includes the drive letter, folder(s), file name, and extension. Suppose that you have stored an MP3 file called *Marley One Love* in the Reggae folder on your hard disk. Its file specification is shown in Figure 4-31.

> **TERMINOLOGY NOTE**
>
> Drive letter assignments are based on conventions that date back to the first PCs. The original IBM PCs shipped with a single floppy disk drive and it was designated drive A. An enhanced PC later shipped with two floppy disk drives, designated A and B. When hard disk drives were eventually added to PC systems, they were designated drive C.

> **TRY IT!**
>
> Look at the directory listing for your computer's hard disk. How many folders does the root directory contain?
>
> [   ]

FIGURE 4-31

A file specification provides the name and location of a file.

C:\Music\Reggae\Marley One Love.mp3

| Drive letter | Primary folder | Secondary folder | File name | File extension |

FILE FORMATS

▶ **What is a file format?** The term **file format** refers to the organization and layout of data that is stored in a file. As you might expect, music files are stored differently than text files or graphics files; but even within a single category of data, there are many file formats. For example, graphics data can be stored in file formats such as BMP, GIF, JPEG, or PNG.

The format of a file usually includes a header, data, and possibly an end-of-file marker. A **file header** is a section of data at the beginning of a file that contains information about a file, such as the date it was created, the date it was last updated, its size, and its file type.

The remaining contents of a file depend on whether it contains text, graphics, audio, or multimedia data. A text file, for example, might contain sentences and paragraphs interspersed with codes for centering, boldfacing, and margin settings. A graphics file might contain color data for each pixel, followed by a description of the color palette. Figure 4-32 illustrates the format for a Windows bitmap (BMP) file and contrasts it with the format of a GIF file.

TRY IT!

What happens to the contents of a file if you change its file name extension?

○ Nothing happens

○ The contents are erased

○ The contents are converted into a format that corresponds to the extension

○ The extension is added to the file header

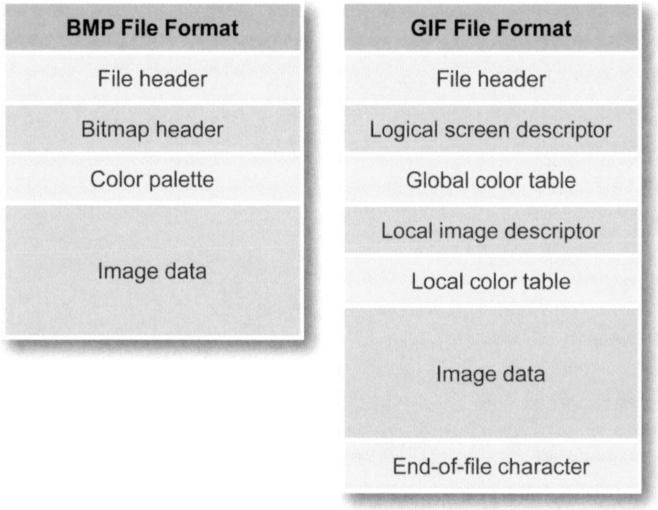

4

BMP File Format	GIF File Format
File header	File header
Bitmap header	Logical screen descriptor
Color palette	Global color table
Image data	Local image descriptor
	Local color table
	Image data
	End-of-file character

FIGURE 4-32

Although BMP and GIF file formats contain graphics, the file layouts differ.

▶ **Is a file extension the same as a file format?** No. Although a file extension is a good indicator of a file's format, it does not really define the format. You could use the Rename command to change a QuickTime movie called *Balloons.mov* to *Balloons.docx*. Despite the .docx extension, the file is still in QuickTime format because the data elements in the file are arranged in a specific configuration unique to QuickTime.

▶ **What should I know about file formats?** Each software application works with specific file formats. When you use the Open dialog box, most applications automatically comb through your files to display a list of files that are stored in file formats they can use.

Some operating systems also do a fairly good job of shielding users from the intricacies of file formats. For example, Windows uses a file association list to link file formats with corresponding application software so that when you double-click a file name, your computer automatically opens a software application that works with the correct file format.

With all this help from the operating system and your application software, it might seem that knowing about file formats is unimportant. However, understanding file formats is useful for accomplishing tasks such as those listed in Figure 4-33.

FIGURE 4-33

Understanding file formats helps you perform the following tasks:

▶ Figure out the correct format for e-mail attachments that you send to friends or colleagues.

▶ Find the right player software for music and media files that you download from the Web.

▶ Discover how to work with a file that doesn't seem to open.

▶ Convert files from one format to another.

Which file formats am I most likely to encounter? A Windows software program consists of at least one executable file with an .exe file extension. It might also include a number of support programs with extensions such as .dll, .vbx, and .ocx. Configuration and startup files usually have .bat, .sys, .ini, and .bin extensions. In addition, you'll find files with .hlp and .tmp extensions. Files with .hlp extensions hold the information for a program's Help utility.

Files with .tmp extensions are temporary files. When you open a data file with software applications, such as word processors, spreadsheets, and graphics tools, your operating system makes a copy of the original file and stores this copy on disk as a temporary file. It is this temporary file that you work with as you view and revise a file.

To the uninitiated, the file extensions associated with programs and the operating system might seem odd. Nevertheless, executable and support files—even so-called temporary files—are crucial for the correct operation of your computer system. You should not manually delete them. The table in Figure 4-34 lists file extensions associated with the Windows operating system and executable files.

TRY IT!

Suppose your friend sends you a file with an .ods extension. You can probably open it with what?

❍ Graphics software

❍ LibreOffice

❍ Microsoft Publisher

❍ iTunes

FIGURE 4-34

Executable File Extensions

Type of File	Description	Extension
Batch file	A sequence of operating system commands executed automatically when the computer boots	.bat
Configuration file	Information about programs the computer uses to allocate the resources necessary to run them	.cfg .sys .mif .bin .ini
Help	The information displayed by on-screen Help	.hlp
Temporary file	A sort of scratch pad that contains data while a file is open, but is discarded when you close the file	.tmp
Support program	Program instructions executed along with the main .exe file for a program	.ocx .vbx .vbs .dll
Program	The main executable files for a computer program	.exe .com .app (Mac OS)

The list of data file formats is long, but becoming familiar with the most popular formats (shown in Figure 4-35) and the type of data they contain is useful, whether you are using a PC or Mac.

FIGURE 4-35

Data File Extensions

Type of File	Extensions
Text	.txt .dat .rtf .docx (Microsoft Word) .doc (Microsoft Word 2003) .odt (OpenDocument text) .wpd (WordPerfect) .pages (iWork)
Sound	.wav .mid .mp3 .m4p .aac
Graphics	.bmp .tif .wmf .gif .jpg .png .eps .ai (Adobe Illustrator)
Animation/video	.flc .swf .avi .mpg .mp4 .mov (QuickTime) .wmv (Windows Media Player)
Web page	.htm .html .asp .vrml .php
Spreadsheet	.xlsx (Microsoft Excel) .xls (Microsoft Excel 2003) .ods (OpenDocument spreadsheet) .numbers (iWork)
Database	.accdb (Microsoft Access) .odb (OpenDocument database)
Miscellaneous	.pdf (Adobe Acrobat) .pptx (Microsoft PowerPoint) .qxp (QuarkXPress) .odp (OpenDocument presentations) .zip (WinZip) .pub (Microsoft Publisher)

How do I know which files a program will open? A software application can open files that exist in its **native file format**, plus several additional file formats. For example, Microsoft Word opens files in its native DOCX (.docx) format, plus files in formats such as HTML (.htm or .html), Text (.txt), and Rich Text Format (.rtf).

Within the Windows environment, you can discover which formats a particular software program can open by looking at the list of file types in the Open dialog box, as shown in Figure 4-36.

FIGURE 4-36

An application's Open dialog box usually displays a list of file formats the program can open. You can also look for an Import option on the File menu.

4

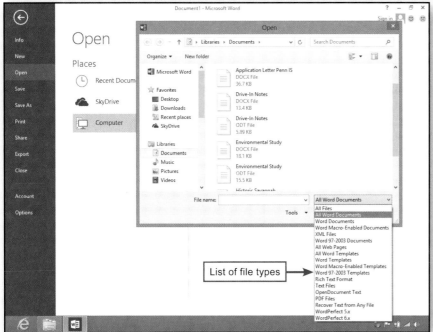

List of file types

Why can't I open some files? Suppose you receive an e-mail attachment called *Cool.tif*. "Aha!," you say to yourself, "My Photoshop software ought to open that file." You try—several times—but all you get is an error message. When a file doesn't open, one of three things probably went wrong:

▶ The file might have been damaged—a techie would call it corrupted—by a transmission or disk error. Although you might be able to use file recovery software to repair the damage, it is usually easier to obtain an undamaged copy of the file from its original source.

▶ Someone might have inadvertently changed the file extension. While renaming the Cool file, perhaps the original .bmp extension was changed to .tif. If you have a little time, you can change the file extension and try to open the file. If a file contains a graphic, chances are that it should have the extension for one of the popular graphics formats, such as .bmp, .gif, .jpg, .tif, or .png. Otherwise, you should contact the source of the file to get accurate information about its real format.

▶ Some file formats exist in several variations, and your software might not have the capability to open a particular variation of the format. You might be able to open the file if you use different application software. For example, Photoshop might not be able to open a particular file with a .tif file extension, but Corel PaintShop Pro might open it.

TRY IT!

Check your word processing software. If a friend sends you a file in .doc format, can you open it? _____

▶ What if all my software fails to open a particular file format? Although a computer might be able to discover a file's format, it might not necessarily know how to work with it. Just as you might be able to identify a helicopter, you can't necessarily fly it without some instructions. Your computer also requires a set of instructions to use most file formats. These instructions are provided by software. To use a particular file format, you must make sure your computer has the corresponding software.

Many files downloaded from the Web require special player or reader software. For example, PDF files require software called Adobe Reader, Flash video files require the Adobe Flash Player, and OGG music files require a player such as Winamp. Suppose you download a file with an .ogg extension and none of your current software works with this file format (Figure 4-37).

FIGURE 4-37

A download from the music group Epoq is in OGG format. To play the file, you'll need software that works with the OGG file format.

Typically, you can follow a link from the Web page that supplied your file download to find a site from which you can download the necessary player or reader software. When such a link is not provided, you can google the file type or extension. Several Web sites provide lists of file formats and corresponding software. By looking up a file extension in one of these lists, you can find out what application software you'll need to download and install.

TRY IT!

Check your computer. Do you have software that reads PDF files? [   ]

▶ How do I know what kinds of file formats I can send to other people? Unless you know what application software is installed on your friends' computers, you won't know for certain whether they can open a particular file you've sent. There's a good chance, however, that your friends can open files saved in common document formats such as Microsoft Word's DOCX or Adobe Reader's PDF format; graphics formats such as PNG, TIFF, or JPEG; and music formats such as MP3 and WAV. You should check with the recipient before sending files in less common, proprietary formats, such as Adobe Illustrator's AI format and QuarkXPress's QXP format.

▶ Is it possible to convert a file from one format to another? Perhaps you created a Word document on your PC, but you need to convert it into a format that's usable by your colleague who is using LibreOffice Writer. Or suppose you want to convert a Word document into HTML format so that you can post it on the Web. You might also want to convert a BMP graphic into JPEG format so that you can include it on a Web page.

The easiest way to convert a file from one format to another is to find application software that works with both file formats. Open the file using that software, and then use the Export option, or the Save As dialog box, to select a new file format, assign the file a new name, and save it (Figure 4-38).

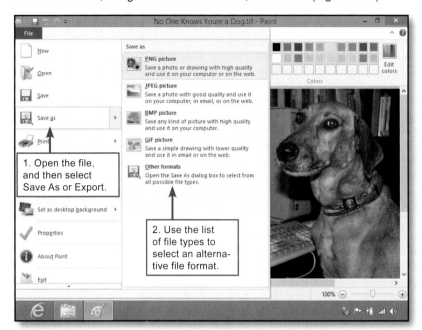

FIGURE 4-38

An easy way to convert a file from one format to another is to open it with an application that supports both file formats, and then use the Save As dialog box to select an alternative file format. ▶ Discover the native file formats for Adobe Reader and Windows Paint. Your interactive eBook also shows you how to adjust the Windows setting for showing or hiding file extensions.

▶ **Will a converted document be identical to the original?** Many file formats convert easily to another format, and the resulting file is virtually indistinguishable from the original. Some conversions, however, do not retain all the characteristics of the original file. When you convert a DOCX file into HTML format, for example, the HTML page does not contain any of the headers, footers, superscripts, page numbers, special characters, or page breaks that existed in the original DOCX file.

When you need a conversion routine for an obscure file format, or if you need to make conversions between many different file formats, consider specialized conversion software, available through commercial or shareware outlets.

QuickCheck

1. .bmp, .docx, .exe, and .mov are examples of file [_____] .

2. When using Windows, you cannot use a(n) [_____] word, such as Aux, as a file name.

3. A disk [_____] is a section of a hard disk drive that is treated as a separate storage unit.

4. A software application automatically stores files in its [_____] file format unless you specify otherwise.

5. When you convert a DOCX file into HTML format, the resulting file is virtually indistinguishable from the original. True or false? [_____]

 CHECK ANSWERS

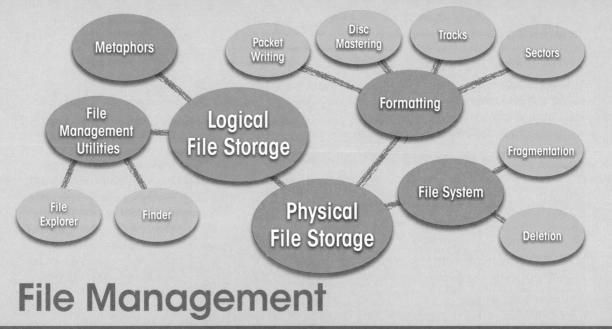

File Management

FILE MANAGEMENT ENCOMPASSES any procedure that helps you organize your computer-based files so that you can find and use them more efficiently. Depending on your computer's operating system, you can organize and manipulate files from within an application program or by using a special file management utility provided by the operating system. Section D offers an overview of application-based and operating system–based file management.

APPLICATION-BASED FILE MANAGEMENT

▶ **How does a software application help me manage files?** Applications generally provide a way to open files and save them in a specific folder on a designated storage device. Some applications also allow you to delete and rename files.

▶ **What should I know about saving files?** Saving files is easy. Simply use the Save option provided by your application, specify a location for the file, and give it a name. Some applications allow you to add a **file tag** that describes the file's contents (Figure 4-39).

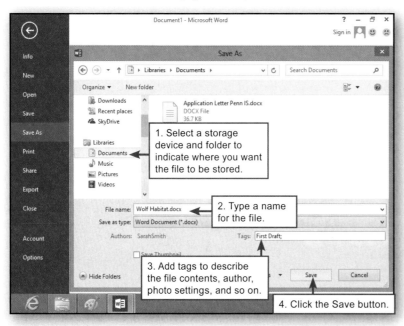

FIGURE 4-39

Some PC applications, such as Microsoft Word, let you enter file tags when you save a file. ▶ Learn more about the Save As dialog box and sort out the differences between it and the Save option.

212

▶ What's the difference between the Save option and the Save As option? The Save As option allows you to select a name and storage device for a file, whereas the Save option simply saves the latest version of a file under its current name and at its current location.

A potentially confusing situation occurs when you try to use the Save option for a file that doesn't yet have a name. Because you can't save a file without a name, your application displays the Save As dialog box, even though you selected the Save option. So when do you use Save and when do you use Save As? Consider the alternatives in Figure 4-40.

Save or Save As When saving a file for the first time, you can use Save or Save As.

Save When you've revised a file and want to save just the newly revised file with the same name and on the same storage device, use Save.

Save as When you've revised a file and want to save the original version in addition to the newly revised version, use Save As, give the file a different name, and/or select a different storage location.

▶ Can I create a new folder while saving a file? Your computer's operating system supplies a ready-made set of folders for storing documents, music, videos, and downloads. You might want to better organize the files in these folders by creating subfolders.

When saving a file, if you don't see a suitable folder for it, create a new folder as shown in Figure 4-41.

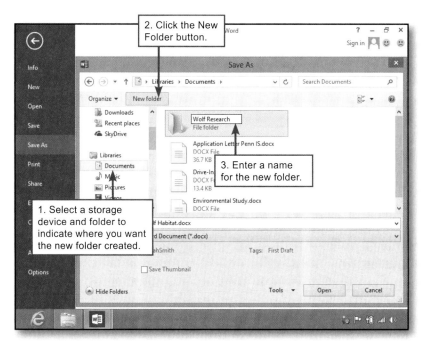

▶ **How about saving files on Macs?** The latest versions of Mac OS have no Save As command. Figure 4-42 details how to use the Save, Duplicate, and Rename commands to accomplish file saving tasks.

FIGURE 4-42

Command Options for Saving Files Under Mac OS

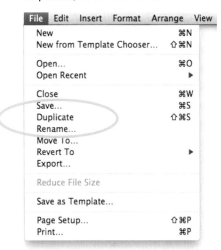

Save Use this option when saving a file for the first time or after you've revised a file and want to save the revisions.

Duplicate Use this option when you want to save a copy of a file, such as when you've revised a document but want to keep the original version in addition to the revised version.

Rename Use this option along with the Duplicate option to give your revised version a different name than the original.

▶ **Can I add tags to Mac files?** File tags are a type of **metadata** that describes the contents of a file. The term **metadata** essentially means "data about data." File tags are metadata that describe the data contained in a file.

You can use tags to specify keywords for a file that will later help you search for it; for example, if you can't remember the file name. Tags can also be used to annotate the file with information you want to remember, such as the status of a document that is in process, or the camera setting you used to create a particularly stunning photo.

Whereas Windows applications let you add tags as you save a file, Mac applications are tagged after they've been created using the Spotlight Comments field of the Get Info dialog box. Figure 4-43 explains how.

FIGURE 4-43

Use Get Info to add tags to Mac files.

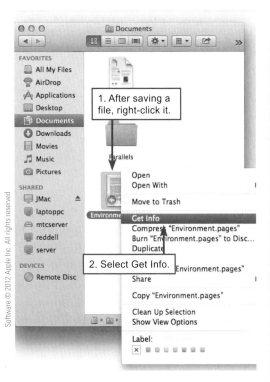

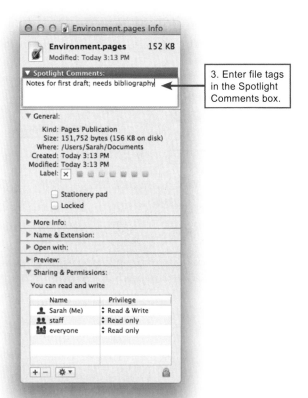

FILE MANAGEMENT METAPHORS

▶ **How does the operating system help me manage files?** Although most application software gives you access to commands you can use to open, save, and rename files, you might want to work with groups of files or perform other file operations that are inconvenient within the Open or Save dialog boxes.

For these other tasks, you can use a **file management utility**, such as the Windows File Explorer or the Mac OS X Finder.

▶ **How can a file management utility help me visualize my computer's file storage?** File management utilities often use some sort of storage metaphor to help you visualize and mentally organize the files on your disks and other storage devices. These metaphors are also called **logical storage models** because they are supposed to help you form a mental (logical) picture of the way in which your files are stored.

▶ **What storage metaphors are typically used for personal computers?** After hearing so much about files and folders, you might have guessed that the filing cabinet is a popular metaphor for computer storage. In this metaphor, each storage device corresponds to one of the drawers in a filing cabinet. The drawers hold folders and the folders hold files.

Another storage metaphor is based on a hierarchical diagram that is sometimes referred to as a tree structure. In this metaphor, a tree represents a storage device.

The trunk of the tree corresponds to the root directory. The branches of the tree represent folders. These branches can split into small branches representing folders within folders. The leaves at the end of a branch represent the files in a particular folder (Figure 4-44).

The tree structure metaphor offers a useful mental image of the way in which files and folders are organized. It is not, however, particularly practical as a user interface. For practicality, storage metaphors are translated into more mundane screen displays. Figure 4-45 shows how Microsoft programmers combined the filing cabinet metaphor to depict a tree structure in the Windows file management utility.

FIGURE 4-44

You can visualize the directory of a disk as a tree on its side. The trunk corresponds to the root directory, the branches to folders, and the leaves to files.

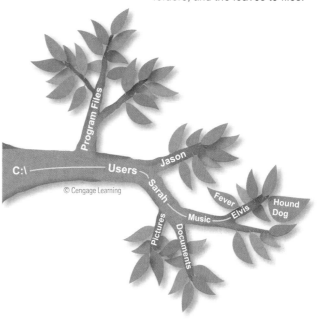

4

FIGURE 4-45

File Explorer borrows folders from the filing cabinet metaphor and places them in a hierarchical structure similar to a tree on its side.

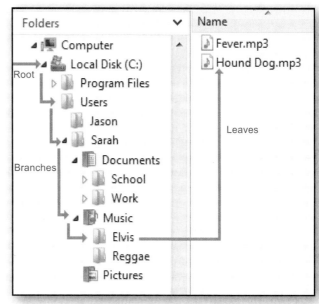

FILE EXPLORER

▶ **How do I use a file management utility?** As an example of a file management utility, take a closer look at **File Explorer**, a utility program bundled with the Windows operating system and designed to help you organize and manipulate the files stored on your computer.

The File Explorer window is divided into several window panes. The pane on the left side of the window lists each of the storage devices connected to your computer, plus several important system objects, such as Desktop and Computer.

An icon for a storage device or other system object can be expanded by clicking its corresponding ▷ symbol. Expanding an icon displays the next level of the storage hierarchy—usually a collection of folders.

A device icon or folder can be opened by clicking directly on the icon rather than on the ▷ symbol. Once an icon is opened, its contents appear in the pane on the right side of the File Explorer window. Figure 4-46 illustrates how to manipulate the directory display.

FIGURE 4-46

File Explorer makes it easy to drill down through the levels of the directory hierarchy to locate a folder or file.
▶ Learn how to navigate through the hierarchy of folders by watching the tour for this figure in your interactive eBook.

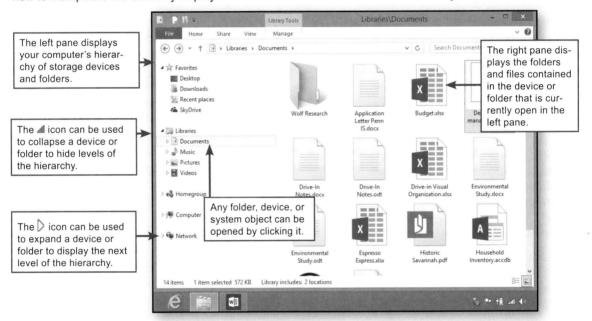

The left pane displays your computer's hierarchy of storage devices and folders.

The ◢ icon can be used to collapse a device or folder to hide levels of the hierarchy.

The ▷ icon can be used to expand a device or folder to display the next level of the hierarchy.

Any folder, device, or system object can be opened by clicking it.

The right pane displays the folders and files contained in the device or folder that is currently open in the left pane.

▶ **What can I do with the folders and files that are listed in File Explorer?** In addition to locating files and folders, File Explorer helps you manipulate files and folders in the following ways:

▶ **Rename.** You might want to change the name of a file or folder to better describe its contents.

▶ **Copy.** You can copy a file from one device to another—for example, from a USB drive to the hard disk drive. You can also make a copy of a document so that you can revise the copy and leave the original intact.

▶ **Move.** You can move a file from one folder to another or from one storage device to another. When you move a file, it is erased from its original location, so make sure you remember the new location of the file. You can also move an entire folder and its contents from one storage device to another storage device, or move it to a different folder.

▶ **Delete.** You can delete a file when you no longer need it. You can also delete a folder. Be careful when you delete a folder because most file management utilities also delete all the files within a folder.

TRY IT!

In Figure 4-46, what is the status of the Favorites folder?

○ Expanded

○ Collapsed

○ Deleted

○ Restored

◗ Can I work with more than one file or folder at a time?
To work with a group of files or folders, you must first select them. You can accomplish this task in several ways. You can hold down the Ctrl key (Command key on the Mac) as you click each item. This method works well if you are selecting files or folders that are not listed consecutively.

As an alternative, you can hold down the Shift key while you click the first item and the last item you want to select. By using the Shift key method, you select the two items that you clicked and all the items in between. After a group of items is selected, you can use the same copy, move, or delete procedure that you would use for a single item.

◗ What are personal folders?
Windows offers a set of preconfigured personal folders, such as My Documents and My Music, for storing your personal data files. Windows also supplies preconfigured Public folders, such as Public Documents and Public Pictures, that can be used to store files you want to share with other network users (Figure 4-47).

◗ What is a library?
In addition to folders, Windows 7 and 8 offer libraries that are handy for organizing and accessing the files you use for projects. A **library** is similar to a folder only in the sense that it can be used to group similar files; however, a library doesn't actually store files. Instead, it contains a set of links to files that are stored on various devices and in various folders.

Macs also have a Library folder, but its purpose is quite different from the Windows Library folder. The Mac Library folder is used for system files and should not be used for your data files.

To understand how you might use libraries in Windows, think about a collection of music files. Some files might be stored on your hard disk in the My Music folder. You might be using other music files for the soundtrack of a movie project stored in a folder called Soundtracks that is stored along with the video footage. Your Music library can contain links to the music files in both folders so that you can access them all from the same list (Figure 4-48).

FIGURE 4-47

Windows supplies a set of pre-configured personal folders and a corresponding set of Public folders.

◢ 📁 Libraries
   ◢ 📄 Documents
      ▷ 📋 My Documents
      ▷ 📁 Public Documents
   ◢ 🎵 Music
      ▷ 📁 My Music
      ▷ 📁 Public Music
   ◢ 🖼 Pictures
      ▷ 📋 My Pictures
      ▷ 📁 Public Pictures
   ◢ 🎬 Videos
      ▷ 📋 My Videos
      ▷ 📁 Public Videos

FIGURE 4-48

A library is not a "real" location; it is more like an index in a book because it points to the location of a file.
◗ Find out how to use libraries to organize files for your projects.

TERMINOLOGY NOTE

In Windows, libraries and personal folders have similar names, which can be confusing. Personal folders are labeled with "My" as in My Documents. The name of the corresponding library is simply Documents.

FILE MANAGEMENT TIPS

A file management utility provides tools and procedures to help you keep track of your program and data files, but these tools are most useful when you have a logical plan for organizing your files and when you follow some basic file management guidelines. Consider the following tips for managing files on your own computer. When working with files on lab computers, follow the guidelines from your instructor or lab manager.

▶ **Use descriptive names.** Give your files and folders descriptive names, and avoid using cryptic abbreviations.

▶ **Maintain file extensions.** When renaming a file, keep the original file extension so that it can be opened with the correct application software.

▶ **Group similar files.** Separate files into folders based on subject matter. For example, store your creative writing assignments in one folder and your MP3 music files in another folder.

▶ **Organize your folders from the top down.** When devising a hierarchy of folders, consider how you want to access files and back them up. For example, it is easy to specify one folder and its subfolders for a backup. If your important data is scattered in a variety of folders, however, making backups is more time consuming.

▶ **Consider using default folders.** You should use personal folders, such as My Documents and My Music, as your main data folders. Add subfolders to these personal folders as necessary to organize your files.

▶ **Use Public folders for files you want to share.** Use the Public folders for files that you want to share with other network users.

▶ **Do not mix data files and program files.** Do not store data files in the folders that hold your software—on Windows systems, most software is stored in subfolders of the Program Files folder; on Macs, in the Applications folder.

▶ **Don't store files in the root directory.** Although it is acceptable to create folders in the root directory, it is not a good practice to store programs or data files in the root directory of your computer's hard disk.

▶ **Access files from the hard disk.** For best performance, copy files from USB drives or CDs to your computer's hard disk before accessing them.

▶ **Follow copyright rules.** When copying files, make sure you adhere to copyright and license restrictions.

▶ **Delete or archive files you no longer need.** Deleting unneeded files and folders helps keep your list of files from growing to an unmanageable size.

▶ **Be aware of storage locations.** When you save files, be sure to specify the correct storage device and folder.

▶ **Back up!** Back up your folders regularly.

PHYSICAL FILE STORAGE

▶ **Is data stored in specific places on a disk?** So far, you've seen how an operating system such as Windows can help you visualize computer storage as files and folders. This logical storage model, however, has little to do with what actually happens on your disk. The structure of files and folders you see in File Explorer is called a logical model because it is supposed to help you create a mental picture. A **physical storage model** describes what actually happens on the disks and in the circuits. As you will see, the physical model is quite different from the logical model.

TRY IT!

Check the root directory of your computer. Does it contain any data files? [   ]

Before a computer can store a file on a disk, CD, DVD, or BD, the storage medium must be formatted. The **formatting** process creates the equivalent of electronic storage bins by dividing a disk into **tracks** and then further dividing each track into **sectors**.

Tracks and sectors are numbered to provide addresses for each data storage bin. The numbering scheme depends on the storage device and the operating system. On hard disks, tracks are arranged as concentric circles; on CDs, DVDs, and BDs, one or more tracks spiral out from the center of the disk (Figure 4-49).

FIGURE 4-49

A process called formatting prepares the surface of a disk to hold data in storage areas called sectors.

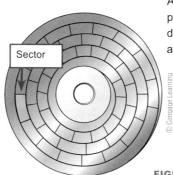

Sector

© Cengage Learning

How does a disk get formatted? Today, most hard disks are preformatted at the factory. CDs, DVDs, and BDs are formatted by the utilities that you use when you copy data files to them. Before you write data to a CD, DVD, or BD, you usually have the option of formatting it for mastering or for packet writing (Figure 4-50).

FIGURE 4-50

CDs and DVDs can be created using mastering or packet-writing techniques. Mastering creates discs that can be used more reliably on a wide variety of computers and standalone players. Packet writing is more flexible for discs that you plan to use only on your own computer.

- **Disc mastering** is the process of creating a CD, DVD, or BD by selecting all the files and then copying them in a single session. The process can take some time—especially when burning a full DVD or BD. Mastered discs are compatible with the largest number of computer optical drives and standalone players. Mastering also works well if you want to burn several copies of a disc.

- **Packet writing** is a recording technology that lets you record in multiple sessions. For example, you can copy a few files to a CD during one session, and then at a later date record additional files to the same CD. In Windows terminology, CDs, DVDs, and BDs formatted for packet writing are referred to as Live File System discs.

Packet writing is faster and more flexible than mastering, but discs created with packet writing might not work on all computers. A process called closing helps make the discs more compatible; but once a disc is closed, no more data can be added to it.

Burn a Disc   ✕

How do you want to use this disc?

Disc title: Soundtrack

● **Like a USB flash drive**
   Save, edit, and delete files on the disc anytime. The disc will work on computers running Windows XP or later. (Live File System)

○ **With a CD/DVD player**
   Burn files in groups and individual files can't be edited or removed after burning. The disc will also work on most computers. (Mastered)

Which one should I choose?

Next   Cancel

How does the operating system keep track of a file's location? The operating system uses a **file system** to keep track of the names and locations of files that reside on a storage medium, such as a hard disk. Different operating systems use different file systems. For example, Mac OS X uses the Macintosh Hierarchical File System Plus (HFS+). Ext3fs (Third Extended File System) is the native file system for Linux. Microsoft Windows 8, 7, NT, 2000, XP, and Vista use a file system called NTFS (New Technology File System).

To speed up the process of storing and retrieving data, a disk drive usually works with a group of sectors called a **cluster** or a block. The number of sectors that form a cluster varies, depending on the capacity of the disk and the way the operating system works with files. A file system's primary task is to maintain a list of clusters and keep track of which are empty and which hold data. This information is stored in a special index file. If your computer uses NTFS, the index file is called the Master File Table (MFT).

TRY IT!

Which formatting option should you use to burn a DVD that can be used in the largest number of computers?

○ Disc mastering

○ Packet writing

○ Live File system

○ iTunes

Each of your disks contains its own index file so that information about its contents is always available when the disk is in use. Unfortunately, storing this crucial file on disk also presents a risk because if the index file is damaged by a hard disk head crash or corrupted by a virus, you'll generally lose access to all the data stored on the disk. Index files become damaged all too frequently, so it is important to back up your data.

When you save a file, your PC's operating system looks at the index file to see which clusters are empty. It selects one of these empty clusters, records the file data there, and then revises the index file to include the new file name and its location.

A file that does not fit into a single cluster spills over into the next contiguous (meaning adjacent) cluster, unless that cluster already contains data. When contiguous clusters are not available, the operating system stores parts of a file in noncontiguous (nonadjacent) clusters. Figure 4-51 helps you visualize how an index file, such as the MFT, keeps track of file names and locations.

FIGURE 4-51

Each colored cluster on the disk contains part of a file. *Bio.txt* is stored in contiguous clusters. *Jordan.wks* is stored in noncontiguous clusters. A computer locates and displays the *Jordan.wks* file by looking for its name in the Master File Table.

Master File Table

File	Cluster	Comment
MFT	1	Reserved for MFT files
DISK USE	2	Part of MFT that contains a list of empty sectors
Bio.txt	3, 4	Bio.txt file stored in clusters 3 and 4
Jordan.wks	7, 8, 10	Jordan.wks file stored noncontiguously in clusters 7, 8, and 10
Pick.bmp	9	Pick.bmp file stored in cluster 9

© Cengage Learning

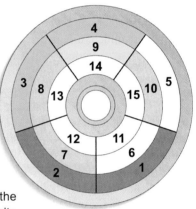

When you want to retrieve a file, the operating system looks through the index for the file name and its location. It moves the disk drive's read-write head to the first cluster that contains the file data. Using additional data from the index file, the operating system can move the read-write heads to each of the clusters containing the remaining parts of the file.

▶ **What happens when a file is deleted?** When you click a file's icon and then select the Delete option, you might have visions of the read-write head somehow scrubbing out the clusters that contain data. That doesn't happen. Instead, the operating system simply changes the status of the file's clusters to "empty" and removes the file name from the index file. The file name no longer appears in a directory listing, but the file's data remains in the clusters until a new file is stored there.

TRY IT!

In Figure 4-51, the Bio.txt file is stored in contiguous _____ .

You might think that this data is as good as erased, but it is possible to purchase utilities that recover a lot of this supposedly deleted data. Law enforcement agents, for example, use these utilities to gather evidence from deleted files on the computer disks of suspected criminals.

To delete data from a disk in such a way that no one can ever read it, you can use special **file shredder software** that overwrites supposedly empty sectors with random 1s and 0s. This software is handy if you plan to donate your computer to a charitable organization and you want to make sure your personal data no longer remains on the hard disk.

▶ Can deleted files be undeleted? The Windows Recycle Bin and similar utilities in other operating systems are designed to protect you from accidentally deleting hard disk files you actually need. Instead of marking a file's clusters as available, the operating system moves the file to the Recycle Bin folder. The deleted file still takes up space on the disk, but does not appear in the usual directory listing.

Files in the Recycle Bin folder can be undeleted so that they again appear in the regular directory. The Recycle Bin can be emptied to permanently delete any files it contains.

▶ How does a disk become fragmented? As a computer writes files on a disk, parts of files tend to become scattered all over the disk. These **fragmented files** are stored in noncontiguous clusters. Drive performance generally declines as the read-write heads move back and forth to locate the clusters containing the parts of a file. To regain peak performance, you can use a **defragmentation utility**, such as Windows Disk Defragmenter, to rearrange the files on a disk so that they are stored in contiguous clusters (Figure 4-52).

FIGURE 4-52

Defragmenting a disk helps your computer operate more efficiently. Consider using a defragmentation utility at least once a month to keep your computer running in top form. ▶ Your interactive eBook shows you how to defragment your computer's hard disk and how to find out how much space is available for storing files.

4

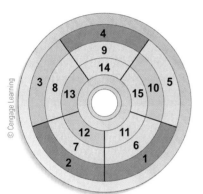

Fragmented disk

On the fragmented disk (left), the purple, orange, and blue files are stored in noncontiguous clusters.

When the disk is defragmented (right), the sectors of data for each file are moved to contiguous clusters.

Defragmented disk

© Cengage Learning

QuickCheck   SECTION D

1. Suppose you open a file and edit it, and then want to save it with a different name. You can use the Save option from the File menu. True or false? [ ]

2. [ ] file storage models, such as a filing cabinet or tree metaphor, help you visualize the organization of your computer files.

3. Windows 8 offers a preconfigured Documents [ ] that's designed to hold links to document files stored in various folders.

4. A hard disk stores data in concentric circles called [ ], which are divided into wedge-shaped [ ].

5. The acronyms NTFS, HFS+, and MFT pertain to [ ] file storage models.

 CHECK ANSWERS

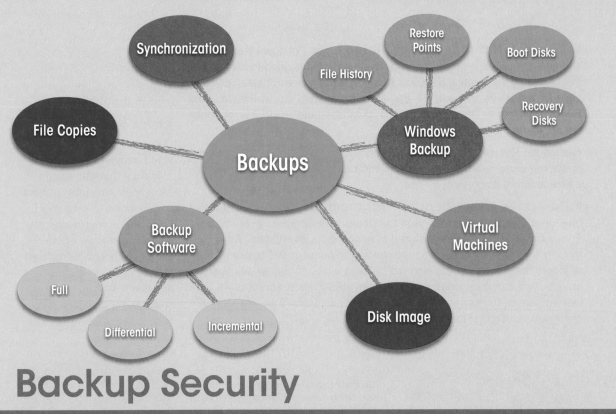

Backup Security

COMPUTER EXPERTS UNIVERSALLY recommend that you back up your data. It sounds pretty basic, right? Unfortunately, this advice tells you what to do, not how to do it. It fails to address some key questions, such as: Do I need special backup equipment and software? How often should I make a backup? How many of my files should I back up? What should I do with the backups? In this section, you'll find the answers to your questions about backing up data that's stored on personal and handheld computers.

BACKUP BASICS

▶ **Why do I need to make backups?** Have you ever mistakenly copied an old version of a document over a new version? Has your computer's hard disk drive gone on the fritz? Did a virus wipe out your files? Did your smartphone fail? These kinds of data disasters are not rare; they can happen to everyone.

You can't always prevent data disasters, so you should have a **backup** that stores the files needed to recover data that's been wiped out by operator error, viruses, or hardware failures. Backups allow you to **restore** data from a backup to the original storage location or to a replacement device.

▶ **How often should I back up my data?** Your backup schedule depends on how much data you can afford to lose. If you're working on an important project, you might want to back up the project files several times a day. Under normal use, however, most people schedule a once-a-week backup. If you work with a To Do list, use it to remind yourself when to make a backup or verify that your automated backup has been completed.

▶ **How can I be sure that my backup works?** You should test your backup by trying to restore one file. Restore the test file to a different drive or folder to avoid overwriting the original file.

▶ Where should I store my backups? You can choose to store backups on local devices such as an external hard disk or a USB flash drive, or you might consider storing your backup on a server in a local network or on an Internet-based server (Figure 4-53).

FIGURE 4-53

The device that holds your backups depends on what you want to back up.

4

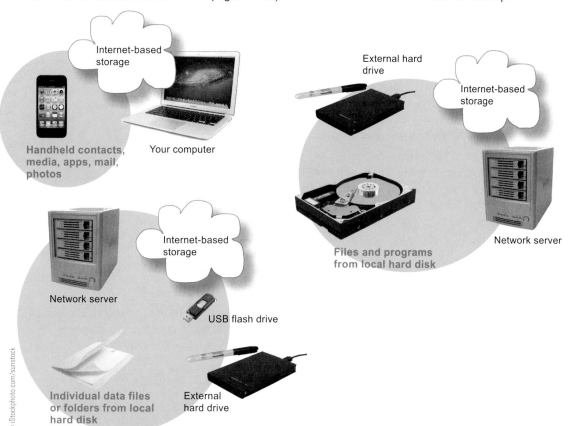

▶ What's better: online backups or local backups? There are advantages and disadvantages for each. Local storage is the traditional route. Your backups are under your control, but they are vulnerable to theft and damage.

If your backups are local, keep them in a safe place. Don't leave them on your computer desk because a fire or flood that damages your computer could also wipe out your backups. In addition, a thief who steals your computer might also scoop up nearby equipment and media. Storing your backups at a different location is the best idea. If off-site storage isn't practical, at least move them to a room apart from your computer.

Web sites that offer storage space for backups are called **online backup services**. The cost of these services usually depends on the amount of storage space that's allocated to you.

Before depending on remote backups, however, be aware that the speed for backing up and restoring your data is only as fast as your Internet connection. Also, remote data is more prone to snooping by employees, hackers, and overzealous government agents; you might want to encrypt your remote backup data, but make sure you don't lose your encryption key or your backup data will be useless.

You should also be aware that a backup service might close down without giving much notice to its users. Use an additional backup location for your really important files.

TERMINOLOGY NOTE

Online backup services are also referred to as remote backup services or managed backup services.

TRY IT!

You'll have the most flexible access to your backup data but the least control over it when you put your backup:

○ on your local hard drive

○ on an external hard drive

○ on a flash drive

○ on a managed backup service

FILE COPIES

▶ **What's the easiest way to back up important files?** The most important files on your computer contain the documents, images, and other data that you've created. These files are unique and might be difficult to reproduce. An easy way to back up your data is simply by copying selected files to a USB flash drive, to an external hard disk, or to cloud-based storage. To copy important files manually, you can use the Copy and Paste commands supplied by your computer's file management software.

▶ **Which data files should I back up?** If your strategy is to back up important data files, the procedure can be simplified if you've stored all these files in one folder and its subfolders. For example, Windows users might store their data files in the preconfigured folders for their user accounts.

Folders such as My Documents, My Music, and My Pictures are all stored as subfolders of your user folder. With your data files organized under the umbrella of a single folder, you are less likely to omit an important file when you make backups.

Some applications, such as financial software, create files and update them without your direct intervention. If you have the option during setup, make sure these files are stored in one of your personal folders. Otherwise, you must discover the location of the files and make sure they are backed up with the rest of your data.

In addition to data files you create, a few other types of data files might be important to you. Consider making backups of the files listed in Figure 4-54.

FIGURE 4-54

Back up these files in addition to your documents, graphics, and music files.

▶ E-mail folders. If you're using local e-mail software, your e-mail folder contains all the messages you've sent and received, but not deleted. Check the Help menu on your e-mail program to discover the location of these files.

▶ E-mail address book. Your e-mail address book might be stored separately from your e-mail messages. To find the file on a Windows computer, search for "Contacts."

▶ Favorite URLs. If you're attached to the URLs you've collected in your Favorites or Bookmarks list, you might want to back up the file that contains this list. To find the file, search your hard disk for "Favorites" or "Bookmarks." As an alternative method, check your browser for an option that exports your favorite URLs.

▶ Internet connection information. Your ISP's phone number and IP address, your user ID, and your password are often stored in an encrypted file somewhere in the Windows\System folder. Your ISP can usually help you find this file.

▶ Downloads. If you paid to download software, you might want to back it up so that you don't have to pay for it again. Downloaded software usually arrives in the form of a compressed .zip file. For backup purposes, the .zip file should be all you need.

▶ Validation codes and other configuration information. If you keep a running list of validation or activation codes that correspond to your software, then it is important to copy this information in case your hard disk crashes and you have to reinstall your software.

▶ **How do I restore files from my data file backups?** Restoring from a data file backup is easy. You simply copy files from your backup to your hard disk.

▶ **Are file backups sufficient protection against data disasters?** Your computer system contains programs and configuration settings in addition to your data files. Your computer setup is unique and you can't capture it by simply backing up your data files. If you want to be able to restore your computer to its current state, you need to back up all of its files using synchronization software, backup software, imaging software, or virtual machine technology.

TRY IT!

Check your computer. Do you have files for downloaded software in your Downloads folder?

SYNCHRONIZATION

▶ **What is synchronization?** **Synchronization** compares the content of files on two devices and makes them the same. It can be used for backup because it dynamically maintains a parallel set of files on your computer's hard disk and your backup device.

▶ **How does synchronization software work?** A program called Time Machine supplied with Mac OS X is a good example of synchronization software. It works by first making a backup of every file from the computer's primary storage device. Every hour, Time Machine checks the files on your computer's primary storage device and synchronizes any files that have been changed. This procedure ensures that your backup is never more than an hour old.

The number of backups you can retain—days', weeks', or months' worth—depends on the capacity of your storage device, the size of your data files, and the frequency at which you make changes. For best results, use an external hard disk drive that's at least the same capacity as your computer's internal hard disk. Time Machine and similar synchronization software can store backups on network file servers and on Internet-based storage services.

▶ **Can I restore individual files from these backups?** Yes. Time Machine displays a window for each hour's backup. You can go back in time to any hour or day, select a file, and restore it to your computer's primary storage device.

▶ **What about restoring the entire computer?** Suppose your computer's hard disk fails and you have to replace it. Once you've installed a new, blank hard disk, you can insert the Mac OS setup CD and select the Time Machine option to restore the operating system, programs, preferences, and data files that existed at the time of the last Time Machine backup. Figure 4-55 explains the elements of Time Machine's interface.

FIGURE 4-55

Time Machine saves hourly backups for the past 24 hours, daily backups for the past month, and weekly backups for data older than a month. When the backup device runs out of space, Time Machine deletes the oldest weekly backup.

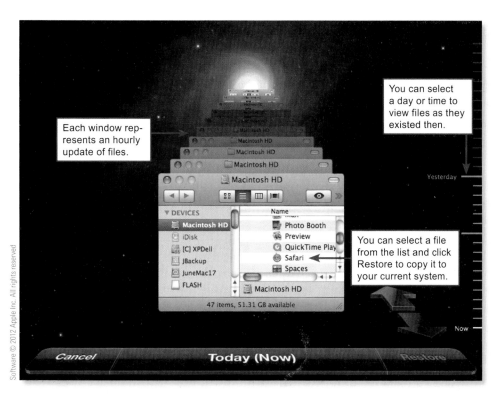

Each window represents an hourly update of files.

You can select a day or time to view files as they existed then.

You can select a file from the list and click Restore to copy it to your current system.

WINDOWS BACKUP

▶ Does Windows include backup software? Windows 8 includes a synchronization utility called File History. It is designed to back up the files stored in your Libraries, Desktop, Favorites, and Contacts folders. Once you activate File History, it checks hourly for files that have changed and copies those files to the backup device. Figure 4-56 explains how to activate File History.

FIGURE 4-56

Microsoft Windows 8 includes the File History utility to back up important files. ▶ Discover how to activate it.

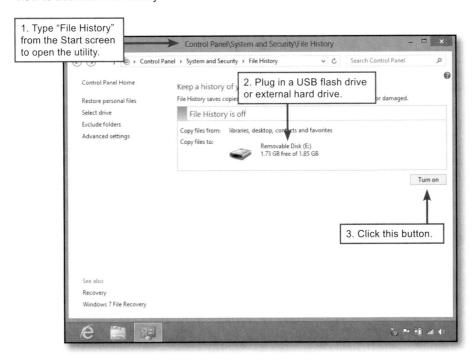

1. Type "File History" from the Start screen to open the utility.

2. Plug in a USB flash drive or external hard drive.

3. Click this button.

▶ How much of my computer is backed up? A **full system backup** includes a copy of every file stored on your computer's hard drive. In addition to data files, a full system backup includes copies of all installed programs, settings, and the operating system. File History is not a full system backup. If your hard drive crashes, the files stored by File History are not sufficient to configure a new drive. To restore your hard drive, you'll need to use a boot disk, a recovery disk, and copies of your application software.

▶ What is a boot disk? A **boot disk** is a removable storage medium containing the operating system files needed to boot your computer without accessing the hard disk. CDs, DVDs, and even USB flash drives can be used as boot disks. With current versions of Windows, the Windows installation CD is configured as a boot disk and can be used if your computer does not boot normally. When you insert the installation CD, you'll have the option of repairing Windows or reinstalling it. Try the repair option first.

▶ What is a recovery disk? A **recovery disk** (sometimes referred to as a recovery CD) is a bootable CD, DVD, or other media that contains a complete copy of your computer's hard disk as it existed when the computer was new. It contains the operating system, device drivers, utilities, and even software that was bundled with your computer.

You can use a recovery disk to return your computer to its factory default state. However, a recovery disk will not restore your data files, any software that you installed, or any configuration settings you've made since you unwrapped your computer from its shipping box.

TERMINOLOGY NOTE

The contents and capabilities of recovery disks vary. Some are designed to restore your computer to its like-new state and wipe out all your data. Others attempt to restore user settings, programs, and data. Before you depend on a recovery disk, make sure you know what it contains and how to use it in case of a system failure.

▶ **Where can I get a recovery disk?** The installation instructions for new computers explain how to make a recovery disk, usually by copying files stored in a **recovery partition** on the computer's hard disk. Be sure to create your recovery disks right away and then store them in a safe place.

Recovery partitions are convenient for restoring a corrupted device driver or software module because you can simply copy or reinstall the file from the recovery partition to the main partition. The files in the recovery partition are not accessible, however, if your computer's hard disk fails. Therefore, don't be misled into thinking that a recovery partition can help you restore your computer after a hard disk failure.

▶ **What about backing up the Windows Registry?** The **Windows Registry**, or Registry as it is usually called, is an important group of files used by the Windows operating system to store configuration information about all the devices and software installed on a computer system. If the Registry becomes damaged, your computer might not be able to boot up, launch programs, or communicate with peripheral devices. It is a good idea to have an extra copy of the Registry in case the original file is damaged.

As simple as it sounds, backing up the Registry can be a problem because the Registry is always open while your computer is on. Some software that you might use for backups cannot copy open files. If you use such software, it might never back up the Registry. To get periodic copies of your computer's Registry settings, you can create restore points.

▶ **What is a restore point?** A **restore point** is a snapshot of your computer settings. Restore points are essentially backups of the Windows Registry. If a hard disk problem causes system instability, you might be able to roll back to a restore point when your computer was operational.

Restore points are set automatically when you install new software. You can manually set restore points, too. For example, you might want to set a restore point before updating a program, setting up a network, or installing new hardware (Figure 4-57).

4

FIGURE 4-57

Restore points can be set by accessing the Control Panel and then searching for "Restore Point." ▶ Use this figure in your interactive eBook to learn how to work with restore points.

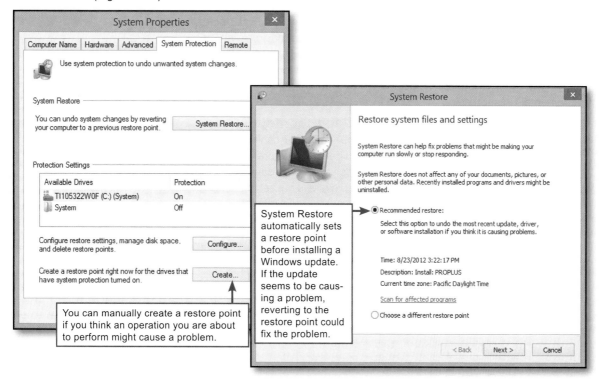

BACKUP SOFTWARE

▶ Are there third-party backup utilities? Yes. Windows users, especially those in a small business or corporate environment, can select from a variety of third-party options for backup that create full system back-ups and disk images.

Backup software is a set of utility programs designed to back up and restore some or all of the files on a computer's primary storage device. Backup software usually includes options that make it easy to schedule periodic backups, define a set of files that you want to regularly back up, and automate the restoration process.

Backup software differs from most copy and synchronization routines because it compresses all the files for a backup and places them in one large file. The backup file is indexed so that individual files can be located, uncompressed, and restored.

▶ How do I use backup software? To use backup software, you specify which files you want to back up, select the location of the backup device, and select the days and times for automatic backups to proceed. Because the backup process uses system resources, most people schedule backups for times when their computer is on, but when they are not using it.

Backup software is usually used for copying the entire contents of a hard disk. A backup made by copying all the files to a backup device is called a full backup. Full backups take lots of time; alternative options that take less time include differential and incremental backups.

▶ What is a differential backup? A **differential backup** makes a backup of only those files that were added or changed since your last full backup session. After making a full backup of your important files, you can make differential backups at regular intervals. If you need to restore all your files after a hard disk crash, first restore the files from your full backup, and then restore the files from your latest differential backup.

▶ What is an incremental backup? An **incremental backup** backs up files that were added or changed since the last backup—not necessarily the files that changed from the last full backup, but the files that changed since any full or incremental backup. To restore a set of incremental backups, you must first install a full backup, then install each of the incrementals in succession.

▶ How do I avoid backing up files that contain viruses? Viruses can damage files to the point that your computer can't access any data on its hard disk. It is really frustrating when you restore data from a backup only to discover that the restored files contain the same virus that wiped out your original data. If your antivirus software is not set to constantly scan for viruses on your computer system, you should run an up-to-date virus check as the first step in your backup routine.

▶ How do I recover from a hard disk crash? To recover from a hard disk crash, you have to get your computer booted up so that you can run your backup software. If your computer won't boot from the hard disk, you can use a boot disk or a recovery disk. Next, use the Restore option from your backup utility to install your applications, settings, and data files.

TRY IT!

You're using third-party backup software, and you want a set of backups that are easy to restore and won't take long to make. What option should you use?

○ Full system backup

○ Incremental backup

○ Differential backup

▶ Can I restore my computer in one simple operation?

Restoring a computer usually entails several steps that can require a boot disk, a recovery disk, backup disks, and file backups. The objective of this extended and sometimes frustrating process is to get optical and hard drive device drivers running so the computer can access its storage devices to get the operating system running, which can then run backup and restore software.

Some backup systems streamline the process by restoring a computer's operating system, device drivers, settings, and data in a single step—a process called **bare-metal restore**.

Bare-metal restore backup software stores the operating system, boot program, drivers, software applications, and data necessary to restore a backed up system to an entirely new computer, without requiring intermediate steps to install the operating system and device drivers. Bare-metal restore software usually works with a disk image.

▶ What is a disk image?

A **disk image** is a bit-by-bit copy of the data from all sectors of a disk. Disk imaging utilities create an exact clone of the original disk, unlike most backup software that makes file-by-file copies. The advantage of disk imaging is that it includes all the data from a disk, even boot information and other data locked by the operating system.

The disadvantage of disk imaging is that it copies data from the entire disk; it generally cannot be configured like traditional backup software to copy only selected files. Disk imaging takes time and is best used while other applications are not running. It is valuable for periodic backups, but cumbersome for daily backups.

Popular Mac disk imaging utilities include SuperDuper! and Carbon Copy Cloner. Popular Windows disk imaging utilities include Paragon Drive Backup, Norton Ghost, and Acronis True Image (Figure 4-58).

TRY IT!

The advantage of a disk image is that it contains a bit-for-bit copy of the operating system, settings, software, and data files on your computer. What is the disadvantage?

○ You can't back up the Windows Registry

○ You can't restore individual files

○ You can't restore it

○ You have to put it on a cloud server

4

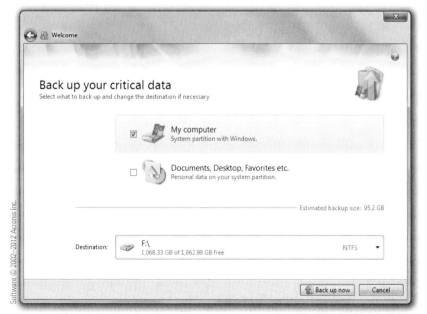

Software © 2002–2012 Acronis Inc.

FIGURE 4-58

Disk imaging software, such as Acronis True Image, creates a bit-by-bit copy of all the data on your computer's hard disk that can be used to restore all operating system, program, and data files.

VIRTUAL MACHINES

▶ Are there any other backup options? Today's trend toward the use of virtual machines offers another option for backups. Reinstalling an operating system on a blank hard disk can be tricky, but you can avoid that hassle if you run your operating system as a virtual machine.

For example, if you run Windows as a virtual machine on a Mac, you can simply back up the entire Windows machine as one folder or file. If a virus or corrupted file begins to disrupt the operation of Windows, instead of reformatting your hard disk and reinstalling Windows, you can simply copy the image of your Windows virtual machine from your backup device to your primary storage device and continue working (Figure 4-59).

FIGURE 4-59

When you run Windows as a virtual machine, the Windows operating system, program files, and settings, along with your data files, are stored in a folder. The entire Windows computer runs essentially like any other software application on the host machine.

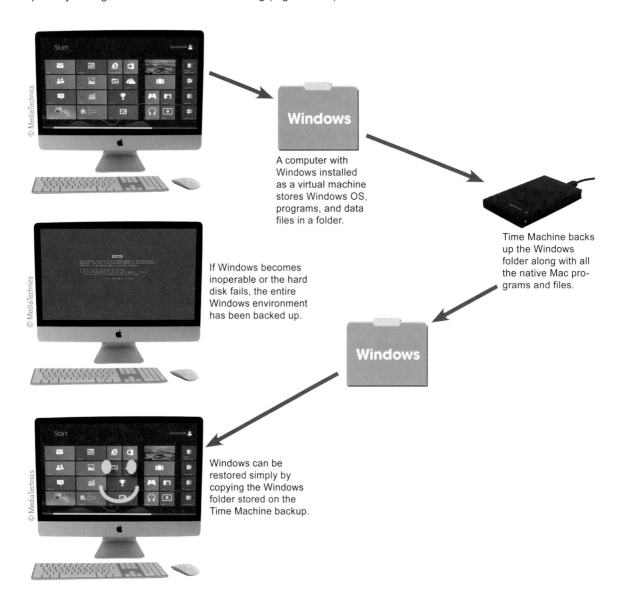

A computer with Windows installed as a virtual machine stores Windows OS, programs, and data files in a folder.

Time Machine backs up the Windows folder along with all the native Mac programs and files.

If Windows becomes inoperable or the hard disk fails, the entire Windows environment has been backed up.

Windows can be restored simply by copying the Windows folder stored on the Time Machine backup.

TABLET AND SMARTPHONE BACKUP

▶ What about my handheld device? Handheld devices are usually backed up by synching them to a desktop or laptop computer. The procedure is a legacy from the days of personal digital assistants that used synchronization as a mechanism to update contacts and appointments from a handheld device to those on a desktop computer.

Synching is usually initiated by tethering your handheld device to a full-size computer using a USB cable. Synchronization software examines files on both devices and asks you which files you want to sync.

iPhones, iPods, and iPads synch with iTunes software, and you have the option to encrypt the backup to prevent your data from exposure if your computer falls victim to an unauthorized intrusion (Figure 4-60).

FIGURE 4-60

iTunes creates a backup of the data stored on your iPad, iPod, or iPhone.

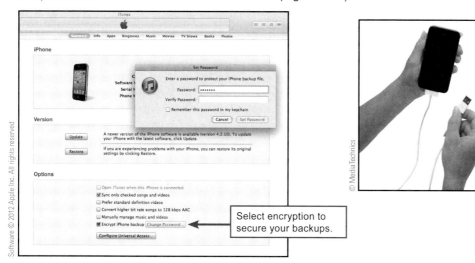

Select encryption to secure your backups.

© MediaTechnics

▶ Can I back up my Android device? Many Android devices include backup software, usually accessible from the Settings icon. Generally, backups from Android devices are stored in the cloud on Google servers. If your Android device accepts SD cards, you may also be able to make backups of individual files.

If you want to go beyond data backup and back up your Android system files, you can use third-party backup software, such as Titanium Backup or Backup Master.

QuickCheck

SECTION E

1. _____ software, such as Time Machine, keeps your backup files up to date with the original files on your hard disk.

2. One of the best devices for home backup is a(n) _____ hard drive.

3. A(n) _____ backup makes copies of only those files that have changed since your last full backup.

4. A(n) _____ point is essentially a backup of the settings in the Windows Registry.

5. A bare- _____ restore includes the operating system, boot program, drivers, software applications, and data necessary to rebuild a replacement hard disk in one easy operation.

▶ CHECK ANSWERS

Issue: Cyberterrorists or Pranksters?

Mikkel William Nielsen/iStockpho

SOME COMPUTER CRIMES require no special digital expertise. Setting fire to a computer doesn't require the same finesse as writing a stealthy virus, but both can have the same disastrous effect on data. Old-fashioned crimes, such as arson, that take a high-tech twist because they involve a computer can be prosecuted under traditional laws.

Traditional laws do not, however, cover the range of possibilities for computer crimes. Suppose a person unlawfully enters a computer facility and steals backup drives. That person might be prosecuted for breaking and entering. But would common breaking and entering laws apply to a person who remotely accesses a corporate computer system without authorization? And what if a person copies a data file without authorization? Has that file really been stolen if the original remains on the computer?

Many countries have computer crime laws that specifically define computer data and software as personal property. These laws also define as crimes the unauthorized access, use, modification, or disabling of a computer system or data. But laws don't necessarily stop criminals. If they did, we wouldn't have to deal with malicious code and intrusions.

One of the first computer crime cases involved a worm unleashed on the ARPANET in 1988 that quickly spread through government and university computer systems. The worm's author, Robert Morris, was convicted and sentenced to three years of probation, 400 hours of community service, and a US$10,000 fine.

A 1995 high-profile case involved a computer hacker named Kevin Mitnick, who was accused of breaking into dozens of corporate, university, government, and personal computers. Although vilified in the media, Mitnick had the support of many hackers and other people who believed that the prosecution grossly exaggerated the extent of his crimes. Nonetheless, Mitnick was sentenced to 46 months in prison and ordered to pay restitution in the amount of $4,125 during his three-year period of supervised release.

Forbes reporter Adam L. Penenberg took issue with the 46-month sentence imposed by Judge Mariana

Pfaelzer and wrote, "Mitnick's crimes were curiously innocuous. He broke into corporate computers, but no evidence indicates that he destroyed data. Or sold anything he copied. Yes, he pilfered software—but in doing so left it behind. This world of bits is a strange one, in which you can take something and still leave it for its rightful owner. The theft laws designed for payroll sacks and motor vehicles just don't apply to a hacker."

The USA PATRIOT Act and the Cybersecurity Enhancement Act carry stiff penalties for cybercrimes—ranging from ten years to life in prison. CNET editor Robert Vamosi questions the harshness of such penalties: "What bothers me most is that here in the United States, rapists serve, on average, ten years in prison. Yet if, instead of assaulting another human being, that same person had released a virus on the Net, the criminal would get the same or an even harsher sentence."

> *This world of bits is a strange one, in which you can take something and still leave it for its rightful owner.*

Modern society has an ambivalent attitude toward computer hackers. On the one hand, they are viewed as evil cyberterrorists who are set on destroying the glue that binds together the Information Age.

From this perspective, hackers are criminals who must be hunted down, forced to make restitution for damages, and prevented from creating further havoc.

From another perspective, hackers are viewed more as Casper the Friendly Ghost in our complex cybermachines—as moderately bothersome entities whose pranks are tolerated by the computer community, along with software bugs and hardware glitches.

Seen from this perspective, a hacker's pranks are part of the normal course of study that leads to the highest echelons of computer expertise. "Everyone has done it," claims one hacking devotee, "even Bill Gates and Steve Jobs."

●TRY IT! Which perspective is right? Are hackers dangerous cyber-terrorists or harmless pranksters? Before you make up your mind about computer hacking and cracking, here's more for you to explore.

1 After the publicity from Kevin Mitnick's trial, consumers might expect corporate databases to be rigorously guarded; but hacking incidents continue to escalate. To find information about recent data breaches, check the Wikipedia article on data breaches or sites such as DatalossDB (*datalossdb.org*). What were the three largest data breaches in the past five years, how many accounts were exposed, and did you have accounts with any of the breached organizations?

2 Data breaches are a major source of information used for identity theft. You probably know basic steps to take to avoid identity theft, but there's always more to learn. Check sites such as *www.identity-theft.org/protect.htm* or the National Crime Prevention Council's online booklet *Preventing Identity Theft*. What are five identity-protection techniques that you didn't know about before this project?

3 In 2010, a mysterious computer worm spread across the Internet and targeted industrial equipment that happened to be used in Iran's nuclear program. According to one security expert, Stuxnet was designed to probe the security of a wide variety of crucial industrial plants throughout the world and gauge potential weaknesses for future cyberwarfare attacks. Use Web resources to learn more about Stuxnet and recent attacks against RSA, a cyber security company, and Google's Gmail system. What is the difference between cyber-warfare and cybercrime?

4 The media labeled an attack against the country of Estonia a "cyber war." Use Web resources to explore this incident. How might a similar incident affect your country?

5 The world of cybercrime has a jargon all its own. What do the following terms mean?

a. Zero-day attack	e. Denial of service
b. Data diddling	f. Man-in-the-middle
c. Salami shaving	g. Dead drop
d. Vandalism	h. Honeypot

4

INFOWEBLINKS

You can check the **NP2014 Chapter 4** InfoWebLink for updates to these activities.

 CLICK TO CONNECT
www.infoweblinks.com/np2014/ch04

What Do You Think?

ISSUE

1. Should a computer virus distribution sentence carry the same penalty as manslaughter?

2. Should it be a crime to steal a copy of computer data while leaving the original data in place and unaltered?

3. Should hackers be sent to jail if they cannot pay restitution to companies and individuals who lost money as the result of a prank?

4. Do you think that a hacker would make a good computer-security consultant?

Information Tools: Fact Checking

These days, you have to be a skeptic. Bloggers have opinions that are not always based on facts. Scam artists say anything to get your money. Even reputable journalists sometimes make mistakes.

Before you form an opinion, make a decision, or take action based on what you read, see, or hear, you can easily use your computer or smartphone to verify facts and look up background information.

Search Google. You can use Google or a similar search engine to find information from all corners of the Web. You can search for information in specific formats, such as videos, images, and news reports. Check out Google Scholar for links to authoritative information in peer-reviewed journals, theses, and other professional publications. Remember that you can formulate searches such as "Define zero-day attack" to learn the meaning of technical terms and find the meaning of acronyms.

Search within sites. Rather than conducting a wide-ranging Google search, you can go to a specific Web site and search within it. Search Wikipedia for definitions and topic overviews. Search a news site for articles and video footage about current events. Start at Snopes.com or *www.hoaxbusters.org* to identify e-mail scams. Try LexisNexis for links to authoritative primary and secondary source material.

When you check facts or use them in your own research papers, primary sources tend to be more reliable than secondary or tertiary sources. How can you tell the difference?

PRIMARY SOURCES	SECONDARY SOURCES	TERTIARY SOURCES
Original material such as speeches, interviews, letters, photos, e-mail messages, tweets, artwork, diaries, laws, database reports, and accounting records	Reviews, critiques, panel discussions, biographies, and other sources that analyze, summarize, or otherwise repackage information from primary sources	A list or compilation of material that pertains to a topic; from sources that include bibliographies, dictionaries, almanacs, indexes, timelines, and inventory lists
Example: A video of Apple's CEO announcing a new music product for the iPhone and iPad	Example: An article on Google News that describes Apple's new music product	Example: Apple's e-commerce site that lists and sells all versions of its new music product

FACT CHECKING TIPS

▶ **Two sources are better than one.** Cross-check facts between two or more sites.

▶ **Use common sense.** Claims that seem outlandish require extra verification.

▶ **Understand your priorities.** For example, you can go to YouTube and view the trailer for Live Free or Die Hard. That might be fun, but it might not be relevant for a term paper on cyberterrorism.

▶ **Use primary sources when possible.** Go to the original text of a speech, check the product manufacturer's Web site, or watch the video clip.

▶ **Use reputable sources.** The Web contains billions of documents; few of them follow strict journalistic standards for accuracy. Check the author's credentials, look at the general quality of the Web site, and make sure the information is up to date.

▶ **Maintain a list of the sites you frequently use for fact checking.** You can create a Fact Check folder in your browser's Bookmarks or Favorites list.

▶ **Nail down your search terms.** When using voice search on your mobile phone, think about an exact set of keywords before you launch Speak Now.

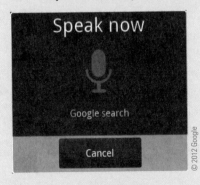

◉TRY IT! Fact checking can be fun and it can lead you to all sorts of intriguing factoids as well as to substantive information. Practice your fact-checking skills by completing the following activities.

❶ After investigating a worm that infiltrated U.S. Army networks, the NSA (National Security Agency) and Department of Defense banned USB flash drives from military computers. From which one of the following sources are you most likely to obtain primary source information about the USB flash drive ban?

Under Worm Assault, Military Bans Disks, USB Drives | Danger ...
www.wired.com/dangerroom/2008/11/army-bans-usb-d/ - Cached

Nov 19, 2008 – Under Worm Assault, Military Bans Disks, USB Drives ...
The ban comes from the commander of U.S. Strategic Command, according to an...

[PDF] USB Storage Drives
www.nsa.gov/ia/_files/factsheets/I731-002R-2007.pdf

File Format: PDF/Adobe Acrobat - Quick View
of devices not described by other policy settings". To allow administrators to ...
www.nsa.gov. Information ... cameras, and USB hard drives. Windows. Linux ..

Judging the cyber war terrorist threat : The New Yorker
www.newyorker.com/reporting/2010/11/.../101101fa_fact_hersh

Subscribe to New Yorker ... by Seymour M. Hersh ... N.S.A. unit commanders, facing penetration of their bases' secure networks, concluded that the break-in was caused by a disabling thumb drive...

❷ Suppose that you receive an e-mail message warning of a zero-day cyberwar worm called Storm that is spreading rapidly. The message warns that your security software doesn't yet have the ability to identify and quarantine this virus. According to the e-mail, it is your civic duty to stop this virus by following a set of instructions to alter the Windows Registry or Mac OS kernel. Of the following options, which would be the best way to find out if this warning is legitimate?

a. Use Google to search for "Storm worm."

b. Go to the Web site Snopes.com and search for "Storm."

c. Reply to the e-mail and ask for the app's security certificate.

❸ Suppose you're gathering information for a term paper about enforcement efforts to catch cybercriminals, and you come across the following short article posted on a security blog. Operation Shady RAT sounds intriguing; but before you add material from this article to your research notes, you should do a fact check by answering the questions in the diagram below.

Operation Shady RAT Exposed

a. Was the sting operation called Shady RAT?

b. Were the hackers based in Romania?

In a massive sting operation called Shady RAT, a U.S. security firm raided the command and control server used by a group of Romania-based hackers.

An extensive investigation led up to the discovery of the clandestine server and the passwords necessary to gain entry. Data gathered from this server revealed hundreds of active targets and terabytes of illicit data waiting to be claimed by hackers.

c. Are these statistics accurate?

Victims ranged from the U.S. Olympic Committee to government agencies in the U.S., Canada, India, South Korea, Taiwan, Pakistan, and Vietnam.

d. Is this list of victims correct?

Dmitri Alperovitch of McAfee, the security firm spearheading the investigation, describes the discovery "even we were surprised by the enormous diversity of the victim organizations and were taken aback by the audacity of the perpetrators."

e. Check the primary source: Is this quote correct?

Technology in Context: Law Enforcement

SIRENS WAIL. Blue lights flash. A speeding car slows and pulls off to the side of the road. It looks like a routine traffic stop, but the patrol car is outfitted with a mobile data computer. The police officers on this high-tech force have already checked the speeding car's license plate number and description against a database of stolen cars and vehicles allegedly used in kidnappings and other crimes.

Mounted in the dashboard of marked and unmarked police cars, a mobile data computer resembles a laptop computer with its flat-panel screen and compact keyboard. Unlike a consumer-grade laptop, however, the computers in police cruisers use hardened technology designed to withstand extreme conditions, such as high temperatures in parked vehicles. The dashboard-mounted computer communicates with an office-based server using a wireless link, such as short-range radio, mobile phone technology, or Wi-Fi. With this wireless link, police officers can access data from local, state, and national databases.

One national database, the National Crime Information Center (NCIC), is maintained by the FBI and can be accessed by authorized personnel in local, state, and federal law enforcement agencies. The system can process more than 5 million queries per day related to stolen vehicles, wanted criminals, missing persons, violent gang members, stolen guns, and members of terrorist organizations. The officers who pulled over the speeding car received information from the NCIC that the car was stolen, so they arrested the car's occupant and took him to the police station for booking.

At the police station, digital cameras flash and the suspect's mug shot is automatically entered into an automated warrants and booking system. The system stores the suspect's complete biographical and arrest information, such as name, aliases, addresses, Social Security number, charges, and arrest date. The system also checks for outstanding warrants against the suspect, such as warrants for other thefts. Booking agents can enter those charges into the system, assign the new inmate to a cell, log his or her personal items, and print a photo ID or wrist band.

Automated warrants and booking systems have been proven to increase police productivity. New York City's system handles more than 300,000 bookings per year, with gains in productivity that have put nearly 300 officers back into action investigating crimes and patrolling neighborhoods.

As part of the booking process, the suspect is fingerprinted. A standard fingerprint card, sometimes called a ten-print card, contains inked prints of the fingers on each hand, plus name, date of birth, and other arrest information. Now, however, instead of using ink, a biometric scanning device can electronically capture fingerprints. Text information is entered using a keyboard and stored with digital fingerprint images.

The fingerprint information can be transmitted in digital format from local law enforcement agencies to the FBI's Integrated Automated Fingerprint Identification System (IAFIS). This biometric identification system uses digital imaging technology and sophisticated algorithms to analyze fingerprint data. IAFIS can classify arriving prints for storage or search for a match in its database containing 66 million criminal prints, 25 million civilian prints, and prints from 73,000 known and suspected terrorists.

Conventional crimes, such as car theft, are often solved by using standard investigative techniques with information from computer databases. To solve cybercrimes, however, the special skills of computer forensic investigators are often required.

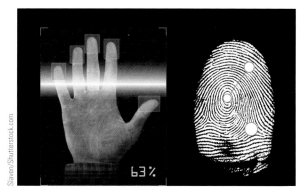

Computer forensics is the scientific examination and analysis of data located on computer storage media, conducted to offer evidence of computer crimes in court. Computer crimes can be separated into two categories. The first includes crimes that use computers, such as transmitting trade secrets to competitors, reproducing copyrighted material, and distributing child pornography. The second includes crimes targeted at computers, such as denial-of-service attacks on servers, Web site vandalism, data theft, and destructive viruses. Computer forensics can be applied to both categories.

Whether investigators suspect that a computer is the origin of a cyber-attack or contains evidence, the first step in the forensic process is to use disk imaging software to make an exact replica of the information stored on the hard disk. The disk image is collected on a write-once medium that cannot be altered with planted evidence, and the forensic scientist begins analyzing the disk image data with simple search software that looks through files for keywords related to the crime. In the case of the Gap-Toothed Bandit who was convicted for robbing nine banks, analysis of the disk image revealed word processing files containing notes he handed to tellers demanding money.

Criminals might attempt to delete files with incriminating evidence, but a good forensic scientist can retrieve data from deleted files with undelete software or data recovery software. Temporary Internet or cache files can also yield evidence, pointing law enforcement officers to Web sites the suspect visited that might be fronts for illegal activity.

When a computer is a target of a cyber-attack, forensic investigators use three techniques to track the source. The first option is to make an immediate image of the server's hard disk and look through its log files for evidence of activity coming from unauthorized IP addresses. A second technique is to monitor the intruder by watching login attempts, changes to log files, and file access requests. Sophisticated intruders might be able to detect such monitoring, however, and cover their tracks. A third technique is to create a honeypot—an irresistible computer system or Web site containing fake information that allows investigators to monitor hackers until identification is possible.

Despite the many techniques and tools available to forensic investigators, they have three main constraints. First, they must adhere to privacy regulations and obtain warrants to set up wiretaps or gather information from ISPs about their customers. Second, they must scrupulously document their procedures so that the evidence they produce cannot be discredited in court as planted or fabricated. Third, forensic investigators must examine a wide range of alternatives pertaining to the crime, such as the chance that an IP or e-mail address used to commit a cybercrime might belong to an innocent bystander being spoofed by the real hacker.

Privacy, documentation, and evidentiary constraints cost forensic investigators time, and failure to adhere to strict standards can sometimes allow criminals to avoid conviction and penalties. But even within these constraints, careful forensic investigation is an important aspect of catching and convicting high-tech criminals.

New Perspectives Labs

To access the New Perspectives Labs for Chapter 4, open the NP2014 interactive eBook and then click the icon next to the lab title.

▶ MANAGING FILES

IN THIS LAB YOU'LL LEARN:

- How to access File Explorer
- How to expand and collapse the directory structure
- How to rename or delete a file or folder
- The basic principles for creating an efficient directory structure for your files
- How to create a folder
- How to select a single file or a group of files
- How to move files from one folder to another

LAB ASSIGNMENTS

1. Start the interactive part of the lab. Make sure you've enabled Tracking if you want to save your QuickCheck results. Perform each lab step, and answer all the lab QuickCheck questions.

2. Use File Explorer or Finder to look at the directory of the disk or USB flash drive that currently contains most of your files. Draw a diagram showing the hierarchy of folders. Write a paragraph explaining how you could improve this hierarchy, and draw a diagram to illustrate your plan.

3. On a blank USB flash drive, create three folders: Music, Web Graphics, and Articles. Within the Music folder, create four additional folders: Jazz, Reggae, Rock, and Classical. Within the Classical folder, create two more folders: Classical MIDI and Classical MP3. If you have Internet access, go on to #4.

4. Use your browser software to connect to the Internet, and then go to a Web site, such as *www.zdnet.com* or *www.cnet.com*. Look for a small graphic (perhaps 100 KB or less) and download it to your Web Graphics folder. Next, use a search engine to search for "classical MIDI music." Download one of the compositions to the Music\Classical\Classical MIDI folder. Open File Explorer and expand all the directories for your USB flash drive. Open the Music\Classical\Classical MIDI folder and make sure your music download appears. Capture a screenshot. Follow your instructor's directions to submit this screenshot as a printout or an e-mail attachment.

▶ BACKING UP YOUR COMPUTER

IN THIS LAB YOU'LL LEARN:

- How to work with restore points
- How to create a recovery disk
- How to create a disk image
- How to make a Windows backup
- How to restore files from a backup

LAB ASSIGNMENTS

1. Start the interactive part of the lab. Make sure you've enabled Tracking if you want to save your QuickCheck results. Perform each lab step as directed, and answer all the lab QuickCheck questions. When you exit the lab, your answers are automatically graded and your results are displayed.

2. Describe where most of your data files are stored, and estimate how many megabytes of data (not programs) you have in all these files. Next, take a close look at these files and estimate how much data (in megabytes) you cannot afford to lose. Would your data fit on a USB flash drive? If so, what capacity?

3. Start the backup software that is provided for your computer, specify its name, and list which of the following features it provides: file backup, system image, disk image, automatic backup, manual backup. If an automatic backup is available, list the user-definable options for selecting backup intervals, days, and times.

4. Explore your computer to discover how its recovery disk is provided. For example, is it a partition, a download, or a utility? Use the built-in Help provided by your computer manufacturer or go to its Web site to learn how to make a recovery disk. Write a short summary of the procedure.

Key Terms

Make sure you understand all the boldfaced key terms presented in this chapter. With the NP2014 interactive eBook, you can use this list of terms as an interactive study activity. First, try to define a term in your own words, and then click the term to compare your definition with the definition presented in the chapter.

4

Android, 201
Application windows, 191
Backup, 222
Backup software, 228
Bare-metal restore, 229
BlackBerry OS, 203
Boot disk, 226
Boot process, 188
Bootstrap program, 188
Buffers, 187
Button, 192
Cluster, 219
Command-line interface, 190
Data fork, 199
Defragmentation utility, 221
Desktop, 191
Desktop operating system, 188
Dialog box, 193
Differential backup, 228
Directory, 206
Disc mastering, 219
Disk image, 229
Disk partition, 206
Dock, 191
DOS, 194
Dual boot, 198
File Explorer, 216
File extension, 204
File format, 207
File header, 207
File management utility, 215
File shredder software, 220
File specification, 206
File system, 219
File tag, 212
File-naming conventions, 204
Folder, 206

Formatting, 219
Fragmented files, 221
Full system backup, 226
Graphical user interface, 190
Icon, 192
Incremental backup, 228
iOS, 200
Kernel, 188
Library, 217
Linux, 202
Linux distribution, 202
Logical storage models, 215
Mac OS, 197
Memory leak, 187
Menu, 192
Menu bar, 192
Metadata, 214
Microsoft Windows, 194
Mobile operating system, 188
Multiprocessing, 186
Multitasking, 186
Multithreading, 186
Multiuser operating system, 187
Native file format, 209
Online backup services, 223
Packet writing, 219
Path, 206
Physical storage model, 218
Push technology, 203
Recovery disk, 226
Recovery partition, 227
Reserved words, 205
Resource, 185
Resource fork, 199
Restore, 222
Restore point, 227
Ribbon, 192

Root directory, 206
Sectors, 219
Server operating system, 187
Single-user operating system, 187
Start screen, 191
Subdirectory, 206
Submenu, 193
Synchronization, 225
Taskbar, 191
Tiles, 192
Toolbar, 192
Tracks, 219
UNIX, 202
User interface, 190
Virtual machine, 198
Windows Registry, 227
Windows RT, 196

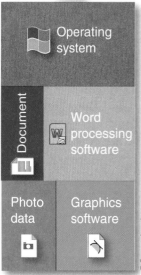

Interactive Summary

To review important concepts from this chapter, fill in the blanks to best complete each sentence. When using the NP2014 interactive eBook, click the Check Answers buttons to automatically score your answers.

SECTION A: An operating system interacts with application software, device drivers, and hardware to manage a computer's [_____], such as the processor, memory, and input/output devices. To allow two or more programs to run simultaneously, an OS can offer [_____] services. Within a single program, [_____] allows multiple parts, or threads, to run simultaneously. An operating system's [_____] capability supports a division of labor among all the processing units. An operating system might have to deal with a memory, [_____], a situation caused by an application that requests memory, but never releases it. Operating systems are informally categorized and characterized using one or more of the following terms: A(n) [_____]-user operating system expects to deal with one set of input devices—those that can be controlled by one person at a time. A(n) [_____]-user operat-

ing system is designed to deal with input, output, and processing requests from many users. A(n) [_____] operating system provides management tools for distributed networks, e-mail servers, and Web site hosting. A(n) [_____] operating system is one that's designed for a personal computer. A(n) [_____] operating system is designed for devices such as iPhones and Droids.

The core part of an operating system is called the [_____], which is loaded into RAM during the [_____] process. In addition to behind-the-scenes activities, operating systems also provide tools, called operating system [_____], that you can use to control and customize your computer equipment and work environment. Many operating systems also influence the "look and feel" of your software, or what's known as the user [_____].

▶ CHECK ANSWERS

SECTION B: Popular [_____] operating systems include Microsoft Windows, Mac OS, and Linux. Windows has evolved to keep pace with 16-bit, 32-bit, and [_____]-bit architectures. Its strengths include a huge library of Windows [_____], support for a variety of peripheral devices, and plenty of documentation. Two of the weakest features of Microsoft Windows are reliability and [_____]. Windows [_____] is the mobile version of Windows 8, designed to run on devices with ARM processors. Mac OS evolved from the original Classic Mac OS designed for [_____] computers based on the Motorola 68000 microprocessor. In 2001, Mac OS X was released for Apple's new line of computers using IBM's PowerPC processor. OS X was again revised for a line of computers using [_____] processors. These Macs can be set up to dual [_____] Mac OS and Windows. Intel Macs also

offer a good platform for [_____] machine technologies that allow you to use one computer to simulate the hardware and software of another. One of the potential problems with Mac OS is its use of [_____] forks, which make cross-platform file sharing clumsy. Apple also has a mobile operating system called [_____] used on iPhones, iPads, and iPod Touches. Linux is a(n) [_____] source operating system that is used extensively for servers. One of the reasons it has not become a popular desktop OS is that it requires a bit more technical savvy than Windows or Mac OS. Developed by Microsoft and supplied on the original IBM PCs, [_____] was one of the first operating systems for personal computers. [_____] is a mobile operating system developed by Google and used extensively for tablets and smartphones.

▶ CHECK ANSWERS

4

SECTION C: A computer _____ is a named collection of data that exists on a storage medium, such as a hard disk, CD, DVD, or USB drive. Every file has a name and might also have a file extension. The rules that specify valid file names are called file-naming _____ . These rules typically do not allow you to use certain characters or _____ words in a file name. A file _____ is usually related to a file format—the arrangement of data in a file and the coding scheme used to represent the data. A software program's _____ file

format is the default format for storing files created with that program. A file's location is defined by a file _____ (sometimes called a path), which includes the storage device, folder(s), file name, and extension. In Windows, storage devices are identified by a drive letter, followed by a(n) _____ . Every storage device has a(n) _____ containing a list of files stored on the device. The top-level list of a device is referred to as the _____ directory, which can be subdivided into several smaller lists called subdirectories that are depicted as _____ . ▶ CHECK ANSWERS

SECTION D: File _____ encompasses any procedure that helps you organize your computer-based files so that you can find them more effectively. _____-based file management uses tools provided with a software program to open and save files. Additional tools might also allow you to create new folders, rename files, and delete files. The Save and Save As dialog boxes are examples of these file management tools. Most operating systems provide file management _____ that give you the "big picture" of the files you have stored on your disks. The structure of folders that you envision on your disk is a(n) _____ model, which is often represented by a storage _____ , such as a tree structure or filing cabinet. Windows File Explorer and the Mac _____ are examples of file management utilities provided by operating systems. These utilities allow

you to find, rename, copy, move, and delete files and folders. In addition, they allow you to perform file management activities with more than one file at a time. The way that data is actually stored is referred to as the _____ storage model. Before a computer stores data on a disk, CD, or DVD, it creates the equivalent of electronic storage bins by dividing the disk into _____ , and then further dividing the disk into _____ . This dividing process is referred to as _____ . Each sector of a disk is numbered, providing a storage address that the operating system can track. Many computers work with a group of sectors, called a(n) _____ , to increase the efficiency of file storage operations. An operating system uses a file _____ to track the physical location of files. ▶ CHECK ANSWERS

SECTION E: A backup is a copy of one or more files that have been made in case the original files become damaged. A good backup plan allows you to _____ your computing environment to its pre-disaster state with a minimum of fuss. Your personal backup plan depends on the files you need to back up, the hardware you have available to make backups, and your backup software. In any case, it is a good idea to back up the Windows _____ and make sure your files are free of _____ . Backups should be stored in a safe place, away from the computer. Personal computer backups are typically recorded on _____ hard drives, USB flash drives, network servers, and online storage services.

An easy way to get a backup of important data files is to use a _____ management utility to select important files and copy them to a USB flash drive. _____ compares files on two devices and makes them the same. Backup software differs from most copy routines because it _____ all the files for a backup into one large file. A(n) _____ backup saves time by backing up only those files that have been changed since the last backup. Restoring a Windows computer usually requires several steps, such as reinstalling the operating system, before a backup can be restored. The process can be simplified by using a backup system that offers bare-_____ restore. ▶ CHECK ANSWERS

Interactive Situation Questions

Apply what you've learned to some typical computing situations. When using the NP2014 interactive eBook, you can type your answers, and then use the Check Answers button to automatically score your responses.

1. While using several Windows programs at the same time, your computer displays an error message that refers to a program that is not responding. You recognize this message as one that might result from a(n) [_____] leak and decide to close the non-responding program using the Task Manager.

2. Your friend wants to open a window on his Mac computer in which he can run Microsoft Windows and play some games designed for the Windows platform. You tell your friend to create a(n) [_____] machine using software such as Parallels Desktop.

3. Suppose you are using Microsoft Word and you want to open a file. When your software lists the documents you can open, you can expect them to be in Word's [_____] file format, which is DOCX.

4. Can you use a Windows application, create a document, and store it using the file name *I L*ve NY*? Yes or no? [_____]

5. When you want to work with several files—to move them to different folders, for example—it would be most efficient to use a file management utility, such as the Windows File [_____] or the Mac Finder.

6. When specifying a location for a data file on your hard disk, you should avoid saving it in the [_____] directory.

7. Your computer seems to be taking longer to store and retrieve files. You use a(n) [_____] utility to rearrange the files in contiguous clusters.

8. You have an old computer that you will donate to a school, but you want to make sure its hard disk contains no trace of your data. To do so, you use file [_____] software that overwrites empty sectors with random 1s and 0s.

9. You just finished copying data files to an external USB hard disk. Before you depend on these files as a backup, you should test to make sure you can [_____] the data in the event of a hard disk crash.

10. Your hard disk crashed for some unknown reason. Now when you switch on the computer power, all you get is an "Error reading drive C:" message. You use a(n) [_____] CD that contains the operating system files and device drivers needed to start your computer without accessing the hard disk.

▶ CHECK ANSWERS

Interactive Practice Tests

Practice tests that consist of ten multiple-choice, true/false, and fill-in-the-blank questions are available in the NP2014 interactive eBook. Test questions are selected at random from a large test bank, so each time you take a test, you'll receive a different set of questions. Your tests are scored immediately, and you can print study guides that help you find the correct answers for any questions that you missed.

▶ CLICK TO START

Learning Objectives Checkpoints

Learning Objectives Checkpoints are designed to help you assess whether you have achieved the major learning objectives for this chapter. You can use paper and pencil or word processing software to complete most of the activities.

1. List and describe the four main resources that an operating system manages.

2. Explain the significance of multitasking, multithreading, and multiprocessing.

3. Explain the term *memory leak*, and describe what you can do if one occurs on your PC.

4. Watch your computer while it boots, and then revise the list on page 188 so that it reflects what happens when your computer boots.

5. Describe five tasks for which you must interact directly with the operating system.

6. Describe the basic elements of a graphical user interface and contrast them with the elements of a command-line interface.

7. List four operating systems used on personal computers, two operating systems used on servers, and four operating systems used on handheld devices. List advantages and disadvantages of the three most popular personal computer operating systems.

8. Explain the difference between dual booting and virtual machine technology. Give examples of tasks that might benefit from dual booting or virtual machine capability.

9. Make a list of five file names that are valid under the file-naming conventions for your operating system. Also, create a list of five file names that are not valid, and explain the problem with each one.

10. Pick any five files on the computer that you usually use, and write out the full path for each one.

11. Describe the significance of file formats. List at least ten common formats and their extensions. Make a list of at least 20 file extensions you find on the computer you use most often. Group these extensions into the following categories: system files, graphics files, sound files, text files, other.

12. Demonstrate that you can manage files on a computer by looking at the files on your computer and locating at least five files or folders that should be renamed or relocated to improve the organization and make it easier to locate information on your computer.

13. Describe what happens in the MFT when a file is stored or deleted. Explain what it means when a file is fragmented.

14. Discuss the pros and cons of using an external hard drive, USB flash drive, network server, or online storage service for backups.

15. Describe how synchronization software works and give two examples of synchronization utilities. Describe the way backup software deals with the files in the backup. Explain the differences between full, differential, and incremental backups.

16. Describe the significance of restore points, bare-metal restore, disk imaging, virtual machines, boot disks, and recovery disks.

17. Describe the basic technique for backing up an iPhone, iPad, or iPod Touch.

Study Tip: Make sure you can use your own words to correctly answer each of the purple focus questions that appear throughout the chapter.

4

Concept Map

Fill in the blanks to illustrate the hierarchy of OS resource management activities.

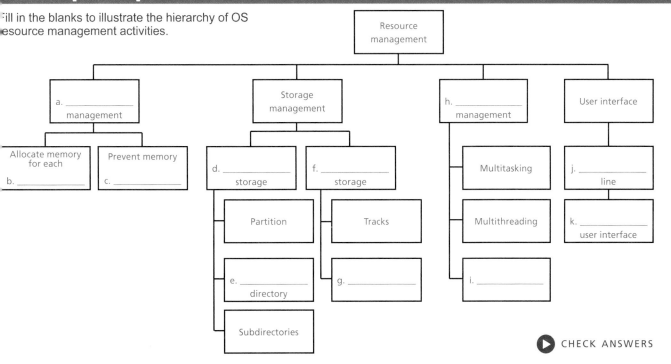

- Resource management
  - a. _____ management
    - Allocate memory for each
      - b. _____
    - Prevent memory
      - c. _____
  - Storage management
    - d. _____ storage
      - Partition
      - e. _____ directory
      - Subdirectories
    - f. _____ storage
      - Tracks
      - g. _____
  - h. _____ management
    - Multitasking
    - Multithreading
    - i. _____
  - User interface
    - j. _____ line
    - k. _____ user interface

▶ CHECK ANSWERS

5

Local Area Networks

Chapter Contents

INFOWEBLINKS

You'll find updates for chapter material by connecting to the **NP2014 Chapter 5** InfoWebLink.

🅦 CLICK TO CONNECT
www.infoweblinks.com/NP2014/ch05

Learning Objectives

After reading this chapter, you will be able to answer the following questions by completing the outcomes-based Learning Objectives Checkpoints on page 299.

1. What are PANs, LANs, MANs, and WANs?
2. What are the advantages and disadvantages of LANs?
3. Which devices are included in a typical LAN?
4. What is the purpose of a communications protocol?
5. Why do most networks transmit digital rather than analog signals?
6. How does data find its way over a network to a specified destination?
7. What are the characteristics of Ethernet that make it a popular network technology?
8. How are data signals sent wirelessly?
9. What are the major differences between Bluetooth and Wi-Fi?
10. How do you configure a router for your LAN?
11. What sort of security is available for wireless routers?
12. How do you join a wireless network?
13. What are the easiest ways to share files on a LAN?
14. What are the threats to LAN security?
15. How does encryption work?

Apply Your Knowledge

The information in this chapter will give you the background to:

▮ Select equipment for building a local area network

▮ Assemble a basic network

▮ Configure a network router

▮ Use a Bluetooth device

▮ Share files, printers, and an Internet connection over a network

▮ Join a Wi-Fi network using a smartphone or other handheld device

▮ Troubleshoot problems with your network

▮ Implement measures to secure your network

▮ Use encryption software

●TRY IT!

IS MY COMPUTER CONNECTED TO ANY NETWORKS?

Chapter 5 introduces computer networks and explains how handy they are for sharing files and accessing the Internet at home, at school, or in a business. Your computer might be connected to a home network or it might have access to a campus network or a local wireless hotspot. To discover the networks that your computer can access, complete the following steps:

View your basic network information and set up connections

1. Open your computer's network utility.
   Windows 8: From the Start screen, type **Control** and access the Control Panel. Under the Internet and Network heading, select **View network status and tasks** to view the Network and Sharing Center.
   Windows 7: Click **Start**, then select **Control Panel**. Click the **View network status and tasks** link to view the Network and Sharing Center.
   Mac: Click the 🍎 **Apple** icon on the menu bar, then select **System Preferences**. Click the **Network** icon.
2. Study the information displayed by your computer.
   How many networks are available? _____
   How many networks are connected? _____
   Is your connection Wi-Fi or Ethernet? _____
3. Check the status of your local network.
   Windows 7 and 8: Look for Connections, then click the Wi-Fi or Ethernet link next to it. Using the applicable red lines shown on the screen at right, write down the status information for the network.
   Mac: If you have a Wi-Fi or Ethernet connection, it should have an IP address. What is the IP address for your network connection?

   _____

Windows 7 and 8

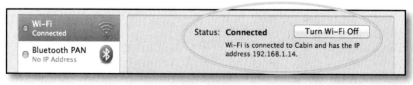

Mac OS X

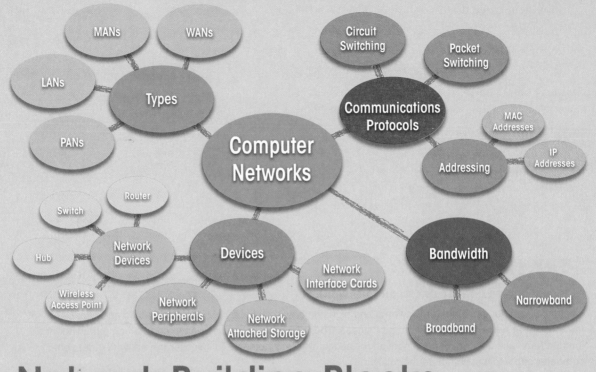

Network Building Blocks

TODAY, NETWORKS ARE EVERYWHERE and everyone wants to be connected. If you understand the network building blocks introduced in Section A, working with network technologies will be a piece of cake.

NETWORK CLASSIFICATIONS

▶ **What's the purpose of a network?** In the early years of personal computers, networks were scarce. Most personal computers functioned as standalone units, and computing was essentially a solitary activity in which one person interacted with one computer.

Some computer engineers, however, had the foresight to anticipate that personal computers could be networked to provide advantages not available with standalone computers. One of the most significant network ideas was conceived by Bob Metcalfe in 1976. His plan for transporting data between computers, shown in Figure 5-1, has become a key element in just about every computer network.

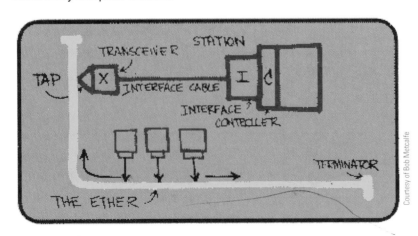

FIGURE 5-1

In 1976, Bob Metcalfe drew this diagram of network technology, which he called Ethernet.

▶ **How are computer networks classified?** Networks can be classified according to their size and geographic scope.

PAN (personal area network) is a term sometimes used to refer to the interconnection of personal digital devices or consumer electronics within a range of about 30 feet (10 meters) and without the use of wires or cables. For example, a PAN could be used to sync data from a handheld device to a desktop computer, ship data wirelessly to a printer, or transmit data from a smartphone to a wireless headset.

A **LAN** (local area network) is a data communications network that connects personal computers within a very limited geographical area—usually a single building. LANs use a variety of wired and wireless technologies. School computer labs and home networks are examples of LANs.

A **MAN** (metropolitan area network) is a public high-speed network capable of voice and data transmission within a range of about 50 miles (80 km). Examples of MANs include local Internet service providers, small cable television companies, and local telephone companies.

A **WAN** (wide area network) covers a large geographical area and usually consists of several smaller networks, which might use different computer platforms and network technologies. The Internet is the world's largest WAN. Networks for nationwide banks, large cable television companies, and multi-location superstores can also be classified as WANs.

▶ **Why is geographic scope important?** Localized networks normally include a small number of computers, which can be connected using basic equipment. As the area of network coverage expands, the number of workstations grows, specialized devices are sometimes required to boost signals, and the diversity of devices requires sophisticated management tools and strategies.

The focus of this chapter is on LANs because you are most likely to encounter this type of network in a school lab or small business. Also, if you intend to set up or upgrade a network in your home or dorm room, you will be working with LAN technologies (Figure 5-2).

5

TRY IT!

A university that offers wireless Internet access to students and the local community is operating what type of network?

○ PAN

○ LAN

○ MAN

○ WAN

FIGURE 5-2

The computer network in a dorm room is a LAN.

© iStockphoto.com/sturti

LAN ADVANTAGES AND DISADVANTAGES

▶ **Why are LANs advantageous?** Today, the pervasiveness of LANs and other types of networks has dramatically changed the face of computing by offering **shared resources**—hardware, software, and data made available for authorized network users to access. LANs offer the following advantages:

▶ **LANs enable people to work together.** Using groupware and other specialized network application software, several people can work together on a single document, communicate by e-mail and instant messaging, take part in multiplayer computer games, and participate in online conferences and Webcasts (Figure 5-3).

FIGURE 5-3

LANs can be used for intra-LAN collaboration, or they can be connected to other networks for broader participation.

▶ **Sharing networked software can reduce costs.** Although purchasing and installing a single software copy for an entire LAN might be technically possible, it is generally not allowed under the terms of a single-user license agreement. However, software site licenses for network use are usually less expensive than purchasing single-user versions of a product for each network user.

▶ **Sharing data on a LAN can increase productivity.** To transfer data between standalone computers, a file is usually copied to some type of removable storage media, and then carried or mailed to the other computer where it is copied onto the hard disk. LANs can provide authorized users with access to data stored on network servers or workstations.

▶ **Sharing networked hardware can reduce costs.** In an office environment, for example, a single expensive high-speed color printer can be purchased and attached to a LAN, instead of the costly alternative of purchasing color printers for each employee who wants to generate color printouts.

▶ **Sharing an Internet connection can be cost-effective and convenient.** A LAN allows all connected devices to access a single Internet connection, so each device is not required to have a separate Internet service contract. Devices sharing the connection have access to a variety of Internet services, such as Google, Skype, and Facebook.

TRY IT!

What type of license is required for multiple computers to simultaneously run the same software on a LAN?

○ An Internet service pack

○ A standard EULA

○ A volume license

○ A LAN copyright

▶ **Sharing networked hardware can provide access to a wide range of services and specialized peripheral devices.** Networked peripheral devices, such as scanners, photo printers, plotters, and high-capacity storage devices, can be accessed by any authorized LAN users. In a home environment, a LAN can offer access to surveillance and monitoring devices from inside or outside the home. LANs can control entertainment devices, and supply them with downloaded music and videos (Figure 5-4).

FIGURE 5-4

Music and video can stream over a LAN to projectors, speakers, and televisions when devices are equipped for wireless networking.

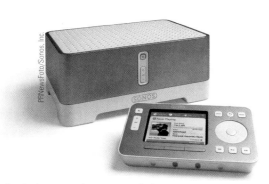

A wireless projector streams video signals from a remote PC.

A wireless receiver connects to an audio system, so you can listen to music from your PC in any room.

A wireless media player can stream video to your television, and play digital music on your stereo system.

▶ **Do LANs have disadvantages?** LAN users need to be aware of several disadvantages that have the potential to compromise privacy and security.

▶ **Malfunctions limit access to data.** One disadvantage of LANs is that when a network malfunctions, many of the resources you're accustomed to accessing are unavailable until the network is repaired.

▶ **LANs are vulnerable to unauthorized access.** Whereas a standalone computer is vulnerable to on-premises theft or access, network computers are vulnerable to unauthorized access from many sources and locations. Through unauthorized use of a LAN workstation, intruders can access data stored on the network server or other workstations. LANs connected to the Internet are vulnerable to intrusions from remote computers in distant states, provinces, or countries. Unsecured wireless connections can be tapped from any computers within range of the wireless signal.

▶ **LANs are vulnerable to malicious code.** LANs are also more vulnerable than standalone computers to malicious code. Whereas the most prevalent threat to standalone computers is disk-borne viruses, networks are susceptible to an ever-increasing number of worms, Trojan horses, and blended threats. If a worm gets through LAN security, every computer on the network is at risk.

▶ **Is it worth the risk?** Most computer owners are enthusiastic about the benefits provided by LANs and believe that those benefits outweigh the risks of intrusions and viruses—especially if their computers can be protected by security tools, such as antivirus software and firewalls. You'll learn more about LAN security threats and countermeasures later in this chapter.

TRY IT!

When a network becomes inoperable:

○ it is easier for hackers to steal data

○ users don't have access to network resources

○ viruses start to spread

○ all of the above

NETWORK DEVICES

▶ **What devices can be attached to a network?** You can think of a network as a spider web with many interconnecting points. Each connection point on a network is referred to as a **node**. A network node usually contains a computer, networked peripheral, or network device.

▶ **How do computers connect to LANs?** A desktop or laptop computer connected to a network is sometimes called a workstation. Other classes of computers, such as mainframes, supercomputers, servers, tablets, and smartphones, can also connect to LANs.

To connect to a LAN, a computer requires network circuitry, sometimes referred to as a **network interface card** (NIC). Network circuitry is built into the main system board of most personal computers. If not, a NIC can be added to a slot in the system board or to a USB port.

▶ **What is a networked peripheral?** A **networked peripheral**, or network-enabled peripheral, is any device that contains network circuitry to directly connect to a network. Printers, scanners, and storage devices are examples of devices that can be equipped to directly connect to a network instead of connecting to a workstation.

A storage device that directly connects to a network is called **network attached storage** (NAS). Networked peripherals are sometimes described as being "network ready" or as having "built-in networking." Some devices offer networking as an optional add-on.

▶ **What are network devices?** A **network device** (sometimes referred to as a network appliance) is any electronic device that broadcasts network data, boosts signals, or routes data to its destination.

The most important network device is a **router**, which acts as a central distribution point for getting data to its destination. Network devices also include hubs, switches, gateways, bridges, wireless access points, and repeaters. You will learn more about these devices later in the chapter. In the meantime, study Figure 5-5 for an example of a LAN that connects a variety of computers, networked peripherals, and network devices.

FIGURE 5-5

A small LAN uses a network device, such as a router, to connect computers and peripherals.

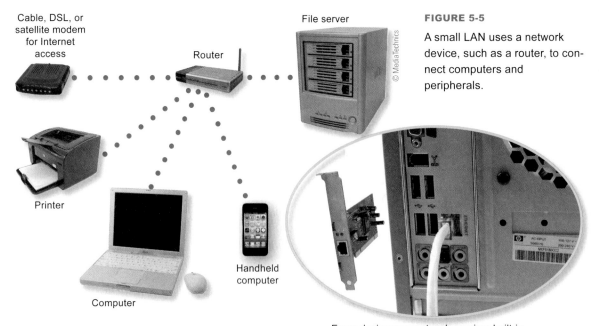

Every device on a network requires built-in network circuitry or a network interface card.

NETWORK LINKS

▶ **What connects network nodes?** Data in a network with wired connections travels from one device to another over cables. A network without wires transports data through the air, eliminating the need for cables.

A **communications channel**, or link, is a physical path or a frequency for signal transmissions. You're probably familiar with channels, such as 101.5, on your car radio that carry the signals from your favorite radio station. Links in a computer network are also considered communications channels.

▶ **Do networks require special cables?** Wired network devices are usually connected using Category 5 (Cat 5) or Category 6 (Cat 6) cables terminated at each end with a plastic **RJ45 connector** (Figure 5-6).

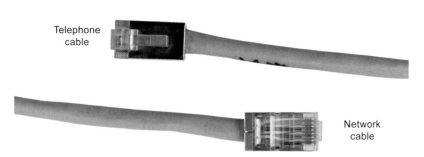

Telephone cable

Network cable

FIGURE 5-6

Network cables are terminated with plastic RJ45 connectors that are similar to, but slightly larger than, the connectors used for telephones.

Network cables contain four pairs of copper wires. Each pair of wires is independently insulated and then twisted together, which is why network cable is sometimes referred to as twisted-pair cable. Shielded twisted-pair (STP) cable contains shielding, which reduces signal noise that might interfere with data transmitted over unshielded twisted-pair (UTP) cable. The shielded cable is not significantly more expensive. Cat 5 and Cat 6 cables have a maximum length of 328 feet (100 meters).

MANs and WANs often use optical fiber cables to carry network signals. An **optical fiber cable** is composed of many strands of glass tubes that are not much wider than a human hair. Data signals speed through these tubes as rays of light.

▶ **What's bandwidth?** Network links must move data and move it quickly. **Bandwidth** is the transmission capacity of a communications channel. Just as a four-lane freeway can carry more traffic than a two-lane street, a high-bandwidth communications channel can carry more data than a low-bandwidth channel. For example, the coaxial cable that brings you more than 100 channels of cable TV has a higher bandwidth than your home telephone line.

The bandwidth of a channel carrying digital data is usually measured in bits per second (bps). For example, your wireless LAN might be rated for an average speed of 27 Mbps. The bandwidth of a channel carrying analog data is typically measured in hertz (Hz). For example, the copper wires that carry voice-grade telephone signals are often described as having 3,000 Hz bandwidth.

High-bandwidth communications systems, such as cable TV and DSL, are sometimes referred to as **broadband**, whereas systems with less capacity, such as dial-up Internet access, are referred to as **narrowband**. Broadband capacity is essential for networks that support many users, and those that carry lots of audio and video data, such as music and movie downloads.

TERMINOLOGY NOTE

Hz is an abbreviation for hertz, which refers to the number of times a wave oscillates, or peaks, per second. Telephone signals are transmitted in the 1,200 Hz range. Many wireless networks transmit a 2.4 GHz signal that peaks 2.4 billion times per second.

TRY IT!

The speed of a computer network connection is usually rated in:

○ Mbps

○ Hz

○ KB

○ GB

5

COMMUNICATIONS PROTOCOLS

▶ What is a protocol? A protocol is a set of rules for interacting and negotiating. In some respects, it is like signals between the pitcher and catcher in a baseball game. Before the ball is thrown, the catcher and pitcher use hand signals to negotiate the speed and style of the pitch.

In the context of networks, a **communications protocol** refers to a set of rules for efficiently transmitting data from one network node to another. Just as a pitcher signals the catcher in baseball, two computers on a network might negotiate their communications protocols through a process called **handshaking**. The transmitting device sends a signal that means "I want to communicate." It then waits for an acknowledgement signal from the receiving device. The two devices negotiate a protocol that both can handle. The sounds you hear as two fax machines connect are examples of handshaking.

The best-known communications protocol is probably TCP/IP. It is the protocol that regulates Internet data transport and has become a standard for LANs as well.

▶ What can communications protocols do? Protocols set standards for encoding and decoding data, guiding data to its destination, and mitigating the effects of interference. Specifically, protocols are responsible for the following aspects of network communications:

▶ Dividing messages into packets

▶ Affixing addresses to packets

▶ Initiating transmission

▶ Regulating the flow of data

▶ Checking for transmission errors

▶ Acknowledging receipt of transmitted data

▶ How does data travel over a network? In 1948, Claude Shannon, an engineer at Bell Labs, published an article describing a communications system model applicable to networks of all types, including today's computer networks.

In Shannon's model, data from a source, such as a network workstation, is encoded and sent as signals over a communications channel to a destination, such as a network printer, storage device, server, or workstation. When data arrives at its destination, it is decoded. Transmission signals can be disrupted by interference called noise, which has the potential to corrupt data, making it erroneous or unintelligible (Figure 5-7).

FIGURE 5-7

A communications system basically sends information from a source to a destination. Although the path between the source and destination might appear to be straight in the diagram, the data can pass through several devices, which convert it to electrical, sound, light, or radio signals; beam it up to satellites; route it along the least congested links; or clean up parts of the signal that have been distorted by noise.

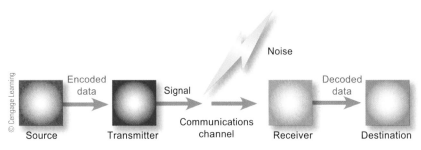

▶ What kind of signals travel over computer networks? When data is transmitted over a network link, it usually takes the form of an electromagnetic signal. You can think of these signals as waves that ripple through cables or through the air. Digital signals are transmitted as bits using a limited set of frequencies. Analog signals can assume any value within a specified range of frequencies. Figure 5-8 helps you visualize the difference between digital and analog waves.

▶ How can a network detect if a signal has been corrupted? Digital networks—those that transmit digital signals—can be easily monitored to determine if interference has corrupted any signals. At its most primitive level, digital equipment is sensitive to only two frequencies—one that represents 1s and one that represents 0s.

Suppose that a 0 is sent as -5 volts and a 1 is sent as +5 volts. What if, during transmission, some interference changes the voltage of a "perfect" 1 from +5 volts to +3 volts? When the signal is received, the receiving device realizes that +3 volts is not one of the two valid voltages. It guesses that a 1 bit (+5 volts) was actually transmitted, and cleans the signal by reestablishing its voltage to +5. Correcting errors is one of the responsibilities of protocols.

▶ What's a packet? When you send a file or an e-mail message, you might suppose that it is transmitted as an entire unit to its destination. This is not the case. Your file is actually chopped up into small pieces called packets.

A **packet** is a parcel of data that is sent across a computer network. Each packet contains the address of its sender, the destination address, a sequence number, and some data. When packets reach their destination, they are reassembled into the original message according to the sequence numbers (Figure 5-9).

FIGURE 5-8

Digital and Analog Waves

The signals carried on a digital channel are depicted as squared waves.

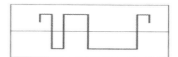

An analog signal is depicted as smoothly curved waves.

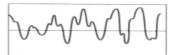

FIGURE 5-9

Before transmission, communications software divides messages into packets. Upon arriving at their destination, packets are reassembled into the original message.

▶ Why not just send an entire message? Some communications networks, such as the telephone system, use a technology called **circuit switching**, which essentially establishes a dedicated, private link between one telephone and another for the duration of a call. This type of switching provides callers with a direct pipeline over which a stream of voice data can flow. Unfortunately, circuit switching is rather inefficient. For example, when someone is on hold, no communication is taking place—yet the circuit is reserved and cannot be used for other communications.

A more efficient alternative to circuit switching is **packet switching** technology, which divides a message into several packets that can be routed independently to their destination. Messages divided into equal-size packets are easier to handle than an assortment of small, medium, large, and huge files.

Packets from many different messages can share a single communications channel, or circuit. Packets are shipped over the circuit on a first-come, first-served basis. If some packets from a message are not available, the

TRY IT!

In a digital network, a 0 or 1 bit might be sent as:

○ a packet

○ a +5 or -5 voltage signal

○ a protocol

○ an analog wave

5

© Cengage Learning

system does not need to wait for them. Instead, the system moves on to send packets from other messages. The end result is a steady stream of data (Figure 5-10).

FIGURE 5-10

Packet switching networks (bottom) provide a more efficient communications system than circuit switching networks (top). To see the differences between these technologies in action, click the Start icons in your interactive eBook.

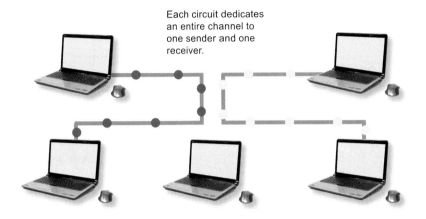

Each circuit dedicates an entire channel to one sender and one receiver.

CIRCUIT SWITCHING NETWORK

▶ CLICK TO START

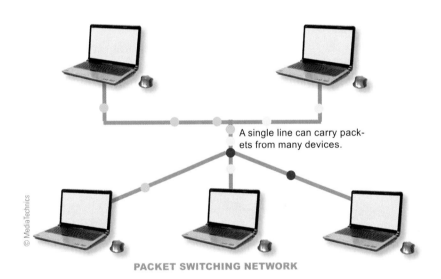

A single line can carry packets from many devices.

© MediaTechnics

PACKET SWITCHING NETWORK

▶ CLICK TO START

▶ **How are packets routed to their destinations?** Every packet that travels over a network includes the address of its destination device, similar to the way a letter contains the address of a house or mailbox. Communications protocols specify the proper format for addresses within a network. When a packet reaches a network node, a routing device examines the address and sends the packet along to its destination.

▶ **How do devices get an address?** Network addresses are a potential source of confusion. Network devices can have a variety of addresses used for different purposes. Two commonly used addresses are MAC addresses and IP addresses.

▶ **What is a MAC address?** In the context of networking, *MAC* stands for Media Access Control. A **MAC address** is a unique number assigned to a network interface card when it is manufactured. MAC addresses are used for some low-level network functions and can also be employed to establish network security.

▶ What is an IP address? An **IP address** is a series of numbers used to identify a network device. IP addresses were originally used on the Internet, but now are the standard for assigning addresses to devices in virtually every type of computer network.

IP addresses are assigned to network computers, servers, peripherals, and devices. When written, an IP address such as 204.127.129.1 is separated into four sections by periods for the convenience of human readers. Each section is called an **octet** because in binary it is represented by eight bits.

▶ Where do IP addresses come from? IP addresses can be assigned by Internet service providers or system managers. Assigned IP addresses are semi-permanent and stay the same every time you boot your computer. If you use an assigned IP address, you have to enter it when you configure your network access.

IP addresses can also be obtained through **DHCP** (Dynamic Host Configuration Protocol), a protocol designed to automatically distribute IP addresses. Most computers are preconfigured to get an IP address by sending a query to the network device acting as the DHCP server.

The IP address assigned by DHCP is good for that session. The next time you boot up, you might be assigned a different address. The fact that your IP address changes each time you boot up isn't a problem. Your network keeps track of your IP address behind the scenes; and unlike an e-mail address, your IP address is not publicized as a permanent address that people use to send files and messages to you.

▶ What happens when data reaches its destination? Even on a small home network, packets might not travel from the source directly to their destination. Like travelers routed from one airline hub to another, network traffic often travels through intermediary routing devices.

When data reaches its destination, it is checked for errors one last time and then the packets are reassembled into their original configuration. Tracking data is appended or stripped off, depending on the application, and then the newly delivered file is ready to be stored or viewed on the destination device.

5

TRY IT!

Check your computer. Does it have a fixed IP address or one handed out by DHCP? (Hint: For Windows, use the Control Panel to access the Network Sharing center; click your network connection and then look at details. For Macs, open System Preferences and select Network.)

○ My computer has a fixed IP address

○ My computer gets its address from DHCP

QuickCheck   SECTION A

1. A dorm-room network covers a limited area and is an example of a(n) [_____] area network.

2. Each connection point on a network is referred to as a network [_____].

3. Communications [_____], such as TCP/IP, set standards for encoding and decoding data, guiding data to its destination, and mitigating the effects of noise.

4. A(n) [_____] switching network establishes a dedicated connection between two devices, whereas a(n) [_____] switching network divides messages into small parcels and handles them on a first-come, first-served basis.

5. IP addresses can be assigned by an ISP or system manager, or can be automatically obtained from a(n) [_____] server. (Hint: Use the acronym.)

▶ CHECK ANSWERS

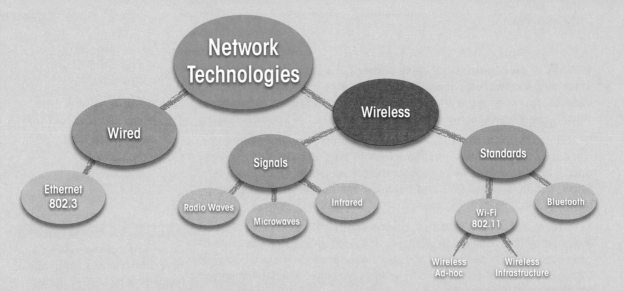

Wired and Wireless Technologies

NETWORK DEVICES CAN BE CONNECTED using wired or wireless technologies. When should you use wired connections? How do they stack up against wireless connections? This section compares the two technologies side by side.

WIRED BASICS

▶ **What is wired technology?** Wired network technology uses cables to connect network devices. Familiar technologies such as telephone and cable television make extensive use of wired connections. Much of the Internet infrastructure is also wired. Before wireless technologies became available, local area networks were exclusively wired.

Today, wired connections are used less frequently for home, school, and business networks. They remain the network technology of choice, however, for LANs that require fast and secure connectivity.

▶ **What are the advantages of wired technology?** Wired connections are fast, secure, and simple to configure. Wired connections transfer data over cables, which have high bandwidth and are shielded against interference.

The speed of a wired connection is useful when accessing large files from a local server. Wired connections also offer a faster infrastructure for playing multiplayer computer games within a LAN (Figure 5-11). For Internet-based multiplayer games, however, the speed of the Internet connection rather than the LAN is usually the limiting factor.

Wired connections are more secure than their wireless counterparts because a computer can only join a network if it is physically connected by a cable. When you set up a wired connection, you don't have to worry about hackers intercepting your data from the sidewalk outside your house, or your neighbor stumbling across your files because your wireless signal reaches past your property line.

FIGURE 5-11

Discerning multiplayer game players prefer a fast wired connection when playing head to head on a LAN.

© Caro/Alamy

256

▶ **What are the disadvantages of wired connections?** The cables that offer speed and security for a wired connection are also its main weakness. Devices tethered to cables have limited mobility. Desktop computers tend to be better candidates for wired connections, whereas laptop computers, tablets, and handheld devices can retain their mobility when they are not tethered to a cable.

Cables are unsightly, tend to get tangled, and collect dust. Running cables through ceilings, walls, and floors can be tricky or banned by your landlord. Some building codes prohibit network cables from running through air conditioning and heating ducts. When drilling holes for network cables, installers should take care to avoid electrical wires and other hazards.

ETHERNET

▶ **What is Ethernet?** **Ethernet** is a wired network technology that is defined by IEEE 802.3 standards. It was first deployed in 1976 and has since emerged as the dominant standard for wired connections in local area networks.

▶ **Why is Ethernet so popular?** Ethernet's success is attributable to several factors:

▶ Ethernet is easy to understand, implement, manage, and maintain.

▶ As a nonproprietary technology, Ethernet equipment is available from a variety of vendors, and market competition keeps prices low.

▶ Current Ethernet standards allow extensive flexibility in network design to meet the needs of small and large installations.

▶ Ethernet is compatible with popular Wi-Fi wireless technology, so it is easy to mix wired and wireless devices on a single network.

▶ **How does Ethernet work?** Ethernet simultaneously broadcasts data packets to all network devices. A packet is accepted only by the device to which it is addressed (Figure 5-12).

> **TERMINOLOGY NOTE**
>
> IEEE (Institute of Electrical and Electronics Engineers) is a nonprofit professional association dedicated to advancing technological innovation. The organization publishes standards, which in networking ensure that devices interoperate.

FIGURE 5-12

On an Ethernet, a packet is broadcast to every device, but is accepted only by the device to which it is addressed.

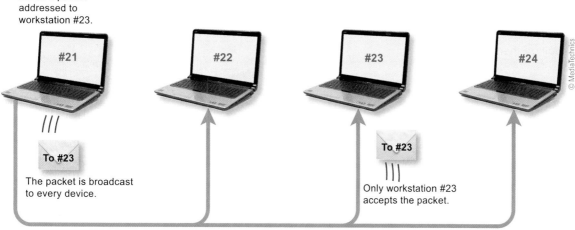

This workstation sends a packet addressed to workstation #23.

#21   #22   #23   #24

To #23

The packet is broadcast to every device.

To #23

Only workstation #23 accepts the packet.

© MediaTechnics

▶ **How fast is Ethernet?** The original Ethernet standard carried data over a coaxial cable at 10 Mbps. Ethernet encompasses a family of LAN technologies that offer various data transmission rates as shown in Figure 5-13. Today, most personal computers and LAN equipment work with Gigabit Ethernet.

Ethernet Standard	IEEE Designation	Speed
10BaseT Ethernet	IEEE 802.3i	10 Mbps
Fast Ethernet	IEEE 802.3u	100 Mbps
Gigabit Ethernet	IEEE 802.3z	1,000 Mbps
10 Gigabit Ethernet	IEEE 802.3ae	10 Gbps
40/100 Gigabit Ethernet	IEEE 802.3ba	40 or 100 Gbps

FIGURE 5-13

Ethernet Standards

▶ **How can I tell if a device is Ethernet ready?** Many computers have a built-in Ethernet port located on the system case. The port looks very similar to an oversized telephone jack (Figure 5-14).

© MediaTechnics

An Ethernet port is slightly larger than a telephone jack.

FIGURE 5-14

Many computers have a built-in Ethernet port.

▶ **What if a computer doesn't have an Ethernet port?** If you want a wired network connection, but your computer has no Ethernet port, you can purchase and install an **Ethernet adapter** (also called an Ethernet card or NIC). A USB Ethernet adapter plugs into a USB port and can be used with laptop and desktop computers. You also have the option of installing an Ethernet card in an expansion slot inside the system unit of a desktop computer. Figure 5-15 illustrates two types of adapters for adding Ethernet ports.

FIGURE 5-15

Ethernet Adapters

© MediaTechnics

Sergei Devyatkin

Ethernet adapter for USB port   Ethernet adapter for expansion slot

TRY IT!

Check your computer. Does it have an Ethernet port for wired network connections?

○ Yes, it is built in

○ Yes, it is an Ethernet adapter in my USB port

○ No, there isn't one

WIRELESS BASICS

▶ **What is wireless technology?** Wireless network technology transports data from one device to another without the use of cables or wires. Although we use the term *wireless connection*, there is no physical connection between wireless devices in a network. Their connection is conceptual in the sense that data can travel between "connected" devices.

Networks of all sizes, from PANs to LANs and WANs, can use wireless technologies, such as radio signals, microwaves, and infrared light.

▶ **How do radio signals transport data?** Most wireless connections transport data as RF signals (radio frequency signals). **RF signals**— commonly called radio waves—are sent and received by a **transceiver** (a combination of a transmitter and a receiver) that is equipped with an antenna. Workstations, peripheral devices, and network devices can be equipped with transceivers to send and receive data on wireless networks (Figure 5-16).

▶ **How do microwaves transport data? Microwaves** (the waves themselves, not your oven!) provide another option for transporting data wirelessly. Like radio waves, microwaves are electromagnetic signals, but they behave differently.

Microwaves can be aimed in a single direction and have more carrying capacity than radio waves. However, microwaves cannot penetrate metal objects and work best for line-of-sight transmission when a clear path exists between the transmitter and receiver. Microwave installations usually provide data transport for large corporate networks.

▶ **How does infrared transport data?** Today, most people are familiar with television remote controls that use **infrared light** beams. Infrared can also carry data signals, but only for short distances and with a clear line of sight. Its most practical use seems to be for transmitting data between devices connected to a PAN.

▶ **What are the advantages of wireless connections?** The main advantage of wireless connections is mobility. Wireless devices are not tethered to network cables, so battery-operated workstations can be easily moved from room to room, or even outdoors. With wireless networks, there are no unsightly cables, and power spikes are much less likely to run through cables to damage workstations.

▶ **Do wireless networks have disadvantages?** In the past, wireless network equipment was more expensive than equivalent wired equipment. With the current popularity of wireless technologies, however, prices have equalized. When compared to wired networks, the main disadvantages of wireless networks are speed, range, licensing, and security.

▶ **Why is wireless slower than wired?** Wireless signals are susceptible to interference from devices such as microwave ovens, cordless telephones, and baby monitors. When interference affects a wireless signal, data must be re-transmitted, and that takes extra time.

FIGURE 5-16

Wireless equipment often sports an antenna for transmitting and receiving data signals. The antenna is not always visible; it can be incorporated within the body of the device.

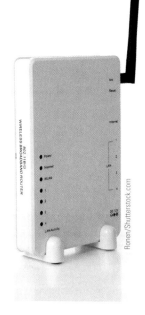

5

TRY IT!

The wireless signals that travel over a home network are most similar to:

○ the emissions from a microwave oven

○ the signals that travel within a fiber-optic cable

○ the interference from an electrical outlet

○ the signals from a car radio

Despite interference, wireless connections are fast enough for most applications, such as sharing files and browsing the Web. But when lots of computer game players compete against each other over a LAN, a fast, wired connection is desirable.

▶ **What limits the range of a wireless network?** The range of a wireless signal can be limited by the type of signal, the transmitter strength, and the physical environment. Just as radio stations fade as you move away from their broadcasting towers, data signals fade as the distance between network devices increases. Signal range can also be limited by thick walls, floors, or ceilings.

As signal strength decreases, so can speed. A weak signal usually means slow data transfers. You can get a rough idea of signal strength for your desktop, laptop, tablet, or smartphone by checking the network signal strength meter (Figure 5-17).

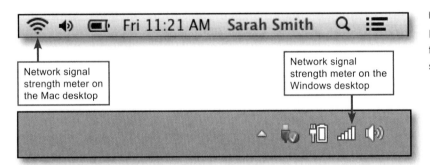

FIGURE 5-17

If your computer is connected to a wireless network, an icon shows the signal strength.

▶ **What's wrong with wireless security?** Wireless signals float through the air and penetrate walls. The signals that carry your wireless data can be accessed from outside your premises. Someone outside of your house, for example, could surreptitiously join your network, access files, and piggyback on your Internet connection. To make wireless data useless to intruders, it should be encrypted. Later in the chapter, you'll learn how to use encryption to secure data sent over wireless connections.

▶ **How does licensing affect wireless connections?** Government agencies, such as the Federal Communications Commission (FCC), regulate signals that are sent through the air. To broadcast at most frequencies, including those used by radio and television stations, a license is required. Only certain frequencies are unlicensed and available for public use.

Unlicensed frequencies include 2.4 GHz and 5.8 GHz used by cordless telephones and baby monitors, and the 460 MHz frequency used for two-way CB (Citizens Band) radios. Wireless connections use unlicensed frequencies so that they can be set up without applying to the FCC for permission. The few unlicensed frequencies are crowded, however, and neighboring networks that are forced to use the same frequencies pose security risks.

▶ **What are the most popular technologies for wireless connections?** By far the most popular wireless LAN technology is Wi-Fi. Additional wireless technologies such as Bluetooth, Wireless USB (WUSB), and Wireless HD (WiHD) are useful for PANs that include wireless game controllers, MP3 players, televisions, printers, digital cameras, and scanners. Other wireless technologies, such as WiMAX, are MAN or WAN technologies commonly used for fixed Internet access. Let's take a brief look at Bluetooth technology and then examine Wi-Fi in more detail.

TRY IT!

Check your computer. Do you have a strong wireless signal?

○ Yes, I have lots of bars

○ I have good, but not full, signal strength

○ I have low signal strength

○ My computer doesn't seem to have a wireless connection

BLUETOOTH

▶ **What is Bluetooth?** **Bluetooth** is a short-range wireless network technology that's designed to make connections between two devices. Bluetooth is not commonly used to connect a collection of workstations into a LAN. Instead, Bluetooth connectivity replaces the short cables that would otherwise tether a mouse, keyboard, game controller, or similar device to a computer.

Bluetooth can be used to link devices in a PAN, connect home entertainment system components, provide hands-free cell phone operation in an automobile, connect game controllers to videogame base stations, synchronize handheld devices with desktop computers, and link a cell phone to a wireless headset (Figure 5-18).

Bluetooth operates at the unlicensed 2.4 GHz frequency, so it is open to public use.

▶ **How does Bluetooth work?** Bluetooth links devices through a process called pairing. **Pairing** creates a persistent link between two devices, usually through the exchange of an authentication code called a passkey.

Devices equipped with Bluetooth capability can be set into **discovery mode**, in which they are open for pairing. Two devices in discovery mode can "discover" each other and exchange passkeys. Once pairing is complete, the two devices can share data without exchanging passkeys again.

▶ **What are the speed and range of Bluetooth?** Bluetooth offers peak transmission rates of only 3 Mbps, and devices should be within about 30 feet of each other. It is one of the slowest wireless technologies, so it is suitable for sending small bursts of data, rather than large files.

▶ **Can I tell if my computer has Bluetooth?** Bluetooth is built into many desktop, portable, and handheld computers. If your computer does not have built-in Bluetooth, you can plug a Bluetooth antenna into a USB port. You can look for the Bluetooth logo on your computer's task bar (Windows) or menu bar (Mac). Figure 5-19 illustrates Bluetooth icons and what they mean.

FIGURE 5-18

Bluetooth technology is used for wireless keyboards and mice, but it is also the technology used for wireless headsets and devices like Motorola's Bluetooth headset, which clips to a motorcycle helmet so you don't miss important cell phone calls.

© iStockphoto.com/muratkoc

Norman Chan/ Shutterstock.com

FIGURE 5-19

Bluetooth status icons appear on an iMac's menu bar at the top of the screen.

© MediaTechnics

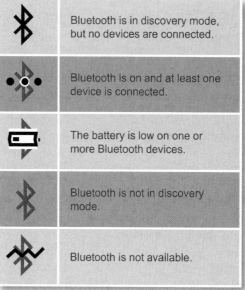

✳	Bluetooth is in discovery mode, but no devices are connected.
•◦•	Bluetooth is on and at least one device is connected.
▭	The battery is low on one or more Bluetooth devices.
✳	Bluetooth is not in discovery mode.
⋇	Bluetooth is not available.

5

WI-FI

▶ **What is Wi-Fi?** **Wi-Fi** refers to a set of wireless networking technologies defined by IEEE 802.11 standards. A Wi-Fi device transmits data as radio waves and is compatible with Ethernet, so you can use the two technologies in a single network.

▶ **How does Wi-Fi work?** You can set up Wi-Fi in two ways. One option is to use **wireless ad-hoc protocol** in which devices broadcast directly to each other (Figure 5-20).

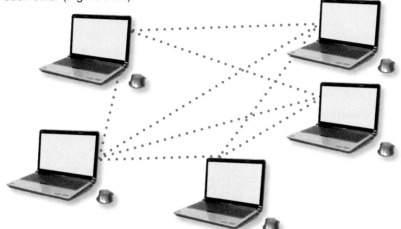

FIGURE 5-20

Wireless ad-hoc networks are conceptually simple, but provide few security safeguards. This type of connection is best limited to occasional use when you want to temporarily connect two computers to share a few files.

A second option uses **wireless infrastructure protocol** in which a centralized broadcasting device coordinates communication among network devices (Figure 5-21). Later in the chapter, you will see how this configuration offers more security than ad-hoc connections.

FIGURE 5-21

Wireless infrastructure networks use a centralized device to handle data that travels from one device to another.

▶ **Are there different types of Wi-Fi?** Wi-Fi encompasses several standards, designated by the letters *b*, *a*, *g*, *n*, and *y*. The current standard is n; so when you purchase Wi-Fi devices, make sure they are compatible with 802.11n.

▶ **How can I tell if a device is Wi-Fi ready?** Today, Wi-Fi capability is included with just about every desktop, laptop, tablet, and smartphone. Don't worry if your device has no visible antenna for transmitting and receiving data; the antenna is likely integrated into the case. Legacy equipment without Wi-Fi can be outfitted with a **Wi-Fi adapter** that plugs into a USB port or an internal expansion slot.

▶ **What should I know about buying a Wi-Fi router?** The key piece of equipment in a Wi-Fi network is a router. The price of a router depends on its range and speed. When comparing routers, you'll see specifications for speed, bands, and antennas similar to those in Figure 5-22.

TRY IT!

What is the standard for most of today's wireless network equipment?

○ 802.11n

○ 803N

○ Ethernet

○ Wi-Fi b, a, g, n, and y

FIGURE 5-22

Router Specifications

	Speed	Bands	Range	Antennas	Uses
Basic Router	300 Mbps	2.4 GHz		1	Browsing, e-mail, voice chat
Basic Dual-band Router	450 Mbps	150 Mbps at 2.4 GHz 300 Mbps at 5 GHz		2 MIMO	Online gaming, simultaneous music downloads
Full-featured Router	600 Mbps	300 Mbps at 2.4 GHz 300 Mbps at 5 GHz		4 MIMO	Video streaming, multiple-story buildings

Speed: Router speed can be designated by a single number or a combination of numbers. A single number, such as 300 Mbps, means that the router transmits one set of signals at a given bit rate. A combination of numbers, such as 300+300, means that the router can transmit more than one set of signals. Such a router might be sold as a 600N router, but savvy consumers understand that no single device connected to such a modem can use all 600 Mbps; each connection is limited to 300 Mbps.

Bands: Wi-Fi can be transmitted over 2.4 GHz or 5 GHz frequencies. When a router uses both frequencies, it is referred to as **dual-band**. Dual-band offers flexibility to support various network devices and also can overcome interference on either of the bands.

Antennas: Devices with one or more antennas use **MIMO** (multiple-input multiple-output) technology to boost signals and spread them more evenly over the signal range. Routers usually have 1–4 antennas; more antennas generally mean more coverage area and good speed even as devices get farther from the router.

▶ **How do the speed and range of Wi-Fi compare to other network technologies?** With wired connections, the rated speed and range are usually quite close to actual performance. Wireless connection speed and range, however, are often theoretical maximums because signals can easily deteriorate. Although Wi-Fi 802.11n is capable of 600 Mbps speeds, its actual performance is normally 144 Mbps, which is far slower than Gigabit Ethernet.

In a typical office environment, Wi-Fi's actual range varies from 25 to 150 feet (8 to 45 meters). Thick cement walls, steel beams, and other environmental obstacles can drastically reduce this range to the point that signals cannot be reliably transmitted.

TRY IT!

Suppose your LAN has a 600 Mbps router. What is the maximum bandwidth available to each workstation?

○ 600 Mbps

○ 300 Mbps

○ 150 MIMOs

○ 600 MIMOs

QuickCheck

SECTION B

1. Today's most popular wired network technology is _____ and is defined by IEEE 802.3 standards.

2. A short-range, wireless network technology primarily used for PANs is called _____ .

3. _____ is today's most popular wireless network technology for LANs.

4. In a network that uses Wi-Fi wireless _____ protocol, a centralized device broadcasts data to all of the workstations.

5. Routers with _____ technology maintain good data speeds even as devices get farther from the router.

▶ CHECK ANSWERS

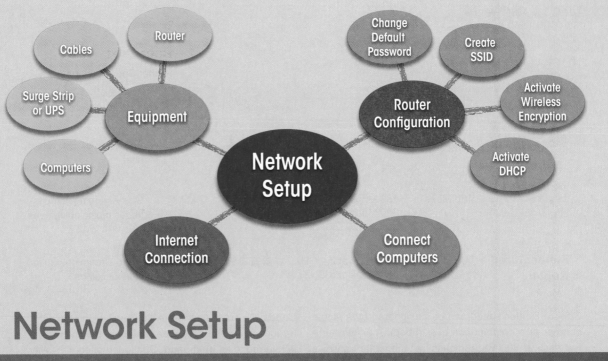

Network Setup

SETTING UP A NETWORK is easy. Whether you want to set up a simple home network to access the Internet, a lightning-fast network for playing games with your friends, or a serviceable network for your small business, use this section as a guide.

SETUP OVERVIEW

▶ **What is the basic plan?** A versatile and secure network should be configured with a centralized network device that supports both wired and wireless connections. Figure 5-23 illustrates a general network plan that can be modified by switching out workstations, printers, or file servers.

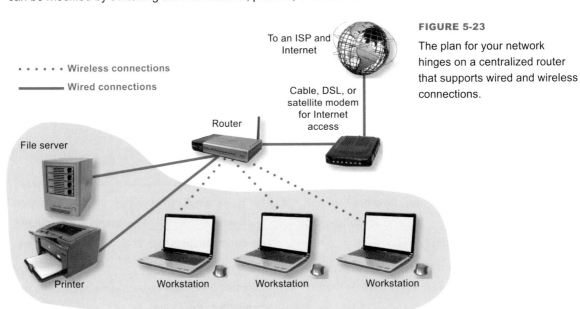

FIGURE 5-23

The plan for your network hinges on a centralized router that supports wired and wireless connections.

❱ **What equipment do I need?** Network equipment is widely available and fairly inexpensive. To get started, you'll need the gear shown in Figure 5-24.

FIGURE 5-24

Wireless Networking Equipment

Wireless-ready devices, such as computers and printers

Short piece of network cable to run between the router and one computer

Surge strip or UPS

Wireless router

❱ **What's the general procedure for setting up a network?** The key to setting up a network is to configure the router, which involves the following steps:

❱ Plug in the router.

❱ Connect the router to a computer.

❱ Configure the router.

❱ Access the router setup utility.

❱ Create a new router password.

❱ Enter an SSID for the network.

❱ Activate WEP, WPA, or PSK and create an encryption key.

❱ Connect an Internet access device.

❱ Set up the wireless workstations.

ROUTER INSTALLATION

❱ **What kind of router do I need?** Look for a Wireless-N router like the one in Figure 5-25 that includes a Gigabit Ethernet switch. The wireless capacity handles Wi-Fi connections, whereas the Ethernet capacity handles wired connections.

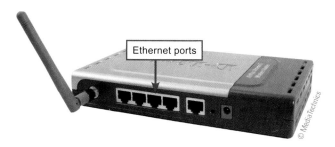

Ethernet ports

© MediaTechnics

FIGURE 5-25

Most wireless routers (note the antenna) also include ports for wired Ethernet connections. ▶ Take a look at the key features of a router.

Make sure the number of Ethernet ports is sufficient for the number of wired devices that you intend to connect. For most home networks, four Ethernet ports are sufficient; you'll likely need one for your Internet connection, one for a network printer, and perhaps one for a file server. If you have lots of friends who like to play games over a wired connection, you might want additional Ethernet ports.

In the previous section, you learned that there are several variations of Wi-Fi, including 802.11a, 802.11b, 802.11g, and 802.11n. Most Wireless-N routers allow you to connect devices that use any of these Wi-Fi standards.

TRY IT!

Check your router. How many Ethernet ports does it have?

▶ **What's the difference between a router and a switch?** In addition to routers, there are several types of network devices, including hubs, switches, gateways, bridges, wireless access points, and repeaters. Each device serves a slightly different purpose.

Modern network equipment often combines the functions of two or more network devices, such as a router that also functions as a switch and a gateway. For a typical home network, all that's needed is a wireless router that includes an Ethernet switch and Internet gateway. Extended networks in businesses and organizations might need additional devices, such as those described in Figure 5-26.

FIGURE 5-26

Network devices serve different purposes.

Network Device	Purpose	
Hub	Extends a wired network by adding additional ports	
Switch	Intelligently facilitates communication among multiple devices on a network	
Gateway	Joins two different types of networks, such as your home network and the Internet	
Bridge	Connects two similar networks	
Repeater	Extends the range of a network by restoring signals to maximum strength and retransmitting them	
Wireless access point (WAP)	Allows wireless devices to connect to a wired network	

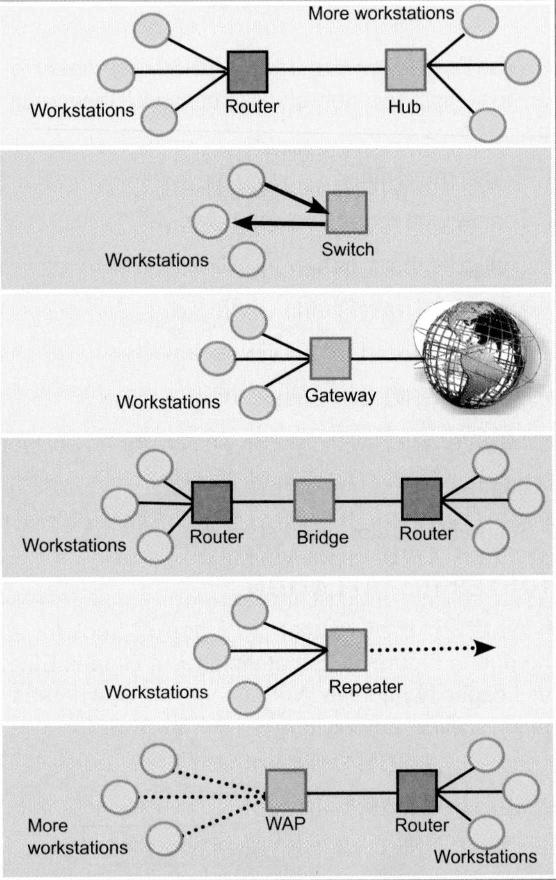

▶ **How do I power up a router?** Place the router in a central location relative to the network devices. Connect the router to a power outlet through a surge strip or UPS.

A UPS will keep your network operational during a power outage. Your ability to access the Internet during a power outage depends on the power situation at your Internet service provider, however. A network that consists of battery-operated laptop computers and a router connected to a UPS should be able to run for several hours during a blackout.

Some routers power up as soon as they are plugged in, whereas other routers have an on/off switch. Make sure your router is powered on by confirming that the power light is lit.

TRY IT!

Suppose all the Ethernet ports of your router are full, but you need to add a few more wired devices to your LAN. What can you use?

○ A hub

○ A switch

○ A bridge

○ A WAP

ROUTER CONFIGURATION

▶ **How do I access the router?** Before using your network, you should adjust the router's configuration settings to make sure your network is secure. The configuration settings are stored in the router's EEPROM memory. You'll need to log in to the configuration software to adjust the settings.

A router has no screen or keyboard of its own; so to access the router's configuration software, you have to connect a computer to the router. The easiest way to make this connection is with a short Ethernet cable (Figure 5-27). The wired connection is detected automatically by the computer's networking utilities, and that connection can provide a direct link to the router without any additional setup.

If your computer has no Ethernet port or you don't have an Ethernet cable, you might be able to activate the router wirelessly. Refer to the router's setup instructions.

▶ **How do I start the router's configuration utility?** You can use your computer's browser to access the router configuration utility. Documentation for the router supplies an IP address for the router and might also supply a default administrator password. Your router's IP address is likely to be something like 192.168.1.1 or 192.168.1.100. After opening your browser, type http:// and the router's IP address in the Address box (Figure 5-28).

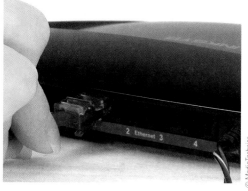

FIGURE 5-27

To connect a computer to the router, plug an Ethernet cable into one of the router's ports. Plug the other end of the cable into a computer.

© MediaTechnics

FIGURE 5-28

To access your router's configuration utility, open a browser and enter the router address.

TRY IT!

To access a router's setup utility, what do you use?

▶ **How do I change the default password?** Your first step after logging on to your router's configuration utility is to change the default password so that hackers can't gain access to your network and reconfigure it for their own malevolent schemes.

Locate the setting for the administrator password and create a new one (Figure 5-29). Follow the recommendations in earlier chapters for creating a strong password. This password is only used to configure the router. It does not need to be conveyed to network users who simply want to set up their computers to send and receive data over the network.

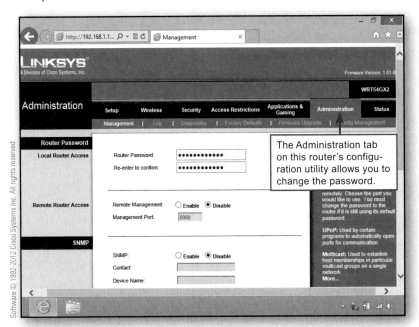

FIGURE 5-29

Change the default password for your router when you install a wireless network. ▶ Your digital textbook shows you how to access router settings and change the default password.

▶ **What is an SSID?** An **SSID** (service set identifier) is the name of a wireless network. In areas where there are overlapping wireless networks, such as in a city or on a college campus, SSIDs help you log in to the right network, rather than a network run by a hacker who will try to suck important information off your computer as soon as you connect.

▶ **How do I set the SSID?** Most routers ship with an SSID predefined by the manufacturer. Predefined SSIDs are typically very simple and publicly known.

As shown in Figure 5-30, use the router configuration software to change the default SSID. When you create an SSID, think of it as a user ID, rather than a password. Examples of SSIDs would be Cabin, Acme Company, Java Joe Coffee Shop, Planters Inn of Miami, or Alpha Kappa Delta Phi.

TRY IT!

Check your computer. What is the SSID for the network you're currently using? (Hint: Click the Wi-Fi icon.)

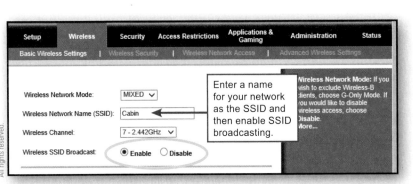

FIGURE 5-30

Create an SSID for your network so that it can be differentiated from other nearby networks.

❱ Should I broadcast my SSID? When SSID broadcasting is turned on, any wireless device passing by can see that a network exists. Legitimate users can easily find the network and connect to it. With SSID broadcasting turned off, the public can't see it. Unfortunately, hackers armed with the right tools can see the network even if the SSID is not broadcast.

Turning off SSID is a very weak form of security. Experts disagree about broadcasting your network's SSID. If you believe the potential for drive-by hacking is high, then you might not want to broadcast the SSID. In any case, SSID should be left on until you configure the rest of the devices that you plan to use on your network.

❱ How do I set the addresses for my network workstations? Each workstation requires a unique address for sending and receiving data. When you configure your router to act as a DHCP server, it will automatically assign an address to each workstation that joins your network. Figure 5-31 illustrates how to set up DHCP.

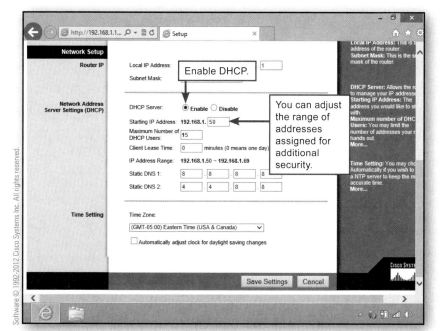

FIGURE 5-31

Enable DHCP so that the router automatically assigns an IP address to each workstation.

❱ Do I need to take any special steps to secure my network? Networks with wireless connections are much more susceptible to unauthorized access and use than networks that have only wired connections. A wireless router is not secure until you activate encryption.

❱ How does encryption secure my network? Preventing Wi-Fi signal interception is difficult, but encrypting transmitted data makes it useless to intruders. **Wireless encryption** scrambles the data transmitted between wireless devices and then unscrambles the data only on devices that have a valid encryption key. Several types of encryption are available; some are more effective than others.

TRY IT!

On a LAN, each workstation has a unique address. Where does it come from?

○ The Internet

○ Your ISP

○ The router's DHCP server

○ Your login name

▶ **What are the options for wireless encryption?** The original wireless encryption protocol was called **WEP** (Wired Equivalent Privacy) because it was designed to provide a level of confidentiality similar to that of a wired network. WEP is very easy to bypass, so it is a weak security measure.

WPA (Wi-Fi Protected Access) and its follow-up version, WPA2, offer stronger protection by making sure that packets have not been intercepted or tampered with in any way. **PSK** (pre-shared key), also referred to as personal mode, is a type of WPA used on most home networks.

▶ **Which type of encryption should I use?** All devices on a network must use the same encryption protocol. If you have even one device on your network that only supports WEP, for example, you will have to use WEP for the entire network. Although WEP is fairly easy for hackers to neutralize, it is better than leaving a network totally unprotected. If available, you'll get better security with WPA2 or PSK2.

▶ **How do I activate encryption?** To activate encryption, open the router's configuration software. Earlier in the chapter, you learned that most wireless routers can be configured by opening a browser and entering the router's IP address. Use the router configuration utilities to select an encryption protocol. In addition, you must create a wireless encryption key.

A **wireless encryption key** (sometimes referred to as a network security key) is the basis for scrambling and unscrambling the data transmitted between wireless devices. All workstations use the same key to scramble and unscramble data.

The key is similar to a password, only it is often longer. Instructions for creating a valid key are usually given in the router's documentation or on-screen Help file. For example, you might be limited to using only numbers 0 to 9 and letters A to F. Alternatively, you might be allowed to use a passphrase, such as notrespassingthismeansu, as the key.

Don't use a key or passphrase that's easy for an intruder to guess. Remember the key or passphrase you use to configure the router. Later, when you set up computers and other network devices, you will enter the same key so that every device on your network can encrypt and decrypt the data flowing on the network. Figure 5-32 illustrates how to activate wireless encryption.

TRY IT!

Which type of wireless encryption offers the most security?

○ WEP

○ WPA

○ WPA2

○ PS2

FIGURE 5-32

The configuration utility used to set up wireless security is supplied by the router manufacturer. In this example, encryption is being configured for a Linksys router.

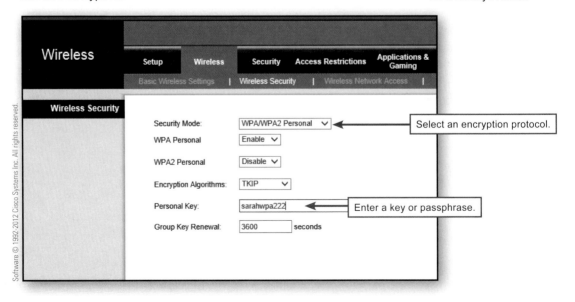

INTERNET CONNECTION

▶ **How do I connect my network to the Internet?** When you've completed the steps to configure the router password, SSID, DHCP, and encryption, make sure you save the configuration settings, then you can close the browser.

Before you connect additional computers to your network, you can connect the router to your Internet service. In the next chapter, you'll survey all the options for Internet connections; but assuming you have Internet service, you can link the router to it.

Your Internet service provider supplies a device called a modem that is designed to carry data to and from the Internet. This device usually has a standard Ethernet port that can be connected to a router (Figure 5-33).

FIGURE 5-33

Your Internet modem should have one or more Ethernet ports.

▶ **Is there a special router port for Internet connections?** Most routers supply a WAN port designed for an Internet connection. The WAN port looks like a standard Ethernet port (Figure 5-34).

FIGURE 5-34

Look for a port labeled "WAN" or "Internet" on your router. If one does not exist, then use any of the other Ethernet ports.

▶ **How do I connect the ports?** Plug a standard network cable into the router's WAN port and connect the other end of the cable into the Internet modem. Turn the modem on and wait a few seconds for it to communicate with the router.

To test the connection, open a browser to access the Internet. If you see a message like the one in Figure 5-35, you might have to check with your Internet service provider for additional instructions.

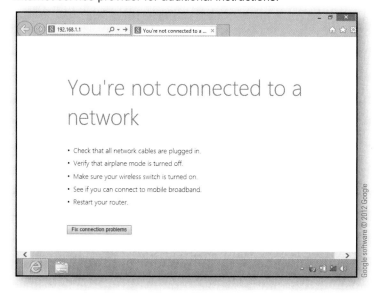

FIGURE 5-35

After you connect the router to the Internet modem, your computer should be able to connect to the Internet and browse to your favorite Web sites. If you see this screen, your connection is not set up correctly.

DEVICE CONNECTION

▶ **How do I make a wireless connection with a Windows computer?** Simply turn on any Windows computer with wireless capability and make sure that it is in range of your router. Windows should automatically find the network SSID and ask you to enter the wireless encryption key or passphrase (Figure 5-36).

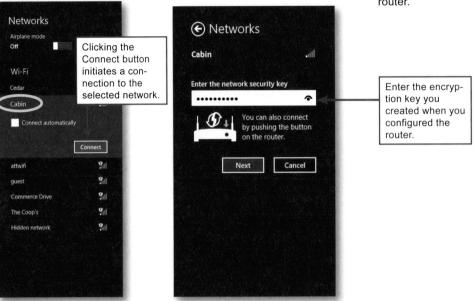

FIGURE 5-36

Windows automatically senses nearby networks and displays their SSIDs. If you choose to connect, you must enter the correct encryption key for the router.

▶ **How about connecting a Mac?** Like Windows, Macs automatically sense available networks and give you the option of connecting to them. Make sure that Wi-Fi wireless networking is turned on, then enter the encryption key when asked for the password (Figure 5-37).

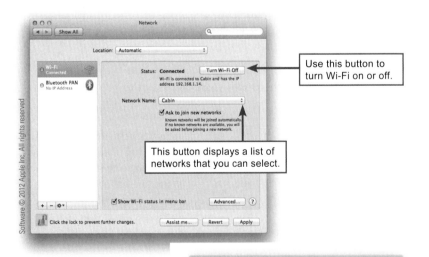

FIGURE 5-37

To make sure Wi-Fi is on, click the Apple icon, select System Preferences, and then select Network. You can connect to a network from this window or by clicking the Wi-Fi icon on the desktop menu bar.

❱ **Will my phone, tablet, and media player connect to LANs?**
Any device that has Wi-Fi capability should be able to connect to your network or any LAN. All use a similar procedure.

First, make sure that Wi-Fi is enabled, then wait for the device to sense the network. When asked, enter the encryption key (Figure 5-38).

FIGURE 5-38

On an iPhone, use the Settings icon to make sure Wi-Fi is enabled. When your phone is within range of a network, you'll see the SSID and can enter the encryption key to join.

❱ **How can I set up a printer for network access?** There are three ways to set up a printer so it can be accessed from any workstation. You can set up printer sharing using a workstation printer, set up printer sharing using a print server, or install a printer with built-in networking (Figure 5-39).

FIGURE 5-39

The easiest way to connect a printer to your network is to purchase a network-ready printer that connects to the router.

Printer attaches to one workstation

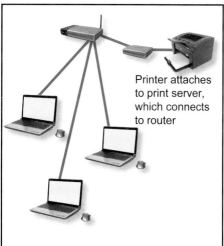

Printer attaches to print server, which connects to router

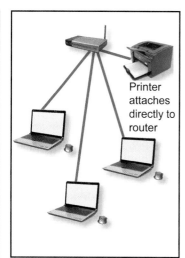

Printer attaches directly to router

QuickCheck   SECTION C

1. For flexibility when using wired and wireless connections, choose a Wireless-N router with a Gigabit _____ switch.

2. To keep your network devices powered on during an electrical outage, you can connect your router to a(n) _____ . (Hint: Use the acronym.)

3. A(n) _____ is the name given to a wireless network.

4. WEP, WPA, and PSK are examples of wireless _____ .

5. To access a router's configuration utility, you can open a(n) _____ and enter the router's network address in the address bar.

▶ CHECK ANSWERS

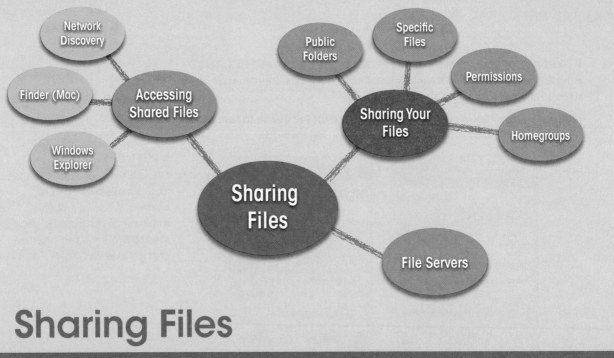

Sharing Files

SECTION **D**

LANS HAVE BECOME an integral part of computing environments at home, at school, and at work. Many LANs are installed solely for sharing access to an Internet connection or printer. What else can you do with a LAN? Section D provides practical tips on how to share files.

FILE SHARING BASICS

▶ **What is file sharing?** **File sharing** allows files containing documents, photos, music, and other data to be accessed from computers other than the one on which they are stored.

On a home network, file sharing allows you to view and copy photos, for example, from your desktop computer to a tablet computer. Or, you can use your laptop to access your course syllabus from the server in your school lab.

▶ **How does file sharing work?** Once your network gives you access to other computers on the network, you can view a list of files stored there. If you have permission, you can open files, view them, edit them, and save them back to the original location. You can also copy them to your own computer and work with them there.

▶ **Are there restrictions on file sharing?** Your ability to share files with other devices on a network depends on several factors:

▶ Which devices your computer can discover

▶ Whether other network devices can discover your computer

▶ Whether you are allowed to access files on other computers

▶ What you are allowed to do with files on other computers

▶ Whether you allow other computers to access files on your computer

▶ Which files you allow others to access

▶ What others are allowed to do with the files they can access

ACCESSING SHARED FILES

▶ **How can I see all of the devices that are connected to my network?** To see a list of devices on your network, you can use your operating system's file management utility, such as File Explorer or Finder (Figure 5-40).

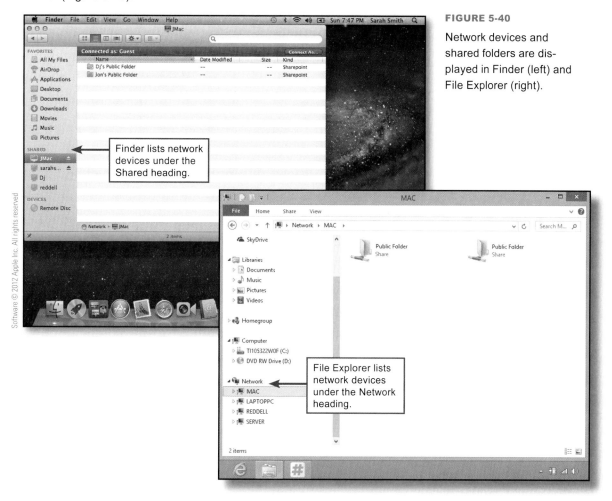

Finder lists network devices under the Shared heading.

File Explorer lists network devices under the Network heading.

FIGURE 5-40

Network devices and shared folders are displayed in Finder (left) and File Explorer (right).

5

▶ **What if other network devices aren't listed?** The network utilities provided by operating systems such as Windows and Mac OS automatically detect other devices when network discovery is turned on. **Network discovery** is a setting that affects whether your computer can see other computers on a network, and whether your computer can be seen by others.

Network discovery is usually turned on as a standard setting. If you connect to a network and don't get a list of other devices, check your computer's network discovery setting.

▶ **How do I access folders located on other computers?** You can double-click any folder to open it. Folders on some computers require a valid password for access. Your file sharing user ID and password are usually the same as the password you use to log in to your computer.

▶ **How do I access files?** Files on other computers can be accessed just as you would access files on your own computer. Double-click a file to open it. As with all files, your computer must have software that is able to open the file. For example, to open *MySong.band*, your computer has must have software that opens GarageBand files.

TRY IT!

How many devices are set to discovery mode on the Windows network shown in Figure 5-40?

SHARING YOUR FILES

▶ **Do I have to turn file sharing on?** Yes. On Windows and Mac OS, a global setting can be used to turn file sharing on or off (Figure 5-41).

FIGURE 5-41

If you want to share files, make sure that the global file sharing setting is turned on.

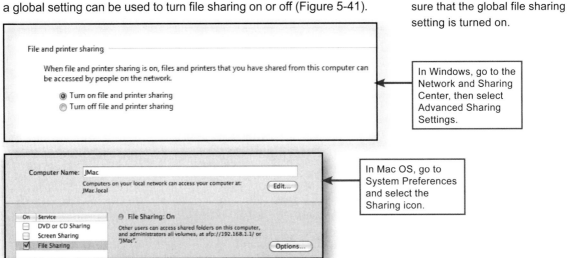

In Windows, go to the Network and Sharing Center, then select Advanced Sharing Settings.

In Mac OS, go to System Preferences and select the Sharing icon.

▶ **How do I specify which of my files can be shared by other workstations?** When you activate file sharing, files in Public folders can be accessed by other network users. You can also make specific files shareable.

▶ **Public folders.** A **Public folder** is designed to hold files and folders that you want to share with other people on your network. Windows and Mac OS are preconfigured with Public folders—for example, the Public Documents folders in Windows. When you want to share a file or folder, simply store it in a Public folder.

▶ **Specific files.** You can designate any file or folder on your computer as shared. This option is the most versatile, but the least secure.

Figure 5-42 illustrates two methods for sharing files in Windows.

FIGURE 5-42

You can share files in your Public folders, or designate specific files that you want to share.

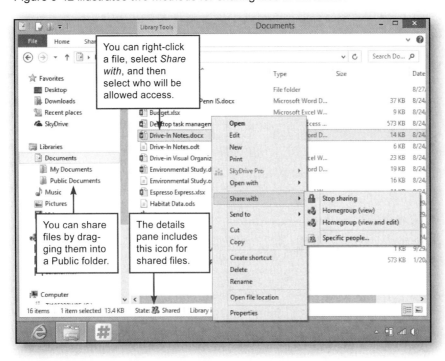

You can right-click a file, select *Share with,* and then select who will be allowed access.

You can share files by dragging them into a Public folder.

The details pane includes this icon for shared files.

▶ **How secure is file sharing?** File sharing poses security risks that have several dimensions. Shared files are subject to misuse, inadvertent modifications, and intentional alterations by those who have access to them. In addition, security holes in file sharing routines are notorious for providing Internet-based hackers with unauthorized access to computers. If you don't need to share files, turn off file sharing globally. If you want the convenience of sharing files, limit what you share and who you share it with by doing the following:

▸ Assign permissions to files.

▸ Limit sharing to specific people.

▸ Remove sharing from files you no longer want to share.

▸ Use a homegroup if your network is composed of Windows computers.

▶ **How do I assign permissions?** Use your computer's sharing utilities to select shared folders and assign permissions to files or folders.

▸ **Read and write permission** allows access for opening, viewing, modifying, or deleting files.

▸ **Read permission** allows authorized people to open a file and view it, but they cannot modify it or delete it.

▸ **Write only permission** works like a drop box, allowing people to put files in one of your folders, but not open, copy, or change any files that you have stored there (Figure 5-43).

▶ **What is a homegroup?** A **homegroup** is a collection of trusted Windows computers that automatically share files and folders. Access to the homegroup can be protected by a password. To join a homegroup, double-click the Homegroup option in File Explorer's navigation pane. Figure 5-44 shows how to set homegroup permissions.

FIGURE 5-43

On a Mac, permissions can be easily changed by clicking a user or group of users and selecting the level of access from a list.

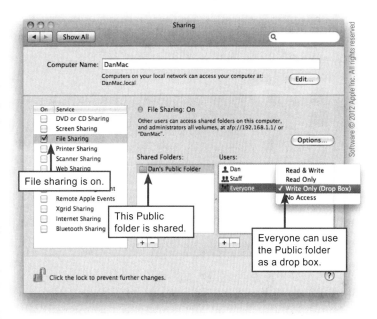

FIGURE 5-44

Right-clicking the Homegroup link takes you to settings. Your digital textbook shows you how to set up a homegroup.

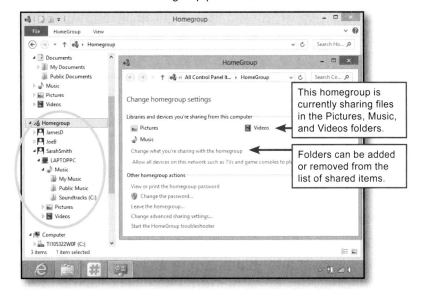

FILE SERVERS

▶ **What is a file server?** A **file server** is a computer whose primary purpose is to be a repository for files that can be accessed by network workstations. A file server can reside on any personal computer. For example, you might designate one of your old desktop computers as a file server and use it to store lots of big video files that you don't want clogging up your local hard disk.

A file server connects to a LAN's router just like any other network device. You can also purchase a computing device advertised as a server. A server normally has no monitor or keyboard; its system unit contains a microprocessor, memory, high-capacity hard disk, and built-in network adapter. File servers are available as tower units or rack-mounted blade servers (Figure 5-45).

FIGURE 5-45

Servers are sold as tower units (left) or as rack-mountable units (right), typically used for business applications.

▶ **Are file servers a good idea for home networks?** Whereas file servers are an essential component of most business networks, in many home networks, files are stored on workstations in shared folders rather than on a file server. A potential problem with this arrangement is that workstations must be turned on in order to access their files over a network.

If you find yourself running all over the house turning on computers in order to find files, your network could be more effective with a file server. File servers are designed to run continuously day and night, so they are always on and their files are always accessible.

Another reason to consider a file server for a home network is backup. Rather than purchasing external hard disk drives for each workstation's backup, one low-cost file server can supply enough space to back up files for several workstations.

▶ **Do file servers require any special setup?** If you're using a file server without its own keyboard or monitor, server configuration software is accessible using a browser. The process is similar to configuring a router. To configure a file server, open a browser from any workstation, enter the file server's IP address, and provide the administrator ID and password. The server's documentation can provide additional setup advice.

TRY IT!

Which one of the following is not a common reason to add a file server to a home LAN?

○ To back up workstation files

○ To have better access to files stored on other computers

○ To increase security

○ To save storage space on LAN workstations

NETWORK TROUBLESHOOTING

▶ **What if my network stops working?** If network discovery and file sharing are on but you cannot share files, your network might not be functioning properly.

Network problems can stem from a variety of sources. Symptoms of network malfunctions are slow response time, intermittent outages, failure to access files from one workstation, and non-availability of network services to all workstations.

To troubleshoot network problems, you have to consider the possibility of a problem with a workstation's hardware or settings; network links including cables and wireless signal strength; or network devices such as routers, servers, or network adapters. When troubleshooting network problems, consider the following possibilities:

▶ Cables. Make sure all network cables are firmly connected. If only one workstation is not accessing the network, you can try swapping cables with another workstation.

▶ Security. Make sure you are using the correct password and that your password has not expired.

▶ Interference. If you have intermittent network outages, look for sources of interference, such as cordless phones, baby monitors, or construction equipment.

▶ Settings. Make sure the network is enabled and then use the Control Panel (Windows) or System Preferences (Mac) to check the drivers for your network equipment.

▶ Switches. Many laptop computers include a physical switch that turns wireless networking on or off. Make sure this switch is in the On position for networking.

▶ Signal strength. For wireless connections, check signal strength. If the signal is weak, move the workstation closer to the router, if possible.

▶ Network devices. Make sure your network hub, switch, router, or wireless access point is plugged in and functioning properly. Check the activity lights to determine if data is being sent and received (Figure 5-46).

FIGURE 5-46

The activity lights on a router can help you determine if the router is sending and receiving data.

▶ Can I monitor network activity? Most computer operating systems provide tools for monitoring the number of packets sent, received, and dropped from your network connection. This information helps you determine if data is flowing over your network.

On Macs, you can view this information using the Network Utility application (Figure 5-47).

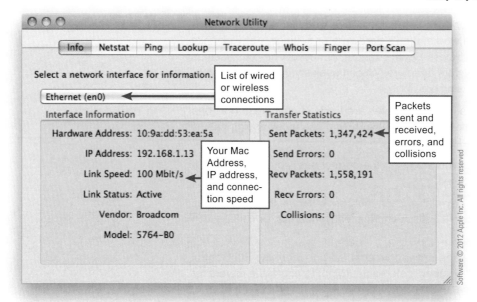

On a PC, the Network and Sharing Center is your one-stop shop for information about your LAN. To access it, open the Control Panel. Look for the link labeled *View network status and tasks* or the Network and Sharing Center icon (Figure 5-48).

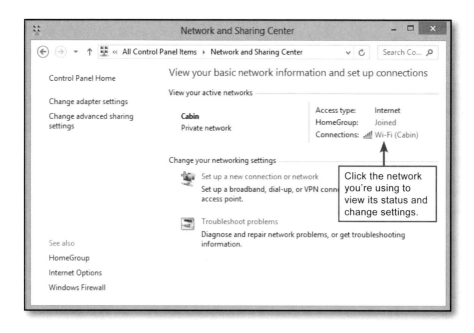

▶ **Where can I find troubleshooting utilities?** Several third-party vendors offer network monitoring and troubleshooting utilities, but check your operating system first. Windows, for example, offers a set of basic troubleshooters from the Network and Sharing Center (Figure 5-49).

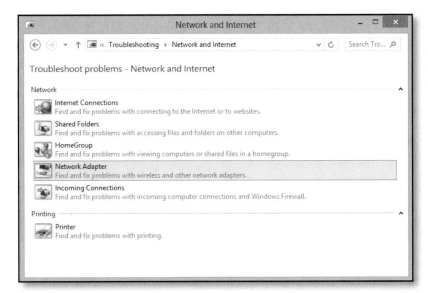

FIGURE 5-49

To access the network trouble-shooters in Windows, go to the Network and Sharing Center and click *Troubleshoot problems*.

▶ **Can I reboot my network?** Yes. When a network is not function-ing correctly, you can try rebooting it. First, make sure all applications on workstation computers are closed. Then turn off the router and your Internet modem. To restart, first turn on the Internet modem. If it has a ready-to-send (RTS) status light or similar indicator, make sure it is lit. Next, turn on your network router. Give the router a few seconds to boot, then check your network connections by trying to access another worksta-tion or the Internet.

QuickCheck   SECTION D

1. Network [_____] is a setting that affects whether your computer can see other computers on a network, and whether your com-puter can be seen by others.

2. A(n) [_____] folder is designed to hold files and folders that you want other people on your network to access.

3. With Windows, network users can join a(n) [_____] that automatically allows them to share files located in designated folders.

4. A(n) [_____] server is a computer whose primary purpose is to be a repository for files that can be accessed by network worksta-tions.

5. Many laptop computers have a physical [_____] that turns wireless network-ing on or off.

▶ CHECK ANSWERS

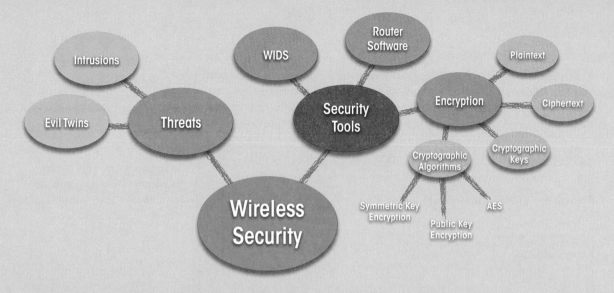

Wireless Security

JUST HOW IMPORTANT is encryption for Wi-Fi connections? Earlier in the chapter, you learned how to activate wireless encryption on your network router. In this section, you'll find out why you don't want to skip that important step.

WI-FI SECURITY

▶ **What are the threats to my network?** Networks with wired or wireless connections are vulnerable to a variety of threats, including viruses, theft, and equipment failure. Many threats can be handled using techniques for standalone computers. Network equipment should be connected to power strips to prevent damage from power spikes. Data should be backed up in case of a hard drive failure, and workstations should be protected by antivirus software.

▶ **Why are wireless connections more vulnerable than wired connections?** Wireless signals are broadcast through the air; and like the signals from a radio station, they can be picked up by any device equipped with a receiver tuned to the right frequency.

Wired connections funnel data through a cable, not through the air. Barring sophisticated eavesdropping techniques, wired signals can be intercepted only by physically tapping into the cable or router.

▶ **Is it easy to tap into wireless signals?** When network discovery is turned on, any Wi-Fi enabled device within range of your network can see its SSID. In addition, most devices indicate whether the network is secured by encryption (Figure 5-50).

▶ **So if I find unsecured networks, can I just sneak in?** When a network is not secured, any Wi-Fi enabled device can access it. You might be tempted to connect to one of these networks, maybe while traveling, to get an Internet connection. Some unsecured networks are legitimate. They are offered by coffee shops, libraries, hotels, and other businesses. Be careful, however, of random unsecured networks. They could be run by hackers who will intercept your transactions or infect your wireless device with malware.

FIGURE 5-50

Any Wi-Fi enabled device can detect wireless connections.

The lock icon indicates a network secured with WEP, WPA, or other wireless encryption.

▶ **What about protecting my network?** If your network is not secured, hackers can easily connect to it, monitor transmitted data, access connected devices, spread viruses, and use your network as a launching pad for spam.

Hackers can also set up an "evil twin"—a network with the same or similar SSID that's designed to fool users into thinking they are logging on to a legitimate network. Hackers lurking on the evil twin network can extract passwords and credit card information from unsuspecting users.

Hackers can use a variety of off-the-shelf tools to uncover information about your network, such as the type of router you use, the channels on which it transmits, and the type of security you have in place (Figure 5-51).

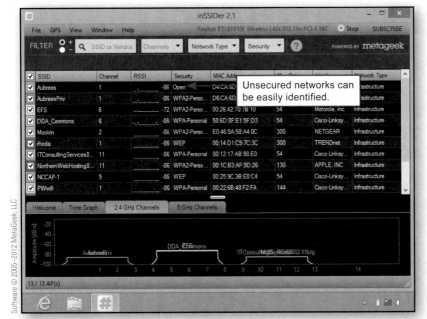

FIGURE 5-51

Software tools such as InSSIDer help locate and identify secured and unsecured networks. Once logged on to an unsecured wireless network, hackers are free to do anything from stealing the network owner's credit card or bank information to attacking computers in other networks.

▶ **How does that information help hackers?** When hackers see a network secured with weak WEP encryption, they know it is an easy target. If there are not unsecured networks in the area, networks with WEP encryption are the easiest to breach.

Suppose a hacker learns that you've installed a Linksys router on your network and that you've activated WPA-TKIP encryption. That network should be pretty secure unless you forgot to change the default administrator password. Hackers know the standard password for every type of router, and it's easy for them to try it just in case you forgot to change it.

Sophisticated hacking tools can also pinpoint the location of a network using GPS tracking. Bank of America might not use BofA as its SSID, but a hacker looking for a juicy target might be able to determine that a network called FI998 is broadcasting from the building that houses a local Bank of America branch.

TRY IT!

In Figure 5-51, what kind of security does the NCCAP-1 network have?

▶ **Can I tell if someone is hacking my network?** Yes. Your network router maintains a list of clients that are accessing your network using wired or wireless connections. You can view a list of current connections as in Figure 5-52, or you can set up your router software to maintain a log over a period of hours or days.

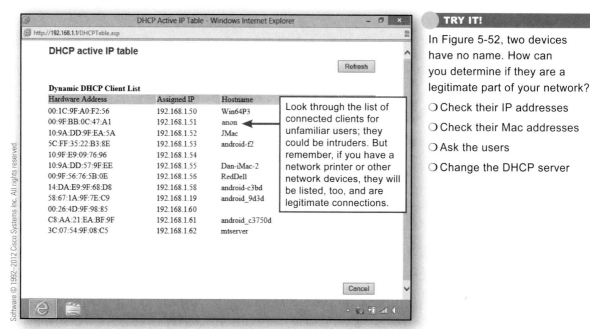

FIGURE 5-52

Router software keeps track of everyone who is accessing a network, and it can be used to uncover intrusions.

TRY IT!

In Figure 5-52, two devices have no name. How can you determine if they are a legitimate part of your network?

○ Check their IP addresses

○ Check their Mac addresses

○ Ask the users

○ Change the DHCP server

You can also use a wireless intrusion detection system (WIDS) to spot unusual activity on your network. Software, such as Who Is On My Wifi and AirSnare, can compile a list of computers that are connected to your network and warn you when unknown computers have joined (Figure 5-53).

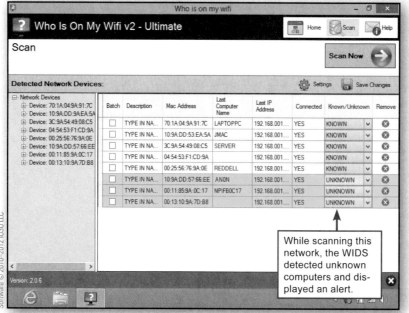

FIGURE 5-53

WIDS software runs in the background, periodically scans your network, and alerts you if unknown computers are detected.

ENCRYPTION

▶ **Exactly what is encryption?** **Encryption** transforms a message in such a way that its contents are hidden from unauthorized readers. Encryption is designed to keep messages secret. In the context of computing, encryption can be used in many ways, including the following:

▶ Scrambling data sent over wired or wireless networks to prevent intrusions

▶ Securing credit card numbers and other personal information transferred from shoppers' computers to e-commerce sites

▶ Encrypting computer files and databases so that data they contain is unusable if the device containing the data is lost or compromised

▶ Scrambling the contents of e-mail messages to maintain privacy

▶ **How does encryption work?** An original message—one that has not yet been encrypted—is referred to as **plaintext** or cleartext. An encrypted message is referred to as **ciphertext**. The process of converting plaintext into ciphertext is called encryption. The reverse process—converting ciphertext into plaintext—is called **decryption**.

Messages are encrypted by using a cryptographic algorithm and key. A **cryptographic algorithm** is a procedure for encrypting or decrypting a message. A **cryptographic key** (usually just called a key) is a word, number, or phrase that must be known to encrypt or decrypt a message.

For example, Julius Caesar made extensive use of an encryption method called simple substitution, which could have been used to turn the plaintext message "Do not trust Brutus" into "GRQRWWUXVWEUXWXV." The cryptographic algorithm was to offset the letters of the alphabet. The key was 3 (Figure 5-54).

FIGURE 5-54

The algorithm for Caesar's encryption technique was to offset the letters of the alphabet—in this case, by three letters. A simple transformation table was used to encrypt or decrypt a message. For example, if a G appears in the encrypted message, it would be a D in the original plaintext message.

CIPHERTEXT LETTERS:

D E F G H I J K L M N O P Q R S T U V W X Y Z A B C

EQUIVALENT PLAINTEXT LETTERS:

A B C D E F G H I J K L M N O P Q R S T U V W X Y Z

▶ **What's the difference between strong and weak encryption?** Caesar's simple substitution key is an example of **weak encryption** because it is easy to decrypt even without the algorithm and key. Unauthorized decryption is sometimes referred to as breaking or cracking a code. You could crack Caesar's code in several ways.

You could discover the key by making 25 different transformation tables, each with a different offset (assuming that the encryption method uses the letters of the alphabet in sequence and not at random). You could also analyze the frequency with which letters appear—in English documents, *E*, *T*, *A*, *O*, and *N* appear most frequently—and you can piece together the message by guessing the remaining letters.

Strong encryption is loosely defined as "very difficult to break." **AES** (Advanced Encryption Standard), the technology used for WPA2, is one of the strongest cryptographic algorithms. With continuous advances in technology, however, strong encryption is a moving target. Several encryption methods that were considered impossible to break ten years ago have recently been cracked.

TRY IT!

Crack this code:
RUDQJHMXOLXV

How long does it take to break strong encryption? Encryption methods can be broken by the use of expensive, specialized, code-breaking computers. The cost of these machines is substantial, but not beyond the reach of government agencies, major corporations, and organized crime. Encryption methods can also be broken by standard computer hardware—supercomputers, mainframes, workstations, and even personal computers. These computers break codes using a brute force attack, which consists of trying all possible keys (Figure 5-55).

The length of a computer-readable encryption key is measured in bits. A 32-bit key, for example, could be one of 4.2 billion (2^{32}) numbers. Surprisingly, it would be possible to try all these numbers and discover the key in less than a day by using an average personal computer.

To discover a 40-bit key, you would have to try about 1 trillion possible combinations—less than a week's worth of processing time on a personal computer. 768-bit encryption—once thought to be unbreakable by any computer in the private sector—requires a lot of computing power, but has been broken by combining the power of many personal computers connected over the Internet. Most encryption today uses a 128-bit key, which is secure from casual hackers.

Another way to understand how the length of a key affects the strength of encryption is to consider this guideline: Beginning with a 40-bit key, each additional bit doubles the time it would take to discover the key. If a personal computer takes one week to crack a 40-bit key, it takes two weeks to crack a 41-bit key, four weeks to crack a 42-bit key, and eight weeks to crack a 43-bit key. A 128-bit key takes $2^{(128-40)}$ times longer to crack than a 40-bit key—that's 309,485,009,821,345,068,724,781,056 times longer!

What's public key encryption? Caesar's encryption method is an example of **symmetric key encryption** in which the key used to encrypt a message is also used to decrypt the message. Symmetric key encryption is used to encrypt stationary data, such as corporate financial records. It is also used to encrypt the data that travels over wireless LANs.

Symmetric keys are not practical for e-mail and other situations in which the person receiving encrypted data does not have the key beforehand. E-mailing the key would be a major security problem because of the potential for a hacker to intercept it.

Public key encryption (PKE) eliminates the key-distribution problem by using one key to encrypt a message, but another key to decrypt the message. Figure 5-56 illustrates how public key encryption works.

FIGURE 5-55

To discover a four-digit PIN by brute force, a criminal must try, at most, 10,000 possibilities. Finding the key to computer data encrypted using a 32-bit key would involve about 4.2 billion possibilities.

Kathleen Finlay/Radius Images/Masterfile

FIGURE 5-56

Public key encryption uses two keys. A public key can only encrypt a message. A private key is required to decrypt the message.

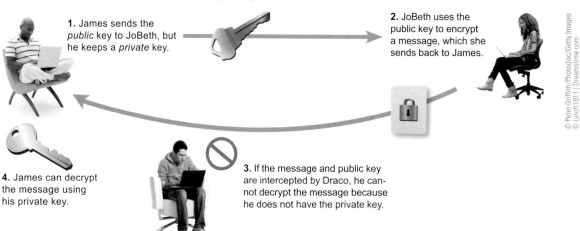

1. James sends the *public* key to JoBeth, but he keeps a *private* key.

2. JoBeth uses the public key to encrypt a message, which she sends back to James.

4. James can decrypt the message using his private key.

3. If the message and public key are intercepted by Draco, he cannot decrypt the message because he does not have the private key.

© Peter Griffith/Photodisc/Getty Images
© Leloft1911 | Dreamstime.com

Public key encryption is a crucial technology for e-commerce and e-mail. When you use a secure connection to transmit a credit card number, the server sends a public key to your browser. Your browser uses this public key to encrypt the credit card number. After it is encrypted, no one—not even you—can use the public key to decrypt the message. The encrypted message is sent to a Web server, where the private key is used to decrypt it.

When personal computer users want to encrypt e-mail or other documents, they turn to public key encryption software, such as PGP (Pretty Good Privacy), GnuPG, or AxCrypt. When you first use PKE software, it generates a private key and a public key. You must keep your private key hidden. You can then e-mail the public key to the people you have authorized to send encrypted messages to you.

The people who receive your public key can store it and use their PKE software to encrypt messages. When they send these messages to you, you can decrypt them using your private key. Figure 5-57 contains an example of a public key generated by PGP software.

```
-----BEGIN PGP PUBLIC KEY BLOCK-----

Version: 5.0

mQCNAi44C30AAAEEAL1r6BylvuSAvOKIk9ze9yCK+ZPPbRZrpXIRFBb
e+U8dGPMb9XdJS4L/cy1fXr9R9j4EfFsK/rgHV6i2rE83LjWrmsDPRPSaiz
z+EQTIZi4AN99jiBomfLLZyUzmHMoUoE4shrYgOnkc0u101ikhieAFje77j
/F3596pT6nCx/9/AAURtCRBbmRyZSBCYBNhcmQgPGFiYWNhcmRAd2
VsbC5zZi5jYS51cz6JAFUCBRAuOA6O7zYZz1mqos8BAXr9AgCxCu8C
wGZRdpfSs65r6mb4MccXvvfxO4TmPi1DKQj2FYHYjwYONk8vzA7XnE5
aJmk5J/dChdvfIU7NvVifV6of=GQv9

-----END PGP PUBLIC KEY BLOCK-----
```

Using public key encryption, you encrypt your Social Security number. Who can decrypt it?

○ I can decrypt it

○ Anyone with a browser can decrypt it

○ The person who has the private key can decrypt it

○ The person who has AES can decrypt it

5

FIGURE 5-57

PGP software generates a huge public key. Each person's public key is unique. You can e-mail this key to anyone who might want to send you an encrypted message.

QuickCheck   SECTION E

1. The term [_____] *twin* refers to a network with the same or a similar SSID that's designed to fool users into thinking they are logging on to a legitimate network.

2. A cryptographic [_____] is a word, number, or phrase that must be known to encrypt or decrypt a message.

3. A cryptographic [_____] is the process used to encrypt or decrypt a message.

4. [_____] key encryption uses one key to encrypt a message, but another key to decrypt the message.

5. [_____] key encryption uses the same key to encrypt a message as it does to decrypt the message.

 CHECK ANSWERS

Issue: Who's Tracking You?

IN THE MOVIE *Harry Potter and the Prisoner of Azkaban*, Harry acquires a magical item called the Marauder's Map, which shows the location of every teacher and student at the Hogwarts School of Witchcraft and Wizardry.

In the context of Harry Potter, tracking technology seems fun; but real-life tracking technologies have a dark side, which privacy advocates fear might be misused by governments, corporations, and possibly criminals to monitor the daily activities of ordinary people.

According to the EFF (Electronic Frontier Foundation), "Tracking is the retention of information that can be used to connect records of a person's actions or reading habits across space, cyberspace, or time."

Two broad categories of tracking are behavioral tracking and locational tracking. Behavioral tracking accumulates information about what you do: the Web sites you visit, the merchandise you purchase online, and the people with whom you correspond. Locational tracking records your physical location: where you live and work, where and when you shop, and the route you take to get to school.

Tracking made headlines in 2011 when Pete Warden and Alasdair Allan discovered that iPhones collect and store date-stamped information that triangulates the phone's location. A simple software application called iPhone Tracker can retrieve this data and display it on a map.

The iPhone tracking story spread like wildfire over the mainstream media, blogs, and social networks. Privacy advocates pointed out that govern-ment agencies, disgruntled spouses, parents, and criminals could easily trace a person's whereabouts.

Apple responded with a press release explaining the need to collect location data for LBS (location-based service) applications to work efficiently. The press release also apologized for a "bug" that allowed tracking data to be collected even when location-based service was turned off.

Copyright © ©Warner Bros/courtesy Everett Collection/Everett Collection

The technology that makes it easy for a cell phone to track your movements can be incorporated into other handheld devices and tucked into vehicles, identification badges, pet collars, clothing, and even tiny chips that can be implanted under the skin. Tracking is controversial, especially when it occurs without the consent or control of the trackee.

Privacy advocates want strict protocols for collecting, using, storing, and distributing location information. They face opposition, however, from law enforcement officials who would like to explore ways location technology can be used to track criminals and prevent terrorism.

Commercial interest in tracking technology for marketing and advertising is also high and consumers seem willing to give up some privacy for the convenience offered by location-based services, such as Yelp and Gowalla.

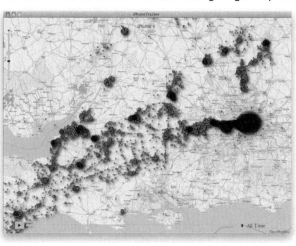

The outcome of conflicting interests will determine if location-tracking technology can be implemented in such a way that the rights and privacy of individuals are protected.

●TRY IT! Locational tracking is kind of creepy. The idea that some-one can pinpoint where you regularly use your desktop computer is one thing, but knowing that someone might be tracking your movements as you travel from home to school, to the mall, to the doctor, and to the movies might give you more than a moment of concern. Explore tracking technolo-gies to arm yourself with knowledge that can help protect your privacy.

❶ Just how detailed is the data about your location? As an experiment, a German privacy advocate named Malte Spitz obtained his personal records from his cell phone carrier, which in six months had amassed over 35,000 usage data points. Spitz made the information public and you can trace his movements on an interactive map at *www.zeit.de/ datenschutz/malte-spitz-data-retention*. What did Mr. Spitz do on Christmas day, December 25?

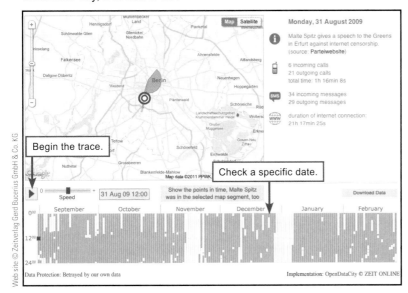

❷ Privacy advocates support Do Not Track regulations. You can explore this concept by looking for "Do Not Track" at *www.eff.org* or Wikipedia. What are the similarities and differences between Do Not Track and Do Not Call?

❸ The location of digital devices can be pinpointed using three different, but complementary, technologies: GPS, cell-tower triangulation, and WPS. Use Wikipedia and other online resources to explore these tech-nologies. How would you describe each technology?

❹ Tracking usually happens behind the scenes, often without a user's knowledge or approval. However, information that people intentionally post online can also be used to track their locations. Think about the information that you post on your social networking and media sharing sites. How might that information be used to determine your location or track your movements?

> **INFOWEBLINKS**
>
> You can check the **NP2014 Chapter 5** InfoWebLink for updates to these activities.
>
> **Ⓦ** CLICK TO CONNECT
> www.infoweblinks.com/NP2014/ch05

What Do You Think?

1. Do you worry about behavioral tracking based on your Internet use?

2. Do you have a device that can track your physical location?

3. Do you support efforts to institute Do Not Track?

Information Tools: Wikipedia

Wikipedia describes itself as "a multilingual, web-based, free-content encyclopedia project based on an openly editable model." Each Wikipedia article is compiled by volunteers who write, edit, and comment without pay. Except for entries prone to vandalism or disruption, Wikipedia articles can be edited by anyone who visits the site. Every edit and comment is tracked, and contributors are asked to conform to guidelines for style and content.

Wikipedia is a controversial resource for information and facts. Some librarians disapprove of its use, and many instructors discourage students from citing Wikipedia as a research source in footnotes or endnotes.

Said one librarian: "I do not allow students to use Wikipedia as a source. Since it can be edited by anyone, one cannot verify if the information is correct." However, that statement is in itself disinformation. The information in Wikipedia articles can and should be fact-checked just as you would check information from any other source.

A contrasting viewpoint is that Wikipedia offers some of the most dependable information available anywhere because it is vetted by a large and diverse audience.

Three core content principles shape the information that is acceptable for Wikipedia articles. Those principles are neutral point of view (NPOV), no original research (NOR), and verifiability.

Neutral Point of View (NPOV)

Avoid stating opinions as facts.

Avoid stating seriously contested assertions as facts.

Avoid presenting uncontested assertions as mere opinion.

Use non-judgmental language.

Accurately indicate the relative prominence of opposing views.

No Original Research (NOR)

Avoid any facts, allegations, ideas, and stories for which no reliable published source exists.

Verifiability

Any quotation or statement that might be challenged must be substantiated by an inline citation to a reputable source.

Many professionals and students make extensive use of Wikipedia as a resource for learning the meaning of technology terms and for getting an overview of a topic. At the college level, Wikipedia can be a useful research tool if you follow these guidelines:

▶ Do not quote Wikipedia directly.

▶ Cross-check before using facts from Wikipedia articles.

▶ Follow links in citations, or use Google to locate original sources for information you want to include in your research papers.

▶ Don't list Wikipedia articles in bibliographies; work with original sources.

▶ Never "lift" citations from the References section of a Wikipedia article; use citations only if you have examined the source document.

▶ Make sure that you go beyond Wikipedia to research your topic in sufficient depth.

TRY IT! Wikipedia includes tools that help you gauge the accuracy and neutrality for most of its articles. Exploring these tools will make you a more professional Wikipedia researcher.

1 Wikipedia is not Facebook or Twitter; articles are much more substantive than a tweet or status. Connect to the pages *Wikipedia: List of bad article ideas* and *Wikipedia: Avoiding common mistakes*. What is an "AfD"?

2 Wikipedia articles are usually written by more than one author, and articles are revised by yet another set of contributors. Just to get an idea of the amount of revision that takes place on Wikipedia, connect to the *Angry Birds* article and click the View History tab. How many revisions were made in the last week?

3 Wikipedia articles undergo constant revisions and some are controversial. If you have doubts about the material presented in an article, you can look at the discussion tab. Connect to the Wikipedia article *Hacker (term)* and click the Discussion tab. What is the major controversy behind this article?

4 While looking at the Hacker article, click the Edit tab. Scroll down, if necessary, until you can see the text for the first paragraph. This text is marked up with symbols that create bold text, links, citations, and headings when the full article is displayed. List three of the symbols used for markup.

5 Although the general public is free to make contributions to Wikipedia, new contributors are encouraged to review the site's tutorial about editing, and experiment with the sandbox area before making edits to live pages. Connect to *en.wikipedia.org/wiki/Wikipedia:Tutorial/Editing* and follow the steps on the Editing tab to use the sandbox, and then record your answers to the following questions:

a. What is the five-step editing process?

b. Continue with the editing tutorial by clicking the Formatting tab. How do you specify the text you want in a heading?

c. Continue to the Wikipedia Links tab. How would you create a bold link to the Wikipedia page about Ethernet?

6 Use Wikipedia to look up a technology topic related to the network concepts presented in this chapter. Read the article and use Wikipedia resources to answer the following questions:

a. In your opinion, what were the three most important facts in the article?

b. Did the article contain any statements that appear to violate the NPOV or NOR principles?

c. What topics are contributors discussing about the article?

d. Select two statements from the article that include references. Follow the reference links. Do the references clearly support the corresponding statements in the Wikipedia article?

INFOWEBLINKS

You can check the **NP2014 Chapter 5** InfoWebLink for updates to these activities.

W CLICK TO CONNECT
www.infoweblinks.com/NP2014/ch05

Technology in Context: Education

© Jenkedco/Shutters

THE FIRST EDUCATIONAL application of computers emerged in the 1960s, when huge mainframes with clunky interfaces introduced students to computer-aided instruction (CAI). Based on operant conditioning research by B. F. Skinner and Ivan Pavlov—remember dogs salivating when a bell rings?—CAI uses basic drill and practice: The computer presents a problem, the student responds, and the computer evaluates the response.

Studies in the 1970s indicated that CAI systems, such as PLATO (Programmed Logic for Automated Teaching Operations), improved student test scores, but students found the mainframe's monochrome display and the CAI's regimented drill format boring. Recent incarnations of CAI, such as an alien-invader style elementary math program, use snazzy graphics and arcade formats to grab learners' attention.

Courtesy of the University of Illinois at Urbana-Champaign Archive

Educators looking for ways to harness computers' interactive and programmable nature arrived at the idea of computer-based training (CBT). CBT is formatted as a series of tutorials, beginning with a pretest to see whether students have the prerequisite skills and ending with a CAI-style drill and practice test to determine whether students can move on to the next tutorial segment. Today, CBT is a popular approach to learning how to use computer software.

Another educational approach, called computer-aided learning (CAL), uses the computer more as a source of information than an assessment mechanism. Students using CAL make decisions about their level of expertise, what material is relevant, and how to pace their own learning. Exploratory CAL environments include Seymour Papert's Logo programming language; students can investigate geometry concepts by using Logo to program a graphical turtle on the screen.

In addition to CAI, CBT, and CAL, simulations have become a popular educational tool. The computer mimics a real-world situation through a narrative description or with graphics. Students are given options and respond with a decision or an action. The computer evaluates each response and determines its consequences. Oregon Trail, a simulation popular with elementary school students, describes events that beset a group of pioneers traveling in a wagon train. Students respond to each event, while learning a little about history, money-handling skills, conservation, and decision making.

Most educators believe that computers can help create an individualized and interactive learning environment, which can make learning more effective and efficient. Although 99% of American public schools have computers and 93% of students use them in some way, these statistics can be deceiving. The reality falls far short of the ideal situation in which every student has access to a computer throughout the school day.

The challenge for K–12 schools is to figure out how to achieve the computers' potential in an educational setting when supplying computers for every student is often cost prohibitive. Compromise solutions have been tried with varying degrees of success. Some schools have installed learning labs where students go for scheduled lab time. In elementary schools, often a few computers are placed in special work areas of classrooms and used for small group projects or individual drill and practice. Some schools have relegated most computers to the library, where they are connected to the Internet and used for research. In some classrooms, a single computer can be used as an effective presentation device.

Some schools—primarily colleges—have tackled the problem of computer access by requiring all incoming first-year students to purchase laptop computers. Many colleges, for example, provide Internet connections in dorm rooms and library study carrels or offer campuswide Wi-Fi service. Students can tote their laptop computers to class and take notes. They can contact instructors via e-mail, use the Internet as a research resource, and run educational software.

The proliferation of tablet computers has led to a bevy of experiments under the umbrella of mLearning, a buzzword for *mobile learning* and defined as learning that happens across locations, or that takes advantage of learning opportunities offered by portable technologies.

Another educational use of computers can be seen in distance education (DE) courses (also called distance learning). Historically, distance education meant correspondence study or courses delivered by radio or television, but the meaning has been broadened to encompass any educational situation in which students and instructors aren't in the same place. Therefore, most DE courses today require students to have access to a computer and an Internet connection. DE courses are offered to K–12 students, college students, military personnel, businesspeople, and the general public.

Most students who choose DE courses do so because they want to learn at their own pace, at a convenient time, and in a location close to home. Single parents who deal with the realities of child care, working professionals who cannot relocate to a college town, and physically disabled students find distance education handy. Distance education has the potential of increasing the pool of students for a course by making it financially feasible; for example, an advanced Kanji course could be offered at a Midwestern university with only ten on-campus Japanese majors if enough distance education students can boost enrollment.

The Internet hosts a wide variety of DE courses, both credit-earning and noncredit courses. Online courses can be presented to a small group of enrollees or to huge numbers of students. The trend toward MOOCs (massive open online courses) gained momentum when 160,000 students enrolled in an online course in artificial intelligence offered by Sebastian Thrun and Peter Norvig. This and similar non-credit courses are currently offered by Udacity, edX, Coursera, and Udemy. They are "open" to enrollments by anyone; students do not have to be formally admitted to a university to participate. Courses are offered by instructors from Stanford, MIT, and other prestigious schools, so they attract students from all over the world.

MOOCs tend to be offered in real time, whereas other online courses are posted on the Web and can be accessed at any time. Khan Academy, with its distinctively colorful instructional "chalkboard," is representative of this type of online course. Its video lessons (left) cover a wide range of topics.

Courtesy of Kahn Academy

Several learning management systems (LMSs), such as Blackboard and Moodle, help teachers prepare and manage DE courses. Learning management software typically runs from a server maintained by a school system, college, or university. Using Web browsers, teachers access the LMS to post an online syllabus, develop Web pages with course content, create a database of questions for online assessment, manage e-mail, set up online discussion groups, and maintain a gradebook. Students using Internet-connected computers and standard Web browsers can access course materials, submit assignments, interact with other students, and take tests.

Computers and the Internet have opened opportunities for lifelong learning. Prospective students can use a search engine to easily find non-credit courses and tutorials for a wide range of topics, including pottery, dog grooming, radio astronomy, desktop publishing, and drumming. Some tutorials are free, and others charge a small fee.

In a society that promotes learning as a lifelong endeavor, the Internet has certainly made it possible for students of all ages to pursue knowledge and skills simply by using a computer and an Internet connection.

New Perspectives Labs

To access the New Perspectives Lab for Chapter 5, open the NP2014 interactive eBook and then click the icon next to the lab title.

▶ LOCAL AREA NETWORKS

IN THIS LAB YOU'LL LEARN:

- When to use wired connections and when to use wireless connections
- The equipment needed to create a LAN
- How to install a router
- How to open the router configuration utility
- How to change a router's default password
- How to create an SSID
- The advantages and disadvantages of WEP, WPA, and WPA2 encryption
- How to enable wireless encryption
- How to set DHCP to automatically hand out local addresses
- How to check network settings from a PC or Mac
- How to connect to a wireless network
- How to connect a LAN to the Internet
- How to connect to a mobile hotspot

LAB ASSIGNMENTS

1. Start the interactive part of the lab. Perform each lab step as directed, and answer all the lab QuickCheck questions.

2. Use your computer's networking utilities to find out if your computer is equipped for wired or wireless connections. Make a note of the type and specifications of any network adapters installed in your computer.

3. Using the information you gathered from assignment 2, draw a sketch showing how your computer could be linked into a LAN.

4. Examine the networking utilities installed on your computer. If you are using Windows, don't forget to look at the HomeGroup utility as well as the Network and Sharing Center. Look at each utility and write a one-paragraph description for each.

© MediaTechnics

Key Terms

Make sure you understand all the boldfaced key terms presented in this chapter. With the NP2014 interactive eBook, you can use this list of terms as an interactive study activity. First, try to define a term in your own words, and then click the term to compare your definition with the definition presented in the chapter.

AES, 285
Bandwidth, 251
Bluetooth, 261
Bridge, 266
Broadband, 251
Ciphertext, 285
Circuit switching, 253
Communications channel, 251
Communications protocol, 252
Cryptographic algorithm, 285
Cryptographic key, 285
Decryption, 285
DHCP, 255
Discovery mode, 261
Dual-band, 263
Encryption, 285
Ethernet, 257
Ethernet adapter, 258
File server, 278
File sharing, 274
Gateway, 266
Handshaking, 252
Homegroup, 277
Hub, 266

Infrared light, 259
IP address, 255
LAN, 247
MAC address, 254
MAN, 247
Microwaves, 259
MIMO, 263
Narrowband, 251
Network attached storage, 250
Network device, 250
Network discovery, 275
Network interface card, 250
Networked peripheral, 250
Node, 250
Octet, 255
Optical fiber cable, 251
Packet, 253
Packet switching, 253
Pairing, 261
PAN, 247
Plaintext, 285
PSK, 270
Public folder, 276
Public key encryption, 286

Repeater, 266
RF signals, 259
RJ45 connector, 251
Router, 250
Shared resources, 248
SSID, 268
Strong encryption, 285
Switch, 266
Symmetric key encryption, 286
Transceiver, 259
WAN, 247
Weak encryption, 285
WEP, 270
Wi-Fi, 262
Wi-Fi adapter, 262
Wireless access point (WAP), 266
Wireless ad-hoc protocol, 262
Wireless encryption, 269
Wireless encryption key, 270
Wireless infrastructure protocol, 262
WPA, 270

Interactive Summary

To review important concepts from this chapter, fill in the blanks to best complete each sentence. When using the NP2014 interactive eBook, click the Check Answers buttons to automatically score your answers.

SECTION A: Networks can be classified by geographical scope as PANs, [_____], MANs, and WANs. LANs allow people to share network resources, such as files, printers, and Internet connections. LAN technologies are standardized by the [_____] organization. Each connection point on a network is referred to as a(n) [_____] and can contain computers, networked [_____], or network devices. Computers connected to a network require network circuitry, often housed on a network [_____] card (NIC). Network nodes are linked by communications channels. High-bandwidth channels are referred to as [_____], whereas low-bandwidth channels are referred to as [_____]. Communications [_____], such as TCP/IP, divide messages into [_____], handle addressing, and manage routing. Most computer networks use packet-switching technology, rather than [_____]-switching technology. Computers on a network have a variety of addresses; the two most common are IP addresses and [_____] addresses. IP addresses can be assigned or they can be automatically distributed by [_____].

▶ CHECK ANSWERS

SECTION B: Wired networks are fast, secure, and simple to configure, but installing [_____] can be a nuisance. [_____] is a fast and secure wired network technology defined by IEEE 802.3 standards. Most wireless routers transport data using [_____] frequency signals. The most popular wireless technology is Wi-Fi, but [_____] is used for PANs and other short-range connections. Wi-Fi is defined by the IEEE [_____] standards, and there are versions denoted by the letters *a*, *b*, *g*, *n*, and *y*. Computers on a Wi-Fi network must have wireless circuitry, such as a Wi-Fi adapter. Wireless networks can be set up as [_____] networks in which devices broadcast directly to each other. Alternatively, a wireless [_____] network uses a centralized broadcasting device, such as a wireless [_____] point or a wireless router. The speed of a router is measured in [_____]. Many routers use [_____] technology to boost signals and spread them over a wider coverage area.

▶ CHECK ANSWERS

SECTION C: Most LANs support both wired and wireless connections because they include a(n) [____] that has a Wi-Fi antenna and [____] ports. LANs can include other network devices, such as hubs, switches, gateways, bridges, and repeaters. After you plug in a router and connect it to a computer, you should configure the router by changing the default administrator [____]. To access the configuration utility, open a(n) [____]

and enter the router's IP address. You should also create a(n) [____] so your network has a name. If your network uses a wireless router, you should also activate wireless [____] to enhance security. Once the router is configured, you can connect it to an Internet modem. Wi-Fi equipped computers and handheld devices can join your LAN, but they have to enter the wireless encryption [____]. ▶ CHECK ANSWERS

SECTION D: You can access other computers in a LAN, and those computers can see yours if network [____] is turned on. In addition, the global setting for file [____] has to be turned on. If you have permission, you can open files from other computers on the network, view them, edit them, and save them back to the original location. You can also [____] files to your own computer and work with them there. You can share folders and files on your own computer if you want to allow other workstations to access them, but sharing is a(n) [____] isk. You should assign [____] to limit who can access your files and whether they are allowed to modify and delete them. Windows users can set up a(n) [____] to create a trusted collection of comput-

ers that can share files. If you have many files that need to be accessed from various workstations, you might want to add a(n) [____] server to the network. Network problems can stem from a variety of sources. Symptoms of network malfunctions are slow response time, intermittent outages, failure to access files from one workstation, and non-availability of network services to all workstations. To troubleshoot network problems, you have to consider the possibility of a problem with a workstation's hardware or settings; network links including cables and wireless signal strength; or network devices such as routers, servers, or NICs. Network problems can sometimes be solved if you [____] the network by turning off the router and Internet modem, then restarting them. ▶ CHECK ANSWERS

SECTION E: Compared to wired networks, wireless networks are much more susceptible to unauthorized access and use. Hackers have an easy time intercepting signals by cruising through a business district or neighborhood with a Wi-Fi enabled laptop computer. Software tools help hackers identify the type of [____] you have, the channels on which it transmits, and the type of security you have in place. Hackers use exploits such as the evil [____] to steal passwords and account numbers. If a hacker can guess the administrator password, your network could get hijacked and be used to spread spam and malware. An original message—one that has not yet been encrypted—is referred to as

[____] or cleartext. An encrypted message is referred to as [____]. Messages are encrypted by a cryptographic [____], which is a specific procedure for encrypting or decrypting a message. A cryptographic [____] is a word, number, or phrase that must be known to encrypt or decrypt a message. [____] key encryption uses the same key to encrypt and decrypt a message. [____] key encryption eliminates the key-distribution problem by using one key to encrypt a message, but another key is used to decrypt the message. ▶ CHECK ANSWERS

Interactive Situation Questions

Apply what you've learned to some typical computing situations. When using the NP2014 interactive eBook, you can type your answers, and then use the Check Answers button to automatically score your responses.

1. You just bought a new Blu-ray player and it mentions that you can access the Internet to view Netflix movies. You assume that the player is equipped with [_____] so that it can connect wirelessly to your LAN's router.

2. You're setting up an Ethernet wired network using a router. To access the router and its configuration software, you open your [_____] and type the router's IP address.

3. You're trying to figure out if your computer has a built-in Ethernet port. You see the port pictured to the right. Is that the port you should use for your RJ45 connector? Yes or no? [_____]

4. You're shopping for a new router and are attracted by the advertising for a 600N model. On examining the specifications, you see that it transmits 300+300, so you know the router is using [_____] broadcast channels.

5. Your computer is connected to a LAN, and you want easy access to files stored on several other computers on the LAN. Because all of the computers use Windows, you can set up a(n) [_____].

6. You arrive at work and one of your co-workers tells you that the router is down. Is it correct to surmise that your workstation will not be able to access other workstations, but will be able to access the Internet? Yes or no? [_____]

7. You have a small network in your house that uses a wireless router. For the past week, you've seen a black SUV parked outside and its occupant seems to be using a laptop computer. The first step you should take to discover if this person has hacked into your network is: a) knock on the car window and ask; b) call the police; or c) use your router utilities to check who is connected to your network. [_____]

8. You've set up a network using some new equipment and a few old Wi-Fi adapters given to you by your roommates. One of the adapters is equipped only for WEP, whereas all the other adapters support WPA2. Your roommate tells you that in order to use all the adapters, you'll have to disable wireless encryption. Is your roommate right? [_____]

 CHECK ANSWERS

Interactive Practice Tests

Practice tests that consist of ten multiple-choice, true/false, and fill-in-the-blank questions are available in the NP2014 interactive eBook. Test questions are selected at random from a large test bank, so each time you take a test, you'll receive a different set of questions. Your tests are scored immediately, and you can print study guides that help you find the correct answers for any questions that you missed.

CLICK TO START

Learning Objectives Checkpoints

Learning Objectives Checkpoints are designed to help you assess whether you have achieved the major learning objectives or this chapter. You can use paper and pencil or word processing software to complete most of the activities.

1. Describe the characteristics of PANs, LANs, MANs, and WANs, plus provide an example of each.

2. List five advantages and three disadvantages of computer networks.

3. Create a list of network devices mentioned in this chapter. Write a brief description of each one.

4. Draw a diagram of Shannon's communications model and explain how it relates to communications protocols. Apply Shannon's model to a Wi-Fi LAN by indicating which real-world devices would exist at various points in the model to originate data, encode it, transmit signals, and so on.

5. Explain the difference between an analog signal and a digital signal. Explain why most modern communications systems use digital signals.

6. Explain the difference between packet switching and circuit switching. Describe the differences between IP addresses and MAC addresses.

7. List five characteristics of Ethernet that make it a popular network standard.

8. List the technologies that carry wireless signals and give an example of where each is commonly used.

9. Describe the differences between Wi-Fi and Bluetooth technologies, and give two examples of where you would expect to find each in use.

10. Draw a storyboard to illustrate the steps you would take to set up a LAN and configure the router so that you can use wired and wireless connections.

11. List four kinds of wireless encryption and indicate which ones provide the best security.

12. Suppose you've set up a wireless router. Create a quick guide that instructs authorized users how to join it using their smartphones.

13. Describe the steps required to turn on file sharing for one specific file that is stored on your computer.

14. Make a list of security concerns that are related to local area networks. Describe the steps that you would take to secure your LAN.

15. Describe the difference between symmetric encryption and public key encryption. List five uses for each one.

Study Tip: Make sure you can use your own words to correctly answer each of the purple focus questions that appear throughout the chapter.

5

Concept Map

Fill in the blanks to show the hierarchy of LAN technologies.

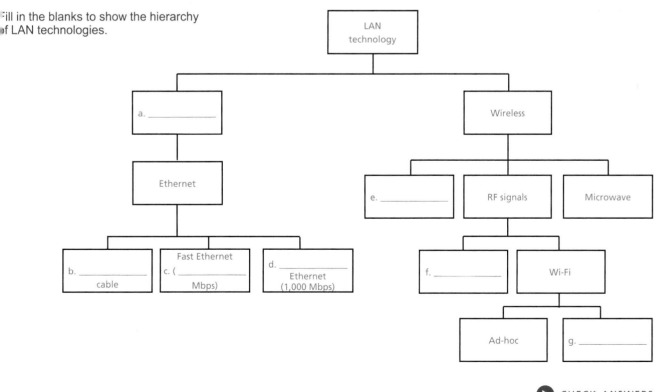

 CHECK ANSWERS

6

The Internet

Chapter Contents

INFOWEBLINKS

You'll find updates for chapter material by connecting to the **NP2014 Chapter 6** InfoWebLink.

Ⓦ CLICK TO CONNECT
www.infoweblinks.com/NP2014/ch06

Learning Objectives

After reading this chapter, you will be able to answer the following questions by completing the outcomes-based Learning Objectives Checkpoints on page 357.

1. Who created the Internet?

2. How does the Internet work?

3. What is TCP/IP?

4. What are the differences between static IP addresses, dynamic IP addresses, private IP addresses, and domain names?

5. Can I find the actual speed of my Internet connection?

6. What is the best type of Internet service?

7. Is there a difference between portable Internet access and mobile Internet access?

8. How do cell phones and other handheld devices access the Internet?

9. How do chat, instant messaging, and other Internet-based communications work?

10. How does Voice over IP work?

11. What are grid and cloud computing?

12. How is FTP different from file sharing technologies such as BitTorrent?

13. How do hackers break into computers?

14. How can I protect my computer from intrusions?

Apply Your Knowledge

The information in this chapter will give you the background to:

▶ Find your computer's Internet address

▶ Get a domain name for your Web site

▶ Measure the speed of your Internet connection

▶ Select the best Internet access services for your location and budget

▶ Access the Internet from a Wi-Fi hotspot

▶ Access the Internet from a mobile phone

▶ Use Internet services such as instant messaging, chat, FTP, Voice over IP, and BitTorrent

▶ Protect your computer from online intrusions

●TRY IT!

HOW FAST AND DEPENDABLE IS MY INTERNET CONNECTION?

You can access the Internet in various ways—using your phone line, your cable TV connection, or a personal satellite dish. Is your Internet connection fast enough for activities such as downloading DVDs and playing online multiplayer games? You can discover the speed of your Internet connection by completing the following steps:

1. Ping Google.

   Windows 7: Click the **Start** button, point to **All Programs**, click **Accessories**, and then select **Command Prompt** from the list. This action opens a DOS box. Type **Ping www.google.com** and then press the **Enter** key.

   Windows 8: From the Start screen, type **Command**, and then select **Command Prompt**. This action opens a DOS box. Type **Ping www.google.com** and then press the **Enter** key.

   Mac: Click the **Finder** icon. Select **Applications**, **Utilities**, and **Terminal**. This action opens the Terminal window. Type **Ping -c 4 www.google.com** and then press the **Enter** key.

2. Your computer makes four attempts to access Google and measures the time required for each attempt. Fill in the blanks below with the Ping statistics for your computer. When you read the chapter, you'll learn how those statistics stack up for videoconferencing, Voice over IP, and online multiplayer gaming.

3. Close the DOS box or Terminal window.

```
Command Prompt                                    –  □  ×

Microsoft Windows [Version 6.2.9200]
(c) 2012 Microsoft Corporation. All rights reserved.

C:\Users\SarahSmith>ping www.google.com

Pinging www.google.com [173.194.64.104] with 32 bytes of data:
Reply from 173.194.64.104: bytes=32 time=122ms TTL=44
Reply from 173.194.64.104: bytes=32 time=126ms TTL=44
Reply from 173.194.64.104: bytes=32 time=141ms TTL=44
Reply from 173.194.64.104: bytes=32 time=147ms TTL=44

Ping statistics for 173.194.64.104:
    Packets: Sent = 4, Received = 4, Lost = 0 (0% loss),
Approximate round trip times in milli-seconds:
    Minimum = 122ms, Maximum = 147ms, Average = 134ms

C:\Users\SarahSmith>_
```

Packets sent: _____

Packets received: _____

Packets lost: _____

Round-trip minimum: _____ ms

Round-trip maximum: _____ ms

Round-trip average: _____ ms

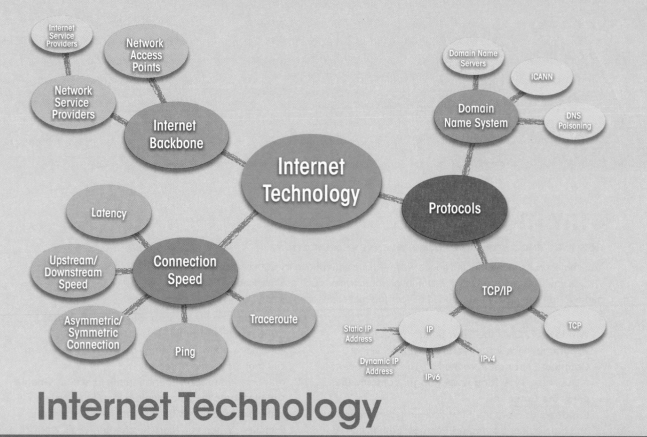

Internet Technology

TO MOST PEOPLE, the Internet seems old hat. Using the Internet is quite easy. Browsing Web sites, shopping at Amazon.com, sending e-mail, and tweeting? No problem. But what makes the Internet "tick"? How can one network offer so much information to so many people? Section A pulls back the curtain and gives you a glimpse of what happens behind the scenes on the Net.

BACKGROUND

▶ **How did the Internet get started?** The history of the Internet begins in 1957 when the Soviet Union launched Sputnik, the first man-made satellite. In response to this display of Soviet superiority, the U.S. government resolved to improve its scientific and technical infrastructure. One of the resulting initiatives was the Advanced Research Projects Agency (ARPA).

ARPA swung into action with a project designed to help scientists communicate and share valuable computer resources. The ARPANET, created in 1969, connected computers at UCLA, Stanford Research Institute, University of Utah, and University of California at Santa Barbara (Figure 6-1).

In 1985, the National Science Foundation (NSF) used ARPANET technology to create a larger network, linking not just a few mainframe computers, but entire LANs at each site. Connecting two or more networks creates an internetwork, or internet. The NSF network was an internet (with a lowercase *i*). As this network grew throughout the world, it became known as the Internet (with an uppercase *I*).

FIGURE 6-1

An original diagram of the ARPANET included four nodes, depicted as circles.

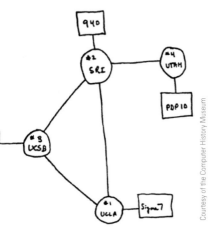

302

▶ How did the Internet become so popular? Early Internet pioneers used primitive command-line user interfaces to send e-mail, transfer files, and run scientific calculations on Internet supercomputers. Finding information was not easy and access was limited to a fairly small group of educators and scientists.

In the early 1990s, software developers created new user-friendly Internet access tools, and Internet accounts became available to anyone willing to pay a monthly subscription fee.

▶ How big is the Internet today? With an estimated 500 million nodes and more than 2 billion users, the Internet is huge. Although exact figures cannot be determined, it is estimated that the Internet handles more than an exabyte of data every day. An exabyte is 1.074 billion gigabytes, and that's a nearly unimaginable amount of data.

INTERNET INFRASTRUCTURE

▶ How is the Internet structured? Surprisingly, the Internet is not owned or operated by any single corporation or government. It is a data communications network that grew over time in a somewhat haphazard configuration as networks connected to other networks and to the Internet backbone.

▶ What is the Internet backbone? The **Internet backbone** is a network of high-capacity routers and fiber-optic communications links that provides the main routes for data traffic across the Internet. At one time, the Internet backbone and interconnected networks might have resembled a spine with ribs connected along its length. Today, however, it more resembles a map of interstate highways with many junctures and redundant routes.

▶ How does the backbone tie the Internet together? Backbone links and routers are maintained by **network service providers** (NSPs), such as AT&T, Cogent Communications, Hurricane Electric, Sprint, and Verizon.

NSP equipment and links are tied together by **network access points** (NAPs), so that, for example, data can begin its journey on a Verizon link and then cross over to a Sprint link, if necessary, to reach its destination.

NSPs supply Internet connections to large Internet service providers, such as EarthLink, Time Warner Cable, AT&T, and Comcast. An **Internet service provider** (ISP) is a company that offers Internet access to individuals, businesses, and smaller ISPs. Figure 6-2 shows a simplified conceptual diagram of the Internet backbone and its components.

FIGURE 6-2

The Internet backbone includes high-speed routers and high-speed fiber-optic links. Data traveling on the Internet (in red) can pass from one NSP to another at network access points.

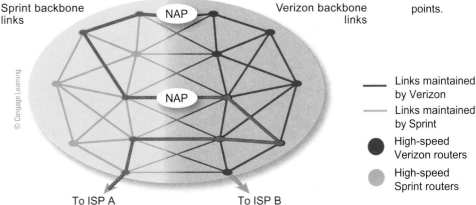

Sprint backbone links · NAP · Verizon backbone links · NAP · To ISP A · To ISP B

Links maintained by Verizon
Links maintained by Sprint
● High-speed Verizon routers
● High-speed Sprint routers

© Cengage Learning

6

▶ What kinds of network devices are part of an ISP? An ISP operates routers, communication equipment, and other network devices that handle the physical aspects of transmitting and receiving data between their subscribers and the Internet. Many ISPs also operate e-mail servers to handle incoming and outgoing mail for their subscribers. Some ISPs have Web servers for subscriber Web sites.

An ISP might operate a server that translates an address, such as *www. google.com*, into a valid IP address, such as 208.50.141.12. ISPs can also maintain servers for online discussions, instant messaging, music file sharing, FTP, streaming video, and other file transfer services (Figure 6-3).

FIGURE 6-3

ISP Equipment

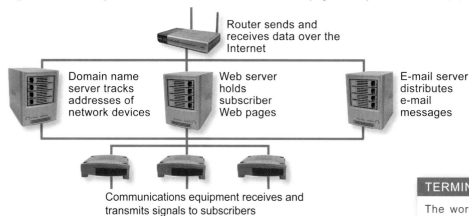

Router sends and receives data over the Internet

Domain name server tracks addresses of network devices

Web server holds subscriber Web pages

E-mail server distributes e-mail messages

Communications equipment receives and transmits signals to subscribers

▶ How does my computer fit into the structure of the Internet? To communicate with an ISP, your computer uses some type of communications device, such as a modem. A **modem** contains circuitry that converts the data-carrying signals from your computer to signals that can travel over various communications channels. The kind of modem you use depends on whether you are connecting to a dial-up, wireless, cable, satellite, or DSL Internet service.

A standalone computer can communicate with an ISP directly through a modem, or through a combination of a router and modem. If your computer is part of a network, the network's router communicates with a modem to handle the Internet connection. Figure 6-4 illustrates the difference between standalone and LAN Internet access.

TERMINOLOGY NOTE

The word *modem* is derived from the words *modulate* and *demodulate*. In communications lingo, modulation means changing the characteristics of a signal, as when a dial-up modem changes a digital pulse into an analog audio signal that travels over telephone lines. Demodulation means changing a signal back to its original state.

FIGURE 6-4

Your computer can connect to the Internet as a standalone device or part of a LAN. Your data first travels to your ISP, then to an NSP and out over the Internet backbone.

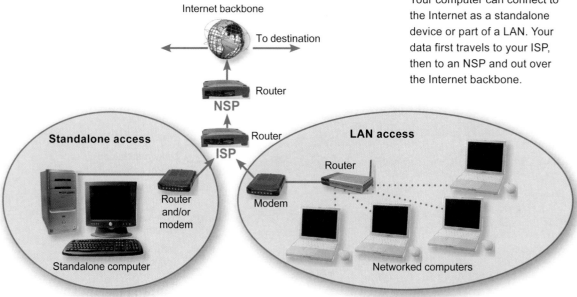

Internet backbone

To destination

Router

NSP

Standalone access

Router

ISP

LAN access

Router

Router and/or modem

Standalone computer

Modem

Router

Networked computers

INTERNET PROTOCOLS, ADDRESSES, AND DOMAINS

▶ **What protocols are used by the Internet?** The Internet uses a variety of communications protocols to support basic data transport and services, such as e-mail, Web access, and downloading. Figure 6-5 briefly describes some of the main protocols used on the Internet.

FIGURE 6-5

Protocols Used on the Internet

6

Protocol	Name	Function
TCP	Transmission Control Protocol	Creates connections and exchanges packets of data
IP	Internet Protocol	Provides devices with unique addresses
UDP	User Datagram Protocol	An alternative data transport to TCP used for DNS, Voice over IP, and file sharing
HTTP	Hypertext Transfer Protocol	Exchanges information over the Web
FTP	File Transfer Protocol	Transfers files between local and remote host computers
POP	Post Office Protocol	Transfers mail from an e-mail server to a client Inbox
SMTP	Simple Mail Transfer Protocol	Transfers e-mail messages from client computers to an e-mail server
VoIP	Voice over Internet Protocol	Transmits voice conversations over the Internet
IRC	Internet Relay Chat	Transmits text messages in real time between online users
BitTorrent	BitTorrent	Distributes files using scattered clients rather than a server

▶ **How significant is TCP/IP?** **TCP/IP** is the primary protocol suite responsible for message transmission on the Internet. A **protocol suite** is a combination of protocols that work together. **TCP** (Transmission Control Protocol) breaks a message or file into packets. **IP** (Internet Protocol) is responsible for addressing packets so that they can be routed to their destination. From a practical perspective, TCP/IP provides a protocol standard for the Internet that is public, free, extensible, and easy to implement.

▶ **Does the Internet use a special addressing scheme?** In the previous chapter, you learned that IP addresses can be assigned to LAN workstations. IP addresses originated on the Internet as part of the TCP/IP protocol. IP addresses are used to uniquely identify computers on the Internet as well as on LANs. In the context of the Internet, IP addresses are sometimes referred to as TCP/IP addresses or Internet addresses.

▶ **How do IP addresses work on the Internet?** Every device on the Internet has an assigned IP address such as 128.110.192.40. In binary, the addresses are 32 bits long, but they are usually written as decimal numbers and divided by periods into four groups called octets.

The numbers in each octet correspond to network classes. For example, an IP address that begins with a number between 128 and 191 corresponds to a Class B network, such as a large college campus. When delivering a packet of data, Internet routers use the first octet to get a general idea of where to send the packet. The rest of the IP address is used to drill down to the exact destination.

TRY IT!

In Figure 6-5, which protocol is used at file sharing sites such as TorLock, where downloads are obtained from distributed clients? [   ]

TERMINOLOGY NOTE

32-bit IP—referred to as IPv4—offers about 4 billion unique addresses. When even more addresses are needed, IPv6 can offer billions and billions of addresses. An IPv6 address is 128 bits and usually written as eight groups of four hexadecimal digits, such as 2001:0db8:0: 0:1319:8a2e:0370:57ab.

▶ Do octets correspond to the parts of e-mail or Web site addresses? E-mail addresses such as *imastudent@uga.edu* and Web site addresses such as *http://www.uga.edu* are separated into parts with periods, similar to the octets in an IP address. The octets do not, however, map to the parts of a Web site address or an e-mail address. So, although *http://www.uga.edu* has an IP address of 128.192.1.9, the first octet, 128, does not correspond to *http://*. Nor does the second octet map to *www*.

▶ What's my Internet address? Although the terms *IP address* and *Internet address* are technically the same, in practice they can be different. Your computer's local IP address might not be the same as the address that is publicly available for sending and receiving data.

In the previous chapter, you found out how to use the Network and Sharing Center (Windows) or the Network utility (Macs) to find your computer's IP address within a LAN. That address is private. The LAN's public address is the one used by your router. Figure 6-6 explains how to find your public IP address, also referred to as your Internet address.

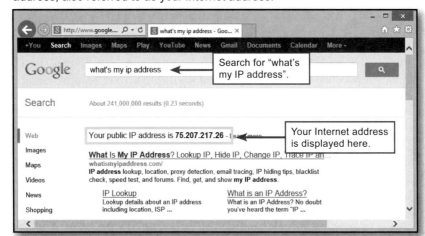

FIGURE 6-6

To find your public Internet (IP) address, start your browser and search for "what's my IP address".

▶ Do I need a permanent IP address? A computer can have a permanently assigned **static IP address** or a temporarily assigned **dynamic IP address**. As a general rule, computers on the Internet that act as servers use static IP addresses. ISPs, Web sites, Web hosting services, and e-mail servers that always need to be found at the same address require static IP addresses. Most other Internet users have dynamic IP addresses.

TRY IT!

Use Google to find your computer's public Internet address. What is it?

▶ Why doesn't everyone have a static IP address? The use of 12-digit IPv4 addresses such as 128.192.100.100 provides approximately 4.3 billion unique addresses; but many of these are reserved for special purposes and devices, leaving a meager number of IP addresses for billions of Internet users. To avoid running out of static IP addresses, dynamic addresses are used whenever possible. Dynamic IP addresses can be handed out as necessary and reused as needed.

▶ How do I get a dynamic IP address? Every ISP controls a unique pool of IP addresses, which can be assigned to subscribers. If you have the type of Internet connection that requires a modem to make a telephone connection, for example, your ISP's DHCP server assigns a temporary IP address to your computer for use as long as it remains connected. When you end a session, that IP address goes back into a pool of addresses that can be distributed to other subscribers when they log in.

Your computer is rarely assigned the same dynamic IP address it had during a previous session. As an IP nomad with no permanent address, you can't feasibly run a Web site or perform other server-related activities on your computer. For example, if you try to run an online store, its address would change every time you connect to the Internet and customers would not be able to find it.

If you want to operate a server, your ISP should be able to supply you with a service plan that includes a static IP address and adequate bandwidth for server activity.

How does a dynamic IP address relate to an always-on connection? Most high-speed Internet connections use always-on technology. An **always-on connection** is linked to your ISP and is online whenever your computer and modem are on, even if you are not actively accessing the Internet. An always-on connection can have a static or dynamic IP address. With an always-on connection, your dynamic IP address might remain the same unless you turn off your modem, or your service provider might randomly change your IP address from time to time.

TRY IT!

If you want to operate an e-commerce site from your home, you'll need all of the following except:

- ❍ a dynamic IP address
- ❍ an always-on connection
- ❍ a static IP address
- ❍ a domain name

Always-on connections are convenient. You don't have to wait for a connection to be established before using your browser or sending e-mail. If you have an always-on connection, however, you should be aware that it poses a security risk. With an always-on connection, your computer is connected to the Internet for long periods of time with the same IP address, making it particularly vulnerable to hackers. In Section E, you'll learn how routers and firewalls can protect computers that have always-on Internet connections.

What's a domain name? People find it difficult to remember the string of numbers in an IP address. Therefore, most Internet servers also have an easy-to-remember name, such as *nike.com*. The official term for this name is *fully qualified domain name (FQDN)*, but most people just refer to it as a **domain name**. A domain name is a key component of Web page addresses and e-mail addresses (Figure 6-7).

www.msu.edu/infotech **jbillings@msu.edu**

Web address E-mail address

FIGURE 6-7

Domain names are part of the addresses for servers that handle e-mail and Web sites.

A domain name ends with an extension that indicates its **top-level domain**. For example, in the domain name *msu.edu*, *edu* indicates that the computer is maintained by an educational institution. Country codes also serve as top-level domains. Canada's top-level domain is ca; the United Kingdom's is uk; Australia's is au; and the European Union uses eu as a top-level domain. Some of the most commonly used top-level domains are listed in Figure 6-8.

FIGURE 6-8

Top-level Domains

Domain	Description
biz	Unrestricted use; usually for commercial businesses
com	Unrestricted use; usually for commercial businesses
edu	Restricted to North American educational institutions
gov	Restricted to U.S. government agencies
info	Unrestricted use
int	Restricted to organizations established by international treaties
mil	Restricted to U.S. military agencies
mobi	Available for sites that cater to mobile devices such as smartphones
net	Unrestricted use; traditionally for Internet administrative organizations
org	Unrestricted use; traditionally for professional and nonprofit organizations

▶ **How are domain names related to IP addresses?** Every domain name corresponds to a unique IP address that has been entered into a huge database called the **Domain Name System** (DNS). Any computer that hosts this database is referred to as a **domain name server**.

A domain name, such as *travelocity.com*, must be converted into an IP address before packets can be routed to it. Figure 6-9 illustrates what happens when you type *www.travelocity.com* into your browser.

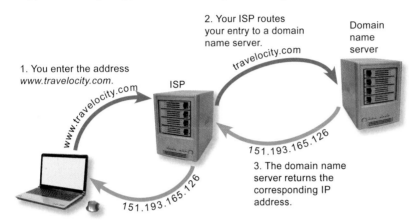

FIGURE 6-9

A domain name request is routed through your ISP to your designated domain name server, which searches through its database to find a corresponding IP address. The IP address can then be attached to packets, such as requests for Web pages.

▶ **Why don't I notice a pause when I enter a domain name?** Although it seems as if you might have to wait quite a while to receive an IP address after you enter a domain name, that is not the case. Popular domain names are "cached" at your ISP; so in practice, you usually don't have to wait for an IP address from a domain name server.

▶ **The DNS seems technical; why worry about it?** The DNS is at the heart of the Internet. There are currently 13 domain name server systems that translate, or "resolve," human-readable domain names into IP addresses. The DNS keeps track of every domain and every static IP address worldwide. When new addresses are added, they take a day or two to "propagate," or arrive, at all the domain name servers. Until domain names are added to the DNS database, new sites can be accessed only by entering their numeric IP addresses.

If a domain name server malfunctions or is hacked, Internet users can get directed to the wrong Web site. This misdirection, called **DNS cache poisoning**, has been used by governments to keeps citizens away from Web sites that supply politically or culturally inflammatory information. DNS cache poisoning is also a tool of hackers who want to direct users to sites infected with worms or keyloggers (Figure 6-10).

TRY IT!

What's the purpose of a domain name server?

○ To hand out IP addresses

○ To translate domain names into IP addresses

○ To route packets to their destination

○ To encrypt data that is sent over the Internet

FIGURE 6-10

After a hacker poisoned this domain name server, requests for Travelocity are routed to the IP address of the hacker's malicious site.

▶ **Do I need my own domain name?** For client-style Internet activities, such as Web browsing, e-mail, and chat, you do not need your own domain name. You might, however, want a domain name if you plan to operate your own Web server or if you establish a Web site using a server provided by a Web site hosting service.

▶ **How do I get a domain name?** An organization called **ICANN** (Internet Corporation for Assigned Names and Numbers) is recognized by the United States and other governments as the global organization that coordinates technical management of the Internet's Domain Name System.

ICANN supervises several for-profit Accredited Domain Registrars, which handle domain name requests. You can select a domain name and register it for a minimal annual fee—currently between US$10 and $50, depending on the registration service (Figure 6-11).

FIGURE 6-11

The first step in registering a domain name is to find out whether the name is currently in use or reserved for future use. If a domain name is not available, consider using a different top-level domain, such as biz instead of com. After you've found an available domain name, you can continue the registration process by filling out a simple online form. ▶ You can learn more about selecting a domain name when you access this figure in your interactive eBook.

CONNECTION SPEED

▶ **How fast is the Internet?** Data travels over the Internet at an incredible speed. On average, data usually arrives at its destination in less than a second after it is sent. Data transport can slow down, however, when usage peaks during breaking news events, or when denial-of-service attacks break through security. Such slowdowns are temporary, however, and usually last only a few hours.

The elapsed time for data to make a round trip from point A to point B and back to point A is referred to as **latency**. Latency generally averages less than 100 ms (milliseconds) in North America. Latency increases slightly for overseas transmissions. If you want to play online multiplayer games, it is best to have less than 100 ms latency. Good-quality Voice over IP and videoconferencing require latency rates of 200 ms or less.

▶ **Can I measure speed and latency?** In the TRY IT! activity at the beginning of this chapter, you used a local Internet utility called **Ping** (Packet Internet Groper), which sends a signal to a specific Internet address and waits for a reply. When a reply arrives, Ping reports that the computer is online and displays the elapsed time for the round-trip message. You can use Ping before playing online games, using Voice over IP, joining an online videoconference, or streaming a Netflix movie to make sure you have adequate speed for everything to run smoothly.

TRY IT!

In the TRY IT! at the beginning of the chapter, you used Ping to measure the speed of your Internet connection. What was your average latency?

Web site © 1995–2012 by Register.com ®

Ping also shows whether packets were lost in transmission. Packets can become lost when signal interference or network congestion overwhelms Internet servers and routers. Lost packets can degrade the quality of Voice over IP communications and videoconferencing. Too many lost packets during an online gaming session can cause the game to stutter or stall. And if packets don't arrive in the correct order, your game character might seem to act randomly for a few seconds.

Another utility called **Traceroute** records a packet's path in addition to its round-trip speed. You can use Traceroute to analyze the latency of your data as it hops from one Internet router to the next (Figure 6-12).

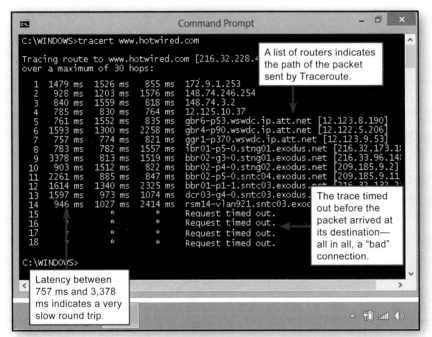

FIGURE 6-12

In this example, Traceroute is used to monitor an Internet connection between a small lakeside cabin in northern Michigan and the HotWired Web site. The satellite connection has extremely high latency and timed out before the Web site could be accessed. ▶ Click to learn how to launch Ping and Traceroute from the Windows command line and interpret the results.

▶ How fast is a typical Internet connection? The connection speeds advertised by ISPs refer to the amount of data that travels between a subscriber's computer and an ISP within a given time period. Connection speed is measured in Kbps (kilobits per second) or Mbps (megabits per second).

Slow dial-up connections top out at 56 Kbps. High-speed (also called broadband) connections at 10,000 Kbps (10 Mbps) are common. High-speed connections can display graphics quickly, show smoothly streaming video, handle Net-based videoconferences, and deliver high-quality Voice over IP.

▶ What factors affect connection speed? Your connection speed depends on whether you connect to your ISP using a telephone, cable television, satellite, or wireless link. Actual speed can differ from maximum speed because links are susceptible to interference that can hinder signals. Upstream speed can also differ from downstream speed.

▶ What are upstream and downstream speeds? **Upstream speed** is the rate of data that is uploaded from your computer to the Internet. **Downstream speed** is the rate of data downloaded to your computer. Many ISPs limit these speeds to make sure everyone gets an equal share of the bandwidth. Usually, upstream speed is slower than downstream speed.

When upstream speeds differ from downstream speeds, you have an **asymmetric Internet connection**. When upstream and downstream

TRY IT!

In Figure 6-12, how many nodes did the data pass through before the connection timed out?

speeds are the same, you have a **symmetric Internet connection**. Asymmetric connections discourage subscribers from setting up Web and e-mail servers that would transmit lots of upstream data. For most users, however, an asymmetric connection is sufficient.

You can use an Internet-based utility, such as Speedtest.net, to see if your Internet connection achieves the speed advertised by your ISP (Figure 6-13).

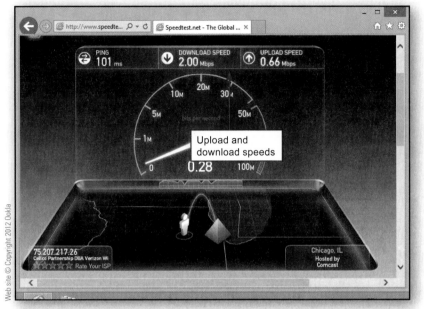

FIGURE 6-13

Speed tests measure the average number of bits that are transmitted per second, whereas utilities such as Ping and Traceroute measure the time required for a packet to make a round trip from your computer and back. ▶ Click to learn how to use Speedtest.net to compare the speed of your Internet connection with your ISP's advertised speed.

▶ **What are my connection options?** Consumers have several options for connecting to the Internet. **Fixed Internet access** links your computer to an ISP from a stationary point, such as a wall socket or roof-mounted antenna. **Portable Internet access** allows you to easily move your access device, as in the case of vehicle-mounted satellite dishes that can be deployed when the vehicle is parked. **Mobile Internet access** allows you to use the Internet as you are on the go, such as using a cell phone to collect your e-mail while you are traveling by train.

You're not necessarily limited to a single Internet access option. Many consumers find it convenient to maintain fixed Internet access for home use, but use a portable or mobile method of Internet access while out and about. In Sections B and C, you'll learn more about Internet access options.

TRY IT!

Check your computer. According to Speedtest.net, what is your actual download speed?

QuickCheck

1. TCP/[_____] is the primary protocol suite used on the Internet.

2. 204.127.129.1 is an example of an IPv4 address. True or false? [_____]

3. A(n) [_____] name server maintains a database of IP addresses that correspond to addresses such as *www.nike.com*.

4. If you ping Google from your computer and get a result of 46 ms, you have a relatively slow Internet connection. True or false? [_____]

5. Most ISPs offer [_____] Internet connections, meaning the downstream speed is faster than the upstream speed.

 CHECK ANSWERS

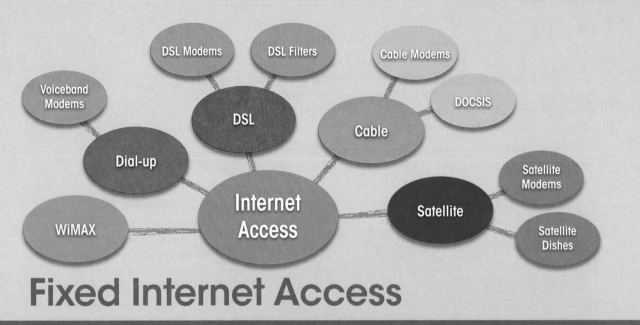

Fixed Internet Access

ONE OF THE MOST challenging aspects of the Internet is selecting a service provider. In this section of the chapter, you'll learn about fixed Internet access, which is typically your main link to the Internet. You'll learn to evaluate the pros and cons of various fixed Internet options, and discover why online interactive game players shun satellite Internet connections but love cable Internet service. Plus, you'll find out which types of Internet access work best for Voice over IP and teleconferencing.

DIAL-UP CONNECTIONS

▶ **What is a dial-up connection?** A **dial-up connection** is a fixed Internet connection that uses a voiceband modem and telephone lines to transport data between your computer and your ISP. ISPs, such as NetZero, AOL, and EarthLink, still offer dial-up Internet access. The service ordinarily costs less than $10 per month, but access speed is slow.

▶ **How does a dial-up connection work?** When you use a dial-up connection, your computer's modem places a regular telephone call to your ISP. When the ISP's computer answers your call, a dedicated circuit is established between you and your ISP—just as though you had made a voice call and someone at the ISP had picked up the phone.

The circuit remains connected for the duration of your call and provides a communications link that carries data between your computer and the ISP. As your data arrives at the ISP, a router sends it out over the Internet (Figure 6-14).

FIGURE 6-14

When you use a dial-up connection to access the Internet, your data travels over local telephone lines to your ISP, which sends it onto the Internet.

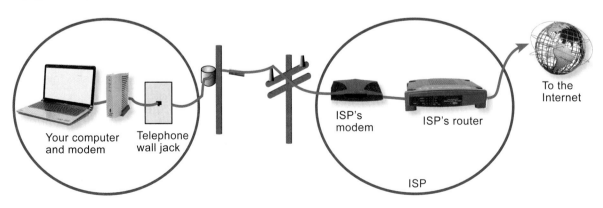

▶ How does a voiceband modem work? The signals that represent data bits exist in your computer as digital signals. The telephone system, however, expects to work with human voices, so it carries analog audio signals. A **voiceband modem**—usually referred to simply as a modem—converts the signals from your computer into audible analog signals that can travel over telephone lines. A modem transmits a 1,070 Hz tone for a 0 data bit and a 1,270 Hz tone for a 1 data bit.

When your computer's modem initiates a connection, it sends a signal that is equivalent to picking up the receiver of a telephone to get a dial tone. It then dials the ISP by emitting a series of tones—the same tones you'd produce if you punched in the ISP's number using a phone keypad.

The modem then waits for the ISP's modem to answer the call. After the ISP's modem answers, the two modems begin to negotiate communications protocols, such as transmission rate. The series of beeps, tones, and whooshing sounds you hear when you connect to your ISP is the sound of your modem "talking" to the ISP's modem. This process of negotiation is sometimes called handshaking. When the negotiation is complete, data transmission can begin (Figure 6-15).

FIGURE 6-15

When you transmit data, your voiceband modem modulates the signal that carries your data. A modem at the other end of the transmission demodulates the signal.

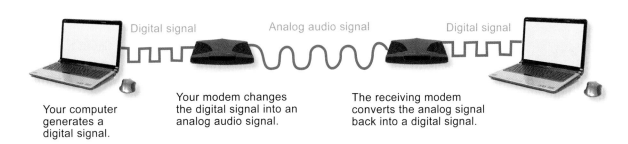

Your computer generates a digital signal.

Your modem changes the digital signal into an analog audio signal.

The receiving modem converts the analog signal back into a digital signal.

▶ How fast is a voiceband modem? Modem speeds are measured in bits per second. (If you're a stickler for details, you'll realize that bps is actually a measure of capacity, but everyone calls it speed.) Most modems use a standard called V.90 to provide a theoretical maximum speed of 56 Kbps. Actual data transfer speeds are affected by factors such as the quality of your phone line and connection. Even with an excellent connection, however, a 56 Kbps modem tops out at about 44 Kbps.

Dial-up connections are asymmetrical; 44 Kbps is a typical download speed for a 56 Kbps modem. For uploads, the data rate drops to about 33 Kbps or less.

▶ Can I use an analog modem if my phone service is digital? In many areas of the world, the telephone system uses digital rather than analog signals to send voice conversations. You can still use an analog modem because the sounds it emits are transported just as if they were voices.

Digital telephone systems opened up the possibilities for digital data transport options such as ISDN and DSL. ISDN service offered slightly faster service than dial-up but has today been replaced by DSL.

TRY IT!

With a dial-up connection:

○ your modem converts analog signals to tones

○ your computer stores 1 bits as a 1,070 Hz tone

○ your voiceband modem has a theoretical downstream speed of 56 Kbps

○ your telephone line must be upgraded to digital or ISDN

DSL

▶ What is DSL? **DSL** (digital subscriber line) is a high-speed, digital, always-on, Internet access technology that runs over standard phone lines. It is one of the fastest Internet connections that's affordable to individual consumers.

Several variations of this technology exist. ADSL (asymmetric DSL) offers faster speeds for downloads than for uploads. SDSL (symmetric DSL) offers the same speed for uploads as for downloads. HDSL (high bit rate DSL), VDSL (very high bit rate DSL), and DSL lite are also available.

▶ How does DSL work? DSL data is transmitted to and from your local telephone switching station in pure digital form, bypassing the bottleneck of analog-to-digital-to-analog conversion and escaping the requirement to use the narrow bandwidth allocated to voice transmissions. The result is fast data transmission over standard copper telephone cable.

DSL uses some fairly sophisticated technology to superimpose digital signals over the unused frequency spectrum of an ordinary telephone line. A DSL connection can simultaneously carry voice and data, if permitted by your DSL provider. Voice and data signals travel over telephone lines to your telephone company's local switching station. There, the voice signals are separated from the data signals. Voice signals are routed to the regular telephone system; data signals are routed to your ISP and then to the Internet (Figure 6-16).

TERMINOLOGY NOTE

The acronym *xDSL* refers to the entire group of DSL technologies (including SDSL, HDSL, and so on). xDSL is not a separate variation of DSL.

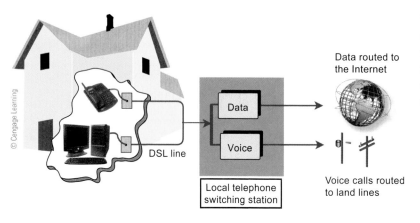

FIGURE 6-16

Voice and data signals travel over DSL to a special device at the local telephone switching station, where they are divided and routed to an ISP or to the regular telephone network.

▶ How fast is DSL? The speed of a DSL connection varies according to the characteristics of your telephone line and your distance from the telephone company's switching station. Current DSL technology can transport data at speeds up to 6 Mbps downstream for a distance of about 1.25 miles (2 km).

DSL signals deteriorate over distance, however. For DSL to work, your connection must be within about 3 miles (5 km) of your telephone company's switching station. The distance requirement only pertains to the distance between you and the switching station. Once the signal arrives at the switch and is handed off to the ISP, it can travel the Internet backbone anywhere in the world.

TRY IT!

What's the similarity between dial-up and DSL?

○ Both use telephone lines

○ They have similar speeds

○ They both operate well over any distance

○ Neither one is as fast as satellite Internet service

▶ **How do I get DSL service?** The first step is to find out if DSL is available in your area. Contact your telephone company or check its Web site (Figure 6-17).

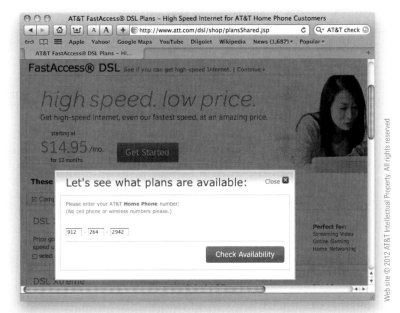

FIGURE 6-17

To find out if DSL is available in your area, check with local carriers and national carriers, such as AT&T.

6

▶ **What equipment do I need for DSL?** Most DSL installations can be handled by consumers. Your DSL service provider will supply you with the necessary instructions and equipment. In general, DSL installations require a modem and filters.

A **DSL modem** (Figure 6-18) is a device that connects a computer to a telephone line and converts computer data signals into signals compatible with DSL. DSL is digital, so data doesn't need to be changed into analog signals and then back to digital as it does when you use a dial-up connection. DSL signals have to be modulated, however, so they can travel on non-voice frequencies.

FIGURE 6-18

A DSL modem connects your computer to a telephone wall jack. You can plug the modem into your computer's USB or Ethernet port.

A **DSL filter** (Figure 6-19) prevents voiceband signals from interfering with DSL signals. Professionally installed business DSL systems often use a single external filter. Self-installed DSL kits provide filters that you connect to every device in your home that uses the telephone line.

FIGURE 6-19

A DSL filter connects to lines used for handsets, answering machines, and similar devices. For example, to filter a telephone, unplug the phone, plug the filter into the wall jack, and plug the phone cable into the filter.

CABLE INTERNET SERVICE

▶ **What is cable Internet service?** **Cable Internet service** is a means of distributing always-on broadband Internet access over the same infrastructure that offers cable television service. Local and national cable companies, such as Comcast, Cox, and Charter, offer cable Internet service for a monthly subscription. Of all Internet services, cable Internet currently offers the fastest access speeds.

▶ **How does cable Internet service work?** The cable television system was originally designed for remote areas where TV broadcast signals could not be received in an acceptable manner with an antenna. These systems were called community antenna television, or CATV. The CATV concept was to install one or more large, expensive satellite dishes in a community, catch TV signals with these dishes, and then send the signals over a system of cables to individual homes.

The topology of a CATV system looks a lot like the physical topology for a computer network. And that is just what is formed when your cable TV company becomes your Internet provider. Your computer becomes part of a neighborhood LAN joined by wiring for the cable TV infrastructure.

▶ **Are television and data signals carried over the same cable?** CATV coaxial and fiber-optic cables have plenty of bandwidth to carry television signals for hundreds of channels in addition to digital data. CATV cables provide bandwidth for television signals, incoming data signals, and outgoing data signals (Figure 6-20).

© Cengage Learning

FIGURE 6-20

A CATV cable has enough bandwidth to support TV channels and data flowing downstream as well as data flowing upstream.

▶ **How fast is cable Internet service?** Most cable Internet service is asymmetric, with upload speeds considerably slower than download speeds to discourage subscribers from setting up public Web servers. A standard home service plan offers speeds of 12 Mbps for downloads and 2 Mbps for uploads. Some premium plans offer even faster connections with speeds of 50 Mbps for downloads and 10 Mbps for uploads.

Cable signals are not particularly vulnerable to environmental interference, but data transport speeds are affected by subscriber use. The cable you share with your neighbors has a certain amount of bandwidth. As more and more neighbors use the service, it might seem to get slower and slower.

As an analogy, consider the luggage conveyor belt in an airport, which moves at a constant speed. If you have three pieces of luggage and you are the only passenger on the plane, your bags arrive one right after another. However, if you just arrived on a full 747, your bags are intermixed with those of hundreds of other passengers, and it takes longer to collect them.

Your cable company's network carries packets at a constant speed. However, if many of your neighbors are sending and receiving packets at the same time, your packets seem to arrive more slowly. Cable Internet subscribers notice that their connection speed seems slower during peak usage times.

TRY IT!

What can limit the speed of a cable Internet connection?

○ Environmental factors

○ Your ISP

○ High traffic from other users

○ Watching TV shows

▶ **Do I need special equipment for cable Internet service?** When you set up your computer for cable Internet service, you are essentially linking to the cable network's Ethernet-style LAN that connects a neighborhood of cable subscribers. The two requirements for this type of connection are circuitry to handle Ethernet protocols and a **cable modem**, which converts your computer's signal into one that can travel over the CATV network.

Most subscribers rent a cable modem from their cable company, and the rental fee is included in the monthly bill. Third-party cable modems manufactured by Linksys, Motorola, D-Link, and other companies can be purchased from electronics stores, but it is a good idea to check with your cable company first to make sure the modem you select is compatible.

A cable modem can plug directly into a coaxial cable wall jack. If you need to connect your cable set-top box and cable modem to a single wall jack, you can use a cable splitter as shown in Figure 6-21.

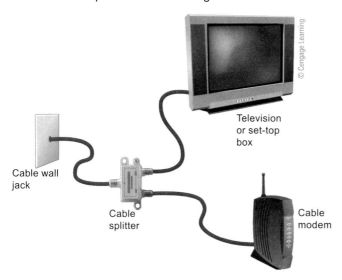

FIGURE 6-21

If your home has only one CATV cable outlet, you might need to use a splitter to link it to your cable modem and television. If you have multiple cable outlets, you can connect your cable modem directly to any one of them.

Most cable modems have USB and Ethernet ports, and you can use one or the other. Some cable companies instruct subscribers to connect the modem directly to a computer. However, as you'll learn in the Internet Security section, the safest way to connect your computer to a cable modem is through a router.

▶ **How secure are cable Internet connections?** In the early days of cable Internet service, some cable Internet subscribers were unpleasantly surprised when they happened to open Windows Network Neighborhood, only to be greeted with a list of their neighbors' computers! When you boot a PC, Windows automatically connects to available LANs and looks for shared files, folders, and printers on LAN workstations. Because cable Internet service uses LAN technology, computers in different households were treated as workstations on a shared LAN.

Today, most cable companies use DOCSIS-compliant cable modems that block crossover traffic between subscribers. **DOCSIS** (Data Over Cable Service Interface Specification) is a data transport technology that includes security filters. DOCSIS secures your computer from your neighbors, but it does not close up all the security holes that are opened when you use an always-on connection. When you use cable Internet service, be sure your computer is running security software.

TRY IT!

What about security on a cable Internet connection?

○ It is an always-on connection, which is vulnerable to intrusions

○ It is vulnerable to DOCSIS

○ It is secure if you've locked your modem

○ It is secure if your computer uses Windows

SATELLITE INTERNET SERVICE

▸ **What is satellite Internet service?** Most people are familiar with services that provide access to television programming over a personal satellite dish. Many companies that provide satellite TV also offer Internet access. **Satellite Internet service** is a means of distributing always-on, high-speed asymmetric Internet access by broadcasting signals to and from a personal satellite dish. In many rural areas, satellite Internet service is the only alternative to a dial-up connection.

▸ **How does satellite Internet service work?** Satellite Internet service uses a geostationary satellite to transmit computer data directly to and from a satellite dish owned by an individual (Figure 6-22).

TERMINOLOGY NOTE

Communications satellites in geostationary orbits move in synchronization with the Earth's rotation and always appear to be in the same location of the sky.

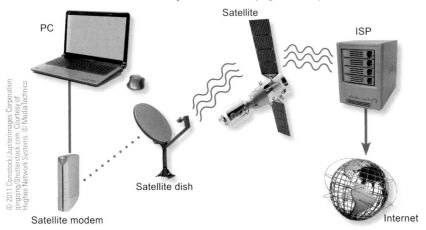

FIGURE 6-22

Satellite Internet services can be beamed to customers whose property offers an unobstructed view of the orbiting satellite. Signals are captured by a satellite dish and relayed to a satellite modem connected to a computer.

▸ **How fast is satellite Internet service?** Satellite service averages 1.0 to 1.5 Mbps for downloads but only 100 to 256 Kbps for uploads. Satellite signals can be slowed or blocked by adverse weather conditions, such as rain and snow, which makes this type of data transport less reliable than wired Internet access services, such as cable and DSL.

Satellite data transport is subject to latency delays of one second or more, which occur as your data is routed between your computer and a satellite that orbits 22,200 miles above the Earth. Latency might not pose much of a problem for general Web surfing and downloading files, but it can become a showstopper for interactive gaming that requires quick reactions, and for video calling with Skype, FaceTime, and similar services.

As with cable Internet service, satellite data transport speeds might seem to decline during peak usage hours because the satellite's bandwidth is shared among all users.

▸ **Does satellite Internet service require special equipment?** A satellite dish and modem are the two pieces of equipment required for satellite Internet access. If you already have a dish for satellite television, you might need a second dish for Internet service. A standard television dish does not provide the signal strength required for a high-speed two-way Internet connection.

A **satellite modem** is a device that modulates the data signals from a computer into a frequency band that can be carried to the satellite dish, where it is converted to another frequency, amplified, and transmitted. The modem connects to the satellite dish using two coaxial cables: one to transmit and one to receive. The modem then can be connected to the Ethernet port of a computer, or for better security, to a router.

A dish for satellite Internet service is slightly larger than the dish for satellite TV.

Satellite modem front (left) and rear (right)

FIXED WIRELESS SERVICE

▶ **What is fixed wireless Internet service?** Fixed wireless Internet service (also called wireless broadband service) is designed to offer Internet access to homes and businesses by broadcasting data signals over areas large enough to cover most cities and outlying areas.

Fixed wireless technologies are MAN (metropolitan area network) standards, in contrast to technologies such as Wi-Fi, which are LAN (local area network) standards. One of the most well-known fixed wireless standards is WiMAX, currently offered by a variety of local service providers.

▶ **What is WiMAX?** WiMAX, which stands for Worldwide Interoperability for Microwave Access, is an Ethernet-compatible network standard designated as IEEE 802.16. Its popularity is growing because it offers an alternative to wired technologies, such as DSL and cable Internet service, that require expensive infrastructures.

WiMAX can be deployed in rural areas where cable service is not available and where customers are too far away from a telephone switching station for DSL service. In an urban environment, WiMAX can offer healthy competition to other Internet service providers.

▶ **How does WiMAX work?** A WiMAX system transmits data to and from WiMAX antennas mounted on towers. A single tower, such as the one in Figure 6-23, can serve a large geographical area.

Towers can transmit data to subscribers, they can relay data to other towers using microwave links, and they can connect directly to the Internet backbone by cable. Within 3 miles/8 km of the tower, signals are strong enough to be picked up by subscribers on a non-line-of-sight device, similar to a Wi-Fi access point. Beyond that range, a line-of-sight antenna is required.

FIGURE 6-23

A WiMAX tower broadcasts signals over a wide area. Subscribers close to the tower can use non-line-of-sight modems to pick up the signal.

▶ **What is the speed of WiMAX?** Under ideal conditions, WiMAX can transmit data at 70 Mbps. Actual speed, however, is affected by distance, weather, and usage. Current services claim speeds of 1 to 5 Mbps for downloads. WiMAX can be distributed as symmetrical or asymmetrical service.

Fixed wireless technologies have less latency than satellite Internet service and can usually offer connection speeds suitable for online gaming and video calling.

▶ **What equipment do I need for WiMAX access?** Your wireless service provider supplies a wireless modem that connects to your computer. The modem includes a transceiver to send and receive signals to a wireless point of access, usually located on a nearby communications tower. Subscribers on the outlying edges of the network's range might also require an antenna mounted on a window or roof, and a line-of-sight to the WiMAX tower.

TRY IT!

Which two of the following fixed Internet connections use wireless technologies?

◯ Dial-up

◯ DSL

◯ Cable

◯ Satellite

◯ WiMax

FIXED INTERNET CONNECTION ROUNDUP

▶ **What's the best Internet connection for my PC?** The best Internet connection depends on your budget, what's available in your area, and what you do while connected. For fixed Internet access, cable Internet service is usually the first choice, when available. If cable Internet service is not available, or proves slower or less dependable than expected, the next choice would be DSL or fixed wireless service, if available.

If several fixed Internet services are offered in your area, the table in Figure 6-24 can help you evaluate their requirements, costs, advantages, and disadvantages.

FIGURE 6-24

Fixed Internet Access Options

	Dial-up	DSL	Cable	Satellite	WiMAX
Download speed (max.)	56 Kbps	384 Kbps– 6 Mbps	5–50 Mbps	1–1.5 Mbps	70 Mbps
Upload speed (max.)	33 Kbps	128 Kbps– 6 Mbps	256 Kbps– 10 Mbps	100–256 Kbps	70 Mbps
Download speed (actual)	44 Kbps	2–5 Mbps	3–10 Mbps	400–800 Kbps	1–5 Mbps
Latency	100–200 ms	10–20 ms	10–20 ms	1–3 seconds	10–50 ms
Short video (72 MB) download	4 hours	5 minutes	3.2 minutes	24 minutes	6.4 minutes
Requirements	Telephone line, ISP, voiceband modem	Computer located within 3 miles of local telephone switch; DSL modem	CATV service that provides Internet access; cable modem	Clear view of southern sky; satellite dish and modem	WiMAX modem, line-of-sight to WiMAX tower for distances > 3 miles
Monthly fee	$	$$	$$	$$	$$
Installation cost	$0	$	$	$$	$
Always-on	N	Y	Y	Y	Y

QuickCheck   SECTION B

1. Dial-up and DSL Internet access use the telephone cables already installed in a home or business. True or false? [_____]

2. Always-on connections are not a security risk because they use DOCSIS. True or false? [_____]

3. The two requirements for cable Internet service are circuitry to handle [_____] protocols and a cable modem.

4. Satellite Internet service has a fairly high [_____] rate, which is unsuitable for some online gaming and video calling.

5. [_____], which adheres to IEEE 802.16 standards, is one of the most promising fixed wireless Internet technologies.

▶ CHECK ANSWERS

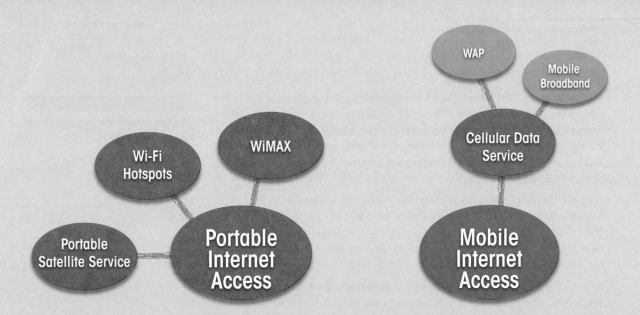

Portable and Mobile Internet Access

SECTION **C**

WHEN YOU'RE ON THE GO and away from your fixed Internet connection, you are not necessarily cut off from your e-mail and other Internet activities. Portable and mobile Internet technologies can provide Internet access while you visit friends, commute to work or school, or take a vacation. In this section, you'll find out what's available for portable and mobile access today and what's on the drawing board for the future.

INTERNET TO GO

▶ **What is portable Internet access?** Portable Internet access can be defined as the ability to easily move your Internet service from one location to another. It is portable in the sense that a hot plate is portable. It is light and compact enough to easily carry, even though you have to remain in one spot when it comes time to use it. Portable Internet access services include Wi-Fi, portable satellite, and portable WiMAX.

▶ **What is mobile Internet access?** Mobile Internet access offers a continuous Internet connection as you are walking or riding in a bus, car, train, or plane. It is very similar in concept to cellular phone service that allows you to move freely within coverage areas as the signal for your connection is seamlessly handed off from one tower to the next. Mobile Internet access includes mobile WiMAX and cellular broadband service (Figure 6-25).

FIGURE 6-25

Using mobile Internet access, you can find the location of the nearest coffee shop.

WI-FI HOTSPOTS

▶ **What is a Wi-Fi hotspot?** In addition to being popular for home networks, Wi-Fi is also used for public networks operated by merchants, hotels, schools, and municipalities. If your computer is equipped for Wi-Fi, as are most of today's laptops, tablets, and smartphones, you have a portable means of accessing the Internet by carrying your digital device to any Wi-Fi hotspot.

A **Wi-Fi hotspot** is an area in which the public can access a Wi-Fi network that offers Internet service. You can find hotspots in locations such as coffee shops, RV parks, hotels, community centers, college campuses, and airports. Wi-Fi hotspot availability is expanding even in small towns and rural areas.

Some Wi-Fi hotspots offer free service that might or might not require a password; others require a service plan or one-time use fee. These fees can be expensive.

▶ **How fast is hotspot access?** The speed of a hotspot is related to the speed of the wired line that connects it to the Internet. A hotspot that goes through a 1 Mbps DSL line will be slower than a hotspot that goes through a 22 Mbps cable Internet connection. You can expect speeds of 2–8 Mbps, but speed can vary depending on your distance from the access point, the number of people logged in, and interference from other networks.

▶ **How do I access a Wi-Fi hotspot?** Accessing a Wi-Fi hotspot is similar to making a wireless connection to a LAN. In a typical scenario, you might take your laptop computer—equipped with Wi-Fi capability—to your local Starbucks cafe. You buy a cup of cappuccino, sit down in a comfortable chair, and switch on your computer.

Your computer's networking utilities automatically sense a Wi-Fi network and add it to the list of available connections. You can view the list of available networks and connect to one as shown in Figure 6-26.

Wi-Fi is considered what type of Internet access?

○ Fixed

○ Portable

○ Mobile

○ DSL

FIGURE 6-26

When connecting to a Wi-Fi hotspot, pay attention to signal strength and security. Secure networks are safest.

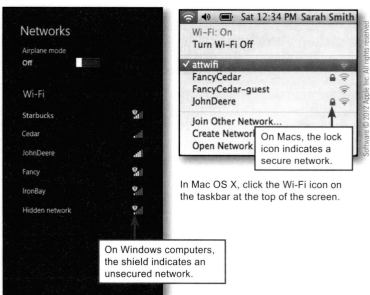

To connect to a hotspot in Windows 7, click the Internet Access icon on the taskbar.

In Windows 8, click the taskbar icon or point to the lower-right corner of the Start screen and select the Settings icon.

In Mac OS X, click the Wi-Fi icon on the taskbar at the top of the screen.

▶ **Is hotspot access secure?** Public hotspots are not typically protected by WPA or other encryption because it is not feasible to hand out passwords and user IDs to every person who wants access. Hotspots are not secure, and Wi-Fi eavesdroppers can easily tap into most of the data that flows over the network.

When using a Wi-Fi hotspot for simple browsing activities such as checking sports scores, reading Google news, and looking for directions, your security risk is fairly low if your computer's antivirus software is up to date.

Your security risk is also low when you are accessing secured Web sites that have addresses beginning with HTTPS. These secured sites, used for activities such as online banking and credit card purchases, encrypt the data that you enter to keep it safe from eavesdroppers.

When you log in to unsecured sites while using public Wi-Fi hotspots, however, a wireless eavesdropper could potentially snag your user ID and password information, then use it later to access your accounts. Logging in to your Webmail account, for example, could be risky if your user ID and password are transmitted over an unsecured connection.

Eavesdroppers might also be able to access the files on your computer if you have file sharing turned on. When using public networks, you should turn file sharing off. You can do so manually if your operating system does not offer that option when you connect (Figure 6-27).

TRY IT!

When using a public Wi-Fi hotspot, how can you tell if it is secured?

○ Look at the connection icon to see if it has a shield or lock

○ Look for HTTPS

○ Make sure it requires a password to log in

○ Check the IP address that you're assigned for a security code

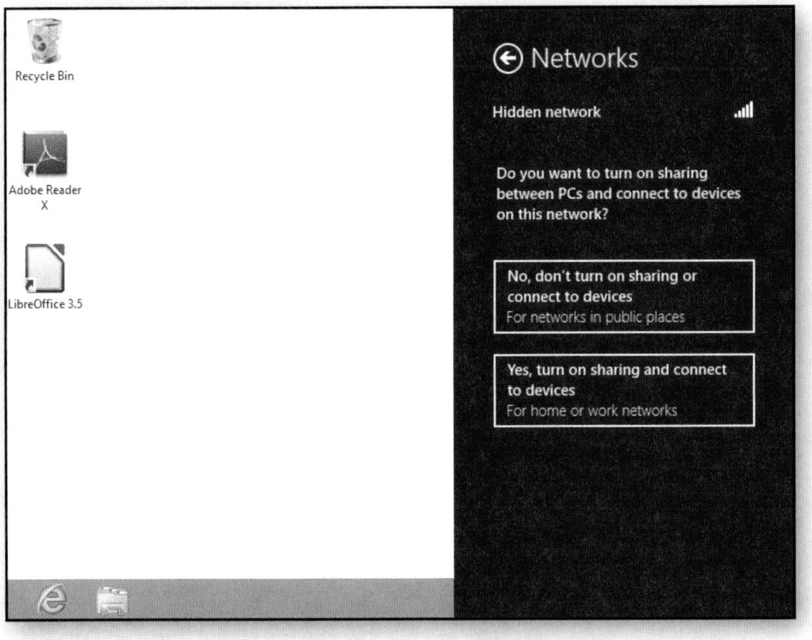

FIGURE 6-27

When connecting to a new network, Windows gives you an opportunity to turn file sharing off. If the network is private and secure; you can leave file sharing on, but if the network is public or unsecured, then select the option to disable sharing.

▶ **Can I use public hotspots for mobile Internet access?** Although Wi-Fi is popular for portable Internet access, public hotspots do not provide acceptable mobile Internet access because you can only remain connected within range of the network's hotspot.

The current model for using most Wi-Fi hotspots is that you enter the area of coverage, find a location with a strong signal, and remain there while accessing the Internet. Wi-Fi handoffs from one Wi-Fi network to another are clumsy and prone to packet loss, which is unacceptable for Voice over IP or streaming video applications. Later in this section, you'll read about cellular-based hotspots that you can set up privately to get mobile Internet access.

PORTABLE AND MOBILE WIMAX

▶ **What is portable WiMAX?** WiMAX can be used as a portable technology because Internet access is available to subscribers anywhere within a tower's coverage area. WiMAX subscribers who use non-line-of-sight modems with an integrated antenna (Figure 6-28) can easily relocate their modems anywhere within the service provider's coverage area.

▶ **What are the pros and cons of portable WiMAX?** The big bonus of portable WiMAX is that you use the same Internet service provider whether you are at home or on the road. You do not need supplemental service contracts or day passes as you do for Wi-Fi hotspots. On the downside, WiMAX is not yet in widespread use and coverage is limited.

▶ **What about mobile WiMAX?** Mobile WiMAX is an up-and-coming standard destined to be deployed by ISPs and cell phone carriers because it is designed to offer Internet access with seamless hand off from the coverage area of one tower to the coverage area of another tower. Mobile WiMAX could make it possible for you to deal with a single service provider for all your cell phone and Internet access needs.

For example, Dell offers a 4G WiMAX plan with average speeds of 3–6 Mbps. Computers equipped with a WiMAX adapter card can pick up the Wi-Fi signal and get Internet access anywhere in the coverage area. However, the coverage area is limited to big cities at present.

PORTABLE SATELLITE SERVICE

▶ **What if I travel to remote areas?** WiMAX and Wi-Fi hotspots provide coverage in cities and small towns, but rarely extend out to sparsely populated areas. If you plan to remain in a single remote location, fixed satellite Internet service is a good option. If, however, Internet access is required as you travel to various remote locations to hike, ski, or conduct research, then portable satellite technology is available.

▶ **How does portable satellite technology work?** For portable satellite Internet service, a satellite dish can be mounted on a vehicle. The disk is stowed while the vehicle is in motion, but can be quickly deployed when the vehicle stops.

Like a fixed satellite dish, a portable dish transmits signals to and receives signals from a geostationary satellite. If a fixed satellite dish moves out of alignment, signals can no longer be captured dependably. The challenge with mobile satellite service is to make sure the dish is correctly aimed from the location where it is used. High-end portable satellite systems have self-aiming hardware that automatically deploys and rotates the dish until it locks onto the satellite signal (Figure 6-29).

▶ **How fast is portable satellite service?** Portable satellite service providers advertise download speeds of 400 Kbps to 5 Mbps and upload speeds of 50 to 500 Kbps. Larger dishes offer faster speeds. Portable satellites work well for browsing the Web and checking e-mail.

FIGURE 6-28

WiMAX modems are easy to transport and can be plugged in anywhere within the coverage area of a WiMAX tower.

FIGURE 6-29

A vehicle-mounted satellite dish can be deployed from a control panel inside the vehicle. As with fixed satellite service, however, latency becomes a factor for real-time applications such as videoconferencing, streaming movies, and online gaming.
▶ See how it works.

CELLULAR DATA SERVICE

▶ **How can I use my cell phone service to access the Internet?** In many countries, including the U.S., cell phone coverage is extensive and the technology is truly mobile; you can use cell phone service while walking or in a moving vehicle. The hand off as you travel from one cell area to another is seamless.

Using cell phone technology to access the Internet offers mobility that is not possible with other wired or wireless computer network technologies. And though in the past cellular-based Internet access was slower than dial-up, new technologies offer speeds that are more competitive with high-speed broadband offerings.

▶ **How fast is cellular data transport?** Data transport speed depends on the technology of the cellular system. Cellular technology is classified by the following generations:

▶ **1G (First-generation)** technology was analog and offered few features beyond voice communications.

▶ **2G** replaced analog technology with digital technology and added support for basic data transport in the form of text messages. Sending computer data over a 1G or 2G system required a voiceband modem to convert digital data into audible signals. Transmission rates were glacially slow.

▶ **3G** technologies offered by many of today's cellular service providers support digital transmission for both voice and data. 3G technologies have speeds ranging from 200 Kbps to 5 Mbps, so they are similar to satellite Internet service, and can potentially match DSL speeds. Cellular phone companies use a variety of 3G technologies, such as EDGE, EV-DO, and HSUPA.

▶ **4G** technology is the next step forward in mobile technology. It is designed to provide peak data rates of 100 Mbps while a device is in motion, or 1 Gbps rates when a device is stationary. Although interim 4G technologies such as LTE (Long Term Evolution) have been deployed since 2009, 4G is not yet available in many countries or in parts of the U.S.

▶ **Can I get to the Internet from any cell phone?** Most cellular service providers offer e-mail and Internet services. Basic phones can access a limited number of specially designed Web sites using WAP.

▶ **What is WAP? WAP** (Wireless Application Protocol) is a communications protocol that provides Internet access from handheld devices, such as cell phones.

WAP-enabled devices contain a microbrowser that displays simplified versions of popular Web sites, such as CNN, Google, Yahoo!, ESPN, UPS, FedEx, The Weather Channel, and MapQuest. WAP devices also include e-mail software formatted for small, low-resolution screens (Figure 6-30).

FIGURE 6-30

The advantages of WAP-enabled devices include their portability and low price. The disadvantage is their small, low-res screens. Although various schemes for scrolling over a full-sized Web page have been tried, most WAP users stick to Web sites specially designed for small screens.

6

▶ Can I use a cell phone to access regular Web sites and other Internet services? Accessing the "real" Internet requires a different approach than is offered by WAP. For the real Internet, cellular service providers offer data services, sometimes referred to as **mobile broadband**. Broadband access requires a fast connection, a data service subscription, and mobile broadband equipment.

Broadband data access is not available in all of a cellular service provider's coverage area. Coverage maps can give you an idea of the service area, but actual coverage and speeds can vary. Where broadband coverage is not available, your device might operate at a much slower speed or might not have access to data services.

▶ What is a data service plan? Most cellular service providers offer a data service plan for accessing the Internet. Prices for these plans range from $20 per month and up. Less expensive plans commonly limit the amount of data you can send and receive, treating megabytes like minutes. Make sure you understand the terms of your service contract. Some data service contracts prohibit users from streaming or downloading music, movies, or games; making Voice over IP phone calls; and using file sharing networks.

▶ What equipment do I need for mobile broadband Internet access? For mobile access the Internet, you'll need a mobile broadband–enabled device. Smartphones and many tablet computers have built-in mobile broadband circuitry.

▶ How do I access the Internet with a handheld device? You can use a smartphone to access, the Internet by subscribing to a data service plan offered by a mobile phone provider such as AT&T, Verizon, or Sprint.

Smartphones include browser and e-mail software (Figure 6-31). Some devices, such as the iPhone, include specialized software to access popular Web sites such as Google Maps and YouTube.

TRY IT!

Check your mobile phone. What browser does it use?

FIGURE 6-31

Many smartphones offer a large color screen, and can connect to Wi-Fi hotspots and cellular data services to access the Internet.

▶ Can I add mobile broadband capability to my laptop?

Most cellular service providers offer wireless modems for broadband data access. These modems are sometimes called aircards or connect cards. A USB modem, like the one in Figure 6-32, slides into the USB port of your laptop computer and is installed following the manufacturer's instructions.

FIGURE 6-32

It looks like a USB flash drive, but it is a modem that gives your computer Internet access using a cell phone network.

© MediaTechnics

After the card has been installed, you can use it to connect to the Internet via your mobile broadband data service. You can use the same set of tools that work with your cable or DSL Internet connection, including your Web browser and e-mail software. With your laptop computer's full-size screen, you'll have the "real" Internet experience anywhere in your mobile service provider's coverage area.

FIGURE 6-33

MiFi routers run on batteries, so they can be used to construct portable networks.

▶ What is MiFi?

MiFi is a brand name for a compact, mobile, wireless router offered by Novatel Wireless. The term is sometimes applied to similar routers produced by other manufacturers. A MiFi router like the one in Figure 6-33 is about the size of a cell phone and runs on batteries.

© MediaTechnics

With MiFi, you can easily assemble a small network just about anywhere. For example, you can use your mobile network even when you are traveling in an RV or a train.

These routers connect to a mobile carrier's broadband data service and provide a wireless hotspot for up to five devices. Wireless routers have a range of about 30 feet, so the devices that you want to use to access the Internet can be placed anywhere within that range (Figure 6-34).

FIGURE 6-34

A MiFi router creates a Wi-Fi hotspot with Internet access for up to five devices via cellular service.

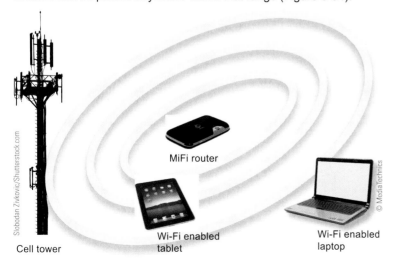

Cell tower

MiFi router

Wi-Fi enabled tablet

Wi-Fi enabled laptop

Slobodan Zivkovic/Shutterstock.com

© MediaTechnics

❱ Can I use my phone as a wireless hotspot? Some cell phones, such as Droids and iPhones, can act as a Wi-Fi hotspot by becoming the router for a wireless network. The ability to serve as a Wi-Fi hotspot is referred to as **tethering**.

You can set up your phone's mobile hotspot anywhere you have data service, but hotspot capability might entail additional monthly service charges.

When in Wi-Fi hotspot mode, your mobile phone can provide portable Internet access to other Wi-Fi enabled devices, such as laptop computers, iPods, iPads, and other smartphones.

Setting up a mobile Wi-Fi hotspot is similar to setting up a router for a private Wi-Fi network. You begin by entering an SSID as the unique network name, then select an encryption method, such as WPA2, to secure the data flowing over the network. When your hotspot is configured and active, other Wi-Fi enabled devices can connect to access the Internet and share files (Figure 6-35).

FIGURE 6-35

Some cell phones can be deployed as the router and modem for a small wireless network that you can use while traveling in a car or an RV.

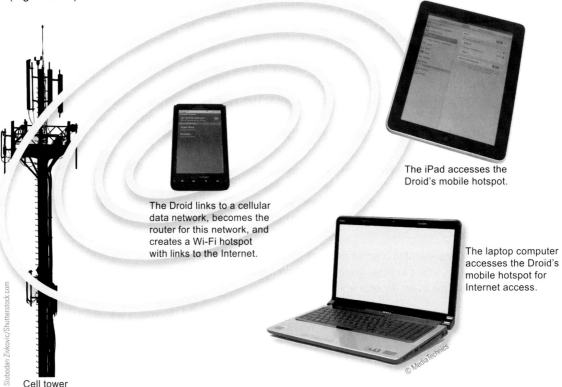

The iPad accesses the Droid's mobile hotspot.

The Droid links to a cellular data network, becomes the router for this network, and creates a Wi-Fi hotspot with links to the Internet.

The laptop computer accesses the Droid's mobile hotspot for Internet access.

Cell tower

Slobodan Zivkovic/Shutterstock.com

QuickCheck

1. _____ Internet access can be defined as the ability to use the Internet while walking or traveling in a moving vehicle.

2. A Wi-Fi _____ is an area in which the public can access a Wi-Fi network that offers Internet service.

3. _____ G technologies include EV-DO, HSUPA, and EDGE.

4. WAP devices have been replaced by devices that use mobile _____ technologies offering the full Internet experience.

5. Portable _____ technology can be used to access the Internet from remote locations where there are no cable, WiMAX, or cellular networks.

 CHECK ANSWERS

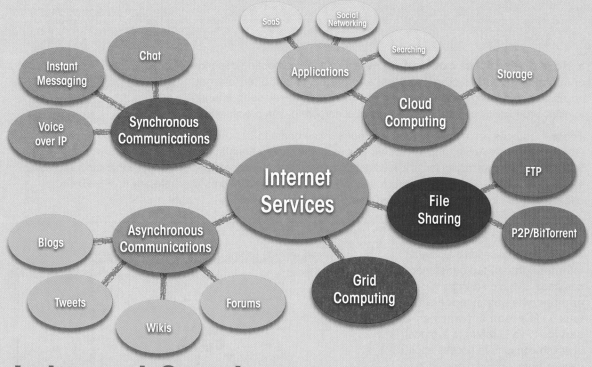

Internet Services

AN INTERNET CONNECTION offers access to a global data communications system. You know that protocols such as TCP/IP and UDP handle basic data transport; but additional protocols, sometimes referred to as application protocols, make possible a variety of useful Internet applications, such as cloud computing, real-time messaging, Voice over IP, blogging, tweeting, grid computing, FTP, and file sharing.

CLOUD COMPUTING

▶ **How does cloud computing relate to the Internet?** There's a lot of buzz about cloud computing these days, and its scope continues to evolve. Cloud computing is a concept, rather than a specific technology. It is the idea that consumers use their computers or handheld devices to access applications, storage, and other computing resources supplied by Internet-based servers, rather than from their local devices.

Under the umbrella of this broad definition, cloud computing encompasses most Internet-enabled activities including Webmail, Google searching, social networking, blogging, and photo sharing. The concept of cloud computing is that apps and data are available any time, from anywhere, and on any device (Figure 6-36).

FIGURE 6-36

Google Apps provides a glimpse of what cloud computing has to offer. Users can access productivity applications as well as their e-mail, blog, and social networking service from a desktop computer or a handheld device. Files created with these applications are also stored in the cloud for easy access.

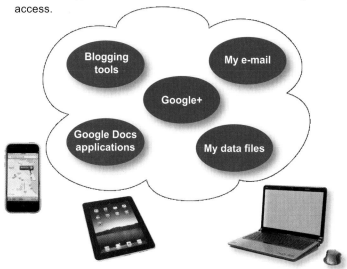

▶ **How does cloud computing work?** Cloud computing depends on a grid of servers, storage devices, and protocols that offer Internet-accessible computing services ranging from consumer-level media sharing to office productivity applications and complex corporate data processing.

These resources are maintained by Internet service companies, such as Google, Amazon, Apple, and Microsoft. For example, Apple maintains a 500,000-square-foot facility for its iCloud data center where subscribers can store music, photos, data files, backups, reminders, and contacts. Microsoft offers a similar cloud service called SkyDrive (Figure 6-37).

▶ **Are cloud services free?** Servers in a cloud data center host a variety of applications. Using an Internet connection, consumers can access these services. Some are free whereas others are fee based. The term **software as a service** (SaaS) refers to a model in which consumers access applications from a cloud provider over the Internet, usually by using a browser. Most SaaS services are offered through paid subscriptions or corporate leases.

▶ **How does the cloud work for enterprise applications?** Many years ago, when the Internet was just becoming popular, Victoria's Secret publicists came up with the innovative idea of holding an online fashion show. Only minutes after the show began, however, the host servers crashed as millions of viewers tried to access the Victoria's Secret site.

If today's cloud resources had been available, those viewers wouldn't have been disappointed. Victoria's Secret could have used Amazon's Elastic Compute Cloud, which instantly scales to respond to spikes in customer traffic.

Cloud computing offers Internet-based resources such as servers, software, and storage space on demand. The concept is similar to a temporary employment agency that provides office assistants, accountants, programmers, and other temporary workers as a business needs them. With cloud computing, Internet resources can be contracted as needed, and released when they are no longer needed.

Cloud computing helps businesses save money and offers scalable solutions that can quickly meet changing needs. For example, a startup e-commerce business might not know the server capacity required to handle its Web site traffic. The business can contract with a cloud service to obtain server capacity that scales as necessary to handle customers.

FIGURE 6-37

With a SkyDrive account, you can store your data on a cloud-based server and access it from any device. You can also specify files and folders on your local computer that can be accessed remotely from SkyDrive.

TRY IT!

E-textbooks are becoming more and more popular. Suppose that you access your computing textbook from the publisher's site using a browser. Is that an example of cloud computing?

○ Yes, it would be

○ Yes, but only if the publisher used a SkyDrive or iCloud server

○ No, the textbook does not qualify as an application

○ No, cloud computing does not make use of browsers

REAL-TIME MESSAGING

▶ **What is real-time messaging?** A network-based **real-time messaging system** allows people to exchange short messages while they are online. One-on-one messaging is referred to as **instant messaging** (IM) and group communications are referred to as **chat**.

Every day, millions of people use messaging systems, such as Facebook Chat, Yahoo! Messenger, Apple iChat, and Windows Messenger, to communicate with friends, family, and coworkers. Some systems offer voice messaging and video options, so that participants can speak to each other using computer-based microphones and cameras.

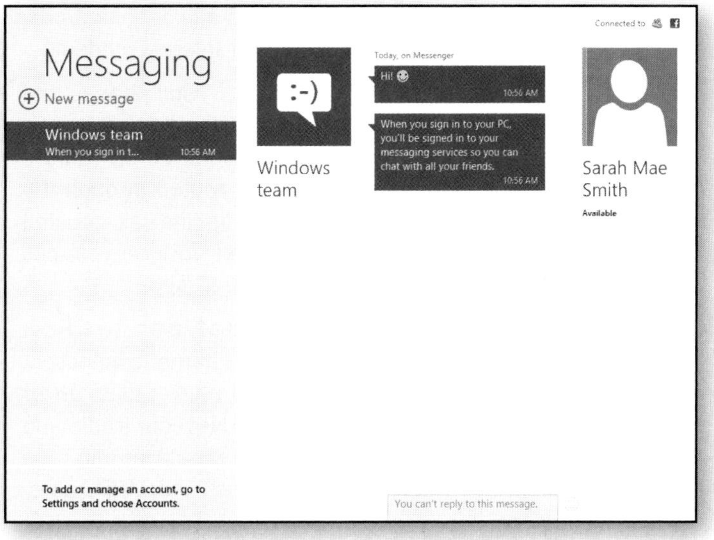

FIGURE 6-38

IM client software displays windows for typing and viewing messages.

▶ **How does real-time messaging work?** Most messaging is based on a client/server model that uses a server to handle communication packets between the participants (clients). When participants log on, they connect to the messaging server, which authenticates their user IDs and passwords. The server then sends back a list of participants who are currently online.

Messages are typed into client software (Figure 6-38), which uses messaging protocols to break the message into packets and ship them to the server for distribution or directly to the recipient. Some protocols encrypt messages before they are transmitted. Messaging and chat protocols include IRC (Internet Relay Chat), MSNP (Microsoft Notification Protocol), and Jabber.

VOICE OVER IP

▶ **What is Voice over IP?** **VoIP** (Voice over Internet Protocol), or Voice over IP, is a technology in which a broadband Internet connection is used to place telephone calls instead of the regular phone system. It is based on SIP (Session Initiation Protocol), so VoIP software is sometimes referred to as a SIP client.

The earliest VoIP connections were computer-to-computer connections. Both the person initiating the call and the person receiving the call had to have computers with microphones and headsets or speakers. You could only call people who were using the same VoIP software and who happened to be online when you wanted to call them. These early VoIP systems worked more like instant messaging with voice than a traditional phone call.

You can still use VoIP to make calls from one computer to another, but today VoIP systems, offered by companies such as AT&T, Comcast, magicJack, and Vonage, allow you to use a standard telephone handset to make or receive calls. They also allow you to receive calls from landline telephones and to place calls to these telephones.

▶ **How do today's VoIP systems work?** Today's VoIP systems convert voice communications to data packets. An IP address is attached to each packet. If you are calling a friend with computer-based VoIP, for example, your friend's IP address will be attached to the packets. If you are

TRY IT!

In what way are Apple iChat and VoIP similar?

○ They both use SIP clients

○ They are both synchronous technologies

○ They use the same protocols

○ They are both susceptible to jitter from low-bandwidth connections

calling a land line or other destination without its own IP address, your VoIP packets will carry an IP address of a service that can route your packets to their destination using land lines where necessary.

▶ How do I set up VoIP? If you want to set up free computer-to-computer VoIP, you and the people you communicate with can download and install freeware or open source VoIP clients, such as Google Talk or Blink. You can also use any messaging service that supports audio transmission. For the most basic setup, you can simply use your computer's built-in microphone and speakers instead of connecting a phone handset.

When you subscribe to a VoIP service, follow your service provider's setup instructions. For example, magicJack provides a small USB device that you plug into your computer and then connect to a telephone. Vonage supplies you with an adapter that you connect to your Internet modem.

▶ Can I use VoIP on a cell phone? Cell phones that offer Wi-Fi as well as cellular phone service can be used to make VoIP calls if permitted by your service provider. When you are within range of a Wi-Fi hotspot, the call is routed through the Internet as a VoIP call. If no hotspot is in range, the call is routed through the standard cellular service. To get VoIP on your cell phone, find and install a compatible mobile VoIP app.

▶ Do I need a high-speed Internet connection for VoIP? In addition to the speed of your Internet connection, VoIP audio quality is affected by jitter and packet loss. **Jitter** measures the variability of packet latency. Network traffic and interference can delay some packets and create erratic data flow. If the variation between packets exceeds 5 ms, VoIP quality is likely to be poor.

Packet loss refers to data that never reaches its destination or gets discarded because it arrives too late to be of any use. Packet loss of less than 2% is required for acceptable VoIP (Figure 6-39).

▶ What about Skype? Skype offers video calling in addition to voice calls using a proprietary technology that's similar to VoIP protocols. As with VoIP, Skype requires a fast Internet connection with minimal latency and packet loss.

FORUMS, WIKIS, BLOGS, AND TWEETS

▶ What about asynchronous communications? Instant messaging, chat, and VoIP are forms of **synchronous communications**; the people communicating have to be online at the same time and the conversation happens in real time. The Internet also supports several types of asynchronous communications, including forums, wikis, blogs, and tweets.

The basic idea behind **asynchronous communications** is that one person posts a message using the Internet. That message can later be read by designated recipients or by the public, depending on the limitations set by the poster.

▶ How do forums work? An **Internet forum** is a Web-based online discussion site where participants post comments to discussion threads. Those comments can be read at a later time by other participants. Most forums have a moderator who monitors discussion threads, weeds out disruptive participants, and handles membership requests.

FIGURE 6-39

You can test your Internet connection to determine if it is suitable for VoIP by connecting to Web sites such as *myspeed.visualware.com*.

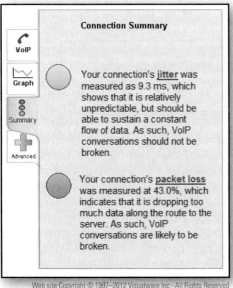

TRY IT!

In Figure 6-39, will the connection work for VoIP?

○ Yes, it is fast and secure

○ Yes, it can work for VoIP and Skype

○ No, there is too much jitter

○ No, the rate of packet loss is too high

▶ Are forums the same as wikis? No. Forums allow participants to comment on the material posted by other participants, but those comments are separate posts and the original post is not modified. A **wiki** allows participants to modify posted material.

Wikipedia is the best known wiki. Participants can post material pertaining to a topic, and other participants can modify it. Wikis can also include discussion pages where participants comment on topic material. For example, in a wiki topic about climate change, the discussion page might contain comments pointing out statements in the original post that cannot be verified.

FIGURE 6-40

Technorati helps you locate popular blogs or write one yourself.

6

▶ How do blogs work? A **blog** (short for Web log) is similar to an online diary; it is maintained by a person, a company, or an organization, and contains a series of entries on one or more topics. Blog entries are text-based, but can also include graphics and video. They are usually displayed in reverse chronological order on one long Web page.

Most blogs are open to the public, so blogging has become a form of personal journalism; a way to make your views public. They have been used extensively for political commentary. Some bloggers have been tapped to be commentators on headline news shows on CNN and FOX. To set up your own blog, you can use a blog hosting service such as Blogger or WordPress. For a list of popular blogs, check out Technorati (Figure 6-40).

Web site © Technorati, Inc

▶ What's a tweet? A **tweet** is a short message of 140 characters or less that is posted to the Twitter Web site (Figure 6-41). Twitter is sometimes referred to as a microblogging service because tweets are similar to blog entries, except for their length. Your tweets are displayed in reverse chronological order on your profile page. By default, your tweets are open to the public, but you can restrict access to a list of approved viewers. Viewer comments on your tweets are also posted on your profile page.

Twitter participants can subscribe to other people's tweets, a process referred to as "following." When you are a follower, you can quickly access tweets from the people you are following to find out what they are doing and thinking.

FIGURE 6-41

Twitter is the platform for short messages called tweets.

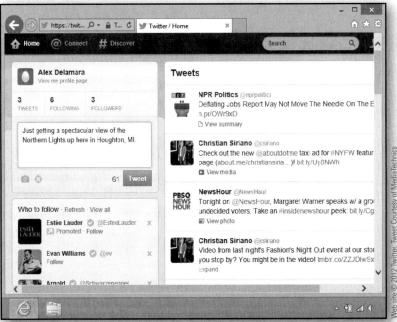

Web site © 2012 Twitter, Tweet Courtesy of MediaTechnics

GRID COMPUTING

▶ What is a grid computing system? In the days when the Internet was really taking off, computer scientists noticed that thousands of computers connected to the Internet sit idle for hours while the people who own them are in meetings, talking on the telephone, sleeping, or otherwise occupied. If these idle processing cycles could be harnessed, they could supply a tremendous amount of computing power.

A **grid computing system** is a network of computers harnessed together to perform processing tasks. Grid computing systems can be public or private. Some grid systems use computers connected to the Internet as resources; others operate on private networks.

▶ What is a distributed grid? Distributed grids (sometimes referred to as CPU scavenging grids) tap into thousands of PCs and Macs with Internet connections whose owners donate their computers' idle hours to a grid processing task. Grid management software divides computational problems into pieces that are farmed out to computers on the grid for processing.

Each computer on the grid runs grid client software that contains the program necessary to process a piece of the problem. In this manner, complex calculations or tasks can be performed in parallel by using as many computers as are available on the grid. Results are sent back to the grid management software for consolidation. Figure 6-42 illustrates the basic architecture of a grid computing system.

▶ Where are distributed grid systems used? Because of their scalability, low cost, and high performance, distributed grids play a central role in scientific high-performance computing. One of the most famous examples of a distributed grid is the SETI@home project, which analyzes radio telescope data to search for signals that might originate from extraterrestrial life. People who wish to donate their computers' idle processing cycles to the SETI@home project can download and install grid client software (Figure 6-43) that processes signals when the computer is idle.

FIGURE 6-42

A distributed grid uses a diverse variety of computers as generic and equal resources.

A server running grid management software farms out pieces of a problem to computers in the grid.

Computers in the grid run grid client software and send results back to the server.

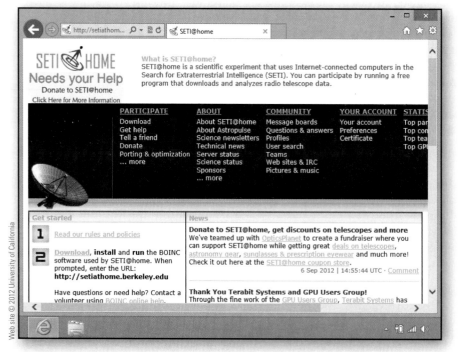

FIGURE 6-43

SETI@home consists of a grid management system and millions of privately owned personal computers whose owners donate idle processing time to the project. The SETI@home grid management system receives and stores raw data from the Arecibo radio telescope in Puerto Rico, divides this data into small segments for analysis, and farms out each segment to one of the privately owned computers.

FTP

▶ **What is FTP?** FTP (File Transfer Protocol) provides a way to transfer files from one computer to another over any TCP/IP network, such as a LAN or the Internet. The purpose of FTP is to make it easy to upload and download computer files without having to deal directly with the operating system or file management system of a remote computer. FTP also allows authorized remote users to change file names and delete files.

▶ **Do I need to use FTP?** Many people use FTP without even knowing it. When you download an updated device driver from a technical support site, access a document in PDF format from a corporate Web site, or pull down an MP3 file from your favorite music site, FTP is in action—although the mechanics of it are incorporated into other applications.

People who use FTP are often sharing large files stored on a file server in conjunction with a project. Files can be uploaded to the server by one participant and downloaded by others. An alternative to FTP, sending files as e-mail attachments, is not practical with very large files or for participants with slow Internet connections.

▶ **How does FTP work?** An **FTP server** resides on a computer containing files that remote users might want to access. The server runs software that listens on ports 20 and 21 for requests coming in from other computers. When a request arrives, the server makes sure the user who made the request has rights to access the file. If the request is valid, the file is transferred over the Internet as a series of packets to the requesting computer, where it is saved in a designated location on a local storage device.

▶ **How can I access FTP servers?** You can access FTP servers with FTP client software or with a browser. To use a Web browser to download a file, simply enter the address of the FTP server as shown in Figure 6-44.

6

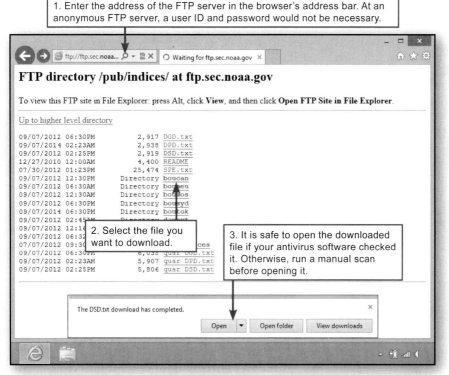

1. Enter the address of the FTP server in the browser's address bar. At an anonymous FTP server, a user ID and password would not be necessary.

2. Select the file you want to download.

3. It is safe to open the downloaded file if your antivirus software checked it. Otherwise, run a manual scan before opening it.

FIGURE 6-44

A browser can provide access to FTP downloads. ▶ Click to see how it works.

Not every FTP server is accessible from a browser, and those that are might work only for downloading files, not uploading them. If you plan to work extensively with FTP, you should get FTP client software. An **FTP client**, such as WS_FTP, CuteFTP, or open-source FileZilla, offers an easy-to-use interface for accessing FTP servers.

Convenient features of FTP clients allow you to save a list of server addresses and their corresponding user IDs and passwords, so you can connect to an FTP server with one click. FTP clients also allow you to download more than one file at a time, and they can pick up where they left off if the transfer is interrupted by a glitch in your Internet connection (Figure 6-45).

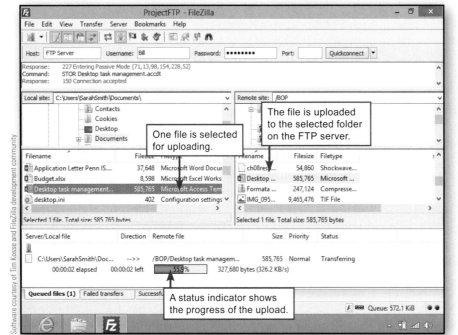

Software courtesy of Tim Kosse and FileZilla development community

FIGURE 6-45

FTP clients such as FileZilla make it easy to upload and download files from an FTP server. ▶ Use your interactive eBook to find out how to use an FTP client to upload and download files from an FTP site.

▶ **Does FTP include security to prevent unauthorized access?** Some FTP sites require remote users to log in before accessing files. A login ID and password can be obtained from the FTP site operator. Access rights can be configured in various ways to allow or prevent remote users from changing file names, deleting files, uploading files, or downloading files.

▶ **What is anonymous FTP? Anonymous FTP** can be accessed by logging in without a password by using the user ID "anonymous." Some anonymous sites request users to enter their e-mail addresses as a password, but rarely is that piece of information used for verification or tracking.

FILE SHARING NETWORKS

▶ **What is file sharing?** File sharing, sometimes called **P2P file sharing**, allows users to obtain files from other users located anywhere on the Internet. In the late 1990s, file sharing burst onto the national scene when college students became aware of a technology called Napster that provided free access to hit songs. Today, file sharing networks such as BitTorrent facilitate movie and music downloads.

▶ **What is BitTorrent?** **BitTorrent** is a file sharing protocol that distributes the role of a file server across a collection of dispersed computers. BitTorrent is, in some sense, an offshoot of grid computing concepts, in which an ad-hoc collection of personal computers located anywhere on the Internet can cooperate to complete a task normally handled by monolithic servers or supercomputers.

A BitTorrent network is designed to reduce the bandwidth bottleneck that occurs when many people attempt to download the same very large file, such as a feature-length film, application software, or an interactive 3-D computer game.

▶ **How does BitTorrent work?** Suppose that 100 computers request the newly released sequel to the film *The Hunger Games* at about the same time. A server breaks the movie file into pieces and begins to download those pieces to the first computer that requested the movie.

As more computers request the file, they become part of a "swarm" that uses peer-to-peer technology to exchange file pieces with each other. After the server has downloaded all the file pieces to the swarm, its job is complete and it can service other requests. The swarm continues to exchange file pieces until every computer in the swarm has the entire file (Figure 6-46).

> **TERMINOLOGY NOTE**
>
> *P2P* stands for peer-to-peer, a network model in which workstations exchange data with each other. It is the opposite of the client/server model in which workstations exchange data with a server.

6

FIGURE 6-46

BitTorrent protocols dissect files into small chunks that might reside on different computers. Source computers have received parts of a file from a server. They then distribute these parts to other computers in the swarm.

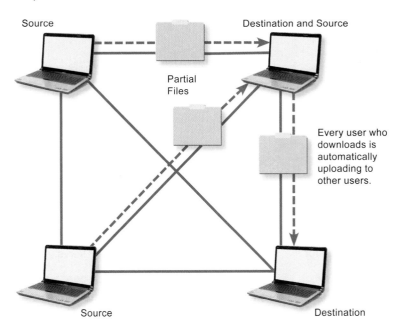

Source

Destination and Source

Partial Files

Every user who downloads is automatically uploading to other users.

Source

Destination

▶ How do I use BitTorrent? BitTorrent client software is currently available from several Web sites. After installing the client, you can use it to download from any BitTorrent-enabled site simply by clicking the file you want. The BitTorrent client handles the entire file-swapping procedure. After getting the entire file, good etiquette requires clients to remain connected to the swarm so that they can "seed" file pieces to others.

▶ Are BitTorrent and similar file swapping networks legal? File sharing originated on FTP-style servers, which held huge collections of popular music stored as digital MP3 files that could be easily downloaded and played on a computer or transferred to CDs. Free distribution of music without the copyright holder's permission is illegal, and file sharing server operators quickly encountered the legal ramifications of their computers' shady dealings.

Peer-to-peer file sharing networks and distributed technologies like BitTorrent have legitimate uses for distributing music, images, videos, and software with the approval of copyright holders. Peter Jackson's production diaries for *King Kong* have been posted for download using BitTorrent technology. Universal Studios and several independent film companies have released movie trailers with BitTorrent technology. The technology itself is not illegal; it is the use of the technology that is subject to legal scrutiny.

▶ Is BitTorrent safe? Because BitTorrent files are assembled from little segments that come from a jumble of computers, they would seem on first thought to be bad candidates for distributing malware. Intelligent hackers would realize that their malicious code could easily be chopped up, too, and that pieces of it might not be delivered. And yet, BitTorrent files have become a source of adware and spyware. If you use BitTorrent, make sure your computer is protected with a security software suite that offers good spyware protection.

QuickCheck   SECTION D

1. _____ computing offers Internet-based computer resources on demand so that individuals and businesses can contract for access as these resources are needed.

2. Instant messaging, chat, and VoIP are classified as _____ communications because both parties have to be online.

3. VoIP quality can be affected by _____ that results from too much packet latency.

4. On some sites, _____ FTP can be used to upload and download files even if you don't have an account on the FTP server.

5. _____ is a peer-to-peer file sharing protocol that uses a "swarm" of computers to exchange chunks of data that can eventually be assembled into complete files.

▶ CHECK ANSWERS

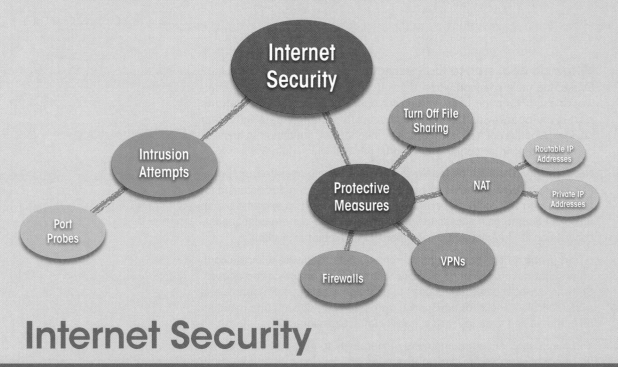

Internet Security

WHEN COMPUTERS are connected to a network, the risk of intrusion must be taken seriously. With Internet-based connections, billions of people are just an IP address away from your computer and its valuable, personal, and confidential data. Section E explains the mechanics of intrusion attempts, and offers some practical advice for securing your computer against unauthorized access.

INTRUSION ATTEMPTS

▶ **Should I worry about intrusions?** Suppose you live in a really dangerous neighborhood where gangs roam the streets, painting every available surface with graffiti, and randomly attacking residents. Burglars creep from house to house looking for unlocked doors and windows, and occasionally trying to pick a lock or two. Dark figures sift through your garbage cans searching for scraps of information that can be pieced together to steal your identity (Figure 6-47).

Unfortunately, this dangerous neighborhood has many similarities to the Internet where gangs of hackers deface Web sites, look for backdoors left open by network administrators, crack passwords to gain access to your data, and probe ports looking for ways to sneak bots into your computer.

Your Internet connection puts you right in the middle of this dangerous neighborhood any time you are connected—and with always-on connections like DSL and cable Internet service, that means any time your computer is turned on.

In the context of computers, an **intrusion** is any access to data or programs by hackers, criminals, or other unauthorized persons. As the result of an intrusion, data can be stolen or altered, system configurations can be changed to allow even more intrusions, and software can be surreptitiously installed and operated under the remote control of a hacker.

Without any visible sign or warning, hackers can infiltrate your computer to obtain personal information or use your computer as a launching pad for attacks on other machines. Yes, you should worry about intrusions!

FIGURE 6-47

The Internet offers a wealth of useful tools and services, but it can be a very dangerous neighborhood.

339

◗ How do hackers use the Internet to infiltrate my computer?

One of the most common ways of gaining unauthorized access to a net-work-based computer is by looking for open ports. A **communications port** is the doorway that allows a computer to exchange data with other devices. A port is not a physical circuit or mechanism, but rather an abstract concept of a door, an opening, or a portal through which data flows.

Network services, such as the Web, FTP, and e-mail, operate from ports. For example, Web requests use port 80. If a port is open and listening for requests—on any computer, even your own—a hacker can exploit it like an unlocked door to gain access to your computer. Hackers are continuously canvassing the Internet and probing ports to find their next victims.

A **port probe** (or port scan) is the use of automated software to locate computers that have open ports and are vulnerable to unauthorized access. Software called a port scanner goes to a randomly selected IP address and systematically checks for a response from each port. Open ports can then be further tested to gauge their suitability for exploitation.

You might scoff at your computer's vulnerability to port probes. After all, there are millions and millions of computers on the Internet and a limited number of hackers. The chances of your computer becoming a target would seem to be slim, but the opposite is true.

Port scanning software can examine more than 30,000 computers per minute. If you use security software to monitor port probes on an unprotected computer, you would see probes within seconds of going online. According to researchers, the average "survival time" for an unprotected computer to remain uncompromised is only nine minutes.

◗ How do I know if ports are open?

You can check your computer for open ports using software tools such as Steve Gibson's ShieldsUP! at *www.grc.com*. You can initiate an "innocent" port probe to discover vulnerabilities. A security report like the one in Figure 6-48 is your goal.

FIGURE 6-48

Your computer's ports are most secure if they don't even appear to exist when probed using a port scanner. ▶ Use your interactive eBook to see how ShieldsUP! checks your computer's ports and learn what the results mean.

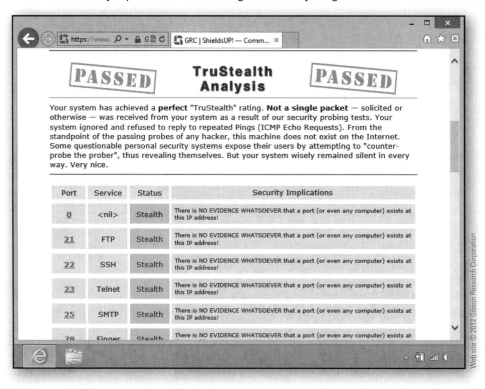

SECURING PORTS

▶ **How do I secure the ports on my computer?** One of the easiest steps to enhance your computer's security is to turn it off when you aren't using it. When your computer is turned off, its ports are inactive and they are not vulnerable to intrusions. Putting your computer into sleep mode or activating a screensaver is not sufficient protection. Your computer must be shut down and turned off.

You should also keep your computer up to date with the latest operating system security patches and service packs. Operating systems are closely linked to port activity. Known vulnerabilities in Windows and Internet Explorer can be exploited to access ports or launch additional attacks once a port is breached.

FIGURE 6-49

To configure a Windows computer for Automatic Updates, use the Security Center option in the Control Panel.

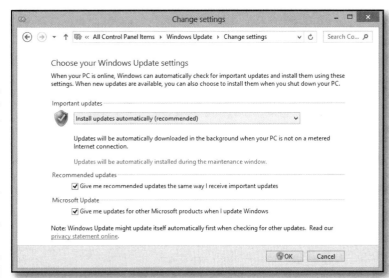

Operating system developers provide useful security tools to their customers. Microsoft's security site is *www.microsoft.com/security*. Apple's security site is *ssl.apple. com/support/security/*.

When operating system developers, such as Microsoft and Apple, produce security patches, they are available for download. You can configure your operating system to automatically check for and install patches (Figure 6-49).

▶ **What about firewall protection?** In the context of networking, a **firewall** is software or hardware designed to filter out suspicious packets attempting to enter or leave a computer.

Firewall software helps keep your computer secure in several ways. It ensures that incoming information was actually requested and is not an unauthorized intrusion. It blocks activity from suspicious IP addresses and—best of all—it reports intrusion attempts so that you can discover whether hackers are trying to break into your computer.

FIGURE 6-50

Windows includes a built-in firewall that can be activated to monitor intrusion attempts. Do not enable it, however, if your antivirus software firewall is activated.

You can use firewall software to open and close ports on your computer. Although it might seem safest to close all the ports, doing so would prevent you from accessing many Internet services, such as the Web, e-mail, instant messaging, and FTP.

Most firewall software is preconfigured to block only unnecessarily open ports targeted by hackers. Windows includes firewall software that you can access and configure from the Security Center (Figure 6-50).

▶ **What other security options should I use?** Sharing printers or files on a LAN or the Internet requires open ports so the data can be transferred to and from your computer. Those open ports can be a potential entryway for hackers. If no one else needs access to your printer, do not configure it for sharing. If you don't need to share files with other network users, you can turn off file sharing. You can also turn off network discovery so your computer is not visible to other devices (Figure 6-51).

FIGURE 6-51

When you turn off file sharing and network discovery, the ports used for those activities are closed to potential intruders.

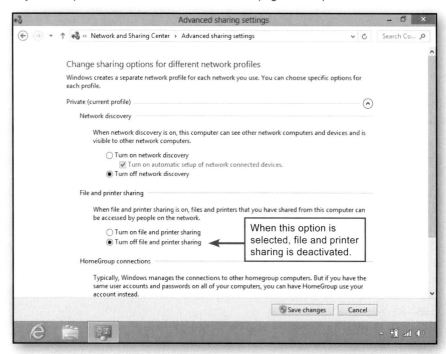

NAT

▶ **How does a router affect security?** One of the most effective steps you can take to secure your computer from intrusions is to install a router. In the chapter on networking, you learned that a router can tie a LAN together and provide a portal to the Internet. Even if you have only one computer, however, a router can offer excellent security.

▶ **How does a router work?** Routers are intended to work within LANs to monitor and direct packets being transported from one device to another. A router can also connect to the Internet through a DSL, cable, or satellite modem.

Routers are handy because they screen IP addresses to keep locally addressed packets within the LAN so that they are delivered without traveling a circuitous route over the Internet and back (Figure 6-52).

FIGURE 6-52

A router monitors the IP addresses of packets on a LAN. Packets with local addresses (green) are kept within the LAN. Packets with external addresses (red) are routed out to the Internet. ▶ See how it works.

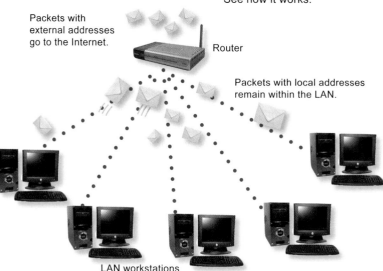

Packets with external addresses go to the Internet.

Router

Packets with local addresses remain within the LAN.

LAN workstations

Your router has its own IP address, typically obtained from your Internet service provider's DHCP server. (Recall that a DHCP server assigns dynamic IP addresses to devices that request them.) It is also possible for your router to have a fixed IP address set up by you or an installer. The key point about your router's IP address is that it is routable. A **routable IP address** is one that can be accessed by packets on the Internet.

When you connect your computer to a router and request an IP address, your router answers your request, not the ISP. Most routers are configured to assign private IP addresses. A **private IP address** is a non-routable IP address that can be used within a LAN, but not for Internet data transport.

When the IP addressing scheme was devised, three ranges of addresses were reserved for internal or private use: 10.0.0.0 to 10.255.255.255, 172.16.0.0 to 172.31.255.255, and 192.168.0.0 to 192.168.255.255. If your computer has a private IP address, its real address is essentially hidden from hackers (Figure 6-53).

FIGURE 6-53

The computers in a LAN have non-routable IP addresses.

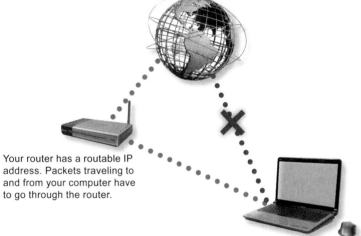

Your router has a routable IP address. Packets traveling to and from your computer have to go through the router.

Your computer has a non-routable address such as 192.168.1.1. That address is not routable; your computer is not reachable directly from the Internet.

▶ **But how do packets with private IP addresses get out to the Internet?** Let's review the scenario. You have a router connected to an Internet device, such as a DSL or cable modem. The router has a routable IP address, visible to any device (and hackers) on the Internet. Your router isn't vulnerable to attacks because it doesn't store any data. You've connected your computer to a router. Your computer has been assigned a private IP address.

Network address translation (NAT) is the process your router uses to keep track of packets and their corresponding private or public IP addresses. Jeff Tyson writing for HowStuffWorks offers a useful analogy for how NAT works:

"NAT is like the receptionist in a large office. Let's say you have left instructions with the receptionist not to forward any calls to you unless you request it. Later on, you call a potential client and leave a message for that client to call you back. You tell the receptionist that you are expecting a call from this client and to put her through. The client calls the main number to your office, which is the only number the client knows. When the client tells the receptionist that she is looking for you, the receptionist checks a lookup table that matches your name with your extension. The receptionist knows that you requested this call, and therefore forwards the caller to your extension."

TRY IT!

In the previous chapter, you found out how to locate your computer's IP address. Find it again. Is it routable?

○ Yes

○ No, it starts with 10

○ No, it starts with 172

○ No, it starts with 192

A router and the receptionist perform essentially similar tasks. Your private IP address is like a private telephone extension in an office. Your router's public IP address is like the main switchboard number. Your router screens incoming packets and only lets one through to your private extension if you've requested it.

When you use the Internet, you initiate every valid transaction; you ask for a Web site, you ask to retrieve your mail, or you request a file from an FTP server. Only those requests that you initiate are valid.

Suppose you want to download a file. You send a packet containing your request to the FTP server at 69.32.167.20. The packet goes to your router, which replaces your address with its own and makes an internal note that you initiated this FTP request. When the FTP server responds, it sends a packet addressed to the router. The router receives the packet, checks its internal note to see who made the original request, and then ships the FTP packet to your computer (Figure 6-54).

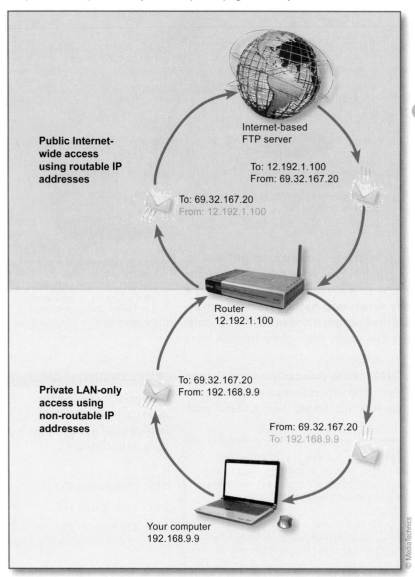

Public Internet-wide access using routable IP addresses

Internet-based FTP server

To: 12.192.1.100
From: 69.32.167.20

To: 69.32.167.20
From: 12.192.1.100

Router
12.192.1.100

To: 69.32.167.20
From: 192.168.9.9

From: 69.32.167.20
To: 192.168.9.9

Private LAN-only access using non-routable IP addresses

Your computer
192.168.9.9

© MediaTechnics

FIGURE 6-54

A router using NAT essentially cloaks your computer and makes it invisible from the Internet.

TRY IT!

Which IP address in Figure 6-54 is not routable?

○ 12.192.1.100

○ 192.168.9.9

○ 69.32.167.20

VIRTUAL PRIVATE NETWORKS

▶ Is it possible to secure connections for remote users?
Sales representatives and telecommuters often access corporate networks from home or from a customer's office by using a secured connection called a **virtual private network** (VPN). You might find a VPN useful when using public computers because it can encrypt the data you transmit, keeping passwords and account numbers safe from hackers.

▶ Who sets up VPNs? On the corporate end, setting up a secure VPN is not a trivial task and it is commonly handled by specialists in the corporation's information technology department. Access to a corporate VPN is usually by invitation only. Employees who need to access a VPN are given the necessary instructions, addresses, and passwords to make connections.

For personal use, you can install personal VPN software such as StrongVPN, WiTopia, or HotSpotVPN. Using a VPN provides an important layer of security when you use public networks, such as Wi-Fi hotspots.

▶ How would I use a personal VPN? Once you've installed VPN software, you'll see its icon in the taskbar. Clicking the icon establishes a connection to the VPN server. When your computer sends or receives data, the VPN software encrypts it and sends it to a special VPN server that decrypts the data and sends it to its destination. Figure 6-55 illustrates how a personal VPN operates.

▶ How important is a VPN? A personal VPN is an important tool when using public networks, but it is not a complete solution. To recap the most important security precautions, you should turn your computer off when not in use, make sure all your computer's unnecessary ports are closed, activate firewall software, turn off file and printer sharing, and install a router. Taking these precautions might not make your computer invincible, but they offer very strong protection against intruders who might steal your identity or hijack your computer for various shady activities.

FIGURE 6-55

A personal VPN offers security for the data that you transmit from public Wi-Fi hotspots.

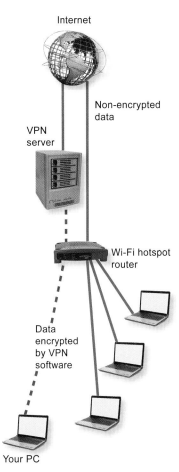

Internet

Non-encrypted data

VPN server

Wi-Fi hotspot router

Data encrypted by VPN software

Your PC

Public Wi-Fi hotspot

6

QuickCheck

1. Hackers use ▭ scanning software to look for computers connected to the Internet that are vulnerable to intrusions.

2. ▭ software monitors network activity, blocks packets from suspicious IP addresses, and reports intrusion attempts.

3. One of the best defenses against intrusions is to install a(n) ▭ between your standalone computer or LAN and your Internet connection device.

4. A(n) ▭ IP address is a non-routable IP address that can be used within a LAN, but not for Internet data transport.

5. When using a public Wi-Fi hotspot, you can use a personal ▭ to encrypt data that travels from your computer. (Hint: Use the acronym.)

 CHECK ANSWERS

Issue: What's a Revolution Without the Internet?

HE CALLED IT REVOLUTION 2.0. From his computer in Cairo, Wael Ghonim, a Google executive-turned-activist, maintained Facebook pages that inspired protests and eventually ended the Egyptian government headed by Hosni Mubarak.

The revolution in Egypt showed the power of the Internet to profoundly influence politics. In an interview, Ghonim said, "If you want to free a society, just give them the Internet."

The Egyptian revolution made extensive use of social media, such as Facebook, Twitter, and blogs. A Web page dedicated to an Egyptian citizen who was beaten to death by police called for demonstrations on January 25, 2011.

Word spread from this site to Facebook and Twitter, prompting hundreds of thousands to march in the streets of Cairo. It was the beginning of widespread demonstrations, strikes, and protests.

The Egyptian government quickly became aware of the Internet's role and took action. On January 27, Egyptian networks began disappearing from the Internet's global routing table, shutting down Internet access to and from Egypt.

Analysis of the event showed that Egypt's ISPs shut down one after another. First, Telecom Egypt, then Raya Telecom, followed by three other ISPs. Analysts speculate that a government agent phoned the ISPs one after another and ordered them to shut down.

According to a Renesys report, "Approximately 3,500 individual BGP routes were withdrawn, leaving no valid paths by which the rest of the world could continue to exchange Internet traffic with Egypt's service providers."

BGP (Border Gateway Protocol) uses a list of routes to transmit data from one router to another. With BGP routes withdrawn, data packets traveling to and from Egypt fell into a digital black hole. As an analogy, imagine the Postmaster General instructing post offices to shred all the mail instead of delivering it.

© 2011 Twitter, Tweet Courtesy of Wael Ghonim

Egypt was not the first country to shut down the Internet, nor was it the last. During the Tunisian revolution, the government blocked access to sites and filtered out dissenting messages in e-mail and blogs.

When Iranian dissidents took to the streets, the Internet remained in operation, but at drastically reduced speed. In Libya, the Internet became a pawn in the conflict between Gaddafi's government and protesters. Rather than a total blackout, however, Gaddafi slowly throttled back on service during critical periods, but periodically restored service.

The idea that Internet communications can be turned off might seem surprising when you consider that the Internet was designed to function even when many of its nodes malfunction or experience denial-of-service attacks.

The Internet as a whole continued to function during the Egyptian revolution, but packets that normally might have routed through Egypt were routed through other countries. Yet, within Egypt, and between Egypt and other countries, there was no service.

The outcome of revolutions in the past century often hinged on who controlled radio and television stations. Today, the outcome of social unrest balances on who controls the Internet—not only because of its role in communication and social media, but because it is the technology essential for banking, national infrastructure, and the stock market.

The effect of an Internet shutdown in any technological society would be chaos. Major communications channels would be unavailable. Banks would close. Credit card payments could not be processed. Airports and train stations would be mobbed by people forced to make travel reservations in person. An Internet outage could even have a cascading effect on the electrical grid, knocking out power to homes and businesses.

Despite the ensuing chaos, governments seem willing to cut off the Internet. Where might it happen next?

TRY IT! The Internet has become so integrated into our everyday lives that we take it for granted. That is a mistake. Our dependence on the Internet makes us vulnerable to cyberthreats that have far greater repercussions than leaving us without access to ESPN sports scores. Here's your chance to explore the relationship between the Internet and fundamental principles of democracy.

In the play, *It Can't Happen Here*, based on a 1935 Sinclair Lewis novel, a populist candidate is elected President of the United States. He makes sweeping changes to the Constitution, abolishes Congress, and forms a jack-booted secret police force. Protesters are thrown in jail while most Americans reassure themselves that "fascism can't happen here."

Work Projects Administration Poster Collection, Prints & Photographs Division, Library of Congress, LC-USZC2-921

1 Watching events in the Arab world and the extensive role of social media, we might be reassured that democracy is safe in America. We all have social media accounts; we're masters of the Information Age. But will the Internet be there if and when we need it? Could an unpopular president use a "kill switch" to censor information about demonstrations and protests?

2 Even if the government doesn't have the power to turn off the entire Internet, suppose it has the power to shut down particular sites, but makes a mistake and inadvertently turns off a big swath of the Internet. Search for "DHS Operation Save the Children 84,000 kill switch." What happened?

3 Suppose the U.S. government has the legal authority to shut down the Internet. You might wonder if it is technically possible to do so. Egypt had only a handful of ISPs; in the U.S., there are many more. But are there chokepoints where the U.S. Internet infrastructure is vulnerable? See what you can find when you search for "Internet Shutdown technically possible U.S. DNS." Pay attention to the origin of the sites you visit; some are likely to contain opinions and misinformation.

INFOWEBLINKS

You can check the **NP2014 Chapter 6** InfoWebLink for updates to these activities.

W CLICK TO CONNECT
www.infoweblinks.com/np2014/ch06

What Do You Think?

ISSUE

1. Does it seem plausible that your government would attempt to shut down the Internet to curtail civil unrest?

2. Do you use the Internet to access political news?

3. Should your government have legal power to shut down the Internet?

4. Have you experienced an Internet outage that lasted longer than 24 hours?

Information Tools: Citations

You can use other people's ideas in your own research papers and presentations, but you must cite the source for any information that is not common knowledge. A citation is a formal reference to a published work, like this:

> "It Can't Happen Here." *Encyclopædia Britannica. Encyclopædia Britannica Online*. Encyclopædia Britannica, 2011. Web. 13 Sep. 2014. <http://www.britannica.com/EBchecked/topic/297133/It-Cant-Happen-Here>.

A collection of citations is called a bibliography.

Use an approved citation style, such as MLA, APA, or Chicago. Several Web sites, such as the Purdue Online Writing Lab, include detailed style guides.

Papers on technology topics frequently contain material from books, magazines, journals, news reports, press releases, and court decisions. Make sure you understand the citation data that you need to collect for each of these formats, both in print and online.

Articles from Print Sources

Author, article title, periodical title, date of publication, page numbers

Books

Author, book title, edition, publisher, place and date of publication, ISBN

(If referencing a section of a book, note page numbers, chapter title, and chapter author, if applicable.)

Journals

Same information as a periodical with the addition of the volume and issue numbers

Legal Decisions

Case name; the volume, abbreviation, and page reference for the legal reporter where the case was reported; the date of the case

Web Pages

Author, title of Web page, title of Web site, complete URL, date of publication (sometimes there will not be a publication date; some citation styles use "n.d." in this case), sponsoring organization (look for it on the copyright line at the bottom of the page), date visited

A publication might have several unique identifying numbers. Stay alert so that you use the correct one.

ISBN (International Standard Book Number): A unique number given to a book or monograph

DOI (Digital Object Identifier): A unique number assigned to journal articles and other online documents

LCCN (Library of Congress Control Number): A unique number assigned to each publication in the Library of Congress

Desktop software such as EndNote, RefWorks, and Zotero helps you create citations and manage all the citations for your bibliographies.

Mobile apps, such as QuickCite, read bar codes and accept manual entries to automatically create citations on the go.

TRY IT! Let's go beyond the basics and work with some advanced citation tools. Use any word processor and create a document called Citation Project [Your Name], and then complete the following steps:

1 Suppose that you'd like to include information from press releases in a research paper. How do you format the citations? Use a search engine to look for "How do I cite a press release." Next, search for a recent press release from Apple. Create a citation for the press release and save it in your Citation Project document.

2 Some academic directories/databases provide citation information for the resources it lists. BibTeX, illustrated at right, is a common format.

Open an academic directory of technology articles, such as Microsoft Academic Search, TDG Scholar, ACM Digital Library, or Odysci. Search for BitTorrent articles and select one. Look for the Bib or BibTeX icon and then click it. Notice that each element of the reference is clearly labeled. Copy the BibTeX data and paste it into your Project document; you'll find out how to format this citation data in the next steps.

> Make sure you collect data for the article itself, not simply the directory that lists the article.

3 Microsoft Word includes a built-in bibliography manager that helps you format citations. To access the citation feature, select References, choose the MLA style, and click Insert Citation. Select Add New Source, then fill in the form. If you have access to Microsoft Word, use its Citation feature to create an MLA citation for the BibTeX data you found for step 2 above.

4 You can use free Web-based citation formatters, such as BibMe, Citation Machine, NoodleBib Express, or EasyBib, to format citations in MLA, APA, or other approved styles. Connect to a Web-based citation formatter, choose Online Journal as the source, select the MLA citation style, and enter the BibTeX data you collected for step 2 above. Paste the formatted citation into your Citation Project document.

5 For some books, Web sites, and journal articles, you can use their ISBN, URL, or DOI instead of manually entering the citation data. Connect to a Web-based citation formatter, such as those listed in step 4. Enter the ISBN 978-1437755824 and use the AutoCite button to search for the citation. Produce the MLA citation, copy it, and paste it into your Citation Project document.

6 The AutoCite button does not always locate the right article. Use EasyBib's Journal tab to Enter the DOI 10.1007/978-3-642-03521-0_9. Describe the result.

> When using automated citation formatters based on ISBN or DOI, look carefully at the citation that is produced to ensure that it contains all required citation information.

BibTeX Citation

```
@article{Thomas:2011:
WWE:1982701.1982999,

author = {Thomas, Christopher
and Sheth, Amit},

title = {Web Wisdom: An essay
on how Web 2.0 and Semantic
Web can foster a global knowl-
edge society},

journal = {Comput. Hum.
Behav.},

issue_date = {July, 2011},

volume = {27},

issue = {4},

month = {July},

year = {2011},

issn = {0747-5632},

pages = {1285--1293},

numpages = {9},

url = {http://dx.doi.org/10.1016/j.
chb.2010.07.023},

doi = {http://dx.doi.
org/10.1016/j.chb.2010.07.023},

acmid = {1982999},

publisher = {Elsevier Science
Publishers B. V.},

address = {Amsterdam, The
Netherlands, The Netherlands},

keywords = {Human and social
computation, Problem solving,
Social networking},

}
```

Technology in Context: Banking

R. F. Davis/Topical Press Agency/Getty Images

FOR MOST OF HISTORY, banks used low-tech methods to track one of the world's most cherished commodities—wealth. Checking accounts were in widespread use as early as 1550, when Dutch traders began depositing money with cashiers for safekeeping. The use of printed checks became popular in England in the late 18th century—so popular that banks found it difficult to process a steadily increasing stream of checks, including those drawn on accounts from other banks.

An unverified story that has become part of bank lore describes the origin of a solution to the check processing problem. As the story goes, a London bank messenger stopped for coffee and got to talking with a messenger from another bank. Realizing that they were delivering checks drawn on each other's banks, the two messengers decided to exchange checks there in the coffee house. This event evolved into a system of check clearinghouses where representatives from various banks met periodically to exchange checks and reconcile totals in cash. By 1839, British clearinghouses were annually processing in excess of £954 million of checks—equivalent to $250 billion in today's money.

Bank clearinghouses were described in an essay, *The Economy of Machinery and Manufactures*, written by computer pioneer Charles Babbage in 1832. He also included a reference to the "possibility of performing arithmetical calculations by machinery"

along with a description of the Difference Engine, then under construction in his workshop.

This dream of automated check clearing did not, however, become reality until more than a century later when S. Clark Beise, senior vice president at Bank of America, contracted with Stanford Research Institute (SRI) to develop a computer system to automate check processing. SRI completed a prototype in 1955 that used mechanical sorting equipment to queue up each check and MICR (Magnetic Ink Character Recognition) technology to read check numbers. In 1959, the first ERMA (Electronic Recording Machine-Accounting) system went into service. With ERMA handling calculations, nine employees could handle the job that once required 50 people. By 1966, 32 regional ERMA systems operated by Bank of America were processing more than 750 million checks per year. ERMA and similar check processing technologies quickly integrated with bank transaction processing systems to become the bedrock of today's banking technology.

Output from check sorting machines can be submitted to the Automated Clearing House (ACH) network, which offers a secure, batch-oriented data exchange system that can be accessed by financial institutions. On a daily basis, banks submit check data and receive a report of balances due to other banks. These balances can be reconciled by electronic funds transfer over the Federal Reserve's Fedwire telecommunications network.

An upswing in check fraud during the 1960s made it increasingly difficult to cash checks at local merchants. As an alternative to trying to cash checks at banks and local merchants, automated teller machines (ATMs) were first installed in the 1970s. A typical ATM connects to a bank's front-end processor—a computer that maintains account balances for in-network customers and monitors suspicious activity. The front-end processor is separated from the bank's main computer system for security.

Some ATMs exchange data with the front-end processor by using dedicated dial-up telephone lines. Other ATMs use always-on leased lines. Legacy protocols, such as SNA and 3270 bisync, are being replaced by the standard Internet Protocol (IP) that can be routed through more affordable connections, such as cable, ISDN, DSL, or Internet VPN.

ATMs are expensive—about $50,000 to purchase a machine, install it, and operate it for one year. Banks have offset this cost by charging transaction fees and reducing the number of bank tellers. Once a promising entry-level occupation, bank tellers today earn less than $30,000 per year. Although tellers continue to accept deposits, process withdrawals, and cash payroll checks, they are increasingly pressed into customer service roles—opening new accounts, issuing ATM cards, resolving disputed transactions, and assisting customers who have lost bank cards or checkbooks. Despite this shift in job description, the number of bank teller jobs is expected to fall at least 10% in the next few years.

© Duncan Smith/Corbis

ATMs offer access to bank services from convenient locations where customers shop, eat, and hang out with friends. The Internet takes banking convenience one step further and provides around-the-clock account access from PCs in customers' homes, schools, and workplaces. Today, most banks and credit unions offer some type of online banking (also called home banking, Internet banking, or electronic banking).

Basic online banking services allow customers to access checking account and bank card activity, transfer funds between checking and savings accounts, view electronic images of checks and deposit slips, download and print monthly statements, and reorder checks. Customers can also pay bills online by scheduling payment dates and amounts. Many credit card and utility companies offer e-billing

services that automatically forward electronic bills to customers' online banking accounts. For monthly fixed-amount bills, such as car loans, online banking offers automatic payment options that deduct funds from specified checking or savings accounts.

For managing assets more effectively, online banking sites also offer sophisticated tools, including account aggregation, stock quotes, rate alerts, and portfolio management programs. Most online banking sites are also compatible with personal finance software, such as AceMoney and Quicken, so that transaction data can be shuttled between customers' local computers and their online banking services.

A cadre of customer support personnel staff online help desks for customers with questions about online banking. Web masters, computer security specialists, and network technicians are also part of banking's new job corps.

Online banking services are housed on a well-secured Web server, and customers are not allowed direct access to the computer system that actually processes transactions. Customer privacy is maintained by the use of passwords and connections that encrypt data as it is sent to and from customers' computers.

Successful banks are built on good business decisions. Bank managers are increasingly working with business intelligence tools to look for trends in customer behavior, analyze competing financial institutions, and examine current business practices. Tools for these activities include data warehouses that collect and organize data, data mining software that organizes and analyzes data in a meaningful way, and statistical tools that formulate comparisons and trendlines.

Today, banking depends on multi-layered technologies that incorporate check processing equipment, transaction processing systems, business intelligence software, ACH networks, Fedwire, ATM networks, the Internet, and Web servers. Many banking practices originated from batch check processing, and only gradually have banks begun to move to more modern online transaction processing (OLTP) systems that store scanned images of checks and instantly update accounts when a purchase is made or a bill is paid.

6

New Perspectives Labs

To access the New Perspectives Labs for Chapter 6, open the NP2014 interactive eBook and then click the icon next to the lab title.

▶ TRACKING PACKETS

IN THIS LAB YOU'LL LEARN:

- How Ping and Traceroute work
- How to use the Ping and Traceroute utilities supplied by Windows
- How to interpret Ping and Traceroute reports to determine the speed and reliability of your Internet connection
- How to access and use a graphical Traceroute utility
- How to find and use Web-based Ping and Traceroute utilities
- The advantages and disadvantages of Web-based Ping and Traceroute utilities
- How to access the Internet Traffic Report Web site and interpret its data and graphs
- How to use Internet traffic data, Ping, and Traceroute to pinpoint problems with your Internet connection

LAB ASSIGNMENTS

1. Start the interactive part of the lab. Make sure you've enabled Tracking if you want to save your QuickCheck results. Perform each lab step as directed, and answer all the lab QuickCheck questions. When you exit the lab, your answers are automatically graded and your results are displayed.

2. Use the Ping utility that's supplied by Windows or OS X to ping *www.abcnews.com*. Record the IP address for the ABC News site, plus the minimum, maximum, and average times. For each time, indicate whether it would be considered poor, average, or good.

3. Use the Tracert command at the Windows command prompt or Mac Terminal to trace a packet between your computer and *www.excite.com*. Print the Traceroute report listing transmission times. Circle any pings on the report that indicate high latency.

4. Locate a Web-based Ping utility and use it to ping *www.gobledegok.com*. Indicate the address for the Web site where you found the Ping utility. Explain the Ping results.

5. Connect to the Internet Traffic Report Web site, make a note of the date and time, and then answer the following questions:

   a. What is the traffic index for Asia?

   b. How does the index for Asia compare with the traffic index for North America?

   c. During the previous 24 hours in Europe, what was the period with the worst response time?

▶ SECURING YOUR CONNECTION

IN THIS LAB YOU'LL LEARN:

- How to use Windows utilities, online utilities, and firewall software to check the security of your Internet connection
- Why an unauthorized intruder might want to gain access to your computer
- The significance of communications ports as an intrusion risk factor
- How to use the Netstat utility to check your computer's open ports
- How to use an online utility to get a hacker's view of your computer
- Why Windows file and printer sharing can make your computer files vulnerable
- How to adjust settings for file and printer sharing
- How firewalls protect computers from intrusions
- How to adjust firewall settings

LAB ASSIGNMENTS

1. Start the interactive part of the lab. Make sure you've enabled Tracking if you want to save your QuickCheck results. Perform each lab step as directed, and answer all the lab QuickCheck questions. When you exit the lab, your answers are automatically graded and your results are displayed.

2. Use the Netstat utility to scan any computer that you typically use. Write out the Netstat report or print it. To print the report, copy it to Paint or Word, and then print. Explain what the Netstat report tells you about that computer's security.

3. Connect to *www.grc.com* and access the ShieldsUP! tests. Test the shields and probe the ports for the same computer you used for Assignment 2. Explain the similarities and differences between the ShieldsUP! report and the Netstat report for this computer. Which report indicates more security risks? Why?

4. In the lab, you learned how to adjust settings for file and printer sharing. Without actually changing the settings, determine the status of file and printer sharing on your computer. Report your findings and indicate whether these settings are appropriate for network access and security.

5. Record the firewall settings on your computer. Indicate whether the settings are optimal for the way you use your computer on networks.

Key Terms

Make sure you understand all the boldfaced key terms presented in this chapter. With the NP2014 interactive eBook, you can use this list of terms as an interactive study activity. First, try to define a term in your own words, and then click the term to compare your definition with the definition presented in the chapter.

6

Always-on connection, 307
Anonymous FTP, 336
Asymmetric Internet connection, 310
Asynchronous communications, 332
BitTorrent, 337
Blog, 333
Cable Internet service, 316
Cable modem, 317
Chat, 331
Communications port, 340
Dial-up connection, 312
DNS cache poisoning, 308
DOCSIS, 317
Domain name, 307
Domain name server, 308
Domain Name System, 308
Downstream speed, 310
DSL, 314
DSL filter, 315
DSL modem, 315
Dynamic IP address, 306
Firewall, 341
Fixed Internet access, 311
Fixed wireless Internet service, 319
FTP, 335

FTP client, 336
FTP server, 335
Grid computing system, 334
ICANN, 309
Instant messaging, 331
Internet backbone, 303
Internet forum, 332
Internet service provider, 303
Intrusion, 339
IP (IPv4 and IPv6), 305
Jitter, 332
Latency, 309
MiFi, 327
Mobile broadband, 326
Mobile Internet access, 311
Modem, 304
Network access points, 303
Network address translation, 343
Network service providers, 303
P2P file sharing, 337
Packet loss, 332
Ping, 309
Port probe, 340
Portable Internet access, 311
Private IP address, 343

Protocol suite, 305
Real-time messaging system, 331
Routable IP address, 343
Satellite Internet service, 318
Satellite modem, 318
Software as a service, 330
Static IP address, 306
Symmetric Internet connection, 311
Synchronous communications, 332
Tethering, 328
TCP, 305
TCP/IP, 305
Top-level domain, 307
Traceroute, 310
Tweet, 333
Upstream speed, 310
Virtual private network, 345
Voiceband modem, 313
VoIP, 331
WAP, 325
Wi-Fi hotspot, 322
Wiki, 333
WiMAX, 319

© MediaTechnics

Interactive Summary

To review important concepts from this chapter, fill in the blanks to best complete each sentence. When using the NP2014 interactive eBook, click the Check Answers buttons to automatically score your answers.

SECTION A: The Internet infrastructure is based on high-capacity communications links referred to as the Internet [_____], tied together at network [_____] points where data can cross over from one NSP's equipment to another's. An Internet [_____] provider offers Internet access to individuals, businesses, and smaller ISPs. The Internet uses several communications protocols, including [_____], which breaks a message or file into packets, and [_____], which is responsible for addressing packets. Every device on the Internet has an IP address. 204.127.128.1 is a(n) [_____] -bit IPv4 address. [_____] IP addresses are permanently assigned to computers, whereas [_____] IP addresses are temporarily assigned by a DHCP server. Most high-speed Internet connections use [_____] technology, and even dynamic IP addresses might seem permanent because they don't change unless you turn off your modem or your ISP has an outage. A(n) [_____] name server converts numeric IP addresses into familiar names, such as Travelocity.com. The speed of an Internet connection measured by utilities such as Ping and Traceroute refers to [_____], the elapsed time for data to make a round trip from point A to point B. The speed advertised by Internet service providers is a measure of the amount of data that travels between two points in a given amount of time. Many Internet connections are [_____], meaning the downstream speed is different than the upstream speed.

▶ CHECK ANSWERS

SECTION B: A(n) [_____] connection is a fixed Internet connection that uses a(n) [_____] modem and telephone lines to transport data between your computer and your ISP. Most modems use a standard called V.90 to provide a theoretical maximum speed of [_____] Kbps. [_____] is a high-speed, digital, always-on Internet access technology that runs over standard phone lines. [_____] Internet service is a means of distributing always-on broadband Internet access over the same infrastructure that offers cable television service. Satellite Internet service is a means of distributing always-on, high-speed asymmetric Internet access by broadcasting signals to and from a personal satellite [_____]. Fixed wireless Internet technologies are [_____] area network standards, in contrast to technologies such as Wi-Fi, which are local area network standards. One of the most well-known wireless wide area network standards is [_____], an Ethernet-compatible network standard designated as IEEE 802.16.

▶ CHECK ANSWERS

SECTION C: [_____] Internet access can be defined as the ability to easily move your Internet service from one location to another. [_____] Internet access offers a continuous Internet connection as you are walking or riding in a bus, car, train, or plane. Wi-Fi is an example of portable Internet access technology that allows public access to the Internet within the network's area of coverage, called a Wi-Fi [_____]. Portable WiMAX and portable satellite offer additional Internet access options in the portable category. Cellular phone service providers offer two ways to access the Internet. [_____] is a communications protocol that provides limited access to e-mail and Internet information from handheld devices with small screens and cell phone keypads. Mobile [_____] services using 3G and 4G technologies offer faster access using conventional browsers and e-mail clients.

▶ CHECK ANSWERS

SECTION D: [   ] computing is the idea

that consumers use their computers or handheld devices to access applications, storage, and other computing resources supplied by Internet-based servers, rather than from their local devices. Network-based one-on-one messaging is usually referred to as [   ] messaging and group communications are referred to as [   ]. Most messaging is based on a client/server model that uses a server to handle communication packets between the participants. Voice over Internet [   ] is a technology in which a broadband Internet connection is used to place telephone calls instead of the regular phone system. In contrast to synchronous communications technologies, such as IM and VoIP, [   ] communications technologies, such as blogs, do not require participants to be online at the same time. [   ] is sometimes referred to as microblogging because messages are limited to 140 characters or less.

A grid computing system is a network of computers harnessed together to perform processing tasks. One of the most famous examples of a grid system is the SETI@home project, but grid technology has also been used to crack codes, analyze earthquake data, and crunch numbers for medical research. File Transfer [   ] provides a way to transfer files from one computer to another over any TCP/IP network, such as a LAN or the Internet. The purpose of FTP is to make it easy to upload and download computer files without having to deal directly with the [   ] system or file management system of a remote computer. [   ] file sharing uses protocols that allow users to obtain files from other users located anywhere on the Internet. [   ] is an example of file sharing technology that links clients in a "swarm" for distributing files.

▶ CHECK ANSWERS

SECTION E: In the context of computers, a(n)

[   ] is any access to data or programs by hackers, criminals, or other unauthorized persons. As the result of an intrusion, data can be stolen or altered, system configurations can be changed to allow even more intrusions, and software can be surreptitiously installed and operated under the remote control of a hacker. One of the most common ways of gaining unauthorized access to a network-based computer is by looking for open [   ]. A port [   ] is the use of automated software to locate computers that have open ports and are vulnerable to unauthorized access. One of the easiest steps to enhance your computer's security is to turn it off when you aren't using it. You should also keep your

computer up to date with the latest operating system security [   ] and service packs. You can also install [   ] software designed to filter out suspicious packets attempting to enter or leave a computer. One of the most effective steps you can take to secure your computer from intrusions is to set up a(n) [   ], which assigns private IP addresses to the computers it controls. The process a router uses to keep track of packets and their corresponding private or public IP addresses is called [   ] address translation. Corporations try to limit intrusions by setting up virtual [   ] networks that offer encrypted connections for access to a remote server.

▶ CHECK ANSWERS

6

Interactive Situation Questions

Apply what you've learned to some typical computing situations. When using the NP2014 interactive eBook, you can type your answers, and then use the Check Answers button to automatically score your responses.

1. A news article states that hackers tried to redirect unsuspecting users to infected sites using a technique called [＿＿＿＿＿] cache poisoning. (Hint: Use the acronym.)

2. You're installing a high-speed Internet connection. The modem has a cable like the one shown at right. This modem is designed to connect to a computer's [＿＿＿＿＿] port.

3. Your Internet access seems very slow one day. You might be able to use a networking utility called [＿＿＿＿＿] to discover the source of the slowdown.

4. Suppose that you decide to open a little Web store to sell handcrafted pottery. Your Web site will need a(n) [＿＿＿＿＿] IP address, and you'll want to register a(n) [＿＿＿＿＿] name.

5. You frequently use public Wi-Fi hotspots in cafes and other locations. To keep your passwords and other confidential data safe, you work with your employer to install a(n) [＿＿＿＿＿] that encrypts the data you transmit over the Internet. (Hint: Use the acronym.)

6. Suppose you have installed a cable modem on a standalone PC. To secure your computer, you should activate [＿＿＿＿＿] software to filter packets entering and leaving your computer.

© MediaTechnics

7. Your friend, a film student, has created a 20-minute short film that she wants to distribute to friends. The file is much too large to be an e-mail attachment and she doesn't have access to a(n) [＿＿＿＿＿] server. You suggest that she try posting it at a(n) [＿＿＿＿＿] P2P file sharing site where a swarm of computers can assist with the downloads.

8. Your friend wants you to follow her tweets and asks if you have a(n) [＿＿＿＿＿] account.

9. Your friend is setting up a cable Internet connection. You recommend that she connect a router between her computer and the cable modem, and explain that network [＿＿＿＿＿] translation can help to secure her computer against intrusions.

▶ CHECK ANSWERS

Interactive Practice Tests

Practice tests that consist of ten multiple-choice, true/false, and fill-in-the-blank questions are available in the NP2014 interactive eBook. Test questions are selected at random from a large test bank, so each time you take a test, you'll receive a different set of questions. Your tests are scored immediately, and you can print study guides that help you find the correct answers for any questions that you missed.

▶ CLICK TO START

earning Objectives Checkpoints

earning Objectives Checkpoints are designed to help you assess whether you have achieved the major learning objectives
or this chapter. You can use paper and pencil or word processing software to complete most of the activities.

. Make a timeline of events associated with the evolution of the Internet.

. Draw a conceptual diagram illustrating the Internet backbone, NAPs, NSPs, routers, and ISPs. Extend the diagram to show how computers on a LAN access the Internet through a single DSL modem.

. List at least five protocols used on the Internet and describe what they are used for.

. Explain the differences between static IP addresses, dynamic IP addresses, private IP addresses, and domain names.

. Describe the difference between Ping and Traceroute by giving an example of when each would be used.

. List the advantages and disadvantages of dial-up, cable, DSL, satellite, and fixed wireless Internet services. List the Internet access methods in which upstream transmission rates differ from downstream rates.

. List the options for mobile and portable Internet access, and explain their strengths and weaknesses.

8. Explain the advantages of mobile broadband services compared to WAP service.

9. Give examples of synchronous and asynchronous communications offered on the Internet.

10. Explain how Voice over IP works, and compare it to cell phone and land line services.

11. List two examples of distributed grid computing and two examples of cloud computing.

12. Draw diagrams to illustrate how FTP, the original Napster, and BitTorrent work.

13. Make a list of security concerns that are related to Internet access.

14. Make a checklist of steps you can take to secure your computer from Internet-based intrusions.

Study Tip: Make sure you can use your own words to correctly answer each of the purple focus questions that appear throughout the chapter.

6

Concept Map

Fill in the blanks to show the hierarchy
of Internet access options.

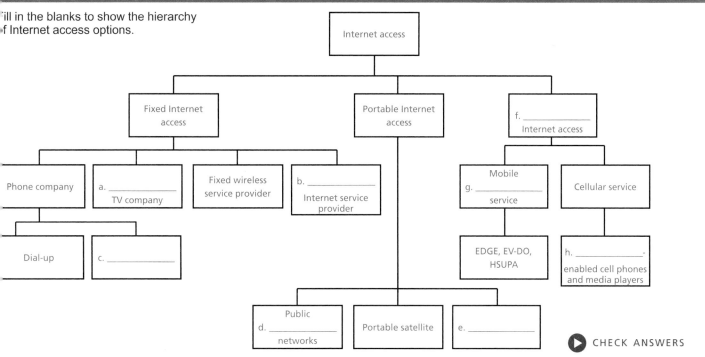

CHECK ANSWERS

7

The Web and E-mail

Chapter Contents

INFOWEBLINKS

You'll find updates for chapter material by connecting to the **NP2014 Chapter 7** InfoWebLink.

Ⓦ CLICK TO CONNECT
www.infoweblinks.com/np2014/ch07

Learning Objectives

After reading this chapter, you will be able to answer the following questions by completing the outcomes-based Learning Objectives Checkpoints on page 419.

1. What is HTML?
2. How does the Web work?
3. What does a browser do?
4. Where do cookies come from?
5. What tools are available for creating Web pages?
6. How do I create a simple Web page?
7. What makes some Web pages interactive?
8. How do search engines work?
9. What is a search operator?
10. What is the correct way to cite Web pages?
11. How do online shopping carts work?
12. How safe is online shopping?
13. Is Webmail better than client-based local e-mail?
14. How do HTML and MIME formats relate to e-mail?
15. What are the security risks of using the Web?

Apply Your Knowledge

The information in this chapter will give you the background to:

▶ Use a browser to view Web pages and the source documents from which they are constructed

▶ Install browser plug-ins necessary to work with a variety of graphics, sound, and video files

▶ Create your own Web pages using a text editor and HTML tags

▶ Use a search engine to locate information on the Web

▶ Formulate advanced search queries

▶ Capture text and graphics from the Web

▶ Know how to keep your credit card information safe when shopping online

▶ Work with Webmail or local e-mail, attachments, and HTML mail formats

▶ Protect yourself from spam, spyware, cookie exploits, phishing, and pharming

TRY IT!

WHAT'S MY BROWSER STATUS?

Chapter 7 focuses on the World Wide Web, or "Web" for short. The most important software tool for accessing the Web is called a browser. To learn about the browser on your computer, follow these steps:

1. Make sure your computer is on and displaying the desktop.
2. Which browser do you usually use to access the Web? _____

   If you don't know, look for browser icons on your desktop. Popular browsers include Internet Explorer, Safari, Firefox, and Chrome.
3. What is the URL that your browser uses as your home page? _____

   The home page is the first Web page displayed and the one displayed when you click the Home button.
4. What is the version number for the browser you are using? _____

   Chrome: Click the  **Settings** icon, then click **About Google Chrome**.

   Firefox on a PC: Click **Help**, and then click **About Firefox**.

   Internet Explorer on a PC: Click the [icon] **Tools** icon, then click **About Internet Explorer**.

   Safari and Firefox on a Mac: Click the browser name on the menu bar, then click the **About** option.

   After you write down the version number, close the dialog box.
5. Find the most recent version for your browser by going to its Web site:

   www.mozilla.org/products/firefox
   www.google.com/chrome
   www.microsoft.com/windows/ie
   www.apple.com/safari
6. Are you using the most recent version of your browser? _____

   Unless you want to download the most recent version of your browser and have permission to do so, exit the download area and close your browser.

About Google Chrome

Google Chrome

21.0.1180.89 m

Copyright © 2006-2012 Google Inc. All Rights Reserved.
Google Chrome is made possible by the Chromium open source project and other open source software.

Google Chrome Terms of Service

☑ Google Chrome is up to date (21.0.1180.89)   OK

About Internet Explorer

Internet Explorer 10

Version: 10.0.9200.16384
Update Versions: RTM (KB2718695)
Product ID: 00150-20000-00003-AA459

☑ Install new versions automatically

© 2012 Microsoft Corporation. All rights reserved.

Close

Safari

Version 5.1.7 (6534.57.2)

Copyright © 2003-2012 Apple Inc.
All rights reserved.

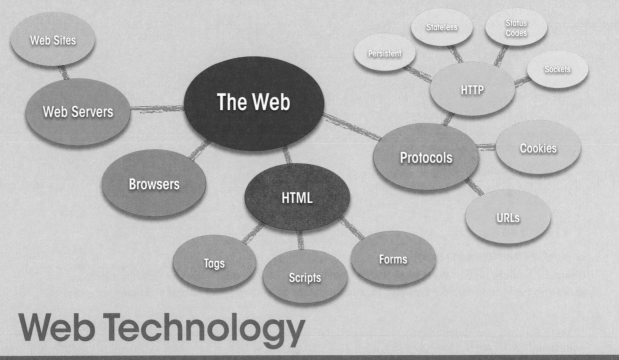

Web Technology

IN 1990, a British scientist named Tim Berners-Lee developed specifications for URLs, HTML, and HTTP; a group of technologies designed to help researchers share information by creating access to a sort of "web" of electronic documents. Berners-Lee's free Web software appeared on the Internet in 1991, but the Web didn't take off until 1993 when Marc Andreessen and his colleagues at the University of Illinois created Mosaic, a graphical browser. Andreessen later formed his own company and produced a browser called Netscape, which put the Web into the hands of millions of Web surfers. In Section A, you'll peel back the layers of Web technologies to take a look at what happens behind your browser window.

WEB BASICS

▶ **What is the Web?** One of the Internet's most captivating attractions, the **Web** (short for *World Wide Web*) is a collection of document, image, video, and sound files that can be linked and accessed over the Internet using a protocol called HTTP.

The concept of interlinking documents to access them pre-dates the Web by almost half a century. In 1945, an engineer named Vannevar Bush described a microfilm-based machine called the Memex that linked associated information or ideas through "trails."

The idea of linked documents resurfaced in the mid-1960s when Harvard graduate Ted Nelson coined the term **hypertext** to describe a computer system that could store literary documents, link them according to logical relationships, and allow readers to comment and annotate what they read. Nelson sketched the diagram in Figure 7-1 to explain his idea of a computer-based "web" of "links."

▶ **What are Web 2.0 and Web 3.0?** Originally, material for the Web was posted as a series of documents that could be accessed using a browser. That model evolved with the introduction of wikis, blogs, and social networking.

TERMINOLOGY NOTE

Although the terms *Internet* and *Web* are sometimes used interchangeably, they are not the same. The Web is an interlinked collection of information; the Internet is a communications system used to transport that information from computers that store it to clients who want to view it.

FIGURE 7-1

Ted Nelson's early sketch of project Xanadu—a distant relative of the Web—used the terms *links* and *web*.

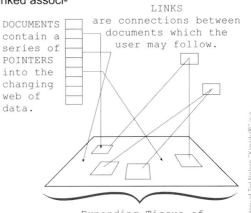

These Web-based applications are sometimes characterized as **Web 2.0**. Cloud computing and other new technologies are likely to further change the way we use the Web, and those innovations are referred to as **Web 3.0**. Although Web 2.0 and Web 3.0 sound like new versions of the Web, they use the same Internet communications infrastructure as the "old" Web.

▶ **What is a Web site?** A **Web site** typically contains a collection of related information organized and formatted so it can be accessed using software called a browser. You are probably familiar with informational Web sites such as HowStuffWorks, CNN, ESPN, and Wikipedia. Web sites can also offer Web-based applications, such as Google Docs, and social networking, such as Facebook.

The activities that take place at Web sites are under the control of Web servers. A **Web server** is an Internet-based computer that accepts requests from browsers. Servers collect the requested information and transmit it back in a format that the browser can display in the form of a Web page.

▶ **What is a Web page?** A **Web page** is the product or output of one or more Web-based files displayed in a format similar to a page in a book. Unlike pages in printed books, however, Web pages can dynamically incorporate videos, sounds, and interactive elements.

A Web page can be based on a document stored as a file or it can be assembled on the fly from information stored in a database. For example, a course syllabus that you view on the Web is probably written with a word processor and stored as a document on a Web server.

In contrast, the Web page you view about a newly released album on iTunes is assembled from a database that contains the album title, artist name, track list, price, release date, album cover art, and other product information.

▶ **How do I access a Web page?** Your main tool for accessing Web pages is browser software, such as Microsoft Internet Explorer, open-source Mozilla Firefox, Google Chrome, or Apple Safari. A **Web browser** (commonly referred to as a browser) is client software that displays Web page elements and handles links between pages. When using a browser, you can access a Web page by clicking a **hypertext link** (usually referred to simply as a link) or by typing a URL (Figure 7-2).

▶ **What is a URL?** Every Web page has a unique address called a **URL** (Uniform Resource Locator, pronounced "You Are ELL"). For example, the URL for the Cable News Network (CNN) Web site is *http://www.cnn.com*. Most URLs begin with http:// to indicate the Web's standard communications protocol. When typing a URL, the http:// can be omitted, so *www.cnn.com* works just as well as *http://www.cnn.com*.

FIGURE 7-2

Browsers display Web pages and the links they contain. When the mouse pointer hovers over a link, it changes from an arrow shape to a hand shape. ▶ For an overview of browser controls, refer to this figure in your interactive eBook.

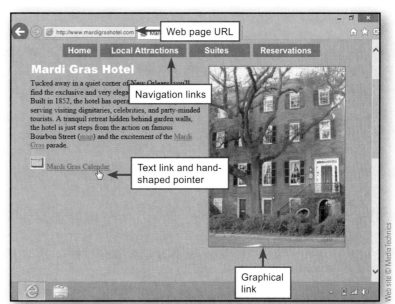

Web page URL

Home　Local Attractions　Suites　Reservations

Mardi Gras Hotel

Tucked away in a quiet corner of New Orleans, you'll find the exclusive and very elegant. Built in 1852, the hotel has opera serving visiting dignitaries, celebrities, and party-minded tourists. A tranquil retreat hidden behind garden walls, the hotel is just steps from the action on famous Bourbon Street (map) and the excitement of the Mardi Gras parade.

Mardi Gras Calendar

Navigation links

Text link and hand-shaped pointer

Graphical link

Web site © MediaTechnics

Most Web sites have a main page that acts as a doorway to the rest of the pages at the site. This main page is sometimes referred to as a home page, although this term can also refer to the page displayed by your browser each time it opens. The URL for a Web site's main page is normally short and to the point, like *www.cnn.com*.

The pages for a Web site are grouped into folders, which are reflected in the URL. For example, the CNN site might include weather information at *www.cnn.com/weather/* and entertainment information at *www.cnn.com/showbiz/*.

The file name of a specific Web page always appears last in the URL. Web page file names usually have an .htm or .html extension, indicating that the page was created with Hypertext Markup Language. You'll learn more about HTML later in the chapter. Figure 7-3 identifies the parts of a URL.

FIGURE 7-3

The URL for a Web page indicates the computer on which it is stored, its location on the Web server, its file name, and its extension.

http://www.cnn.com/showbiz/movies.htm

| Web protocol standard | Web server name | Folder name | File name and file extension |

▶ **What are the rules for correctly typing a URL?** A URL never contains spaces, even after a punctuation mark, so do not type any spaces within a URL. An underline symbol is sometimes used to give the appearance of a space between words; for example, *www.detroit.com/top_10.html*.

Be sure to use the correct type of slash—always a forward slash (/)—and duplicate the URL's capitalization exactly. Some Web servers are case sensitive. On these servers, typing *www.cmu.edu/Info.html* (with an uppercase *I*) will not locate the Web page that's stored on the Web server as *www.cmu.edu/info.html* (with a lowercase *i*).

HTML

▶ **What is HTML?** HTML (Hypertext Markup Language) is a set of specifications for creating documents that a browser can display as a Web page. HTML is called a **markup language** because authors mark up documents by inserting special instructions, called **HTML tags**, that specify how the document should appear when displayed on a computer screen or printed.

Tim Berners-Lee developed the original HTML specifications in 1990. These specifications have been revised several times by the World Wide Web Consortium (W3C). The current version, **HTML5**, was introduced in 2010.

XHTML is a markup language very similar to HTML, but it can be customized with tags that describe the data in databases. XHTML is more rigidly structured than HTML and a bit more complex, however, so XHTML documents are required to be "well-formed" by adhering to a strict set of syntax rules.

▶ **How do HTML tags work?** HTML tags are incorporated into an **HTML document**, which is similar to a word processing file, but has an .htm or .html extension. HTML tags, such as <hr /> and <b>, are enclosed in angle brackets and embedded in the document. These tags are instructions for the browser. When your browser displays a Web page on your computer screen, it does not show the tags or angle brackets. Instead, it attempts to follow the tags' instructions.

TERMINOLOGY NOTE

URLs can get quite long. For tweets and other postings where long URLs are troublesome, short URL nicknames, such as *http://bit.ly/87wbb*, can be supplied by services such as bitly and TinyURL.

TRY IT!

What is the purpose of HTML?

○ To give browsers directions on how to display Web pages

○ To tell your computer how to download files from a Web server

○ To create unique addresses for Web-based information

○ To supply the software used to access the Internet

▶ So HTML documents look a lot different from Web pages, right? Exactly. An HTML document is like a screenplay, and your browser is like a director who makes a screenplay come to life by assembling cast members and making sure they deliver their lines correctly.

As the HTML "screenplay" unfolds, your browser follows the instructions in an HTML document to display lines of text on your computer screen in the right color, size, and position.

If the screenplay calls for a graphic, your browser collects it from the Web server and displays it. Although the HTML screenplay exists as a permanent file, the Web page you see on your computer screen exists only for the duration of the "performance."

Technically speaking, you can distinguish HTML documents (the screenplay) from Web pages (the performance). However, in everyday conversation, the term *Web page* is often used for the HTML document as well as the Web page displayed on the screen.

An HTML document is sometimes referred to as a **source document** because it is the source of the HTML tags used to construct a Web page. You can view the HTML source documents for most Web pages if you are curious about how they were constructed. Figure 7-4 illustrates the difference between an HTML source document and the Web page it produces.

7

FIGURE 7-4

An HTML document (top) contains text and HTML tags. Formatting tags are used to change font size and separate paragraphs. Other tags add graphics and links to a page. The HTML document produces a Web page (bottom).
▶ Refer to your interactive eBook to see more examples of HTML source code.

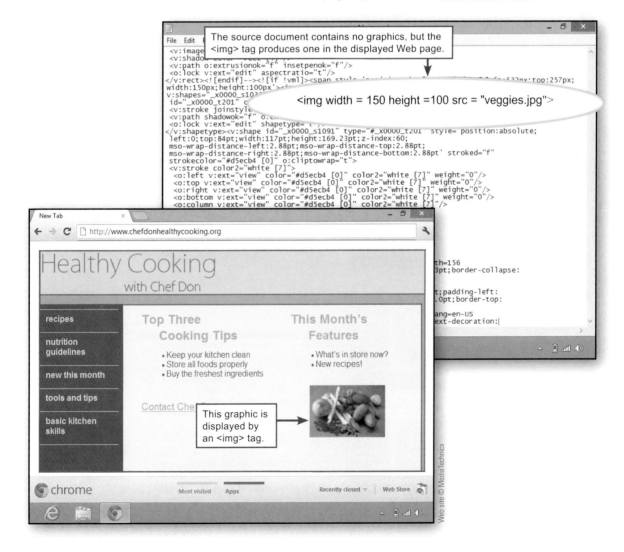

HTTP

▶ **How does HTTP work?** **HTTP** is a protocol that works with TCP/IP to get Web resources to your desktop. A Web resource can be defined as any chunk of data that has a URL, such as an HTML document, a graphic, or a sound file.

HTTP includes commands called methods that help your browser communicate with Web servers. GET is the most frequently used HTTP method. The GET method is used to retrieve text and graphics files necessary for displaying a Web page. This method can also be used to pass a search query to a file server. HTTP transports your browser's request for a Web resource to a Web server. Next, it transports the Web server's response back to your browser.

An HTTP exchange takes place over a pair of sockets. A **socket** is an abstract concept that represents one end of a connection. Although a packet switching network doesn't actually make point-to-point connections between network nodes, many people find it handy to visualize network connections as a communication line with a doorway-like socket at each end. For HTTP, sockets routinely are associated with port 80 on the client and server.

In an HTTP exchange, your browser opens a socket on your PC, connects to a similar open socket at the Web server, and issues a command, such as "send me an HTML document." The server receives the command, executes it, and sends a response back through the socket. The sockets are then closed until the browser is ready to issue another command. Figure 7-5 demonstrates the messages that flow between your browser and a Web server to retrieve an HTML document.

FIGURE 7-5

HTTP messages flow between a browser and a Web server. For an animated view of how HTTP works, take a look at this figure in your interactive eBook.

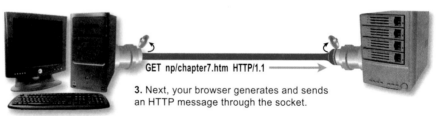

1. The URL in the browser's Address box contains the domain name of the Web server that your browser contacts.

Address www.infoweblinks.com/np/chapter7.htm

2. Your browser opens a socket and connects to a similar open socket at the Web server.

GET np/chapter7.htm HTTP/1.1 ⟶

3. Next, your browser generates and sends an HTTP message through the socket.

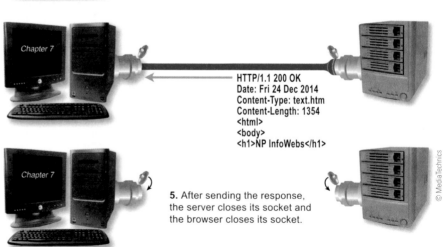

4. The server sends back the requested HTML document through the open sockets.

HTTP/1.1 200 OK
Date: Fri 24 Dec 2014
Content-Type: text.htm
Content-Length: 1354
<html>
<body>
<h1>NP InfoWebs</h1>

5. After sending the response, the server closes its socket and the browser closes its socket.

© MediaTechnics

▶ CLICK TO START

▶ Is each Web page element retrieved separately? HTTP initially allowed only one request and response per session. As a result, a browser could open a session and request an HTML document; but as soon as the document was sent, the session was closed. To make additional requests—for example, to request a graphic for the page—the browser had to open another session.

A **persistent HTTP connection** reuses the same HTTP connection to send and receive multiple requests. Today's browsers use persistent connections to obtain text, images, and audio for a Web page during a single session.

▶ What if an element cannot be found? A Web server's response to a browser's request includes an **HTTP status code** that indicates whether the browser's request could be fulfilled. The status code 200 means that the request was fulfilled—the requested HTML document, graphic, or other resource was sent. Anyone who surfs the Web has encountered the "404 Not Found" message. Your browser displays this message when a Web server sends a 404 status code to indicate that the requested resource does not exist (Figure 7-6).

FIGURE 7-6

When a broken link points to a nonexistent HTML document, your browser produces a 404 Not Found error. When a broken link points to a nonexistent graphic or other non-HTML file, your browser usually displays one of the broken link icons shown below.

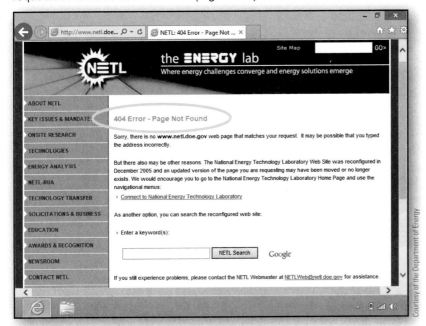

Courtesy of the Department of Energy

▶ What is a Web cache? When your browser fetches pages and graphics to form a Web page, it stores that material on your computer in temporary files referred to as a **Web cache**, browser cache, or browser history.

A Web cache comes in handy if you switch back and forth between pages or sites. Rather than fetch the entire page and all its graphics again, your browser can simply load them from the local cache. Files are deleted from the Web cache within days or weeks, depending on your browser's settings.

A potential problem with your Web cache is that it stores Web page elements from all the sites you've visited. If you use a public or lab computer, the Web page elements are stored there and can be viewed by others. To maintain your privacy, you might consider deleting these files periodically, adjusting browser settings to limit the time these files remain on your computer, or limiting the amount of space they can use on the hard disk.

WEB BROWSERS

▶ What are the most popular browsers? Netscape Navigator was one of the first browsers with a graphical user interface. It has been superseded by today's popular browsers, such as Mozilla Firefox, Microsoft Internet Explorer, Apple Safari, and Google Chrome. Browsers have many similarities, as you can see from examining their toolbars in Figure 7-7.

FIGURE 7-7

Popular browsers include Firefox, Internet Explorer, Safari, and Chrome.

Mozilla Firefox. In 1998, Netscape source code became open source software, managed by an organization known as Mozilla. The organization's main product, a browser called Mozilla, was all but ignored by most computer owners. In 2004, however, a new version of Mozilla, dubbed Firefox, rapidly gained popularity because it offered effective security features.

Microsoft Internet Explorer (IE). The program code for the original IE 1.0 browser was licensed from a Netscape spin-off called Spyglass. Originally developed for Windows, IE has evolved through ten versions since 1995 and is also available for Mac OS, Linux, and several versions of UNIX.

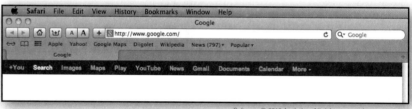

Software © 2012 Apple Inc. All rights reserved

Apple Safari. In 2003, Apple introduced a browser called Safari, which is now included with Macintosh computers and available for PCs. Safari is also available on Apple iPhones and iPads.

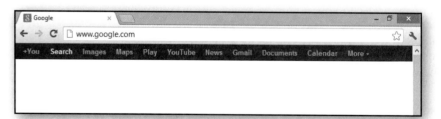

Google Chrome. Developed in 2008, Chrome was engineered specifically to support Web-based e-mail and similar online applications. It is generally considered to have the best support for HTML5.

TRY IT!

You might have more than one browser available. Check your computer. How many browsers are installed?

○ 1

○ 2

○ 3

○ 4

▶ Should I upgrade my browser when new versions become available? It is a good idea to upgrade when a new version of your browser becomes available. Because most browser updates are free, you can get up-to-date functionality simply by spending a few minutes downloading and installing an update.

The problem with using an old browser is that some Web pages depend on new HTML features supported only by the latest browser versions. Without the latest upgrade, you might encounter errors when your browser tries to display a page, but cannot interpret some of the HTML. In other cases, your browser might display the Web page without errors, but you will not see all the intended effects.

Another important reason to upgrade is for increased security. As hackers discover and take advantage of security holes, browser publishers try to patch the holes. Upgrades normally contain patches for known security holes, although new features might sometimes open new holes.

▶ Why do I have to download software to view some Web pages? Browsers were originally limited to displaying documents in HTML format and graphics files in GIF and JPEG formats. Today, however, many additional formats are used for graphics, sound, and video included in Web pages. Browsers do not have built-in support for all these formats.

If your browser does not have built-in support for a file format required to display or play a Web page element, you can download the necessary software. For example, to read a PDF file, you might be directed to the Adobe Web site to download Adobe Reader software that handles PDF files. To display an animation, you might need Adobe's Flash software. The software your browser calls upon to work with additional file formats is referred to as a plug-in, add-on, or player.

▶ What is a plug-in? A **plug-in** is a program that extends a browser's ability to work with file formats. Most plug-ins can be downloaded from the Web. Plug-ins come in different versions for different browsers. When looking for plug-ins, let your browser do the searching and it will find the correct version.

The process of installing a plug-in application creates an association between the browser and a file format, such as PDF, SWF, or MOV. Whenever your browser encounters one of these file formats, it automatically runs the corresponding plug-in, which in turn opens the file.

You can download, install, and delete plug-ins for your browser. Figure 7-8 shows a list of plug-ins installed for use with Internet Explorer.

TERMINOLOGY NOTE

The term *player* is sometimes used to refer to plug-ins, but it can also refer to standalone software that does not require a host program. For example, Adobe Flash Player is a stand-alone application that you run to view Flash video and animations. The player is also available as a plug-in that is installed in your browser.

7

FIGURE 7-8

You can usually find a list of plug-ins installed for use with your browser. If you use Internet Explorer, look for a Manage Add-ons option on the Tools menu. ▶ For more information about managing plug-ins, refer to this figure in your interactive eBook.

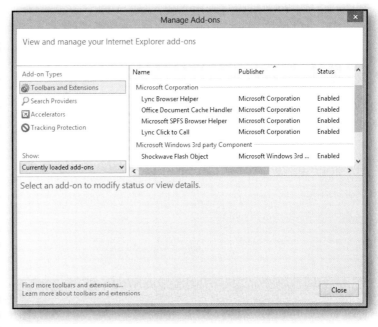

COOKIES

▶ **What is a cookie?** A **cookie** (technically an HTTP cookie) is a small chunk of data generated by a Web server and stored in a text file on your computer's hard disk. Cookies allow a Web site to store information on a client computer for later retrieval. Web sites use cookies to:

▶ Monitor your path through a site to keep track of the pages you viewed or the items you purchased.

▶ Gather information that allows a Web server to present ad banners targeted to products you previously purchased at that Web site.

▶ Collect personal information you submit to a Web page, and retain it for the next time you visit the Web site.

▶ **Why do Web sites need to use cookies?** In many respects, cookies are the solution for problems caused by HTTP's **stateless protocol**, which maintains no record of the pages you visit at a Web site.

Suppose that you use your browser to visit a popular online music store. You search for your favorite bands, listen to some sample tracks, and put a few albums in your shopping cart.

Because HTTP is a stateless protocol, each time you connect to a different Web page at the site, the server regards it as a new visit. Cookies enable the server to keep track of your activity and compile a list of your purchases.

▶ **What's in a cookie?** Cookies can contain any information that's collected by the host site, such as a customer number, Web page URL, shopping cart number, or access date (Figure 7-9).

▶ **How do cookies work?** When your browser connects to a site that uses cookies, it receives an HTTP "Set-cookie" message from the Web server. This cookie message contains information that your browser stores on your computer's hard disk. The server that creates a cookie can request it any time your browser is accessing a Web page from the Web site server.

▶ **How long do cookies stay on my computer?** A Web developer can program a cookie to time out after a designated date. When a cookie reaches the end of its predefined lifetime, your Web browser simply erases it. Some cookies have no expiration date or expire on a date far into the future, so cookies tend to accumulate on your computer's hard disk.

▶ **Can I see the cookies stored on my computer?** You can view a list of cookies stored on your computer, but first you must find them. Refer to your browser documentation to discover which folder holds your cookies (Figure 7-10).

FIGURE 7-9

When you look at a cookie stored on your computer, most of the information is unintelligible. The cookie below is called ppkcookie, its value is "hello," and it was created at *www. quirksmode.org*. The cookie contains an expiration date, but it is encoded so you can't decipher it.

ppkcookie1hellowww. quirksmode.org/1600 1827327360298117151 14706012829810307*

© MediaTechnics

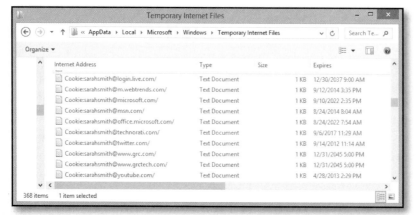

FIGURE 7-10

Internet Explorer stores cookies as individual files in the AppData\Local\Microsoft\ Windows\Temporary Internet Files folder. The information after the @ symbol indicates the domain name of the site that created the cookie.

WEB PAGE AUTHORING

▶ **What tools can I use to create Web pages?** You can create HTML documents for Web pages with an HTML conversion utility, online Web authoring tools, Web authoring software, or a text editor.

An **HTML conversion utility** adds HTML tags to a document, spreadsheet, or other text-based file to create an HTML document that can be displayed by a browser. For example, you can work with Microsoft Word to create a standard DOCX file and then use Word's Save As Web Page option to convert the document into HTML format. The HTML conversion process sometimes produces an unusual result, however, because some of the features and formatting in your original document might not be possible within the world of HTML.

A second option for Web page authors is to use a set of online Web page authoring tools. These template-like tools are provided by some ISPs and other companies that host Web pages for individuals and businesses. Working with these tools is quite simple—you type, select, drag, and drop elements onto a Web page (Figure 7-11).

Does your favorite word processor offer an option to output to HTML format?

○ Yes, under the Export option

○ Yes, under Save As there is an HTML option

○ Yes, when I select the Download option

○ No, it doesn't have an HTML option

7

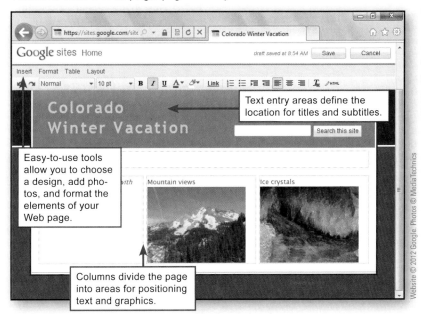

FIGURE 7-11

Many Web hosting sites, such as Google, offer subscribers online tools for creating Web pages. ▶ For a tour of online Web page authoring, activate this figure in your interactive eBook.

Text entry areas define the location for titles and subtitles.

Easy-to-use tools allow you to choose a design, add photos, and format the elements of your Web page.

Columns divide the page into areas for positioning text and graphics.

A third option for creating Web pages is a special category of software, referred to as **Web authoring software** or HTML editors, which provides tools specifically designed to enter and format Web page text, graphics, and links. Popular Web authoring products include Adobe Dreamweaver, and open source KompoZer and Amaya.

▶ **How do I create a Web page with a text editor?** You can use a text editor like Notepad (Windows) or TextEdit (Mac) to create simple HTML documents or to make quick modifications to more complex pages. The first step in the process is to open the editor. Then you can enter text and HTML tags.

▶ **How do I start an HTML document?** The framework for an HTML document consists of two sections: the head and the body. The head section begins with <!DOCTYPE html> and <head> tags. It may also include information that defines global properties, including the Web page title that appears in the browser title bar and information about the page that can be used by search engines.

The body section of an HTML document begins with the <body> HTML tag. This section of the document contains text, HTML tags that format the text, plus a variety of links to graphics, sounds, and videos. Figure 7-12 contains basic HTML for a Web page. You can use it as a template for creating your own pages.

FIGURE 7-12

Using a text editor to create an HTML document requires attention to details, such as including all necessary quotation marks and brackets.

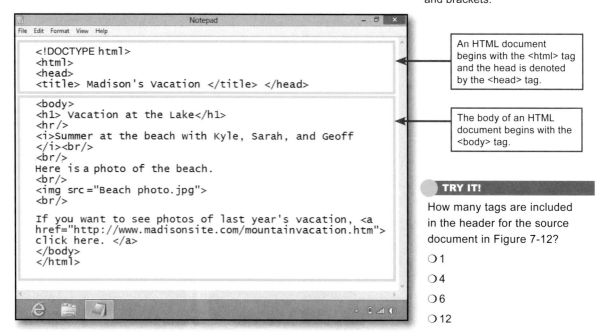

An HTML document begins with the <html> tag and the head is denoted by the <head> tag.

The body of an HTML document begins with the <body> tag.

TRY IT!

How many tags are included in the header for the source document in Figure 7-12?

○ 1

○ 4

○ 6

○ 12

❱ How do I specify the text and graphics for a Web page?

In the body section of your HTML document, you can enter text and HTML tags to format fonts and spacing. You can also specify the images you want to appear on the page, and you can create clickable links to other Web pages. The table in Figure 7-13 provides a list of basic HTML tags that you can use to create your own HTML documents; the HTML lab at the end of the chapter goes into more detail on the use of these tags.

FIGURE 7-13

Basic HTML Tags

HTML Tag	Use	Example
<b> <i>	Bold or italicize text	<b> Hello </b>
<h1> <h2> ... <h6>	Change font size; h1 is largest	<h1> Chapter 1 </h1>
<h1 style="color: ">	Change font color	<h1 style="color:green"> Fir Trees </h1>
<hr/>	Include a horizontal line (no end tag)	Section 2 <hr/>
** **	Line break (no end tag)	This is line one. This is line two.
<p>	Paragraph break	<p>It was the best of times, it ...of comparison only.
<ol> <ul> <li>	Numbered list <ol>; bulleted list <ul>; list items <li>	<ol> <li>First item</li> <li> Second item</li> </ol>
<a href="URL">	Link to another Web page	<a href="www.news.com/today.htm"> Click here </a>
<img src="File">	Include an image	<img src="Photo.jpg">
<table>, <tr>, <td>	Create tables, table rows, and cells	<table>

> **How do I get my Web pages on the Internet?** Whether you work with a text editor or another authoring tool, save your HTML document with an .htm or .html extension.

Creating a Web page is not the end of the publishing process. Additional steps include those shown below.

1. Test each page locally. When you complete the first draft of a Web page, you should test it to verify that every element is displayed correctly by any browsers that visitors to your Web page might use.

You can accomplish this task without connecting to the Web. Simply open a browser, and then enter the local file name of the HTML document you created for your Web page. Repeat this process for any other browsers you expect visitors to use.

One caution: Your hard disk drive is much faster than most Internet connections, so the text and graphics for your Web page are displayed faster during your local test than for someone viewing your page over the Internet.

2. Transfer pages to a Web server. Whether you're publishing a single page, a series of pages, or an entire Web site, you must put your pages on a Web server—a process called posting.

To post Web page files manually, you can use a file transfer utility such as FileZilla or WS_FTP.

Web authoring software provides a menu option that automates the process of posting HTML documents and associated media files.

3. Test all pages and links. After you post your pages on a Web server, make sure you can access each page, and then test the links between your pages as well as any links to pages on other sites.

4. Update your pages to keep them current. Periodically, you should review the information on your Web pages and verify that the links connect to pages that still exist.

INTERACTIVE WEB PAGES

> **How do Web pages become interactive?** Standard HTML provides a way to display text and graphics on a Web page and link to other Web pages. Basic HTML is not a programming language because it lacks a set of logical operations necessary to perform complicated tasks or respond to user actions.

Despite the limitations of HTML, many Web sites are interactive. For example, e-commerce sites validate credit card information when customers make purchases. Online courses include testing modules that score student answers. Cloud-based apps provide interactive tools for creating word clouds, designing logos, and collaborating on projects.

Today's Web sites are also dynamic. Objects move on the page. Hovering over "hotspots" produces tips or other information. Animated ads flash into view.

Interactive and dynamic Web sites are possible when programming and scripting technologies supplement native HTML features, such as forms and canvas.

> **What's an interactive form?** An **HTML form** uses the <form> tag to accept typed input. Chances are good that whenever you enter data at a Web site—your user ID and password, your billing data, a tweet, or the answer to an online quiz—there is a <form> tag involved.

A form can be used to collect the answer to a quiz question, as shown in Figure 7-14.

HTML Source Document (excerpt)

```
<form action="">

What is the tallest mountain in the world? <input type="text" name="response" />

<br/>

</form>
```

Web Page

What is the tallest mountain in the world? [   ]

FIGURE 7-14

The HTML <form> tag is used to display a question and a box into which you can enter an answer. The answer is stored in your computer's memory as a variable called "response."

▶ What happens to the data collected by a form? The basic <form> tag is limited to collecting what you type. Taking action requires additional tools. Form data, other interactions, and animated effects can be handled locally or by a remote server.

When the HTML source document that's received by your local browser handles interactions, the process is referred to as **client-side**. When interactions are handled by a remote server, the process is referred to as **server-side**.

▶ How does client-side interaction work? In the quiz question example, a client-side supplement to the HTML can check the response, compare it to the correct answer, and generate a message or an HTML page that displays "Correct!" or "Not correct."

A computer scripting language called **JavaScript** is commonly used to add logic and other programmable elements to a Web page. JavaScript consists of a series of instructions that can be included in the HTML source document. JavaScript is executed by the browser, as shown in Figure 7-15.

TRY IT!

Where does the <form> tag operate?

○ Client-side

○ Server-side

○ In a word processor

○ On secured sites

HTML Source Document (excerpt)

```
<script type = "text/javascript">

if (response="Everest")

  { display ="Correct!";}

else

  { display = "Not correct.";}

</script>
```

Web Page

What is the tallest mountain in the world? [   ]

Correct!

FIGURE 7-15

JavaScript can be included in an HTML source document. The JavaScript statements are executed client-side by the browser.

▶ **Are there other client-side technologies?** Other client-side technologies exist. Adobe Flash, for example, is a multimedia technology that can be used to create animation and interactive modules. An HTML source document can contain a tag that downloads the Flash module along with other elements for a Web page. Flash, once the dominant tool for interactive Web pages, is gradually being replaced by JavaScript and new features available in HTML5.

▶ **What about server-side?** Server-side scripts or programs run on Web servers. They typically handle requests for data that originates in corporate databases. Server-side scripts accept data submitted by a form, process that data, and then generate a custom HTML document that is sent to the browser for display. A popular server-side activity is verifying billing data at an e-commerce site (Figure 7-16).

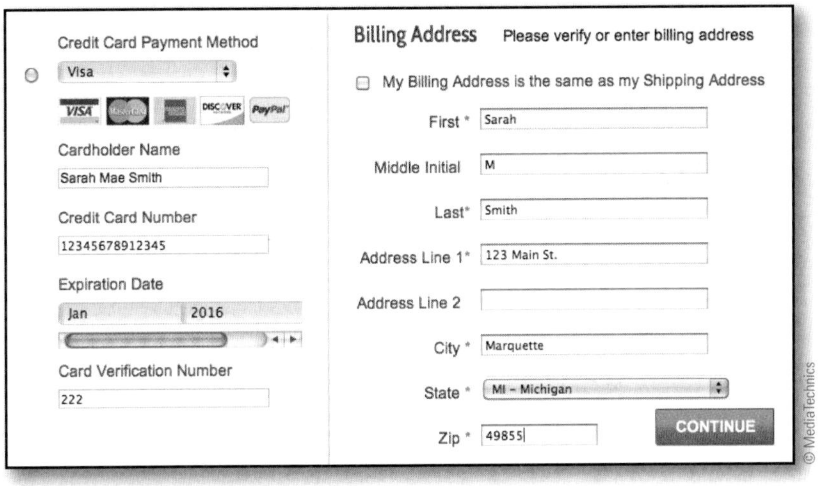

FIGURE 7-16

The data from this form is held in memory until you click the Submit button. Then, your browser sends the data to a program on an HTTP server where it can be processed and stored.

Server-side scripts can be written using a variety of programming and scripting languages, such as Perl, PHP, and Java. Pages produced dynamically by server-side scripts can often be identified because the URL displayed in your browser's Address bar ends in an extension such as .asp or .php.

▶ **Which is better: client-side scripts or server-side programs?** Client-side scripts tend to be used for interactive user interface elements, such as form entry, drop-down menus, rollover buttons, and on-screen drawing. They are not used for secure transactions because all the coding they contain can be viewed on the client computer. For example, if you want to create a full-featured online quiz system, where students can't peek at the answers by viewing the HTML source, then you would use server-side programs.

QuickCheck

1. Ted Nelson coined the term [   ] to describe a web of linked documents, similar to Web pages.

2. Every Web page has a unique address called a(n) [   ] . (Hint: Use the acronym.)

3. The main protocol for sending and receiving Web content is [   ] . (Hint: Use the acronym.)

4. The basic markup language used on the Web is [   ] . (Hint: Use the acronym.)

5. [   ] were developed because HTTP is a stateless protocol; so each time you connect to a different page, the Web server regards it as a new connection.

 CHECK ANSWERS

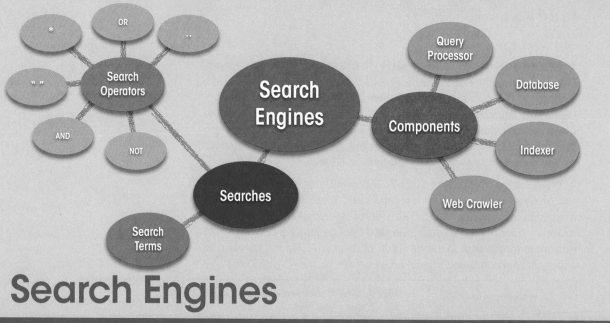

Search Engines

THE WEB ENCOMPASSES hundreds of millions of pages stored on servers scattered all over the globe. To use this information, however, you have to find it. Modern Web surfers depend on search engines to wade through the tsunami of information stored on the Web. In Section B, you'll find out how Web search engines work so that you can use them more efficiently.

SEARCH ENGINE BASICS

▶ **What is a Web search engine?** A **Web search engine** (commonly referred to simply as a search engine) is a program designed to help people locate information on the Web by formulating simple queries consisting of one or more words called keywords or search terms. In response to a query, the search engine displays results, or "hits," as a list of relevant Web sites, accompanied by links to source pages and short excerpts containing the keywords (Figure 7-17).

FIGURE 7-17

A query for *mountain bike trails* returns a list of links to relevant sites.

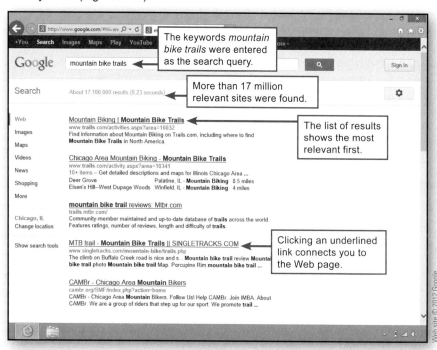

The keywords *mountain bike trails* were entered as the search query.

More than 17 million relevant sites were found.

The list of results shows the most relevant first.

Clicking an underlined link connects you to the Web page.

Popular search engines are located at Web sites such as *www.google.com*, *www.yahoo.com*, *www.bing.com*, and *www.ask.com*. The search engines at these sites build the equivalent of a book index. Just as an index helps readers turn to a page on which they can find a particular word or concept, a search engine helps Web surfers link to pages that contain information they seek. Unlike a book, however, the information on the Web is too vast to catalog manually, so search engine software does it autonomously.

▶ **What is the difference between a search engine and a search engine site?** It is easy to think of *www.google.com* as a search engine; but to be precise, it is a Web site that offers access to a search engine. A search engine is the program that works behind the scenes to gather, index, find, and rank information from the Web.

Some sites, including Google, use their own proprietary search engines, but other sites use third-party search technology. For example, Microsoft's Bing search engine is the underlying technology for Yahoo! searches.

Search engine technology can also be incorporated in e-commerce, informational, and corporate sites, most often taking the form of query toolbars used to search within a single Web site (Figure 7-18).

▶ **How do search engines work?** A search engine contains four components:

▶ **Web crawler:** Combs the Web to gather data that's representative of the contents of Web pages

▶ **Indexer:** Processes the information gathered by the crawler into a list of keywords and URLs stored in a database

▶ **Database:** Stores billions of index references to Web pages

▶ **Query processor:** Allows you to access the database by entering search terms, and then produces a list of Web pages that contain content relevant to your query

Let's take a look at each of these components to find out how they affect your ability to mine information from the Web.

▶ **What is a Web crawler?** A **Web crawler** (also referred to as a Web spider) is a computer program that is automated to methodically visit Web sites. Web crawlers can be programmed to perform various activities as they visit sites; but in the context of search engines, Web crawlers download Web pages and submit them to an indexing utility for processing.

7

FIGURE 7-18

Many Web sites use search engine technology for searching within the site rather than searching the entire Web.

▶ How much of the Web does a Web crawler cover? A Web crawler begins with a list of URLs to visit. After copying the material at a specified URL, the Web crawler looks for hypertext links and adds them to the list of URLs to visit next. To cover the Web as efficiently as possible, a Web crawler can run multiple processes in parallel. Sophisticated algorithms keep processes from overlapping or getting stuck in loops.

High-performance Web crawlers can visit hundreds of millions of Web pages a day. Those pages, however, are only a fraction of the Web. Researchers estimate that the most extensive search engines cover less than 20% of the Web. Each search engine seems to focus on a slightly different collection of Web sites. The same search entered into different search engines can produce different results, so it is sometimes worthwhile to try alternative search engines.

Web crawlers generally do not gather material from the invisible Web, which encompasses pages that require password-protected logins and pages that are dynamically generated with server-side scripts.

The potential volume of dynamically generated pages, such as all the possible pages that Amazon.com could generate from its inventory database, is just too great to feasibly index. To access information related to e-commerce merchandise or library catalogs, you might have to go directly to the merchant's or library's Web site and use its local search tools.

▶ How frequently do Web crawlers revisit sites? When you query a search engine, you want the results to be up to date so that you don't waste time trying to link to pages that have changed or been deleted. Search engines use various algorithms to refresh their indexes.

The number of times a search engine's crawler visits a Web page varies, depending on several factors such as how often the page tends to change and its popularity. Obscure pages might be visited only once a month, whereas the pages at a news site would be visited daily (Figure 7-19).

FIGURE 7-19

Google's crawler collects entire Web pages, so its database contains a copy of the page as it existed when the crawler last visited.

▶ How do search engine indexers work? A **search engine indexer** is software that pulls keywords from a Web page and stores them in an index database. The purpose of the indexer is to make pages easy to find based on their contents. For example, a Web page at a mountain biking site might contain information about bikes, gear, riding, and trail maps. Keywords that might help catalog this page for future access include *mountain*, *bike*, *trail*, *directions*, *gear*, *Colorado*, *bikepacking*, and *bunny hop*.

▶ Which Web sites are shown at the top of the results list? A search engine's **query processor** looks for your search terms in the search engine's indexed database and returns a list of relevant Web sites. The order in which Web sites are listed in response to a search depends on relevancy criteria, such as keyword matches and link popularity.

TERMINOLOGY NOTE

The words you enter for your search can be referred to as queries, search criteria, search terms, or keywords.

7

If a search is based on multiple keywords, pages that contain the most matching words are listed first. **Link popularity** is a measure of the quality and quantity of the links from one Web page to others. Pages with links to and from popular sites tend to get high relevancy ratings.

▶ **Can a search engine be manipulated into giving a high ranking to a page?** Web sites can be added to a search engine index in several ways. Sites can automatically get discovered by a search engine's Web crawler, they can be submitted to a search engine by Web masters who manage various Web sites, they can be submitted for a paid placement, or they can be submitted as banner or pop-up ads.

Most search engines make it easy to submit a Web site URL, so that Web masters don't have to wait for their sites to be discovered by a Web crawler. Manual submissions are added to the crawler's list of sites to visit and the site will eventually be indexed.

Disreputable Web site operators are constantly trying to devise schemes, such as manipulating meta keywords, to move their Web sites up to the top of search engine query results. A **meta keyword** is entered into a header section of a Web page when it is created and is supposed to describe the page contents.

Keyword stuffing is an unethical practice in which meta keywords are manipulated to gain high relevancy rankings. For example, a Web page author might include meta keywords such as *sex* (which happens to be the most frequently used search term) even though the term has little to do with the information on the page.

Socially responsible search engine sites take steps to foil practices that manipulate rankings and make their policies on paid ads clear to users. When you use a search engine, read its About page to learn its ad placement policies and discover whether or not you can trust the search results to be unbiased.

▶ **What are sponsored links?** Some search engines accept paid ads called **sponsored links**, which are bumped to the top positions on the results list. Other search engines also accept paid ads, but place them in a clearly marked area (Figure 7-20).

FIGURE 7-20

Sponsored links on Google are paid ad placements that appear when users make queries using relevant keywords.

FORMULATING SEARCHES

▶ How do I formulate a basic search? Most search engines work with keyword queries in which you enter one or more words, called **search terms**, related to the information you want to find. For example, if you're interested in Batman comics, you can simply type the obvious: *Batman* (Figure 7-21).

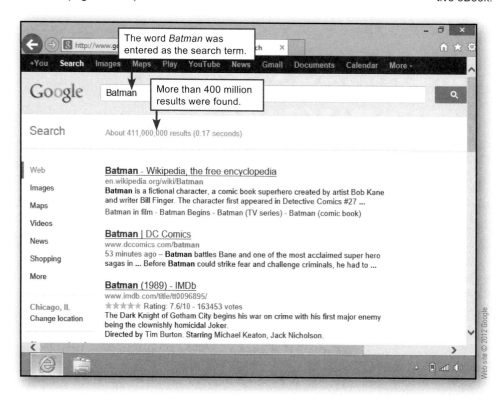

When formulating queries, keep the simple guidelines from Figure 7-22 in mind.

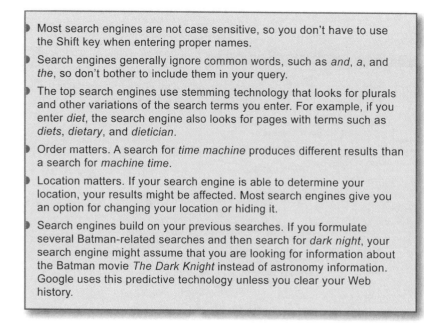

- Most search engines are not case sensitive, so you don't have to use the Shift key when entering proper names.
- Search engines generally ignore common words, such as *and*, *a*, and *the*, so don't bother to include them in your query.
- The top search engines use stemming technology that looks for plurals and other variations of the search terms you enter. For example, if you enter *diet*, the search engine also looks for pages with terms such as *diets*, *dietary*, and *dietician*.
- Order matters. A search for *time machine* produces different results than a search for *machine time*.
- Location matters. If your search engine is able to determine your location, your results might be affected. Most search engines give you an option for changing your location or hiding it.
- Search engines build on your previous searches. If you formulate several Batman-related searches and then search for *dark night*, your search engine might assume that you are looking for information about the Batman movie *The Dark Knight* instead of astronomy information. Google uses this predictive technology unless you clear your Web history.

FIGURE 7-22

Tips for Effective Queries

TRY IT!

Does your search engine know your location?

○ Yes

○ It shows a location, but it is not correct

○ It is not showing a location

▶ **How do I get more targeted results?** Narrowing a search can reduce the number of results and produce a more targeted list. For example, the query *first appearance Batman comic book* produces more than a million results, and those listed first link to information about when Batman first appeared in the May 1939 issue of *Detective Comics*.

Search engine queries rarely produce fewer than a thousand results. A game called Googlewhacking illustrates just how hard it is to create a narrowly targeted query. Googlewhacking challenges you to type a two-word query that produces one and only one result. Try it! You need to choose two fairly unrelated words, but they cannot be totally unrelated or you'll get no results. You can view some successful Googlewhacks at *www.googlewhack.com/tally.pl*.

▶ **What are search operators?** A **search operator** is a word or symbol that describes a relationship between search terms and thereby helps you create a more focused query. Figure 7-23 provides a quick overview of how to use search operators when formulating searches.

FIGURE 7-23

Search Operators

AND	When two search terms are joined by *AND*, both terms must appear on a Web page before it can be included in the search results. The query *railroad AND cars* will locate pages that contain both the words *railroad* and *cars*. Your search results might include pages containing information about old railroad cars, about railroad car construction, and even about railroads that haul automobiles (cars). Some search engines use the plus symbol (+) instead of the word *AND*.
OR	When two search terms are joined by *OR*, either one or both of the search words could appear on a page. Entering the query *railroad OR cars* produces information about railroad fares, railroad routes, railroad cars, automobile safety records, and even car ferries.
NOT	The search term following *NOT* must not appear on any of the pages found by the search engine. Entering *railroad NOT cars* would tell the search engine to look for pages that include *railroad* but not the term *cars*. In some search engines, the minus sign (-) can be used instead of the word *NOT*.
" "	To search for an exact phrase, enter it in quotes. For example, *"Dynamic Duo."*
*****	The asterisk (*) is sometimes referred to as a wildcard character. It allows a search engine to find pages with any derivation of a basic word. For example, the query *medic** would produce pages containing not only the word *medic*, but also the words *medics*, *medicine*, *medical*, *medication*, and *medicinal*.
..	Google lets you use two dots to specify a range of numbers, dates, episodes, or prices. For example, to view Batman episodes 5, 6, 7, and 8, you can enter *Batman episodes 5..8.*

TRY IT!

Which one of the following searches returns the most targeted (fewest) results?

○ racing shell gear

○ "racing shell" gear

○ racing shell -gear

○ racing OR shell OR gear

▶ What is an advanced search? Many search engines provide ways to make your searches more precise and obtain more useful results. You might be able to use advanced search options to limit your search to material written in a specific language or stored in a specific file format. You might be able to specify a date, eliminate results from adult sites, and stipulate whether to look for your search terms in the title, URL, or body of the Web page (Figure 7-24).

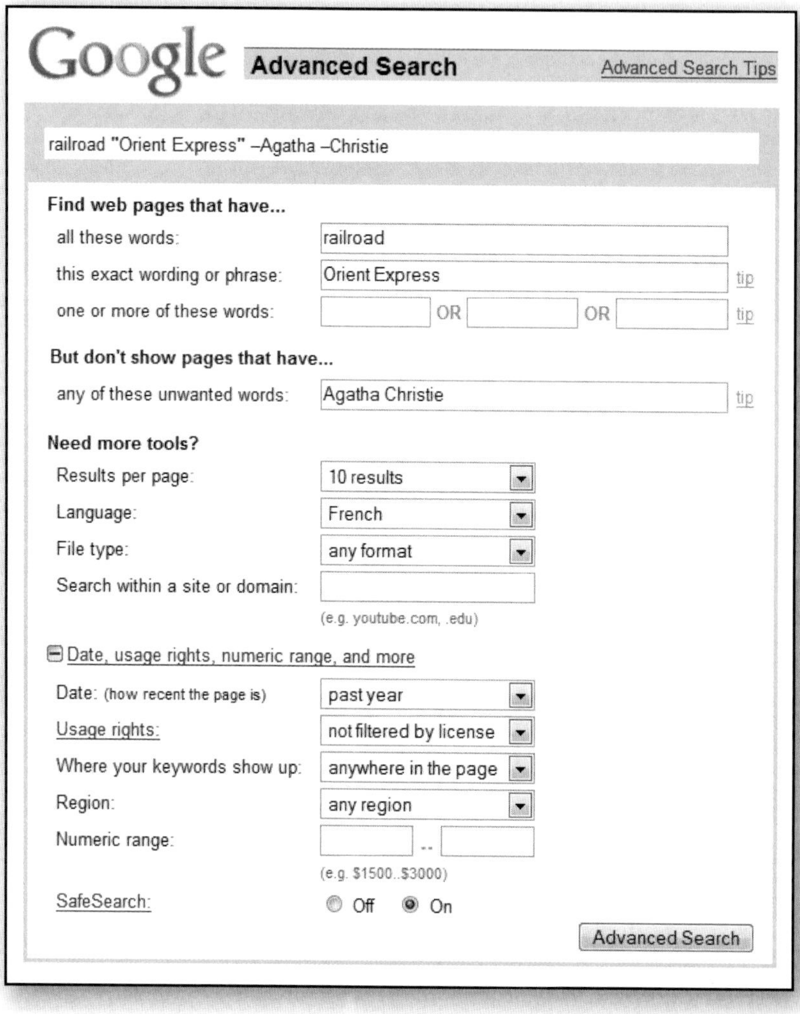

FIGURE 7-24

Many search engines provide forms designed to enhance the search process. These forms are accessible by clicking an Advanced Search link, which is located on the main page of the search engine Web site.

Some search engine sites offer separate searches for academic works, images, videos, news, e-commerce merchandise, and blogs. Look for links to these specialized searches at your favorite search engine sites.

In addition to using search engines, you can also find Web-based information using a **metasearch engine** that searches a series of other search engines and compiles the search results. Popular metasearch sites include *www.ixquick.com*, *www.dogpile.com*, *www.webcrawler.com*, and *www. yippy.com*.

TRY IT!

Try the advanced search shown in Figure 7-24. How many results do you get?

○ About 300

○ About 3,000

○ About 3 million

○ More than 5 million

▶ Are the top results really the most relevant? The links listed on the first page of search results are very often the most relevant, but Figure 7-25 explains how a little detective work can help you home in on the best links to explore.

FIGURE 7-25

Studying search engine results helps you select the best links.

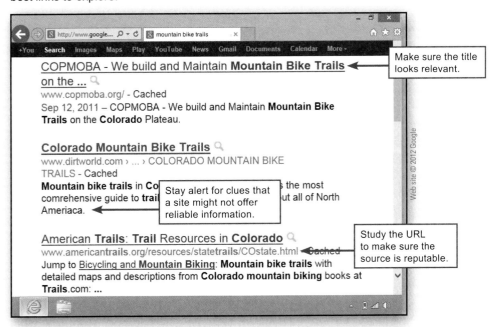

▶ Do search engines keep records of my queries? Considering that a major search engine can receive upward of 100 million queries every day, the surprising answer to this question is "yes." Search engines at major sites such as Google, Bing, and Yahoo! save massive numbers of searches made by site visitors.

Industry analysts believe that some sites retain user queries for at least 30 days, and that at least one search engine site has retained every search ever made at the site.

In 2006, AOL released a database of queries for research purposes. Figure 7-26 illustrates a small section of this database for queries made by users interested in mountain bikes.

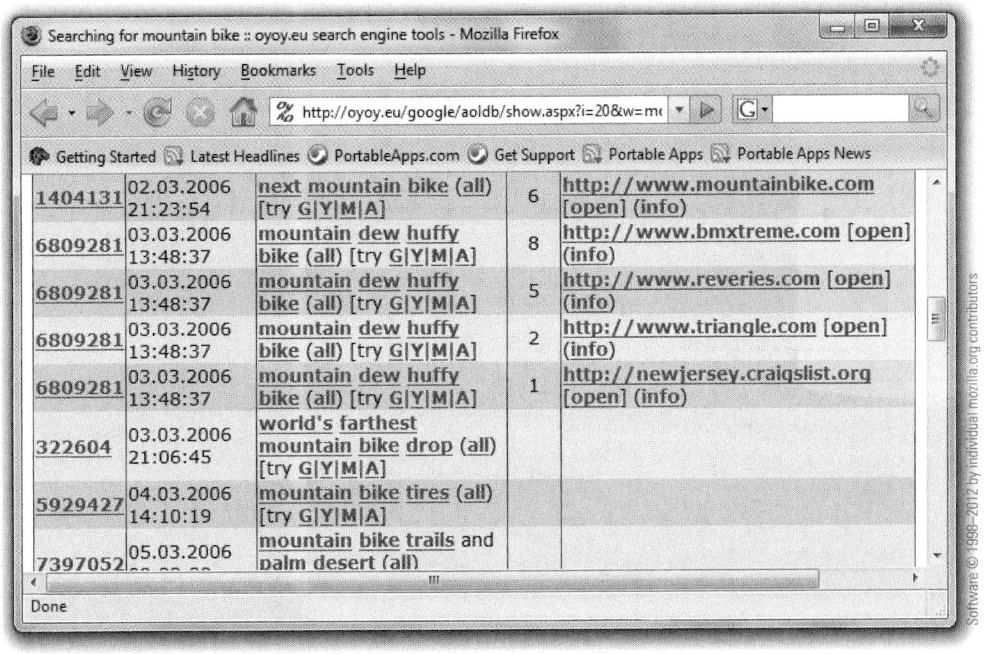

FIGURE 7-26

A database of 20 million AOL queries is available to the public. For example, many people, including user 1404131, entered queries about mountain bikes. From the database, you could also discover other queries made by this user.

Privacy advocates question the wisdom of search engines retaining queries. They can't identify any beneficial uses for such data and fear that it is of potential benefit only to marketing companies. Anyone who uses search engines should be aware that the content of their searches could become public.

▶ What kind of information does a search engine store?

Although your queries do not contain your name, you are assigned a unique ID number that is stored in a cookie on your computer. In addition to storing an ID number, search engines store the IP address from which the query was initiated, the date and time of the query, the search terms, and URLs for any Web sites accessed from the results list.

▶ What can I do to keep my searches confidential? Your

search-engine-assigned ID number is stored in a cookie and remains the same as long as the cookie remains on your computer. If you frequently delete your cookies as explained in Section E, a search engine's query database is unlikely to collect enough information to link back to you.

You can block cookies from a specific search engine site, and that setting will force the search engine to assign a different ID number to you for each session. You can also download and use a cookie anonymizer that sets your Google ID number to 0.

Anonymizer sites, such as *www.torproject.org*, act as relay stations to forward your searches to Google or other search engines without leaving a trail back to a cookie or an IP address. These sites claim to delete all activity logs every day or two, but they are the subject of law enforcement scrutiny.

USING WEB-BASED SOURCE MATERIAL

▶ Can I copy text and graphics that I find on Web pages?

Most browsers provide a Copy command that allows you to copy a section of text from a Web page, which you can then paste into one of your own documents. To keep track of the source for each text section, you can highlight the Web page's URL in the Address box, use the Copy command, and then paste the URL into your document (Figure 7-27).

FIGURE 7-27

To copy a passage of text from a Web page, highlight the text, right-click it, then select Copy. Next, switch to your own document and use the Paste option. ▶ For a demonstration of this process, go to your interactive eBook.

▶ **How do I cite sources?** Presenting someone else's work as your own is plagiarism. If you copy text, pictures, or other works from a Web page, make sure you give credit to the original author. Information that identifies the source of a quotation or excerpted work is called a citation. Written documents, such as reports and projects, generally include footnotes, endnotes, or in-line citations formatted according to a standard style, such as MLA, APA, or Chicago.

When compiling the citation for online sources, be sure to provide sufficient information so readers can locate the source. Also, include the date when you accessed the source and the full URL. According to APA style, a citation to a Web-based source should provide a document title or description; author name, if available; the date of publication, update, or retrieval; and a URL.

▶ **Do I need permission to use material?** In the United States, the Fair Use Doctrine allows limited use of copyrighted material for scholarship and review without obtaining permission. For scholarly reports and projects, for example, you can use a sentence or paragraph of text without obtaining permission if you include a citation to the original source.

Photos and excerpts from music and videos can be used within the context of critique, but their use purely as decorative elements for a document would, in most cases, not be considered fair use.

Some Web sites clearly state allowable uses for material on the site. Look for a link to Terms of Use. For example, the YouTube Web site contains a collection of videos submitted by amateurs and semi-professionals, who retain the copyright to their materials. The Terms of Use section of the site allows the public to access, use, reproduce, distribute, create derivatives of, display, and perform user-submitted works. Even with such broad terms of use, however, it is essential to cite the original source of the material if you incorporate it in your own work.

▶ **How do I get permission?** To obtain permission to use text, photos, music, videos, and other elements you find on the Web, contact the copyright holder by e-mail, and explain what you want to use and how you plan to use it. You can often find contact information on the Web site, if not for the copyright holder, at least for a Web master who can direct you to the copyright holder.

7

TRY IT!

When you incorporate Web-based material in research papers, why is it not necessary to get permission from the source?

○ Because the Fair Use Doctrine allows it

○ Because the material is not copyrighted

○ Because it is on the Web

○ Because your school library has a deal with the content owner

QuickCheck   SECTION B

1. A search engine's [_____] pulls keywords from a Web page and stores them in a database.

2. When you enter search terms, the search engine's [_____] processor looks for the terms in the search engine's database.

3. *AND*, *OR*, and *NOT* are examples of search [_____].

4. Most search engines keep track of users by assigning a unique ID number, which is stored in a(n) [_____] on the hard disk of the user's computer.

5. To keep track of the Web pages where you obtained information or images, you can highlight the Web page's [_____], copy it, and then paste it into a list of sources. (Hint: Use the acronym.)

▶ CHECK ANSWERS

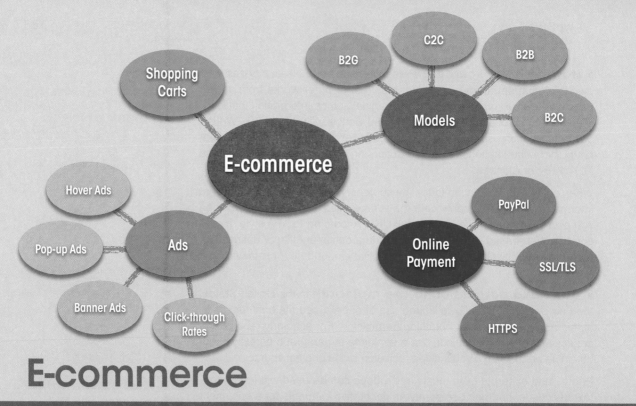

E-commerce

ONE OF THE MOST POPULAR activities on the Web is shopping. Online shopping has the same allure as catalogs—you can shop at your leisure, anonymously, and in your pajamas. But the economics of the Web provide opportunities that go beyond retail catalogs. The Internet was opened to commercial use in 1991. Since then, millions of businesses have set up shop at Web sites. This section of the chapter focuses on e-commerce and the technologies a typical shopper might encounter on the Web.

E-COMMERCE BASICS

▶ **What is e-commerce?** Although the experts don't always agree on its definition, the term **e-commerce** typically refers to business transactions that are conducted electronically over a computer network. It encompasses all aspects of business and marketing enabled by Internet and Web technologies.

E-commerce wares include many kinds of physical products, digital products, and services. Physical products offered at e-commerce sites include such goods as clothing, shoes, skateboards, and cars. Most of these products can be shipped to buyers through the postal service, a parcel delivery service, or a trucking company.

Increasingly, e-commerce goods include digital products, such as news, music, movies, databases, ebooks, and software. The unique feature of these products is that they can be transformed into bits and delivered over the Internet. Consumers can get them immediately upon completing their orders, and there are no shipping costs.

E-commerce merchants also peddle services, such as online medical consultation, distance education, or custom sewing. Some of these services can be carried out by computers. Others require human agents. Services can be delivered electronically, as in the case of a distance education course, or they might produce some physical product, such as a custom-fit boat cover.

TRY IT!

What company is the largest online retailer based on sales in the U.S. and Canada?

○ Overstock.com

○ Amazon

○ Target

○ Walmart

▶ What are the most common e-commerce business models?
E-commerce activities are classified as **B2C** (business-to-consumer), **C2C** (consumer-to-consumer), **B2B** (business-to-business), and **B2G** (business-to-government), as described in Figure 7-28.

E-commerce offers consumers many types of goods and services.

B2C: Online storefronts offer goods, merchandise, and services to consumers.

C2C: Consumers sell to each other at popular auction and list sites such as eBay and craigslist.

B2B and B2G: Businesses sell goods and services to other businesses or to the government.

▶ Is e-commerce more profitable than offline business?
E-commerce enhances traditional business models by offering efficiency and opportunities for automation, computerization, and digitization. As with a traditional brick-and-mortar business, profit in an e-commerce business is the difference between income and expenses.

One of the advantages of e-commerce is its ability to increase profit margins by cutting costs. For example, a typical catalog order placed over the phone costs the merchant $2.50, whereas an online transaction costs about 35 cents. A hotel reservation made online costs the innkeeper 80% less than a booking by phone. A withdrawal or deposit costs a bank about a dollar when handled by a teller, about 25 cents on an ATM, and only a penny on the Web.

E-commerce merchants also generate income by hosting advertising space for marketers, who are creating increasingly hard-to-avoid styles of online advertisements, such as banner and pop-up ads. A **banner ad** is an advertisement embedded at the top of a Web page. A **hover ad** overlays the content on a Web page, sometimes obscuring it until you click the ad or its timer expires and the ad disappears. A **pop-up ad**, such as the one in Figure 7-29, is an advertisement that appears in a separate window when you connect to a Web page. If you click a banner, hover, or pop-up ad, your browser connects directly to the advertiser's Web site, where you can find product information and make a purchase.

Pop-up ads appear as separate windows.

Online ads earn revenue for hosting merchants based on the **click-through rate**—the number of times that site visitors click the ad to connect to the advertiser's site. The hosting merchant is paid a small fee for each click-through. Click-through rates have declined in recent years because most browsers include a configurable feature to block pop-up ads. Consumers simply ignore banner and hover ads or install **ad-blocking software** to prevent ads from appearing on their screens.

▶ Who benefits from e-commerce?
Both merchants and consumers benefit from e-commerce because niche goods and small merchants can reach a global customer base. At online music shops and bookstores, for example, you can find obscure titles and alternative music that brick-and-mortar merchants haven't the space or inclination to stock.

Merchants are always looking for ways to attract customers. The Web and its search engines give small merchants without a budget for national advertising a way to be found by customers. When you're looking for hand-made chainmail, for example, you're unlikely to find it at your local Walmart, but chances are good that you can find a chainmail merchant on the Web.

E-COMMERCE SITE TECHNOLOGY

▶ What makes online shopping so special? E-commerce offers some unique advantages over brick-and-mortar stores and mail-order catalogs. Customers can easily search for specific merchandise. They can configure products online, see actual prices, and build an order over several days.

E-commerce customers can easily compare prices among multiple vendors using Web sites such as Bizrate, Nextag, and PriceGrabber. Many sites also offer product reviews written by consumers.

E-commerce seems simple from the perspective of a shopper who connects to an online store, browses the electronic catalog, selects merchandise, and then pays for it. Behind the scenes, an e-commerce site uses several technologies to display merchandise, keep track of shoppers' selections, collect payment data, protect customers' privacy, and prevent credit card numbers from falling into the wrong hands.

▶ Are there different e-commerce models? There are two popular models for e-commerce stores. The first is the B2C model pioneered by Amazon.com. The second is the C2C model represented by online auction sites such as eBay, and online classified advertisement sites such as craigslist.

▶ What are the important elements of a B2C e-commerce site? Most B2C sites are operated by a single merchant. The business has an inventory of products, such as DVDs, books, clothing, and other merchandise. A key element of this model is that the inventory is usually quite large and contains multiple quantities of each item; for example, Amazon's inventory includes huge quantities of *The Twilight Saga* DVDs. Customers can select several items from the inventory by placing them in shopping carts.

▶ How is a B2C inventory stored? The inventory for a B2C store can be quite large and it would be impractical to create individual Web pages for each item. Instead, inventory items, along with their prices and descriptions, are entered into a database. When you browse through the merchandise at an online store, the site's Web servers and database servers interact to pull information from the database and convert it to Web pages that can be displayed in a browser.

When you view products at a large-scale B2C site, the product pages have been produced on the fly by server-side CGI, PHP, or ASP scripts. The next time you shop online, pay attention to the Address bar of your browser. When product pages are displayed, you'll probably see a ? symbol somewhere in the URL, and the URL might also include *cgi*, *php*, or *asp*—all indicating the Web page you're viewing was assembled by a server-side script from the information in a database (Figure 7-30).

FIGURE 7-30

Product pages that contain a ? symbol are constructed from a database on the fly by server-side scripts.

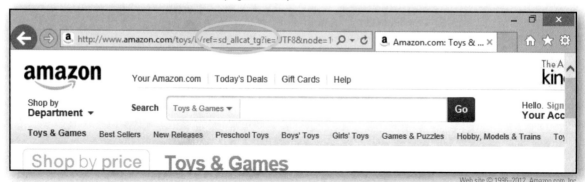

How do shopping carts work? If you've done any shopping online, you've probably used an **online shopping cart**—a cyberspace version of the metal cart you wheel around a store and fill up with merchandise.

As mentioned earlier, HTTP is a stateless protocol, which maintains no record of your browser's previous interactions and handles each browser request based entirely on information that comes with it. Under these circumstances, you might wonder how it is possible for an online retail store to remember the items you put in your shopping cart.

Most shopping carts work because they use cookies to store information about your activities on a Web site. Cookies work with shopping carts in one of two ways, depending on the e-commerce site. An e-commerce site might use cookies as a storage bin for all the items you load into your shopping cart, as shown in Figure 7-31.

FIGURE 7-31

Shopping cart items can be stored in a cookie.

1. When you click the Add to Cart button, the merchant's server sends a message to your browser to add that item number to the cookie, which is stored on your computer.

ITEM # B7655

2. When you check out, the server asks your browser for all the cookie data that pertains to your shopping cart items.

3. Your browser sends those cookies along with a request for an order summary.

Your order:

1 Blender $29.95

1 Wok $38.49

4. The Web server uses the cookies to look up products in its database and produce a Web page listing the items you want to purchase.

Some e-commerce sites use cookies simply as a way to uniquely identify each shopper. These sites generate a unique ID number that is stored along with your item selections in a server-side database (Figure 7-32).

FIGURE 7-32

Shopping cart items can be stored in a server-side database.

1. When you connect to a merchant's site, the server assigns you a unique shopping cart ID number and sends it to your browser in a cookie.

WEB SERVER

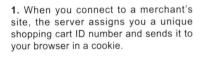

CART # 2098-2

DATABASE

CART # 2098-2

ITEM # B7655

3. The Web server stores this number and your merchandise selection in the merchant's server-side database.

WEB SERVER

CART # 2098-2

2. When you select an item to purchase, your browser reads your shopping cart ID number from the cookie, and then sends this number to the merchant's Web server.

Order for CART # 2098-2

1 Blender   B7655 $29.95

1 Wok   GJK4-31 $38.49

4. When you check out, your browser sends your shopping cart number to the server, which retrieves all your selections from the merchant's database.

▶ **How do C2C sites work?** At C2C auction and online classified advertising e-commerce sites, consumers offer goods and services to other consumers. The key characteristic of C2C sites is that the merchandise is generally individual items, such as a used boat, a collectible stuffed bear, or an antique flower vase. Each item is unique and sellers individually enter information that becomes the product Web page.

C2C sites are hosted by an e-commerce provider such as eBay or craigslist. The host site offers tools for sellers to auction or sell items. Sellers are provided with a way to enter item descriptions, prices, and photos. They might also be provided with tools to track bids, purchases, and other activity. Buyers are provided with tools to locate products and contact sellers with questions. Host sites might also maintain ratings for buyers and sellers to help participants avoid shady deals.

▶ **How do sellers enter product information?** Sellers can enter product information by filling in an online form and uploading photos as shown in Figure 7-33.

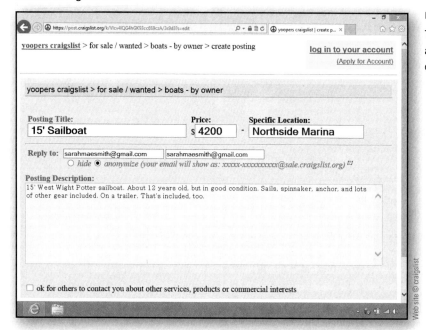

FIGURE 7-33

The craigslist Web site provides a form for entering product descriptions and photos.

▶ **How is product data stored?** Product data is stored in a database at the host site in much the same way as product data is stored at a B2C e-commerce site. Shoppers can enter queries to locate products from the database (Figure 7-34); matching descriptions and photos are retrieved and displayed as Web pages.

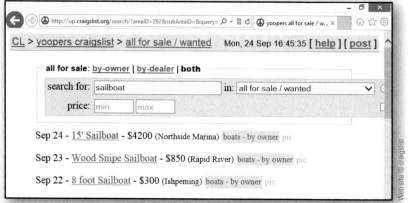

FIGURE 7-34

Buyers can find products by entering search terms.

▶ **How do buyers contact sellers?** Another key characteristic of a C2C site is that buyers interact directly with individual sellers; so if you purchase a used boat advertised on craigslist, you'll likely be interacting with a different seller than when you purchase a classic street bike. C2C sites have to provide a way for buyers and sellers to interact while protecting the privacy of both parties.

Many C2C sites use e-mail forwarding to protect participants' privacy. When you register with a C2C host, you usually receive an e-mail account tied to your user ID. Your e-commerce correspondence is forwarded from that account to your regular e-mail account, which effectively hides your real name and e-mail address from the buyers or sellers you work with at the C2C site (Figure 7-35).

FIGURE 7-35

Communication between sellers and buyers is mediated through protected e-mail forwarding provided by the C2C host provider.

ONLINE PAYMENT

▶ **How can I pay for merchandise from online shopping and auction sites?** The most popular ways to make online payments include submitting your credit card number directly to a merchant and using a third-party payment service such as PayPal.

▶ **Is it safe to use my credit card online?** Online shoppers are justifiably worried that personal information and credit card numbers supplied in the course of an e-commerce transaction might be hijacked and used inappropriately. Many shoppers worry that hackers might use packet sniffers to intercept credit card numbers traveling over the Internet.

To protect your credit card from packet sniffers, you should engage in electronic transactions only over a secure connection. A **secure connection** encrypts the data transmitted between your computer and a Web site. Even if a hacker can capture the packets containing payment data, your encrypted credit card number is virtually useless for illicit purposes. Technologies that create secure connections include SSL/TLS and HTTPS.

> **TERMINOLOGY NOTE**
>
> Secure connections differ from secure Web sites. A secure connection encrypts the data transmitted between your computer and a Web site. A secure Web site, such as an online banking site, uses password security to prevent unauthorized access to pages on the site.

▶ What is SSL/TLS? **SSL** (Secure Sockets Layer) and its successor **TLS** (Transport Layer Security) are protocols that encrypt data traveling between a client computer and an HTTP server. These encryption protocols create a secure connection using a specially designated port. Secure connections commonly use port 443; port 80 is generally used for unsecured HTTP communications.

▶ What is HTTPS? **HTTPS** (Hypertext Transfer Protocol Secure) is a combination of HTTP and SSL/TLS that provides a secure connection for Web-based transactions. Web pages that provide a secure connection start with https: instead of http:.

FIGURE 7-36

Look for https or a padlock icon to ensure you have a secure connection.

▶ How do I know if a connection is secure? Your browser helps you identify when you are using a secure connection. Figure 7-36 explains.

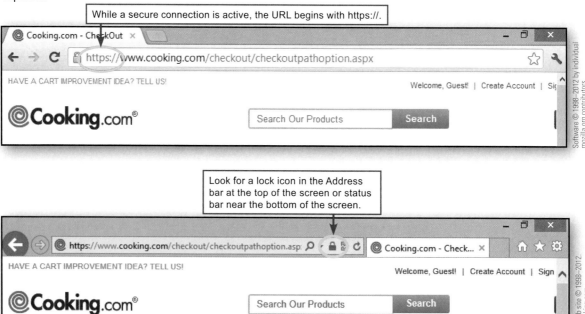

▶ What if the connection is not secure? Pay attention to your browser's Address bar. It can warn you when connections might not be secure by displaying a warning or turning the Address bar yellow (suspicious site) or red (dangerous site). If you link to a site that generates a security warning, do not enter personal data. The following conditions can generate security warnings:

FIGURE 7-37

Google Chrome indicates that some items on this page are not secure. Each browser has a slightly different system of warnings. Check your browser's Help pages to become familiar with its warning system.

▶ **Expired security certificate.** HTTPS checks the Web server's security certificate. If the certificate is out of date, the site might not be legitimate.

▶ **Suspected phishing site.** Browsers check URLs against a list of sites that have been reported to be fakes.

▶ **Partially secured.** Some items on the page are not secured by HTTPS (Figure 7-37).

▶ **What is a person-to-person payment?** A **person-to-person payment** (sometimes called a P2P payment, an online payment, or a third-party payment) offers an alternative to credit cards. It can be used to pay for online auction items and to wire money over the Internet. The online service called PayPal, now owned by eBay, pioneered person-to-person payments. PayPal's model has since been copied by several other service providers.

▶ **How does a person-to-person payment work?** The process begins when you open an account at a person-to-person payment service. You receive a user ID and password that enable you to access your account to make purchases and deposit additional funds. Money can be sent to anyone who has an e-mail account, as shown in Figure 7-38.

FIGURE 7-38

PayPal and other online payment systems offer a method for transferring funds without revealing your credit card number to the payee.

1. To use a person-to-person payment service, simply log in to your account, enter the recipient's e-mail address, and indicate the payment amount.

2. The recipient immediately receives an e-mail notification of your payment.

3. The recipient connects to the payment site to pick up the money by transferring the funds to his or her checking or payment account, requesting a check, or sending the funds to someone else.

▶ **Are person-to-person payments safe?** The major advantage of person-to-person payments is that the payment service is the only entity that sees your credit card number—merchants, auction dealers, and other payment recipients never receive your credit card number and, therefore, can't misuse it or store it on an unsecured computer. Consumer advocates recommend using these services with caution and keeping your account balances low.

QuickCheck   SECTION C

1. Online auction sites such as eBay are examples of B2G e-commerce. True or false? [_____]

2. One factor in the e-commerce economic model is ad revenue based on [_____] rates, the number of times that site visitors click an ad to connect to the advertiser's Web site.

3. Most online shopping carts work because they use [_____] to store information about your activities at a Web site.

4. Product pages at e-commerce sites with URLs that contain a(n) [_____] symbol, cgi, php, or asp are most likely assembled by a server-side script from the information in a database.

5. Web sites that provide a secure connection have URLs that begin with https: instead of http:. True or false? [_____]

▶ CHECK ANSWERS

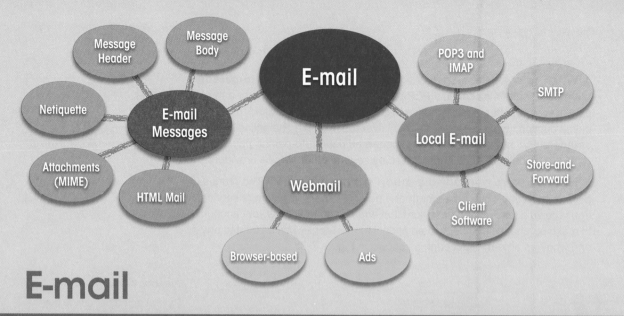

E-mail

THE INTERNET REALLY TOOK OFF when people discovered electronic mail. More than 250 billion e-mail messages speed over the Internet each day. This section of the chapter offers background information about how e-mail works—in particular, the difference between Webmail and client-based local e-mail.

E-MAIL OVERVIEW

▶ **Exactly what is e-mail?** The term *e-mail* can refer to a single message or to the entire system of computers and software that transmits, receives, and stores e-mail messages. An **e-mail message** is an electronic document transmitted over a computer network.

The computers and software that provide e-mail services form an **e-mail system**. At the heart of a typical e-mail system is an **e-mail server**—a computer that essentially acts as a central post office for a group of people. E-mail servers run special e-mail server software, which provides an electronic mailbox for each person, sorts incoming messages into these mailboxes, and routes outgoing mail over the Internet to other e-mail servers.

E-mail messages have a standard format that consists of a **message header** and the message body as shown in Figure 7-39.

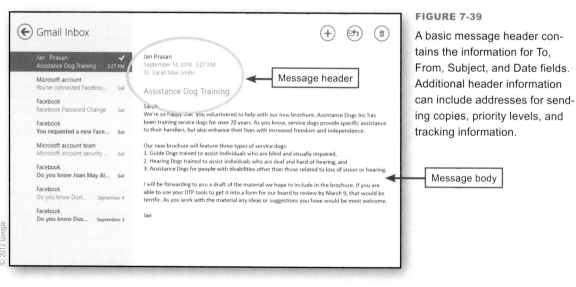

FIGURE 7-39

A basic message header contains the information for To, From, Subject, and Date fields. Additional header information can include addresses for sending copies, priority levels, and tracking information.

392

▶ How do I get access to e-mail? To use an e-mail system, you need an Internet connection, an e-mail account, and software to compose e-mail messages.

▶ **Internet connection.** As you learned in earlier chapters, Internet connections are available from telephone, cable, satellite, and cellular service providers. Wi-Fi hotspots and local area networks at home, school, or work can also provide Internet access. Any of these connections work for e-mail, though a dial-up connection will respond slowly when sending or receiving messages with photos or other large files attached.

▶ **E-mail account.** Obtaining an **e-mail account** gets your electronic mailbox set up on an e-mail server. Your ISP might play the role of postmaster, set up your e-mail account, and provide you with e-mail software. You can also obtain an e-mail account from a Webmail service, such as Hotmail, Gmail, or Yahoo!.

▶ **E-mail software.** The software you use to send, receive, and manage messages is called **e-mail client software**. It is available for desktop, laptop, tablet, and handheld devices. E-mail software can be installed locally on a hard drive, as a portable app on a USB flash drive, or accessed from the Web through a browser. E-mail systems based on local client software are referred to as **local e-mail**. Systems that provide access to e-mail through a browser are called **Webmail**.

Whether you use local e-mail or Webmail, your e-mail account has a unique **e-mail address**. Like the address on a letter, an e-mail address provides the information necessary to route messages to a specified mailbox. An e-mail address consists of a user ID (also called a user name), followed by the @ sign and the name of the e-mail server that manages the user's electronic post office box. For example, the address ann_smith@mtc.com refers to the e-mail account for Ann Smith on the e-mail server named mtc.com.

▶ How do I select an e-mail address? In order for e-mail to be routed correctly, each e-mail address must be unique. Gmail can have only one AnnSmith user ID, which explains the existence of e-mail addresses such as AnnSmith256@gmail.com and ASmithTraverseCity@gmail.com. You can, however, use the same user ID for e-mail accounts on different servers. For example, AlexZ@msu.edu and AlexZ@hotmail.com are perfectly acceptable for a student who has e-mail accounts on a school server and at Hotmail.

E-mail addresses can sometimes tell you a bit about the person who holds the account. The first part of an e-mail address often corresponds to the account holder's name, nickname, or online persona. For example, the address cat_lover32@hotmail.com probably belongs to a person who likes cats. You should be aware of the image that e-mail addresses can project and select one that won't be embarrassing when you correspond with prospective employers.

The second part of an e-mail address is the e-mail server's domain name, which can provide information about the account holder's job or school. An account for jwatson@ibm.com probably belongs to an IBM employee. An account for rbutler@uga.edu probably belongs to a student at the University of Georgia. You can't control the server domain name, but you can establish several e-mail accounts so that your work server handles business mail and a generic provider, such as Gmail, handles your private mail.

TRY IT!

What can you deduce from the e-mail address jbieber@epa.gov?

○ It is Justin Bieber's e-mail address

○ It is probably an e-mail address for a student

○ The owner is probably a politician

○ It is probably a fake address

LOCAL E-MAIL

▶ How does local e-mail work? When you use local e-mail, an Internet-based e-mail server stores your incoming messages until you launch your e-mail client and get your mail. Messages are then downloaded to a folder on a local storage device that serves as your e-mail Inbox. This telecommunications technique is sometimes referred to as **store-and-forward**.

Using your e-mail client, you can read your mail at your leisure. You can also compose new mail and reply to messages. This outgoing mail can be temporarily stored in an Outbox or it can be sent immediately.

The protocols **POP3** (Post Office Protocol version 3) or **IMAP** (Internet Message Access Protocol) are used to manage your incoming mail. POP3 deletes messages from the server after they are downloaded, whereas IMAP leaves messages on the server until you specifically delete them. **SMTP** (Simple Mail Transfer Protocol) handles outgoing mail.

Keep these protocols in mind when setting up local e-mail because the server you specify for outgoing mail might be different than the server for incoming mail (Figure 7-40).

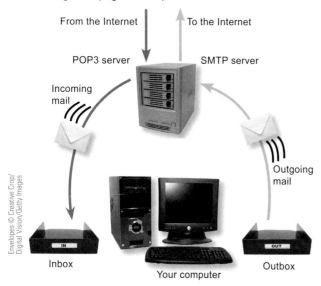

FIGURE 7-40

Outgoing mail can be stored in your Outbox until you connect to the Internet and send it to the SMTP server. Incoming mail can be stored on a POP3 server until it is downloaded to the Inbox on your hard disk.

▶ What are the advantages of local e-mail? Because local e-mail stores your Inbox and Outbox on your computer, you can compose and read mail offline. You are required to go online only to transfer outgoing mail from your Inbox to the e-mail server, and to receive incoming messages. On a slow dial-up connection or in situations where you are charged for dial-up service by the minute, local e-mail might be preferable to Webmail.

Local e-mail also works well with broadband always-on connections, such as DSL, cable Internet, or satellite Internet. When using these connections, you can remain online throughout the entire process of collecting, reading, and sending mail. By configuring your e-mail client to send messages immediately, messages can be sent as they are composed instead of remaining in your Outbox and being sent as a batch.

The major advantage of local e-mail is control. Once your messages are transferred to your computer's hard disk, you can control access to them. With this control, however, comes the responsibility for maintaining backups of your important e-mail messages.

TRY IT!

Which server handles outgoing mail?

○ POP

○ IMAP

○ SMTP

○ Local

▶ How do I set up local e-mail? To set up local e-mail, the first step is selecting a local e-mail client. Macs include a mail client called Mail. Microsoft Outlook is one of the most popular e-mail clients for Windows. Its pared-down cousin, Windows Mail, can be downloaded for free as part of the Windows Live Essentials suite. Thunderbird, a free open source e-mail client, is another popular alternative, and several other very serviceable e-mail clients are available as shareware.

After installing an e-mail client, you can configure it for the e-mail service you're using. Your e-mail provider can supply the information needed for this task. That information can include the following:

▶ Your e-mail user ID, which is the first part of your e-mail address (for example, in AlexHamilton@gsu.edu, the user ID is AlexHamilton)

▶ Your e-mail password, if required to access the e-mail server

▶ An address for the outgoing (SMTP) server, such as *mail.viserver.net* or *smtp.charter.com*

▶ An address for the incoming (POP3) server, such as *mail.gsu.edu* or *pop.media.net*

▶ Port numbers for incoming and outgoing servers, which are usually Port 110 (incoming) and Port 25 or 587 (outgoing)

▶ Whether the servers require secure authentication

▶ The type of connection security used by the servers: STARTTLS or SSL/TLS

Figure 7-41 illustrates basic information necessary to set up a local e-mail account.

7

FIGURE 7-41

When configuring local e-mail, the incoming and outgoing servers might require different settings. ▶ This figure in your interactive eBook guides you through the process of configuring a local e-mail account.

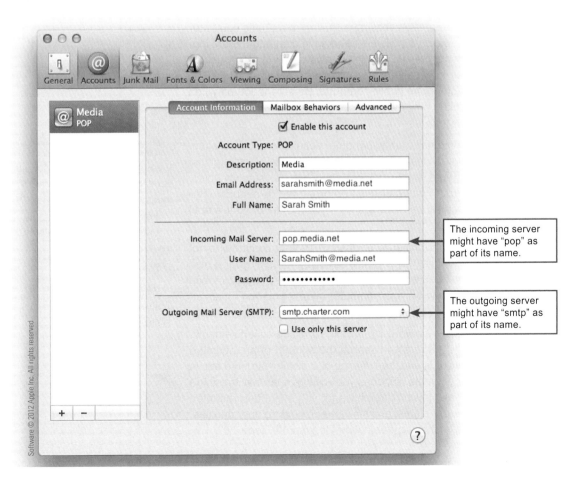

The incoming server might have "pop" as part of its name.

The outgoing server might have "smtp" as part of its name.

WEBMAIL

▶ **How does Webmail work?** Webmail is typically a free service accessed using a browser. Most Webmail services also can be accessed using a local e-mail client, such as Microsoft Outlook, if you prefer a local client's feature set and do not want to remain online while reading and composing messages.

In a classic Webmail configuration, your Inbox is stored on the Web; and because messages are sent immediately, an Outbox is not needed. When you want to read or send mail, use a browser to go to your e-mail provider's Web site and log in. The controls for reading, composing, and managing messages are all presented in the browser window. While reading and composing mail, you generally must remain online (Figure 7-42).

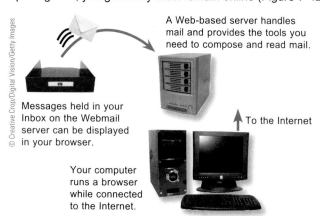

A Web-based server handles mail and provides the tools you need to compose and read mail.

Messages held in your Inbox on the Webmail server can be displayed in your browser.

To the Internet

Your computer runs a browser while connected to the Internet.

© Creative Crop/Digital Vision/Getty Images

FIGURE 7-42

The key characteristic of Webmail is that your messages remain on the Web server, rather than being downloaded to your computer.

▶ **What are the pros and cons of Webmail?** Webmail is ideal for people who travel because accounts can be accessed from any computer connected to the Internet. Accessing e-mail from a public computer can be a security risk, however. If possible, reboot the computer before logging in to your e-mail account. Avoid entering sensitive information, such as your credit card number, in case your keystrokes are being monitored by malicious software lurking on the public computer. Be sure to log off when your session is finished. Log out of Windows and shut down the computer if you are allowed to do so.

Even when accessing Webmail from your home, security can be an issue. Unfortunately, Webmail services are the target of many malicious exploits, which can work their way into your computer through various security holes. When using Webmail, your computer must be protected by security software, and your computer will be more secure if you log out of your e-mail account when you are not using it.

Webmail can be accessed from mobile devices when your computer is not handy. If you opt to use mobile mail, read the options offered by your e-mail service provider and make sure you understand how to sync your mobile e-mail with the mail you view on your computer so that you don't miss an important message.

Free Webmail is supported by advertising, so expect to see advertisements. Today's sophisticated ad servers can search the content of an incoming message looking for keywords and then use them to display targeted ads in your e-mail window. For example, suppose you receive an e-mail message about service dogs. When viewing the message, you might be presented with ads about dog food, pet stores, and similar e-commerce opportunities. Some Webmail services offer an ad-free option for a monthly fee.

TRY IT!

If you have a Webmail account, send yourself an e-mail message that mentions Paris. When you view the message, are there ads about hotels and travel services?

○ Yes

○ No, but there are other unrelated ads

○ There aren't any ads

How do I get a Webmail account? Getting a Webmail account is an automated process that you can complete online. Begin by using a browser to access a Webmail site such as *www.gmail.com*, *www.hotmail.com, or www.yahoomail.com*. Selecting the Sign Up or Register option produces an on-screen form. When you submit the completed form, your e-mail account is created and ready for immediate use (Figure 7-43).

FIGURE 7-43

You can use a browser to access your Webmail account. ▶ This figure in your interactive eBook takes you on a tour of Gmail.

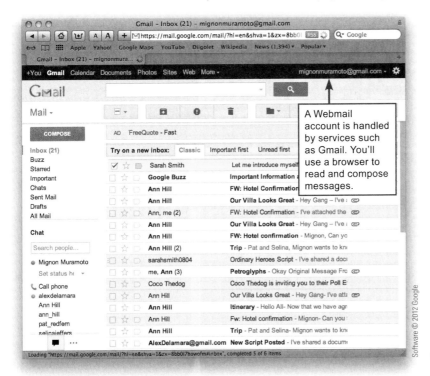

FIGURE 7-44

An e-mail message in HTML format can include graphics in addition to a variety of fonts and font colors.

Is Webmail the same as HTML mail? No. **HTML mail** is a term used for e-mail messages containing HTML tags that produce bold, italicized, and underlined text; fancy fonts; embedded graphics; and various font sizes. Most e-mail software offers a setting for choosing HTML or plain, unformatted ASCII text.

You should be aware that HTML formatted e-mail messages can distribute viruses and open security holes that leave your computer vulnerable to hackers. When working with HTML mail, make sure your antivirus software is checking incoming messages. Figure 7-44 illustrates an e-mail message written in HTML format.

E-MAIL ATTACHMENTS

▶ What is an e-mail attachment? Originally, e-mail messages were stored in a plain and simple format called ASCII text. No fancy formatting was allowed—no variation in font type or color, no underlining or boldface, and, of course, no pictures or sounds. Although you cannot technically insert a digital photo or sound file into a plain ASCII e-mail message, you can send these kinds of files as e-mail attachments.

Any file that travels with an e-mail message is called an **e-mail attachment**. A conversion process called **MIME** (Multipurpose Internet Mail Extensions) provides a clever way of disguising digital photos, sounds, and other media as plain ASCII code that can travel over the Internet with text-based e-mail data. An electronic message incorporated in the e-mail header provides your e-mail software with information that allows it to reconstruct the attachment into its original form (Figure 7-45).

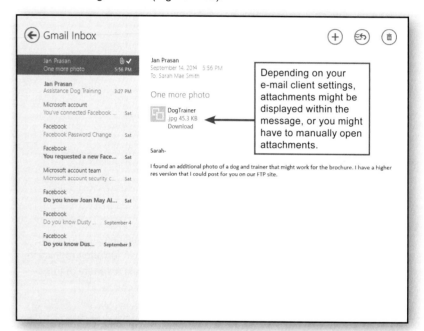

FIGURE 7-45

Attachments ride along with e-mail messages. ▶ For more tips about attachments, refer to this figure in your interactive eBook.

▶ What should I know about attachments? When working with attachments, keep the following points in mind:

▶ Don't send huge attachments. Try to limit the size of attachments to 50 KB or less for recipients who have dial-up connections. If necessary, use a compression program, such as WinZip, to shrink the attachment.

▶ Explain all attachments. To reassure recipients that an attachment is legitimate, include the file name of the attachment, what the attachment contains, and the name of the software you used to create it.

▶ Don't open suspicious attachments. If an attachment arrives from an unknown source, don't open it because it might contain a virus.

▶ You can save attachments. By right-clicking an attachment, you can save it as a separate file.

▶ You might have to download a plug-in or player. Attachments can contain text, music, video, and other types of files stored in a variety of file formats. To open some files, you might need to download a plug-in or player.

TRY IT!

Select an e-mail message that has an attachment. Can you view the MIME source?

○ Yes, by clicking the arrow next to Reply and selecting Show Original

○ Yes, by clicking View, Message, and Raw Source

○ Yes, if I select View, then Message Source

○ No, there doesn't seem to be any way to do it

NETIQUETTE

▶ Is e-mail different from other types of communication?

In some respects, e-mail is similar to an old-fashioned letter because its message is conveyed without the facial expressions, voice inflections, and body gestures that accompany face-to-face conversations. When composing a message, it is important to carefully consider your audience and the message you want to convey.

By understanding netiquette, you can avoid some of the pitfalls and problems of e-mail communications. **Netiquette** is online jargon for Internet etiquette. It is a series of customs or guidelines for maintaining civilized and effective communications in online discussions and e-mail exchanges (Figure 7-46).

FIGURE 7-46

Principles of Netiquette

▶ **Put a meaningful title on the subject line.** The subject line of your message should clearly describe the contents of your e-mail message.

▶ **Use uppercase and lowercase letters.** An e-mail message that's typed in all uppercase means that you're shouting.

▶ **Check spelling.** Most e-mail software offers a Check Spelling command. Use it.

▶ **Be careful what you send.** E-mail is not private, nor is it secure. Treat your messages as though they are postcards that can be read by anyone. Remember that all laws governing copyright, slander, and discrimination apply to e-mail.

▶ **Be polite.** Avoid wording that could sound inflammatory or argumentative. If you would not say it face-to-face, don't say it in e-mail.

▶ **Be cautious when using sarcasm and humor.** The words in your e-mail arrive without facial expressions or voice intonations, so a sarcastic comment can easily be misinterpreted.

▶ **Notify recipients of viruses.** If you discover that your computer sent out infected attachments, use antivirus software to remove the virus, and then notify anyone to whom you recently sent mail.

▶ **Use smileys and text messaging shorthand cautiously. Smileys** are symbols such as :-) that represent emotions. They can help convey the intent behind your words, but use them only in casual messages.

▶ **Use the Bcc function for group mailings.** By placing e-mail addresses for secondary recipients in the Bcc box, the recipients of your message won't have to scroll through a long list of addresses before reaching the meat of your message.

▶ **Don't send replies to all recipients.** Use the Reply All command only when there is a very specific need for everyone listed in the To, Cc, and Bcc boxes to receive the message.

QuickCheck

SECTION D

1. The [_____] of an e-mail message contains recipient addresses, the subject line, and the file names of any e-mail attachments.

2. For most client-based e-mail systems, a(n) [_____] server handles outgoing mail, and a(n) [_____] server or an IMAP server handles incoming mail. (Hint: Use the acronyms.)

3. HTML mail is the same as Webmail. True or false? [_____]

4. Attachments to e-mail messages are encoded in [_____] format. (Hint: Use the acronym.)

5. The rules and suggestions regarding electronic communications such as e-mail are referred to as [_____].

 CHECK ANSWERS

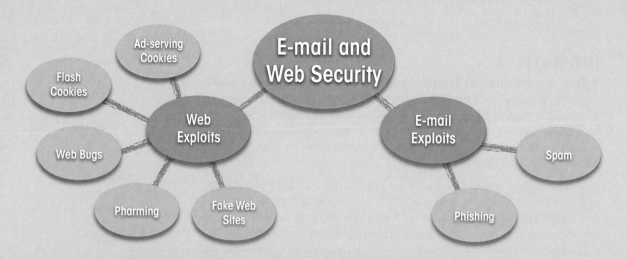

Web and E-mail Security

THE WEB AND E-MAIL abound with spam and scams engineered to monitor your online activities and collect confidential information, such as credit card numbers, passwords, and bank account numbers. You were introduced to spyware in an earlier chapter. Now you'll learn about specific spam and spyware exploits, and find out how to minimize the risk they pose to computer security and your privacy.

COOKIE EXPLOITS

▶ **Can cookies be a security risk?** Cookies have built-in safeguards designed to reduce their abuse, but marketers, hackers, and pranksters have discovered loopholes that twist cookies to serve the dark side. One of the most prevalent cookie exploits involves ad-serving cookies, and Flash cookies pose another potential threat.

▶ **What is an ad-serving cookie?** When you connect to a Web site, you expect it to store an innocuous cookie on your computer's hard disk. Some Web sites, however, feature banner ads supplied by third-party marketing firms. If you click the ad, this third party can surreptitiously create an ad-serving cookie and use it to track your activities at any site containing banner ads from that third party.

The marketing firms that distribute **ad-serving cookies** claim that the data in their cookies is used simply to select and display ads that might interest you. However, privacy advocates worry that shopper profiles can be compiled, sold, and used for unauthorized purposes. Figure 7-47 on the next page illustrates how third parties use ad-serving cookies.

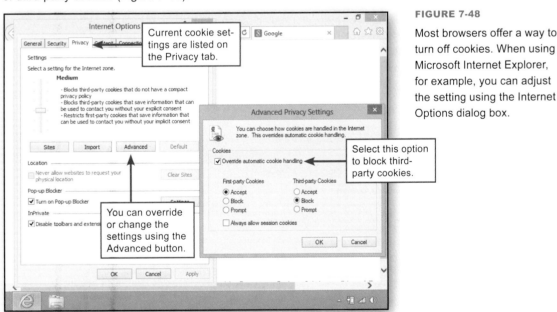

FIGURE 7-47

Ad-serving Cookies

1   You purchase a birth-day gift for a friend at PlusSize.com.

You receive a routine shopping cart cookie from the PlusSize site.

You also receive an ad-serving cookie from UglyAds.com, a firm that runs ads on the PlusSize site.

2   You're working on a report about the cardiovascular system for a biology class and mistakenly end up at a bodybuilding site.

At the Workout site, UglyAds.com reads the ad-serving cookie and changes it to show you've also been to a bodybuilding site.

3   Many e-commerce sites you now visit display banner ads for weight-loss products.

At a third site, the UglyAds cookie is read again, but this time it interacts with the UglyAds server. Based on your previous browsing, it determines that you are a potential customer for weight-loss products.

▶ **Can I turn off cookies to foil ad-serving exploits?** Most browsers include security settings that allow you to block first-party cookies or third-party cookies (Figure 7-48).

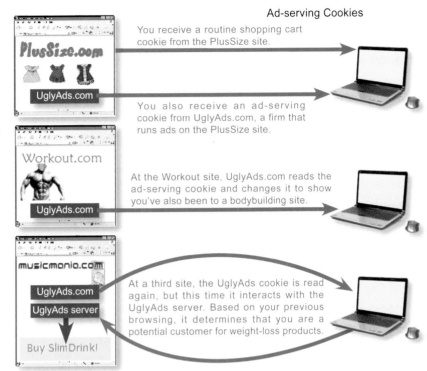

FIGURE 7-48

Most browsers offer a way to turn off cookies. When using Microsoft Internet Explorer, for example, you can adjust the setting using the Internet Options dialog box.

▶ **What is the difference between first-party and third-party cookies?** A **first-party cookie** is created by the Web site that you are visiting. If you visit Amazon.com, for example, and it sets a cookie for your shopping cart, that is classified as a first-party cookie.

A **third-party cookie** is one that is set by an affiliated site. These sites are usually associated with marketing and advertising, so most third-party cookies are not desirable.

▶ Which cookies should I disable? If you disable all cookies, you might not be able to make online purchases, participate in online classes, use Webmail, or register for premium services at search engine sites. Rather than block all cookies, blocking third-party cookies eliminates most ad cookies without disabling cookies required for legitimate Web activities.

You can also block cookies from specific sites. For example, if you'd rather not have your favorite search engine compile and store your searches, you can block its cookies.

Your browser might offer a feature called **private browsing**, which provides additional ways to surf the Web without accumulating a trail of cookies. For example, Internet Explorer's InPrivate Browsing automatically deletes cookies at the end of your browsing session.

▶ Should I delete cookies? Some privacy advocates suggest deleting cookies periodically, rather than blocking them. By deleting cookies, you can still interact with online shopping carts and take part in other activities that require cookies, but deleted third-party cookies won't be able to communicate with their handlers. The downside of deleting cookies is it might disrupt your attempts to opt out of various cookie schemes.

An opt-out function allows you to refuse to participate in an activity or promotion. Similar to the National Do Not Call Registry, several third-party advertising companies, such as Google DoubleClick, ZEDO, and the Network Advertising Initiative (NAI), now provide users with an opt-out mechanism to disallow ad-serving cookies.

Opting out creates an opt-out cookie. If you delete all the cookies on your computer, the opt-out cookie will also be deleted and third-party ads will again start appearing when you use your browser.

▶ What is a Flash cookie? A **Flash cookie**, also called a local shared object, is the Flash equivalent of a conventional Web cookie. Flash cookies are set and used by Adobe's Flash Player, which is installed on many computers to run movies, videos, and games.

Because so many computer users delete or block conventional cookies, some marketers now use Flash cookies as an alternative way to track and target consumers. In the context of running Flash animations, Flash cookies can collect and store personal data, and surreptitiously operate your computer's built-in camera. It is not a bad idea to put a sticker over your computer's camera when it is not in use.

▶ Can I avoid Flash cookies? You can manually delete Flash cookies from your computer. You can also adjust your computer's settings for Flash cookies (Figure 7-49).

How would you activate private browsing on your computer?

○ Click the Tools icon, select Safety, then select InPrivate Browsing

○ Click the browser name, then click Private Browsing

○ Click the wrench icon, then select *New incognito window*

○ Select Preferences, then go to the Privacy tab

FIGURE 7-49

To access settings for Flash cookies, look for Flash Player in the Control Panel (PCs) or in System Preferences (Macs).

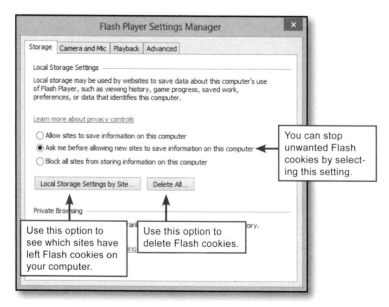

▶ **Can I surf the Internet anonymously?** In addition to tracking cookies, Web sites can track IP addresses of computers that connect to their sites. IP addresses can sometimes be traced back to individuals, especially those who have fixed IP addresses or always-on connections that retain the same IP address for long periods of time.

Individuals who prefer not to leave a trail of their Internet activities surf through an **anonymous proxy service**, which uses an intermediary, or proxy, server to relay Web page requests after masking the originating IP address (Figure 7-50).

Proxy service is similar to a VPN in some respects because they both encrypt data being sent over the Internet. An anonymous proxy service, however, is limited to use with your browser, whereas a VPN can be used with any network application. If you use a VPN, you don't need a proxy service.

A tradeoff to the anonymity offered by anonymous proxies is that they tend not to operate at the same speed as your regular browser. In addition, some Web sites and discussion groups block access from proxy servers because they have been used to spam the site or flood it with traffic. Also, anonymous proxies can be compromised by malicious third parties or monitored under court order, so anonymity is never assured.

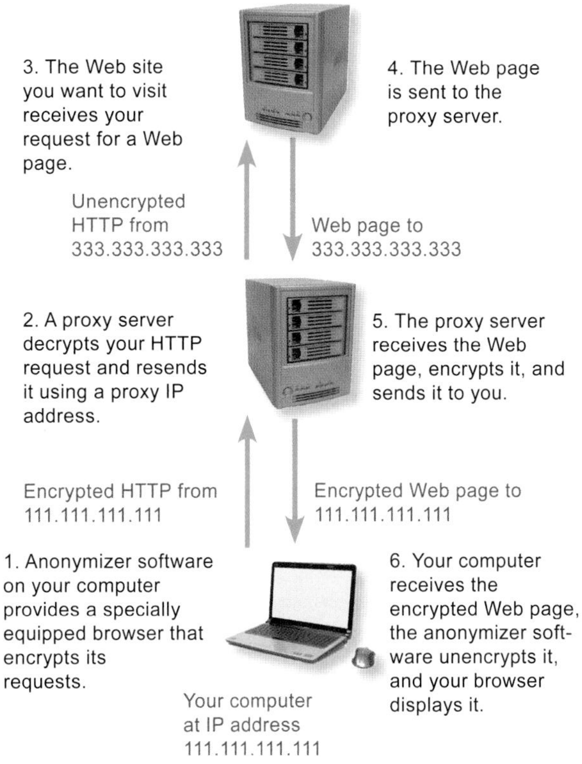

▶ **What is a Web bug?** A **Web bug** (also called a clear GIF or pixel tag) is a 1x1 pixel graphic embedded in a Web page or an e-mail message. It is almost invisible due to its size, and is designed to track who's reading the Web page or e-mail message. Web bugs on a Web page can generate third-party ad-serving cookies.

Unlike cookies that are generated when you click a banner ad, you don't have to click anything to receive a third-party cookie generated by a Web bug. When you view a Web bug infested page, an HTTP set-cookie request automatically goes to a third-party server, which can be the site of a marketer or hacker. The site can set a cookie on your computer for later retrieval, or log the IP address of your computer.

▶ **Is there any way to avoid Web bugs?** A drastic solution is to turn off all the graphics displayed by your browser, but that step makes the Web much less interesting. A better solution is to download a Web bug detector, such as Ghostery, that flags clear GIF images used to set third-party cookies. Clear GIFs are also used legitimately for alignment purposes on Web pages, however, so not all clear GIFs are malware.

Antispyware is a type of security software designed to identify and neutralize Web bugs, ad-serving cookies, and other spyware. Antispyware such as Spy Sweeper, Ad-Aware, Spybot Search & Destroy, SpywareBlaster, and Microsoft Security Essentials can offer some degree of protection against browser parasites and other Web-based nuisances. Avoid responding to or downloading spyware from pop-up ads, however. Those ads often lead to infected software.

3. The Web site you want to visit receives your request for a Web page.

Unencrypted HTTP from 333.333.333.333

4. The Web page is sent to the proxy server.

Web page to 333.333.333.333

2. A proxy server decrypts your HTTP request and resends it using a proxy IP address.

5. The proxy server receives the Web page, encrypts it, and sends it to you.

Encrypted HTTP from 111.111.111.111

Encrypted Web page to 111.111.111.111

1. Anonymizer software on your computer provides a specially equipped browser that encrypts its requests.

Your computer at IP address 111.111.111.111

6. Your computer receives the encrypted Web page, the anonymizer software unencrypts it, and your browser displays it.

FIGURE 7-50

An anonymous proxy server relays your Web page requests after stripping off your IP address. ▶ To see this process in action, activate this figure in your interactive eBook.

TRY IT!

How is a proxy service different from private browsing?

○ A proxy service hides your IP address, but private browsing deletes cookies at the end of a session

○ Private browsing encrypts your connection, but a proxy service does not

○ A proxy service avoids Flash cookies, but private browsing does not

○ They are not different

SPAM

▶ **What is spam?** One of e-mail's main disadvantages is **spam**— unwanted electronic junk mail about medical products, low-cost loans, and fake software upgrades that arrives in your online mailbox. Today's proliferation of spam is generated by marketing firms that harvest e-mail addresses from mailing lists, membership applications, and Web sites.

▶ **Is spam dangerous?** In the past, spam flooding your Inbox with unsolicited and often pornographic messages was merely an annoyance. These days, however, spam has turned into another major hacking tool for cybercriminals. Spam sometimes contains Web bugs, viruses, worms, or keyloggers that can wreak havoc on your computer or steal personal information such as passwords. Spam can also be used for phishing scams, which are described later in this section.

▶ **Can spam be blocked before it gets to my mailbox?** With millions of copies of some spam floating around the Internet, it would seem possible to identify and delete it before individuals have to contend with it. Most ISPs make an effort to block spam by blacklisting known spam servers. However, this method often results in blocking e-mail from legitimate ISPs that just happen to have been the source for dubious e-mail traffic.

▶ **What can I do about spam?** First, you can be aware of spam and delete it without responding to it. You can also install and configure spam filters. A **spam filter** is a type of utility software that captures unsolicited e-mail messages before they reach your Inbox. It works by checking the text of e-mail headers and messages against a series of rules.

For example, a rule such as *The message header contains viagra, v1agra, v.a.gra, or vi@gra* would help identify spam that's trying to hawk cheap pharmaceuticals.

Spam filters periodically download updated rules to catch the latest spams. Some spam filters also allow consumers to create their own rules to target spam that gets through the standard filters (Figure 7-51).

FIGURE 7-51

Spam filters include standard rules that block common spams, but you can create your own rules for spam that standard filters miss. ▶ Activate this figure in your interactive eBook to find out how to create customized spam filters.

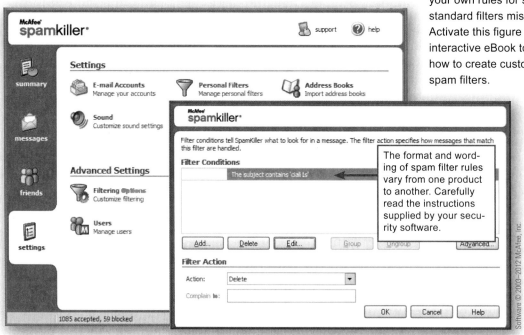

Spam filters are available as standalone software, but often are included in e-mail clients and security suites. Spam filters tend to slow down the process of downloading mail and they sometimes trash legitimate mail. Periodically, you should look in the junk e-mail folder used by your spam filters to retrieve any mail that's not junk.

In addition to using spam filters, you can avoid being a spam victim by following the guidelines in Figure 7-52.

FIGURE 7-52

Guidelines for Avoiding Spam

▶ Never reply to spam when you receive it.

▶ Don't click links in e-mail messages, even if it's an opt-out link.

▶ Give your e-mail address only to people from whom you want to receive e-mail. Be wary of providing your e-mail address at Web sites, entering it on application forms, or posting it in public places such as online discussion groups.

▶ Use a disposable e-mail address when you register for sites that you use only occasionally. You can use this disposable address to set up an account and confirm your registration, but don't use it for regular e-mail correspondence.

▶ If your e-mail provider offers a way to report spam, use it.

▶ When spam gets out of hand, consider changing your e-mail account so that you have a different e-mail address.

PHISHING

▶ **What is phishing?** **Phishing** is an e-mail based scam that's designed to persuade you to reveal confidential information such as your bank account number or Social Security number. Unlike pharming attacks (which you'll read about in a moment), phishing scams require that you reply to an e-mail message or click an embedded Web site link for the scam to unfold.

> **TERMINOLOGY NOTE**
>
> Fake sites, URLs, and even e-mail addresses are often referred to as spoofed, and the process of misdirection is called spoofing.

If you've used e-mail for any length of time, you've probably encountered the granddaddy of all phishing scams: a letter from a Nigerian political refugee who wants to move a large sum of money to a bank in your country and needs a bank account (yours!) to stash it for a few days. Of course you'll get a percentage for your trouble. Don't even think about it. According to the FBI, several gullible individuals have been lured abroad where they've been kidnapped and killed.

More innocuous but potentially damaging spam scams start with an e-mail message that appears to come from a legitimate organization such as a bank, an online payment service, an online store, or even your ISP. The message directs you to click a link to verify confidential data. The link connects you to a bogus site cleverly disguised to look very much like a legitimate Web site. There you are urged to enter your bank account number, PIN, password, credit card number, or other data.

▶ **How do I avoid phishing scams?** If you don't want to become a phishing victim, be suspicious of e-mail messages that supposedly come from banks, ISPs, online payment services, operating system publishers, and online merchants. Even if the messages appear to be legitimate, do not click links in the messages, but instead go to the Web site using your browser and link to your account as you normally would. If your account needs updating, you should see instructions about how to proceed.

FAKE SITES

▶ **What is a fake site?** A fake, or fraudulent, Web site looks legitimate, but has been created by a third party to be a very clever replica of a legitimate Web site, such as eBay or even the White House.

Many fake Web sites are bogus storefronts designed exclusively for collecting credit card numbers from unwary shoppers. These sites might have the trappings of a real site. They might even offer a secure connection for transmitting your credit card number. When your data is received, however, it is stored in a database that belongs to a hacker, who can use the data for unauthorized transactions.

Bogus Web sites aren't limited to fake storefronts. Some are official-sounding sites, such as government agencies, that actually contain sexually explicit material. Other bogus sites simply present totally fabricated information or stories designed to fool the user. Fake sites are a key part of illegitimate pharming schemes.

▶ **What is pharming?** Pharming is an exploit that redirects users to fake sites by poisoning a domain name server with a false IP address. Pharming and phishing are similar in many respects; both take advantage of fake sites. Phishing links, however, often lead to fake sites with URLs that are just slightly different from those of legitimate sites. Hackers depend on victims not paying close attention to the discrepancy when they click links.

Pharming is more sophisticated than phishing because the link appears to be for a legitimate URL. Even a close examination of the URL will not reveal anything suspicious because the URL's IP address has been changed at the domain name server.

▶ **How can I recognize a pharming attack?** Pharming is more surreptitious and tougher to detect than most other hacker schemes. Antipharming tools are emerging in response to growing security threats posed by fake sites. Mainstream browsers now include routines that compare IP addresses to a list of known fake sites and warn you of suspicious sites. Make sure your antipharming and antiphishing filters are activated (Figure 7-53).

TRY IT!

The green Address bar in Figure 7-53 does what?

○ Helps me know that this site is legitimate

○ Reminds me that it is an encrypted connection

○ Tells me that the site is free of spam

○ Tells me that the site has an IP address

FIGURE 7-53

Most browsers include features that can help you avoid pharming and phishing attacks.

▶ **What's the best defense against all the bad stuff on the Web and in e-mail?** First, understand that there is no perfect defense. Then understand that you should do all you can to safeguard your computer and your privacy. Use the list in Figure 7-54 as a starting point.

FIGURE 7-54

Guidelines for Secure and Private Web Surfing

▶ Use antispyware utilities to clean up any spyware that might have infiltrated your computer.

▶ Run antispyware continuously just as you do antivirus software.

▶ Set your browser to reject third-party cookies.

▶ Consider using your browser's private browsing feature when you want cookies deleted at the end of your session.

▶ Check Flash Player settings to make sure you control the sites that store Flash cookies on your computer.

▶ Make sure your browser's antispoofing tools are activated; or install a third-party antispoofing tool to help you identify fake Web sites.

▶ Set up a disposable e-mail address at a site such as Hotmail or Gmail and use it when you don't want to disclose your primary e-mail address.

▶ Do not click links in untrusted e-mail or pop-up ads, and never respond to e-mail offers, especially those that seem too good to be true.

7

QuickCheck   SECTION E

1. A Web [＿＿＿＿＿] embedded in an e-mail message or a Web page can be activated when you view an infested page.

2. If you don't want your IP address tracked as you surf the Web, you can use an anonymous [＿＿＿＿＿] service.

3. A spam [＿＿＿＿＿] can be configured with rules that block messages containing text such as *viagra* or *v1@gra*.

4. A(n) [＿＿＿＿＿] exploit redirects users to fake sites by poisoning a Domain Name Server with a false IP address.

5. Most browsers offer a(n) [＿＿＿＿＿] browsing setting that deletes the cookies accumulated during a session.

▶ CHECK ANSWERS

Issue: Who's Reading Your E-mail?

WHEN YOU DROP an envelope into the corner mailbox, you probably expect it to arrive at its destination unopened, with its contents kept safe from prying eyes.

When you make a phone call, you might assume that your conversation will proceed unmonitored by wiretaps or other listening devices. Can you also expect an e-mail message to be read only by the person to whom it is addressed?

Your e-mail messages can go public in any number of ways. The recipient of your e-mail can forward it to one or more people—people you never intended for it to reach. Your e-mail messages could pop up on a technician's screen in the course of system maintenance, updates, or repairs.

Employers routinely monitor employee e-mail. Government agencies tasked with maintaining national security monitor all types of electronic communications. Schools and organizations sometimes monitor messages that flow over their e-mail systems. You might wonder if such open access to your e-mail is legal. The answer in most cases is yes.

In the United States, the Electronic Communications Privacy Act of 1986 prohibits the use of intercepted e-mail as evidence unless a judge approves a search warrant. That doesn't mean the government isn't reading your mail.

Heightened security concerns after the September 11, 2001 terrorist attacks resulted in a clear pattern of legislation characterized by the American Civil Liberties Union (ACLU) as allowing the federal government to "conduct dragnet surveillance of Americans' international telephone calls and e-mails en masse, without a warrant, without suspicion of any kind, and with only very limited judicial oversight."

According to the American Management Association, 43% of U.S. businesses monitor employee e-mail. Employees generally have not been successful in defending their rights to e-mail privacy because courts have ruled that an employee's right to privacy does not outweigh a company's rights and interests.

You should use your e-mail account with the expectation that some of your mail will be read by someone other than the intended recipient.

Courts seem to agree that because a company owns and maintains its e-mail system, it has the right to monitor the messages carried by the system.

Like employees of a business, students who use a school's e-mail system cannot be assured of e-mail privacy. When a Caltech student was accused of sexually harassing a female student by sending lewd e-mail to her and her boyfriend, investigators retrieved all the student's e-mail from the archives of the e-mail server. The student was expelled from the university even though he claimed that the e-mail had been spoofed to make it look as though he had sent it, when it had actually been sent by someone else.

Why would an employer want to know the contents of employee e-mail? Why would a school be concerned with the correspondence of its students? It is probably true that some organizations simply snoop on the off chance that important information might be discovered.

Most organizations, however, have legitimate reasons for monitoring e-mail. An organization that owns an e-mail system can be held responsible for the consequences of actions related to the contents of e-mail messages on that system. For example, a school has a responsibility to protect students from harassment. If it fails to do so, it can be sued along with the author of the offending e-mail message.

You should use your e-mail account with the expectation that some of your mail will be read by someone other than the intended recipient. Think of your e-mail as a postcard, rather than a letter, and save your controversial comments for face-to-face conversations.

⬤TRY IT! We all use e-mail. Should we be nervous about sending messages such as: "When we meet at the airport, we'll have some time to kill before our flight, so you can tell me your explosive news then." Explore the issue to find out just how cautious you need to be.

1 Many schools and businesses have e-mail privacy policies, which explain the conditions under which you can and cannot expect your e-mail to remain private. Locate your school's e-mail privacy policy. Was it easy to find and what does it say?

2 Webmail services, such as Gmail and Yahoo! Mail, display ads that are related to the content of each e-mail message. For example, if you are e-mailing a friend about spring break in Cancun, your Webmail service might display ads for hotels and other travel deals. To explore how e-mail ad servers work, send a few e-mail messages to yourself that include notable keywords, such as *Cancun*, *motorcycle*, *Chevy Volt*, *diabetes*, or *CIA*. What kinds of ads appear?

3 With increasing frequency, government agencies, such as the U.S. Department of Justice (DOJ), have tried to force e-mail service providers to hand over e-mail messages. The legal debate about e-mail

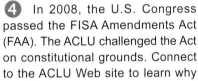

1 Koele/Shutterstock.com

privacy hinges on the Fourth Amendment to the U.S. Constitution. Exactly what does the Fourth Amendment say and how does it relate to the government reading your e-mail?

4 In 2008, the U.S. Congress passed the FISA Amendments Act (FAA). The ACLU challenged the Act on constitutional grounds. Connect to the ACLU Web site to learn why the ACLU believes that FAA is unconstitutional. What is the name of the lawsuit challenging FAA and what is the status of that suit?

5 Google, Yahoo!, and other e-mail service providers receive requests from government agencies, such as the U.S. Department of Justice, to hand over e-mail messages. Some requests are based on a search warrant; others are not. Most e-mail service providers have privacy policies that describe the circumstances under which e-mail messages would be handed over. Find the policy for your e-mail service. How will your service provider respond to government requests to hand over your messages?

INFOWEBLINKS

You can check the **NP2014 Chapter 7** InfoWebLink for updates to these activities.

Ⓦ CLICK TO CONNECT
www.infoweblinks.com/np2014/ch07

What Do You Think?

ISSUE

1. Do you think most people believe that their e-mail is private?

2. Do you agree with Caltech's decision to expel the student who was accused of sending harassing e-mail to another student?

3. Should the laws be changed to make it illegal for employers to monitor e-mail without court approval?

4. Would you have different privacy expectations regarding an e-mail account at your place of work as opposed to an account you purchase from an e-mail service provider?

Information Tools: Your Own Words

© MediaTechnics

PLAGIARISM. Buying a term paper from a company or an individual and turning it in as your own. Copying words directly from someone else's print or online work. Paraphrasing without attribution. That's plagiarism.

COMMON KNOWLEDGE. To avoid plagiarism in your written work, you should include citations for any statements that are not common knowledge. Common knowledge includes ideas and facts that can be found in many places and are known by many people. Material that is based on the work, ideas, or statements of other people is not common knowledge and needs a citation for its source. Include a citation for:

- Any statement that refers to a research study or is based on its conclusions

- Any statement or graph that includes statistics

- Any word-for-word spoken or written quotations

- Any statement that restates or summarizes another person's original ideas

PARAPHRASING. Citations are required even when you paraphrase. Changing the words of an original source is not sufficient. You must cite the source whenever you borrow ideas as well as words.

Acceptable paraphrasing should not be too close to the original wording, yet you must be careful not to change the idea behind the original wording. Your paraphrase also requires a citation to the original source. Suppose you find this passage on Carla Charmer's blog that contains material you'd like to include in a mid-term report:

> A Michigan man who accessed his wife's e-mail account while she was allegedly carrying on an affair faces up to five years in prison. He is being prosecuted for violating a state law typically used against hackers and identity thieves. It is shocking that a person could be charged with a felony for reading his spouse's e-mail.

There are several ways in which you can use this material. Some ways are more ethical than others.

A Michigan man faces five years in prison on charges that he violated a state law by reading his wife's e-mail without permission.	Common knowledge. Okay to use without a citation to the original source.
It is shocking that a person could be charged with a felony for reading his wife's e-mail. A Michigan man who read his wife's e-mail while she was supposedly having an affair faces up to five years in prison for violating a state law usually used for identity thieves and hackers.	This paraphrase is too close to the original and should include a citation.
It came as quite a shock that a Michigan man could be charged with a felony and face up to five years in the slammer simply for reading his wife's e-mail while she was supposedly having an affair with another man.	This paraphrase is unique and maintains the basic idea of the original, but still requires a citation.
Blogger Carla Charmer found it "shocking that a person could be charged with a felony for reading his spouse's e-mail."	This use of a direct quotation includes an in-context citation, but could also use a more complete citation in MLA, APA, or Chicago style.

⬤**TRY IT!** Explore the differences between original and plagiarized material by answering the following questions.

① Which of these statements would not need a citation because it is common knowledge?

    a. While it is fairly easy to build a slow crawler that downloads one or a few pages per second for a short period of time, building a high-performance system that can download hundreds of millions of pages over several weeks presents a number of challenges in system design, I/O and network efficiency, and robustness and manageability.

    b. Search engines, such as Google, include software called a Web crawler that visits Web sites and indexes the material it finds there. This material can later be accessed by entering keywords at a search engine site.

    c. Experimental results show that a distributed Web crawler can more effectively visit Web pages than a single Web crawler.

② Which of these statements would need a citation because they refer to statements based on statistics?

    a. The main problem search engines have to deal with is the size and rate of change of the Web, with no search engine indexing more than one-third of the publicly available Web.

    b. Back in 2004, the average working day consisted of dealing with 46 phone calls, 15 internal memos, 19 items of snail mail, and 22 e-mails.

    c. Search engines deal with a vast amount of material. The process of collecting and organizing that material becomes ever greater as the Web expands.

③ Which of these statements should have citations because they refer to a research study or its conclusions?

    a. We ran a crawl of over 100 million Web pages on about 5 million hosts. The crawl was performed over a period of 18 days; however, the crawler was not continuously in operation during this time. Of the 138 million pages cataloged, more than 400,000 produced a 403 error that access was forbidden.

    b. Given the current size of the Web, even large search engines cover only a portion of the publicly available part. A report from the Websonite Group indicates that large-scale search engines index no more than 40% to 70% of the indexable Web.

    c. You can study the Web all you want, but there will still be more to learn.

> "Can ordinary Americans like you and me sue the government for illegally spying on them? When it comes to the NSA surveillance program, the government itself says the answer is no. After all, since it's a secret program, you don't really know if you're being spied on. And if you don't know you're being spied on, you have no standing to sue."

④ Use a search engine to find the above quotation, then do the following:

    a. Create an MLA citation for the original source.

    b. Create an acceptable paraphrase for the quotation using an in-context citation.

    c. Write at least two sentences on the same topic that would be common knowledge and not need a citation.

⑤ Plagiarism scanning services, such as Turnitin and Viper, make it easy for instructors to check the originality of your work. Before turning in a paper, you can make sure you've cited all relevant sources by running your document through the student version of Turnitin or a free plagiarism scanner such as Viper, Grammarly, Dustball, or Dupli Checker. Copy a page of text from one of your original documents and submit it to a plagiarism checker, then do the same for a page that you copy out of Wikipedia. What are the results?

INFOWEBLINKS

You can check the **NP2014 Chapter 7** InfoWebLink for updates to these activities.

Ⓦ CLICK TO CONNECT
www.infoweblinks.com/np2014/ch07

Technology in Context: Fashion Industry

FASHION IS BIG BUSINESS. Worldwide, clothing sales generate more than $340 billion in revenue. Shoes, accessories, and jewelry bump the industry's revenue even higher. Competition is tough as designers, manufacturers, and retailers compete for customer dollars.

In the fashion industry, trends change quickly. As the saying goes, "Today's style is tomorrow's markdown." Fashion industry players look for every competitive advantage. It is no surprise that technology plays a major role in this glitzy industry.

Fashion begins with designers, such as Miuccia Prada, John Galliano, and Marc Jacobs. Their runway extravaganzas set off fashion trends that eventually work their way to retail stores. Fashion runways went high-tech in 1999 when lingerie manufacturer Victoria's Secret produced a Webcast watched by over 1 million viewers. Bravo television's *Project Runway* show has been one of the top iPod downloads. Fashion podcasts and blogs abound on the Web, as do fashion sites packed with news about the latest trends.

Although runway fashions are often conceived with a sketch and stitched by hand, designs are adapted for the ready-to-wear market by using computer-aided design (CAD) tools, such as pattern-making software.

Garments are constructed by sewing together sections of fabric that form arms, fronts, backs, collars, and so forth. The set of templates used to cut fabric sections is called a pattern. Pattern-making is a tricky 3-D challenge because flat pieces of fabric eventually become garments shaped to conform to curved body contours. Pattern-making software helps designers visualize how flat pieces fit together and drape when sewn. Once a master pattern is complete, pattern-making software automatically generates a set of patterns for each garment size.

Fashion requires fabric, and computers play a major role in fabric design and manufacturing. Computer

software, such as ArahWeave, lets fabric designers experiment with colors, yarns, and weaves while viewing detailed, realistic on-screen samples. Fabric designs can be stored in a variety of formats for weaving machines. A few older mechanical weaving machines are controlled by punched cards. Digital fabric designs can be transferred to punched cards with a dedicated card punch machine.

Most of today's weaving mills use computerized machinery that directly accepts digital input to control threads and patterns. Networks tie looms to CAD stations and to the Internet. Fabric designs can be stored in XML format, transmitted to a fabric manufacturer over the Internet, and used directly by computerized weaving machines.

Clothing production, warehousing, and shipping are also highly automated. Benetton's high-tech facility at Castrette, Italy can produce over 110 million gar-

ments per year. Its automated distribution center uses a workforce of only 24 people to handle 40,000 boxes of merchandise daily. RFID tags—sometimes called smart labels—can be attached to individual garments or to packing boxes as an important tool for controlling inventory.

RFID technology uses an inexpensive, tiny computer chip with a built-in antenna and the capacity to store between 64 and 128 bits of data about a garment—its SKU number, size, model, dye lot, manufacturing date, and so on. Tags can be attached to a garment or its label. An RFID reader that can retrieve data from tags is used to track merchandise from the manufacturing plant through the distribution chain to the retailer.

RFID tags are becoming popular for all types of merchandise. Businesses that use them can save time and money. For example, RFID tags can reduce the time it takes to do a physical inventory by a factor of 10. Privacy advocates, however, are worried because these tags remain active even after you bring your merchandise home. Could a thief circle your house with an RFID scanner to find out what's inside? Could a stalker follow your movements by tracking the RFID tag embedded in your sweater?

Next time you buy a garment, check to see if an RFID tag is attached. It would normally be sewn into a seam and may carry a warning "Remove before wearing."

In response to competition from offshore companies, U.S. clothing manufacturers pioneered Quick Response (QR)—a business model for compressing supply chains to quickly obtain raw materials, such as fabric, yarn, buttons, and zippers. Sophisticated software tools, such as the Sourcing Simulator, simplify QR planning.

Online shopping has become routine, but one drawback of catalog and online ordering is the cost associated with restocking returned merchandise. Can an online customer find out how a garment will fit and look before ordering it? Can in-store customers find their correct size without trying multiple sizes?

In 1998, Lands' End introduced My Virtual Model technology that allows shoppers to create a custom model of themselves by choosing from a variety of hair colors and styles, face shapes, and body types. The model can "try on" clothes to show online customers how they would look when wearing the garments.

More recently, a company called Unique Solutions is setting up full-body scanners in malls all over the country. According to the company's Web site, the scanning process takes about 15 seconds and produces 200,000 data points that can be used to match your body's contours with actual clothing sizes for different brands.

No discussion of fashion and computers would be complete without highlighting wearable technology. MIT's Media Lab has been a hotbed of wearable technology development. A recent student project uses a Webcam, a battery-powered projector, and an Internet-enabled mobile phone, and allows wearers to use hand gestures in 3-D space to conjure up information from the phone and project it on any surface.

Some wearables have even emerged from the laboratory and onto store shelves.

Originally popular with Secret Service agents, the SCOTTEVEST is a jacket with pockets for cell phone, MP3 player, iPad, and built-in wiring to connect these devices into a personal area network (PAN). Available as a jacket or vest and in men's and women's sizes, the jacket and vest can now be purchased by civilians.

With a growing emphasis on the use of technology in fashion design and manufacturing, fashion degree programs at colleges and technical schools have added courses such as computer-aided fashion design, computer-based pattern drafting, pattern grading and computer-aided drafting, and wearable computers.

7

New Perspectives Labs

To access the New Perspectives Labs for Chapter 7, open the NP2014 interactive eBook and then click the icon next to the lab title.

▶ BROWSER SECURITY & PRIVACY

IN THIS LAB YOU'LL LEARN:

- How to adjust the security settings for Internet Explorer's security zones
- How your browser can help you avoid phishing scams
- Why Web-based images and active content can pose a security risk
- The safest way to close pop-up ads and the most effective way to block them
- How to adjust security settings for active content
- How to delete or block Flash cookies
- How to secure the camera and microphone on your computer
- How to prevent Web sites from determining your location, or allow them to do so

LAB ASSIGNMENTS

1. Perform each lab step as directed, and answer all the lab QuickCheck questions.
2. Identify which browser you usually use and look at its security settings. Does your browser allow you to select an overall security level, such as low, medium, or high?
3. Look at your browser's security settings and record the current settings for its phishing filter, pop-up blocker, ActiveX controls, JavaScript, and Java. Would you make any changes to these settings?
4. Connect to the Flash Player Settings Manager and count the number of Flash cookies you have. Next, record the security settings for your computer's camera and microphone.

▶ WORKING WITH COOKIES

IN THIS LAB YOU'LL LEARN:

- How Web servers use cookies
- Why cookies might pose a threat to your privacy
- How to locate, view, block, and delete cookies
- How to limit the space allocated to cookies created by Internet Explorer
- What a session cookie is
- How to set cookie prompts and use the cookie prompt dialog box
- How to take advantage of P3P and Compact Privacy Policies
- The differences between first-party and third-party cookies

LAB ASSIGNMENTS

1. Perform each lab step as directed, and answer all the lab QuickCheck questions.
2. Use your browser to look at the cookies on your computer. Indicate how many cookies are currently stored. Examine the contents of one cookie, and indicate whether you think it poses a threat to your privacy.
3. Indicate the name and version of the browser you generally use. Next, look at your browser's cookie settings. Describe how you would adjust these settings to produce a level of privacy protection that is right for your needs.
4. Adjust your browser settings so that you are prompted whenever a Web server attempts to send a cookie to your computer. Go to your favorite Web sites and watch for third-party cookies. When you receive a message from a third-party Web site, record the name of the third-party site and the contents of the cookie it is attempting to send. Finally, indicate whether you would accept such a cookie.

▶ WORKING WITH HTML

IN THIS LAB YOU'LL LEARN:

- How to use a text editor such as Notepad to create a basic HTML document
- Which HTML tags to use to format text
- How to use HTML for numbered and bulleted lists
- How to add graphics to your Web pages
- How to add hyperlinks to a Web page
- Methods for testing Web pages locally
- How to post your Web page

LAB ASSIGNMENTS

1. Perform each lab step as directed, and answer all the lab QuickCheck questions.
2. Use a text editor such as Notepad to create a Web page that contains your name as the title and at least two paragraphs of text.
3. Use the heading, bold, and horizontal rule HTML tags to add interest to your page.
4. Add at least one hyperlink to the page, making sure that you include explanatory link text.
5. Select a graphic to add to your page. Make sure that it is stored in a file that's not too big to load quickly. Designate alternative text for the graphic for accessibility.
6. Test your Web page locally. Print your HTML document and then make a screen capture of your Web page as it appears in the browser.
7. If your instructor so specifies, post your Web page to a Web site, test it, and supply the page's URL to your instructor using e-mail.

Key Terms

Make sure you understand all the boldfaced key terms presented in this chapter. With the NP2014 interactive eBook, you can use this list of terms as an interactive study activity. First, try to define a term in your own words, and then click the term to compare your definition with the definition presented in the chapter.

7

Ad-blocking software, 385
Ad-serving cookies, 400
Anonymous proxy service, 403
Antispyware, 403
B2B, 385
B2C, 385
B2G, 385
Banner ad, 385
C2C, 385
Click-through rate, 385
Client-side, 372
Cookie, 368
E-commerce, 384
E-mail account, 393
E-mail address, 393
E-mail attachment, 398
E-mail client software, 393
E-mail message, 392
E-mail server, 392
E-mail system, 392
First-party cookie, 401
Flash cookie, 402
Hover ad, 385
HTML, 362
HTML conversion utility, 369
HTML document, 362
HTML form, 371
HTML mail, 397
HTML tags, 362
HTML5, 362
HTTP, 364
HTTP status code, 365

HTTPS, 390
Hypertext, 360
Hypertext link, 361
IMAP, 394
JavaScript, 372
Keyword stuffing, 377
Link popularity, 377
Local e-mail, 393
Markup language, 362
Message header, 392
Meta keyword, 377
Metasearch engine, 380
MIME, 398
Netiquette, 399
Online shopping cart, 387
Persistent HTTP connection, 365
Person-to-person payment, 391
Pharming, 406
Phishing, 405
Plug-in, 367
POP3, 394
Pop-up ad, 385
Private browsing, 402
Query processor, 376
Search engine indexer, 376
Search operator, 379
Search terms, 378
Secure connection, 389
Server-side, 372
Smileys, 399
SMTP, 394
Socket, 364

Source document, 363
Spam, 404
Spam filter, 404
Sponsored links, 377
SSL, 390
Stateless protocol, 368
Store-and-forward, 394
Third-party cookie, 401
TLS, 390
URL, 361
Web, 360
Web 2.0, 361
Web 3.0, 361
Web authoring software, 369
Web browser, 361
Web bug, 403
Web cache, 365
Web crawler, 375
Web page, 361
Web search engine, 374
Web server, 361
Web site, 361
Webmail, 393
XHTML, 362

Don Farrall/Getty Images

Interactive Summary

To review important concepts from this chapter, fill in the blanks to best complete each sentence. When using the NP2014 interactive eBook, click the Check Answers buttons to automatically score your answers.

SECTION A: The Web, one of the Internet's hottest attractions, is a collection of document, image, video, and sound files that can be linked and accessed over the Internet via the [   ] protocol. The Web is an interlinked collection of information; whereas the [   ] is the communications system used to transport Web information from computers that store it to client computers that request it. An Internet-based computer that stores and distributes Web files is called a Web [   ]. It can host one or more Web [   ] such as *www.wikipedia.com* or *www.facebook.com* containing HTML [   ] documents, which can be accessed and displayed using client software called a Web [   ]. Each Web page has a unique address called a(n) [   ]. [   ] Markup Language is a set of specifications for creating documents that a browser can display as a Web page. To create HTML documents, you can use a variety of Web authoring tools, such as a text [   ], an HTML conversion utility, an online Web authoring tool, or Web authoring software. Web designers can collect user input with the < [   ] > tag. To enable Web pages to perform tasks beyond what HTML can do, Web page designers can add interactivity by embedding or linking to instructions created with [   ].

▶ CHECK ANSWERS

SECTION B: To sift through the massive amounts of information available on the Web and locate pertinent information about a topic, Web surfers utilize programs called search [   ]. These special programs have four major components. A Web [   ], also called a Web spider, is automated to methodically visit Web sites and gather Web pages. A search engine [   ] culls keywords from the gathered pages and stores them in a(n) [   ]. The search engine's query [   ] accepts one or more words called search [   ], looks them up in the database, and produces a list of relevant Web sites. There are a number of ways to narrow searches and produce more targeted results, such as using [   ] operators or putting exact phrases in [   ]. The order in which Web sites are returned in response to your query is dependent on relevancy criteria, such as keyword matches and [   ] popularity.

▶ CHECK ANSWERS

SECTION C: Any business transaction that is conducted electronically over a computer network is typically referred to as a(n) [   ] transaction. The most common business models are business-to- [   ], consumer-to-consumer, business-to-business, and business-to-government. E-commerce merchants cut costs by taking advantage of the efficiencies and opportunities offered by [   ], computerization, and digitization. They also increase their profits by providing space for third-party hover, pop-up, and [   ] ads on their Web pages. Online stores use [   ] to track customers' online shopping carts. B2C e-commerce sites usually store product descriptions in a(n) [   ]. Product information is assembled into Web pages on the fly by [   ]-side programs. Online purchases can be paid for by submitting a credit card number directly to a merchant or using a person-to- [   ] payment service, such as PayPal.

▶ CHECK ANSWERS

7

SECTION D: E-mail is an electronic version of the postal system that transmits messages from one computer to another, usually over the [_____] . Obtaining an e-mail [_____] gets your electronic mailbox set up on an e-mail server. The software you use to send, receive, and manage messages is called e-mail [_____] software. E-mail systems based on client software that's installed locally are referred to as [_____] e-mail. Systems that provide access to e-mail through a(n) [_____] are called Webmail. Incoming mail can be handled by one of two protocols. [_____] deletes messages after they are downloaded, whereas [_____] leaves messages on the server until you specifically delete them. The protocol that handles outgoing mail is [_____] .

[_____] mail is a term used for e-mail messages that contain tags that produce bold, italicized, and underlined text; fancy fonts; embedded graphics; and various font sizes. Any file that travels with an e-mail message is called an e-mail attachment. A conversion process called [_____] provides a clever way of disguising digital photos, sounds, and other media as plain ASCII code that can travel over the Internet as e-mail attachments. Attachments can harbor computer [_____] . Do not open attachments from an unknown source. [_____] is online jargon for Internet etiquette. It is a series of customs or guidelines for maintaining civilized and effective communications in online discussions and e-mail exchanges.

▶ CHECK ANSWERS

SECTION E: When you surf the Web or work with your e-mail, you need to be aware of potential spyware exploits, such as [_____] cookies from third parties. While browsers and marketing firms are now providing opt-out mechanisms to block third-party cookies, it is not as easy to turn off all kinds of cookies. [_____] cookies, also called local shared objects, are used as an alternative to conventional cookies, and most users are not aware of their existence. Web [_____] , or clear GIFs, are practically invisible 1x1 pixel graphics embedded in a Web page or an e-mail message that can be used to set cookies for third-party Web sites. [_____] redirects users to fake sites by

tampering with the information in a(n) [_____] name server. While these attacks don't need any action on your part to be effective, [_____] scams require you to respond to an e-mail message or click an embedded link in your e-mail. [_____] is unsolicited e-mail that you can avoid by practicing safe e-mail techniques such as using a spam [_____] . You can also use a(n) [_____] e-mail address to receive confirmation for online purchases without getting added to a spam mailing list. A safe bet for combating most forms of spyware is using a type of security software called [_____] .

▶ CHECK ANSWERS

Interactive Situation Questions

Apply what you've learned to some typical computing situations. When using the NP2014 interactive eBook, you can type your answers, and then use the Check Answers button to automatically score your responses.

1. Suppose that you are about to check out at an online store, but you don't see any indication that your transaction data will be protected by a secure connection. It would be best, under these circumstances, to use PGP software to encrypt your shipping and billing data. True or false? [   ]

2. Your friend, who is a little computer phobic, is going to be creating his first Web page and asks you to recommend some software for the task. Which one requires the least knowledge of HTML tags: Notepad or LibreOffice Writer? [   ]

3. Suppose you visit a Web site that has eye-catching pages. You want to know how these pages were formatted, so you use one of the options on your browser's menu to take a look at the HTML [   ] document.

4. Suppose you click a link at a Web site and get a message that the file cannot be displayed because it is in PDF format. To view the file, you need an updated version of your browser. True or false? [   ]

5. Suppose you're performing a local test of a Web page you created. All the page elements appear to be correctly positioned and formatted. You're also happy to discover that your large graphics files are displayed quite quickly by your browser. Can you expect similar performance after you post the page on a Web site? Yes or no? [   ]

6. You'd prefer not to have the search engine you use maintain accumulative records of your searches. You can block [   ] from a specific search engine site, and that setting will force the search engine to assign a different ID number to you for each session.

7. You're getting ready for a week-long trip. You'd rather not take your computer, but you'll have access to public computers. Rather than use Webmail while you're away from home, you decide to use your familiar POP e-mail [   ] software by storing it and your e-mail files on a portable USB flash drive.

8. One of your relatives wants to try online shopping, but is suspicious that her credit card number might get stolen from a merchant's server by a hacker using a packet sniffer. Is it correct to tell her that she can best avoid these potential rip-offs by using a secure connection, such as HTTPS? Yes or no? [   ]

9. Your Inbox is getting more and more unsolicited messages with "fisd foos" in the header. You decide to generate a new rule for your security software's spam [   ] to block those irritating messages.

10. You're conducting a research project that requires you to visit sites with lots of pop-up ads and other junk that you don't want accumulating in your Temporary Internet Files folder. You remember that you can turn on [   ] browsing to delete all that junk when you end your session. ▶ CHECK ANSWERS

Interactive Practice Tests

Practice tests that consist of ten multiple-choice, true/false, and fill-in-the-blank questions are available in the NP2014 interactive eBook. Test questions are selected at random from a large test bank, so each time you take a test, you'll receive a different set of questions. Your tests are scored immediately, and you can print study guides that help you find the correct answers for any questions that you missed.

▶ CLICK TO START

Learning Objectives Checkpoints

Learning Objectives Checkpoints are designed to help you assess whether you have achieved the major learning objectives for this chapter. You can use paper and pencil or word processing software to complete most of the activities.

7

1. Explain the relationship between an HTML source document and a Web page. List five HTML tags and describe how each is used.

2. Draw a multi-panel cartoon that shows how a Web server and a browser interact. Include the following terms: *Web server*, *browser*, *HTTP*, *HTML*, *port*, *socket*, *HTML document*, *graphic file*, and *URL*.

3. Briefly sketch the evolution of Web browsers. Describe how browsers use plug-ins.

4. Explain why cookies are useful in an environment that is based on a stateless protocol, and provide some concrete examples of their use.

5. Describe the advantages and disadvantages of each type of Web page development tool discussed in this chapter.

6. Create a short tutorial explaining how to create, test, and post a Web page using a text editor such as Notepad or TextEdit.

7. Explain the purpose of JavaScript.

8. Create a comic-strip like sequence of diagrams that illustrates how the following technologies interact: Web crawler, search engine database, indexer, query processor.

9. Use a search engine and search operators to formulate a search for information about your favorite era in history. Can you make a more targeted search to find out what kind of slang was used during that time period?

10. List the three most commonly used styles of citation and demonstrate how to correctly format a citation to a Web page using each style.

11. Explain two ways that shopping carts can work with cookies.

12. List three threats to the security of credit card numbers and other sensitive data during e-commerce transactions. Describe how the following e-commerce technologies work: SSL/TLS, HTTPS, and person-to-person payment systems.

13. Create a table that compares and contrasts local mail with Webmail.

14. List the advantages and disadvantages of HTML formatted mail. Explain how MIME works.

15. Make a list of security and privacy concerns discussed in this chapter. Describe each one and then list procedures and technologies available to make your online experience more secure and private.

Study Tip: Make sure you can use your own words to correctly answer each of the purple focus questions that appear throughout the chapter.

Concept Map

Fill in the blanks to show the hierarchy of Web technology concepts presented in this chapter.

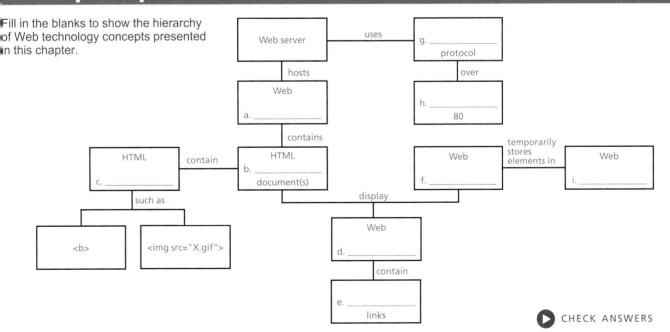

CHECK ANSWERS

Digital Media

INFOWEBLINKS

You'll find updates for chapter material by connecting to the **NP2014 Chapter 8** InfoWebLink.

Ⓦ CLICK TO CONNECT
www.infoweblinks.com/np2014/ch08

Learning Objectives

After reading this chapter, you will be able to answer the following questions by completing the outcomes-based Learning Objectives Checkpoints on page 483.

1. How do computers and portable media players such as iPods store digital music?
2. Why are some digital audio files so huge?
3. What is the difference between digital audio and MIDI?
4. What are bitmap graphics, where are they used, and how can they be identified?
5. How are images transferred from digital cameras to computers?
6. What affects the quality of a bitmap graphic and its suitability for Web pages, e-mail attachments, printed photos, or desktop-published documents?
7. Can compression play a role in reducing the size of graphics files?
8. How do vector graphics differ from bitmaps?
9. Is it possible to convert vector graphics into bitmap graphics?
10. What tools and techniques are used to create 3-D graphics?
11. What affects the amount of video that can be stored on a hard disk or portable media player?
12. How is digital video deployed on the Web?
13. What are the most popular digital media file formats and software players?
14. Is a special procedure required to make DVDs that work on standalone DVD players?
15. How do digital rights management technologies restrict the ways in which I can use digital media?
16. How are time shifting, place shifting, and format shifting related to digital media?

Apply Your Knowledge

The information in this chapter will give you the background to:

▶ Recognize digital media files by their extensions

▶ Manipulate music and video files on your computer and handheld devices

▶ Add WAV or MIDI music to Web pages

▶ Manipulate software with voice commands

▶ Create digital photos with a camera or scanner and then edit them

▶ Create vector and 3-D graphics

▶ Process photos to make them suitable for e-mail attachments, Web pages, or printing

▶ Create and edit digital video

▶ Turn your digital video into a DVD

▶ Legally use digital content, including content that is controlled by digital rights management

DIGITAL MEDIA

TRY IT!

WHAT KINDS OF GRAPHICS, AUDIO, AND VIDEO FILES ARE ON MY COMPUTER?

You can use your computer to work with many types of media, such as photos, music, and videos. Your computer stores media that you've created and downloaded. It also stores images from Web sites you've recently visited. To discover what sort of media is stored on your computer, follow these steps:

Windows 8:
1. From the Start screen, type **pic** as shown below to display Search. Click **Files** for a list of pictures.
2. Search again for **music** and then search once more for **video**.

Windows 7:
1. Click the **Start** button. Type **pictures** into the search box as shown below. Click the **See more results** option above the search box.
2. Repeat step 1 to search for **music** and then again to search for **video**.

Mac (Lion):
1. Click the **Finder** icon located on the dock.
2. Click **Pictures** on the left side of the Finder window. If your Mac displays file names but you'd prefer to see the images, click the **View** menu and then select **as icons**.
3. Click **Movies** to see a list of video files.
4. Click **Music** to see a list of music files.

Mac (Leopard):
1. Click the **Finder** icon, located on the dock.
2. Use the SEARCH FOR listing on the left side of the Finder window to select **All images**. If your Mac displays file names but you'd prefer to see the images, click the **View** menu and then select **as icons**.
3. Use the SEARCH FOR listing to select **All Movies**.
4. To find music on your Mac, type **music** in the search box, located in the upper-right corner of the Finder window.

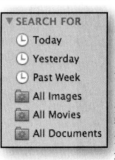

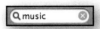

Software © 2012 Apple Inc. All rights reserved

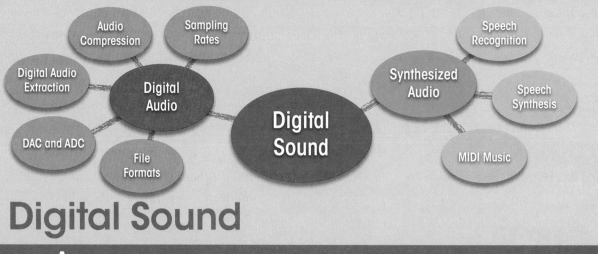

Digital Sound

COMPUTERS CAN RECORD, store, and play sounds, such as narrations, sound effects, and music. Downloading music files over the Internet is currently the most popular use of digital audio, but audio technology plays a key role in other interesting applications. This section of the chapter covers a wide-ranging selection of digital audio concepts and technologies that you're likely to find handy for personal and professional use.

DIGITAL AUDIO BASICS

▶ **What is digital audio?** **Digital audio** is music, speech, and other sounds represented in binary format for use in digital devices. Sound is produced by the vibration of matter such as a violin string or a drum head. This vibration causes pressure changes in the surrounding air, creating waves.

The smooth, continuous curve of a sound wave can be directly recorded on analog media, such as vinyl records. To digitally record sound, samples of the sound wave are collected at periodic intervals and stored as numeric data. Figure 8-1 shows how a computer digitally samples a sound wave.

FIGURE 8-1

Sampling a Sound Wave

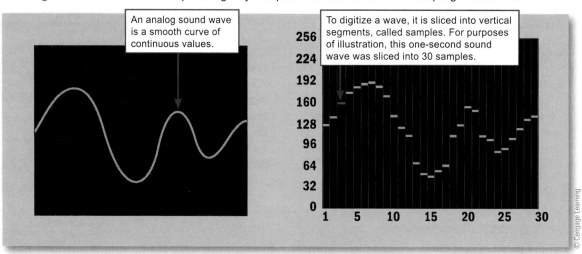

An analog sound wave is a smooth curve of continuous values.

To digitize a wave, it is sliced into vertical segments, called samples. For purposes of illustration, this one-second sound wave was sliced into 30 samples.

© Cengage Learning

Sample	Sample Height (Decimal)	Sample Height (Binary)
1	130	10000010
2	140	1000110
3	160	10100000
4	175	10101111

The height of each sample is converted into a binary number and stored. The height of sample 3 is 160 (decimal), so it is stored as its binary equivalent—10100000.

▶ Does sampling rate affect sound quality? Sampling rate

refers to the number of times per second that a sound is measured during the recording process. It is expressed in hertz (Hz). One thousand samples per second is expressed as 1,000 Hz or 1 kHz (kilohertz). Higher sampling rates increase the quality of the sound recording but require more storage space than lower sampling rates.

To conserve space, applications that do not require high-quality sound use low sampling rates. Voice-overs and narrations are often recorded with sampling rates of 11 kHz (11,000 samples per second). This rate results in lower quality sound, but the file is about one-fourth the size of a file for the same sound recorded at 44.1 kHz. Figure 8-2 illustrates how sampling rate affects sound quality.

FIGURE 8-2

A higher sampling rate produces more true-to-life sound quality. Use your interactive eBook to compare the quality of these audio clips, which were digitized at different sampling rates. You'll have to listen carefully to notice the differences.

8

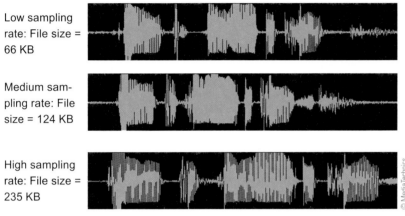

Low sampling rate: File size = 66 KB

CLICK TO START

Medium sampling rate: File size = 124 KB

CLICK TO START

High sampling rate: File size = 235 KB

CLICK TO START

© MediaTechnics

▶ How much space is required to store an audio file? When

you sample stereo CD-quality music at 44.1 kHz, one second of music requires about 0.176 MB of storage space. Forty-five minutes of music—the length of a typical album—require about 475 MB. You might wonder how audio files rack up so much space.

The height of each sound sample is saved as an 8-bit number for radio-quality recordings, or a 16-bit number for high-fidelity recordings. The audio CDs you buy at your favorite music store are recorded at a sampling rate of 44.1 kHz, which means a sample of the sound is taken 44,100 times per second.

Sixteen bits are used for each sample. To achieve stereo effects, you must take two of these 16-bit samples. Therefore, each sample requires 32 bits of storage space (Figure 8-3).

TRY IT!

Study Figure 8-3 below. How many bytes are required to record a three-minute high-fidelity stereo song?

FIGURE 8-3

To get an idea of the space required to store digital audio, just look at the number of bytes required to sample one second of music.

ILYA AKINSHIN/Shutterstock.com

01001011
01000101

01001011
01000101

One stereo
sample = 32 bits

✕

44,100
samples per
second

=

1,411,200 bits
(176,400 bytes)
per second

❱ Is there any way to shrink audio files? Regardless of sampling rate, digital audio file size can be reduced using audio compression techniques. **Audio compression** reduces the size of a sound file by removing bits that represent extraneous noise and sounds that are beyond the frequencies of normal hearing.

In addition, general-purpose compression techniques explained later in the chapter can be applied to sound files. A compressed audio file requires less storage space than an uncompressed file and can be transmitted faster over a network. Most of the music for portable media players is stored in compressed audio file formats.

❱ How does a computer produce digital audio? Your computer's sound card is responsible for transforming the bits stored in an audio file into music, sound effects, and narrations. A **sound card** is a device that contains a variety of input and output jacks, plus audio-processing circuitry.

A desktop computer's sound card is usually plugged into an expansion slot inside the system unit. Alternatively, sound card circuitry referred to as **integrated audio** can be built into a computer's system board. Portable computers rarely feature a separate sound card because manufacturers save space by using integrated audio.

A sound card is equipped to accept input from a microphone and send output to speakers or headphones. For processing digital audio files, a sound card contains two types of circuitry. A **digital-to-analog converter** (DAC) transforms digital bits into analog waves when you play an audio file. An **analog-to-digital converter** (ADC) samples live sounds and converts them into digital signals.

To play a digitally recorded sound, the bits from an audio file are transferred to your computer's sound card, where they are converted into signals that can be output to speakers or a headset. When you speak into your computer's microphone while Skyping or recording the narration for a soundtrack, the analog-to-digital converter samples the sound many times per second to create a list of digital values that represent the sound wave. Figure 8-4 illustrates the input and output from a sound card.

If you have a laptop computer, the sound card:

○ is likely to be built into the circuitry of the main board

○ is part of the microprocessor

○ is used to output integrated audio

○ prevents audio from becoming compressed and taking up too much space

FIGURE 8-4

Most sound cards have DAC and ADC circuitry to handle audio input and output.

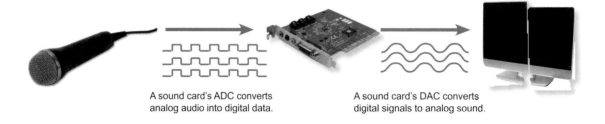

A sound card's ADC converts analog audio into digital data.

A sound card's DAC converts digital signals to analog sound.

❱ What type of hardware do I need for digital audio?

Your PC outputs sound to headphones or speakers. The speakers on your laptop computer are fine for listening to music; but when you're giving presentations or showing movies, you're likely to need external speakers to generate adequate volume.

Some speakers draw power from the computer, but they are limited in volume. Speakers that plug into a wall outlet offer much more versatile audio output, especially in situations that require high volume.

Most portable computers include a built-in microphone. If you're not picky about sound quality, you'll find the bundled microphone suitable for radio-quality voice recording and sound effects destined for Web pages or presentations. For multimedia or professional audio projects, you'll want to shop for a better-quality "mic." You can connect most standard microphones to your computer through the microphone socket or USB port.

DIGITAL AUDIO FILE FORMATS

❱ How can I recognize a digital audio file? You can recognize

a digital audio file by looking at its file extension. Digital audio is stored in a variety of file formats. The table in Figure 8-5 provides an overview of the most popular digital audio formats, including **AAC** (Advanced Audio Coding), **MP3** (also called MPEG-1 Layer 3), **Ogg Vorbis**, **WAV**, and **WMA** (Windows Media Audio).

FIGURE 8-5

Popular Digital Audio File Formats

Audio Format	File Extension	Advantages	Disadvantages
AAC	.aac, .m4p, or .mp4	Very good sound quality based on MPEG-4; compressed format; used for iTunes music	Files can be copy protected so that use is limited to approved devices
MP3 (also called MPEG-1 Layer 3)	.mp3	Good sound quality even though the file is compressed; can be streamed over the Web	Might require a standalone player or browser plug-in
Ogg Vorbis	.ogg	Free, open standard; supported by some browsers; supplies audio stream for Google's WebM format	Slow to catch on as a popular standard
WAV	.wav	Good sound quality; supported in browsers without a plug-in	Audio data is stored in raw, uncompressed format, so files are very large
WMA (Windows Media Audio)	.wma	Compressed format; very good sound quality; used on several music download sites	Files can be copy protected; requires Windows Media Player 9 or above

❱ What type of software is required to play digital audio

files? To play a digital audio file, you must use audio or media player software. Audio software might be included with your computer's operating system, packaged with your sound card, installed in a handheld device, or available on the Web. Popular audio and media players include iTunes, Windows Media Player, and open source offerings such as QuickAudio and Audacity.

Audio player software tends to support several audio file formats. In the Windows environment, for example, you can use Windows Media Player to play audio formats such as WAV, WMA, and MP3.

▶ **What about Web-based audio?** WAV, MP3, and Ogg files can be embedded into a Web page using the HTML5 <audio> tag. WAV files are supported by most Web browsers, so it is a popular audio file format. Other audio formats can be delivered over the Web, but require plug-ins.

Suppose that you want to listen to some free tracks at a jazz Web site where files are stored in Ogg format. Firefox and Chrome offer built-in support for Ogg audio. If you use Internet Explorer, however, you'll have to download and install a plug-in before you can listen to the jazz tracks.

Web-based digital audio is often delivered in streaming format to avoid lengthy delays while the entire audio file is downloaded. **Streaming audio** plays as its file is downloaded (Figure 8-6).

▶ **Can I convert audio files from one format to another?** Imagine that you find a cool MIDI ring tone on the Web, but your iPhone won't play MIDI music. You can use audio converter software to change audio files from one format to another. Your audio player software might provide tools for opening a file stored in one format and saving it in another format. If not, a quick Google search can provide links to free audio converters.

Suppose you want your iPod to play tracks from one of your audio CDs. You can use audio software to rip tracks into a format that's supported by your iPod. *Ripping* is a slang term that refers to the process of importing tracks from a CD or DVD to your computer's hard disk. The technical term for ripping is **digital audio extraction**.

Music is stored on CDs in a digital format called CDDA. The format offers high fidelity; but as with WAV files, one minute of CDDA music requires in excess of 10 MB of storage space. During the ripping process, music in CDDA format is converted into a compressed format such as MP3, AAC, or WMA to reduce file size.

Many software tools are available for converting audio files from one format to another and ripping CD tracks. One of the most versatile tools is Apple iTunes software (Figure 8-7).

FIGURE 8-6

Streaming audio provides the technology for real-time Internet radio broadcasts, podcasts, and voice chat sessions.

TRY IT!

Which digital audio format is not supported by the <audio> tag?

○ WAV

○ Ogg

○ WMA

○ MP3

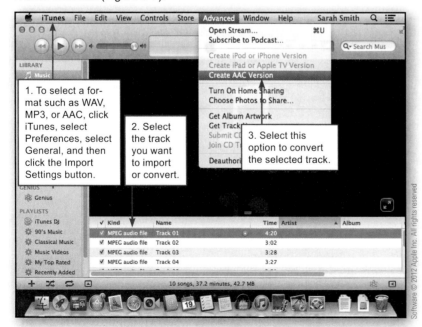

FIGURE 8-7

iTunes software makes it easy to convert audio files into other formats.

MIDI MUSIC

▶ What is MIDI music? Digital audio is a recording of real analog sound signals. In contrast, **synthesized sound** is an artificially created, or synthetic, sound. Synthesized sound can be classified as MIDI music or synthesized speech.

MIDI (Musical Instrument Digital Interface) specifies a standard way to store music data for synthesizers, electronic MIDI instruments, and computers. Unlike digital audio files, which contain digitized recordings of real performances, MIDI files contain instructions for creating individual notes that sound like various musical instruments.

MIDI music is encoded as a **MIDI sequence** and stored as a file with a .mid, .cmf, or .rol file extension. A MIDI sequence is analogous to an old player-piano roll that contains punched information indicating which musical notes to play. A MIDI sequence contains instructions specifying the pitch of a note, the point at which the note begins, the instrument that plays the note, the volume of the note, and the point at which the note ends.

▶ Is special hardware needed for MIDI music? Most computer sound cards are equipped to generate music from MIDI files, and many can capture music data from a MIDI instrument as well.

A MIDI-capable sound card contains a **wavetable** (sometimes called a patch set), which is a set of prerecorded musical instrument sounds. The sound card accesses these sounds and plays them as instructed by the MIDI file. For example, if a sound card receives a MIDI instruction for a trumpet to play middle C, it accesses the trumpet's middle C patch and routes it to the speaker until it receives a MIDI instruction to stop the note.

▶ What are the advantages and disadvantages of MIDI? MIDI files are much more compact than digital audio files. Depending on the exact piece of music, three minutes of MIDI music might require only 10 KB of storage space, whereas the same piece of music stored in a high-quality, uncompressed digital audio file might require 30 MB of storage space.

One of the big disadvantages of MIDI is that it does not produce high-quality vocals. Another disadvantage is that it does not have the full resonance of real sound. Most musicians can easily identify MIDI recordings because they simply lack the tonal qualities of symphony-quality sound. You can compare the differences by using the CLICK TO START buttons in Figure 8-8.

FIGURE 8-8

MIDI music tends not to have the full resonance of digital audio. Use your interactive eBook to listen to these two sound clips and see if you can hear a difference.

▶ CLICK TO START

▶ CLICK TO START

▶ When would I use MIDI? Classic computer games used MIDI music for their soundtracks; but today, MIDI is used less frequently for sound effects and more often as a tool for creating music. For example, several apps available for desktops, laptops, and handhelds turn the device's keyboard or touchscreen into a MIDI instrument.

Music composition software offers MIDI support, so you can use music editing tools to place notes on a screen-based music staff, then play back the composition on a MIDI keyboard. You can also input notes from a MIDI instrument directly to your computer. The input is handled by music composition software (Figure 8-9), which allows you to edit notes and combine the parts for several instruments.

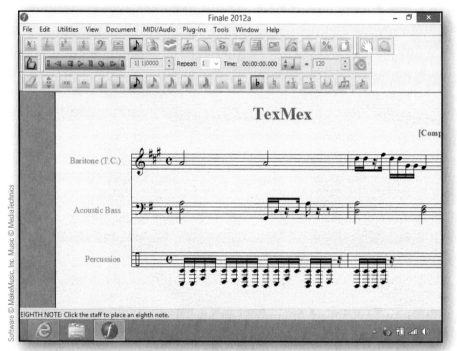

FIGURE 8-9

Music composition software provides tools for entering notes, specifying instruments, printing sheet music, and saving compositions in formats such as MIDI. ▶ You can use your interactive eBook to take a tour of music composition software and see how the TexMex music was created.

SPEECH RECOGNITION AND SYNTHESIS

▶ **What's the difference between speech synthesis and speech recognition?** **Speech synthesis** is the process by which machines, such as computers, produce sound that resembles spoken words. **Speech recognition** (or voice recognition) refers to the ability of a machine to understand spoken words.

Speech recognition is used to automate telephone-based services such as Directory Assistance and interactive voice response systems such as Google Voice Search and Siri.

The use of digital spectrographic analysis to identify human speakers is an emerging part of law enforcement and homeland security. Not only can digitized samples of voices be analyzed to confirm identity, but real-time voice print identification can match speakers with known recordings of their voices.

Speech synthesis is a key technology in mobile communication, such as accessing your e-mail using a cell phone—a speech synthesizer reads your e-mail messages to you. A speech synthesizer can also read a computer screen aloud, which unlocks access to computers and the Internet for individuals with visual disabilities.

▶ **How does speech synthesis work?** A basic sound unit, such as "reh" or "gay," is called a **phoneme**. Most speech synthesizers string together phonemes to form words. For example, the phonemes "reh" and "gay" produce the word "reggae." A basic speech synthesizer consists of **text-to-speech software**, which generates sounds that are played

TRY IT!

Which one of the following requires digital-to-analog conversion?

○ Speech synthesis

○ Speech recognition

○ Entering a Google Voice command

○ Voice dialing

through your computer's standard sound card. As an alternative, some speech synthesizers are special-purpose hardware devices.

▶ **How does speech recognition work?** On a personal computer or smartphone, a speech recognition system collects words spoken into a microphone that's connected to the sound card. The sound card's analog-to-digital converter transforms the analog sound of your voice into digital data. This data is then processed by speech recognition software.

Speech recognition software analyzes the sounds of your voice and converts them to phonemes. Next, the software analyzes the content of your speech. It compares the groups of phonemes to the words in a digital dictionary that lists phoneme combinations along with their corresponding English (or French, Spanish, and so on) words. When a match is found, the software can display the word on the screen or use it to carry out a command.

Speech recognition software can be integrated with word processing software so that you can enter text simply by speaking into a microphone. Going beyond word processing, speech recognition can be used to activate Windows controls instead of using a mouse. Most speech recognition software also works with your browser, allowing you to "voice surf" the Web (Figure 8-10).

FIGURE 8-10

The Windows Speech Recognition Wizard displays short text passages. As you read each passage, the computer listens to the way you pronounce each word and stores it in your speech profile.

You can voice surf with a handheld device, too. ▶ Find out how Google Voice Search works.

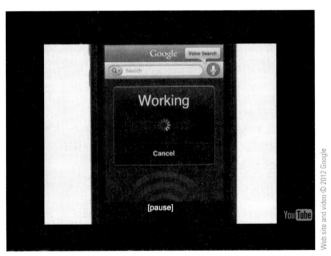

QuickCheck

1. [_____] rate refers to the number of times per second that a sound is measured during the recording process.

2. When sound card circuitry is incorporated into a computer system board, it is often referred to as [_____] audio.

3. The process of ripping tracks from an audio CD to a digital format such as MP3 is called digital audio [_____].

4. MIDI sound is generated from a(n) [_____] (or patch set), which is a set of prerecorded musical instrument sounds.

5. When a telephone-based airline voice response system asks you to say your flight number, it processes your response using speech [_____] software.

 CHECK ANSWERS

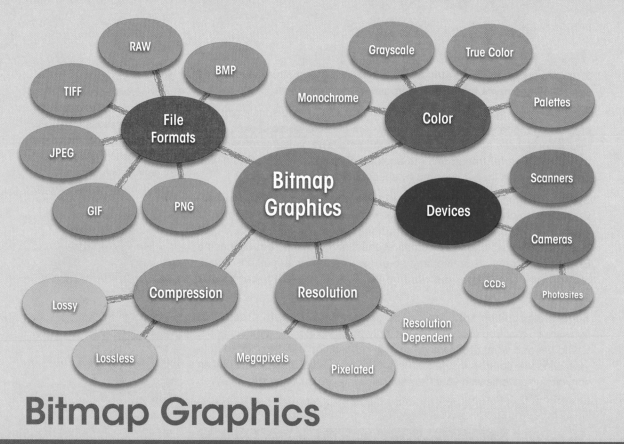

Bitmap Graphics

A DIGITAL CAMERA seems easy to use. Point it, shoot the photo, and…what next? How do you transfer digital photos from camera to computer? How can you print them? How do you get them ready to become e-mail attachments? How do you prepare them for inclusion on Web pages? To understand the wide range of possibilities for digital photos, you'll need some background information about bitmap graphics.

BITMAP BASICS

▶ **What is a bitmap graphic?** A **bitmap graphic**, also called a raster graphic or simply a bitmap, is composed of a grid of dots. The color of each dot is stored as a binary number. Think of a grid superimposed on a picture. The grid divides the picture into cells, called pixels. Each pixel is assigned a color, which is stored as a binary number. Figure 8-11 illustrates these basic characteristics of a bitmap graphic.

> **TERMINOLOGY NOTE**
>
> The term *pixel* is derived from *picture element*. It is the smallest element that can be manipulated on a computer display or printer.

FIGURE 8-11

A bitmap graphic is divided into a grid of individually colored pixels. The color number for each pixel is stored in binary format. ▶ Learn how to use Windows Paint to create bitmap graphics and see how to work pixel by pixel to edit an image.

▶ Are there different kinds of bitmap graphics? Many graphics file formats exist, and most graphics software works with several popular formats, such as BMP, RAW, TIFF, JPEG, GIF, and PNG. Selecting the best graphics file format to use depends on what you intend to do with the image. Figure 8-12 summarizes popular formats and their uses.

FIGURE 8-12

Bitmap Graphics Formats

	Format	Use
 © MediaTechnics	**BMP**, pronounced "bee-em-pee" or "bump," is the native bitmap graphics file format of the Microsoft Windows environment. Microsoft Paint, included as part of Microsoft Windows, creates BMP graphics files. The BMP format supports True Color and can be used for a wide variety of graphics applications, such as photographs, illustrations, and graphs. BMP files are often too large for e-mail attachments. BMP graphics are not supported by most browsers, so they are not used on the Web.	Graphical elements, such as buttons and other controls for graphical user interfaces
 © MediaTechnics	**RAW** image formats contain the unprocessed pixel data generated directly by a digital camera's sensor. Up to 12 bits of data can be stored for each of the red, blue, and green values for a pixel, so RAW files are very large. Cameras that offer a RAW format also supply proprietary software to convert RAW data to JPEG or TIFF.	Photographic images before they are stored in other formats
 © MediaTechnics	**TIFF** (Tagged Image File Format), or TIF, is a flexible and platform-independent graphics file format supported by most photo-editing software packages. Scanners and digital cameras commonly store bitmaps in TIFF format because it supports True Color and can be easily converted into other graphics file formats.	Desktop publishing and any projects that require high-resolution graphics; not supported by browsers
 © MediaTechnics	**JPEG** (pronounced "JAY-peg"), which stands for Joint Photographic Experts Group, is a graphics format with built-in compression that stores True Color bitmap data very efficiently in a small file. The JPEG format is popular for Web graphics and for photos attached to e-mail messages. When creating a JPEG or converting an image to JPEG format, you can control the level of compression and the resulting file size. The compression process eliminates some image data, however, so highly compressed files suffer some quality deterioration.	General use, such as desktop publishing or Web pages, where flexibility in file size is important
 JPL/NASA	**GIF** (Graphics Interchange Format), pronounced "GIF" or "JIFF," was specifically designed to create images that can be displayed on multiple platforms, such as PCs and Macs. GIF graphics are limited to 256 colors, but the format supports simple animations. Once a popular format for Web pages, GIF is being replaced by JPEG and PNG.	Web graphics and simple animations
 © MediaTechnics	**PNG** (Portable Network Graphics), pronounced "ping," is a graphics format designed to improve on the GIF format. A PNG graphic can display up to 48-bit True Color (trillions of colors). Unlike JPEG, PNG compresses bitmap files without losing any data, so compressed images retain the same high quality as the originals. PNG was developed as a public domain format without any restrictions on its use.	Web graphics and other general uses

8

▶ **Where would I encounter bitmap graphics?** Bitmap graphics are used to create realistic images, such as photographs. You might also encounter bitmaps in the form of cartoons, images that appear in computer games, the desktop images displayed by your computer or smartphone, and rendered images produced by 3-D graphics software.

When you use a digital camera or camera-enabled cell phone, your photos are stored as bitmaps. A scanner produces bitmaps. The photos you send or receive as e-mail attachments are bitmaps, as are most Web page graphics.

▶ **How do I create bitmap images?** You can create a bitmap graphic from scratch using the tools provided by graphics software—specifically a category of graphics software referred to as paint software. You might be familiar with paint software such as Adobe Photoshop, Corel Painter, and Microsoft Paint (included with Windows).

Paint software includes tools for freehand sketching, filling in shapes, adding realistic shading, and creating effects that look like oil paints, charcoal, or watercolors. If your freehand sketching talent maxes out with stick figures, you can also create bitmap graphics by using a scanner or digital camera.

SCANNERS AND CAMERAS

▶ **How do I convert a printed image into a bitmap?** When you have a printed image, such as a photograph, a page from a magazine, or a picture from a book, you can use a **scanner** to convert the printed image into a bitmap graphic.

A scanner essentially divides an image into a fine grid of cells and assigns a digital value for the color of each cell. As the scan progresses, these values are transferred to your computer's hard disk and stored as a bitmap graphics file. Scanners, such as the one pictured in Figure 8-13, are inexpensive and easy to use.

© MediaTechnics

▶ **When should I use a digital camera rather than a scanner?** Whereas a scanner is designed to digitize printed images, a **digital camera** creates a digital image of real objects. Although you could take a photo with a conventional camera, develop the film, and then digitize the photo with a scanner, it is much simpler to use a digital camera to take a photo in digital format, which you can then transfer directly to your computer or print directly to a photo printer.

TRY IT!

Which one of the following formats would not be used for bitmap graphics?

○ JPEG

○ PNG

○ TIFF

○ XLXS

FIGURE 8-13

To scan an image, turn on the scanner and start your scanner software. Place the image face down on the scanner glass, and then use the scanner software to initiate the scan. The scanned image is saved in RAM and can then be saved on your computer's hard disk.
▶ Learn the difference between scanning an image and scanning a document into an editable word processing file.

▶ **How does a digital camera capture an image without using film?** The lens of a film camera captures the light from an image onto a light-sensitive roll of film, which is developed to produce a photographic print. In a digital camera, the lens focuses light from the image onto a small image sensor called a **CCD** (charge-coupled device). A CCD contains a grid of tiny light-sensitive diodes called **photosites**.

The number of photosites depends on the size of the CCD. A one-half-inch square CCD can contain more than 500,000 photosites. Each photosite detects the brightness and color for its tiny piece of the image (Figure 8-14).

A CCD's photosites correspond to pixels. The more pixels used to capture an image, the higher its resolution, and the better the resulting picture. Cameras with larger CCDs produce higher quality images. Some cameras contain multiple CCDs, which enhance the color quality of a camera's output.

▶ **How does a digital camera store images?** Some digital cameras store photos on CDs, mini CDs, or microdrives, but the most popular digital camera storage is solid state memory cards. Like RAM, memory cards can be erased and reused. Unlike RAM, however, solid state storage holds data without consuming power, so it doesn't lose data when the camera is turned off.

▶ **How can I get images out of the camera?** Digital cameras allow you to preview images while they are still in the camera and delete those you don't want. The photos you want to keep can be transferred directly to a properly equipped printer or transferred to your computer's hard disk. Depending on your camera, this transfer can be achieved in several ways:

▶ Card readers. A card reader is a small device designed to read data contained in a solid state memory card. To transfer photo data from a memory card, remove it from the camera and insert it into the card reader, as shown in Figure 8-15.

▶ Direct cable transfer. If your computer and your camera have FireWire ports or USB ports, you can connect a cable between these two ports to transfer the photo data.

▶ Infrared port. Some cameras can beam photo data to your computer's infrared port. This method eliminates the need for a cable but is much slower than using FireWire or USB.

▶ Media transfer. If your camera stores data on CDs or similar optical media, you can simply remove the media from your camera and insert it into the appropriate drive of your computer.

▶ Docking station. Some camera manufacturers offer a camera docking station that connects to a computer by cable. A camera can be placed in the docking station to transfer photos to the computer's hard disk.

▶ E-mail. Cell phone photos can be transferred to a computer by e-mailing the photo to your e-mail account. The photo arrives as an attachment, which can be saved as a separate file.

FIGURE 8-14

A digital camera's CCD converts the image captured by the camera lens into a grid of colored pixels, which are stored as bits. ▶ Watch the video for this figure in your interactive eBook for an overview of digital camera features, file formats, and the process of transferring photos from a camera to your computer.

Courtesy of Learning Technology Services, University of Wisconsin-Stout

FIGURE 8-15

Card readers can be connected to your computer's USB port, built into a computer system unit, or built into a photo printer.

© MediaTechnics

8

▶ How do I access the memory card? Your computer treats memory cards essentially like any other storage device. After inserting a memory card, you can use File Explorer or Finder to copy photo files from the card to your computer's hard disk. Files copied in this way retain their original file names, such as *img00030*, which can be fairly cryptic.

You can also handle photo transfer with photo software, which might be supplied along with your camera, with your card reader, or by a stand-alone graphics software package, such as Adobe Photoshop. This software allows you to select a file format, specify a file name, and determine the location for each image file.

After you store your digital photos on your computer's hard disk, you can modify them, send them as e-mail attachments, print them, post them on Web pages, or archive them on a CD or DVD.

▶ What characteristics of a bitmap can I modify? Because bitmap graphics are coded as a series of bits that represent pixels, you can use graphics software to modify or edit this type of graphic by changing individual pixels.

You can modify photos to wipe out red eye or erase the "rabbit ears" that ruined an otherwise good family portrait. You can design eye-catching new pictures with images digitally cut out from several photos or scanned images. You can even retouch old photographs to eliminate creases, spots, and discoloration (Figure 8-16).

Whether you acquire an image from a digital camera or a scanner, bitmap graphics tend to require quite a bit of storage space. Although a large graphics file might provide the necessary data for a high-quality printout, these files take up space on your hard disk and can require lengthy transmission times that clog up mailboxes and make Web pages seem sluggish.

The size of the file that holds a bitmap depends on its resolution and color depth. Read on to see how these factors affect file size and how you can alter them to create smaller graphics files, suitable for e-mail attachments and Web pages.

IMAGE RESOLUTION

▶ How does resolution pertain to bitmap graphics? The dimensions of the grid that forms a bitmap graphic are referred to as its resolution. The resolution of a graphic is usually expressed as the number of horizontal and vertical pixels it contains. For example, a small graphic for a Web page might have a resolution of 150 x 100 pixels—150 pixels across and 100 pixels high.

▶ How does resolution relate to image quality? High-resolution graphics contain more data than low-resolution graphics. With more data, it is possible to display and print high-quality images that are sharper and clearer than images produced using less data. For example, a photograph taken with an inexpensive camera might produce a graphic with a resolution of 1600 x 1200, but a more expensive camera with 3888 x 2592 resolution contains more pixels and produces a higher-quality image.

Camera manufacturers sometimes express the resolution of digital cameras as megapixels. A **megapixel** is 1 million pixels. A camera with a resolution of 1600 x 1200 has the capability of producing photos containing 1.9 megapixels (1600 multiplied by 1200). A camera with 3888 x 2592 resolution is technically 10.1 megapixels, but might be rounded off and called a 10 megapixel camera by its manufacturer.

Which one of the following is a characteristic of low-quality digital images?

○ They are taken with a camera that has a large CCD

○ They contain a low number of pixels

○ They have to be edited in Photoshop

○ Their resolution is measured in megapixels

FIGURE 8-16

Bitmap graphics can be easily modified. Many graphics software products include wizards that help you retouch photographs.

Before

After

▶ How does resolution relate to the file size of a graphic?

Each pixel in a bitmap graphic is stored as one or more bits. The more pixels in a bitmap, the more bits needed to store the file.

▶ How does resolution relate to the physical size of an image?

A bitmap graphic is simply a collection of data. Unlike a printed photograph, a bitmap has no fixed physical size. The size at which a bitmap is displayed or printed depends on the density as well as the resolution (dimensions) of the image grid.

Imagine that each bitmap image and its grid come on a surface that you can stretch or shrink. As you stretch the surface, the grid maintains the same number of horizontal and vertical cells, but each cell becomes larger and the grid becomes less dense. As you shrink the surface, the grid becomes smaller and more dense. The graphic retains the same resolution no matter how much you stretch or shrink the graphic's physical size, as shown in Figure 8-17.

Reduced size
remains at
24 x 24 resolution

Original graphic at
24 x 24 resolution

Enlarged graphic still
has 24 x 24 resolution

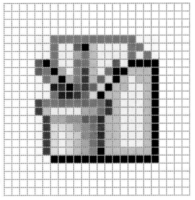

FIGURE 8-17

When a bitmap graphic is enlarged or reduced in size, it still retains its original resolution—24 x 24.

This concept of stretching and shrinking without changing resolution is important for understanding what happens when bitmaps are displayed and printed. The denser the grid, the smaller the image will appear. The density of an image grid can be expressed as dots per inch (dpi) for a printer or scanner, or as pixels per inch (ppi) on a display device.

▶ How do I specify the size of a printed image?

Most graphics software allows you to specify the size at which an image is printed without changing the resolution of the bitmap graphic. You'll get an acceptable image if you print 400 dpi or more. So, if a photo's resolution is 1600 x 800 pixels, it will look fine as a 4" x 2" print. As you enlarge the image beyond this size, it will start to appear somewhat fuzzy because the pixels will begin to become visible.

As a general rule, when you incorporate an image in a desktop-published document, or when you print photographs, you should work with high-resolution bitmaps so that you can produce high-quality output. To capture high-resolution bitmaps, use the highest resolution provided by your digital camera. When scanning an image, choose a dpi setting on your scanner that is at least as high as the dpi for the printout.

▶ How does a bitmap's resolution relate to what I see on the screen?

In Chapter 2, you learned that you can set your computer display to a particular resolution, such as 1024 x 768. When you display a bitmap graphic on the screen, each pixel of the graphic usually corresponds to one pixel on the screen. If the resolution of your graphic is 1024 x 768 and your display is set at 1024 x 768 resolution, the image

TRY IT!

Suppose you want to display a photo so it fills your screen, and the screen resolution is set at 1280 x 720. Which of the following produces the highest quality image?

○ A 1280 x 720 graphic

○ A 1.9 megapixel graphic

○ A bitmap with 100 x 150 resolution

○ A WUXGA bitmap

appears to fill the screen. If you view a 4.0 megapixel image on the same display device, the image is larger than the screen, and you have to scroll or change the zoom level to view it (Figure 8-18).

▶ Can I change a graphic's file size? The resolution and corresponding file size of a graphic might not be right for your needs. For example, if you take a photo with a 10.0 megapixel camera, it is unsuitable for a Web page. Not only would it take a long time to download, but it would be larger than most screens.

A 10.0 megapixel graphic is also not suitable for an e-mail attachment. Uploading and downloading such a large file—especially over a dial-up connection—would take much too long. Reducing the resolution of a bitmap can reduce its file size and on-screen display size. Most experts recommend that Web graphics not exceed 100 KB and that e-mail attachments not exceed 1 MB.

You can reduce the size of a bitmap by cropping it. **Cropping** refers to the process of selecting part of an image—just like cutting out a section of a photograph.

▶ What happens if I try to change the overall resolution? Bitmap graphics are **resolution dependent**, which means that the quality of the image depends on its resolution. If you reduce the overall resolution of an image, the computer eliminates pixels, which reduces the size of the image grid.

Suppose you reduce the resolution from 2160 x 1440 (3.1 megapixels) to 1080 x 720 (0.8 megapixels). The image grid becomes a quarter of its original size, and the file size is reduced by a similar amount. However, the computer threw away data with the pixels, which can reduce image quality.

If you attempt to enlarge a bitmap by increasing its resolution, your computer must somehow add pixels because no additional picture data exists. But what colors should these additional pixels become? Most graphics software uses a process called **pixel interpolation** to create new pixels by averaging the colors of nearby pixels.

For some graphics, pixel interpolation results in an image that appears very similar to the original. Other images—particularly those with strong curved or diagonal lines—develop an undesirable **pixelated**, or "bitmappy," jagged appearance (Figure 8-19).

FIGURE 8-18

When viewing an image larger than the screen, you must scroll to see all parts of the image or set the zoom level of your graphics software to less than 100%. You should understand, however, that changing the zoom level stretches or shrinks only the size of the image grid. It has no effect on the printed size of a graphic or the graphic's file size.

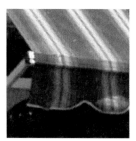

The figure above has a resolution of 130 x 130. The figure at right was enlarged to a resolution of 260 x 260, but it has a rough, pixelated appearance.

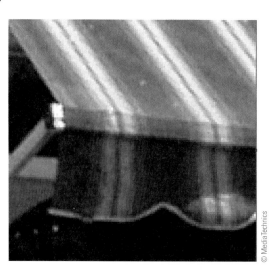

FIGURE 8-19

When you increase the resolution of an existing graphic, the file size increases, but the quality might deteriorate.

COLOR DEPTH AND PALETTES

▶ **What is color depth?** As you learned in Chapter 2, color depth is the number of colors available for use in an image. As the number of colors increases, image quality improves, but file size also increases. You can limit color depth to decrease the file size required for a graphic. To find out how this works, first take a look at the storage requirements for various color depths.

▶ **How does color depth relate to file size?** To answer this question, consider a simple monochrome display device. Each screen pixel can be either "on" or "off." A **monochrome bitmap** is displayed by manipulating the pattern of "off" and "on" pixels displayed on the screen. To store the data for a monochrome bitmap, an "on" pixel is represented by a 1 bit. An "off" pixel is represented by a 0 bit. Each row of the bitmap grid is stored as a series of 0s and 1s, as shown in Figure 8-20.

FIGURE 8-20

Each pixel in a monochrome bitmap graphic is stored as a bit.

1. This image originated as a black-and-white silhouette.

2. The computer divides the picture into a matrix.

3. If a cell is white, it is coded as a 1. If a cell is black, it is coded as a 0.

© MediaTechnics

Monochrome bitmaps require very little storage space. Suppose you create a full-screen monochrome bitmap with your screen resolution set to 1024 x 768. Your screen displays 786,432 pixels (that's 1,024 multiplied by 768). Each pixel is set to display a black dot or a white dot. When you store the graphic, each dot requires only one bit. Therefore, the number of bits required to represent a full-screen picture is the same as the number of pixels on the screen.

At a resolution of 1024 x 768, a full-screen graphic requires 786,432 bits of storage space. The number of bytes required to store the image is 786,432 divided by 8 (remember that there are eight bits in a byte). Your full-screen monochrome bitmap would, therefore, require only 98,304 bytes of storage space.

TRY IT!

What is the resolution of the cat's ear shown in image number 2 of Figure 8-20?

○ 13 x 16

○ 1 x 0

○ 1 megapixel

○ 208 megapixels

▶ How about black and white images? What we call "black and white" photos are actually grayscale images, which are formed from shades of gray (Figure 8-21).

FIGURE 8-21

A "black and white" photograph is depicted in shades of gray.

Rather than each pixel simply being designated as black or white, in a grayscale image, each pixel is represented by an intensity of light, ranging from bright to dark.

Grayscale images are commonly stored using eight bits per pixel, in which case a pixel can be one of 256 shades of gray. These shades of gray are collectively referred to as a **grayscale palette** (Figure 8-22).

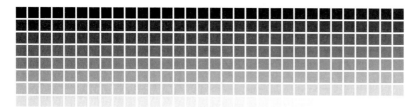

FIGURE 8-22

A grayscale palette includes many intensities or "shades" of gray.

▶ What is a color palette? Just as artists use a kidney-shaped palette to hold the selection of colors for a painting, digital artists can use a digital **color palette** to define a selection of colors for an on-screen image.

In addition to grayscale palettes, digital artists can use full palettes containing all possible colors, or limited palettes containing a subset of colors. A **system palette** is the collection of colors used for interface elements in an operating system, such as Windows 8. A **Web palette** is a collection of colors that display without distortion even on legacy screens that display only 256 colors. Today, however, even mobile devices have sophisticated displays, so Web-safe palettes and several other limited palettes have fallen into disuse.

TRY IT!

How many bits are used to represent each pixel in the photo shown in Figure 8-21?

○ 2

○ 8

○ 16

○ 256

▶ **How do computers handle color?** Today's color display devices represent color using the **RGB color model**. The color displayed for a pixel is based on the intensity of red, green, and blue signals received by the screen's color elements.

Each red, green, and blue signal is assigned a value ranging from 0 to 255: 0 represents the absence of color, and 255 represents the highest intensity level for that color. A pixel appears white if the red, green, and blue signals are set to maximum intensity. If red, green, and blue signals are equal but at a lower intensity, the pixel displays a shade of gray. A pixel appears purple if it receives red and blue signals (Figure 8-23).

FIGURE 8-23

Look at the center where the circles intersect to see the color that is generated.

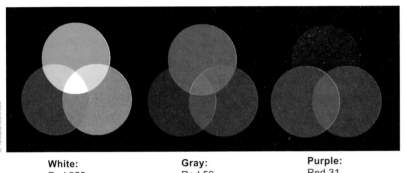

© MediaTechnics

White:
Red 255
Blue 255
Green 255

Gray:
Red 50
Blue 50
Green 50

Purple:
Red 31
Blue 255
Green 35

▶ **How does color affect image file size?** With three color signals that are each able to produce 256 values, the number of possible colors is 16.7 million (256 x 256 x 256). A graphic that uses this full range of colors is referred to as a **True Color bitmap** or a 24-bit bitmap.

You might be able to guess where the term *24-bit* comes from. The highest value for each component of the RGB signal is 255, which is 11111111 in binary. The binary representation for the red signal, for example, requires 8 bits. So, if the computer requires 8 bits for blue, 8 bits for green, and 8 bits for red, that's a total of 24 bits for each pixel.

Using 24 bits for every pixel, True Color bitmaps produce very large files. For example, a 3 megapixel True Color bitmap requires a 9 MB file! These files contain high-quality images, but they are too large to efficiently send as e-mail attachments or post on Facebook.

You might occasionally encounter a 32-bit bitmap. Just like a 24-bit bitmap, it displays 16.7 million colors. The extra bits are used to define special effects, such as the amount of transparency, for a pixel. These files are even larger than those containing 24-bit bitmaps. A 3 megapixel 32-bit bitmap would be about 10 MB.

▶ **How are colors specified in HTML?** When you examine the <color> tags in an HTML source document, you'll notice that some colors have names and others are specified by a hexadecimal (base 16) triplet such as #FFC057.

Each pair of digits refers to the intensity of the red, blue, or green signal. Therefore, #FFC057 would be Red FF (255 decimal), Blue C0 (192 decimal), and Green 57 (87 decimal). You can find lists of colors and their hexadecimal triplets on the Web.

TRY IT!

Wait! Each RGB value can have 256 different values, but 11111111 is only 255. What's the story?

○ 11111111 is really 256

○ The values are numbered from 0–255, so counting 0 there are 256

○ The values are in base 16, so there are really 256 of them

○ There are three pixels, so 11111111 plus 11111111 plus 11111111 is 256

IMAGE COMPRESSION

▶ What is image compression? **Image compression** refers to any technique that recodes the data in an image file so that it contains fewer bits. Smaller files produced as a result of image compression require less storage space and can be transmitted more rapidly than the larger, original files. Images can be compressed using lossless or lossy compression.

▶ What is the difference between lossless and lossy compression? **Lossless compression** provides the means to compress a file and then reconstitute all the data into its original state. TIFF, PNG, and GIF graphics formats offer lossless compression.

In contrast, **lossy compression** throws away some of the original data during the compression process. In theory, the human eye won't miss the lost information. JPEG files are compressed using lossy compression. Most lossy compression techniques have adjustable compression levels so that you can decide how much data you can afford to lose.

▶ How does lossless compression shrink a file without throwing away data? Various techniques exist for lossless image compression. As a simple example, consider a type of lossless compression called run-length encoding. **Run-length encoding** (RLE) replaces a series of similarly colored pixels with a binary code that indicates the number of pixels and their colors.

Suppose that a section of a picture has 167 consecutive white pixels, and each pixel is described by one byte of data, as in a 256-color bitmap image. RLE compresses this series of 167 bytes into as few as two bytes, as shown in Figure 8-24.

FIGURE 8-24

In an uncompressed file, each pixel of a 256-color bitmap requires one byte to indicate its color. For example, a white pixel might be coded 11111111. Run-length encoding compresses graphical data by recoding like-colored pixels when they appear in a series.

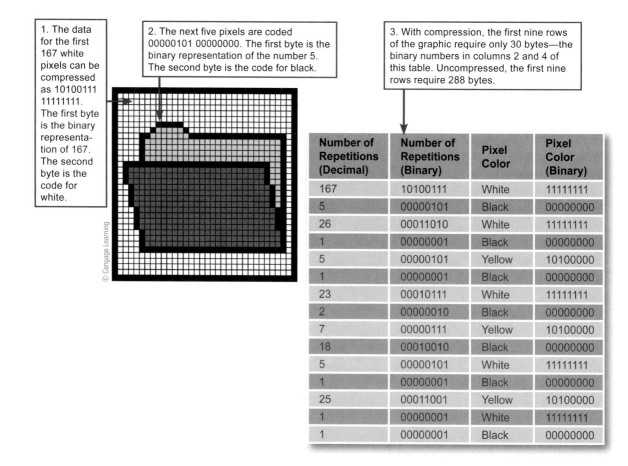

1. The data for the first 167 white pixels can be compressed as 10100111 11111111. The first byte is the binary representation of 167. The second byte is the code for white.

2. The next five pixels are coded 00000101 00000000. The first byte is the binary representation of the number 5. The second byte is the code for black.

3. With compression, the first nine rows of the graphic require only 30 bytes—the binary numbers in columns 2 and 4 of this table. Uncompressed, the first nine rows require 288 bytes.

© Cengage Learning

Number of Repetitions (Decimal)	Number of Repetitions (Binary)	Pixel Color	Pixel Color (Binary)
167	10100111	White	11111111
5	00000101	Black	00000000
26	00011010	White	11111111
1	00000001	Black	00000000
5	00000101	Yellow	10100000
1	00000001	Black	00000000
23	00010111	White	11111111
2	00000010	Black	00000000
7	00000111	Yellow	10100000
18	00010010	Black	00000000
5	00000101	White	11111111
1	00000001	Black	00000000
25	00011001	Yellow	10100000
1	00000001	White	11111111
1	00000001	Black	00000000

▶ What happens during lossy compression? Lossy compression techniques discard some data from an image to shrink its file size. JPEG is a lossy version of run-length encoding that can be applied to images, such as photographs, that don't have large areas of solid color.

A True Color photograph might not have any adjoining pixels of the same color. Applying RLE to such a photo would not result in any compression whatsoever. JPEG preprocesses an image by tweaking the colors in adjoining pixels so that they are the same color whenever possible. After this preprocessing is complete, run-length encoding can be applied with more success.

For many images, lossy compression results in only a minor reduction in the sharpness of the image. The reduction in quality can be unnoticeable in many circumstances. Figure 8-25 illustrates a section of a noncompressed image and a section of that same image after JPEG compression has been applied. Can you see any difference?

FIGURE 8-25

JPEG compression can slightly adjust the colors of adjacent pixels to make them the same. These like-colored pixels can then be compressed with RLE.

Non-compressed JPEG image

JPEG image with 35% compression

▶ How do I compress image files? Some graphics file formats automatically compress file data. You can also compress files using a general-purpose file compression utility.

GIF, JPEG, PNG, and TIFF file formats include compression options. Software that works with these file formats might allow you to select compression levels before saving a graphics file. For example, when saving an image in JPEG format, you might be given the option of selecting compression settings from 1 (worst quality) to 10 (best quality) as shown in Figure 8-26.

FIGURE 8-26

When saving an image in JPEG format, you can specify the level of compression.

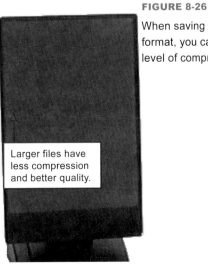

Larger files have less compression and better quality.

▶ What about file formats without compression options?

Formats such as BMP and RAW do not include compression options. If you want to compress these types of image files, you can do so manually using a file compression utility.

A **file compression utility** uses lossless compression to shrink file size. You can compress any kind of file, including programs and data files, graphics, and document files.

BMP file sizes might shrink by as much as 70% when compressed. Image files stored in formats such as PNG, GIF, and JPEG hardly shrink at all when you use compression utilities because they are already stored in a compressed format.

Compressing files is sometimes called zipping. The compression utilities supplied with Windows and Mac OS produce compressed folders. These folders can contain a single file or a combination of several files and folders.

For example, suppose you want to send two files and a folder to your boss. The original files are called *Rowing book.indd* and *Rowing book3.pdf*. The folder is called *Rowing Photos*. You can zip the folder and files into a single compressed folder called *Rowing Book First Draft* (Figure 8-27).

Which file is likely to shrink the most when you zip it?

○ Skateboard.jpg

○ Motocross.bmp

○ ATV.png

○ Crew.gif

FIGURE 8-27

File compression with Finder on a Mac (top) and File Manager on Windows (below) zips one or more files into a new compressed folder with a .zip extension. ▶ Watch how to zip multiple files into a single compressed folder.

▶ **How do I access the files in a compressed folder?** Folders that display a zipper contain compressed files and should be unzipped before any of the files are opened. Reversing the compression process is called unzipping or extracting.

On a Mac, simply double-clicking a zipped folder extracts its contents to a new folder. In Windows, you can click the folder and use the Compressed Folder Tools, or you can right-click the zipped folder and select Extract All (Figure 8-28).

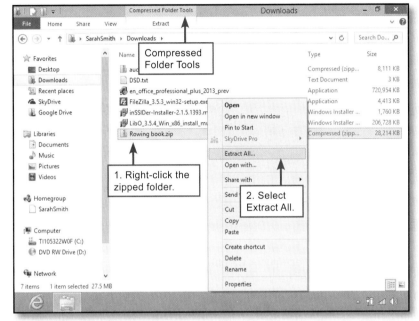

FIGURE 8-28

With Windows, use the Compressed Folder Tools or Extract All option to unzip a compressed folder.

▶ Learn how to extract files from a zipped folder.

Compressed folder icons feature a zipper. The folder name has a .zip extension, which is visible only if you have file extensions turned on in Windows.

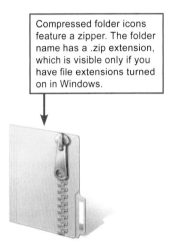

8

QuickCheck

1. A digital camera captures images on the photosites of a(n) [_____] . (Hint: Use the acronym.)

2. A characteristic of bitmap graphics is that they are resolution [_____] , so that reducing the resolution also reduces the image quality.

3. Graphics stored in True Color format require [_____] bits for each pixel.

4. The most popular True Color formats for Web graphics include [_____] and JPEG. (Hint: Use the acronym.)

5. Unlike [_____] compression, [_____] compression shrinks a file without throwing away any data.

 CHECK ANSWERS

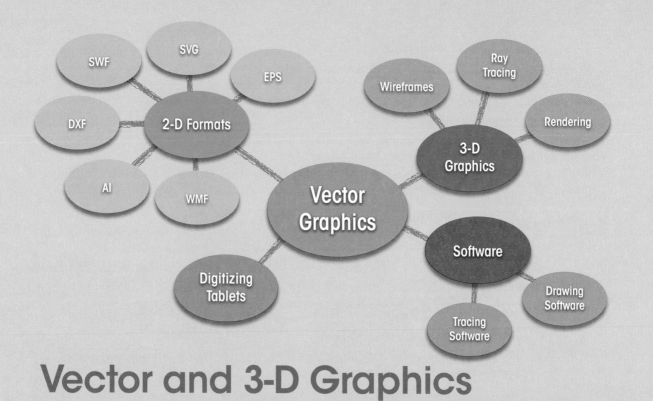

Vector and 3-D Graphics

SECTION **C**

IF YOU'VE PLAYED any computer games recently or watched an animated movie, you've seen the product of computer-generated animated graphics. This section begins with two-dimensional vector graphics. You'll find out how they differ from bitmaps and why you might want to use them. After covering the basics for two-dimensional graphics, the section progresses to static 3-D graphics and then to animated 3-D graphics.

VECTOR GRAPHICS BASICS

▶ **What is a vector graphic?** Unlike a bitmap graphic created by dividing an image into a grid of pixels, a **vector graphic** consists of a set of instructions for re-creating a picture. Instead of storing the color value for each pixel, a vector graphics file contains instructions the computer needs to create the shape, size, position, and color for each object in an image.

These instructions are similar to those a drafting teacher might give students: "Draw a 2-inch (or 112-pixel) circle. Locate this circle 1 inch down and 2 inches in from the right edge of the work area. Fill the circle with yellow."

▶ **How can I identify vector graphics?** It can be difficult to accurately identify a vector graphic just by looking at an on-screen image. Some have a flat, cartoon-like quality (Figure 8-29), but others can look fairly realistic. For a more definitive identification, you should check the file extension. Vector graphics files have file extensions such as .wmf, .ai, .dxf, .eps, .swf, and .svg.

FIGURE 8-29

The parts of a vector graphic are created as separate objects. This image was created with a series of roughly rectangular objects for the stones and a circular object for the sun. The objects are layered and can be manipulated individually. This characteristic of vector graphics gives artists flexibility in arranging and editing image elements.

444

▶ **How do vector graphics compare with bitmap graphics?** Vector graphics are suitable for most line art, logos, simple illustrations, and diagrams that might be displayed and printed at various sizes. You should take the following distinctions into account when deciding which type of graphic to use for a specific project.

▶ **Vector graphics resize better than bitmaps.** When you change the size of a vector graphic, the objects change proportionally and maintain their smooth edges. In contrast, bitmap graphics might appear to have jagged edges after they are enlarged, as shown in Figure 8-30.

FIGURE 8-30

Unlike bitmaps, vector graphics can be resized without becoming pixelated and blurry.

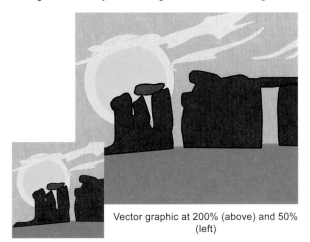

Vector graphic at 200% (above) and 50% (left)

Bitmap graphic at 200% (above) and 50% (right)

▶ **Vector graphics usually require less storage space than bitmaps.** The storage space required for a vector graphic reflects the complexity of the image. Each instruction requires storage space; so the more lines, shapes, and fill patterns in the graphic, the more storage space it requires. The Stonehenge vector graphic used as an example in this chapter requires less than 4 KB of storage space. A True Color photograph of the same image requires 1,109 KB.

▶ **Vector graphics are not usually as realistic as bitmap images.** Many 2-D vector images have a cartoon-like appearance instead of the realistic appearance you expect from a photograph. This cartoon-like characteristic of vector images results from the use of objects filled with blocks of color.

▶ **It is easier to edit an object in a vector graphic than an object in a bitmap graphic.** In some ways, a vector graphic is like a collage of objects. Each object can be layered over other objects, but moved and edited independently. You can individually stretch, shrink, distort, color, move, or delete any object in a vector graphic. Figure 8-31 illustrates the difference between vector and bitmap graphics when you try to edit out parts of the Stonehenge image.

FIGURE 8-31

Vector graphic objects are layered, so it is easy to move and delete objects without disrupting the rest of the image. In contrast, deleting a shape from a bitmap image leaves a hole because the image is only one layer of pixels.

Stones in this vector image are a separate layer that can easily be removed.

A bitmap graphic is not layered, so removing the stones leaves a hole.

▶ **What tools do I need to create vector graphics?** Neither scanners nor digital cameras produce vector graphics. Architects and engineers might use a digitizing tablet to turn a paper-based line drawing into a vector graphic. A **digitizing tablet** (sometimes called a 2-D digitizer) is a device that provides a flat surface for a paper-based drawing and a pen or mouse-like puck that you can use to click the endpoints of each line on the drawing. The endpoints are converted into vectors and stored.

Usually, vector graphics are created from scratch with vector graphics software, referred to as drawing software. Popular drawing software includes Adobe Illustrator, Corel DESIGNER, LibreOffice Draw, and open source Inkscape. Drawing software is sometimes packaged separately from the paint software used to produce bitmap graphics. In other cases, it is included with bitmap software as a graphics software suite.

Vector graphics software provides an array of drawing tools that you can use to create objects, position them, and fill them with colors or patterns. For example, you can use the filled circle tool to draw a circle filled with a solid color. You can create an irregular shape by connecting points to outline the shape. Figure 8-32 illustrates how to use drawing tools to create a vector graphic.

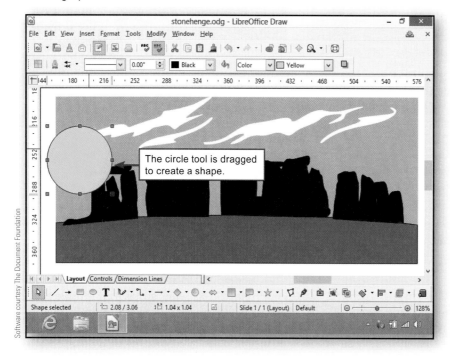

Software courtesy The Document Foundation

FIGURE 8-32

To draw a circle, select the filled circle tool, and then drag the mouse pointer to indicate the circle's location and size. A color palette allows you to select the circle color. After you create the circle object, you can move it and change its size or color. You can also create irregular shapes for objects, such as clouds, by connecting short line segments. ▶ Learn the basics of drawing vector images by accessing this figure in your interactive eBook.

The clouds are created as a series of short line segments and filled with color.

The stones are created as a series of short line segments and filled with black.

The sun is two circles, each filled with a slightly different shade of yellow.

Vector graphics software helps you easily edit individual objects within a graphic by changing their sizes, shapes, positions, or colors. For example, the data for creating a circle for the sun is recorded as an instruction, such as CIRCLE 40 Y 200 150, which means create a circle with a 40-pixel radius, color it yellow, and place the center of the circle 200 pixels from the left of the screen and 150 pixels from the top of the screen.

If you move the circle to the right side of the image, the instruction that the computer stores for the circle changes to something like CIRCLE 40 Y 500 150, which reflects its new position at 500 pixels from the left instead of 200.

When filling a shape with color, your graphics software might provide tools for creating gradients. A **gradient** is a smooth blending of shades from one color to another or from light to dark. Gradients, as shown in Figure 8-33, can be used to create shading and three-dimensional effects.

Some vector graphics software provides tools that apply bitmapped textures to vector graphics objects, giving them a more realistic appearance. For example, you can create a vector drawing of a house, and then apply a brick-like texture derived from a bitmap photograph of real bricks. A graphic that contains both bitmap and vector data is called a **metafile**.

VECTOR-TO-BITMAP CONVERSION

❱ Is it possible to convert a vector graphic into a bitmap?

A vector graphic can be converted quite easily into a bitmap graphic through a process called rasterizing. **Rasterization** works by superimposing a grid over a vector image and determining the color for each pixel. This process can be carried out by graphics software, which allows you to specify the output size for the final bitmap image.

On a PC, you can rasterize a vector graphic by using the Print Screen key to take a screenshot of a vector image. On a Mac, the Command-Shift-3 key combination takes a screenshot. It is important to rasterize images at the size you ultimately need. If you rasterize a vector image at a small size and then try to enlarge the resulting bitmap image, you will likely get a poor-quality pixelated image, such as the one in Figure 8-34.

After a vector graphic is converted to a bitmap, the resulting graphic no longer has the qualities of a vector graphic. For example, if you convert the Stonehenge vector graphic into a bitmap, the sun is no longer an object that you can easily move or assign a different color.

❱ How about converting a bitmap graphic into a vector graphic? Converting a bitmap graphic into a vector graphic is more difficult than converting from a vector to a bitmap. To change a bitmap graphic into a vector graphic, you must use tracing software. **Tracing software** locates the edges of objects in a bitmap image and converts the resulting shapes into vector graphics objects.

Tracing software works best on simple images and line drawings. It does not usually produce acceptable results when used on complex, detailed photos. Tracing capabilities are included in some general-purpose graphics software, but standalone tracing software offers more flexibility and usually produces better results.

FIGURE 8-33

Gradients can create the illusion of three dimensions, such as making this shape appear to be a tube.

8

FIGURE 8-34

When vector images are rasterized, they become bitmaps and can't be enlarged without becoming pixelated.

© MediaTechnics

VECTOR GRAPHICS ON THE WEB

▶ **Do vector graphics work on the Web?** Web browsers were originally designed to support a limited number of graphics formats—GIF and JPEG—and these formats were exclusively bitmaps. Today, vector graphics such as **SVG** (Scalable Vector Graphics) and **Flash** can also be used on the Web (Figure 8-35).

FIGURE 8-35

The two most pervasive vector formats on the Web are SVG and Flash.

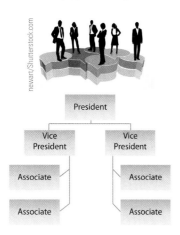

SVG is supported by most modern browsers without requiring a plug-in. It supports gradients, drop shadows, multiple levels of transparency, and animation effects, along with portability to other platforms, such as handheld computers and cellular phones.

Adobe's Flash software creates vector graphics that are stored in files with .swf extensions. Flash graphics can be static or animated. Flash was once the dominant technology for vector graphics and animation, but its use has declined since Apple announced that Flash would not be supported on iOS devices.

▶ **What are the advantages of using vector graphics on the Web?** Vector graphics have several advantages:

▶ **Consistent quality.** On Web pages, vector graphics appear with the same consistent quality on all computer screens. This capability makes it possible for browsers to adjust the size of an image on the fly to fit correctly on a screen, regardless of its size or resolution.

▶ **Searchable.** Text contained in a vector image is stored as actual text, not just a series of colored dots. This text can be indexed by search engines so that it can be included in keyword searches.

▶ **Compact file size.** A third advantage of vector graphics on the Web is their compact file sizes. A fairly complex graphic can be stored in a file that is under 30 KB—that's kilobytes, not megabytes. These files require little storage space and can be transmitted swiftly from a Web server to your browser.

▶ **What about animated Web graphics?** For many years, Adobe Flash technology was the gold standard for Web-based animation, as well as the tool of choice for animated television cartoons and commercials. Sophisticated Flash animations can be scripted to allow user interactions, such as controlling game characters or exploring educational diagrams.

An alternative to Flash gained popularity with the introduction of HTML5 and its <canvas> tag. The **HTML5 canvas** is a container for graphics that are drawn and animated using a scripting language such as JavaScript. Elements on the canvas are drawn with vector-like instructions. Once drawn, however, graphical elements on the canvas become bitmaps, though they can be manipulated with JavaScript.

TRY IT!

What technology seems to be having an effect on the tools and techniques used for Web graphics?

○ Microsoft Office

○ Flash

○ HTML5

○ GIF

3-D GRAPHICS

▶ **How do vector graphics relate to 3-D graphics?** Like vector graphics, **3-D graphics** are stored as a set of instructions. For a 3-D graphic, however, the instructions contain the locations and lengths of lines that form a wireframe for a three-dimensional object.

A **wireframe** acts in much the same way as the framework of a pop-up tent. Just as you would construct the framework for the tent and then cover it with a nylon tent cover, a 3-D wireframe can be covered with surface texture and color to create a graphic of a 3-D object.

The process of covering a wireframe with surface color and texture is called **rendering**. The rendering process, shown in Figure 8-36, outputs a bitmap image.

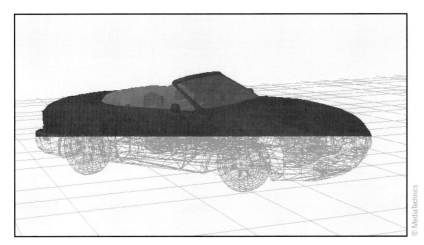

FIGURE 8-36

3-D graphics are based on a wireframe, which can be rendered into a bitmap image that looks three-dimensional.

For added realism, the rendering process can take into account the way that light shines on surfaces and creates shadows. The technique for adding light and shadows to a 3-D image is called **ray tracing**.

Before an image is rendered, the artist selects a location for one or more light sources. The computer applies a complex mathematical algorithm to determine how the light source affects the color of each pixel in the final rendered image. Figure 8-37 shows the image from the previous figure rendered with an additional light source and ray tracing.

FIGURE 8-37

Ray tracing adds realism to 3-D graphics by adding highlights and shadows that are produced by a light source.

8

▶ What tools do I need to create 3-D graphics? 3-D graphics software runs on most personal computers, although some architects, designers, special effects artists, and engineers prefer to use high-end workstations. A fast processor, lots of RAM, and a fast graphics card with its own video RAM all speed up the rendering process.

To create 3-D graphics, you need 3-D graphics software, such as Autodesk AutoCAD or Caligari trueSpace. This software has tools for drawing a wireframe and viewing it from any angle. It provides rendering and ray tracing tools, along with an assortment of surface textures that you can apply to individual objects. Figure 8-38 takes you on a tour of a popular 3-D graphics software package.

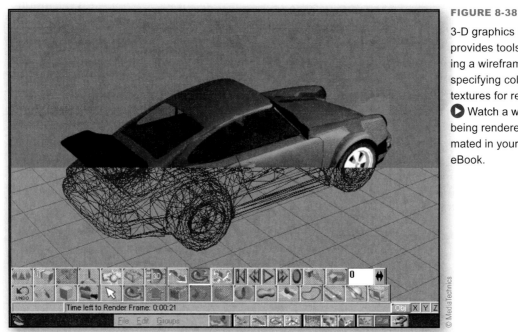

FIGURE 8-38

3-D graphics software provides tools for drawing a wireframe and then specifying colors and textures for rendering. ▶ Watch a wireframe being rendered and animated in your interactive eBook.

▶ Is it possible to animate 3-D graphics? 3-D graphics can be animated to produce special effects for movies or to create interactive, animated characters and environments for 3-D computer games. Animated special effects, such as massive battle scenes, are created by rendering a sequence of bitmaps, in which one or more objects are moved or otherwise changed between each rendering.

In traditional hand-drawn animation, a chief artist draws the keyframes, and then a team of assistants creates each of the in-between images—24 of these images for each second of animation. For 3-D computer animation, the computer creates the in-between images by moving the object and rendering each necessary image. All the images are then combined into a single file, creating essentially a digital movie.

Graphics design companies such as Pixar Animation Studios and DreamWorks Studios use 3-D animation techniques to produce animated feature films as well as special effects. The first full-length animated 3-D movie was *Toy Story*, released in 1995 by Walt Disney Studios and Pixar. Digitally animated films, such as *Avatar* and *Monsters University*, illustrate the growing sophistication of 3-D animation.

▶ **Do game and movie animation require similar tools and techniques?** An important characteristic of special effects and animated films is that rendering can be accomplished during the production phase of the movie and incorporated into the final footage. In contrast, 3-D computer game animation happens in real time. Each frame that makes the image seem to move must be rendered while you are playing the game—a process that requires an incredible amount of computer power (Figure 8-39).

To give you a handle on the immensity of the processing power required to render the real-time images for computer games, consider a classic game like *Doom* displayed on a screen that's set at 1024 x 768 resolution. At this resolution, the screen contains 786,432 pixels (1,024 multiplied by 768). If the game is presented in 32-bit color, each frame of the animation requires 25,165,824 bits (multiply 786,432 times 32).

Computer game designers believe that on-screen animation looks smoothest at 60 frames per second, which means your computer must handle 1,509,949,440— that's more than 1 billion—bits of information every second just to display the 3-D image on the screen. In addition, the computer must process even more data to keep track of the movements of each player.

To handle all the data required for game play, your computer's main processor gets help from a graphics processor located on your computer's graphics card. These graphics processors vary in their capabilities. For the fastest graphics capability, some computers can accept two graphics cards that work in tandem as 3-D accelerators.

▶ **Can I create my own animated 3-D graphics?** You can create 3-D animations on a standard PC or Mac with commercially available software; but professional 3-D software products, such as Autodesk Maya and 3ds Max, are expensive and have a steep learning curve.

If you want to dabble with 3-D animations before making an expensive software investment, you might try Smith Micro Poser, DAZ Studio, or Alice. Whether you use a commercial or shareware package, be prepared to spend lots of time with the manual before you are able to produce your own original animations.

FIGURE 8-39

Classic computer games established building blocks for animation technologies used to create today's fast-action, visually detailed computer games, such as *Call of Duty*.

© Jamaway/Alamy

TRY IT!

Connect to the Web site *www. alice.org* and watch one of the introductory videos. What do you think?

○ Looks like fun

○ Looks like work

○ I'm not sure how it relates to 3-D graphics

○ It's not my cup of tea

QuickCheck

SECTION C

1. Vector graphics require more storage space than bitmaps, but vectors can be enlarged without becoming pixelated. True or false? [_____]

2. A process called [_____] converts vector graphics into bitmap images.

3. With the decline of browser support for Flash, [_____] is a popular format for vector graphics on the Web.

4. A 3-D image is based on an assemblage of vectors called a(n) [_____] .

5. The technique of adding light and shadows to a 3-D image is called ray [_____] .

 CHECK ANSWERS

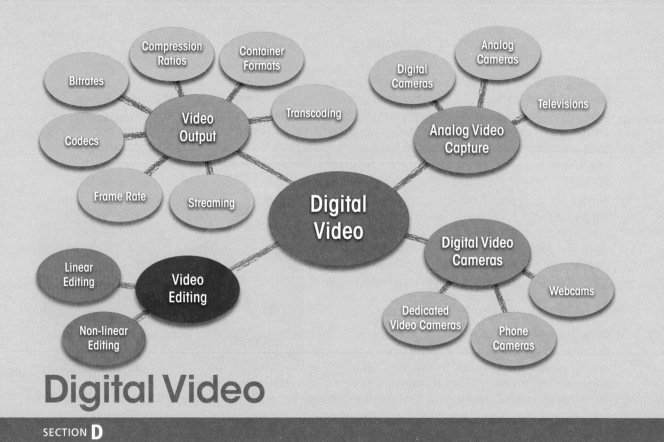

Digital Video

DIGITAL VIDEO IS EVERYWHERE. It encompasses several technologies, including those that produce theater-quality DVD movies, desktop video that you edit on your computer, and quick clips that you shoot with the camera on your smartphone. In this section, you'll take a look at what you can do with affordable, easy-to-use desktop video tools.

DIGITAL VIDEO BASICS

▶ **What is digital video?** A video is a series of still frames, like those in Figure 8-40, projected at a rate fast enough to fool the human eye into perceiving continuous motion. **Digital video** uses bits to store color and brightness data for each video frame. The process is similar to storing the data for a series of bitmap images in which the color for each pixel is represented by a binary number.

▶ **Where does digital video footage originate?** Footage for digital videos can be supplied from digital or analog sources, but analog video requires conversion. You can shoot footage with a consumer-quality camcorder, webcam, or cell phone camera. Some cameras designed for still photography can also capture short videos. Footage can also originate from a videotape, television, DVD, or even a digital video recording device.

▶ **How is digital video used?** You can use your personal computer to edit footage into videos suitable for a variety of personal and professional uses, such as video wedding albums, product sales videos, training videos, video holiday greeting cards, documentaries for nonprofit organizations, and video scrapbooks. Video that is created on a personal computer and designed to be played back on a similar device is sometimes referred to as **desktop video**.

In addition to its use to create personal videos, digital video is also used in the movie industry. Digital cinematography and editing have been used for many award-winning films, such as *Cold Mountain*, *Slumdog Millionaire*, and *The Social Network*. Outside of the context of Hollywood, digital video

FIGURE 8-40

A video is composed of a series of bitmap graphics, each one called a frame.

is a core technology for HDTV, videoconferencing systems, and video messaging. Real-time video even allows deaf people to sign over cell phones.

Digital videos can be stored on a hard disk or distributed on CDs, DVDs, videotapes, memory cards, file sharing networks, or the Web. Popular software for playing digital video on computers includes Apple QuickTime Player, Windows Media Player, and Adobe Flash Player.

▶ **How do I create digital videos?** To understand how you can create your own digital videos, you'll need information about four procedures summarized in Figure 8-41 and explained in the rest of this section.

FIGURE 8-41

Creating digital videos requires a few fairly simple steps.

8

1. **Produce video footage.** Select equipment for filming videos and use effective filming techniques.

2. **Transfer video footage to a computer.** Use a cable, a video capture card, or an SD card to move video footage from cameras, videotapes, television, and DVDs to your computer's hard disk.

3. **Edit video footage.** Use software to select video segments, arrange them into a video, and add a soundtrack.

4. **Store and play.** Select digital video file formats for playback on desktop, Web, portable, and DVD platforms.

PRODUCING VIDEO FOOTAGE

▶ **What kinds of video cameras are available?** You can shoot video footage using standalone video cameras and cameras embedded in computers and handheld devices.

As you might expect, digital video cameras capture footage as a series of bits. Most of today's standalone digital video cameras store data on solid state memory cards, but storage options also include solid state drives, miniDVDs, digital tape, or built-in hard drives. Cameras run the gamut from sub-US$150 consumer minicams to professional quality shoulder-mount camcorders costing more than $20,000 and high-definition Hollywood-style cameras priced over $100,000 (Figure 8-42).

FIGURE 8-42

Digital video cameras are available in many sizes and prices.

▶ **Can I use an analog camera?** You can use an analog video camera to shoot footage that eventually becomes digital video. Analog footage is stored on tape as a continuous track of magnetic patterns. To use your computer to store and edit analog footage, you'll have to convert it into digital format.

▶ **How about webcams?** Another option for shooting video footage is a small, inexpensive **webcam** that is built in above the screen of a laptop computer or attached as a peripheral device (Figure 8-43). These cameras capture a series of still photos, which are stored in digital format directly on your computer's hard disk or transmitted over a network.

Webcams can be controlled by various software applications, including instant messenger clients and specialized webcam software that is bundled with new computers and add-on webcams. Webcams tend to produce low-quality video. Most webcams must remain tethered to your computer, which tends to limit your videos to "talking heads."

▶ **Can I get digital footage from my cell phone camera?** Most mobile phones and handheld devices include a camera. Many of these cameras are equipped to shoot video footage and store it on the device's internal hard drive or memory card. The video quality produced by these cameras is not usually as high as the footage produced by standalone digital video cameras, and storage space is usually more limited.

Cameras embedded in handheld devices tend to have fewer options and features than standalone cameras. For example, most cameras included with handheld devices lack an image stabilization feature that compensates for hand vibration.

▶ **Do I need a fancy camera?** Most people agree that an inexpensive camera is better than nothing, but the quality of your camera can make a difference in the quality of the finished footage.

A common misconception is that a cheap camera won't make a difference for videos shown on small screens at a fairly low resolution. Just the opposite is true: The higher the quality of the original video, the better the final video will look, regardless of the size of the screen on which it is shown.

▶ **Does digital video require special filming techniques?** When videos are processed and stored on a personal computer, some of the image data is eliminated to reduce the video file to a manageable size. Simpler videos tend to maintain better quality as they are edited, processed, and stored. Camera movements, fast actions, patterned clothing, and moving backgrounds all contribute to the complexity of a video and should be minimized. The techniques listed in Figure 8-44 can help you produce video footage that maintains good quality as it is edited and processed.

FIGURE 8-43

A Web camera can be built into a computer display device or can be attached as shown. It is designed mainly for "talking head" applications, such as online video chats and video-conferences.

Andresr/Shutterstock.com

FIGURE 8-44

Video Filming Tips

© MediaTechnics

▶ Use a tripod to maintain a steady image.

▶ Move the camera slowly if it is necessary to pan from side to side.

▶ Zoom in and out slowly.

▶ Direct your subjects to move slowly, when possible.

▶ Position your shot to eliminate as much background detail and movement as possible.

▶ Ask the subjects of your video to wear solid-colored clothing, if possible.

VIDEO TRANSFER

▶ **What can I do with my video footage?** Video footage can be transferred to a computer for editing, streamed out during synchronous communications sessions, e-mailed, or uploaded to file sharing sites. Some cameras automate these transfers, whereas transferring footage from other types of cameras requires several manual steps.

▶ **What are my options for webcam footage?** The footage captured by webcams is often immediately streamed to your computer's hard disk or out over a network during a video chat session or videoconference. If you've stored webcam footage on your computer, you can view and edit it using video editing software.

▶ **How about video from handheld devices?** Video from handheld devices can be e-mailed directly to friends or to yourself. E-mailing footage to yourself is an easy way to get it to your computer for editing. Alternatively, your handheld device might store video footage on a memory card that you can transfer to your computer. Most handheld devices also allow you to directly upload videos to cloud-based storage, YouTube, and other video sharing sites.

▶ **How do I transfer video footage from a video camera to my computer?** The basic method for transferring digital video footage to your computer's hard disk for editing is to remove the SD card from the camera and insert it into a card reader on your computer.

Your digital camera might provide other ways to transfer data to a computer. You can connect the camera to your computer with a cable and fire up video editing software to control the transfer. This method is used for cameras that store video on non-removable media, such as a built-in hard drive or digital videotape, but you might also use this method if you want a lengthy video divided into several smaller clips.

▶ **How do I transfer video from analog devices?** Analog video footage from TV, videotape, and analog video cameras must be converted into digital format before it can be stored on your computer's hard disk. The process of converting analog video signals into digital format is referred to as **video capture** and requires a video capture device and software.

Your computer's graphics card might include video capture capabilities. If not, you can purchase a separate video capture device that connects to your computer's USB port or a video capture card that plugs into an expansion slot (Figure 8-45).

© MediaTechnics

▶ **How much hard disk space is required to store video files?** Video files are large, but just how large depends on the video format used by your camera. Video files produced from digital tape usually are largest, whereas videos stored on memory cards are somewhat smaller, and videos from cell phones and webcams are usually small enough to e-mail.

If you collect lots of video footage, consider using an external hard disk drive to hold video and sound files for projects that you're not actively editing.

TRY IT!

How many devices do you own that can take digital photos?

8

FIGURE 8-45

After it has been installed in your computer, a video capture card can be connected to the video-out and audio-out ports on an analog camera, a television, a VCR, or a DVD player.

VIDEO EDITING

❯ Do I need special equipment for video editing?

Before camcorders went digital, editing a video consisted of recording segments from one videotape onto another tape. This process, called **linear editing**, required a minimum of two VCRs. Professional video editors used expensive editing equipment that was beyond the budget of most consumers.

Today's **nonlinear editing** simply requires a computer hard disk and video editing software. The advantage of nonlinear editing is that you can use a random-access device to easily edit and arrange video clips. Video editing requires lots of hard disk space, however. So before you begin an editing session, make sure your computer's hard disk has several gigabytes of available storage space. It is also a good idea to have at least 1 GB of RAM—professionals opt for at least 4 GB.

❯ How do I edit a video?

After your video footage is transferred to your computer and stored on the hard disk, you can begin to arrange your video clips by using video editing software, such as Adobe Premiere, Apple iMovie, Windows Movie Maker, or Corel VideoStudio.

Videos are easier to edit if you divide them into several files, each containing a one- or two-minute video clip. Some video capture software automatically creates clips by detecting frame changes, such as when you turn your camera off, pause, or switch to a new scene.

Video editing software allows you to further crop clips and add transitions between them. You can also overlay video clips with one or more audio tracks containing music or narrations.

Your completed video consists of video tracks containing video segments and transitions, plus audio tracks containing voices and music. Figure 8-46 illustrates how to lay out video and audio tracks.

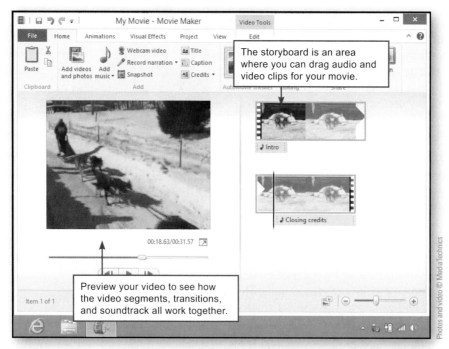

FIGURE 8-46

Simple video editing software combines video clips, sounds, and transitions into movies. ▶ Learn the basics of Windows Movie Maker and see how to create a short movie about sled dogs, complete with a soundtrack. (This tour might take a few moments to begin. Please be patient.)

VIDEO OUTPUT

▶ **How does video footage become a digital video?** Your video editing software combines the data from all the video and audio files you selected into a single file, which is stored on your computer's hard disk. During the output process, you can select settings for aspect ratio, frame size, and compression so that the resulting video quality and file size are appropriate for the video's intended use.

Aspect ratio refers to the relative width and height of the video frame; widescreen is 16:9 and fullscreen is 4:3. Most computers, televisions, and handheld devices are designed for widescreen format, though the screens for a few devices, such as iPads, are sized for fullscreen formats.

Frame size defines the resolution of a video window. Small Web videos have a frame size of 320 x 240. The frame size for fullscreen DVD video is 720 x 480; whereas high-definition video is 1280 x 720 or 1920 x 1080.

▶ **How is video compressed?** Raw video requires vast amounts of storage space, so videos are usually compressed to create files that can be conveniently stored and transmitted. Video compression can be achieved by decreasing the frame rate (number of frames per second), reducing the frame size, and using techniques similar to JPEG to compress the data stored for each frame.

A **codec** (compressor/decompressor) is the software that compresses a video stream when a video is stored, and decompresses the file when the video is played. Popular codecs include MPEG, DivX, H.264, Theora, and Windows Media Video. Each codec uses a unique algorithm to shrink the size of a video file, so they are not interchangeable. When creating videos, you should use one of the codecs included in popular video players.

Video compression can be expressed as a compression ratio or as a bitrate. A **compression ratio** indicates the ratio of compressed data to uncompressed data. A video file with a high compression ratio, such as 35:1, has more compression, a smaller file size, and lower image quality than a file with a smaller compression ratio, such as 5:1.

Bitrate refers to the amount of data transferred per second as a video plays. Higher bitrates produce better quality video. Click the CLICK TO START buttons in Figure 8-47 to compare video and audio quality produced by different compression settings.

8

FIGURE 8-47

Different compression ratios can have a remarkable effect on video quality and file size.

Bitrate: 90 Kbps
Frame rate: 10
File size: 359 KB

 CLICK TO START

Bitrate: 448 Kbps
Frame rate: 15
File size: 1177 KB

 CLICK TO START

Bitrate: 928 Kbps
Frame rate: 30
File size: 2448 KB

 CLICK TO START

© MediaTechnics

▶ How can I specify a compression level? Some entry-level video editing software allows you simply to select a use for your video, such as sending it as an e-mail attachment, posting it on the Web, publishing it on YouTube, or viewing it from your local hard disk. The software automatically applies an appropriate level of compression to the video data.

Alternatively, your software might offer the option of selecting a maximum file size. For example, if you are planning to send a video as an e-mail attachment, you might limit the size to 1 MB, and your video data will be compressed to that specified size.

Some video editing software allows you to select a bitrate for your final video. Uncompressed video files contain a huge number of bits per frame, so smooth playback requires a high bitrate, such as 340 Kbps. Compressed files contain fewer bits per frame and play back more smoothly at lower bitrates, such as 38 Kbps, offered by slower Internet connections.

As another option, your video editing software might offer a selection of compression ratios, such as 5:1 or 35:1. You can experiment with various compression ratios to find the best balance between file size and image quality.

▶ What is the best video file format? Many video file formats are available; the format you use should be compatible with the device on which it is played and its browser or player software. Video file formats are sometimes referred to as **container formats** because they hold the compressed video and audio data streams that form a video (Figure 8-48).

Figure 8-49 describes some popular video container formats—**AVI**, **MOV**, **MPEG**, **WebM**, **ASF**, **Flash video**, **VOB**, and **Ogg Theora**.

FIGURE 8-48

Codecs and video formats are easily confused, especially because some containers have the same names as codecs. A codec, such as H.264, is software that compresses the video stream, whereas a container format, such as MOV, is a method of storing video data in a file.

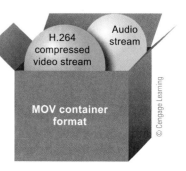

FIGURE 8-49

Popular Digital Video Formats

Format	Extension	Platform	Description and Use
AVI (Audio Video Interleave)	.avi	PC	A format sometimes used for storing digital clips from video cameras; used for desktop video on the PC platform
MOV (QuickTime Movie)	.mov	PC, Mac, UNIX, Linux	A popular format for desktop video and streaming Web videos
MPEG (Moving Picture Experts Group)	.mpg or .mpeg	PC, Mac, UNIX, Linux	Versions include MPEG-1, MPEG-2, and MPEG-4; used for desktop video and streaming Web video
WebM	.webm	PC, Mac, UNIX, Linux	Royalty-free, high-quality open format for use with HTML5
ASF (Advanced Systems Format)	.asf or .wmv	PC	Container format for Microsoft's Windows Media Video (WMV) desktop video and streaming Web video
Flash video	.flv	PC, Mac	Popular for Web-based video; requires Adobe Flash Player
VOB (Video Object)	.vob	Standalone DVD player, PC, Mac, Linux	Industry-standard format for stand-alone DVD players
Ogg Theora	.ogg	PC, Mac	A non-proprietary container (Ogg) and video codec (Theora)

▶ Can I change videos from one format to another? Digital videos can be converted from one file format to another through a process called **transcoding**. If you want to move a video into a different file format, you can check to see if your video editing software offers a conversion, export, or transcoding option. If not, you can find transcoding software on the Web. Transcoding can cause loss of quality, so avoid transcoding an already transcoded video file.

WEB VIDEO

▶ **How do Web-based videos work?** A video for a Web page is stored on a Web server in a file. Usually, a link for the video file appears on the Web page. When you click the link, the Web server transmits a copy of the video file to your computer. If your browser has a plug-in that corresponds to the video format, the video is displayed on your computer screen.

The transfer of a digital video file from the Web to your computer can happen in one of two ways, depending on the video format. In one case, your computer waits until it downloads the entire video file before starting to play it. This technology is typically used for movie downloads.

An alternative video delivery method, called **streaming video**, sends a small segment of the video to your computer and begins to play it. While this segment plays, the Web server sends the next part of the file to your computer, and so on, until the video ends. With streaming video, your computer essentially plays the video while it continues to receive it. Videos intended to be viewed in the context of a Web page are routinely delivered by streaming video technology.

▶ **How do I post a video to YouTube or a similar file sharing site?** YouTube is a video sharing Web site that encourages members to upload, view, and rate video clips. YouTube and similar sites accept most popular video file formats directly from digital cameras, camcorders, cell phones, and webcams (Figure 8-50).

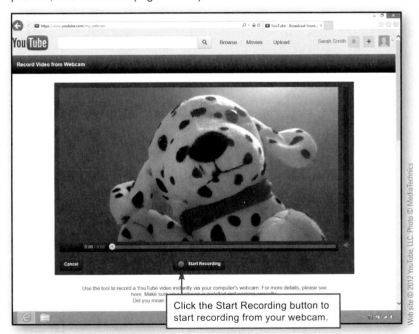

Click the Start Recording button to start recording from your webcam.

TRY IT!

How are YouTube videos supplied to consumers?

○ As a download

○ As JPEGs

○ As .zip files

○ As streaming video

8

FIGURE 8-50

You can use YouTube to capture footage on your computer's webcam and upload it to the YouTube Web site.

Before uploading videos, you can edit them and save them in a standard video format, such as WebM, MPEG, MOV, AVI, WMV, or Flash video. YouTube imposes a length and time limitation, so you should check the current regulations before you finalize your video.

After your file is uploaded, it is converted into the standard formats used by YouTube. Originally, all YouTube videos were converted into Flash format. Later, a format for mobile phones was added, as was an HD widescreen format. In conjunction with the move to HTML5, WebM format was also added. In order to make YouTube videos more accessible to the deaf and hearing impaired, some videos can be automatically captioned.

▶ **How are videos added to Web pages?** On today's Web, most videos are embedded in Web pages so that they appear to play in place. For browsers that support HTML5, the <video> tag can be used to specify the name of the video file and a message to display if someone tries to access the video without the corresponding plug-in. The <object> and <iframe> tags can be used in HTML5 or earlier versions of HTML.

A simple HTML5 snippet using the <video> tag for adding a video might look like this:

```
<video src="myvideo.webm" controls>
If the video doesn't begin, you might need to download a plug-in.
</video>
```

▶ **What are the best formats for Web videos?** The HTML5 <video> tag supports several video formats, but it does not designate a common video format for all HTML5-compliant browsers. Web site developers sometimes have to provide a video in multiple formats to make it accessible to a variety of browsers and hardware devices.

At the time this book was published, there was no single video format supported by all browsers. But Ogg Theora, H.264, and WebM formats appear to be the best candidates for widespread Web use with HTML5.

▶ **Can I incorporate videos from the Web into my own Web site and social networking pages?** There are several ways to reuse and share videos that you find on the Web. When using videos created by others, make sure you give the authors credit, adhere to originating sites' usage policies, and abide by copyright law.

Video sharing sites, such as YouTube, include tools for e-mailing videos, sharing videos on social networking sites, and including them in blogs. You can embed videos from these sites by copying HTML code into the source code for your own Web pages. You can also copy video links into e-mail messages and Web page source documents so that readers can quickly connect to the original video source on YouTube, Facebook, or other Web sites (Figure 8-51).

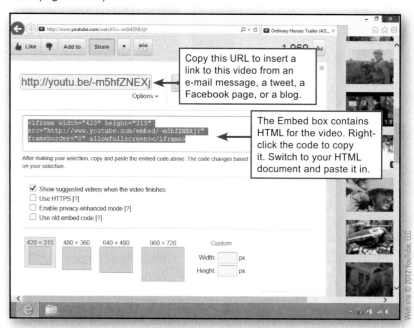

FIGURE 8-51

YouTube provides source code for embedding a video into your own Web page or sharing links on Facebook, Twitter, and other social networking sites.

DVD-VIDEO

▶ **Can I burn my digital videos onto DVDs with interactive menus like commercial movies?** Suppose you've used video editing software to create a short documentary on sled dogs. You can package the completed video footage into a professional-style DVD that can be played on computer DVD drives (if your computer is equipped with DVD player software) or standalone DVD players. It can include interactive menus with options, such as Play Video, Select a Scene, and Special Features, that viewers can select using their DVD remote controls.

▶ **What equipment do I need?** To create video DVDs, you need a writable DVD drive (sometimes called a DVD burner) plus software that includes tools for DVD menu creation and writing data onto a DVD-Video—a process sometimes called burning. Basic DVD tools are included with Windows and Mac OS. Full-featured tools are offered by video editing software and specialized DVD authoring software, such as Adobe Encore, Sonic MyDVD, Nero, and Corel DVD MovieFactory.

▶ **What's the process for making a video DVD?** To create a video DVD, you usually begin by selecting one or more completed videos that include soundtracks, transitions, titles, special effects, and so on. You then use DVD authoring software to design menus and buttons that viewers can use to navigate to specific parts of your video. To complete the project, you can test your project and then burn it to DVD.

▶ **What are my options for creating interactive DVD menus?** A DVD menu is a screen that provides viewers with navigation tools to start a video, skip to specific scenes, play special features, and link to other menus. A typical DVD menu consists of a decorative background and option buttons that viewers can select using their DVD player's remote control. Some DVD authoring software offers a selection of predesigned menu and button templates that you can easily incorporate with your videos (Figure 8-52).

FIGURE 8-52

DVD authoring software offers a selection of backgrounds and themes styles for creating DVD menus. ▶ Your interactive eBook demonstrates how to create a DVD menu and generate a standalone iDVD.

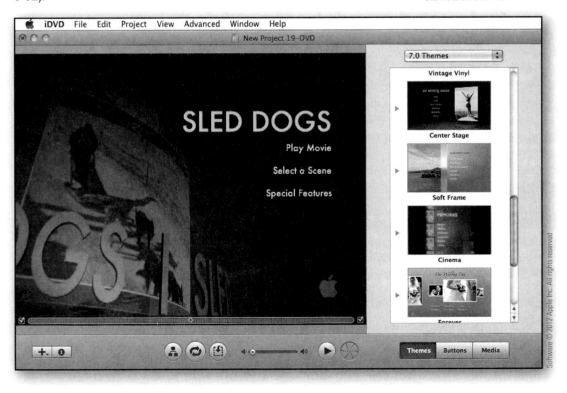

8

▶ **Are menus easy to create?** Yes, they just require a little advance planning. As you design the menu flow, remember that you want to provide viewers with a way to return to the main menu from each submenu. You might also want viewers to return to the main menu after viewing individual clips. If a submenu offers options for outtakes or other special features, you should provide a way for viewers to return to the submenu when the special feature ends. To help visualize the way your menus will work, you can draw a diagram similar to the one in Figure 8-53.

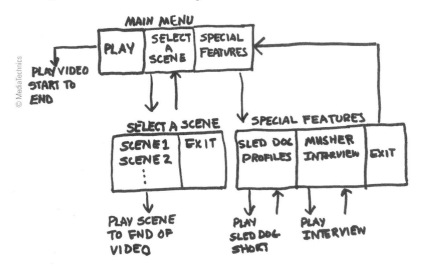

© MediaTechnics

FIGURE 8-53

Sketching a diagram of the menus for your DVD can help you envision how viewers will navigate to selected scenes and special features.

▶ **How do I output my video to DVD?** To create a DVD that can be viewed on a standalone DVD player, you have to output your video in DVD-Video format, which requires video encoded with MPEG-2 and stored in VOB files. Your DVD authoring software can generate MPEG-2 video clips and menus, store them in VOB files, and lay them out on a DVD according to industry standards.

Most DVD authoring software can accomplish the MPEG encoding on the fly as it burns the DVD. However, this process takes time. So if you are burning more than one copy, or if you want to test your menu structure before burning the video onto a DVD, you might want to consider creating a DVD image.

▶ **What's a DVD image?** A **DVD image** (sometimes called a DVD volume) is essentially a prototype of your DVD, but it is stored on your computer's hard disk. If you have space to store a DVD image, it is a good idea to make one before burning a DVD. You can use a DVD image for testing. You can also use the image to burn multiple DVDs without waiting for your software to prepare the files for each burn.

▶ **Can I simply copy a desktop video to a DVD using the Copy command?** Desktop videos are usually stored in WMV or MOV format, and some standalone DVD players are not equipped to handle those formats. So, although you can use the Copy command to copy MOV and WMV files to a DVD and distribute them, these files can be viewed on most computers, but not on all DVD players.

TRY IT!

If you want to burn a DVD with a menu that works with any DVD player's remote control, what format should you use?

○ HTML5

○ JPEG

○ H.264

○ VOB

Even copying files stored in MPEG format might not produce a DVD that works in a standalone player. The DVD-Video format specification requires a specific layout for data on the DVD surface. Simply copying computer data files does not produce the required layout, so most DVD players will not be able to play the video.

▶ **How do I test my DVD image?** Your DVD is ready for production and distribution if the video quality looks good and the menus work correctly. Use the tips listed below to test your DVD on your computer before you burn a DVD:

▶ Test each button to make sure it links to the correct clip.

▶ Play each clip to the end and make sure it returns to the correct menu when completed.

▶ Watch the video carefully and look for any poor quality segments with distracting artifacts, such as blurs or halos. Artifacts can sometimes be removed by revisiting your MPEG coding options.

▶ Listen to the soundtrack to make sure the audio is clear, smooth, and synchronized with the video.

▶ **Does it make a difference if I use recordable or rewritable DVDs?** Commercial DVD movies are stamped onto DVD-ROM discs during the manufacturing process—something you can't do with your computer's DVD drive. Your computer can burn data on DVD-R, DVD+R, or DVD-RW discs.

Because the DVD industry has not achieved a single media standard, some standalone DVD players—particularly those manufactured before 2004—are not able to read one or more of these disc types. DVD+R and DVD-R seem to be compatible with the widest variety of DVD players, whereas DVD-RW seems to be the least compatible. Before you distribute your DVDs, make sure you test them in a standalone DVD player.

> **TERMINOLOGY NOTE**
>
> In the world of video production, an artifact is any visible degradation in the image quality, such as shimmering where contrasting colors meet or backgrounds that become wavy during fast pans or zooms.

8

QuickCheck   SECTION D

1. The process of converting analog video signals into digital format is referred to as video [_____].

2. A(n) [_____] is the software that compresses a video stream when a video is stored, and decompresses the file when the video is played.

3. Compressed files contain less data per frame and play back more smoothly at lower [_____] rates.

4. Digital videos can be converted from one file format to another through a process called [_____].

5. Before you create a DVD video, it is a good idea to create a DVD [_____] on your computer's hard disk.

 CHECK ANSWERS

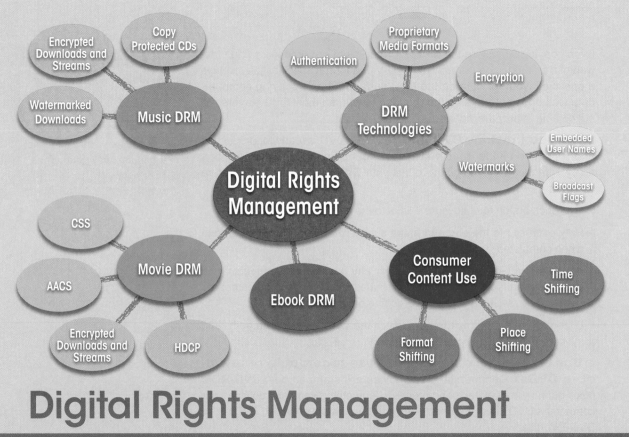

Digital Rights Management

THE SECURITY SECTIONS of earlier chapters looked at security from the user perspective. In contrast, the security section for this chapter examines the techniques used by content providers to protect digital media from unlicensed duplication and use. In this section, you'll learn about DRM technologies you may have already encountered and some that are likely to affect your ability to use digital media in the future.

CONTENT BASICS

▶ **What is "content"?** **Media content** (or simply content) includes television shows, movies, music, and books. **Digital content** is a term used for movies and other content that is stored digitally.

Content is accessed by means of a player. Keep in mind that the term *player* can refer to a hardware device or software.

▶ Software players include familiar media players, such as iTunes, Windows Media Player, and QuickTime.

▶ Hardware players include standalone devices such as CD players, VCRs, DVD players, Blu-ray players, ebook readers, and portable media players.

▶ Computer devices, such as CD, DVD, and Blu-ray drives, are also considered players, though they require software to play back content.

▶ **How do consumers expect to use media content?** Consumers expect to be able to manipulate media content so that they can use it on multiple devices at a convenient time and place (Figure 8-54 on the next page).

▶ **Time shifting** is the process of recording a broadcast, such as a television show, so that it can be played back at a more convenient time.

myosotisrock/Shutterstock.com

FIGURE 8-54

Consumers want to be able to engage in time, place, and format shifting.

▶ **Place shifting** allows media that originates in one place to be accessed from another place without changing the device on which it is stored.

Place shifting is often achieved using computer networks, as when you stream a movie from your computer to your Wi-Fi equipped DVD player to your Wi-Fi equipped HDTV.

▶ **Format shifting** is the process of converting media files from a format suitable for one device to a format suitable for a different kind of device.

A common use of format shifting is ripping audio tracks from a CD and converting them into MP3 format for playback on a portable media device, such as an iPod.

© Media Technics

▶ **What's the problem?** Pirating music and movies is a multibillion-dollar worldwide activity that is increasingly controlled by organized crime. Yet individuals also contribute to the high incidence of movie and music piracy.

File-sharing sites entice consumers with free, but illegal, downloads. Audio extraction software makes it easy to rip tracks from an audio CD and hand them out to friends.

Every hardware device and software program that interacts with digital content poses a potential vulnerability that can be exploited by pirates. Software that encrypts content can be cracked, signals that travel from one device to another can be intercepted, and when all else fails, the **analog hole** allows pirates to capture content by using a microphone to record songs as they are output to speakers or using a camcorder to film movies as they are projected in a movie theater.

Content providers use digital rights management to reduce piracy, but it can limit the way ordinary consumers use digital content that they purchase, rent, subscribe to, or download.

TRY IT!

Converting a YouTube video into a file that you can store on your computer is an example of:

○ time shifting

○ place shifting

○ format shifting

○ the analog hole

DRM TECHNOLOGIES

▶ **What is DRM?** **Digital rights management** (DRM) is a collection of techniques used by copyright holders to limit access to and use of digital content.

You've probably encountered DRM systems, such as Apple's FairPlay and Microsoft's Windows Media DRM, that are designed to protect music, movies, ebooks, and even television shows. DRM systems often consist of several layers of technology, which means that a movie, for example, might be protected by multiple types of DRM.

DRM technologies include authentication, proprietary media formats, encryption, and watermarks.

▶ **What is authentication?** Authentication is a very simple form of digital rights management that allows content to be accessed only by authorized individuals. It is commonly one aspect of digital rights management for cloud-based content. Very simply, you are required to log in with a valid user ID and password before you can access movies, music, or other digital content.

Authentication provides weak protection unless combined with encryption and other DRM technologies. Additional DRM is necessary to prevent customers from copying content and sharing their IDs with friends who can then access content without paying any fees.

▶ **What are proprietary media formats?** Digital content that is distributed on physical media, such as CDs, DVDs, or Blu-ray discs, can be **copy protected** by proprietary media formats that intentionally vary from standard formats. Proprietary formats have been used with music CDs and with DVD movies. Figure 8-55 illustrates how a proprietary media format was used to protect music CDs.

What is the DRM status of MP3 files?

○ They have DRM encryption

○ They require authentication

○ They are protected by CSS

○ The MP3 format includes no DRM

FIGURE 8-55

Copy protected CDs contain a software program that strips out intentionally corrupted data.

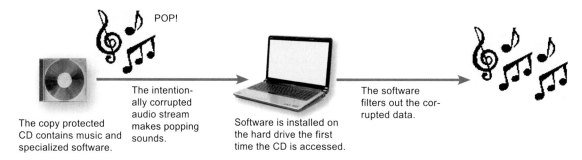

POP!

The copy protected CD contains music and specialized software.

The intentionally corrupted audio stream makes popping sounds.

Software is installed on the hard drive the first time the CD is accessed.

The software filters out the corrupted data.

▶ **How is encryption used for DRM?** Encryption is the gold standard of DRM. Data for a television show, movie, song, or ebook is encrypted so that the file cannot be viewed without a valid encryption key. Keys and decryption are usually handled behind the scenes, so users don't need to know the keys or enter them. DRM encryption can be handled by software or hardware. Software-based DRM encryption is the easier solution (Figure 8-56).

FIGURE 8-56

With software-based DRM, player software is required to decrypt encrypted content.

Player software, such as Windows Media Player or iTunes, decrypts the media file and plays it.

Software-based DRM encryption can be circumvented by routing content to a recording device as it is decrypted during playback. To close the loophole created by routing playback to a recorder, DRM encryption is also necessary within the devices used for playback.

CSS, AACS, HDCP, and similar DRM technologies are built into devices such as microprocessors, computers, DVD players, and televisions. These technologies protect content from unauthorized playback, recording, or transmission (Figure 8-57).

FIGURE 8-57

With hardware-based DRM, all playback devices are required to be compliant.

8

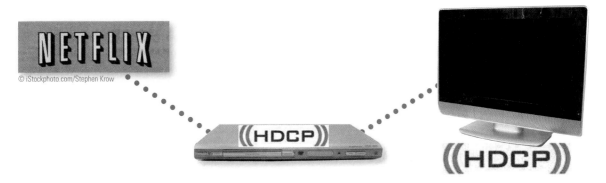

© iStockphoto.com/Stephen Krow

▶ **What are watermarks?** A **digital watermark** is a pattern of bits, inserted at various places in an image or a content stream, that can be used to track, identify, verify, and control content use. Watermarks are usually imperceptible to viewers, readers, or listeners, but can be picked up by compliant devices.

Watermarks can be used to identify content owners or authorized users. For example, iTunes embeds your name in the content stream for the music and movies that you download.

Some watermarks are classified as broadcast flags. A **broadcast flag** is a set of bits inserted into the data stream that specifies how the stream can and cannot be used. A broadcast flag can:

▶ Limit the resolution or sound quality of playback

▶ Prevent fast-forwarding during commercials

▶ Limit content use to specific regions

▶ Prohibit copying or limit the number of copies that can be made (Figure 8-58)

FIGURE 8-58

Watermarks are read by devices that comply with the limitations embedded in the content stream.

Original DVD with one-copy-only watermark

Compliant DVD burner

DVD copy now contains do-not-copy watermark

Compliant DVD burner will not copy the DVD

MUSIC DRM

▶ Can I copy tracks from an old CD? Suppose you get your hands on a classic Garth Brooks CD and you'd like to add the tracks to your iTunes collection. You might assume that you can use audio extraction software to rip the tracks from the CD and save them in MP3 format.

Music CDs adhere to a standardized Red Book format, which implements DRM with a data bit that can be set to "no-copy." The Red Book no-copy bit is easy to defeat, so between 2000 and 2005, the recording industry produced copy protected CDs that did not play correctly on computers or when copied. Ripping tracks from these CDs is difficult, but not impossible. Most people prefer to avoid the aggravation and simply purchase a digital version of the music.

▶ How does DRM affect the way I can use music downloads? Downloading pulls a music file to your local device and stores it there before playing it. With downloads, you have to wait for the file to arrive; but once it is there, playback can proceed without interruption. Downloads are used at online music stores where you purchase or rent music.

Because downloaded files are stored locally, you have the potential to access them multiple times and copy them to other devices. Further, you don't have to be connected to the Internet when you want to access your music, so you can listen to downloaded music at a remote beach or with a device that doesn't have an Internet connection.

In practice, your ability to play downloaded content can be restricted by DRM that limits the devices on which you can play it, prevents you from making copies, or prohibits you from converting the music to a non-protected format.

Some music sites offer DRM-free downloads, but copyright law remains in effect. Technically, you might be able to make a copy and distribute it to your friends, but it is illegal to do so. Consumers should be aware that downloads from iTunes have the purchaser's name embedded in the file. If you give one of your music files to a friend who gives it to another friend, and it eventually winds up on a file sharing network, you could be liable for copyright violation.

▶ Is streaming music protected by DRM? Streaming music is transmitted to your computer and played immediately. It is the technology used for Internet radio, subscription music services, and some services that offer cloud-based music storage (Figure 8-59).

It is easier to protect streamed content than downloaded content, but streaming is not an effective DRM technology by itself because the stream can be captured using various software tools. Streaming music can be protected by authentication DRM that requires you to log in when you want to access music. It can also be encrypted using software-based DRM, or DRM that requires a compliant radio or other device.

TRY IT!

Which of the following is easiest to pirate?

○ Music downloads
○ Streaming music
○ AACS Blu-ray discs
○ Streaming video

FIGURE 8-59

Streaming music is not stored on your local device; so every time you want to listen to a song, it has to be re-streamed. Also, because the content never exists as a local file, you cannot copy it.

MOVIE DRM

▶ **Can I make a copy of a DVD movie?** The first DVD players were introduced primarily as a distribution medium for mainstream movies. Based on prior experience with CD and VHS piracy, a DRM technology called CSS was built into the DVD standard from its inception.

CSS (Content Scramble System) is a digital rights management technology designed to encrypt and control the use of content stored on DVDs. It is intended to render DVD copies nonfunctional and enforces additional restrictions, such as region coding.

A key aspect of CSS is the use of an authentication key that allows a DVD disc and player to prove to each other that they are legitimately licensed to use CSS. CSS was introduced in 1996. Only four years later, tools for disabling it began to emerge. Although tools such as DeCSS are readily available, in many countries including the U.S., it is illegal to use them to circumvent DRM.

▶ **Are Blu-ray movies copy protected?** The primary DRM technology for Blu-ray discs is **AACS** (Advanced Access Content System). Like CSS, AACS works with an encrypted content stream. AACS, however, uses a much stronger encryption key, which makes it quite difficult for hackers to break the encryption using brute force methods.

FIGURE 8-60

AACS depends on authentication and revocation built into devices and content.

Another difference between the two methods is that CSS uses a shared set of encryption keys, and all devices of a specific model use the same key. In contrast, AACS compliant devices each contain their own unique set of keys, and these keys can be revoked if a player is found to be compromised.

The concept of authorization and revocation can be applied to hardware devices and software players to give licensing bodies the means to keep non-complying players off the market and deny further access to complying devices that have become compromised (Figure 8-60).

Despite its complexity, AACS has been broken. Just knowing the key, however, is not enough to proceed with Blu-ray copying; so as with other anti-DRM hacks, most users find it easier to simply pay to get content in the format and on the devices they desire.

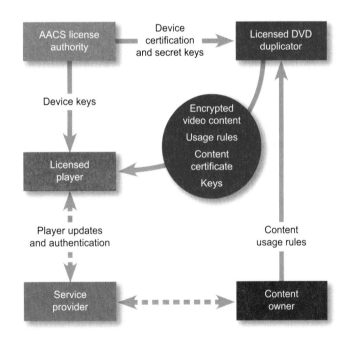

▶ **Are movie downloads copy protected?** Movie downloads tend to have more rigorous DRM protection than music downloads. Whereas music stores such as iTunes and Amazon MP3 allow you to make copies of music, change its format, and burn it to CDs for your own use, there are tighter restrictions on movies.

Downloaded movies that you rent or buy are generally protected by DRM software and hardware encryption. They require authorized devices and proprietary player software, which are all designed to deter digital pirates.

▶ **What about streaming movies?** The technology for streaming movies is the same as for streaming music, but movies are much longer and require more bandwidth. Movie streams are buffered when the amount of data exceeds the carrying capacity of your network connection.

For example, suppose you're streaming a Netflix movie over a basic cable Internet connection. Before the movie begins, Netflix takes a minute or so to check your connection speed and transmit the first few minutes of the movie to a memory area of your computer called a buffer. When the buffer is filled, the movie begins.

While data from the buffer is processed to display the movie, additional data is streamed to the buffer. If the buffer doesn't get filled fast enough because your Internet connection is too slow or because the Netflix server is overloaded, then the movie pauses for a period of time while it refills the buffer. During this time, you'll see a "rebuffering" or "loading" message.

Buffers open a potential hole for movie pirating, so streaming movies are usually protected by additional DRM technologies, such as encryption and HDCP. **HDCP** (High-bandwidth Digital Content Protection) is a hardware-based DRM technology that requires compliant devices for content playback. When working with HDCP-protected content, you'll have to make sure that your computer, DVD player, television, and handheld are all compliant. Look for the HDCP label when you purchase new media devices.

EBOOK DRM

▶ **Are ebooks protected?** Early DRM efforts for ebooks tied books to dedicated ebook readers, such as the Kindle and Nook, which were designed to decrypt ebook files and display them (Figure 8-61).

In response to consumer demand, ebook distributors expanded the platforms on which digital books can be read. Now, when you purchase a digital book from Amazon, Barnes & Noble, or iTunes, you can read it on devices that include computers, tablets, and smartphones. Ebook DRM technologies have evolved to allow this flexibility, yet retain control over copying and unauthorized distribution.

The power of digital rights management is illustrated by an incident that took place in 2009 when Amazon deleted copies of George Orwell's *1984* and *Animal Farm* that Kindle users had legitimately purchased and stored on their devices. According to an Amazon press release, those titles had been added to the Kindle store by a company that did not have the right to distribute them.

Customers were credited for their purchases, but many Kindle users were uncomfortable with the idea that Amazon was able to reach across the Internet and pull content from their personal Kindles.

ENFORCEMENT

▶ **How do I know if I am breaking the law?** The person who creates a film, an album, a television show, or a book automatically receives the copyright to that work. The copyright can be transferred to a second party such as a publisher or distributor. By law, the copyright holder is the only entity that can make copies of the work and distribute them, but license agreements and usage policies might allow you to make copies under certain circumstances.

When using digital content, make sure you know the rules. Check the license agreement and usage policy to find out if you are allowed to make

When shopping for media devices, such as a DVD player, what should you look for if you want to make sure the device will play movies protected by DRM?

○ HD

○ HDMI

○ HDCP

○ AACS

FIGURE 8-61

Ebooks can be displayed on a dedicated reader, such as the Kindle, which handles digital rights.

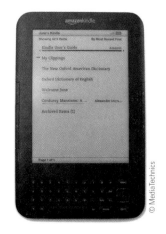

copies for your own use and if there are limitations on what you can do with those copies.

▶ **What are the penalties?** The copyright owner is entitled to recover monetary damages resulting from infringement, and any profits made from illegal sales of the work. Under U.S. law, copyright holders may also be awarded statutory damages up to $250,000. You've seen the warnings displayed while waiting for your movie to start (Figure 8-62).

FIGURE 8-62

Unauthorized copying of movies, music, and books is illegal.

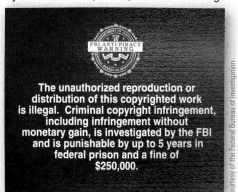

▶ **Who will know if I copy a few songs?** Copyright holders periodically crack down on infringers. In the past decade, the music industry has singled out over 30,000 alleged music pirates and threatened them with astronomical fines.

A current initiative called Six Strikes takes a slightly different approach to curtailing infringement. Copyright holders, such as music companies, scan the Internet for IP addresses that initiate suspicious activity. For example, suppose the music watchdogs see your IP address participating in a swarm for *The Lone Ranger*. Your ISP will receive a notice about your alleged infringement and that notice will be forwarded to you.

After the fifth or sixth alert (hence the "Six Strikes" name), your ISP can institute mitigation measures, such as directing you to educational information about copyright, or temporarily reducing your Internet connection speed.

Although ISPs have agreed to participate in Six Strikes, it is unclear how aggressively they will monitor and punish their subscribers.

▶ **It sounds like I don't have to worry?** Not only is it against the law to make unauthorized copies of music, movies, and books, it is unethical. Copyright infringers have a whole host of excuses for what they do, but don't get caught up in that vibe.

Happily, the most draconian digital rights management schemes have failed. Today's digital content distributors maintain fairly reasonable prices and policies that allow consumers to download content and play it back on multiple devices. Copyright holders are watching the situation, however. If copying gets out of control, content providers will certainly crack down by raising prices, harassing consumers, and re-instituting intrusive digital rights management systems.

QuickCheck   SECTION E

1. _____ shifting is the process of converting media files from a format suitable for one device to a format suitable for a different kind of device.

2. A digital _____ can be inserted into a music or video file to specify the number of times a content stream can be duplicated.

3. HDCP is a(n) _____ -based DRM technology.

4. _____ is the primary technology used to protect DVDs, but it was cracked soon after it was introduced. (Hint: Use the acronym.)

5. Streaming movies are temporarily held in a(n) _____ that opens a potential hole for illegal copying.

▶ CHECK ANSWERS

Issue: What Happened to Fair Use?

FAIR USE is the right to use portions of copyrighted material without the permission of the copyright holder for purposes such as review, criticism, or parody. Under certain circumstances, Fair Use is also a successful defense for practices, such as time shifting, in which whole works are copied for limited personal use.

Exactly what does or does not constitute Fair Use, however, is only sketched out in copyright law. The precise nature of Fair Use is shaped by court decisions covering situations and devices as disparate as vinyl records, printer toner cartridges, videotape recorders, and file sharing networks.

It seems incredible, but there once were no restrictions on copying sound recordings. "Record pirates" could legally copy and distribute, say, an Elvis Presley recording.

In 1971, the U.S. Congress passed the Sound Recording Act that prohibited copying music for commercial use. The law was not, however, aimed at prohibiting consumers from making copies for their own use.

The legal precedent that gave consumers a green light for time shifting is the landmark 1984 Betamax case in which Universal Studios attempted to hold Sony Corp. of America liable for copyright infringement by people who used video recorders to tape movies from their televisions. The U.S. Supreme Court sided with Sony and concluded that some instances of time shifting were legal.

The court's decision, however, was based on a definition of time shifting as "the practice of recording a program to view it once at a later time." Note the word "once." The Betamax case did not offer legal precedent for copying and saving content for viewing multiple times.

The proliferation of computer networks and streaming media has made place shifting a reality. You can, for example, view a cable television broadcast sent from your Wi-Fi equipped set-top box in your living room to your Wi-Fi equipped laptop out on the deck.

"Specifically, it is not the intention of Congress to restrain the home recording, from broadcasts or from tapes or records, of recorded performances, where the home recording is for private use and with no purpose of reproducing or otherwise capitalizing commercially on it."

U.S. Judiciary Committee statement regarding the Sound Recording Act of 1971

Your network, however, is transmitting a copy of the broadcast, a use of copyrighted work that is not explicitly allowed by copyright law in most countries. Therefore, unless a user agreement extends the basic rights granted by copyright law, place shifting would be considered a questionable practice.

So how about format shifting? Surely, it must be legal to rip tracks from a CD that you own, save them as an MP3 file, and play them on your iPod. Many consumers believe that they have a right to use a legally purchased song or video in any manner they please short of redistributing it for profit.

Consumers are familiar with copyright restrictions on printed books and have an expectation that digital media can be legally used in parallel ways.

Readers expect to be able to carry a book with them to any location, read it at any time, use any type of reading light or reading glasses, loan the book to friends, and sell the book when they have finished using it.

No wonder consumers are peeved when ebook vendors and other digital content providers use DRM technology to limit how much of an ebook can be viewed, whether the text can be printed or shared, and how long it can be viewed.

Although it is convenient to focus on the "once I buy it I can use it as I like" rationale, we tend to ignore situations in which our expectations about content use are more limited. For example, we do not expect that after attending a Widespread Panic concert, we are entitled to a free DVD or video of the performance. If we pay to see a movie at a theater, we don't then expect to get the DVD or soundtrack CD for free when they are released.

From rock concerts to theaters, consumers are familiar with the idea that different venues and formats might require separate payments. Digital rights management technologies simply enforce this idea in practice.

TRY IT! Do you know how to legally use music, movies, ebooks, and other media? Here's a chance for you to explore Fair Use and content usage policies.

1 Fair Use is defined in Section 107 of U.S. copyright law. It includes four factors designed to determine whether a use is fair. Look up Section 107 of the U.S. Copyright Law. In your own words, what are those four factors?

2 The book *Grateful Dead: The Illustrated Trip* included concert posters and ticket images used without approval of the copyright holder. In a subsequent suit, courts decided the use was fair and transformative, based on a four-factor analysis. Look up the results of this case by searching for the article, *Grateful Dead Posters' Re-publication Held to Be a Transformative, Fair Use* by Martine Courant Rife. In your own words, what did the court say about each of the four factors?

Charlie Gillett/Redferns/Getty Images

3 "Transformative use" means that you change a work enough to make it your own. Collages, music remixes, and video parodies can fall into this category. Find an example of a transformative work on YouTube and list the original works from which it is derived. In your opinion, what makes this a transformative work?

4 Digital content providers such as iTunes, Amazon, and Google each have their own rules about how you can use the content you purchase, rent, or subscribe to. To get an idea of a typical usage policy, search for "Amazon Instant Video Usage Rules," and then answer the following questions:

a. Are you allowed to stream more than one video at a time?

b. Are you allowed to stream the same video to two devices at the same time?

c. Are you allowed to stream videos to any digital device?

d. Are you allowed to save rented content to a handheld device so that you can watch it after the viewing period has ended?

5 The Digital Millennium Copyright Act (DMCA) makes it illegal to circumvent a technological measure that controls access to a work, but this law is reviewed every three years. Search the Web for the latest DMCA review (2010 or 2013). Which changes are beneficial to consumers?

INFOWEBLINKS

You can check the **NP2014 Chapter 8** InfoWebLink for updates to these activities.

W CLICK TO CONNECT
www.infoweblinks.com/np2014/ch08

What Do You Think?

ISSUE

1. Have you ever had trouble using software, music CDs, or movie DVDs because of copy protection?

2. In your opinion, do sites like the iTunes Store provide consumers with enough flexibility for copying files and creating playlists?

3. Do you think digital rights management technologies are justified because of the high rate of piracy?

Information Tools: Media Attribution

You can easily copy music, photos, and video clips for use in reports, on your blog, on YouTube, and on your Facebook page. If you are not creating a transformative work or a critical work that would be covered by Fair Use, what steps must you take to use "borrowed" content correctly?

As a general rule, assume that all images and media are copyrighted. Media elements on the Web are covered by the same copyrights as works in print and in other formats. When using copyrighted media, you should seek permission and you should provide attribution that identifies the copyright holder. Permission and attribution are not the same.

▶ **Permission** means obtaining rights for a specific use, such as on a Web site.

▶ **Attribution** means acknowledging the person who holds the copyright, usually by including a tagline under a media element or a citation in a bibliography.

You can obtain permission by asking the copyright holder. Most media sharing sites provide links to copyright holders. Supply the copyright holder with information about the item you want to use and how you intend to use it.

You might not have to contact the copyright holder for permission if the media element is covered by a license. Look for a license or rights link near the media element, or a site-use policy near the bottom of a Web page.

You can place your photo attribution in a small font directly under the photo or on its side, or you can include it in the bibliography. Video and music attributions should be placed near the "Play" link or in a bibliography.

The copyright holder might specify the text you should use for the attribution. For example, "Courtesy IBM" or "Jerry Harris Photography."

If the wording for an attribution is not specified, then you should include the following:

▶ Copyright holder's name

▶ License type, such as "with permission" or "Creative Commons"

▶ URL (optional)

The easiest media elements to use legally have a Creative Commons license for "Attribution."

These licenses clearly specify whether the element can be used for personal or commercial use, and only require you to provide an attribution crediting the source.

> For academic work, such as term papers and theses, you must include attributions for any media elements that you use, even though academic work falls under the umbrella of Fair Use. As with citations for quoted and paraphrased material, media attribution helps to establish the legitimacy of your work.

Courtesy of NASA

Courtesy of Creative Commons

TRY IT! The more you learn about copyright, citations, and attributions, the more complex these topics seem. Here's your chance to track down a few more concepts pertaining to media citations and then summarize what you've learned. For this project, create a document called Chapter 8 Media Project.

1. Photographers sometimes give permission to use images that are not free from other copyright and legal restrictions. For example, if a photographer takes a photo of a painting, it is considered a derivative work and it is subject to the painting's copyright. Link to the Shutterstock photo site and search for photos of the Mona Lisa. Can you find any photos of the actual painting? Why do you think this is the case?

2. Some museums and libraries allow personal, educational, and non-commercial use of digital images and other media. What is the policy for personal and educational use of digital versions of works from the Smithsonian American Art Museum's collection?

3. Media elements that include images of identifiable people are subject to complex legal issues, depending on the subject, the subject's age, and the element's intended use. To be on the safe side, photos or videos that contain images of identifiable people should be used only if the license includes a model release. Link to Shutterstock and Flickr and search for images of businessmen. Which site provides clear information about model releases?

4. Go to the Flickr site and link to the Advanced Search. Enter "Pyramids" in the search field, then select the options for Creative Commons-licensed content and for content to use commercially. Select an image with an "Attribution" license. Download the smallest resolution and paste the image into your Media Project document.

   Add the appropriate attribution under the Pyramids photo in your Media Project document.

5. Fill in the following table to summarize what you've learned about media attributions and citations.

SITUATION	FAIR USE?	IS THIS USE CORRECT? WHY OR WHY NOT?
You use a photo from an online magazine in a research paper without seeking permission and you do not attribute the source.		
You use a photo from an online magazine in a research paper without seeking permission, but you do attribute the source.		
You use a photo from an online magazine in a poster for an event without seeking permission, but you attribute the source.		
You use a photo from an online magazine in a poster for an event, but you get permission to do so and follow the photographer's instructions for attribution.		
A photo from Shutterstock is royalty free, so you use it on your Facebook page.		
You use a photo from the Smithsonian American Art Museum for a background in an app that you sell on iTunes.		

Technology in Context: Film

IN 1895, eager Parisians crowded into a busy cafe to watch the first public presentation of an exciting new invention—the Cinematograph. The 10-minute film, mostly scenes of everyday life, was a smashing success and ushered in the motion picture era. Early films were short, grainy, grayscale, and silent, but technology quickly improved. In the New York debut of *The Jazz Singer* (1927), Al Jolson spoke the first words in a feature film, "Wait a minute, wait a minute. You ain't heard nothin' yet!"

Even before "talkies" and Technicolor, filmmakers sought ways to escape the bounds of reality through special effects. As early as 1925, directors such as Willis O'Brien used stop-motion photography to animate dinosaurs, giant gorillas, and sword-wielding skeletons. Special-effects technologies—miniatures, blue screens, puppets, Claymation, 3-D, and composite shots—were used with varying degrees of skill over the next 50 years. Films such as Stanley Kubrick's masterpiece, *2001: A Space Odyssey* (1968), and George Lucas's original *Star Wars* (1977) stretched these technologies to their limits, but audiences demanded even more spectacular, yet "realistic," effects.

In 1982, Disney released *TRON*, a movie about a computer programmer who becomes trapped in the depths of a computer where programs are human-like creatures that serve every whim of an evil Master Control Program. The movie included the first primitive attempts at computer-generated footage—30 minutes of computer-generated imagery (CGI) created by two Cray X-MP supercomputers.

CGI uses rendering techniques to create a 3-D scene from a 2-D image, a camera angle, and a light source. Sophisticated algorithms determine how textures, colors, and shadows appear in the rendered scene. Camera angles can be changed at will, and fantastic effects can be created by bending or stretching the image, manipulating light, creating textures, and adding movement to the scene.

Rendered scenes can be set in motion with computer animation techniques. Manual animation requires a painstaking process called in-betweening, in which an artist draws a series of incrementally different images to produce the illusion of movement.

Computers can easily generate in-between images and free up human animators for more challenging work.

A captivating animation special effect called morphing was first seen on the big screen in James Cameron's *The Abyss* (1989), and was later used in *Terminator 2* (1991) and other movies. Like in-betweening, morphing starts out with animators defining the morph's start and end points—for example, in *Terminator 2*, the liquid metal face of the T-1000 robot and actor Robert Patrick's face. The start and end points are rendered into digital images, and then the computer generates all the in-between images. Human animators tweak the images by inserting small discrepancies for a touch of less-than-perfect realism in the final footage.

© Disney/Pixar/Photofest

Although the process might sound simple, morphing complex objects realistically and believably takes a tremendous amount of time and computer power. The five-minute morphing sequence in *Terminator 2* took special-effects company Industrial Light & Magic a year to create.

Memorable computer-generated scenes from classic blockbusters include the breathtaking aerial scenes in *Spiderman*, a furry blue monster called Sully careening downhill in *Monsters, Inc.*, the endless army of Uruk-hai marching down the valley toward Helm's Deep in *The Lord of the Rings: The Two Towers*, and Princess Merida unfurling her wildly curly locks in *Brave*.

Spiderman's acrobatic swing through Manhattan was generated with three professional rendering products: Maya, Houdini, and RenderMan. The Uruk-hai were created with MASSIVE, a custom program that gave each computer-generated warrior a unique sequence of actions. To individually animate each of Sully's 2,320,413 blue hairs, animators developed software called Fizt, a dynamic simulator.

Animation took another leap forward when Pixar's team of artists and engineers developed a computer program called Taz to realistically depict Princess Merida's flowing, curly hair.

Rendering, morphing, and other special effects require sophisticated computer systems. Pixar Animation Studios, the company that provided the technology behind *Toy Story*, *Up*, *Ratatouille*, *WALL-E*, and many other feature-length animated films, uses a cluster of computers called a renderfarm.

The film *Toy Story* took more than 800,000 computer hours to produce using the renderfarm. That might seem like a long time; but if Pixar animators had used a single-processor computer, it would have taken 43 years to finish the job!

Other CGI variations are being used for increasingly sophisticated effects. Special-effects guru John Gaeta developed bullet time and image-based rendering for *The Matrix* (1999). Bullet time produces reality-defying action sequences that slow time to a tantalizing crawl and then crank it back up to normal speed as the camera pivots rapidly around the scene. The effect requires a computer to meticulously trigger a circular array of more than 100 still cameras.

Films such as *Sky Captain and the World of Tomorrow* (2004) and *Sin City* (2005) took green screen special effects to a new level. Filmed entirely indoors on a sound stage, these movies used a technique called compositing that layers two or more video clips over each other and merges them into one image. Actors were filmed against a green background screen. During post-production, video editing software removed the background and layered in scenery created with CGI or from real footage on location.

Sin City is also notable as one of the first fully digital live action motion pictures. It was filmed in full color with high-definition digital cameras. The footage was converted to black and white, and then color was reintroduced digitally with the use of a DLP Cinema projector.

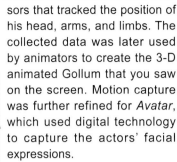
Copyright © 20th Century Fox Licensing/Merchandising/Everett Collection

Motion capture suits were put to award-winning use for Peter Jackson's *The Lord of the Rings*. The actor who played Gollum was outfitted with sensors that tracked the position of his head, arms, and limbs. The collected data was later used by animators to create the 3-D animated Gollum that you saw on the screen. Motion capture was further refined for *Avatar*, which used digital technology to capture the actors' facial expressions.

Avatar also reignited the popularity of the 3-D film genre, which had been languishing as a small niche market since the 1950s. 3-D has gone mainstream and is now available on consumer televisions and computers.

Sophisticated animation and rendering techniques now come close to producing realistic human figures. Animations were once clearly two-dimensional and far from lifelike, but CGI renderings are becoming more difficult to distinguish from real actors.

What might happen in the future is the subject of *Simone* (2002), starring Al Pacino as a washed-up director who is given a hard disk containing code for a computer-generated movie star. Pacino uses her as the leading lady in a string of hits, all the while keeping her identity secret. According to reviewer Leigh Johnson, it becomes clear that Simone, a computer-generated image, is more authentic than the people watching her. It is one of the film's main themes, expressed by Pacino's character: "Our ability to manufacture fraud now exceeds our ability to detect it."

The implications of computer-generated actors are just emerging. Not only do they blur the line between reality and fiction, but they also raise puzzling questions for actors and their agents, directors, and programmers. Is it possible to create CGI doubles for long-dead actors, such as Marilyn Monroe and James Dean? If so, who controls their use and profits from their work? Can aging actors sign contracts for use of their "young" CGI counterparts? Would it be legal and ethical for programmers to create and market virtual characters based on real actors or a compilation of the best traits of popular stars? As is often the case, new technologies present issues along with their benefits—issues you might want to consider the next time you watch a movie.

8

New Perspectives Labs

To access the New Perspectives Lab for Chapter 8, open the NP2014 interactive eBook and then click the icon next to the lab title.

▶ WORKING WITH BITMAP GRAPHICS

IN THIS LAB YOU'LL LEARN:

- How to identify common bitmap graphics file extensions
- How to capture an image from the Web
- How to find the properties of a graphic
- How to eliminate red eye and manipulate the brightness, contrast, and sharpness of photos
- How to make a photo look old
- How to prepare graphics for the Web and e-mail attachments
- The effects of lossy compression

LAB ASSIGNMENTS

1. Start the interactive part of the lab. Make sure you've enabled Tracking if you want to save your QuickCheck results. Perform each lab step as directed, and answer all the lab QuickCheck questions. When you exit the lab, your answers are automatically graded and your results are displayed.

2. Make a list of the available bitmap graphics software.

3. Capture a photographic image from a digital camera, scanner, or Web page. Save it as "MyGraphic." Open the image using any available graphics software. Use this software to discover the properties of the graphic. Indicate the source of the graphic, and then describe its file format, file size, resolution, and physical size.

4. Prepare this graphics file to send to a friend as an e-mail attachment that is smaller than 200 KB. Describe the steps that were required.

5. Select a high-resolution image and then convert it to two other file formats. For example, if the original image is a BMP file, you might convert it to a PNG and a JPEG graphic. List the size of each file and then indicate which image is the best quality and why.

Key Terms

Make sure you understand all the boldfaced key terms presented in this chapter. With the NP2014 interactive eBook, you can use this list of terms as an interactive study activity. First, try to define a term in your own words, and then click the term to compare your definition with the definition presented in the chapter.

8

Interactive Summary

To review important concepts from this chapter, fill in the blanks to best complete each sentence. When using the NP2014 interactive eBook, click the Check Answers buttons to automatically score your answers.

SECTION A: Music, voice, and sound effects can all be recorded and stored on a computer as [   ] audio. To digitally record sound, [   ] of the sound are collected at periodic intervals and stored as numeric data. High-quality sound is usually sampled at 44.1 [   ], and each stereo sample requires 32 bits of storage space. To conserve space, radio-quality recordings of speaking voices are often recorded at lower sampling rates. A computer's [   ] card is responsible for transforming the bits stored in an audio file into music, sound effects, and narrations. It contains [   ] circuitry that transforms bits into analog sound, and [   ] circuitry that samples live sounds and converts them into digital signals, and records analog sounds as digital bits. Digital audio file formats include WAV, AAC, WMA, Ogg, and MP3.

Most portable media players work with MP3 format or with the [   ] format, used for .m4p files at the iTunes Store. MIDI music is [   ] sound that is artificially created. Unlike digital audio sound files, which contain digitized recordings of real sound passages, MIDI files contain [   ] for creating the pitch, volume, and duration of notes made by musical instruments. MIDI files are typically much smaller than digital audio files for similar musical passages. However, MIDI music tends to lack the full resonance of symphony-quality sound that can be achieved with digital audio. Speech [   ] is the process by which machines, such as computers, produce sound that resembles spoken words. Speech [   ] refers to the ability of machines to "understand" spoken words.

▶ CHECK ANSWERS

SECTION B: A(n) [   ] graphic is composed of a grid of dots, and the color of each dot is stored as a binary number. Popular bitmap graphics formats include BMP, TIFF, GIF, JPEG, RAW, and PNG. Of these formats, GIF, JPEG, and PNG are supported by most Web browsers. Both scanners and cameras produce images in bitmap format. The dimensions of the grid that forms a bitmap graphic are referred to as its [   ]. High-resolution graphics typically produce better image quality than low-resolution graphics, but require more storage space. It is possible to change the resolution and/or the file size of a bitmap graphic; but because bitmaps are resolution [   ], these changes can reduce image quality. For example, enlarging a bitmap requires your computer to fill in missing pixels, which often results in a jagged or [   ] image. As a general rule, images

that you intend to print should remain at full size and resolution. When sending bitmap files as e-mail attachments, they can be [   ] in size or resolution to produce a file that is less than 1 MB. Color [   ] refers to the number of colors available for use in an image. For example, a bitmap graphic composed of 256 colors requires only [   ] bits to store the data for each pixel, whereas 24 bits are required for each pixel in a(n) [   ] Color graphic. Grayscale, system, and Web palettes use eight bits to represent each pixel. Image [   ] shrinks the size of a graphics file. [   ] compression permanently removes data, but [   ] compression shrinks files without removing any data.

▶ CHECK ANSWERS

SECTION C:
Unlike a bitmap graphic, created by superimposing a grid of pixels over an image, a(n) [_____] graphic consists of a set of instructions for creating a picture. These graphics are created by using a type of graphics software called [_____] software. They are stored as a collection of [_____] and their corresponding sizes, colors, and positions. You can identify these graphics by their flat, cartoon-like appearance and their file extensions: .wmf, .ai, .dxf, .eps, .swf, and .svg. A vector graphic can be converted into a bitmap by a process called [_____]. Once converted, however, the resulting graphic loses the object-editing qualities it had in its vector state. Two vector graphics formats, [_____] and Flash, are popular for Web-based graphics. 3-D graphics are stored as a set of instructions that contain the locations and lengths of lines that form a(n) [_____] for a 3-D object. This framework then can be covered by colored, patterned, and textured surfaces. This process, called [_____], produces a bitmap image of the 3-D object. [_____] tracing adds highlights and shadows to the image. 3-D graphics can be animated to produce special effects for movies and animated characters for 3-D computer games.   ▶ CHECK ANSWERS

SECTION D:
Footage for digital videos can be supplied from a digital source, or from a(n) [_____] source that requires conversion. In addition to standalone digital cameras, digital footage can also be obtained from cameras embedded in handheld devices and from [_____] built in above a computer screen. Video stored on a computer hard disk can be edited using a technique called [_____] editing, which does not require moving segments from one VCR to another. After editing, you can prepare to output your video by selecting settings for [_____] ratio, display size, and compression so that the resulting video quality and file size are appropriate for its intended use. Software, such as MPEG, DivX, Theora, and H.264, that compresses the video stream is referred to as a(n) [_____]. A compression [_____] indicates the degree of compression. A video file compressed at 35:1 has more compression, a smaller file size, and lower image quality than a file compressed at 5:1. Video and audio streams are combined into the final video file and stored using a(n) [_____] format, such as AVI, MOV, or WebM. Video can be included in HTML5-compliant Web pages using the <video> HTML [_____]. Videos can also be burned onto DVDs for playback in a standalone DVD player that requires data in [_____] format.   ▶ CHECK ANSWERS

SECTION E:
Digital [_____] management is a collection of techniques used by copyright holders to limit access to and use of digital content. DRM technologies can limit or prevent convenient [_____], place, and format shifting. A digital [_____] is a DRM technology inserted into the content stream in such a way that it is imperceptible to users, but can be recognized by complying devices. In the past, music CDs were [_____] protected by DRM technology, but that technology was not very effective. The major DRM technology for DVD content, called [_____], was cracked shortly after it was introduced. A somewhat more sophisticated DRM technology called [_____] is used on Blu-ray and HD-DVD. A hardware-based DRM technology called [_____] requires all devices involved in content playback to be compliant. Content downloaded from online music and video stores might be protected by DRM technologies, such as Apple's [_____] and Microsoft's Windows Media DRM. [_____] content is somewhat easier to protect than downloaded content because it is never stored in a file on a local device.   ▶ CHECK ANSWERS

Interactive Situation Questions

Apply what you've learned to some typical computing situations. When using the NP2014 interactive eBook, you can type your answers, and then use the Check Answers button to automatically score your responses.

1. Suppose you are creating an English-as-a-Second-Language Web page and you want to add links to sound files that pronounce English phrases. Would it be better to store the files in WAV or MIDI format? _____

2. Imagine that you're a musician and you are asked to synthesize some upbeat music for a modern ballet. For this project, you would most likely work with _____ music.

3. Suppose you visit a Web site that allows you to enter sentences, and then it reads the sentences back to you. The site even gives you a choice of a female or male voice. You assume that this site uses speech _____ technology.

4. You have an old photograph that you want to incorporate in a brochure for your antiques business. To convert the photo into digital format, you use a(n) _____.

© MediaTechnics

5. Imagine that you are preparing a series of bitmap graphics for a Web site. To decrease the download time for each graphic, you can use a compressed format such as GIF, PNG, TIFF or _____.

6. You've taken a photo with a high-resolution digital camera and you want to send it as an e-mail attachment. You decide to _____ it to reduce the image to a more manageable size.

7. Suppose you are designing a logo for a client. You know the design will undergo several revisions, and you understand that the logo will be used at various sizes. You decide it would be best to use drawing software to create the logo as a(n) _____ graphic.

8. After you finish arranging video clips and adding a soundtrack, you can select a video file format and a compression technique. For example, you might store the video in WebM container format and use the MPEG _____ to compress the file.

9. After purchasing a CD of your favorite rock group, you try to rip one of the tracks to your computer and convert it to MP3 format. When you play the file on your computer, you notice loud pops in the audio that indicate that the CD was probably copy _____.

10. You've downloaded a movie from a new online store. You can watch it on your computer; but when you try to watch it on a large-screen television, you don't get a picture. You know the television is working, so you guess that the movie is protected by _____ that requires all devices to be compliant.

▶ CHECK ANSWERS

Interactive Practice Tests

Practice tests that consist of ten multiple-choice, true/false, and fill-in-the-blank questions are available in the NP2014 interactive eBook. Test questions are selected at random from a large test bank, so each time you take a test, you'll receive a different set of questions. Your tests are scored immediately, and you can print study guides that help you find the correct answers for any questions that you missed.

▶ CLICK TO START

Learning Objectives Checkpoints

Learning Objectives Checkpoints are designed to help you assess whether you have achieved the major learning objectives for this chapter. You can use paper and pencil or word processing software to complete most of the activities.

8

1. Draw a diagram to show how the smooth curve of an analog sound wave is divided into samples and stored digitally.

2. Explain the relationship between sampling rate, audio quality, and file size.

3. Make a list of ten digital audio applications and indicate whether each one would use WAV or MIDI.

4. Use the file manager on your computer to locate five bitmap graphics. List the file name and extension for each one, and where possible identify whether it originated from a digital camera, a scanner, or some other source.

5. Describe six ways to transfer photos from a digital camera to a computer.

6. Explain how resolution, image size, color depth, and color palettes can be manipulated to adjust the file size of a bitmap graphic. Summarize how you would prepare bitmap graphics for the following uses: e-mail attachment, Web page, desktop publishing, and printed photo.

7. Recap key points about image compression, explaining the difference between lossy and lossless compression and listing file types with built-in compression.

8. Describe differences in the ways that vector and bitmap graphics are created, stored, and used. Explain how the concept of layering relates to your ability to modify a vector graphic.

9. Describe the procedures used to convert bitmap graphics into vector graphics, and to convert vector graphics into bitmaps.

10. Make a series of quick sketches that illustrates the evolution of a 3-D graphic from wireframe to rendered image, and to ray-traced image.

11. Explain how compression affects the file size of a digital video.

12. Explain how streaming audio and video work, and contrast them with non-streaming technology.

13. Use your own words to make a list of the steps required to burn video onto a DVD that can be viewed on standalone DVD players.

14. Make a list of the file extensions that were mentioned in this chapter and group them according to digital media type: bitmap graphic, vector graphic, digital video, digital audio, and MIDI. Circle any formats that are used on the Web and put a star by formats that typically require you to download a player.

15. Explain how specific DRM technologies are used to prevent consumers from a) making a copy of a music CD, b) ripping tracks from a music CD, c) copying a DVD movie, and d) watching a streaming movie.

16. Give examples of time shifting, place shifting, and format shifting.

Study Tip: Make sure you can use your own words to correctly answer each of the purple focus questions in the chapter.

Concept Map

Fill in the blanks on the concept map to show the hierarchy of digital media formats.

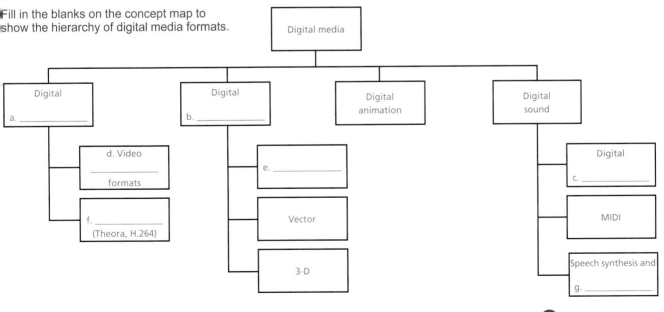

CHECK ANSWERS

GLOSSARY

3-D graphics A type of digital graphics format that displays a three-dimensional image on a two-dimensional space. 449

3-D graphics software The software used to create three-dimensional wireframe objects, then render them into images. 124

64-bit processor A microprocessor with registers, an address bus, and a data bus that holds 64 bits of data, in contrast to 32-bit processors that hold 32 bits of data. 68

AAC (Advanced Audio Coding) A file format that provides highly compressed audio files with very little loss of sound quality, and is promoted by Apple on its iTunes Web site. 425

AACS (Advanced Access Content System) A digital rights management system that uses encryption to restrict access and copying content from optical media. 469

Absolute reference In a worksheet formula, cell references (usually preceded by a $ symbol) that cannot change as a result of a move or copy operation. 138

Access time The estimated time for a storage device to locate data on a disk, usually measured in milliseconds. 77

Accounting software A category of software that includes accounting, money management, and tax preparation software. 126

Ad-blocking software A type of software that prevents ads from appearing on your computer screen. 385

Ad-serving cookie A cookie installed by a marketing firm to track user activities on Web sites containing its ads. 400

Adaptive utilities Utility software that alters a device's user interface to create an accessible environment for individuals with disabilities. 130

AES (Advanced Encryption Standard) An encryption standard that uses three separate key sizes and is based on the Rijndael encryption algorithm. 285

All-in-one computer A desktop computer form factor in which the system unit and screen are integrated into a single unit. 58

ALU (Arithmetic Logic Unit) The part of the CPU that performs arithmetic and logical operations on the numbers stored in its registers. 31

Always-on connection In the context of Internet access, a permanent connection, as opposed to a connection that is established and dropped as needed. 307

Analog data Data that is measured or represented on a continuously varying scale, such as a dimmer switch or a watch with a sweep second hand. 22

Analog hole Any device or technique that allows digital content to be copied legally or illegally from an analog device. 465

Android An open source operating system used primarily for handheld devices. 201

Anonymizer tools Software and/or hardware that cloaks the origin of an e-mail or a Web page request. 11

Anonymous FTP A type of FTP access that requires no account on a server, but rather can be accessed using "anonymous" as the user ID. 336

Anonymous proxy service A server on the Internet that can be used to forward Web requests after cloaking the originating address for users who want to surf anonymously. 403

Antispyware Software that blocks spyware from entering a computer. 403

Antivirus software A computer program used to scan a computer's memory and disks to identify, isolate, and eliminate viruses. 167

Application software Computer programs that help you perform a specific task such as word processing. Also called application programs, applications, or programs. 16

Application windows Rectangular-shaped areas on a computer desktop that hold program menus and workspaces. 191

Apps Short for applications; popularly used to refer to applications available for the iPhone, iPad, and other mobile devices. 16

ASCII (American Standard Code for Information Interchange) A code that represents characters as a series of 1s and 0s. Most computers use ASCII code to represent text, making it possible to transfer data between computers. 24

ASF (Advanced Systems Format) Microsoft's proprietary container format for streaming digital multimedia; typically holds WMV and WMA files. 458

Asymmetric Internet connection Any connection to the Internet in which the upstream speed differs from the downstream speed. 310

Asynchronous communications A communications mode, such as forums, e-mail, blogs, and tweets, in which participating parties do not have to be online at the same time. 332

Audio compression Techniques used to reduce the size of files that contain audio data. 424

Audio editing software A program that enables users to create and edit digital voice and music recordings. 121

Authentication protocol Passwords, user IDs, and biometric measures used to verify a person's identity. 34

Automatic recalculation A feature found in spreadsheet software that automatically recalculates every formula after a user makes a change to any cell. 138

AVI (Audio Video Interleave) A video file format, developed by Microsoft, that was once the most common format for desktop video on the PC. 458

B2B (business-to-business) An e-commerce exchange of products, services, or information between businesses. 385

B2C (business-to-consumer) An e-commerce exchange of products, services, or information between businesses and consumers. 385

B2G (business-to-government) An e-commerce exchange of products, services, or information between businesses and governments. 385

Backup A duplicate copy of a file, disk, or tape. Also refers to a Windows utility that allows you to create and restore backups. 222

Backup software A set of utility programs that performs a variety of backup-related tasks, such as helping users select files for backup, copying, and restoring. 228

Bandwidth The data transmission capacity of a communications channel. Digital signals are measured in bits per second; analog signals in Hertz. 251

Banner ad A type of advertisement typically embedded at the top of a Web page. 385

Bare-metal restore A process by which a backup is restored to a hard disk without first reinstalling the operating system and device drivers. 229

Benchmarks A set of tests used to measure computer hardware or software performance. 70

Binary number system A method for representing numbers using only two digits: 0 and 1. Contrast to the decimal number system, which uses ten digits: 0, 1, 2, 3, 4, 5, 6, 7, 8, and 9. 23

Biometrics The use of physical attributes, such as a fingerprint, to verify a person's identity. 34

BIOS A small set of basic input/output system instructions stored in ROM. 74

Bit The smallest unit of information handled by a computer. A bit is one of two values, either a 0 or a 1. Eight bits constitute a byte, which can represent a letter or number. 23

Bitmap graphic An image, such as a digital photo, that is stored as a grid work of colored dots. 430

Bitrate A ratio such as 5:1 that indicates the ratio of compression that has been applied to a file. High compression ratios such as 35:1 indicate more compression so data can be contained in smaller files. 457

BitTorrent A peer-to-peer technology in which pieces of files are distributed to and from a collection of networked computers; used for distributing music and movies over the Internet. 337

BlackBerry OS The operating system software designed for handheld BlackBerry devices. 203

Blog (Web log) A publicly-accessible personal journal posted on the Web. Blogs often reflect the personality of the author and are typically updated daily. 333

Blu-ray A high-capacity storage technology that stores up to 25 GB per layer on Blu-ray discs (BDs). 81

Blue screen of death An error condition in which a PC "freezes" and displays a blue screen (black screen in some versions of Windows); usually turning the computer off and turning it on again clears the error. 103

Bluetooth A wireless technology used in conjunction with standard Ethernet networks that allows data transfer rates between 200 and 700 Kbps up to a maximum range of 35 feet. 261

BMP The native bitmap graphic file format of the Microsoft Windows OS. 431

Boot disk A floppy disk or CD that contains the files needed for the boot process. 226

Boot process The sequence of events that occurs within a computer system between the time the user starts the computer and the time it is ready to process commands. 188

Bootstrap loader A program that automatically runs when a computer is first turned on in order to load the operating system. 74

Bootstrap program A program stored in ROM that loads and initializes the operating system on a computer. 192

Bot An intelligent agent that autonomously executes commands behind the scenes. Sometimes used to refer to a remote access Trojan horse that infects computers. 164

Botnet A group of bots under the remote control of a botmaster, used to distribute spam and denial-of-service attacks. 164

Bridge A device that connects two similar networks by simply transferring data without regard to the network format. 267

Broadband A term used to refer to communications channels that have high bandwidth. 251

Broadcast flag A status flag inserted into the data stream of digital television to indicate whether it can be copied. 467

Brute force attack A method of breaking encryption code by trying all possible encryption keys. 37

BSD license (Berkeley Software Distribution license) An open source software license patterned on a license originally used by the University of California. 160

Buffers Memory that is temporarily used to store input or other data until the processor is ready to use it. 187

Button An on-screen graphical control that can be clicked to initiate an action or a command. 192

Byte An 8-bit unit of data that represents a single character. 26

C2C (consumer-to-consumer) An e-commerce exchange of products, services, or information between consumers; for example, online auctions. 385

Cable Internet service A type of Internet connection offered to subscribers by cable television companies. 316

Cable modem A communications device that can be used to connect a computer to the Internet via the cable TV infrastructure. 317

CAD software (computer-aided design software) A program designed to draw 3-D graphics for architecture and engineering tasks. 124

Capacitors Electronic circuit components that store an electrical charge; in RAM, a charged capacitor represents an "on" bit, and a discharged one represents an "off" bit. 72

Card reader A device that can be used to read and record data on solid state storage devices, such as flash memory cards. 84

Case sensitive A condition in which uppercase letters are not equivalent to their lowercase counterparts. 35

CCD (charge-coupled device) One of the components in a digital camera that captures light from an image and converts it into color data. 433

CD (compact disc) An optical storage medium used to store digital information. CD-ROMs are read only. CD-Rs and CD-RWs can be used to record data. 81

Cell In spreadsheet terminology, the intersection of a column and a row. In cellular communications, a limited geographical area surrounding a cellular phone tower. 136

Cell references The column letter and row number that designate the location of a worksheet cell. For example, the cell reference C5 refers to a cell in column C, row 5. 137

Central processing unit (CPU) The main processing circuitry within a computer or chip that contains the ALU, control unit, and registers. 15

Character data Letters, symbols, or numerals that will not be used in arithmetic operations (name, Social Security number, etc.). 24

Chat Interactive real-time person-to-person communication over a network. 331

Ciphertext An encrypted message. 285

Circuit switching The method used by the telephone network to temporarily connect one telephone with another for the duration of a call. 253

CISC (complex instruction set computer) A general-purpose microprocessor chip designed to handle a wider array of instructions than a RISC chip. 69

Click-through rate The number of times Web site visitors click an ad to connect to an advertiser's site. 385

Client A computer or software that requests information from another computer or server. 18

Client-side Scripts and other activities that are executed by a client's browser, as opposed to being executed by the server. 372

Cloud computing A type of computing in which local devices access applications that run on an Internet-based server, where data can also be stored. 9

Cluster A group of sectors on a storage medium that, when accessed as a group, speeds up data access. 219

Codec Short for compressor/decompressor; a hardware or software routine that compresses and decompresses digital graphics, sound, and video files. 457

Color depth The number of bits that determines the range of possible colors that can be assigned to each pixel. For example, an 8-bit color depth can create 256 colors. 90

Color palette The selection of colors used in a graphic; also called a color lookup table or a color map. 438

Command-line interface A style of user interface that requires users to type commands, rather than use a mouse to manipulate on-screen controls. 190

Commercial software Copyrighted computer applications sold to consumers for profit. 159

Communications channel Any pathway between the sender and receiver; *channel* may refer to a physical medium or a frequency. 251

Communications port In the context of computer networking, a virtual location for data that arrives or leaves the device; common ports include 21 for FTP, 110 for e-mail, and 80 for Web data. 340

Communications protocol A set of rules that ensures the orderly and accurate transmission and reception of data. 252

Compiler Software that translates a program written in a high-level language into low-level instructions before the program is executed. 30

Compression ratio A ratio such as 5:1 that indicates the ratio of compression that has been applied to a file. High compression ratios such as 35:1 indicate more compression so data can be contained in smaller files. 457

Compute-intensive Refers to any task, problem, or product that is able to handle massive amounts of data and complex mathematical calculations. 19

Computer A device that accepts input, processes data, stores data, and produces output according to a stored program. 14

Computer network A collection of computers and related devices connected in a way that allows them to share data, hardware, and software. 8

Computer program A detailed set of instructions that tells a computer how to solve a problem or carry out a task. 15

Computer virus A program designed to attach itself to a file, reproduce, and spread from one file to another, destroying data, displaying an irritating message, or otherwise disrupting computer operations. 163

Computer worm A software program designed to enter a computer system, usually a network, through security "holes" and then replicate itself. 163

Container formats File formats, typically for storing sound and video, that contain one or more types of data that is compressed using standard codecs. 458

Control unit The part of the microprocessor that directs and coordinates processing. 31

Convergence In the context of technology, the melding of digital devices into a single platform that handles a diverse array of digital content, such as cell phones that also play digital music and display digital video. 9

Cookie A message sent from a Web server to a browser and stored on a user's hard disk, usually containing information about the user. 368

Copy protected Any digital rights management technology designed to prevent duplication of digital content; also referred to as copy prevention or copy restriction. 466

Copyright A form of legal protection that grants certain exclusive rights to the author of a program or the owner of the copyright. 156

Copyright notice A line such as "Copyright 2014 by ACME CO" that identifies a copyright holder. 156

CPU (central processing unit) The main processing circuitry within a computer or chip that contains the ALU, control unit, and registers. 15

CPU cache Special high-speed memory providing the CPU rapid access to data that would otherwise be accessed from disk or RAM. 68

Cropping The process of selecting and removing part of an image. 436

Cryptographic algorithm A specific procedure for encrypting and decrypting data. 285

Cryptographic key A specific word, number, or phrase that must be used to encrypt or decrypt data. 285

Data In the context of computing and data management, *data* refers to the symbols that a computer uses to represent facts and ideas. 15

Data bus An electronic pathway or circuit that connects the electronic components (such as the processor and RAM) on a computer's system board. 94

Data fork An element of the Macintosh file system that comprises the part of the file that contains the text, audio, or video data; contrast with resource fork. 199

Data processing An input-processing-output cycle that converts data into information. 6

Data representation The use of electronic signals, marks, or binary digits to represent character, numeric, visual, or audio data. 22

Data transfer rate The amount of data that a storage device can move from a storage medium to computer memory in one time unit, such as one second. 77

Database A collection of information that might be stored in more than one file or in more than one record type. 139

Database software Software designed for entering, finding, organizing, updating, and reporting information stored in a database. 139

Decryption The process of converting ciphertext into plaintext. 285

Dedicated graphics Circuitry for graphics that is supplied on an expansion card rather than integrated into the main system board of a digital device. 91

Defragmentation utility A software tool used to rearrange the files on a disk so that they are stored in contiguous clusters. 221

Demoware Commercial software that is distributed for free, but expires after a certain time limit and then requires users to pay to continue using it. 159

Desktop A term used to refer to the main screen of a graphical user interface that can hold objects such as folders and widgets. 191

Desktop computer A computer that is small enough to fit on a desk and built around a single microprocessor chip. 58

Desktop operating system An operating system specifically designed for use on personal computers, such as Microsoft Windows or Mac OS X. 188

Desktop publishing software (DTP) Software used to create high-quality output suitable for commercial printing. DTP software provides precise control over layout. 127

Desktop video Videos stored in digital format on a PC's hard disk or CD. 452

Device driver A type of system software that provides the computer with the means to control a peripheral device. 131

DHCP (Dynamic Host Configuration Protocol) A set of rules that allow network client computers to find and use the Internet address that corresponds to a domain name. 255

Dial-up connection A connection that uses a phone line to establish a temporary Internet connection. 312

Dialog box An element of graphical user interfaces that appears in a window and requests information, such as command parameters, from a user. 193

Dictionary attack A method of discovering a password by trying every word in an electronic dictionary. 36

Differential backup A copy of all the files that changed since the last full backup of a disk. 228

Digital audio Music or voice that has been digitized into files using sampling techniques; sometimes referred to as waveform audio. 422

Digital audio extraction The process of copying files from an audio CD and converting them into a format that can be stored and accessed from a computer storage device, such as a hard disk; sometimes referred to as ripping. 426

Digital camera A camera that takes and stores a digital image instead of recording onto film. 432

Digital content Media content that is stored in digital format. 464

Digital data Text, numbers, graphics, or sound represented by discrete digits, such as 1s and 0s. 22

Digital divide A gap between those who have access to digital technologies and those who do not. 13

Digital revolution A set of significant changes brought about by computers and other digital devices during the second half of the 20th century. 4

Digital rights management (DRM) A set of techniques and technologies designed to discourage and prevent unauthorized duplication of digital content. 466

Digital signal processor Circuitry that is used to process, record, and play back audio files. 424

Digital video A series of still frames stored sequentially in digital format by assigning values to each pixel in a frame. 452

Digital watermark A digital rights management technology that inserts a hidden signal into multimedia content as an identifying marker that can be tracked or verified. 467

Digitization To convert non-digital information or media to a digital format through the use of a scanner, sampler, or other input device. 5

Digitizing tablet A device that provides a flat surface for a paper-based drawing and a "pen" used to create hand-drawn vector drawings. 446

Directory In the context of computer file management, a list of files contained on a computer storage device. 206

Disc mastering The process of creating a CD or DVD by selecting all the files to be copied and then writing them in a single session. Contrast with packet writing. 219

Discovery mode The status of a Bluetooth device that is open for pairing. 261

Disk image A bit-by-bit copy of the contents of a disk created for backup, archiving, or duplication of data. 229

Disk partition An area of a hard disk created by dividing a large hard disk into several smaller virtual ones, such as when using two operating systems on a single computer. 206

DNS cache poisoning An exploit in which the DNS database is changed in such a way that a URL no longer connects to the correct Web site. 308

Dock The area of a Mac desktop (usually at the bottom on the screen) that displays program icons. 191

DOCSIS (Data Over Cable Service Interface Specification) A security technology used for filtering packets and maintaining customer privacy on cable Internet services. 317

Document formatting The specifications applied to fonts, spacing, margins, and other elements in a document created with word processing software. 135

Document production software Computer programs that assist the user in composing, editing, designing, and printing documents. 125

Domain name Short for *fully qualified domain name*; an identifying name by which host computers on the Internet are familiarly known (for example, nike.com). 307

Domain name server A computer that hosts the Domain Name System database. 308

Domain Name System (DNS) A large database of unique IP addresses that correspond with domain names. 308

DOS (Disk Operating System) The operating system software shipped with the first IBM PCs, then used on millions of computers until the introduction of Microsoft Windows. 194

Dot matrix printer A printer that creates characters and graphics by striking an inked ribbon with small wires called pins, generating a fine pattern of dots. 93

Dot pitch (dp) The diagonal distance between colored dots on a display screen. Measured in millimeters, dot pitch helps to determine the quality of an image displayed on a monitor. 90

Download The process of transferring a copy of a file from a remote computer to a local computer's storage device. 18

Downstream speed The rate at which transmitted data flows from a host or server to a local computer (contrast with upstream speed). 310

Drawing software Programs that are used to create vector graphics with lines, shapes, and colors, such as logos or diagrams. 123, 446

Drive bays Areas within a computer system unit that can accommodate additional storage devices. 86

DSL (digital subscriber line) A high-speed Internet connection that uses existing telephone lines, requiring close proximity to a switching station. 314

DSL filter Devices that are commonly used to prevent interference from analog devices, such as telephones, that use the same line as DSL devices. 315

DSL modem A device that sends and receives digital data to and from computers over telephone lines. 315

Dual band The capability of a communications device, such as a router, to use two communications frequencies. 263

Dual boot A computer that contains more than one operating system and can boot into either one. 198

Duplex printer A printer that prints on both sides of the paper in a single pass. 94

Duty cycle A measurement of how many pages a printer is able to produce per day or month. 93

DVD (digital video disc or digital versatile disc) An optical storage medium similar in appearance and technology to a CD but with higher storage capacity. 81

DVD authoring software Computer programs that offer tools for creating DVD menus and transferring digital video onto DVDs that can be played in a computer or standalone DVD player. 122

DVD image A series of files containing the data needed for a video DVD. The image is typically stored on a hard disk for testing before the image is transferred or "burned" to the DVD. 462

DVI (Digital Visual Interface) A standard type of plug and connector for computer display devices. 96

Dynamic IP address A temporarily assigned IP address usually provided by an ISP. 306

Dynamic RAM (DRAM) Random access memory that requires a power source to hold data; used as main memory on most computers. 72

E-commerce Short for *electronic commerce*, it is the business of buying and selling products online. 384

E-mail account A service that provides users with an e-mail address and a mailbox. 393

E-mail address An identifier that includes a user name, an @ symbol, and an e-mail server; used to route e-mail messages to their destination. 393

E-mail attachment A separate file that is transmitted along with an e-mail message. 398

E-mail client software Software that is installed on a client computer and has access to e-mail servers on a network. This software is used to compose, send, and read e-mail messages. 393

E-mail message A computer file containing a letter or memo that is transmitted electronically via a communications network. 392

E-mail server A computer that uses special software to store and send e-mail messages over the Internet. 392

E-mail system The collection of computers and software that works together to provide e-mail services. 392

EBCDIC (Extended Binary-Coded Decimal Interchange Code) A method by which digital computers, usually mainframes, represent character data. 25

EEPROM (electrically erasable programmable read-only memory) A type of non-volatile storage typically used in personal computers to store boot and BIOS data. 74

Encryption The process of scrambling or hiding information so that it cannot be understood without the key necessary to change it back into its original form. 285

Enhanced media player Handheld devices designed to play music, but with enhanced features, such as a browser and apps. 65

eSATA A standard for high-speed ports, plugs, and connectors typically used to connect external hard drives to computers. 96

Ethernet A popular network technology in which network nodes are connected by coaxial cable or twisted-pair wire. 257

Ethernet adapter A type of network interface card designed to support Ethernet protocols. 258

EULA (end user license agreement) A type of software license that appears on the computer screen when software is being installed and prompts the user to accept or decline. 157

Executable file A file, usually with an .exe extension, containing instructions that tell a computer how to perform a specific task. 146

Expansion bus The segment of the data bus that transports data between RAM and peripheral devices. 94

Expansion card A circuit board that is plugged into a slot on a computer system board to add extra functions, devices, or ports. 95

Expansion port A socket into which the user plugs a cable from a peripheral device, allowing data to pass between the computer and the peripheral device. 95

Expansion slot A socket or "slot" on a computer system board designed to hold a circuit board called an expansion card. 95

Extended ASCII Similar to ASCII but with 8-bit character representation instead of 7-bit, allowing for an additional 128 characters. 24

Field The smallest meaningful unit of information contained in a data file. 139

File A named collection of data (such as a computer program, document, or graphic) that exists on a storage medium, such as a hard disk or CD. 15

File compression utility A type of data compression software that shrinks one or more files into a single file occupying less storage space than the files did separately. 442

File Explorer A file management utility included with Windows 8 that helps users manage their files. 216

File extension A set of letters and/or numbers added to the end of a file name that helps to identify the file contents or file type. 204

File format The method of organization used to encode and store data in a computer. Text formats include DOCX and TXT. Graphics formats include BMP, TIFF, GIF, and PNG. 207

File header Hidden information inserted at the beginning of a file to identify its properties, such as the software that can open it. 207

File management utility Software, such as Finder and File Explorer, that help users locate, rename, move, copy, and delete files. 214

File server A network computer that is dedicated to storing and distributing files to network clients. 278

File sharing The process of allowing access to document, photo, video, and other files from a computer other than the one on which they are stored. 274

File shredder software Software designed to overwrite sectors of a disk with a random series of 1s and 0s to ensure deletion of data. 220

File specification A combination of the drive letter, subdirectory, file name, and extension that identifies a file (such as C:\Pictures\Photo.jpg); also called a path. 206

File system A method that is used by an operating system to keep files organized. 219

File tag In the context of Windows, a piece of information that describes a file. Tags, such as Owner, Rating, and Date Taken, can be added by users. 212

File-naming conventions A set of rules, established by the operating system, that must be followed to create a valid file name. 204

Firewall Software or hardware designed to analyze and control incoming and outgoing packets on a network; used to enhance security by filtering out potential intrusion attempts. 341

FireWire A standard for fairly high-speed ports, plugs, and connectors typically used to connect external storage devices, and for transferring data from cameras to computers. 96

First-party cookie A cookie that is generated by the Web page that is shown in the browser. 401

Fixed Internet access Any Internet access service designed to be used from a fixed, non-portable location (i.e., dial-up, DSL, and cable Internet service). 311

Fixed wireless Internet service A high-speed, wide area Internet service alternative to cable and DSL that transmits data wirelessly using RF signals. 319

Flash A file format developed by Macromedia and marketed by Adobe that has become popular for animations on Web pages. 448

Flash cookie A cookie-like object that is created and used by Adobe Flash Player; also referred to as a local shared object. 402

Flash video A popular video file format developed by Adobe Systems and used for Web-based video at sites such as YouTube. 458

Floppy disk A removable magnetic storage medium, typically 3.5" in size, with a capacity of 1.44 MB. 80

Folder The subdirectories, or subdivisions of a directory, that can contain files or other folders. 206

Font A typeface or style of lettering, such as Arial, Times New Roman, and Gothic. 135

Footer Text that appears in the bottom margin of each page of a document. 135

Form factor The configuration of a computer's system unit; examples include tower, mini-tower, and cube. 58

Format shifting The process of converting media into a different file format to use it on a device other than the original one. 465

Formatting The process of dividing a disk into sectors so that it can be used to store information. 219

Formula In spreadsheet terminology, a combination of numbers and symbols that tells the computer how to use the contents of cells in calculations. 137

Fragmented files Files stored in scattered, noncontiguous clusters on a disk. 221

Freeware Copyrighted software that is given away by the author or copyright owner. 161

Front side bus (FSB) The data bus that carries signals between the CPU and RAM, disks, or expansion slots. 68

FTP (File Transfer Protocol) A set of rules for uploading and downloading files between a client computer and a remote server. 335

FTP client The computer or software that is used to access an FTP server and transfer files to it or from it. 336

FTP server A computer that stores and distributes files to remote client computers. 335

Full system backup A copy of all the application, system, and data files that exist on a computer's hard disk. 226

Fully justified The horizontal alignment of text where the text terminates exactly at both margins of the document. 135

Function (1) In the context of spreadsheet software, a built-in formula for making a calculation. (2) In the context of programming, a section of code that manipulates data, but is not included in the main sequential execution path of a program. 137

Game controllers Devices such as joysticks, wands, and steering wheels; used to control on-screen action in computer games. 88

Gateway A network device that connects two dissimilar networks even if the networks use different protocols. 266

GIF (Graphics Interchange Format) A bitmap graphics file format, popularized by CompuServe, for use on the Web. 431

Gigabit (Gb or Gbit) Approximately 1 billion bits, exactly 1,024 megabits. 26

Gigabyte (GB) Approximately 1 billion bytes; exactly 1,024 megabytes (1,073,741,824 bytes). 26

Gigahertz (GHz) A measure of frequency equivalent to 1 billion cycles per second. 67

Globalization A group of social, economic, political, and technological interdependencies linking people and institutions from all areas of the world. 12

GPL (General Public License) A software license often used for freeware that insures it will be distributed freely whether in its original form or as a derivative work. 160

Gradient A smooth blending of shades of different colors, from light to dark. 447

Grammar checker A feature of word processing software that coaches the user on correct sentence structure and word usage. 134

Graphical user interface (GUI) A type of user interface that features on-screen objects, such as menus and icons, manipulated by a mouse. 190

Graphics Any picture, photograph, or image that can be manipulated or viewed on a computer. 123

Graphics card A circuit board inserted into a computer to handle the display of text, graphics, animation, and videos. Also called a video card or graphics board. 91

Graphics processing unit (GPU) A microprocessor dedicated to rendering and displaying graphics on personal computers, workstations, and videogame consoles. 91

Graphics software Computer programs for creating, editing, and manipulating images; types include paint software and drawing software. 123

Grayscale palette Digital images that are displayed in shades of gray, black, and white. 438

Grid computing system A network of computers harnessed together to perform processing tasks; distributed grids like the SETI@home project use ad hoc and diverse Internet connected computers; also see *cloud computing*. 334

Handshaking A process where a protocol helps two network devices communicate. 252

Hard disk drive A computer storage device that contains a large-capacity rigid storage surface sealed inside a drive case. Typically used as the primary storage device in desktop and laptop computers. 78

Hard disk platter The component of a hard disk drive on which data is stored. It is a flat, rigid disk made of aluminum or glass and coated with a magnetic oxide. 78

Hash value A number produced by a hash function to create a unique digital "fingerprint" that can be used to allow or deny access to a software application. 161

HDCP (High-bandwidth Digital Content Protection) A form of copy protection designed to prevent digital content from being transmitted over a DVI interface to a non-complying display device. 470

HDMI (High-Definition Multimedia Interface) A standard type of plug and connector for computer display devices. 96

Head crash A collision between the read-write head and the surface of the hard disk platter, resulting in damage to some of the data on the disk. 79

Header Text that is placed in the top margin of each page of a document. 135

Home computer system A personal computer designed for use with mainstream computer applications such as Web browsing, e-mail, music downloads, and productivity software. 60

Homegroup A feature of Windows that quickly creates a peer-to-peer network for sharing files and printers. 277

Horizontal market software Any computer program that can be used by many different kinds of businesses (for example, an accounting program). 126

Hot-plugging The ability of a component, such as a USB flash drive, to connect to or disconnect from a computer while it is running; also referred to as hot-swapping. 97

Hover ad An advertisement, created using interactive Web tools such as DHTML, that appears on top of Web pages, sometimes obscuring parts of them. 385

HTML (Hypertext Markup Language) A standardized format used to specify the layout for Web pages. 362

HTML conversion utility Utility software that converts documents, spreadsheets, and databases into HTML files that can be posted on the Web. 369

HTML document A plain text or ASCII document with embedded HTML tags that dictate formatting and are interpreted by a browser. 362

HTML form An HTML document containing blank boxes that prompt users to enter information that can be sent to a Web server. Commonly used for e-commerce transactions. 371

HTML mail E-mail messages that contain formatting, such as bold and italics, by turning on the HTML mail function. 397

HTML tags A set of instructions, such as <B>, inserted into an HTML document to provide formatting and display information to a Web browser. 362

HTML5 The version of HTML that was in the final stages of the approval process as of 2012. 362

HTML5 canvas A container for graphics defined by the HTML scripting language and used to create graphics and animations for Web pages. 448

HTTP (Hypertext Transfer Protocol) The communications protocol used to transmit Web pages. HTTP:// is an identifier that appears at the beginning of Web URLs (for example, *http://www.fooyong.com*). 364

HTTP status code A code used by Web servers to report the status of a browser's request. The HTTP status code 404 means document not found. 365

HTTPS (Hypertext Transfer Protocol Secure) The protocol used to create secure connections for e-commerce by adding a layer of encryption. 390

Hub A network device that connects several nodes of a local area network. 266

Hypertext A way of organizing a collection of documents by assigning an address to each and providing a way to link from one address to another. 360

Hypertext link Also referred to simply as a link; an underlined word or phrase on a Web page that, when clicked, takes you to a designated URL. 361

ICANN (Internet Corporation for Assigned Names and Numbers) A global organization that coordinates the management of the Internet's domain name system, IP addresses, and protocol parameters. 309

Icon A graphical object, such as those that represent programs or folders on a computer desktop. 192

Identity theft An illegal practice in which a criminal obtains enough information to masquerade as someone. 36

Image compression Any technique that is used to reduce the size of a file that holds a graphic. 440

IMAP (Internet Message Access Protocol) A protocol similar to POP that is used to retrieve e-mail messages from an e-mail server, but offers additional features, such as choosing which e-mails to download from the server. 394

Incremental backup A backup that contains files that changed since the last backup. 228

Infrared light A transmission technology that uses a frequency range just below the visible light spectrum to transport data. 259

Ink jet printer A non-impact printer that creates characters or graphics by spraying liquid ink onto paper or other media. 92

Input As a noun, the information that is conveyed to a computer. As a verb, to enter data into a computer. 15

Instant messaging A private chat in which users can communicate with each other in real time using electronically transmitted text messages. 331

Instruction cycle The steps followed by a computer to process a single instruction: fetch, interpret, execute, then increment the instruction pointer. 32

Instruction set The collection of instructions that a CPU is designed to process. 30

Integrated audio Sound card circuitry that is built into the circuitry of a digital device, in contrast to the use of an add-on sound card. 424

Integrated circuit (IC) A thin slice of silicon crystal containing microscopic circuit elements such as transistors, wires, capacitors, and resistors; also called chips and microchips. 27

Integrated graphics Circuitry for graphics processing that is integrated into the mainboard rather than as an expansion card. 91

Intellectual property A legal concept that refers to ownership of intangible information, such as ideas. 12

Internet The worldwide communication infrastructure that links computer networks using the TCP/IP protocol. 8

Internet backbone The major communications links that form the core of the Internet. 303

Internet forum An asynchronous online discussion in which participants post comments to discussion threads, which can be read at a later time by other participants. 332

Internet service provider (ISP) A company that provides Internet access to businesses, organizations, and individuals. 303

Interpreter A program that converts high-level instructions in a computer program into machine language instructions, one instruction at a time. 30

Intrusion In the context of computer security, the unauthorized access to a computer system. 339

iOS The operating system used for iPhones, iPods, and iPads. 200

IP (Internet Protocol) One of the main protocols of TCP/IP; responsible for addressing packets so that they can be routed to their destinations; IPv4 offers 32-bit addresses whereas IPv6 offers 128-bit addresses. 305

IP address Unique identifying numbers assigned to each computer connected to the Internet. 255

Jailbreak Making unauthorized changes to an iPod, iPhone, or iPad to get apps from a source other than the official iTunes App Store. 145

JavaScript A scripting language used to develop interactive and animated Web pages. 372

Jitter Deviations in the timing of a digital signal that can interfere with communications, especially voice over IP. 332

JPEG (Joint Photographic Experts Group) A format that uses lossy compression to store bitmap images. JPEG (pronounced "JAY-peg") files have a .jpg extension. 431

Kernel The core module of an operating system that typically manages memory, processes, tasks, and storage devices. 188

Keylogger A program, sometimes part of a Trojan horse, that records a person's keystrokes, saves them, and then sends them to a system administrator or remote hacker. 37

Keyword search The process of looking for information by providing a related word or phrase. 141

Keyword stuffing The practice of including a huge variety of keywords in the header of an HTML document in the hopes that a search engine will display it even when the content of the page is not relevant to the search. 377

Kilobit (Kbit or Kb) 1024 bits. 26

Kilobyte (KB) Approximately 1,000 bytes; exactly 1,024 bytes. 26

Label In the context of spreadsheets, any text used to describe data. 136

LAN (local area network) An interconnected group of computers and peripherals located within a relatively limited area, such as a building or campus. 247

Lands Non-pitted surface areas on a CD that represent digital data. (See also *pits*.) 81

Laptop computer A small, lightweight, portable computer that usually runs on batteries. Sometimes called a notebook computer. 59

Laser printer A printer that uses laser-based technology, similar to that used by photocopiers, to produce text and graphics. 92

Latency The elapsed time it takes for a packet of data to arrive at its destination. 309

LCD (liquid crystal display) Technology used for flat panel computer screens typically found on laptop computers. 90

Leading Also called line spacing, the vertical spacing between lines of text. 135

LED (light-emitting diode) Either a display technology that uses LEDs to produce an image on the screen, or one that uses LEDs as backlighting. 90

Library In the context of Microsoft Windows, a superfolder that contains pointers to various folders and files; examples include Documents, Pictures, and Videos. 217

Linear editing A video editing technique involving recording segments of video from one tape to another. 456

Link popularity A metric used by some search engines to rank the sites that are relevant to a query. 377

Linux An operating system that is a derivative of UNIX, available as freeware, and widely used for servers though it is also used on personal computers and workstations. 202

Linux distribution Usually a download that includes the Linux operating system, a Linux desktop, and other Linux utilities. 202

Linux platform A computer that is running the Linux operating system. 64

Local e-mail An e-mail system that requires users to install e-mail client software on their computer hard disk or flash drive; messages are held on a server until the client software downloads them to the local computer. 393

Local software Computer applications that are installed on and run from a local device, usually a computer hard drive. 7

Location-based software Applications that are able to access your current location using, for example, a smartphone's GPS or nearby LAN signals. 125

Logical storage models Any visual or conceptual aid that helps a computer user visualize a file storage system. Also called a storage metaphor. 215

Lossless compression A compression technique that is able to reconstitute all of the data in the original file; hence *lossless* means that this compression technique does not lose data. 440

Lossy compression Any data compression technique in which some of the data is sacrificed to obtain more compression. 440

MAC address (Media Access Control address) A unique identifier similar to a serial number assigned to networking equipment at the time of manufacture. 254

Mac OS The operating system software designed for use on Apple Macintosh computers. 197

Mac platform A family or category of Macintosh-compatible personal computers designed and manufactured by Apple Computer. 64

Machine code Program instructions written in binary code that the computer can execute directly. 30

Machine language A low-level language written in binary code that the computer can execute directly. 30

Magnetic storage A technology for recording data onto disks or tape by magnetizing particles of an oxide-based surface coating. 78

Mainframe computer A large, fast, and expensive computer generally used by businesses or government agencies to provide centralized storage, processing, and management for large amounts of data. 18

Malicious software Any program or set of program instructions, such as a virus, worm, or Trojan horse, designed to surreptitiously enter a computer and disrupt its normal operations. 162

Malware Programs such as viruses, worms, and bots designed to disrupt computer operations. 162

MAN (metropolitan area network) A public, high-speed network that can transmit voice and data within a range of 50 miles. 247

Mapping application An application that displays satellite, aerial, or street maps that can be used to locate places and get directions. 125

Markup language A language that provides text and graphics formatting through the use of tags. Examples of markup languages include HTML, XML, and SGML. 362

Mass-mailing worm A worm that sends itself to every e-mail address in the address book of an infected computer. 163

Mathematical modeling software Software for visualizing and solving a wide range of math, science, and engineering problems. 126

Mathematical operators Symbols such as + - / * that represent specific mathematical functions in a formula. 137

Media content A term popularized in the context of multimedia that refers to music, movies, television shows, and books. 464

Megabit (Mb or Mbit) 1,048,576 bits. 26

Megabyte (MB) Approximately 1 million bytes; exactly 1,048,576 bytes. 26

Megahertz (MHz) A measure of frequency equivalent to 1 million cycles per second. 68

Megapixel 1 million pixels; expresses the resolution and quality of an image; usually used in reference to digital cameras. 434

Memory The computer circuitry that holds data waiting to be processed. 15

Memory card A small, flat, solid state storage medium, frequently used to store data on cameras and handheld devices. 84

Memory leak An undesirable state in which a program requests memory but never releases it, which can eventually prevent other programs from running. 187

Menu In the context of user interfaces, a list of commands or options often displayed as a list. 192

Menu bar A standard component of most graphical user interfaces that is displayed as a strip of clickable options, that in turn display a list of commands. 192

Message header The section of an e-mail file that contains address, subject, and file attachment information. 392

Meta keyword A word that is included in the header of an HTML document in order to describe the document's contents. 377

Metadata Data that contains information about other data; file tags are an example of metadata. 214

Metafile In the context of graphics, a file that contains both vector and bitmap data. 447

Metasearch engine A search engine that searches other search engines. 380

Microcontroller A special-purpose microprocessor that is built into the device it controls. 20

Microprocessor An integrated circuit that contains the circuitry for processing data. It is a single-chip version of the central processing unit (CPU) found in all computers. 15

Microprocessor clock A timing signal that sets the pace for executing instructions in a microprocessor. 67

Microsoft Windows An operating system, developed by Microsoft Corporation, that provides a graphical interface. Versions include Windows 3.1, 95, 98, Me, NT, 2000, XP, Vista, 7, and 8. 194

Microwaves Electromagnetic waves with a frequency of at least 1 gigahertz; one type of channel for transmitting data over communications networks. 259

MIDI (Musical Instrument Digital Interface) A standardized way in which sound and music are encoded and transmitted between digital devices that play music. 427

MIDI sequence Digitally encoded MIDI music stored on a digital device, such as a computer or MIDI instrument. 427

MiFi A small, wireless router that connects to a cellular data network, creating a mobile Wi-Fi hotspot. 327

MIME (Multi-purpose Internet Mail Extensions) A standard for formatting non-ASCII messages so that they can be sent over the Internet, typically as e-mail messages. 398

MIMO (multiple input multiple output) A wireless communications device that uses an array of antennas to transmit data over more than one channel. 263

Mobile app An application designed to be downloaded to a handheld device, such as a smartphone or tablet computer. 145

Mobile broadband High-bandwidth wireless technology that was developed for sending digital data over cell phone systems. 326

Mobile Internet access Any service that allows subscribers to access the Internet while on the go. 311

Mobile operating system An operating system used by a handheld device, such as a smartphone or tablet computer. 188

Modem A device that modulates and demodulates a signal; typically used to send data from a computer to the Internet over telephone, cable television, or satellite networks. 304

Module A component or part of a software program or an office suite (e.g., a word processing module). 132

Money management software Software used to track monetary transactions and investments. 128

Monochrome bitmap A bitmap image that contains only the colors black and white. 437

Mouse An input device that allows the user to manipulate objects on the screen by clicking, dragging, and dropping. 88

MOV A multimedia file format, popular for digital videos, that works with QuickTime software. 458

MP3 A file format that provides highly compressed audio files with very little loss of sound quality. 425

MPEG (Moving Picture Experts Group) A family of highly compressed container file formats and codecs for digital multimedia; MPEG-1, MPEG-2, and MPEG-4. 458

Multi-core processor A microprocessor that contains circuitry for more than one processing unit. 68

Multiple-user license Legal permission for more than one person to use a particular software package. 157

Multiprocessing The ability of a computer or an operating system to support dual-core processors or multiple processors. 186

Multitasking The ability of a computer, a processor, or an operating system to run more than one program, job, or task at the same time. 186

Multithreading A technology that allows multiple parts or threads from a program to run simultaneously. 186

Multiuser operating system An operating system that allows a single computer to deal with simultaneous processing requests from multiple users. 187

Music software A broad category of software that can be used to play, record, compose, or manipulate sound files. 121

Narrowband A term that refers to communications channels that have low bandwidth. 251

Native file format A file format that is unique to a program or group of programs and has a unique file extension. 209

Natural language query A query formulated in human language as opposed to an artificially constructed language such as machine language. 141

Netiquette (Internet etiquette) A set of guidelines for posting messages and e-mails in a civil, concise way. 399

Network access points (NAPs) Internet nodes that link together different network service providers so that data can be transferred from one service provider to the other. 303

Network address translation (NAT) A security technique that allows a LAN to use one type of IP address for intra-network data and another type of address for data traveling to and from the Internet. 343

Network attached storage (NAS) Storage devices that are designed to be attached directly to a network, rather than to a workstation or server. 248

Network device Any device, such as a gateway, hub, or router, that is used to broadcast network data, boost signals, or route data to its destination. 250

Network discovery A setting that when turned on allows a computer to see other computers on a network and to be seen by those other computers. 275

Network interface card Circuitry, often on an expansion card mounted inside a computer, that transmits and receives data on a local area network. Also called a NIC, network card, or network adapter. 250

Network service providers (NSPs) Companies that maintain a series of nationwide Internet links. 303

Networked peripheral A peripheral device that contains circuitry that allows it to be directly connected to a network, rather than connecting to a computer that transfers data to a network. 250

Node In a network, a connection point; in a hierarchical database, a segment or record type. 250

Non-volatile Any electronic component that does not require a constant supply of power to hold data. 84

Nonlinear editing A digital video editing technique that requires a personal computer and video editing software. 456

Numeric data Numbers that represent quantities and can be used in arithmetic operations. 23

Object code The low-level instructions that result from compiling source code. 30

Octet One of four sections of an IP address. 255

Office suite A collection of productivity programs, typically word processing, spreadsheet, presentation, and database modules. 132

Ogg Theora A non-proprietary container format (Ogg) and video codec (Theora). 458

Ogg Vorbis An open source audio file format. 425

Online backup services Space for backup data provided through a Web site. 223

Online shopping cart A feature of e-commerce sites that stores information about items selected for purchase often by creating a cookie on a shopper's computer. 387

Op code Short for *operation code*; an assembly language command word that designates an operation, such as add (ADD), compare (CMP), or jump (JMP). 31

Open source An approach to developing and licensing software in which source code remains public so it can be improved and freely distributed. 12

Open source software Software that includes its source code, allowing programmers to modify and improve it. 160

Operand The part of an instruction that specifies the data, or the address of the data, on which the operation is to be performed. 31

Operating system The software that controls the computer's use of its hardware resources, such as memory and disk storage space. Also called an OS. 16

Optical fiber cable A high-bandwidth communications cable used for MANs and WANs. 251

Optical storage A technology that records data as light and dark spots on a CD, DVD, or other optical media. 81

Output The results produced by a computer (for example, reports, graphs, and music). 15

Overclocking Forcing a computer component, such as a microprocessor, to run at a higher speed than intended by the manufacturer. 71

P2P file sharing A practice in which individuals can obtain music, video, and other types of files from other users on a network; sometimes the files are shared without authorization from the copyright holder. 337

Packet A small unit of data transmitted over a network. 253

Packet loss A situation in which data bits are lost in transit, requiring them to be resent, which significantly increases the time required for an intact message to arrive at its destination. 332

Packet switching A technology used by data communications networks, such as the Internet, where a message is divided into smaller units called packets for transmission. 253

Packet writing The process of recording data to a CD or DVD in multiple sessions. Contrast with disc mastering. 219

Page layout The physical positions of elements on a document page such as headers, footers, page numbering, and graphics. 135

Paint software Software that creates and manipulates bitmap graphics. 123, 430

Pairing The process of establishing a link between two Bluetooth devices, usually through the exchange of passkeys. 261

PAN (personal area network) An interconnected group of personal digital devices located within a range of about 30 feet. 247

Paragraph alignment The horizontal position (left, right, justified, centered, for example) of the text in a document. 135

Paragraph style A specification for the format of a paragraph, which includes the alignment of text within the margins and line spacing. 135

Parallel processing The simultaneous use of more than one processor to execute a program. 69

Password A special set of symbols used to restrict access to a user's computer or network. 35

Password manager Software that keeps track of sites at which a user has registered and the password that corresponds to each site. 40

Path A file's location specified by the drive on which it is stored and the hierarchy of folders in which it is stored. (See *file specification*.) 206

Payroll software Horizontal market business software used to track employee hours, calculate pay, and print pay checks. 126

PC platform A family of personal computers that use Windows software and contain Intel-compatible microprocessors. 64

PDF (Portable Document Format) A standard format for exchanging files that can be viewed using Adobe Reader software. 129

Peripheral device A component or equipment, such as a printer, that expands a computer's input, output, or storage capabilities. 56

Persistent HTTP connection The process of using the same TCP connection to handle multiple HTTP requests, such as for obtaining the text and then the graphics for a Web page; contrast to stateless protocol. 365

Person-to-person payment A method of e-commerce payment that uses an intermediary or a third party such as PayPal to handle payment between a buyer and seller. 391

Personal computer A microcomputer designed for use by an individual user for applications such as Web browsing and word processing. 17

Personal computing A type of computing characterized by the use of standalone computers designed for single users. 7

Personal finance software Software geared toward individual finances that helps track bank account balances, credit card payments, investments, and bills. 128

Pharming An exploit that redirects users to fake Web sites. 406

Phishing An e-mail based scam that's designed to fool users into revealing confidential information. 37, 405

Phoneme A unit of sound that is a basic component of words and is produced by speech synthesizers. 428

Photo editing software The software used to edit, enhance, retouch, and manipulate digital photographs. 123

Photosites In digital photography, each photosite is a single point in an image, equivalent to one pixel. 433

Physical storage model A representation of data as it is physically stored. 218

Ping (Packet Internet Groper) A command on a TCP/IP network that sends a test packet to a specified IP address and waits for a reply. 309

Pipelining A technology that allows a processor to begin executing an instruction before completing the previous instruction. 69

Pirated software Software that is copied, sold, or distributed without permission from the copyright holder. 156

Pits Spots on a CD that are "burned" onto an optical storage medium to represent digital data. 81

Pixel interpolation A process that is used by graphics software to average the color of adjacent pixels in an image, usually when the image is enlarged. 436

Pixelated Describes the effect of increasing the size and thus decreasing the quality of an image. 436

Pixels Short for *picture elements*; the smallest unit in a graphic image. Computer display devices use a matrix of pixels to display text and graphics. 90

Place shifting The practice of accessing media from a remote location, such as over a network. 465

Plaintext An original, unencrypted message. 285

Plug-in A software module that adds a specific feature to a system. In the context of browsers, a plug-in adds the ability to display or play various additional file formats. 367

PNG (Portable Network Graphics) A type of graphics file format similar to but newer than GIF or JPEG. 431

Point size A unit of measure (1/72 of an inch) used to specify the height of characters in a font. 135

Pointing device An input device, such as a mouse, trackball, pointing stick, or trackpad, that allows users to manipulate an on-screen pointer and other screen-based graphical controls. 88

Pop-up ad A type of advertisement that usually appears in a separate window when you enter a Web site. 385

POP3 (Post Office Protocol version 3) A standard for retrieving e-mail messages from an e-mail server. 394

Port probe An exploit used by hackers to locate computer ports that can be used for surreptitious access; also called a port scan. 340

Portable computer Any type of computer, such as a laptop computer, that runs on batteries and is designed to be carried from one location to another; also called a mobile computer. 59

Portable Internet access Any type of Internet service, such as portable satellite, that can be moved from one place to another. 311

Portable software Software designed to be stored on a flash drive or CD, and that does not require installation before it is used. 151

PostScript A printer language, developed by Adobe Systems, that uses a special set of commands to control page layout, fonts, and graphics. 94

Power surge A spike in electrical voltage that has the potential to damage electronic equipment such as computers. 99

Presentation software Software that provides tools to combine text, graphics, graphs, animation, and sound into a series of electronic "slides" that can be output on a projector, or as overhead transparencies, paper copies, or 35-millimeter slides. 142

Printer Command Language (PCL) A standard for codes embedded within a document that specify how a printer should format each page. 94

Private IP address An IP address that cannot be routed over the Internet. 343

Processing The manipulation of data by a computer's microprocessor or central processing unit. 15

Product activation The process of becoming a registered user of a software product; the process might include entering a validation code to unlock the software. 161

Productivity software Software that helps people work more efficiently; traditionally word processing, spreadsheet, presentation, e-mail, and database software. 132

Programming language A set of keywords and grammar (syntax) that allows a programmer to write instructions that a computer can execute. 29

Project management software Software specifically designed as a tool for planning, scheduling, and tracking projects and their costs. 126

Proprietary software Software that carries restrictions on its use that are delineated by copyright, patents, or license agreements. 159

Protocol suite A group of protocols, such as TCP and IP, that work together. 305

PSK (pre-shared key) A variation of WPA encryption protocol for wireless connections in which the encryption key used by the router is the same for all client computers that connect to the network. 270

Public domain software Software that is available for public use without restriction except that it cannot be copyrighted. 158

Public folder A predefined folder designed to hold files that can be shared over a network. 276

Public key encryption (PKE) An encryption method that uses a pair of keys: a public key (known to everyone) that encrypts the message, and a private key (known only to the recipient) that decrypts it. 286

Push technology Transmitting data initiated by a server, rather than requested by a client, as when e-mail appears automatically. 203

Quarantined file A file suspected to be infected with a virus that antivirus software moves to a special folder to prevent accidental access to it. 169

Query A search specification that prompts the computer to look for particular records in a file. 141

Query by example (QBE) A type of database interface in which the user fills in a field with an example of the type of information that is being sought. 141

Query language A set of command words that can be used to direct the computer to create databases, locate information, sort records, and change the data in those records. 141

Query processor The component of a search engine that examines keywords entered by users and fetches results that match the query. 376

RAM (random access memory) Computer memory circuitry that holds data, program instructions, and the operating system while the computer is on. 72

Random access The ability of a storage device (such as a disk drive) to go directly to a specific storage location without having to search sequentially from a beginning location. 77

Rasterization The process of superimposing a grid over a vector image and determining the color depth for each pixel. 447

RAW In the context of digital graphics, a file that contains unprocessed image data directly from a digital camera's sensors. 431

Ray tracing A technique by which light and shadows are added to a 3-D image. 449

Read-only technology Storage media that can only be read from, but not recorded on. 82

Read-write head The mechanism in a disk drive that magnetizes particles on the storage disk surface to write data, or senses the bits that are present to read data. 78

Readability formula A feature found in some word processing software that can estimate the reading level of a written document. 134

Real-time messaging system Technologies, such as instant messaging and chat, that allow people to exchange messages when they are online. 331

Record In the context of database management, a record is the fields of data that pertain to a single entity in a database. 139

Recordable technology The devices and standards that allow computers to write data permanently on CDs and DVDs, but do not allow that data to be changed once it has been recorded. 82

Recovery disk A CD that contains all the operating system files and application software files necessary to restore a computer to its original state. 226

Recovery partition A section of a hard disk that contains the files necessary to restore a computer's hard disk contents to factory condition. 227

Registers A sort of "scratch pad" area of the microprocessor into which data or instructions are moved so that they can be processed. 31

Relative reference In a worksheet, a cell reference that can change if cells change position as a result of a move or copy operation. 138

Remote Access Trojan (RAT) A type of Trojan horse that provides a "backdoor" into a computer for remote hackers to transmit files, snoop, run programs, and launch attacks on other computers. 163

Rendering In graphics software, the process of creating a 3-D solid image by covering a wireframe drawing and applying computer-generated highlights and shadows. 449

Repeater A network device that can boost signals and retransmit them to extend the coverage area of a network. 266

Reserved words Special words used as commands in some operating systems that may not be used in file names. 205

Resolution dependent Graphics, such as bitmaps, in which the quality of the image is dependent on the number of pixels constituting the image. 436

Resource A component, either hardware or software, that is available for use by a computer's processor. 185

Resource fork A storage characteristic of Mac OS that creates a file containing a description of the data stored in an accompanying raw data file. 199

Response rate In the context of display technology, response rate is the time it takes for one pixel to change from black to white then back to black. 90

Restore The process of copying files from a backup back to a computer's hard disk. 222

Restore point Data stored about the state of files and the operating system at a given point in time, then used to roll back the computer system to that state. 227

Rewritable technology The devices and standards that allow users to write data on a storage medium and then change that data. 82

RF signals (radio frequency signals) Data that is broadcast and received via radio waves with a transceiver. 259

RGB color model The use of red, green, and blue light that can be combined to create the full spectrum of colors. 439

Ribbon An element of the user interface popularized by Microsoft Office 2007 that presents users with multiple tabs instead of menus at the top of the application window. 192

RISC (reduced instruction set computer) A microprocessor designed for rapid and efficient processing of a small set of simple instructions. 69

RJ45 connector A square plastic cable connector that resembles an oversized telephone connector, and is used to connect Ethernet devices. 251

ROM (read-only memory) Refers to one or more integrated circuits that contain permanent instructions that the computer uses during the boot process. 74

Root directory The main directory of a disk. 206

Rooting A process that enables users to gain root access to Android mobile devices with the purpose of overcoming limitations imposed by mobile service providers. 145

Rootkit Software that conceals running processes; used by hackers to disguise security breaches and break-ins. 165

Routable IP address A network address that can be routed over the Internet; contrast to private IP address. 343

Router A device used to make wired or wireless connections and route data to its destination on a network. 250

Run-length encoding (RLE) A graphics file compression technique that looks for patterns of bytes and replaces them with messages that describe the patterns. 440

Safe Mode A boot option that appears when an operating system is unable to complete the boot sequence. By entering Safe Mode, a user can gracefully shut down the computer, and then try to reboot it. 105

Sampling rate The number of times per second a sound is measured during the recording process. 423

Satellite Internet service A high-speed Internet service that uses a geosynchronous or low-earth orbit satellite to send data directly to satellite dishes owned by individuals. 318

Satellite modem A device that connects a computer to a satellite for purposes of accessing the Internet. 318

Scanner A device that converts a printed image into a bitmap graphic. 432

Screen resolution The density of the grid used to display text or graphics on a display device; the greater the horizontal and vertical density, the higher the resolution. 91

Search and Replace A feature of document production software that allows the user to automatically locate all instances of a particular word or phrase and substitute another word or phrase. 133

Search engine indexer The component of a search engine that reviews the Web pages brought back by a crawler and creates pointers to them so that they can be quickly accessed. 376

Search operator A logical search operator such as AND, OR, and NOT that helps form complex queries. 379

Search terms The words entered into a search engine or database to form a query. 378

Sectors Subdivisions of the tracks on a storage medium that provide storage areas for data. 219

Secure connection An Internet connection that encrypts data transmitted between your computer and a Web site. 389

Security software Any software package that is designed to protect computers from destructive software and unauthorized intrusions. 162

Security suite A software suite containing modules to protect computers against viruses, worms, intrusions, spyware, and other threats. 166

Semiconducting materials (semiconductors) Substances, such as silicon or germanium, that can act as either a conductor or an insulator. Used in the manufacture of computer chips. 27

Sequential access A characteristic of data storage, usually on computer tape, that requires a device to read or write data one record after another, starting at the beginning of the medium. 77

Serial processing Processing data one instruction at a time, completing one instruction before beginning another. 69

Server A computer or software on a network that supplies the network with data and storage. 18

Server operating system A type of operating system, sometimes called a network operating system, that provides management tools for distributed networks, e-mail servers, and Web hosting sites. 187

Server-side Scripts and other activities that are executed by a Web server in response to client data. 372

Service pack A collection of patches designed to correct bugs and/or add features to an existing software program. 152

Setup program A program module supplied with a software package for the purpose of installing the software. 148

Shared resources Hardware, software, and data that is available over a network to authorized users. 248

Shareware Copyrighted software marketed under a license that allows users to use the software for a trial period and then send in a registration fee if they wish to continue to use it. 159

Shrink-wrap license A legal agreement printed on computer software packaging, which becomes binding when the package is opened. 157

Single-user license Legal permission for one person to use a particular software package. 157

Single-user operating system A type of operating system that is designed for one user at a time using one set of input devices. 187

Site license Legal permission for software to be used on any and all computers at a specific location (for example, within a corporate building or on a university campus). 157

Slide rule A manual calculator invented by William Oughtred that uses John Napier's logarithms to perform complex engineering and scientific calculations. 487

Smartphone A cellular phone that has a high-resolution color screen, a browser, and the ability to run apps. 65

Smileys Text-based symbols used to express emotion. 399

SMTP (Simple Mail Transfer Protocol) A communications protocol used to send e-mail across a network or the Internet. 394

Sniffing In the context of computer hacking, a technique that uses packet sniffer software to capture packets as they are sent over a network. 37

Social media Online Web sites and services, such as Facebook, Twitter, and LinkedIn, that help users create content and share it with others. 10

Socket A communication path between two remote programs. 364

Software The instructions that direct a computer to perform a task, interact with a user, or process data. 15

Software as a service A cloud computing model in which consumers access applications using a browser; usually fee based. 330

Software installation The process by which programs and data are copied to the hard disk of a computer system and otherwise prepared for access and use. 143

Software license A legal contract that defines the ways in which a user may use a computer program. 157

Software update A section of code or a program module designed to correct errors or enhance security on an already installed software product. 152

Software upgrade A new version of a software product containing new features and designed to replace the entire earlier version of the product. 152

Solid state drive A data storage device that utilizes erasable, rewritable circuitry. 85

Solid state storage A technology that records data and stores it in a microscopic grid of cells on a nonvolatile, erasable, low-power chip. 84

Sound card A circuit board that gives the computer the ability to accept audio input from a microphone, play sound files, and produce audio output through speakers or headphones. 424

Source code Computer instructions written in a high-level language. 29

Source document A file containing the HTML tags or scripts for a Web page. 363

Spam Unsolicited e-mail typically sent as a bulk or mass-mailing and often used for fraudulent or deceptive marketing. 404

Spam filter Software that identifies unsolicited and unwanted e-mail messages and blocks them from the recipient's Inbox. 404

Speech recognition The process by which computers recognize voice patterns and words, and then convert them to digital data. 428

Speech synthesis The process by which computers produce sound that resembles spoken words. 428

Spelling checker A feature of document production software that checks each word in a document against an electronic dictionary of correctly spelled words, and then presents a list of alternatives for possible misspellings. 134

Spelling dictionary A data module that is used by a spelling checker as a list of correctly spelled words. 134

Sponsored links Links displayed by a search engine that have paid placements. 377

Spreadsheet A numerical model or representation of a real situation, presented in the form of a table. 136

Spreadsheet software Software for creating electronic worksheets that hold data in cells and perform calculations based on that data. 136

Spyware Any software that covertly gathers user information without the user's knowledge, usually for advertising purposes. 164

SSID (service set identifier) A code that identifies a network containing wireless connections and is attached to every packet that travels on that network. 268

SSL (Secure Sockets Layer) An older security protocol that uses encryption to establish a secure connection between a computer and a Web server. 390

Start screen The Windows 8 screen that contains all of the tiles for applications. 191

Stateless protocol A protocol, such as HTTP, that allows one request and response per session. 368

Static IP address A permanently assigned and unique IP address, used by hosts or servers. 306

Statistical software Software for analyzing large sets of data to discover patterns and relationships within them. 126

Storage The area in a computer where data is retained on a permanent basis. 15

Storage density The closeness of the particles on a disk surface. As density increases, the particles are packed more tightly together and are usually smaller. 77

Storage device A mechanical apparatus that records data to and retrieves data from a storage medium. 76

Storage medium The physical material, such as a hard disk or CD, on which data is stored. 76

Store-and-forward A technology used by communications networks in which an e-mail message is temporarily held in storage on a server until it is requested by a client computer. 394

Stored program A set of instructions that resides on a storage device, such as a hard drive, and can be loaded into computer memory and executed. 16

Streaming audio An audio file format that allows the audio clip to begin before the file is entirely downloaded. 426

Streaming video An Internet video technology that sends a small segment of a video file to a user's computer and begins to play it while the next segment is being sent. 459

Strong encryption Encryption that is difficult to decrypt or "break" without the encryption key. 285

Style A feature in many desktop publishing and word processing programs that allows the user to apply numerous format settings with a single command. 135

Subdirectory A directory found under the root directory. 206

Submenu A user interface element that emerges after a menu is selected to offer additional options. 193

Supercomputer The fastest and most expensive type of computer, capable of processing trillions of instructions per second. 19

Surge strip A device that filters out electrical spikes that could damage computer equipment. 100

SVG (Scalable Vector Graphics) A graphics format designed specifically for Web display that automatically resizes when displayed on different screens. 448

Switch A network device that sends data to a specific address instead of broadcasting it over an entire network. 266

Symmetric Internet connection Any connection to the Internet in which the upstream speed is the same as the downstream speed. 311

Symmetric key encryption An encryption key that is used for both encryption and decryption of messages. 286

Synchronization The process of updating files so they are the same on two devices; can be used for backup or to update addresses, etc. 225

Synchronous communications A communications mode, such as VoIP, in which participants must be online at the same time. 332

Synthesized sound Artificially created sound, usually found in MIDI music or synthesized speech. 427

System board The main circuit board in a computer that houses chips and other electronic components. 28

System palette A selection of colors that are used by an operating system to display graphic elements. 439

System requirements (1) The minimum hardware and operating system specifications required for a software application to operate correctly. (2) Criteria for developing a successful information system, which are typically compiled into a System Requirements Report at the conclusion of the analysis phase of the SDLC. 155

System software Computer programs, such as an operating system or utility software, that help the computer carry out essential operating tasks. 16

System unit The case or box that contains the computer's power supply, storage devices, main circuit board, processor, and memory. 57

System utilities Utility software that diagnoses and repairs disk errors, corrupted files, and other software or hardware problems. 130

Tablet computer A small, portable computer with a touch-sensitive screen that can be used as a writing or drawing pad. 65

Taskbar A graphical user interface element usually displayed near the bottom of the screen to help users launch and monitor applications. 191

Tax preparation software Software used to help individuals or businesses calculate annual state and federal taxes. 128

TCP (Transmission Control Protocol) The protocol within TCP/IP that is responsible for establishing a data connection between two hosts and breaking data into packets. 305

TCP/IP (Transmission Control Protocol/Internet Protocol) The primary protocol suite for transmitting messages over the Internet. 305

Text-to-speech software Software that generates speech based on written text that is played back through a computer's sound card. 428

Thesaurus A feature of documentation software that provides synonyms. 134

Third-party cookie A cookie that is generated by an ad or an entity other than the Web page that is shown in the browser. 401

Thunderbolt A high-speed expansion port typically used to connect external storage devices to a computer. 96

TIFF (Tagged Image File Format) A bitmap image file format with a .tif extension that automatically compresses the file data. 431

Tiles In the context of Windows 8, tiles are the icons that represent programs on the Start screen. 192

Time shifting The practice of recording digital content for later playback. 465

TLS (Transport Layer Security) An update of the Secure Sockets Layer (SSL) protocol for encrypting data before it is transmitted over a network. 390

Toolbar A component of graphical user interfaces that displays icons representing tools, commands, and other options. 192

Top-level domain A major domain category into which groups of computers on the Internet are divided, such as com, edu, gov, int, mil, net, and org. 307

Touchscreen A display device that accepts input from being touched with a stylus or fingertip. 89

Tower case A desktop computer form factor that stores the system board and storage devices in a tall system unit with detached display and keyboard. 58

Traceroute A network utility that records a packet's path, the number of hops, and the time it takes for the packet to make each hop. 310

Tracing software Software that locates the edges of objects in a bitmap graphic and converts the resulting shape into a vector graphic. 447

Trackpad A touch-sensitive surface on which you slide your fingers to move the on-screen pointer. 89

Tracks A series of concentric or spiral storage areas created on a storage medium during the formatting process. 219

Transceiver A combination of a transmitter and a receiver used to send and receive data in the form of radio frequencies. 259

Transcoding The process of converting audio and video files from one digital format to another, such as converting an MOV file into a Flash video file. 458

Trojan horse A computer program that appears to perform one function while actually doing something else, such as inserting a virus into a computer system or stealing a password. 163

True Color bitmap A color image with a color depth of 24 bits or 32 bits. Each pixel in a True Color image can be displayed using any of 16.7 million different colors. 439

Tweet A short message, sometimes called a microblog, posted on Twitter. 333

Unicode A 16-bit character-representation code that can represent more than 65,000 characters. 25

Uninstall routine A program that removes software files, references, and registry entries from a computer's hard disk. 153

UNIX A multiuser, multitasking server operating system developed by AT&T Bell Laboratories in 1969. 202

Unzipped Refers to files that have been uncompressed. 150

Upload The process of transferring a file from a local computer to a remote computer over a LAN or the Internet. 18

UPS (uninterruptible power supply) A battery-backed device designed to provide power to a computer during blackouts, brownouts, or other electrical disruptions. 100

Upstream speed The rate at which data is transmitted from your home computer to the Internet. 310

URL (Uniform Resource Locator) The address of a Web page. 361

USB (universal serial bus) A high-speed bus commonly used for connecting peripheral devices to computers. 96

USB flash drive A portable solid state storage device nicknamed "pen drive" or "keychain drive" that plugs directly into a computer's USB port. 85

USB hub A device that provides several auxiliary USB ports. 96

User ID A combination of letters and numbers that serves as a user's "call sign" or identification. Also referred to as a user name. 34

User interface The software and hardware that enable people to interact with computers. 190

Utility software A type of system software provided by the operating system vendor or third-party vendors that specializes in tasks such as system maintenance, security, or file management. 129

Value A number used in a calculation. 136

Vector graphic An image generated from descriptions that specify the position, length, and direction in which lines and shapes are drawn. 444

Vertical market software Computer programs designed to meet the needs of a specific market segment or industry, such as medical record-keeping software for use in hospitals. 126

VGA (Video Graphics Array) A screen resolution of 640 x 480. 96

Video capture The process of converting analog video signals into digital data stored on a hard drive. 455

Video editing software Software that provides tools for capturing and editing video from a camcorder. 122

Videogame console A computer specifically designed for playing games using a television screen and game controllers. 17

Viewing angle width The angle at which you can clearly see the screen image from the side. 90

Virtual keyboard A keyboard that is displayed on a touchscreen and used for input on smartphones and tablet computers. 89

Virtual machine Software that creates an operating environment that emulates another computer platform; as an example, Parallels Desktop creates a virtual PC on an Intel Macintosh computer. 198

Virtual memory A computer's use of hard disk storage to simulate RAM. 73

Virtual private network (VPN) A network connection that typically carries encrypted data over the Internet to and from a remote access server. 345

Virus definitions A group of virus signatures used by antivirus software to identify and block viruses and other malware. 168

Virus hoax A message, usually e-mail, that makes claims about a virus problem that doesn't actually exist. 166

Virus signature The unique computer code contained in a virus that security software uses to identify it. 167

VOB (Video Object) An industry-standard video format for standalone DVD players. 458

Voiceband modem The type of modem typically used to connect a computer to a telephone line. 313

VoIP (Voice over Internet Protocol) Hardware, software, and protocols used to make telephone-style calls over the Internet. Also referred to as Internet telephony. 331

Volatile A term that describes data (usually in RAM) that can exist only with a constant supply of power. 72

WAN (wide area network) An interconnected group of computers and peripherals that covers a large geographical area, such as multiple branches of a corporation. 247

WAP (Wireless Access Protocol) A communications protocol that provides Internet access for handheld devices. 325

WAV An audio file format with a .wav extension that was Windows' original "native" sound format. 425

Wavetable A set of pre-recorded musical instrument sounds in MIDI format. 427

Weak encryption Encryption that is relatively easy or simple to decrypt without the encryption key. 285

Web Short for *World Wide Web*; an Internet service that links documents and information from computers located worldwide, using the HTTP protocol. 8

Web 2.0 A group of new and innovative ways to use the Web, such as for social networking, blogging, and wikis. 361

Web 3.0 A group of technologies including cloud computing that extend the ways in which the Internet and Web can be used. 361

Web application Application software that is accessed and used from within a browser. 143

Web browser A program that communicates with a Web server and displays Web pages. 361

Web bug A small graphic on a Web page that installs cookies designed to track your online activities. Also known as a clear GIF or pixel tag. 403

Web cache A collection of Web pages and associated graphics that have been accessed and are temporarily stored locally to speed up subsequent access to them. 365

Web crawler The component of a search engine that autonomously visits Web sites collecting Web page data that will be indexed and available for searching. 375

Web page Information displayed by a Web browser that's produced from an HTML document or generated on the fly from data in a database. 361

Web palette A standard selection of colors that all Internet browsers can display; also called a Web-safe palette or browser palette. 438

Web search engine A program that uses keywords to find information on the Internet and returns a list of links to relevant documents. 374

Web server A computer that listens for queries from Web browsers and transmits HTML documents over the Internet. 361

Web site A Web address that holds a collection of information identified by a common domain name, such as *www.cnn.com*. 361

Webcam An inexpensive digital camera that attaches directly to a computer and creates a video by capturing a series of still images. 454

WebM A multimedia container format designed for HTML5 projects. 458

Webmail An e-mail system that allows users to access e-mail messages using a browser. 393

WEP (Wired Equivalent Privacy) An encryption algorithm used to protect data on Wi-Fi networks. 270

What-if analysis The process of setting up a model in a spreadsheet and experimenting to see what happens when different values are entered. 136

Wi-Fi An Ethernet-compatible wireless connection that uses 802.11a, b, g, and n standards. 262

Wi-Fi adapter A type of network interface card that includes a transmitter and a receiver using Wi-Fi protocols. 262

Wi-Fi hotspot The geographical area in which you can connect to a Wi-Fi signal, such as a Wi-Fi equipped campus or coffeehouse. 322

Wiki Software that allows users to collaborate to create, change, and link Web pages. Used for applications such as Wikipedia and open source project management. 333

WiMAX A fixed wireless Internet service based on Ethernet protocols with a range of 30 miles and a transmission speed of 70 Mbps. 319

Windows Registry A group of files on Windows computers that is used by the operating system to store configuration information about hardware and software. 227

Windows RT The version of Microsoft Windows designed for tablet computers. 196

Wireframe A representation of a 3-D object using separate lines, which resemble wire, to create a model. 449

Wireless access point A network device that connects several devices of a local area network by broadcasting signals to any device with compatible Wi-Fi cards. 266

Wireless ad-hoc protocol Wireless connections in which devices broadcast directly to each other instead of to a central access point. 262

Wireless encryption A security measure for networks containing wireless connections that scrambles data transmitted between network devices. 269

Wireless encryption key The basis for scrambling and unscrambling the data that travels over a wireless connection; sometimes called a network security key. 270

Wireless infrastructure protocol Wireless connections in which devices communicate through a central access point. 262

WMA (Windows Media Audio) A file format with a .wma extension that is promoted by Microsoft and provides highly compressed audio files with very little loss of sound quality. 425

Word processing software Computer programs that assist the user in producing documents, such as reports, letters, papers, and manuscripts. 133

Word size The number of bits that a CPU can manipulate at one time, which is dependent on the size of the registers in the CPU, and the number of data lines in the bus. 68

Word wrap The ability of word processing software to automatically sense the right margin and stream text to the next line. 133

Worksheet A computerized, or electronic, spreadsheet. 136

Workstation (1) A computer connected to a local area network. (2) A powerful desktop computer designed for specific tasks. 17

WPA (Wi-Fi Protected Access) A method for encrypting data transmitted over wireless connections. 270

XHTML A markup language very similar to HTML, but more customizable. 362

Zipped Refers to one or more files that have been compressed. 150

Zombie A computer that has been compromised by malware that allows it to be controlled by a remote user. 164

INDEX

TRY IT! ANSWERS

CHAPTER 1

005

○ No, data processing was associated with business and government computing.

● Correct! CompuServe and AOL had some similarities to today's social media, but were designed for people using desktop computers and dial-up Internet connections.

○ No, CompuServe and AOL were popular in the 1980s and mid-1990s, whereas the first tablet was not introduced until 2000.

○ No, cloud computing became popular long after the heyday of AOL and CompuServe.

007

○ No, the Beatles got together in 1960. Beatlemania was in full swing from 1963-1966, ten years before the age of personal computing.

○ No, the first human spaceflight was in 1961. That's 15 years before the first personal computers hit store shelves.

○ No, Bill Clinton was president from 1993-2001, which was after the personal computing era.

● Correct! The Apple II computer was one of the devices that characterized the personal computing era.

008

● Correct!

○ No, the Web consists of sites, and the Internet is a network that can link devices.

010

● Correct! A Google search for "number of Facebook users" will provide you with an estimate of the current number. It's astoundingly huge.

○ As of this textbook's publication date, Twitter had about half the number of users as Facebook.

011

○ No, although the United States government monitors information on the Internet, it does not officially censor it.

○ No, although Russian law allows the government to shut down Web sites that contain offensive content, Russia is not the country with the most censorship.

● Correct! You can find interesting information about Internet censorship in the Wikipedia article "Internet Censorship by Country."

○ No, in Greece the government may monitor Internet-based communications, but does not engage in full-scale censorship.

012

○ No, more than 25% of the world population has Internet access.

● Correct! In 2012 when this book went to press, about a third of the world population had Internet access.

○ No, when this text went to press this figure was too high.

○ No, when this text went to press, this figure was too high.

015

○ No, an iPad might have 1 GB of memory, called RAM, for temporary storage, but it would require too much battery power to operate 64 GB of memory.

● Correct! The specification of 64 GB refers to storage where you can save programs and data, even when the power is off.

016

● Correct! Microsoft Windows is an operating system.

○ No, Microsoft Word is application software.

● Correct! Apple iOS is the operating system used in iPhones and iPads.

● Correct! Mac OS X is the operating system used in Apple desktop and notebook computers.

○ No, iWork is application software for Apple computers.

○ No, iTunes is application software.

018

○ No, the computer is uploading to a server.

● Correct! The computer is a client because it is uploading and downloading from the YouTube server.

○ No, although the computer shown could be a server, it is acting as a client in this example.

020

○ No, a microcontroller typically has a built-in program, but would not run apps such as Angry Birds.

○ No, some handheld devices, such as GPSs and basic mobile phones, don't allow you to download and run apps.

● Correct! Handheld computers, such as iPods and smartphones, are characterized by their ability to download and run a variety of apps.

021

● The black rectangular chip is correct.

023

○ No, 10111 is binary for 23.

● Correct!

○ No, 10000 is binary for 16.

○ No, 1111 is binary for 15.

024

● 01001000

● 01101001

● 00100001

025

● 00110001

● 00110000

● 00100000 OR 11111111

● 01010011

● 01110100

026

● GB OR gigabytes

● MB OR megabyte OR megabytes

● KB OR kilobytes

027

○ No.

○ No.

○ No.

● Correct!

029

○ No, Bill Gates is the founder of Microsoft.

● Correct! In 1842, Ada devised a way of computing Bernoulli numbers on a proposed computing machine called the Analytical Engine.

○ No, Grace Hopper was a pioneer in computing, and she did program one of the first operational computers in 1944.

○ No, although there is a computer language called Fortran, it is not named after a person.

030

○ No, an interpreter would convert source code into machine code one instruction at a time, and it would not create a file that could be distributed.

● Correct! A compiler will convert all of the source code instructions into a file that contains object code that can be distributed and run as an iPhone app.

○ No, COBOL is an old programming language that's not designed for modern devices such as iPhones.

○ No, ASCII code is not a programming tool.

031

● [The one on the left] op code OR operation code

● [The one on the right] operand

033

● [Accumulator] 9

● [Register 1] 4

● [Register 2] 5

● [RAM] 9

034

○ No, single-factor authentication involves only one means of identification.

○ No.

● Correct!

○ No, password security relies on the complexity of the password you select.

037

● mouse

038

○ No, this password is based on the user's name.

○ No, this password is based on the user's name plus an easy-to-guess sequence of numbers.

○ No, although Gilgamesh is an odd word, it is a historical name listed in most dictionaries.

● Correct! This seems to be a random selection of characters, but it is a passphrase from "It's hard to guess this great password".

○ No, two words are more secure than one, but they can still be found using a dictionary attack.

041

○ iPhones include a browser, so your friend can access Web sites that require logins. A password manager would be a good idea.

● Correct!

CHAPTER 2

058

● Prices may have changed since this book was published, but typically Dell offers a desktop computer for less than $300.

059

● These computers are thinner, lighter, and a bit more expensive than a standard laptop computer.

060

● Correct!

○ No, both have touchscreens.

○ No, both use the slate form factor.

○ No, neither offers mobile phone service.

062

○ No, this price range is typical of enhanced media players, not desktop and laptop computers.

○ No, this price range is typical of tablet computer prices, not desktops and laptops.

● Correct!

○ No, this price range is too high.

063

● Correct!

○ It is possible to install the Mac OS on a PC, but the process is difficult.

○ No, a tablet computer will not allow you to "access Windows" over the Internet.

○ No, it can be done. Read the explanation on this page.

064

○ No, iOS is only used for Apple products, such as iPhones, iPods, and iPads.

● Yes, the Android platform is used for smartphones and tablets from a wide variety of manufacturers.

○ No, Windows 8 RT is not as widely used as Android.

○ No, this platform is used only by BlackBerry brand devices.

068

○ No, faster clock speeds (higher GHz numbers) typically increase performance.

● Correct! Instructions that require multiple cycles will decrease performance.

○ No, a fast front side gets data to the processor faster and increases performance.

○ No, having more cores allows the processor to process more instructions during each clock cycle.

069

○ No, serial processing is slowest because only one instruction is processed at a time.

○ No, pipelining is faster than serial processing, but is not as fast as parallel processing.

● Correct! And if you have a good grasp of this concept, you'll understand that combining pipelining with parallel processing can lead to the best performance.

070

● The correct answer is the line containing *Graphics* in Figure 2-18.

072

○ No, just the opposite is true.

● Correct!

○ No, *volatile* means that it holds data only when the computer is on.

074

○ No.

○ No.

● Correct!

076

○ No, there is not typically a path for data directly between the processor and the storage device.

● Correct!

○ No, computers process data in the microprocessor, not in storage devices.

077

● Correct!

○ No, sequential access was used by old tape drives, not by hard drives, USB drives, and other modern storage devices.

078

● The average price of a 2 TB hard drive is about $100.

079

● Correct!

○ No, drive capacity is measured in GB or TB.

○ No, drive rotation speed is measured in rpms.

○ No, transfer rate is measured in Mbps.

080

○ Try again.

○ That's not correct.

● Correct, USB flash drives use solid state technology.

○ That's not correct.

081

○ No, Blu-ray discs have more capacity than DVDs.

○ No.

● Correct! The capacity of a standard DVD is just about 5 GB, whereas Blu-ray disc capacity is about 25 GB.

082

○ No.

○ No.

○ No.

● Correct!

083

● You should select the row containing DVD-ROM or BD-ROM.

084

● Correct!

○ No, RAM is more temporary.

○ No, RAM is not designed to be easily removable.

○ No, solid state storage typically has more capacity than RAM.

086

● Correct!

○ No, you need access to the drive to insert and remove CDs.

○ No, a USB drive plugs into an external port.

○ No, you need access to the drive to insert and remove Blu-ray discs.

088

● Apple iPad and iPhones use a screen-based QWERTY keyboard as do most tablet computers. Some smartphones use an ABCD layout.

090

○ No, blue and red produce magenta, a reddish purple.

● Correct!

○ No, green and blue produce cyan, a bluish green.

○ No, red, green, and blue at full intensity combine to produce white.

092

● Printers use the CMYK model that has four basic colors, in contrast to the three-color RGB model used by display devices.

093

○ No, laser printers are faster than ink-jet printers, but more costly to operate.

● Correct!

097

● The Windows icon produces a "Safe to remove hardware" message on the screen. The Mac eject button displays the message, "You can remove your USB device."

099

○ Plugging directly into a wall outlet leaves your device vulnerable to power surges.

● Plugging into a surge strip will protect your device while it is charging.

100

○ Try again. A UPS can keep your desktop computer running when the power fails.

● Correct!

○ Try again. A UPS can keep your home network up and running during a power failure.

○ Try again. A UPS can maintain your Internet connection during a power failure.

104

○ No, the blue screen of death is a symptom of a problem, not a solution.

○ No, Safe Mode provides a way to troubleshoot, but it is not a simple process.

● Correct!

○ No, a surge strip can prevent problems, but cannot solve them.

CHAPTER 3

122

● When this book was published, popular DVD authoring software included Final Cut Pro, Roxio Creator, and Windows DVD Maker.

123

○ No, a team logo created with Paint software might not look sharp when you make it larger or smaller.

○ No, photo editing software provides great tools for working with photos, but does not produce sharp logos.

● Correct! Drawing software will create high-quality graphics regardless of how they are enlarged or shrunk.

126

● Correct! This software automates specialized tasks for retail businesses.

○ No, point-of-sale software is not generalized for use across all types of businesses.

○ No, project management software is not used to track sales transactions.

○ No, CAD software is used to create 3-D drawings.

127

○ No, don't forget to count the titles and the photo, which are in separate frames.

○ No, don't forget to count the titles and the photo, which are in separate frames.

○ No, don't forget to count the titles and the photo, which are in separate frames.

● Correct!

128

● The name of the IRS e-filing software is Free File.

129

○ Try again.

● Correct! Paint is an application designed for a human-centric task, rather than a utility designed to adjust computer or software settings.

○ No.

○ No.

131

○ No, device drivers are system software.

○ No, adaptive utilities are usually classified as system software.

○ No, this is system software.

● Correct! Desktop publishing software (DTP) is application software, not system software.

134

● Correct!

○ No, a spelling checker might miss misspellings for place names and technical terms that are not in the dictionary.

○ No, a spelling checker might not catch misused words, such as when you use *their* instead of *there*.

○ No, although a grammar checker might run along with your spelling checker, they are two separate utilities.

136

● Correct! The worksheet looks at two "what-ifs:" Scenario 1 and Scenario 2.

○ Try again.

138

● Correct! These references are relative, so they can automatically change if rows are inserted or deleted. If changed to absolute references, the formula would be =$B$3-$B$4.

○ No, if these were absolute references, the formula would be =$B$3-$B$4.

140

● Correct! There are two tables, but they are included in the same database.

○ No, there is only one database containing the two tables.

○ No, there are four records in each table, but that has nothing to do with how many databases there are.

○ No, there are eight records shown in the figure, but that has nothing to do with how many databases there are.

141

○ No.

○ Try again.

● Correct!

○ No, make sure you read the FAQ "How do I locate specific data?"

143

● The "Remote computer" icon is correct. Web apps run from a remote computer, usually in the Internet cloud.

146

○ No.

○ No.

● Correct! The three files ending in .exe are executable files.

○ No.

147

○ No, .app files are applications.

○ No, .exe files are executable on PCs.

● Correct!

○ No.

151

○ No, portable software does not have to run from the hard disk.

○ No, portable software does not require a setup program.

○ No, portable software does not run from the cloud.

● Correct! Portable software is not installed on a hard disk and no Registry entries are made.

152

○ No, an upgrade is a new version of a software or utility program.

● Correct! Both are designed to correct errors or close security holes.

○ No.

○ No.

156

● Yes, all software is generally copyrighted, even if it is free.

○ No, pirated software might or might not contain a copyright notice.

○ No.

○ No.

157

○ No.

○ No, a site license would allow access to all lab users.

● Correct! Because the license limits the number of copies that can be used simultaneously.

○ No, let's hope not.

158

● You are licensing the software according to the GRANT OF LICENSE.

● The license goes into effect "by installing, copying, or otherwise using the SOFTWARE."

● You can make a copy for use on a portable computer.

● No, the license says, "you may not rent, lease, or lend the software."

● Technically, you can TRANSFER the software to another person if you retain no copies for your own use.

● Yes.

159

● Correct!

○ No, shareware IS copyrighted.

○ No, both shareware and demoware are "free."

○ No, app stores are not set up to allow users to freely exchange shareware.

160

○ No.

● Correct!

○ No.

○ No.

161

○ No, read the definition of freeware carefully.

○ No.

○ No.

● Correct! The licenses for most free apps prohibit their sale and distribution by end users.

164

● When this book was published, Festi was the largest botnet with more than 300,000 infected computers under its control.

167

● Your computer might use popular antivirus software such as avast!, Windows Defender, Norton AntiVirus, Kaspersky Anti-Virus, AVG AntiVirus, or MacKeeper Antivirus.

168

● Your virus definitions should have been updated within the last week. If not, check your settings.

169

● If your antivirus has quarantined files, you might be frequenting dangerous Web sites or downloading infected files. Think about being more careful online.

CHAPTER 4

185

○ [Microprocessor] Although some data is stored temporarily in microprocessor registers, this resource's primary function is processing.

● [RAM] Correct! RAM is a resource that temporarily stores data.

○ [DISK] Disk drives are considered storage resources that hold data on a permanent basis.

○ [PRINTER] A printer is an example of an output resource.

○ [MOUSE] User interface elements do not store data.

186

○ No, read the description of multitasking.

○ No, read the description of multithreading.

● Correct!

187

○ Try again.

● Correct! Although Windows 8 allows more than one user to have an account, only one person can use the computer at a time.

188

○ No, the bootstrap loader remains in ROM

● Correct!

○ No, ROM is hardware and cannot be loaded into RAM.

○ No, the desktop is displayed on the screen, not loaded into RAM.

190

○ No, computers had GUIs back in 1984. Do the math.

○ No, computers had GUIs back in 1984. Do the math.

○ No, computers had GUIs back in 1984. Do the math.

● Correct!

194

● The first PCs used an operating system called DOS that had a command-line user interface.

196

● Correct!

○ No, Windows Pro is designed for desktops, laptops, and tablets with Intel processors.

○ No, Windows Server 2012 is designed for desktops and laptops.

○ No, Windows Enterprise is designed for desktops and laptops.

198

● Virtual machine technology is the correct answer.

199

● The correct answer is forks.

200

○ Try again.

● Correct! The MacBook Air is a laptop computer that uses Mac OS X.

○ Try again.

○ Try again.

201

○ No, there is no Start menu in the Android user interface.

○ No, Apple and Microsoft mobile devices feature a physical Home/Start button.

○ No.

● Correct!

202

○ No.

● Correct!

○ No.

○ No, UNIX predates many of today's operating systems.

205

● Correct! Budget: contains a colon, which is reserved for drive letters.

○ No, "macBook Air" is a perfectly acceptable file name.

○ No, although it contains the reserved word *Aux*, it is acceptable because there are other words in the name.

○ No, Paint.exe is a perfectly acceptable file name.

206

● You should have fewer than 20 folders in the root directory. On a PC, be sure you looked at the Hard Disk Drive C:. On a Mac, you should have looked at the Macintosh HD.

207

● Correct! Changing the file extension does not change the data or its format.

○ No.

○ No.

○ No.

208

○ No, check the list of files in the graphics row of Figure 4-35.

● Correct!

○ No, Microsoft Publisher opens its native .pub format and .docx documents.

209

● Most word processing software can open .doc files, even if its native format is .docx or .odt.

210

● Most computers have Adobe Reader. Look for it on your computer's Start screen (Windows) or in the Applications folder (Mac).

216

● Correct! Its subfolders (Desktop, Downloads, etc.) are displayed.

○ No.

○ No.

○ No.

218

● Your computer's root directory should not contain data files; but if you have a PC, there might be some .txt files containing EULA license agreements. Leave them where you found them.

219

● Correct!

○ No, read the FAQ, "How does a disk get formatted?"

○ No, read the FAQ, "How does a disk get formatted?"

○ No, read the FAQ, "How does a disk get formatted?"

220

● Clusters is the correct answer.

222

● Correct! In a 2012 report, Microsoft study results showed that only 5% of users made backups.

○ No.

○ No.

○ No.

223

○ No, you have the most control over your backup data when it is on a device you own.

○ No, you have the most control over your backup data when it is on a device you own.

○ No, you have the most control over your backup data when it is on a device you own.

● Correct! When you store your data in the cloud, you can access it from anywhere, but do not have full control over who might access it.

224

● If you have files for downloaded software, you should be sure to back up your Downloads folder so you won't have to download all those apps again if your hard disk fails.

227

○ No, File History is the last thing you'll restore.

● Correct! You'll have to boot your computer from a CD using a recovery disk so that you can install Windows on the new hard drive.

○ No, a restore point is useful only if your hard drive hasn't failed.

○ No, Time Machine is for Macs, not PCs.

228

○ No, a full system backup will take lots of time because it copies every file on your hard disk.

○ No, although an incremental backup takes the least time to create, it takes the most time to restore.

● Correct! A differential backup takes less time to make than a full system backup, and requires less time to restore than an incremental backup.

229

○ No.

● Correct!

○ No.

○ No.

CHAPTER 5

247

○ No, a PAN is used for connecting devices that are within a few feet of each other.

○ No, a LAN would not cover enough area to reach the local community.

● Correct!

○ No, a WAN would tend to cover a larger area than a local community.

248

○ No.

○ No, a standard EULA provides a license for only one workstation.

● Correct!

○ No, although software is copyrighted, LANs are not.

249

○ No, when the network is down, hackers cannot steal data from it.

● Correct!

○ No, viruses cannot spread through a network that is inoperable.

○ No.

250

● The correct answer is router.

251

● Correct!

○ No, read the FAQ, "What is bandwidth?"

○ No, read the FAQ, "What is bandwidth?"

○ No, read the FAQ, "What is bandwidth?"

252

○ No, DOS is an operating system, not a protocol.

○ No, Windows is an operating system, not a protocol.

● Correct!

○ No, handshaking is just another word for protocol.

253

○ No, packets consist of many bits.

● Correct!

○ No.

○ No, bits are sent as analog waves only on analog networks, like non-digital telephone networks.

255

● Your computer has a fixed IP address if the network utility says "DHCP Enabled No," "DHCP with manual address," or "Manually."

● Your computer gets its address from DHCP if the network utility says "Using DHCP" or "DHCP Enabled Yes."

258

● Most desktop computers and full-size laptops have built-in Ethernet ports.

● Interesting. That's rare, but an effective way of getting a fast wired connection.

● Tablets and thin laptops, such as the MacBook Air, have no built-in Ethernet ports.

259

○ No.

○ No.

○ No.

● Correct!

260

● That's great!

● Signal strength can be affected by the distance between your computer and the router or interference from electrical devices.

● Signal strength can be affected by the distance between your computer and the router or interference from electrical devices.

● If you have no bars, then you may not have a wireless connection; you might be using a wired connection instead.

262

● Correct!

○ No.

○ No, Ethernet is a wired standard.

○ No, these are Wi-Fi standards, but only "n" is currently popular.

263

○ No, 600 Mbps is the total bandwidth for all channels.

● Correct! Each channel provides 300 Mbps and that is the maximum available to each user.

○ No, MIMO is an antenna technology.

○ No, MIMO is an antenna technology.

265

● Most routers have five Ethernet ports; one might be labeled WAN or Internet.

266

● Correct!

○ No, a switch is used to route data.

○ No, a bridge connects two dissimilar networks.

○ No, WAP handles wireless connections, not Ethernet.

267

● The correct answer is browser.

268

● If the Wi-Fi icon (the one that shows signal strength) does not provide a network name, you might not be using a wireless network.

269

○ No.

○ Not usually. Your ISP might give you an IP address, but it will be used for your router unless you connect directly to your ISP over a dial-up connection.

● Correct!

○ No.

270

○ No, WEP offers the minimum level of security.

○ No, WPA is pretty good, but not the best security.

● Correct!

○ No, PS2 is a PlayStation gaming device.

275

● The correct answer is four; MAC, LAPTOPPC, REDDELL, and SERVER.

278

○ Try again.

● Correct!

○ Try again.

○ No.

283

● The correct answer is WEP.

284

○ No, hackers could have legitimate IP addresses assigned by DHCP even if they sneak onto your network.

● Correct! If you know the MAC address of legitimate devices, then any user with an unknown MAC address does not belong on your network.

○ Ha! A hacker isn't going to admit to breaking into your network.

○ No.

285

● The correct answer is Orange Julius.

287

○ No, with PKE the key used to encrypt data cannot be used to decrypt it.

○ No, PKE will protect encrypted data from unauthorized access.

● Correct!

○ No, AES is a type of encryption, not a key.

CHAPTER 6

303

○ No, but ARPANET technology was used for the NSFNET that was created in 1985.

○ No, ISPs have to get permission to use the backbone from the companies that provide it.

○ No, NAPs are points on the backbone where data is transferred to routes maintained by a different service provider.

● Correct!

305

● The correct answer is BitTorrent.

306

● Your Internet address is displayed as four groups of digits, like 72.200.10.1. If you found an address that begins with 10, 172, or 192, that's your LAN address, not your Internet address.

307

● Correct! A dynamic address changes, and as a result your customers will have a difficult time finding you.

○ Try again. You need an always-on connection for an e-commerce site.

○ Try again. You need a static IP address for an e-commerce site.

○ Try again. A domain is important for an e-commerce site.

308

○ No.

● Correct!

○ No, that's the job of a router.

○ No.

309

● Most connections have less than 100 ms latency.

310

● The correct answer is 14.

311

● Your download speed depends on the type of Internet connection you have. Speeds are measured in Mbps or Mb/s.

313

○ No, a dial-up modem converts the digital signals produced by your computer.

○ No, that's the frequency for a 0 bit.

● Yes, 56 Kbps is the theoretical downstream speed.

○ No, you can use analog service for a dial-up connection.

314

● Correct!

○ No, DSL is much faster than dial-up.

○ No, DSL is limited to about 3 miles from the switching station.

○ No, DSL is faster than satellite Internet service.

316

● Yes! But there are other answers, too.

● Right, but there are even more correct answers.

● Yes!

○ No, your cable connection has enough bandwidth for viewing TV without sacrificing Internet speed.

317

● Correct!

○ No, DOCSIS is not a vulnerability; it is a security measure.

○ No, there is no way to lock your modem.

○ Not necessarily. Windows has security holes that can allow intrusions from a cable Internet connection.

319

○ No.

○ No.

○ No.

● That's one of them.

● That's one of them.

322

○ No.

● Correct!

○ No, moving from one Wi-Fi hotspot to another is not seamless.

○ No.

323

● Correct!

○ No, HTTPS means a secure browser connection, but does not tell you if the wireless LAN is encrypted.

○ Not necessarily. Many secure hotspots require passwords, but you might be asked for the password only the first time you connect.

○ No, IP addresses do not contain security codes.

326

● Your phone might use Safari, IE, Chrome, or Firefox. If you can't find an icon for one of those browsers, your phone probably uses a proprietary browser.

330

● Correct!

○ No, cloud computing is supported by servers at many Internet nodes other than SkyDrive and iCloud.

○ No, cloud computing does not require a local application. The software reader for a cloud-based book might run on the cloud server and be displayed in your browser.

○ No, cloud computing often uses a browser to display content.

331

○ No, VoIP uses SIP, but chat uses IRC.

● Correct!

○ No, they use different protocols.

○ This answer is partially correct. VoIP is susceptible to jitter, but chat is not unless it is voice chat.

332

○ Try again.

○ Try again.

○ Although there is jitter, the test results showed that the connection would work for VoIP anyway.

● Correct!

335

● Correct!

○ No, FTP is used more frequently for downloads than uploads, though you can upload to an FTP server.

○ No.

○ No, streaming technology is different from downloads and FTP.

336

● Hmmm. Something should have been displayed in your browser.

● Yes, that is what happens for most users at this FTP site.

● You were given an option to enter a user ID and password, but you could connect as a guest.

● Your school computer lab might have blocked this site.

337

○ No.

● Correct!

○ No.

○ No.

343

● Your IP address should not be routable. If it doesn't begin with 10, 172, or 192, then make sure you're not looking at your Internet address. If you're sure, then you don't have a router.

● Okay, then your IP address is not routable, which is a security feature.

● Okay, then your IP address is not routable, which is a security feature.

● Okay, then your IP address is not routable, which is a security feature.

344

○ Try again.

● Correct! Make sure you understand why.

○ No.

CHAPTER 7

362

● Correct!

○ No, that would be HTTP.

○ No, that is handled by TCP/IP and HTTP.

○ No, that is a Web browser.

364

○ No, that is simply the first part of the URL.

○ No, HTML is a scripting language.

○ No, FTP is a download protocol.

● Correct!

366

● If you have just one installed, it is probably IE on a PC or Safari on a Mac.

● Chrome and Firefox are popular alternative browsers.

● Okay, it is unusual to have so many.

● That's quite a collection of browsers!

369

● Microsoft Word has an Export option that produces HTML source documents.

● If you select Save As in LibreOffice or OpenOffice, you can choose HTML as the file format.

● Google Drive lets you download a document you've created, putting it into HTML format.

● iWork Pages software does not have an option to save to HTML.

370

○ No, count the tags in <> angle brackets.

○ No, count the tags in <> angle brackets.

● Correct!

○ No, just count the tags in the header area.

372

● Correct!

○ No.

○ Hmmm. You might have a <form> field in your word processor, but it is not an HTML tag.

○ No, although forms can be used as part of a secure transaction, such as getting billing data.

375

○ No.

○ There should be more.

● Correct!

○ That's too many.

376

● Correct!

○ Sorting is too slow for all of the data managed by a search engine.

○ A Web crawler simply gathers the data from Web pages.

○ No, an HTML viewer is just another name for a browser.

377

● Assuming that you are not blocking ads, Bing probably displays more advertising.

378

● Google shows your location.

● The location shown is for your Internet address, which could be your ISP.

● Bing does not show your location, but go to maps and the location it shows is where it expects you to be located.

379

○ No, that's a fairly broad query.

● Yes, that's the one to use if you are seeking gear for your racing shell.

○ No, that query returns a surprising number of results.

○ No, that query returns oodles of results.

380

○ No.

● Correct!

○ Too many.

○ Way too many!

382

○ No.

● Correct!

○ No, though journalists use Tor and other technologies to avoid tracking.

○ No.

383

● Correct!

○ No, most Web-based material is copyrighted.

○ No, just because content is on the Web, it doesn't mean it is in the public domain.

○ Although schools often have an arrangement with academic journals, the right to use excerpts is not necessarily covered.

384

○ No.

● Correct!

○ No.

○ No.

386

○ No, though some businesses use craigslist to market to consumers.

○ No.

○ No.

● Correct!

392

○ No, the sender's name is part of the header, but not the subject line.

○ No, the Gmail Inbox identifies the Web-mail provider.

○ No, Sarah Mae is the recipient.

● Correct! Some, but not all, e-mail clients label the subject line as Subject:, but this e-mail client does not.

393

○ That's unlikely.

○ No, a student's e-mail server would probably have an .edu domain.

○ No, although the domain is .gov, the EPA probably would not supply an e-mail account to a politician.

● Correct! (Unless there is an employee named J. Bieber at the EPA.)

394

○ No.

○ No.

● Correct!

○ No.

395
- Local e-mail clients include Apple Mail, Outlook, and Thunderbird.
- You're using a Web-based e-mail client such as Hotmail, Gmail, Yahoo! Mail, or AOL.
- When you work with e-mail, check to see if it is displayed in a browser window, which means you are using Webmail.

396
- There will be ads pertaining to Paris unless you have ads turned off or blocked.
- There might be some ads related to other aspects of your profile and browsing history.
- If there are no ads, then they are turned off. Good for you!

398
- Great! You found the process for Gmail.
- That's how to see MIME in Apple Mail.
- That works in Thunderbird.
- The mail clients for both Windows 8 and Outlook do not have a way to display the MIME source.

402
- That's how to do it in Internet Explorer.
- That's how it works on the Mac in Safari
- That's how it works in Chrome.
- That's how it works in Firefox.

403
- Correct!
- ○ No, just the opposite.
- ○ No, both should avoid Flash cookies.
- ○ No, they are different.

404
- That is correct for several e-mail clients, such as Yahoo! Mail.
- That is correct for Hotmail, Apple Mail, Outlook, and Gmail.
- That is correct for Thunderbird.
- That would be unusual.

406
- Correct! It means the URL is not a known fake.
- ○ No, the lock icon or HTTPS tells you it is an encrypted connection.
- ○ No.
- ○ Every site, even a fake one, has an IP address.

CHAPTER 8

423
- The answer is 529,200 bytes (that's 176,400 x 3).

424
- Correct!
- ○ No, the microprocessor does not contain audio circuitry.

- ○ No, integrated audio is defined as audio circuitry that's part of the system board.
- ○ No, try again.

426
- ○ Try again.
- ○ That is not the correct answer.
- Correct!
- ○ No.

427
- ○ No, MP3 files don't usually contain synthesized music.
- ○ No, WAV files don't usually contain synthesized sound effects.
- ○ No, Ogg files usually contain digital audio.
- Correct! MIDI music is synthesized and often stored in files with .mid extensions.

428
- Correct!
- ○ No, speech recognition requires analog-to-digital conversion.
- ○ No, processing Google voice commands is an analog-to-digital conversion.
- ○ No, voice dialing requires analog-to-digital conversion.

432
- ○ Try again.
- ○ That's not correct.
- ○ No.
- Correct! XLSX is a format for spreadsheets.

434
- ○ No, large CCDs tend to product high-quality images.
- Correct!
- ○ No, both low-res and high-res images can be edited in Photoshop.
- ○ This is not the best answer. Low-quality images would tend to have fewer than a million pixels.

435
- Correct! A one-to-one correspondence between the pixels on the screen and in the file gives the best resolution on the screen.
- ○ No, this image is larger than the screen. When sized for the screen, some pixels will be discarded.
- ○ No, this image will look pixelated when enlarged to fit the screen.
- ○ No, a WUXGA image is 1920 x 1200 so some pixels will be discarded when it is sized to fit the screen.

437
- Correct!
- ○ No.
- ○ No.
- ○ No.

438
- ○ No, two bits produce an image with pure black and pure white, but no grays.
- Correct! With eight bits, a pixel can have 256 shades of gray.
- ○ No.
- ○ No, there are 256 possible colors, but only eight bits are necessary to produce them.

439
- ○ No, 11111111 is really 255.
- Correct!
- ○ No.
- ○ No.

440
- ○ No, lossy compression loses data.
- Correct!
- ○ No, JPEG compression is lossy so it loses data.
- ○ No, bitmap is not a type of compression.

442
- ○ No, JPEG files are already compressed, so they are not likely to shrink much.
- Correct! Data in BMP files is not compressed, so zipping them tends to substantially reduce the file size.
- ○ No, PNG files are already compressed, so they are not likely to shrink much when you zip them.
- ○ No, GIF files are already compressed, so they are not likely to shrink much when you zip them.

446
- ○ No, bitmaps tend to require lots of storage space.
- Correct!
- ○ No, compressed bitmaps can be small, but a similar image can usually be stored as a vector in less space.
- ○ No, MIDI is an audio format.

448
- ○ No.
- ○ No, Flash was a dominant tool used with HTML 4, but its use is declining with HTML5.
- Correct! HTML5 specifications are encouraging developers to use native features such as the <canvas> tag.
- ○ No, GIF is a legacy file format.

451
- If it looks like fun, you can try a free download and experiment with 3-D animation.
- Animation is not easy, but it is a hot career field.
- Alice is a tool that automates the scripting process for developing animations.
- Yes, it's not for everyone.

455

● Most people have a digital camera, a smartphone, and at least one computer that can take digital photos.

456

● Great!

● Windows computers include Windows Movie Maker, and Macs include iMovie, so you should have one.

● Look in the list of applications for Windows Movie Maker, iMovie, Final Cut Pro, Adobe Premiere, or Roxio Creator.

457

○ No, not technically.

● Correct!

○ No.

○ No, though they are used to compress video files.

459

○ No.

○ No.

○ No.

● Correct!

460

○ No, unfortunately, there is not yet a video standard on the Web.

● Correct!

○ No, Flash video can be referenced by the <video> tag as with other video file formats.

○ No, the <object> tag is still part of HTML5.

462

○ No, that's a Web scripting language.

○ No, that's a format for still images.

○ No, that's a video codec.

● Correct! VOB is the format used for commercial DVDs.

465

○ No, time shifting relates to recording broadcasts.

○ No, with place shifting, a file remains on the original server, but is broadcast elsewhere.

● Correct! It is necessary to change to a non-streaming format.

○ No, the analog hole would require you to film a YouTube video as it is displayed on your screen.

466

○ No.

○ No.

○ No.

● Correct!

468

● Correct!

○ No, streaming music never exists as a file on your computer, so it is more difficult to pirate than downloaded music.

○ No, Blu-ray discs are not easy to pirate even though AACS has been cracked.

○ No, streaming video never exists as a file on your computer, so it is more difficult to pirate than downloaded content.

470

○ No, HD (high-definition) is a screen format.

○ No, HDMI is a type of video port, but it can be part of DRM.

● Correct!

○ No, AACS is the technology used to protect Blu-ray discs.